# American Popular Music and Its Business

## THE FIRST FOUR HUNDRED YEARS

I

The Beginning to 1790

# American Popular Music and Its Business

## THE FIRST FOUR HUNDRED YEARS

Volume I. *The Beginning to 1790*
Volume II. *From 1790 to 1909*
Volume III. *From 1900 to 1984*

# American Popular Music and Its Business

## THE FIRST FOUR HUNDRED YEARS

I

The Beginning to 1790

RUSSELL SANJEK

New York          Oxford
OXFORD UNIVERSITY PRESS
1988

Oxford University Press

Oxford   New York   Toronto
Delhi   Bombay   Calcutta   Madras   Karachi
Petaling Jaya   Singapore   Hong Kong   Tokyo
Nairobi   Dar es Salaam   Cape Town
Melbourne   Auckland

and associated companies in
Berlin   Ibadan

Published by Oxford University Press, Inc.,
200 Madison Avenue, New York, New York 10016

Oxford is a registered trademark of Oxford University Press

Library of Congress Cataloging-in-Publication Data

Sanjek, Russell.
American popular music and its business.

Bibliography: p.
Includes indexes.
Contents: v. 1. The beginning to 1790—v. 2. From
1790 to 1909—v. 3. From 1900 to 1986.
1. Popular music—United States—History and criticism.
2. Music—United States—History and criticism.   3. Music
trade—United States—History and criticism.   I. Title.
ML200.S26   1988      780′.42′0973        87-18605
ISBN   0-19-504028-7

2 4 6 8 9 7 5 3 1
Printed in the United States of America
on acid-free paper

# Preface

This is a life's work, in the truest sense. Russell Sanjek had a seventy-year love affair with America's music, and these three volumes are the product of that infatuation and devotion. By his teenage years, in the late 1920s, he was already a collector of phonograph records, playing popular music, jazz, black and country records at home, to the consternation of his Croatian immigrant parents. During his early twenties, in the Great Depression years, he began to learn the public-relations skills that would become his trade, progressing from runner to writer at a New York City advertising agency. He also earned record money as a Sunday afternoon semi-professional football player, and a stringer for New York City news services.

By the late 1930s he was Associate Editor of the *Hot Record Society Rag,* an early jazz magazine, and worked on several recording sessions with leading jazz musicians. Many of the record hunters and music fans he met during these years were to find work in record companies, broadcasting, trade publications, and other areas of the music industry, and they remained his friends and acquaintances through the next five decades.

In 1940 he joined Broadcast Music, Inc., a performing rights licensing company newly founded by radio broadcasters to counter what they saw as a monopoly by ASCAP. As writer, Director of Special Projects, and eventually Vice President for Public Relations, Russell Sanjek melded vocation and avocation at BMI, working in the "many worlds of music" that he loved. During his BMI years he produced more than 150 concerts and evenings of entertainment, directed the BMI Student Composer Awards program, was chairman of the Lincoln Center for the Performing Arts jazz and folk music advisory committee, and served as a member of the Country Music Hall of Fame advisory committee, a member of the first National Endowment for the Arts jazz panel, and an elector of the National Academy of Recording Arts and Sciences Hall of Fame. He also served as President of the New York NARAS chapter, and on its national board of trustees. Other offices and honors also bore witness to the regard with which Russell Sanjek was held within the music industry.

Aside from his writing for *The Many Worlds of Music,* the BMI magazine he edited and produced, it was his 1972 piece "The War on Rock" that first brought his thinking about American music and its business to a public audience. It was during the next few years that he conceived an historical work; as it was written over a dozen years, it grew from one volume to three. In 1976 the outline of this work was tested in a course of lectures Russell Sanjek presented as Associate Professor of Music Business at Belmont College, in Nashville, Tennessee. His interaction there with students, as well as discussions with music industry friends and colleagues in New York and Nashville, confirmed his instinct that he was on the right course, if the journey might prove to be longer than first expected.

I remember well the work plan he adhered to while writing this book—five pages a day, quit when you finish. He would usually read what he was working on each night to Betty Sanjek, his wife, at the dinner table, and to his sons Rick, David, and myself, and my wife Lani, when we visited. We were all captured by the story, his presentation, and his enthusiasm. He delighted in making connections that other writers and scholars had not seen, or never could, due to their narrower focus of research or experience. I especially enjoyed his confessions of self-discovery, those things he learned that made him understand why events he had lived through had occurred. He was particularly pleased as he pieced together the larger historical contexts and trends that had led to the changes in American music he participated in, from the 1930s, through each following decade, into the 1980s. He loved the earlier periods, but this history was also his history.

In 1981 Russell Sanjek retired from BMI, and began to devote full time, not just weekends and vacations, to writing. That year he was commencement speaker at the Berklee College of Music in Boston, a special honor for a non-musician. He also began a 1981–82 Senior Research Fellowship at the Brooklyn College Institute for Studies in American Music. The two public lectures that he presented under the fellowship were published in 1983 as *From Print to Plastic: Publishing and Promoting America's Popular Music (1900–1980).* Between 1981 and 1986 he spoke widely, at colleges, conferences, and music industry meetings, and devoted much effort to the New York NARAS chapter, serving as President from 1983 to 1985.

The years in which these volumes were written were not easy ones for him. Almost as he began, in 1977 he learned that he had prostate cancer, and that it had already spread to other parts of his body. Perhaps the only thing that took him away from his writing over the next nine years was his periodic hospital visits for radiation treatments, surgery, and chemotherapy, and his recuperative days at home. In the last few years the days of pain became more frequent. This book sustained him. I learned from his doctor in 1986 that her prognosis in 1977 had been that he would live at most five years. That did not happen. His determination to finish the work he had started carried him through. In May 1986 he received the copy-edited version of volume one of this book from

Roberta Leighton. He was satisfied things were now in good hands, and told me later that month, "The book is done." He died June 11, 1986.

I completed the editing and proofreading process, with much help from Roberta Leighton, and support from Leona Capless and Sheldon Meyer of Oxford University Press, and from Betty, Lani, David, and Rick Sanjek. I wish I could also properly acknowledge, as he would have done, the scores, if not hundreds, of Russell Sanjek's friends in music who gave help and support to him, through the dozen years of these volumes' writing, and throughout his life-long career in the music business. But, unfortunately, that part of the finishing up is not something I can do.

In his last, difficult week at home, Russell Sanjek listened to some of the music he loved best. I played Ellington, Red Allen, Peewee Russell, Eddie Lockjaw Davis, Johnny Hodges, Joe Venuti, Paul Desmond, John Lewis, and others. Verbal communication was difficult, but the music played on while he was awake. After playing a Lester Young record, and attempting to express the bond between us that music had always been, I asked, "Did you ever see Lester play?" Words did not come easily by then. "Oh sure," he said, surprising me with his matter-of-fact tone. On June 10, I played John Kirby's 1939 sextet recording of "Blue Skies." He sang along with the intricate, reworked lyrics, both startling and touching me.

The legacy of America's music is one I am privileged to have inherited from Russell Sanjek. That legacy belongs to us all—in recorded and printed form, and through the three volumes that now sit before you.

*New York*                                                                          Roger Sanjek
July 1987

# Contents

# Prologue

## Summer at Drake's Bay, California, 1579

In the early summer of 1579, on the beach of an inlet north of the peninsula on which San Francisco now sits, the crew of the small rib-sprung *Golden Hind* spent four weeks ashore, repairing their battered vessel. During that stay, officers and men entertained a Native American audience with popular and religious music and songs. Thus their captain, Sir Francis Drake, was the first to bring popular music in the English language to the American mainland. There followed a long series of British invasions that shaped the course of American popular music, gave form to its business practices, and established the principle of property rights that makes the music business in America a multibillion-dollar enterprise.

Some fifty years before that summer, a major international crisis had erupted. Great Britain's young King Henry VIII was desperate to divorce the Spanish princess to whom he was married at eleven. She had borne him no sons, only a dark and ill-favored daughter. Anne Boleyn, a lickerish English lady-in-waiting, made pregnant by the royal seed, swore she carried a boy. Only a church-sanctioned divorce could make the embryo legitimate. Although Henry was the Holy Father's true "defender of the faith" and England a devout bastion of the Catholic church, the best efforts of his ambassadors could not move the pope to comply. Frustrated to the point of revolt, Henry sent his queen into rustication and broke with Rome. Within four years he established himself as supreme head of the Catholic church in England; two years later, in 1534, his Act of Supremacy effected a reformation of the church in England and ended nine hundred years of loyalty to Rome. Monasteries and convents were closed, churches and cathedrals seized, all religious property confiscated. Priests and nuns were sent into the streets and fields. An incalculable wealth of buildings and land was redistributed to the stout-hearted middle-class Britons who had put the Tudors on the throne and were resolved to keep them there. In the purging of Latin words and Roman Catholic music from the order of worship, a music-publishing monopoly was created, bringing into being the nation's first merchant stationers, who were made wealthy issuing music by means of the artificial handwriting Gutenberg had devised eighty years earlier.

Spain declared herself the church's military arm, ready to contend with the heretic British on land or water. An army of 50,000, led by chivalric and intrepid commanders, made that country the world's dominant power. Its modern fleet of 150 ships of the line ruled the seas. Its annual gross national product was ten times that of England, underwritten by the riches of the New World, most of which had been ceded by a high-placed native son, Pope Alexander VI, in 1493.

The British grew angrier as each new load of gold and silver was poured into the Spanish treasury, and goods of Spain's manufacture flowed west to supply thriving overseas colonies. Henry's split with Rome had cost them all friends but the Protestant Dutch and the French Huguenots. Matters did not improve under his successors, Edward VI and Mary, and the economic situation was desperate.

One result was a new industry—fathered by a national instinct for commerce that would maintain the English ensign around the world for centuries—piracy, which, when blessed by the state, is called "privateering." Sailing out of the inlets of southern England aboard ships smaller than twentieth-century lifeboats, British seamen combined a taste for plunder with religious fervor, becoming the scourge of Catholic shipping. With Dutch and Huguenot allies, they preyed on papist commerce under whatever flag it sailed.

By the late 1560s, privateering had become international big business of such dimension that aristocratic families invested both their money and their sons in it. Joint-stock companies were formed to finance it, creating a taste for speculation that led to colonization. Dividends were great, and opportunity limitless.

In 1562, Englishmen added a sideline, testing the recent Spanish proscription against the African slave trade. Three hundred blacks were loaded aboard a small flotilla and sold as field hands to West Indian planters in exchange for drugs, sugar, and spices. Two years later, a larger force of British ships used battle-tested gunners to enforce the sale of a cargo of prime African blacks at 150 pounds a head. Elizabeth, the new queen, was an investor in this enterprise. During her reign, her admirals, pirate leaders who became respectable officers of the Royal Navy when need arose, brought home power and riches England had never known.

One of them was a short, tough, socially ambitious captain from Devon, Francis Drake. On December 12, 1577, he had sailed from England in command of five ships and a company of 162 able and efficient men, financed by a joint-stock syndicate in which the queen was a leading investor.

Included in the ship's company were professional musicians, who played nightly during dinner and on other social occasions, such as the entertainment of captured Spanish and Portuguese officers. Drake was devoted to music, as an important facet of the civility to which he was aspiring. He was a capable falsettist, a practitioner of the art of the countertenor. This voice sang parts in popular and religious music that women would otherwise have taken, and was considered the mark of a gentleman. After Drake's death, a chest of musical instruments was listed among his effects found aboard ship. In it were a lute, oboes, sagbuts (ancestors of the modern trombone), cornetts (horns made of wood, which were eventually supplanted by Italian violins), citterns, bandores, and orpharions (from which the contemporary guitar comes).

In the late spring of 1579, the *Golden Hind* was so heavy with plundered gold and silver that the treasure was used for ballast. Drake and his crew were some 16,000 miles and twenty months away from home, separated from the remainder of the fleet, when their ship sprang a leak and her ribs began to separate. That is when they landed in what is now called Drake's Bay, where a fort was hurriedly built against possible enemies and repair work begun. Within a few days, a large number of Native Americans gathered, for the first of many welcoming ceremonies and frenzies of adoration of the godlike white men.

The record of the voyage kept by the fleet chaplain, Francis Fletcher, is almost all that survives in print of this time when English music was first heard in America. He confined his memoirs to matters spiritual, however, omitting mention of any native reaction to the popular music sung and played by the British officers and their rough crew of German, Dutch, and Welsh sailors.

Elizabethan England was a land where a guitar hung in every barbershop window for the pleasure of waiting customers. The music-publishing business was doing a lively trade in printed sheets of love songs, news ballads, and popular gospel songs. The cleverest of the publishers compiled books made up of their best-selling items. Some songwriters were well known, and their hits were circulated beyond London by traveling song-selling peddlers. London's musicians' union had a schedule of prices for weddings, beef breakfasts, parties, and social dances. Two publishers were being made wealthy through a state-granted monpoly to print and sell the Book of Psalms, which every Protestant Englishman was required to bring to church.

Protestant church music was being criticized by a new cult of Puritans chiefly because it was popular in origin and liked by the young. Everybody, these conservative Anglicans pointed out, knew that anything young people liked only made them disorderly and worse.

Blackstone had not yet been born to write about copyright, but publishers were able to protect publication rights in books or music by depositing copies of their works at Stationers' Hall, paying a small fee for the registration. The Stationers' Company included about one hundred publishers, who locked out all other competition, forcing them into job printing, book piracy, and the business of making and selling popular songs printed as broadsides. It was out of this business that the newspaper developed.

Stage personalities were cajoled into featuring new songs between the acts of plays or during the action of contemporary tragedies, comedies, and historical romances. Popular songs were used for political purposes, which provided employment and free drink for some songwriters and prison for others.

Those native Californians were therefore treated to a lively variety of the part songs, rounds, airs, ballads, old favorites, and madrigals that made up Elizabethan popular music.

In the mid-twentieth century a brass plate was found in the sand of Drake's Bay, and treated with considerable suspicion of its authenticity.

Be it known unto all men by these presents June 10, 1579, by the grace of God in the name of Her Majesty Queen Elizabeth of England and her successors forever I take possession of this kingdom whose king and people freely resign their right and title in the whole land to Her Majesty's keeping now named by me and to be known unto all men as Nova Albion

Francis Drake

Only one sentence is missing:

Here English music was heard for the first time in America.

# PART ONE

# The Beginning to 1603

# CHAPTER 1

# Popular Music in Henry's England

The evolution of the language of the Angles and Saxons into a common language in England was temporarily sidetracked after 1066, the year William the Conqueror mounted his successful invasion. For much of the next century, the government did its official business in the victor's Norman French, while a rudimentary English made up of Angle, German, Saxon, French, and Latin components was spoke by the people. Church Latin remained in use as the official language of international business and diplomacy. Only in 1363 was Parliament for the first time opened by an address in native English.

The earliest British entertainers and singers of popular songs did not, like European minstrels of the Dark Ages, wander from the court of one petty noble to that of another performing sophisticated music in several languages for the amusement of the powerful and wealthy. Instead, during the thirteenth century, the first generations of itinerant English musicians, considered to be rogues, vagabonds, and beggars, sang in the vernacular, to audiences knowing only that tongue. The blunt, coarse, and simple songs they performed concerned the things that mattered to these poor and simple folk: life, death, sex, ancient gods, mysteries of magic and religion, heroism, cuckoldry, rape, Mary the mother of Jesus, the foolishness of their betters, hunger, happiness, war, and the man on the hill to whom they owed fealty, taxes, and the right to deflower every new bride. Romantic love was a passion not yet known to them.

The earliest English popular song, "Sumer is icumen in" (c. 1280), is believed to be the work of a monk, but only because the words and the music are in what is recognized as his hand, and the manuscript contains corrections and erasures typical of a songwriter. The directions for singing it as a round, or rota, a four-part canon on a ground bass, were written in Latin. Like "Three Blind Mice," a similar round, it demands audience participation to make it the jolly affair intended by its author.

The growth and spread of a common language made inevitable the traditional true English ballad, that popular narrative poem that is the domain of the folk-

3

lorist. According to the definition of folk music adopted in 1954 by the International Folk Music Council

> Folk music is the product of a musical tradition that has been evolved through the process of oral transmission.
>
> The factors that shape the tradition are
> (a) continuity which links the present with the past;
> (b) variation which springs from the creative impulse of the individual or the group, and
> (c) selection by the community, which determines the form or forms in which the music survives.
>
> The term can be applied to music that has been evolved from rudimentary beginnings by a community uninfluenced by popular and art music and it can likewise be allied to music which has originated with an individual composer and has subsequently been absorbed into the unwritten living tradition of the community.
>
> The term does not cover composed popular music that has been taken over readymade by a community and remains unchanged, for it is the re-fashioning and re-creation of the music by the community that gives it is folk character.

Thus popular music is music growing out of popular culture and art music, originating with an individual, distributed to the community by entrepreneurial, commercial, and mechanical means through human performance, passing into the living tradition of a community in either its original form or one altered by the performers and the public's memory. Sometimes it disappears with the inexorable passage of time and changes in audience tastes.

Until owners of sixteenth-century printing presses discovered a market for the English street ballad, popular songs rarely existed in written form, but went through the process that made them folk music. The scribes working for a selective market—colleges, the church, wealthy collectors of the classics—found little demand for manuscript ballads. Pre-Gutenberg stationers made small profit marketing such ephemera.

Since most Britons were restricted by law to their home villages, except at fair time, early popular ballads traveled by way of that first itinerant music maker, the English-speaking minstrel. The word *minstrel* described all traveling entertainers, whether actors, singers, or musicians, for these early popular entertainers were required to know "how to invent, to make rhymes, to acquit himself well as a swordsman; to know how to play drums, cymbals well; to know how to throw up little apples and to catch them on the point of a knife; to imitate the songs of birds, to perform tricks with cards and jump through hoops, to play the cittern and the mandoline, to accompany well with a fiddle, and to speak and sing pleasantly," according to a fraternity of medieval German minstrels, who drew up these specifications, which continued to serve for centuries.

Until the printing press provided the means for mass duplication of original music in the exact form its author intended, British minstrels served as the principal medium carrying all popular music and entertainment to people in their own environment.

In the late fourteenth century, English minstrels attached to the king's retinue or the entourage of important nobles were granted permission to form a protective trade association. A code of honor bound all members and was enforced by the king of the minstrels and his assistants, who could arrest and try violaters and resolve disputes and complaints. As with twentieth-century protective associations and unions of music makers, two of the principal functions of this group were to control opportunities for employment and to bar competitors.

Richard II commissioned one of his officers "to take and seize for the king all such singing-men expert in the science of music as he could find and think able to do the king's service within all places of the realm, as well as cathedrals, colleges, chapels, houses of religion and all other franchised or exempt places. . . ." One of his successors, Henry V, so loved the minstrels who had shared the campaign against the French that ended with victory at Agincourt in 1415 that he left each of them a bequest of one hundred shillings. Among his favorites was John Lydgate, the monk who entertained the court with satirical ballads, hundreds of which survived in manuscript. For centuries, the oldest British ballad known, "London Lickpenny," was attributed to "Dean John Lydgate, Monk of Bury St. Edmond, minstrel to Henry the Fifth." The Corporation of the City of London commissioned him to preserve in verse accounts of public functions, some of which were modeled after the writing of his friend and mentor Geoffrey Chaucer, the wine merchant's son who ran out of *Canterbury Tales* after he had filled five hundred pages with glorious verse.

As the Chapel Royal, a group of royal vocalists formed in the twelfth century, grew more sophisticated in the music it employed, the minstrels' prestige faded. The group's name referred to no specific building, but to the priests, singers, and musician accompanists who traveled with the king to perform daily religious services. The greatest honor to which a British musician could aspire was membership in this privileged group. Still, royal press gangs roamed the countryside to recruit, by force when necessary, promising musical talent, a practice that persisted for almost two centuries.

The Chapel Royal of Henry VIII numbered seventy-five, including a choir of six men and six boys. For a time the master of boys was William Cornyshe, musician, playwright, and actor, who developed an early form of musical theater by using popular music in dramatic and comedy "interludes." He was represented in *Twenty Songs,* the first printed collection of English popular music, published in 1530. He went with Henry to his famous meeting with the French ruler Francis I, in 1520, at which, on the Field of the Cloth of Gold, medieval art and chivalry enjoyed their last days in the sun. A fountain ran with wine, the kings wrestled, and each nation mounted days and nights of entertainment. Cornyshe produced the British offerings. The entire Chapel Royal entertained, displaying the young, red-haired king's musicians and singers in a sampler of pageants and theatrical shows.

Henry's retinue included the three major composers of the period: Robert Fayrfax, doctor of music from both Oxford and Cambridge and considered to be the best musician in the nation; Hugh Aston, of York Chapel, and Cornyshe. Aston's "Hornpipe," based on a traditional country dance, marked, in a transcription for the virginals, the beginning of English keyboard composition. For most of the next two centuries, *virginals* denoted all quilled keyboards, including the harpsichord and the first spinet, which got its name from its Italian inventor, Giovanni Spinetti.

After wresting control from Richard III in 1485, the Tudor family struggled to rid the nation of the disastrous consequences of the Wars of the Roses. This thirty-year-long civil conflict left Britain an impoverished nation. The music of the culture-loving Anglo-Norman aristocracy placed in power by William the Conqueror was destroyed in the process, and with it much of the nation's genteel art and most original religious composition. Although John Dunstable, a leading composer, had been dead only since 1453, he was remembered but vaguely in his native land, while Italians were boasting that their music was taking "such a wonderful flight because it seems to be a new art which originated with the English under the leadership of Dunstable." His international prestige had been such that the duke of Milan dispatched a court musician to secure the services of Dunstable-trained singers for his chapel. The violent wars destroyed most of Dunstable's manuscripts, and only those preserved in Italy remain to fix his place in history.

When Henry VII took power, a ruined aristocracy could no longer afford to play the role of patron to the arts. A company of household musical servants was an ostentation few could support. Only after the government subsidized the fishing and maritime industries, and the economy improved, did the growth of merchant companies venturing into international trade end England's isolation from the development of polyphonic music in Flanders, Burgundy, and Italy. Musical instruments of Continental manufacture and manuscripts and printed editions of French and Italian love songs and instrumental music slipped into the cargoes brought home by British shipping. The holds also carried European musicians in search of the British ruler's gold, for few native minstrels had survived at court after Henry VIII developed a taste for modern and sophisticated musicianship. Henry spoke French, Latin, and a little Italian, played well on the lute and virginals, sang at sight, and drew the bow with a strength greater than that of any man in England. He was proud of his musical abilities and took every opportunity to demonstrate his skills, playing and singing music of his own writing, though it was known that Cornyshe and other royal musicians often applied their professional competence to its creation. To surround himself with excellent musicians, Henry paid premium wages for daily attendance upon him to foreigners, usually Italians. The average stipend was 112 pence a week, with twenty-eight more for board and an additional annual sixteen pounds for the uniforms that showed their rank to be above that of a household servant but not yet that of a gentleman. Members of what was called the Royal or King's Musick had a virtually tax-free income and performed no other services. Two centuries later Bach extolled the advantages of such an arrangement: they "have no anxiety regarding their livelihood and consequently are relieved of such infelicity, each man is able to cultivate his own instrument and make himself a competent and agreeable performer on it."

Henry could provide any form of music his visitors might wish, performed as competently as in any European palace, and on occasion with extraordinary virtuosity, on the major instruments known to Western civilized man: the virginals, cornett, harp, organ, bagpipes, drums, wind instruments, viol, flute, and lute. He owned the instruments used by his servants and cataloged them among his personal treasures.

The Dutch philosopher Erasmus, who praised folly in wise men and taught Greek at Oxford for fifteen pounds per annum, came to know Henry and saw only good in this swaggering monarch until Henry determined to supplant the pope as head of the Catholic church in England. He wrote to friends at home that the Tudor monarch could "not only sing his part sure, but of himself composed a service of four, five and six parts." He took no pleasure in the course pursued by English music before Henry's apostasy, writing, "There was no music in St. Paul's time, words were then pronounced, but nowadays seem to mean nothing. Modern church music is so fashioned that the worshippers cannot hear one word distinctly. The celebrants do not understand what they are singing. . . . [They are] a set of creatures who ought to be lamenting their sins [and] fancy they can please God by gurgling in their throats."

The course of English music was altered considerably by the closing of monasteries and convents and other religious houses, the dispersal of priests, and the confiscation of church property as Henry consolidated his religious revolution and, in passing, added more than a million pounds to his bankrupt purse. The choir schools that had been attached to cathedrals and religious buildings and the chantry schools supported by bishops had provided the first basic music education most British children received, initiating the training that impelled the most talented to pursue this interest. Now these doors were barred.

Members of the Chapel Royal and those musicians and organists attached to cathedrals now converted to the uses of Protestantism labored to compose new melodies, suited to the meter of an English ritual. The traditional reading and singing of the entire Book of Psalms was continued, but because Latin was proscribed, new English translations were needed, with new music to accompany them. Some Protestants branded the earliest results of this work as "more convenient to minstrels than to devout ministers of the divine service; for plainly as it is used, specially considering the words to be so strange and so diversely descanted, it is more to the outward pleasure of the ear and vain recreation, than to the inward comfort of the heart and mind with good devotion."

The most rabid of these critics was John Taverner, a leading master of English music in Henry's time, who used the British love song "Western Wind" as the central theme of a Catholic mass written when he was in charge of young students at one of Oxford's colleges. Accused of heresy, he was thrown, together with his fellow apostates, into the bowels of a school building where fish had been stored. Being merely a musician, Taverner was pardoned and dismissed from the school. After the Protestant terror began, he was a paid government agent, seeking out and destroying music manuscripts, razing holy shrines and convents, repenting all the while that "he had made songs to Popish ditties in the time of his blindness." Three of his songs were printed in the 1530 edition of *Twenty Songs*.

Henry suppressed the first published Psalms translation, Miles Coverdale's
*Goostly Psalms,* printed in 1528 by the London stationer John Rastell. The royal
objection was tainted by pique; Coverdale was, Henry ranted, infused with the
same Lutheranism as that infecting William Tyndale's first English translation
of the Bible. Some dozen years before, Martin Luther had skewered the Tudor
king for his youthful defense of the pope, which Henry never forgave. Coverdale, too, was an enemy of those "foul and corrupt ballads" being used to
accompany his translations of the "sweet songs of God's honour."

Not until 1562 was a suitable combination of piety and approved melody tolerated in a printed version. This combination of words and music, in the idiom
of popular song, was known as "Singing Psalms" and was circulated in broadside ballad form by wandering entertainers.

During the fifteenth century, minstrel singers, owing allegiance neither to the
King's Musick nor the king of the minstrels, wandered about Britain singing
and entertaining for a night's lodging or small coins. Their playing added to
the gaiety of weddings, social affairs, and civic functions, bringing provincial
audiences a glimpse of the delights for which London was famed. In time, many
of these music makers gave up the uncertainties of life on the open road and
took up permanent residence in some large community, becoming local personalities as they learned the tastes of those who paid them best, the dance and
popular music their patrons preferred, and those tunes that brought an additional flagon of ale or bonus of silver. Local authorities permitted these town
musicians to do business as long as they observed the ordinances and broke no
laws.

Many of them became "waits," a name originally used to mean night watchmen, who walked the streets sounding a horn to mark the hours, usually a shawm,
the loudest and easiest instrument to play. Being trained, the former minstrels
brought new skills to the work and became official civic musicians, providing
all music, public and private.

London's Guild of Waits was chartered before 1330, and Canterbury paid its
night watchmen a pound a year before the fifteenth century. During Tudor times,
seventy communities employed musicians, adding fire watching to their duties
when timber-framed houses began to burn to the ground in minutes. The shawm
had developed into the hautboy, the next step in the life of that double-reed
instrument now called the oboe. Official uniforms were provided, London's being
a gown of blue with red sleeves and a silver chain stamped with the city's arms.
Waits were admitted into the city's Fellowship of Musicians, but, though they
monopolized all official music making, they could not perform at private parties, weddings and funerals, beef breakfasts, banquets, and other social rites for
which a schedule of prescribed minimum rates had been established. A common code of ethics forbade ridicule or abuse of fellow members. The master-
and-apprentice system prevailed, providing a continuing supply of trained
members. It was, however, a practice that effectively shut off any opportunity
for nonmembers to find work, which led to cutthroat competition in the seventeenth century.

The waits of London, Chester, and Norwich were acknowledged to be the finest in all England, the last being famed for their group singing. Each noise, or band, of musicians had its own signature music for identification, Oxford citizens recognizing their town players by the gavotte for which the group was famous, just as early twentieth-century radio audiences knew it was time for Bing Crosby when the first strains of "When the Blue of the Night Meets the Gold of the Day" were heard, or swing fans made ready to jitterbug as the first clarinet notes of Benny Goodman's "Let's Dance" were sounded.

Norwich's waits, who once took strike action, after learning that other groups were receiving higher pay and more privileges, were such fine entertainers that Francis Drake persuaded the town fathers to lend them for one of his voyages, hoping to impress captured Spaniards with their virtuosity. Only two of the six returned; the others died of fever or wounds suffered in an attack on Cadiz. Trainees replaced the dead waits and continued the first free public concerts in Britain, provided by the city of Norwich.

Other cities took up the practice. London's residents and the flood of visitors that poured in to see its wonders were entertained at public expense from March to late September by the waits, eighteen in number, playing from the turret of the recently completed Royal Exchange every Saturday and holiday evening.

Throughout the sixteenth century, antivagabond laws were enacted, to control problems caused by migration of the poor in search of work, to restrict fraud by wandering peddlers, to punish those rascals and rogues thriving on the gullibility of country people, and to regulate the passage of traveling entertainers. Earlier, there had been a realization of the strict requirement binding the lower classes to their place of birth. Not until Elizabeth's Statute of 1572 were musicians named specifically as potential violators of the law. Only that entertainer belonging to "some honorable personage of great degree" was exempt. Teachers and masters of the art of swordplay, keepers of bears trained for baiting, and "common players of interludes" still went about freely, because they provided Elizabethans with their favorite amusements. Ballad singers, who poured through the countryside with packs of little chapbooks (cheap books) and penny broadsheets, could wander about, but only after they had first secured a license or "pass port," signed by two local justices of the peace, exactly as tinkers, other itinerant sellers, repairmen, and off-job workers were required to do. The waits' badge of office was a valuable insigne, providing protection from the vagabondage laws and assuring its bearer of freedom. A musician in search of work and without a badge or a uniform of a company of minstrels was liable to be "grieviously whipped and burnt through the gristle of the right ear with a hot iron of the compass of an inch about" on his first arrest and could be put to death on the third.

By the mid-sixteenth century, big-city waits, who were to provide official music, were paid an annual salary and provided with a uniform, but even so, because their patent had promised full protection against competition from strangers, London's musicians complained about the influx of amateur and wandering players. Tailors, shoemakers, and others, they alleged, were working at weddings, in alehouses and inns, and playing and singing "three man's songs," harmonized popular music, which was supposed to be their exclusive domain. With its population fast approaching 150,000, London had become too large a metropolis to police such infractions, so these rascals continued to work without hindrance. They competed with guild musicians for the best-paying work, weddings, at which music was played from the presentation of the bride to the assembled guests until the blowing of instruments woke the bride and groom from sleep the following day.

The musical abilities of waits, particularly those of London, kept pace with those of the court musicians and the most talented music lovers. Thomas Morley's instruction book for chamber-music ensembles, *First Booke of Consort Lessons* (1598) was intended for those skilled on a "double curtail [bassoon], lyserden [tenor bass tuba], a treble oboe, a cornet and a set of recorders," one of the wind instrumentations most popular in England and the Continent, for which London's waits were famous.

# CHAPTER 2

# Music in Elizabeth's England

The eternally virgin queen Elizabeth Tudor was twenty-five in 1558 when she assumed the throne of England her father had left to a sickly half-brother, Edward VI, and that was occupied on his death by her half-Spanish half-sister, Mary, the "bloody queen." She quickly found management of the national economy a complicated business, and it was far more so than even this shrewd woman would ever truly master. In her father's reign, international bankers had exacted fourteen percent interest on loans guaranteed by the Tudors' family fortune. During one century of their rule, prices increased 400 times, whereas workers' wages went up only twenty percent. The upper class grew rich through control of the country's business and overseas investments. And the middle class, fortified by redistribution of Catholic church lands, eventually became an equally major factor in the national economy. Yet, by 1600, total government revenue was only £500,000, less than the fortune Drake brought home from his single voyage around the world.

The vast majority of Elizabeth's five million subjects were farmers, most of them sharecropping tenants. Three-fourths of all Britons lived in the country; the balance lived in London and the major small cities, Norwich and Bristol, though there were fewer than 20,000 inhabitants in either. No Englishman, unless he was noble or rich, could leave his home area without permission. He could sell the things he made or grew only in the community in which he lived, except on fair days, when he could take his merchandise or produce to any of the hundreds of fairs held throughout the year.

Every Briton wanted to see London before he died, and on foot, on horse or donkey, in vehicles drawn by animals, in small number in fancy coaches, and by river the people came. The Thames was the main thoroughfare of the city until the Industrial Revolution provided other means of transportation. London Bridge, built in 1209, was the only road across the Thames; it connected the south side, where theaters, jails, brothels, and taverns flourished, with the north bank, center of business and commerce. Merchants opened their stores and stalls on the city's muddy, unlighted streets and alleys, and earned fortunes from overseas trade and the letters patent that Elizabeth used to reward her favorites or to pay off obligations without expending any of her shrinking purse. Patents affected every aspect of life, from the licensing of an alehouse, to the manufacture of leather, glass, and yarn, to the production of vinegar, the *Book of Common Prayer,* and its accompanying Singing Psalms. An already precarious economy tottered as price-rigging monopolies drove every cost upward, usually far beyond the reach of the average Londoner, who worked twelve hours a day in summer and through daylight in winter, for twelvepence.

The language spoken in England was an amalgam of words from the Celtic, Roman, Angle, and Saxon past, laced with Norman English and borrowings from Latin, French, and Italian. The spelling of English words was not fixed until 1552, when Richard Huelot's *Abcedarium Anglico-Latinum* appeared in print, a dictionary "for young beginners" containing 26,000 words.

Though the education of young girls came to an end when Henry closed the monastic buildings where priests and nuns had taught them, boys attended the free grammar schools that began to open to fill the void. There they learned to read and write their mother tongue, labored through religious instruction, and sometimes dipped into Greek and Latin classics. Among the skills some of them developed was rapid writing, or shorthand. These picked up such proficiency that visiting orators and preachers marveled at their ability to copy out a sermon as spoken. Playwrights and theater managers learned to their sorrow that the smiling youth with paper and writing tool was often copying down the playscript as spoken, to sell it to a pirating printer or a rival acting company. Only the rich and powerful could send their offspring to the universities at Oxford and Cambridge, where 3,000 were in attendance in 1580.

General music education declined after church-supported singing schools were closed, and instruction in sight reading was given in only a handful of grammar schools. Musicians and singers from the poor classes had to learn through imitation or by sheer innate skills. Wealthy youths had the advantage of access to professional musicians, often in the employ of their parents.

Health in both towns and rural areas was chancy. The increasing number of persons who made London their home brought about a series of plagues that took life on a grand scale, those of 1592 and 1603 leveling man, woman, and child indiscriminately by bubonic infection and smallpox. Urban Britons shared the public well and the public bath, endowing city streets and farm fields with their wastes. Sir John Harrington's invention in 1596 of a flush toilet afforded improved hygiene only to those who had their own source of water.

While the average Englishman had little prospect of wealth in an expanding world economy from which he was barred, sea-roving privateers gave Elizabeth and England the most potent and persuasive claim to a place in the world order. In her grandfather's day, daring sailors had made fishing the nation's most profitable business when they ventured far distances in search of new grounds. In 1496, Henry VII had issued a patent to the Genoese mariner Giovanni Caboto, who made his home in Bristol, where he was known as John Cabot. The grant instructed this brilliant navigator, who had already served many foreign rulers, to "seek out, discover and find, whatsoever Isles, Countries, Regions or Provinces of the Heathens and Infidels, whatsoever they be, which before this time have been unknown to all Christians."

Cabot's small vessel and crew of eighteen sailed some 1,200 miles along the wooded North American coast. The king rewarded him with ten pounds and an annual lifetime pension of twice that. This lasted only a single year, for Cabot disappeared on his second voyage. However, he had established England's claim to the New World, in spite of Pope Alexander VI's 1493 Line of Demarcation, dividing it between Spain and Portugal. As a good Catholic, Henry observed the papal order, and for the next several decades he and his son showed little interest in overseas discovery and colonization. Royal subsidies were expended to build up a proper fleet, and Britain's geopolitical ambitions focused on the markets of West Africa, Morocco, the Baltic, Russia, and the Mediterranean countries. Spain had the New World to itself, with only a little competition from Portugal.

Under Elizabeth, adventurous Britons combined service to God with patriotism and avarice, raiding Spanish possessions in America. They captured Catholic treasure ships and sold African slaves to American plantation and mine owners, all the while tweaking the Spanish monarch's nose by attacking his European coastal cities. Their accomplishments were a matter of national pride to ordinary men, who were unaware of the complexities of world politics, but who exulted in ballads recounting triumphs over Spain.

The extraordinary profits from piracy opened investors' eyes to the reality of gold, silver, and other American resources. As Protestants, and therefore no longer restrained by the papal division of the Americas, they established joint-stock companies, which financed expeditions, most of them unsuccessful, to settle the land called "Terra Florida." Professional ballad writers were hired to stimulate public interest and support with penny broadsides that passed from hand to hand and voice to voice.

Navigational skills and brilliant seamanship were mastered during voyages of piracy. These required, and brought about, improvement in the construction and armament of seagoing ships. The daring competence of her highly professional navy emboldened Elizabeth to challenge Spain on the European mainland. She gave financial aid to Holland's Protestant rebels in a war of liberation, and English soldiers learned the art of modern warfare fighting alongside the Dutch. Philip II of Spain, the husband Bloody Mary had taken by proxy in order to effect a new partnership between the two countries and thus restore England to the Roman faith, had abandoned any notion of conquering Elizabeth in the marriage bed. He now resolved to defeat her by force, as though she were a manly equal.

In 1588, Spain sent her Grand Armada of 130 vessels, 8,050 sailors, and 19,000 soldiers against England. So certain was the prospect of total victory that hundreds of Catholic monks accompanied the forces, ready to convert the heretics after occupation. The entire fleet was imbued with zeal, determined to punish the fallen and set Catholic Britons in the seats of power. Philip, however, vacillated too long with his plots and furtive strategies. Englishmen, both

Protestant and Catholic, rallied to the call to arms, casting aside differences and divisions. English battle tactics and gunnery proved invincible. In less than a month British guns and seamanship, the Channel and Atlantic weather, and Spanish pride itself destroyed over half of the invading fleet.

Thomas Deloney, the most popular songwriter of latter-day Elizabethan England, had long stirred the people's emotions with ballads reporting battles and victories during the Spanish wars. On August 10, 1588, as the Armada was in total rout, a London bookseller published his "O Noble England, fall downe upon thy knee," and the city's streets resounded to its words, sung to a popular French dance tune that had been published on the Continent a half-dozen years before, "Monsieur's Alemaigne." It ended with a prayer.

> Lord God Almighty
> Which hath the hearts in hand
> Of every person to dispose,
> Defend this English land.
> Bless thou our sovereign
> With long and healthy life
> Inbue her council with thy grace,
> And end this mortal strife.
> Give to the rest,
> Of commons more and less,
> Loving hearts, obediant minds,
> And perfect faithfulness.
> That they and we
> And all with one accord:
> On Zion hill may sing the praise
> Of our most mighty Lord.

That prayer was answered, and Spain's control of Atlantic shipping lanes was ended. England was ready for Protestant colonization of the North American mainland. Its mastery of the Atlantic would provide the means; its steadily declining economic condition, both the incentive and the colonists; the thirst for profit of its middle class, its rich, and its bankers and merchants, the financing.

As the upper classes turned their minds to the pursuit of money, trained musicians and singers found work in the households of the nobility and newly rich merchants, providing them with music for the entertainment of family and guests, and teaching their young the "science of music." In this they were aping royalty, as had the Tudor family after it toppled the last of the Plantagenets, Richard III.

When Elizabeth became ruler, some sixty musicians and singers made up her Musick. She soon cut down on that number. Expenditures for her musical entertainment rarely cost more than £3,000 annually, and little was wasted on incompetency. She had been taught to love music and was adept on the virginals, and she once told the French ambassador that in her youth she had "danced very well and composed measures and music and had played them herself and danced them." The changing character of secular art music was reflected in the inventory of her music library. Manuscripts and printed books of music in the new polyphonic style, written by European experimenters and much more complicated and demanding to perform, offered a continuing challenge to the musicianship of the Queen's Musick. Imported dance music for steps with foreign names, French and Italian love songs, complex music for groups of viols and winds in consort, chamber music in "setts and lessons," contributed to the rising tide of musical literacy among the upper classes and their musician servants, spurring English music toward its first golden age.

Elizabeth expected her favorite musicians, William Byrd and Thomas Tallis, to be grateful when she awarded them a monopoly of music printing in lieu of an increase in their daily stipend. It was her shrewd way of rewarding those who pleased her without dipping into her purse. She once gave the royal instrument maker a money-making patent for the exportation of ashes to Europe, where they were an ingredient essential to glassmaking, and one for worn-out English shoes, which were prized by fashion-conscious foreigners, to another favorite.

Though they were underpaid, members of the Queen's Musick had the best of everything, save money, the cream of imported or domestic custom-crafted musical instruments, and a social prestige just under that of the petty aristocracy. Their principal duties were to entertain the queen, providing music on all occasions. Birthdays, funerals, holidays, and festivals were marked by special music. Her dinner was escorted from the kitchen by twelve trumpets and two kettledrums, and the upper classes spent fortunes emulating such pomp.

Byrd, Morley, and other gentlemen of the Chapel Royal were a little below the queen's musicians in rank. Their salary was exactly half, thirty pounds annually, seven and a half pence daily, and a shilling a day for board. Their uniforms were less splendid, refurbished only when the entire royal music massed on public display, dressed in black for funerals and red for special events.

"Twenty gentlemen, eighteen trumpeters, five musicians, four sackbutts, six viols, five flutes, one drummer, a harper, and a bagpiper" had escorted Henry VIII's body to Westminster Abbey and performed the special mass for which he had provided a large sum in his will. They were dressed in surplices of the finest Holland cloth, a holdover from popish ritual that had been adopted by the Church of England.

The composers attached to the Chapel Royal had the finest musicians, men and boy singers, to perform their new works, and the queen's musical establishment set a social and creative tone for all the nation. Its influence spread as organists and choirmasters in large-city cathedrals and hinterland churches bought hand-drawn copies of music written by the court composers and in turn introduced such music to audiences hundreds of miles from London. The music funded by the crown served as a national academy for the nation, supported by a ruler who understood and loved contemporary music.

Opportunity to supplement their income came to court musicians from singing for royal weddings and from bonuses received when the Chapel Royal was transferred from one of Elizabeth's five palaces to another or when they and other musicians went on the "progresses" about the nation during London's hot and unhealthy summer. On these, the queen visited her wealthier subjects, dragging along all her household, and permitted her hosts to entertain them all, at their own expense, in the manner to which she had become accustomed.

Elizabeth's celebrated parsimony came about from the desperate financial state in which she had found her nation. Henry had left a great debt after squandering the family fortune his merchant grandfather built up. Despite continuing inflation, she ran the royal court for one-third of the £120,000 her half-sister had spent in each of the four years of her reign. Elizabeth never asked for more, though prices quadrupled and she had a household of 2,000 to support. She took cunning advantage of the men who vied for her favor or glance, in a manner that would have stunned the Spanish who knew them only as bloodthirsty daredevils.

On her progresses, towns greeted her with speeches and gifts and music, parading their local waits in displays of songs and music. Powerful noblemen showed off their musician servants or imported expensive London and European talent to impress her. Acting companies were called into the country, far from their usual haunts, to be rewarded amply for presentation of a favorite play bearing the stamp of approval from the Office of the Queen's Revels and known to please the queen. Elizabeth's tours, on horseback and in open litters, made English summers times of excitement and opportunity for musicians and entertainers.

The queen's devotion to the secular arts—music, the theater, and even bearbaiting—was a major influence on the evolution of popular culture. She provided employment to a great body of people involved in entertainment—trainers of animals, fireworks makers, players, musicians, singers, dramatists, composers—giving opportunity for self-expression to the best talent in the country. The master of Revels superintended a round of amusements, many of which were musical. As his duties grew, he came to determine the content of various forms of theater, with one eye on the humor of his ruler, but always alert for any tinge of dissentious thinking.

In the last years of his life, Henry VIII had named Thomas Cawarden the first permanent master of Revels, charged to oversee and control all court programs, to provide costumes and necessary stage props to the acting companies, and to ensure a continuing round of music, plays, masques, interludes, athletic competitions, and parlor games. His position soon gave Cawarden power of total censorship of any material considered for presentation before the queen.

In 1581, Elizabeth confirmed the extent of the master's powers in a royal patent to the new incumbent, Edmund Tilney, extending his control to the public theater. Armed with this, Tilney added to his jurisdiction, and that of his successors, by the licensing of all theatrical performances and the public buildings in which they were played. His power made it virtually impossible for any form of popular amusement to be presented without approval and permission. One went to the master of Revels for a license to show such disparate diversions as "feats of discharging of a gun; an Italian showing a musical organ with divers strange and rare motions; tumbling, rope dancing, legerdemain and dancing horses."

In time, he added the authorization of small books and broadside street ballads, printed on one side only. A hundred years later, control of the sale of small books and ballads had become so lucrative a privilege that it was auctioned off to the highest bidder by the master, "according to the old custom," as a notice in the *London Gazette* of April 13, 1682, testifies.

# CHAPTER 3

# English Musical Theater

The roots of modern American musical theater, the stage for *The Black Crook, Little Johnny Jones, Showboat, Oklahoma!, My Fair Lady, Hair,* and *A Chorus Line,* grew deep, springing from the twelfth century, when laymen began to play the role of priest in outdoor religious rites. By the use of the simplest forms of storytelling and music, Holy Scripture was interpreted in terms illiterate people could understand. These mini-dramas moved from the chancel to the street and then to the public square. The mysteries and miracles of the Immaculate Conception, the Nativity, the Passion of Christ, His Resurrection and Incarnation, the conflict between God and the Devil, all were depicted on raised platforms, by townspeople in their perception of the clothes worn in far-off Near Eastern lands.

In the fourteenth century, control of the public theater came into the hands of the guilds, craft associations that vied with one another in the splendor of costumes, and the color of presentation. Scenes from the Bible and legends of saints and martyrs were enacted on makeshift outdoor stages during holidays, when the towns were crowded with visitors. From sunrise to twilight, favorite incidents in the entire cycle from Creation to Resurrection were presented in a blend of serene belief and bawdy humor. Exeter built the first theater in the Western world since Roman times, to house these spectacles, and other large towns erected similar but smaller buildings for the same purpose. The earliest mystery plays relied on Latin chants and church music, into which the rhythmic and melodic songs of the people were gradually interpolated. In time, the sacred music and the Latin phrases were replaced with the "by by lullay, lullay," "terri li, terri lo," and "fa la la, laddigo lay" of British folk song. Musicians accompanied singers and performed the necessary special effects—the sound of thunder, the voice of doom, the music of heaven, and the discord of hell. Adam and Eve sang a lament as they were driven out of Paradise, the story of the Nativity ended with a carol, and Noah's neighbors drowned their fears of a flood in drink with appropriate song.

Gradually, this entertainment for the sake of the soul was spiced by the introduction of scenes reflecting everyday life, the foibles of a local personality, the misdeeds of town characters. Professional entertainers took to pouring in during the seasons of holiday; minstrels, acrobats, jugglers, and other itinerant players joined the celebration. To ensure that the plays would maintain good quality, civic authorities issued ordinances and levied fines against the guilds whose member actors were not well-spoken good players.

As the Renaissance burst over Britain, a new form, the "moral interlude," developed. The miracle pageants had gotten larger and larger, eventually involving hundreds of players and cumbersome sets. The moral interlude reduced the number of actors to a half-dozen and made do with no more scenery than could be transported by cart. Playing on the village green or in the courtyard of a country nobleman, the players engaged in short dramatic debates on "Youth and Riches," "Three Laws of Christ," or "The Treachery of Jews."

Popular music returned to the stage with the appointment of William Cornyshe to the official family of Henry VIII as producer of plays, pageants, and interludes. Casting boy members of the Chapel Royal in his presentations, Cornyshe shaped the moral interlude into a theatrical form, employing music and adding comic elements. From 1509 until his death, about fifteen years later, Cornyshe wrote these short plays with music, sometimes ensuring success by interpolating Henry's songs. A manuscript collection of the time bound together thirty-eight pieces by the king with a modest eleven by Cornyshe, proof of the latter's politic judgment of talent in a court often subject to outbreaks of the monarch's quick temper. It is likely that the 1530 *Twenty Songs* contained many that had been used in court interludes.

On Cornyshe's death, John Heywood was put in charge of official entertainment. He had been a member of the Chapel Royal from boyhood, graduating to the rank of court singer and player of the virginals for Henry's personal pleasure. He introduced and refined the device of dialogue leading into song. Stage directions might require that the play "begin with two actors singing a ballad" or that a character "enter with a song."

Heywood was one of the young princess Mary's few friends at court in her youth and spent much time with the half-Spanish, half-English child, ignoring her sister, Bess. This devotion was rewarded when Mary became queen in 1553, giving him his most glorious days. He was often in the queen's company, and, it is said, was called to her deathbed to sing one of the stories with which he had entertained her as a child. Soon after, he fled the country, fearful that Elizabeth would punish him for past errors of social judgment as well as his Catholicism, but his songs lived long after him. In *Otello,* the doomed Desdemona sings a snatch of his "Green Willow."

In 1512, Cornyshe had introduced another theatrical diversion to the British aristocracy, the masque. A chronicler wrote that "on the day of Epiphany at night the King with eleven other were disguised after the manner of Italy, called a *Masque,* a thing not seen before in England, and desired the ladies to dance. Some were content, and some that knew the fashion of it refused, because it was a thing not commonly seen. And after they danced, commoned together as the fashion of masques is.'' Such opportunity to take part in public entertainment, hidden behind a mask, appealed to the ladies of Henry's court, and this new form of theater became a prominent feature of social life, reaching its greatest vogue in the Jacobean period.

The interpolation of the masque into the interlude created a new form, permitting Heywood and his contemporaries to write farce comedies for the professional company of child actor-singers attached to the Chapel Royal. These performers were usually from seven to twelve years of age and precocious beyond their years from proximity to the royal court. Many of them became members of professional acting companies, playing female parts, until it was impossible to disguise their sex, in this age when women were not permitted to appear on stage.

Talented composers and musicians superintended the activities of private and cathedral singing schools, training young boys in the musical arts as part of their elementary education. John Redford, organist and master of the school at St. Paul's, wrote plays for his child actors. Nicholas Udall served in a similar post at Eton and the Westminster Cathedral school. William Hunnis, compiler of the best-selling *Seven Sobs of a Sorrowful Soul for Sin,* was master of the Children of Her Maiesties Chappel. His predecessor, Richard Farrant, had rented rooms in an abandoned London monastery and opened them as the Blackfriars Theatre for the first public appearance of the chapel's children. Until the great public theaters took away its customers, Blackfriars offered popular entertainment, by companies of boys from the chapel and from the cathedrals, in the form of dramatized popularizations of Greek and Roman legends. These companies of children performed plays by almost every important Elizabethan playwright except William Shakespeare, who refers cynically to them in *Othello.*

The wedding of Mary to Philip of Spain in 1554 gave Udall, the new court poet, an opportunity to present his talent in a series of brilliant productions of music, song, dance, and plays. A few years before, while working as a teacher, from which he was plucked to serve the queen, he had written the first five-act play in English. This comedy, *Ralph Roister Doister,* which smelled of Plautus, was borrowed from that Roman writer as a change for his young pupils from the Latin stage work that tradition demanded. Written in verse and set in London, *Ralph* logically made use of popular street songs, sung by the youthful cast to the accompaniment of a group of musicians. Udall fully exploited the device developed by Heywood of dialogue to introduce his songs.

The author of Britain's next important comedy, *Gammer Gurton's Needle,* may have been any one of three Cambridge scholars, for the play was first performed there sometime between 1552 and 1563. It made even more demands for song upon its actors and musicians than Udall's comedy. Old Grandmother Gurton loses her best needle, and the small town in which she lives splits into quarreling factions, accusing each other of the theft, until the missing article is found in the seat of the servant's trousers Gammer had been mending. Musical interludes were played between all acts, and this knockabout farce was enlivened by street songs, among them England's first lasting drinking song, ''I cannot eat but little meat.''

Dance and popular music found their way into British tragedy in a new play by Thomas Sackville and Thomas Norton, *Gorbeduc.* Borrowing the panto-mime from its Italian innovators to serve as an explanatory prologue to each of the five acts, the authors made a practical extension of the experiments in blank verse being tried then by poets, a style of dramaturgy Shakespeare would raise to its most glorious heights.

The well-to-do first-night London audience of lawyers, friends, and law ap-prentices, sitting in a hall at the Inns of Court on January 18, 1562, watched the play begin with the music of viols. "Six wild men" of the cast of student players leaped onstage to the music, dancing and miming an incident tangent to the action. Cornetts, a sort of woodwind carved from animal horns, preceded the second act, their music heralding the setting of a royal court. Murder was anticipated by the mournful song of flutes and hautboys, accompanying a dumb show that began the fourth act as "furies chastise kings and queens who had unnaturally killed their own children." Shakespeare used the same device in *Hamlet,* when the young prince hopes to "catch the conscience of the king" with a pantomimed re-creation of his father's murder. "Tumults, rebellions and arms and civil war" in the prologue to Act Five used the music of fifes and drums.

Such dumb shows were eventually dropped from the scripts of Elizabethan tragedies except for purposes of dramatic appeal or historical authenticity.

Metropolitan sophistication made its way into the music of traveling enter-tainers as original new lyrics, set to popular tunes, were offered for entertain-ment and to stimulate audience reaction. College students, touring the country-side during vacations, performed at country fairs for a ha'penny or more, offering "London mummery."

The leading London public acting companies of Elizabeth's reign were formed out of the many professional performers who made their living prior to 1574 in the yards of the city's largest inns. This form of open-air diversion was pre-sented on Sundays, just after services had ended and Londoners were in a joy-ous state of mind. Trumpet calls summoned people to the open inn yards. There was no admission charge in the early days, but money was collected midway in each performance, generally before a suspenseful scene was to be played. As the vogue for these presentations grew, audiences were charged a penny at the gate and another for entry to the projecting galleries running along the two sides of the yard. The stage was the floor of a large freight wagon, drawn across the far end.

Theater went unlicensed before 1557, when spies of the Catholic bishop of London viewed a comedy staged at the Boar's Head Inn in Aldgate. The entire company of *A Sack Full of News* was jailed for violating one of Queen Mary's edicts against public subversion. Censorship of the stage was tightened, and all playscripts were shown to a commission appointed by the bishop.

Once innkeepers were required to take out licenses for each performance, posting a bond to ensure order, a wicket was set up at the courtyard entrance to collect fees, a portion of which was an early amusement tax levied by the city government for care of the poor. Servants carried food and drink from the kitchen and aleroom, adding to the landlord's profits. Because of the enclosed nature of their construction, inn yards could serve for public theaters in any but the most severe weather. Public safety soon became a consideration for civic regulation, the Council complaining that "sundry slaughters and maimings of the Queen's subjects have happened by ruins of scaffolds, frames and stages, and by engines, weapons and powder used in plays."

To show off their power and their household servants, wealthy noblemen and successful merchants took actors and musicians into their service, dressing them in household uniforms in emulation of their queen. These players supplemented their earnings by taking to the streets of London and the large inn courtyards, to present plays and variety shows. During the early 1570s, the city's actors succeeded in making the London stage the "arena for adultery, vice and wantonness," as its Puritan enemies dubbed it, affording the newly risen Separatist sect an opportunity thunderingly to denounce the stage of British morality, and force the Common Council to renew that censorship of entertainment which had been allowed to drift after Bloody Mary's death.

Six companies of actors received licenses to appear within city limits. Among them were two groups licensed by the queen: Leicester's Men, the oldest organized body of professional actors, and the servants of Lord Howard, who became known as the "Admiral's Men" because their patron had won that rank for his dashing gallantry against the Armada. London's masses now had an opportunity to see what had been the exclusive domain of castles, palaces, great houses, and the halls of universities. The people showed an immediate affection for the actors, a feeling never abandoned during the succeeding four centuries and carried into movie houses when technology enabled the preservation of images on Celluloid.

Since the art form had achieved great public acceptance, it was time for the entrepreneurial system to go into tentative gear. With £660 borrowed from his father-in-law, James Burbage, leading member of Leicester's Men, built the first public theater in England to be devoted to purely secular art. Because he was an actor, he was regarded as shiftless, and only with difficulty did he manage to persuade property owners to give him a twenty-one-year lease on some houses and land between Finsbury Fields and the public road nearby for the purpose of creating a playhouse. The round and roofless building, called "The Theatre," opened in the autumn of 1576. A penny was charged for a place on the ground and two for room under the roofed-over gallery at the sides. A stool was available for an additional penny. All receipts collected at the entrance went into a locked box, part for the landlord, the remainder to be divided among the actors.

There were no refreshment rooms in the new theater, but food and drink were brought in from an adjoining alehouse, built by owners of the property leased to Burbage. Londoners flocked to the new playhouse to view programs of tragedy and comedy, or displays of quarterstaff and cudgel mastery, or combat with broadsword, sword and dagger, or sword and buckler, fought for a prize by masters in the art of self-defense.

Programs were announced by the music of three trumpets and the raising of a flag, a custom borrowed from the popular outdoor sports of bear- and bull-baiting. This gory combat had been introduced to England in the twelfth century by a company of traveling Italians for the amusement of King John, and remained a national passion until the eighteenth century, when an act of Parliament outlawed it. Bears were maintained by the royal house, the cost of providing their keep and training covered by a tax on the people, who were allowed to view the games without charge. Bulls and bears were chained to a post in the center of the arena and worried by a dog, who was held back by the ears until his trainer thought him ready to attack. Many bears were public favorites, and announcement of their appearance brought out groups of fans to cheer them on to victory. Elizabeth was a great fancier of the spectacle and ordered the public playhouses closed on Thursdays, the traditional time for animal baiting, because ''in divers places the players do use to recite their plays to the great hurt and destruction of the game of bear-baiting and such like pastimes which are maintained for her Majesty's pleasure.'' Fireworks and puppet shows were other features on Thursdays at the Bear Garden, an open amphitheater on the Bankside. Elizabeth became fond of these displays of explosives and combustibles after she had been treated to a demonstration during a progress.

In the face of such competitive spectacles, the acting-company managers attempted to prevent boredom by presenting a wide variety of plays. No play was repeated immediately, and new works were shown only once a week throughout the season. A hit was set aside for several years after its initial success. It quickly became impossible to rely only on the output of amateur authors, even those prominent and politically powerful, and professional playwrights found employment in turning out new repertory. A new piece was ordered as its need became obvious, and delivery was expected promptly. As many as five authors worked on a single play, one on each act, dividing the author's fee of five or ten pounds.

Well aware of the power of popular music to attract audiences, managers encouraged its use. Acting companies retained a small staff of musicians, performers on the viols, citterns, bandores, flutes, cornetts, trumpets, drums, fifes, and still-horns, to accompany interpolated songs or to play incidental music. The musicians also served as actors in crowd scenes or in small bit parts. Elizabethan dramatists had to be well versed in the new music as well as in the old favorites. There was continual reference to old hit songs and interpolation of familiar ballad texts. Beaumont and Fletcher, among the most popular late-sixteenth-century dramatists, used over fifty songs in their tragedies and tragicomedies, and demanded actors who could sing and musicians who could act.

Shakespeare was a master of this practice. Every one of his works except *The Comedy of Errors* made use of popular music or featured dancing to popular melodies. Songs could mirror the madness of their singer, as in *Hamlet*, where Ophelia loses her reason and fondles the memory of a time when she was loved. Men sang as they caroused. Maidens learned of the inconstancy of men and the quick march of time from ballads. Lovers sang the praises of their beloved, and the witches awaited their fated rendezvous with Macbeth to the "additional beauty" of song.

Often his songs were new arrangements of ballads grown old with familiarity, as with Desdemona's willow song. *The Merry Wives of Windsor* is studded with references to "Greensleeves." The Bard puns upon the old tune "Light o' Love" in both *The Two Gentlemen of Verona* and *Much Ado About Nothing*, and in *The Merchant of Venice* declares his love affair with music:

> The man that hath no music in himself,
> Nor is not moved with concord of sweet sounds,
> Is fit for treasons, stratagems and spoils.
> The motions of his spirit are dull night
> And his affections dark as Erebus.

The most successful of the early rapprochements with the songs of the street made by Elizabethan managers and producers was the jigg, a short play concluding every performance. These were usually bawdy farces sung to a popular tune, and they took advantage of every new piece of slang and every new fad, all in a style that forced the ladies who stayed after the featured play to wear masks to hide their identity. Only a few of the jiggs were printed in broadside form, since their authors knew, as did playwrights and managers, that circulation of dialogue staled audience response.

In Richard Tarleton and his successor, Will Kemp, audiences found clowns of such consummate ability that they would roar their approval at the players' first appearance. Tarleton specialized in comic roles, the grave-digger in *Hamlet*, and Bottom, the weaver, in *A Midsummer Night's Dream*. In hayseed's clothing, big nose, and scrawny beard, he also starred in jiggs.

When outbreaks of plague closed London's theaters from 1592 until 1594, many actors went abroad in search of work, taking along the jiggs and popular ballads that had won them fame. In Holland, Germany, and the Scandinavian countries, these sung comedies proved especially popular, in time leading to the singspiels of Hiller and Mozart. During the Jacobean and early Stuart periods, the English jigg became such a favorite that writers of sophisticated plays complained that the theater was being ruined by the jigg after-piece.

For twenty years, Burbage's theater stood on the wrong side of the Thames, beset by sagging receipts and rising costs. When competition from other acting troupes and new theaters—the Curtain, the Rose, the Swan, erected near the more hospitable red-light district on London's Southside—finally became too great, The Theatre was torn down by his son Richard, a well-known actor, and his brother. Its timbers were carried across the river in 1597 to build the Globe. There Shakespeare won his greatest fame, and from an investment in the theater's construction and operation and other real estate profited more than from all the words he ever put to paper.

By 1600, there were eight public and private theaters in London, one of them, the Swan, holding 3,000 people, and another, the Rose, boasting England's first enclosed stage. The private theaters were built in large rooms of residential mansions, where small, elite audiences sat to watch, in artificial light, stage presentations by the choirboys of the Chapel Royal and St. Paul's. These youngsters danced and sang in plays mirroring the sophisticated tastes of the fashionable world watching them. The most popular creator of these stage pieces was John Lyly, who championed alliteration, mythological allusion, and sharp contrast in writing in the English language. Fortunately, Elizabeth continually rejected his application for the post of Revels master. Had she not, Shakespeare might have spent his life rewriting plays to please that master of euphuism. But the English audiences that brought the madrigal into vogue loved Lyly and his style of writing and the hour-long concerts before the plays. A visiting German who was taken to Blackfriars wrote in 1602: "For a whole hour preceding the play one listens to a delightful entertainment on organ, lutes, pandorins, mandolins, violins and flutes, as on the present occasion, indeed, when a boy *voce cum tremulo* sang so charmingly to the accompaniment of a bass-viol that unless possibly the Nuns of Milan may have exceeded him, we had not heard his equal on our journey." Such concerts were to become commonplace in theaters where there was yet no orchestra pit or any curtain or true scenery of any kind. Until the 1667 production of Shakespeare's *Tempest,* altered to suit that day's tastes, theater musicians sat or stood wherever it suited the management. In one playhouse they sat in a back room, going on stage only when the play called for them to sound a flourish of trumpets or a roll of drums to bring on an army, to play melancholy music on the lute for a maid gone mad with love, to support bumpkin villains tampering with the magic of midsummer's night, or to prepare an audience for the ghostly presence of Hamlet's father. In their room backstage, they played "act-time" music, between the acts.

Performances began after the third time a musician came to the front of the curtainless stage playing upon sackbut or trumpet to prepare the audience for the spoken prologue. Music served to indicate changes in location and the passage of time. As the art of ensemble playing was formalized, the musicians were formed into a consort, often broken into combinations of various instruments. Theater musicians found very practical the publication of arrangements of contemporary music, based on European dance music, in part books and "setts" or "lessons," edited by Thomas Morley and Anthony Holborne. These pleasant galliards, allemandes, and solemn dirges and airs were ideal to keep audiences from growing too restive between the acts.

The Elizabethan Briton had an extraordinary outlet for his emotions and sensibilities in the popular music he adored. London dramatists and theatrical managers perceived this and used such music to bring variety and color to the stage. Some used as many as seventeen songs in a single play; a few hesitated, regarding the practice as condescending to the vulgar tastes of the common horde. Still, the theatrical repertory enjoyed lyrics of great beauty and of naïve charm that demand a place among the riches of both our literature and our music.

# CHAPTER 4

# The Music of God's Englishmen

They stood in a sixth-century Roman slave pen, the first Englishmen the young priest Gregory ever saw, with their "white skin and comely countenance and hair of excellent beauty." Asking what they were called, he was told they were Angles from an island off Europe above France. Whereupon, the flag-waving British historian Bede the Venerable later wrote, he said, "Well were they so called, for they have an angel's face, and it is mete that such men were inheritors with the angels in Heaven." When he was elected pope in A.D. 590, Gregory sent a party of missionaries to bring them word of the true Christ. A group of forty monks landed in Kent in 597 and fascinated the pagan Britons with the painted portrait of Christ they carried before them and the Latin litany they chanted "for the eternal salvation of themselves and those for whose sake they had landed."

The local king, Ethelbert, welcomed them and gave food and a base of operations in his chief city, Canterbury. Persuaded to do so by his French Christian wife, the king adopted the new faith, in the company of large numbers of his subjects. Augustine, chief monk of the papal mission, was named first archbishop of Canterbury and there established the capital city of the Christian church in England.

Pope Gregory remained fond of his "angels," permitting them to christen old pagan temples as churches and to transform the ancient custom of sacrificing oxen to the gods into "killing them to the refreshing of themselves in the praise of God." Such a pragmatic use of established belief and comfortable superstition did much to attract other tribes to the new religion, and when nobles and landowners learned they could secure tax abatement by founding monasteries and convents on their property, total evangelization was assured. Talented young people were sent to Rome to learn the art of singing, and on their return were placed in charge of choirs in the larger churches, which sang in both Latin and the vernacular. By the tenth century, the Roman Catholic church had become a major English political, social, and landowning power, educating the young, fostering the arts, supporting the poor, and was thus a dominant force in running the state.

During the first several centuries after the establishment of Christianity in Rome, the litany was sung in Greek. Only after Pope Celestine I, in the early 400's, ordered formation of large congregational choirs of men and women to sing in imitation of the heavenly choruses of angels and saints, alternating leading parts of psalms and celestial hymns of praise, was the Christian world's major language, Latin, substituted for Greek. One fifth-century future saint complained that "there are towns where one can enjoy all sorts of histrionic spectacles from morning to night. And, we must admit, the more people hear lascivious and pernicious songs, which raise in their souls impure and voluptuous desires, the more they want to hear." Musical instruments were forbidden, for did they not "make men behave like pagans rather than Christians?" Clement of Alexandria asked, voicing the church's policy. The tuba, drum, and flute, "which are liked by those who prepare for war," were unwelcome, but church fathers saw worth in the noble lute, lyre, and harp, instruments associated with the heavenly choir. Reform swept religious music in the early centuries after Christ, to rid it of those vulgar traces that made it appealing to worshipers. This paved the way for Gregorian chant, named for Pope Gregory I, who did much to codify church music. Choirs were directed to sing the same notes, the voices of boys and women an octave higher than those of men, a method known as "plain song," as distinguished from florid song and its counterpoint, which had permeated church music.

The central focus of Catholic service remained the mass, the music for which was originally sung by all celebrants. As music became more complex, participation by the entire congregation was ended, and "canonical choristers" sang the responses to the ministrant's chants, and the psalms, hymns, and all other music of the various services.

Only after the eleventh-century development of musical notation into a system resembling the contemporary language of music were composers provided with the means to write, preserve, and transmit their music, and performers with an opportunity to "hear" it with their eyes, to learn to sing it on sight. In 1040, monks revived the ancient Greek system of naming notes by letters, and an Italian Benedictine brother, Guido d'Arezzo, earned the statue still standing in his hometown public square, which heralds him as "inventor musicae," inventor of music. He took, for his system, the first syllables of each half-line in a hymn to John the Baptist:

> UT queant laxis REsonare fibris,
> MIra gestorum FAmuli tuorum,
> SOlve polluti LAbii reatum,
> SAncte JOannes.

*Ut* continued in use as the first note in this method, called "solmization" until it was changed in the middle of the seventeenth century to the more singable *do*. However, the British had already revised his syllables to the more seemly *fa, so, la, fa, so, la, mi,* the "fasola" system, which was taken to the Ameri-

cas by the earliest colonists, and still persists, particularly in small pockets of
the South, where it is the root base of the popular religious shape-note tradition.

The conventional two-line stave used a red line to indicate the F note and
one in yellow and green to represent C. Some innnovator, perhaps the choir-
trainer Guido himself, added two lines; a fifth was added in the following century. Guido and his fellow music teachers were able quickly to transmit to their
eleventh-century pupils what had previously taken hours of patient repetition.
The system used to measure the duration of notes was first detailed in the treatise *Ars Cantus Mensurabilis,* by a French alchemist, astrologer, priest, and
magician, Franco, of Cologne, about 1060. It fixed the exact value, in place of
the fluid time length of earlier music.

The new methodology permitted composers to create polyphonic music, which
asked soloists and performers to sing or play different but harmonizing strains,
and to expect the result to resemble roughly what they had written. Fortunately,
their work found receptivity among sophisticated popes, cardinals, and bishops,
the most important patrons of the newest things in art and letters. Extending
the boundaries of their discipline further, twelfth- and thirteenth-century musicians evolved the motet (from the French *mot,* word), in which voices sang a
complex interlacing of individual lines.

Inevitably, voices rose against these changes in music. Pope John XXII in
1324 complained about modern music and what he called the disorganized fashion
in which composers "chopped up the melodies . . . so that these rush around
ceaselessly, intoxicating the ear without quieting it and disturbing devotion instead of evoking it." Once started, revolutions rarely halt in their tracks, and
these remarkable changes in religious music made their way to England, where
the people were soon observed at worship singing "in many many manners and
many rites."

By Tudor times, British religious music had been fixed in content and com-
prised the Latin motet and mass, the Latin anthem and response. These were
sung by trained choirs, accompanied by large pipe organs, cymbals and musical
instruments. The great organ at Winchester Cathedral, installed in the tenth
century, was powered by "seven strong men laboring with their arms to drive
the wind up with all its strength that the full-bosomed box may speak with its
four hundred pipes which the hands of the organist govern," encased in heavy
gloves in order to manipulate the wide and unwieldly keyboards.

Early in the thirteenth century, the diocese of Sarum created a native Catholic liturgy, the Use of Sarum, or Sarum Rite. The city was slowly destroyed,
and the bishopric was transferred to nearby New Sarum, now Salisbury. There
a cathedral was erected between 1220 and 1260 with the tallest spire in England. The Sarum Rite continued to be the accepted mode of service for most
English Catholics until advisers to the teen-age King Edward VI in 1549 banned
it as the official order of service for the nation and replaced it with the first
*Book of Common Prayer.*

Musical folk elements had been present in Christian religious music from the
start, a source of constant vexation to church authorities, who set about period-

ically to obliterate the use of the simplest language and music, which did so much to attract the masses to the service of a Christian God. In Britain the most tenacious of these were the carols, nonliturgical songs, which Percy Dearmer, in the *Oxford Book of Carols,* describes as containing "a religious impulse . . . simple, hilarious, popular and modern." This body of "pop religioso" music, as the twentieth-century popular music-trade press would call it, was brought to England in 1224 by followers of Saint Francis of Assisi. It became the progenitor of poetical hymns in the English language and of the stream of white popular gospel music that lives in the hymns of Isaac Watts, the Wesley brothers, and their disciples, in the nineteenth-century gospel hymns of Ira Sankey and Dwight Moody, blind Fanny Crosby and Sir Arthur Sullivan, in the work of Homer Rodeheaver, and in the revivalist songs of the 1920s, and exists today in creations of figures commemorated in gospel music's own Hall of Fame, in Nashville, Tennessee.

The word *carol,* dictionaries remind, is from the Middle English *carol, carole,* a dance or round in a ring accompanied by singing, from the Old French *carole,* this in turn from *choraules, choraula,* a flute player who accompanied choral dances, from the Greek *choraules,* the *khoros,* a ring dance.

The small band of Franciscans—they called themselves *fratres,* being brothers rather than priests—who brought Francis's gospel of poverty and divine ignorance to Britain, also carried techniques of religious instruction their founder had developed to spread his message. Francis recognized the appeal of popular verse, in the simplest language, which when set to familiar secular tunes would do more to attract the ignorant than the best-constructed sermons from Rome. His poems were the first popular hymns, mating religious verse to secular music, converting the devil's tunes to God's purpose.

"What are the servants of God if not his minstrels," Francis asked, "who ought to stir and incite the hearts of men to spiritual joy?" Men's hearts were indeed stirred and made glad as he and his followers moved through thirteenth-century Italy into Central Europe, France, and Spain, living and teaching out of doors, usurping the traditionally exclusive privilege of bishops to preach the Word. Long made indifferent to Christianity by the use of religion by church and state to drive men into battle and death in the name of God, medieval Europeans found their faith restored by Francis's message. He and his simple followers probed men's souls to strike lurking racial memory, in which hid the pagan past. In Britain, as they had done on the Continent, the Franciscans seized upon relics of old native myths and celebrations for the songs they created. The shortest day of the year, so near to the birthday of Christ, inspired many of their carols. Easter, in the midst of the ancient festivals of ground-turning and planting, received its name from the old goddess of spring, Eastre. Midsummer's Night, harvest time, and other celebration days were inspiration for their songs, which had uniform stanzas and a refrain or chorus. Though these were chiefly religious, occasionally they had two sets of lyrics. It has been estimated that five of every half-dozen carols were religious in content, the sixth being intransigently secular, ribald or rowdy.

When the church permitted dramatization of Bible stories, performed by members of the trade guilds during thirteenth-century celebrations of holy days, carols were introduced into this form of popular entertainment. They served first as filler between the short plays. Singers with portable organs strapped to their bodies paraded about the stage, playing and singing favorite carols, in which the audience joined lustily. In time, carols serving to move the story line forward were incorporated into scripts. Wynkyn de Worde was the first to publish an English carol, but only after almost 500 had been collected in a handwritten manuscript issued in 1492, a quarter of them credited to James Rymer. Worde's 1521 publication "The Boar's Head Carol" is still sung by Oxford students during the Christmas season.

The first *Book of Common Prayer,* issued to replace Roman Catholic music and Latin texts, provided composers and poets with the form of meter and language in which they were permitted to write English liturgical selections. A few papist rituals were retained, but one new provision was very specific: "for every syllable a note, so that it may be sung distinctly and devoutly." From the first, the new music was sung to organ accompaniment or that of a chest of viols, a set usually kept in a chest. Another charge called for complete public reading of the entire Book of the Psalms of David during the course of a month. Confronted with this order but deprived of the use of those traditional melodies to which the Psalms had long been sung, the Anglican clergy was confused by the variety of new musical settings and often awkward translations.

Once the Reformation was fact, former Catholics looked for new liturgies to take the place of those discarded. Martin Luther, energizer of the rebellion against the papacy, preserved far more of the standard tradition than did other theological radicals. He permitted translation of old Latin hymns and wrote many of his own, settling these to German folk tunes he had known since childhood. His musical liberalism was unique among his contemporaries. He wrote:

> It is not singular and admirable that one can sing a simple tune, while three, four or five other voices, singing along, envelop the simple tune with exultation, playing and leaping around and embellishing it wonderfully through craftsmanship as if they were leading a celestial dance, meeting and embracing each other amiably and cordially. Those who have a little understanding of this art and are moved by it, must express great admiration and come to the conclusion that there is hardly a more unusual thing than such a song adorned with several voices.

Had the British Puritans been inspired to devotion by someone other than John Calvin, the father of French Protestantism, English and American music, both secular and popular, might have taken an entirely different turn. Calvin tolerated music, for "properly practised it affords a recreation," but, he cautioned, "it also leads to voluptuousness." He urged his adherants, therefore, to "take good care that it does not furnish the occasion for dropping the reins to dissoluteness or for causing us to become effiminate in disorderly delights." Puritan America was guided by that stricture for more than a century.

Calvin, a most unseemly ally to Henry VIII in fighting Rome, went into exile from France in the 1530s, eventually finding a home in Geneva, a city already old when Julius Caesar captured it years before Christ. Never deviating from his original concept of the austere simplicity of ritual, he held out for unaffected group singing of the Psalms, unaccompanied and in unison. He did permit his coreligionists to sing contemporary polyphonic music in their homes, though he preferred that they confine themselves to the Psalms.

In 1541, Calvin approved the first of a series of Geneva psalters for his Huguenot Reformed Church members. The Huguenot poet Clément Marot had first translated Hebrew texts into French, a work continued on his death by Théodore de Bèze, or Beza, for which Loys Bourgeois composed most of the 125 single-line tunes approved of by Calvin personally. Only after completing a jail term for rewriting religious music "without leave" and then promising never to do so again did Bourgeois find employment working for the Geneva city council. The best known of his tunes is the popularization of the Dutch melody known as "The Old Hundredth," to which the Doxology is still often sung. A more sophisticated composer, Claude Goudimel, took over from Bourgeois and in 1565 published a complete psalter with chordal harmonizations for groupsinging worship. The chief appeal of this series of influential Genevan church songbooks—more than 100 French editions were printed—was a simplicity lending itself admirably to untutored congregational singing, and resolving some of the confusion following deletion of familiar Catholic melodies in England.

Those English Protestants who fled to escape Queen Mary's persecution, from 1554 to 1558, were prompted by the Calvin books to publish, in Geneva in 1556, their own *One Hundred and Fifty Psalms of David in English*. Once Elizabeth's coronation took place, they returned home, bringing with them the new psalter and its melodies from Geneva and Protestant Europe, which have persisted in Protestant hymnals to the present.

Elizabeth confronted a situation that had her people split between the old faith and the new religion. Two-thirds of them remained faithful to the pope; the remainder practiced her father's form of popeless Catholicism. London and the south were centers of the new Anglican church; other regions remained staunchly Roman. Within the year, she abolished the mass, declared Anglo-Saxon English the only language suitable for worship, and made herself supreme governor of England in matters temporal and ecclesiastical. A national shift to Anglicanism had not developed, and the queen called on her bishops to adapt to English form the best-loved Roman rituals and on English poets and musicians to develop new liturgical music and song.

Though many Protestants were delighted by the vigor of the royal campaign against popery, they were offended by the dogma being applied to persuade people to conversion. They could find no passage in the bible countenancing the leavening of their beliefs by retention of Roman trappings and Latin mummery, no verse that sanctioned the state's authority over the new church. They intended to pursue no way of life other than "Godly living." Inculcated with Calvin's joyless theology, returning Marian refugees brought the inflexible conviction that the Church of England had fallen upon evil ways and must be purified of all papist notions and rid of any theology that could not be substantiated word for word in the Testament.

The queen found pleasure in rising public opinion against these narrow-minded radicals who threatened the progress of Britain's Anglicanization. By 1564, they were being called ''Puritans,'' as a term of derision, for their seemingly paranoiac fixation on purification of the church. The most determined of them proudly adopted the would-be insulting appellation. Elizabeth endured their complaints, for they were as buzzing flies compared to the Spanish-financed native-born papist plotters threatening the nation's very being. She was able to foil most Catholic conspiracies and sent sixty-one priests and forty-nine laymen to the scaffold. Her predecessor, Mary, had been far more bloodthirsty, putting 300 contentious Protestant martyrs to death by fire, hanging, and quartering.

Patient though she may have appeared, the queen saw in the Puritans a challenge to her authority and to the principle of absolute monarchy upon which her tentative hold on power depended. Their struggle to effect self-government in matters of religion would inevitably lead to self-determination in affairs of state. Reluctantly, she permitted independent churches to function. Underground printing presses added Puritan-inspired tracts to the spew of Catholic pamphlets attacking her and the new canons. The government's determination to establish religious conformity incited Puritans to increasing opposition. The most severe of these nonconformists, the Separatists, moved to Holland, where they established new congregations and waited for the day when they and their children would find a place where their concept of separation of church and state would dominate.

The Puritans who remained in Britain, ancestors of the Presbyterians, were, though militant, less radical. Although they appeared reconciled to things as they were, they prayed for a monarch more friendly, who would give them positions of power within the national government. Among men of such mixed loyalty to God and crown was John Stubbs, who, when his right hand was cut off for writing seditious Puritan pamphlets, used the other to doff his hat and cry, ''God save the Queen!''

By 1590, all of Britain's churches were Protestant, forcing recusant Catholics to worship in cellars or caves in fear of their lives, expecting to become Roman martyrs. Three dozen churches, chapels, and cathedrals whose pipe organs and decorations had not been removed in the mad rush during the Reformation's early years to eradicate anything smacking of popery became the showcases of the Anglican church, pulsing with the pomp so pleasing to the church's supreme governor. Boy choristers sang treble parts and gentlemen of the Chapel Royal sang the other voices in newly created Episcopalian litany. The master of boys was paid money for food, drink, and keep, providing his young charges in return with ''convenient meat, drink, lodging, washing, barbering, apparel and other necessities.'' He was also responsible for selection of appropriate and pleasing music for each service. The religious choral music written by the Chapel's gentlemen has been in continuous use since. Thomas Tallis, John Mundy, Christopher Tye, and Thomas Cawston, best-known composers of the first Anglican music, had begun by rewriting Catholic liturgy before offering music of their own composition. The second generation, including William Byrd the ''Shakespeare of British Music,'' Thomas Morley, Thomas Weekles, and Orlando Gibbons, supported themselves as church organists and court musicians while creating major pieces of religious and art music.

In the great cathedrals, massive organs were supported by music of sackbuts, viols, and recorders. The poorer churches, generally away from metropolitan areas, had neither choir nor musical instruments. Though there was printed singing instructions—the *Book of Psalms*—not all Protestants were literate, nor were all clergymen trained in music. Generally, the parish clerk would name the psalm, set the pitch, and chant each line as it was to be sung, a practice known as "lining out." A diarist wrote in the 1580s:

> The people everywhere are exceedingly inclined to the better part. Ecclesiastical and popular music have very greatly helped it on. For, as soon as they had once commenced singing in public, in one little church in London, immediately not only in the neighboring churches, but even far distant cities, began to vie with each other in the same practice. You may sometimes see at St. Paul's Cross, after the sermon, six thousand persons, old men, boys, girls, singing and praising God together. This sadly annoys the mass-priests and the devil. For they perceive that by these means the sacred discourses sink more deeply into the minds of men, and that their kingdom is weakened and shaken at almost every note.

As Tudor Britons set their native echoes flying, whether they knelt before God in a grand cathedral or in a mossy country chapel, the Puritans grew more determined to make some change. The joy with which David's book was sung to the strains of foreign popular music eventually goaded them to action. All but the most liberal dissenters were persuaded that the Protestant church needed to cleanse itself of these unseemly last remnants of the pope. They asserted that the queen's hand-picked archbishop of Canterbury and his assistants had gleaned the *Book of Common Prayer* out of what they insisted was "that popish dunghill, the Mass Book." Opposing the queen's self-declared sovereignty over their faith, they now determined to govern their own churches and establish their own rites and service.

The first Puritan "presbytery" was established in 1572, a local church whose authority and government were shared jointly by minister and lay members. The movement began to grow, until London eventually became a Puritan city, and the House of Commons a Puritan stronghold. Though she had been able to cope with a Catholic majority when she took the throne, Elizabeth found this single-minded band of religious and social zealots too strong for even her political genius. Her advisers resorted to the guild of book printers and publishers, the Stationers' Company, empowered by Philip and Mary to ferret out seditious writings and to destroy presses and type from which came attacks on royal prerogatives. The House of Lords rammed through legislation decreeing that anyone who continued to question Her Majesty's authority had a simple choice if determined not to conform to the law: prison or exile.

A group of the most obdurate Puritans opted for exile. These Separatists, who moved abroad to wait in Dutch cities, grew alarmed as their children began to forget their British heritage and assimilate the foreign culture around them.

Daily, they prayed to their personal God to resolve the problem by taking Elizabeth to His bosom and replacing her with a more amenable monarch.

Those Puritans who remained in England were equally patient, marshaling their growing political strength to increase control of Parliament, meanwhile speculating on the ability of Catholic Mary Stuart's Protestant son, James of Scotland, to govern their country once he succeeded the queen. But they discerned in him neither authority nor divinity and feared his reign would bring back the Catholicism they so despised. Those anticipating the worst planned to find new homes outside Britain.

# CHAPTER 5

# The Business
# of Music Publishing

The invention, around 1450, of artificial writing by means of movable type was the first of a series of technological innovations that created the contemporary music business. It came at a time when public interest made it mandatory and the demands of progress made it inevitable.

Until the thirteenth century, only scholars, the clergy, some international businessmen and government officials, and a few of the nobility could read. Duplication of the English word was, like education, in the domain of the Christian Catholic church. Cloistered in monasteries or the libraries of papal princes, monks made beautiful copies on vellum or parchment of those classic and antique writings permitted by their superiors to remain in circulation, or reproduced new works grounded in acceptable theology and philosophy. These scribes worked slowly, with quills, reed pens, and colored inks. It took a year to duplicate the Latin Bible, which, therefore, only a small minority of English-speaking Britons could afford.

Secular music was circulated by its creators in manuscript, and most of it fell apart or disappeared. Little is known of the complete character of nonreligious music prior to the Renaissance and the age of entrepreneurial printing, and that history has been reconstructed chiefly from those of its popular elements borrowed by religion or vested in folk music. Its image will never be limned fully. The mass duplication on demand that would have preserved this body of our cultural past was impossible before Gutenberg's invention. After it, movable type was used to duplicate music, even before the use of wood blocks or metal plates.

Early religious music has been preserved by tradition and in those magnificent old manuscript books and scrolls found in museums, written in so permanent an ink that its blackness has endured through the centuries. Ornamented with beautifully designed initial letters, with gold and silver used freely, these pages are a miracle of wonder. They are usually very large, with bold letters, big enough to read from a distance. When placed on a support in front of a large cathedral choir, a single copy served many eyes. Smaller books were copied for use by choirmasters, who studied them and then taught their pupils words and music by rote.

With the growth of universities, the need for books increased, a new sort of copyist made his appearance, ready to duplicate textbooks for use by professors and students. Thirteenth-century Oxford and its 3,000 students swelled demand for secular books, as did the newly formed university at Cambridge. By mid-century, a new trade in books copied by hand—law texts and the classics—was flourishing in the two university towns and in London, the center of government and the legal system. The stationer, who derived his name from the fact that his place of business, shop or stall, was fixed in one location, became the middleman in this process. He took orders for copies of books or lent them out of his own stock to be transcribed by his customers. A number of craftsmen worked for him: the writer of the text letter, a scribe, or scrivener, who made the copies; the parchminer, who turned the skin and tissues of animals into parchment and vellum; the limner, who illustrated or illuminated the pages; and the bookbinder, who bound the final set of sheets into a book.

No commodity could be sold in fourteenth-century London except by members of a trade guild. Consequently, stationers and their workmen formed separate associations of people engaged in the supporting crafts. The number of people engaged in the book trade swelled, but it never matched that of France, whose two major university cities alone supported 10,000 copyists.

In the late fourteenth century, a new and inexpensive oily black ink went on the market, and a linen paper made from castoff clothing was manufactured by French and Italian paper mills. The ready availability of these basic staples led to the mass duplication of sheets of words and illustrations, cut into wooden or metal plates.

Johann Gutenberg, born in Mainz, around 1400, was a printer who used this new technology. Two years after he became a citizen of Mainz, in 1448, he borrowed money from a local goldsmith, with his press as collateral, to develop new tools and methods for printing words on paper. Like many Renaissance innovations, printing with separate and movable characters had been well known to East Asians for centuries. Twelfth- and thirteenth-century Chinese and Koreans worked with metal and wooden ideographs to print books. The method was so logical that it may be wondered why it was not discovered by a European much earlier.

Gutenberg began with wood, whittling out each letter in reverse, so that it would appear correctly on the paper, and then fashioned metal cutting punches with raised letters, which were struck against a metal mold. An alloy of lead, tin, and antimony was heated to make it molten and poured into the matrix to form separate individual characters. Next Gutenberg made a type form that was movable, allowing it to be covered with ink and pushed back and forth under an adjustable plate supporting the paper on which the impression was made. Finally, he perfected a moving press, which produced as many impressions as one had ink and paper for.

Gutenberg's first book, the 1456 Bible, contained 1,282 pages of double-

columned type. A few years after its publication, the town of Mainz was pillaged by invading armies, and the printing industry, which had formed around
Gutenberg's shop, was dispersed into France and Italy, bringing the light of
discovery with them. Gutenberg died in 1468, a victim of the financial setbacks
that had plagued him all his life.

The cultural and technological revolution he had set off burst into full blos-
som after his death. Copyists and limners found themselves without work in
the new mass market. A handful of the church's most perceptive thinkers were
soon aware that questioning of theological infallibility would inevitably follow
mass distribution of the printed Word. Statesmen perceived that the combination of ink, paper, and type might soon turn notions into ideas, as half of Europe became avid readers of books. Control of the duplicating process had moved
from the hands of the church into those of the entrepreneur. Literature was becoming secular to meet the demands of its new audience, and music, too, would
soon be laicized as its principal patron, the church, was replaced by the public
consumer.

One of Gutenberg's presses and movable type were sent to Britain by William Caxton, who needed the equipment to satisfy the demands of friends for
copies of his translations of French romantic literature, made as a hobby. The
strain of copying them out by hand had caused his eyes to dim. After marveling
at the work of a printer's shop in Bruges, where he was in the cloth-trading
business for more than two decades, he paid to learn the craft of printing in
Cologne. Within a few years he was qualified to set up his own operation, and
issued English translations for the European trade, copies of which he sent to
London stationers. In 1475, he rented a shop inside Westminster Abbey and set
up his press and equipment to become a full-time book publisher. On December 31, 1476, he produced the first piece of datable printing in England. By the
time of his death in 1491, he had printed ninety-eight books, among them Thomas
Malory's *Le Morte d'Arthur,* Geoffrey Chaucer's *Canterbury Tales,* and poetry
by John Lydgate, who also wrote highly regarded ballads.

Following Caxton's death, the shop was taken over by Wynkyn de Worde,
an Alsation typesetter and proofreader who had been brought to London to train
the staff, most of whom were European, when Caxton set up the shop. In 1484,
government policy was to encourage the importation of foreign printing craftsmen in order to build up the stationers' trade and encourage learning. A half
century later, when the book business was flourishing, influential sellers and
printers prevailed upon the king's advisers to exclude foreign competition by a
strict quota on immigration of printers and typesetters, permitting native-born
and naturalized printers to secure a monopoly over the British book trade, half
of whose output was of a religious nature.

Worde issued the first book to contain music printed from type, a 1495 edition of the *Polychronicon,* a history of the world to 1360, which Caxton had
brought up to 1460. The book contained an illustration showing eight musical
notes of a Pythagorean consonance. In the first, 1482, edition, Caxton had left
the space for the music open, to be filled in by hand. Disdaining this old-fashioned
method, Words contemplated the alternatives in use abroad, where the first true

musical notation was printed in 1480. Seven years later, wood blocks were used for notes and staff lines. Worde could either stamp or print notes by use of a wooden or metal plate and fill in the lines by hand (it was standard practice to print notes in black ink and lines in red), or reverse the process, writing the notes by hand on printed lines, or use two separate blocks, one for notes, the other for lines. Forced to improvise, he used metal letter type turned to print the square bottoms as diagmond-shaped notes and the thin raised metal lines that served as borders or columnar separations for staff lines. Makeshift though this was, it provided England's first printed music notation.

With little public demand for locally printed music, there was no further activity in this field for several decades. Those who wanted music imported it from the Continent, where the beautiful and sophisticated output of printed secular music made by Ottaviano dei Petrucci, of Venice, around 1500 qualified that craftsman as "the father of music publishing." Only a handful of pieces printed from type had been produced when Petrucci received an exclusive monopoly from Venice for publication of popular and nonreligious music. A market for it had surfaced because of improvement in design, quality, and playability of those instruments most closely associated with popular music—lute, viols, harpsichord and its variants, spinet, and virginals. Petrucci's skill as a type cutter, designer, printer, and publisher, coupled with his realistic perception of exactly what music would appeal in the new marketplace, small though it was, emerged in proper time to meet the demand. Using movable metal type of his own making, he lowered the cost of production while sustaining quality. His first publication was a collection of ninety-six popular pieces, four-fifths of them French chansons, a vogue for which was sweeping the sophisticated centers of Europe, and music by Isaac, Obrecht, Ockenheim, and their contemporaries. Between 1504 and 1509, Petrucci published ten artistic books, 600 songs in all, using a triple-impression method: first the staves, then the lyric, and last the notes. With the staff of professional musicians to compile and edit the books, and overcoming the technical difficulties inherent in printing the complicated notation of guitar tablature, Petrucci was the first to publish lute books. These contained popular dance music, precursors of the pavane and galliard that swept the English court during the sixteenth century, when Thomas Morley wrote "next in gravity and goodness is the pavan, a kind of staid music ordained for grave dancing, and most commonly made of three strains, whereof each strain is played or sung twice, a strain they make to contain 8, 12 or 16 semibreves as they list, yet fewer than 8 I have not seen in any pavan . . . after every pavan we usually set a galliard."

His twenty-year Venetian monopoly ended, Petrucci moved into the service of the pope under a patent granted him for publication of Flemish church music approved for use by papal authority. When his final publication appeared, in 1520, this first full-time professional European music publisher could look on a contribution to his trade that had provided more copies of music, to a wider public, than made by virtually all the scriveners, copyists, and composers who had preceded him with their hand-drawn copies.

Petrucci's triple-impression system of music printing was, however, so expensive that few Continental music publishers imitated it, relying instead on the less complicated single or double process. This resulted in products of mixed quality until a more precise technology evolved. Distribution to a market greater than the princes of church and state and their wealthier subjects demanded a less costly system of duplication—the use of movable metal type in a single impression, to produce music and words simultaneously.

In the early years of the sixteenth century, British book publishers sent their work to France, where costs were lower, prices more competitive, and the product as good as that of the best English craftsmen. The London stationer, lawyer, writer, and member of Parliament John Rastell devised an important innovation at almost the same time as the French publisher who is generally credited with the two remaining improvements that shaped the basic form of music publishing to that known for the past 400 years. In the middle 1520s, Pierre Attignant, of Paris, printed each word of a song directly beneath the note to which it was to be sung, at the same time perfecting the process that permitted printing of typeset music from a single impression. Working without any awareness of Attignant's new process, Rastell and the London stationer John Gough published two songs, in about 1525, by means of a single impression. The presumed writer of "Away Mourning" and "Time to Pass with Goodly Sport" was William Cornyshe, Henry VIII's official producer of court entertainment, whose music, including these songs, was interpolated into Rastell's 1515 "moral interlude" *The Four Elements*.

Rastell was a brother-in-law of Sir Thomas More, lord chancellor to Henry VIII. Through this connection, he had access to the highest offices of power and was able to obtain a number of favors. One of these was a printing privilege, the earliest form of protection for published British intellectual property. The growing number of presses owned by that company of printers who were making London their home began to produce surreptitious editions of best-selling texts to meet public demand, cutting into the profits of Rastell and others in the trade. Because only royal action could afford relief, Rastell took his case to the king.

British publishers were late in seeking government protection for their property. Shortly after Caxton introduced the printing press into Britain, Henry's father had licensed the first royal printer, William Faques, to produce statute books, royal proclamations, documents, and other official forms, but gave him no rights in the materials he printed. Faques's successor, Richard Pynson, was the first English publisher to print and sell books of religious music—six missals, processionals, and manuals of the Use of Sarum, the most common Catholic liturgy before the Reformation.

With Pynson, Rastell petitioned for a privilege like those being granted in Europe. Under these, unauthorized printing and the pirating of protected works were forbidden for two to ten years, with a fine ordered for any bootleg copy found or one imported from other countries for local sale. The first British privilege was granted to Pynson in late 1518, covering publication of a sermon in Latin on the recent peace between France and England. No British printer other than Pynson or his assignees could sell or copy that test, and thus the principle of publisher protection for a limited period entered British business and legal practice.

Once Rastell obtained a royal grant, the following notice began to appear in books he issued in 1520:

> Reprinted in London on the south side of Paul's by John Rastell with the privilege of our most sovereign Lord, King Henry VIII, granted to the compiler thereof that no man in this His realm sell none but such as the same copyer maketh printed for the space of two years.

This was soon shortened into "Cum privilegio regali" (with the privilege of the king), assuring the printer of exclusivity under royal protection. Authors had no similar privilege, for printers bought works outright, paying as much as five pounds for a book, less than half that for a pamphlet. Though affirmation of property rights played a part in increasing the flow of textbooks, lawbooks, popular literature, scientific works, and other nonreligious books, only one set of part books of popular music was published in London during the next generation. On October 10, 1530, the collection *Twenty Songs* appeared in London. Like similar books issued by Petrucci and his competitors, the book contained parts for several voices compiled from a number of composers. Struck off metal blocks for staff lines and with notes and words from a handsome type developed in Germany, it contained ten songs for four parts and ten for three, written by William Cornyshe, Robert Fayrfax, Richard Davy, and other members of the King's Musick.

## The Growth of the Stationers' Company

Reformation of the Christian church resulted from the questioning of centuries-held doctrine and the use of the printing press to distribute tracts, pamphlets, and books. When 6,000 copies of an English translation of the New Testament from the original Greek and Latin were smuggled into Britain and distributed to incipient Protestants, authorities seized and burned many, which German Lutheran presses quickly replaced, adding to the flood of schismatical literature pouring into the nation. Government agents were dispatched but failed to either assassinate or kidnap young William Tyndale, the English scholar who was working with Martin Luther on additional texts challenging British Catholicism and King Henry himself.

Parliament issued a number of acts, making possession, circulation, or sale of dissident literature a crime of high treason, punishable by death, but the heresy continued to surface. European texts of any nature were barred from importation without written consent. Six royal proclamations in all, often rewritten by the king in his own hand, were issued during the 1530s affecting printing, publishing, and copyright, as well as popular English ballads.

In 1538, Henry signed the document that first enabled his government to invoke censorship in the guise of licensing printed material, but treasonous, dissenting, or merely irritating publications continued to appear. Acts were issued to suppress "ballads, rymes, and other lewd treatises in the English tongue," and at least one Tudor songwriter, John Hogan, who wrote and sang a political parody of the king's favorite song, "The Hunt Is Up," was prosecuted and barely escaped hanging. In the final year of his reign, Henry issued an order intended to smoke out the mysterious authors of "such English books as contain pernicious and detestable heresies" by requiring that local officials undertake censorship, but few mayors cared to read each new work that appeared. Many printers felt themselves outside these laws, believing them aimed only at works of a religious nature.

It remained for Queen Mary, King Philip, and their advisers finally to delegate enforcement of both old and new acts of censorship to the book publishers. Soon after she came to power in 1553, the Catholic queen signed a proclamation forbidding London's publishers to "print any book, matter, ballad, interlude, process or treatise . . . except they have Her Grace's special license in writing for the same." Censorship grew more rigid, martial law took over, and "anyone found to have any of the said wicked and seditious books shall be reputed and taken for a rebel, and shall without delay be executed for that offense." Then a long-pending application for a royal charter by the stationers' guild gave the state the opportunity to relegate control over printing presses to those with the greatest economic incentive to support and enforce government policies regarding their trade.

In the thirteenth century, the craftsmen engaged in manual duplication of the written word—parchminers, scriveners, limners, and bookbinders—had had separate craft guilds. In 1403, the stationers had joined with them to form a new trade group of all the various artisans involved in the book trade. As the art of printing words from movable type improved, due chiefly to the foreign printers who came to London and trained British apprentices, practitioners of the outmoded and virtually discarded text-writing technology joined other guilds or eventually disappeared. Adding printing presses to their holdings and hiring printers to work for them, members of the stationers' guild soon dominated the book business. Aspiring stationers, often barred from participation, turned to pirating all sorts of material in violation of the privileges that continued to be awarded to the most prominent businessmen book dealers. The various acts of repression of the book trade issued during Henry's reign and enforced in that of Edward winnowed out many of the poorer stationers.

The stationers' guild was anxious to obtain any royal sanction that would maintain the monopolies of its limited membership, and the government was eager for a more efficient method of policing the printing presses. In 1557, both achieved their desires when Mary and Philip issued a royal charter to the Stationers' Company of London. "To satisfy the desire of the Crown for an effective remedy against the publishing of seditious and heretical books," ninety-seven members were given "certain priviliges in addition to the normal rights of a company." These additional powers ensured that only members of the entrenched printing structure would print and sell books, gave them the right of search and seizure of any premises for allegedly pirated or contraband and illegally imported literature, and made fines and imprisonment for three months without trial mandatory for any person whom the company deemed guilty of violation of the law and of their charter. The stationer members were responsible only to the Privy Council.

From the start, the stationers succumbed readily to the Privy Council's demands. A master, two wardens, and a Court of Assistants were elected to govern the company, assign tasks and obligations to members, and mete out punishment for infractions of trade rules and practices. Agents were recruited to seek out and report the printing and sale of seditious books and ballads. Confiscated material was burned in a large fireplace in the kitchen of Stationers' Hall, a building recently purchased in the judicious expectation that the royal charter would be granted. Several persons were executed for violation of the law and of company regulations, and others were imprisoned in the hall's cellars. Publishers of unlicensed ballads were fined fourpence for each copy seized and occasionally were held for a short period in the basement cells.

Members of the Stationers' Company took one copy of each new publication to the hall, and, after paying a fee of fourpence, received in return registration of their ownership of the material, the only form of property protection available to literary works.

Black-letter ballad broadsheets, which sold for a penny in London streets and at printers' stalls, were also required to be registered at Stationers' Hall for the fee of fourpence. From 1557 to 1700, more than 3,000 such registrations were made. These did not include all of the many thousands of those "darling songs of the common people," as Joseph Addison called them. Most were issued by printers denied admission to the company, or were not registered because the fee was considered too high for such ephemera.

Under Queen Mary's order, politically sound and well-connected Catholic stationers were rewarded for their loyalty by the grant of royal monopolies. The system that had been in force since Henry's time continued to indulge and woo major printers and booksellers.

### Religious Music Printing

In his campaign to cleanse the new Church of England of all papist influences, Henry had granted a privilege to Richard Grafton, of London, for the publication and sale of the newly approved English Bible, including the New Testament translation by Tyndale. Presses capable of turning out the large books, with its lavish illustrations, were not available in England, making it necessary for Grafton to send the work to France. While the last sheets were still on the press, officers of the French Catholic Inquisition swooped down on the printing office and confiscated all work that was finished. Fortunately, a few proof copies had been sent to Grafton. After locating some sheets, which had been sold for wrapping paper, and using London presses and working with Dutch typesetters who were unfamiliar with the English language, he eventually brought out an edition of 1,500 copies, at the extremely high cost of £500, more than several hundred thousand dollars in 1980s' currency.

Sales fell below expectation, and the publisher persuaded church authorities to compel every parish to buy one copy and every monastery six. This taught

Grafton and other stationers that state-enforced sales of printed books could make their business viable. Orders from the archbishop of Canterbury, Queen Elizabeth, and, in time, Puritan leaders, requiring that only the Psalms be used during worship and forbidding the singing of any other religious song, made publication of Protestant church music the most profitable aspect of English music publishing for nearly a century.

Grafton brought out seven editions of the new Bible, several service books, and the first edition of the *Book of Common Prayer* with appropriate music, sponsored by Edward VI. He became a wealthy man. When Mary assumed the throne, he was stripped of his monopolies, which were turned over to loyal Catholics.

After reinstalling the Roman order of worship and the Use of Sarum, Mary began reconverting churches and cathedrals to the old religion. Favored London printers issued a number of service manuals and missals in Latin, working with alphabet and letter types made by Flemish and French type cutters. British craftsmen had attempted to duplicate these fine types, but failed, producing at best only crude results and, in the process, winning a shabby international reputation.

For a brief period during Mary's reign, John Day, later a prosperous religious-music book publisher, attempted to work within the new order, even though he was a Protestant. He had been a string maker and then a fishmonger before he apprenticed himself to a London printer. In 1547, he joined William Seres, who handled business matters, while he operated the printing side of their venture. Day was probably responsible for the reintroduction of printed English mensural music, after its first appearance in *Twenty Songs*. The new book, Seres's *Certain Psalms,* selected from "the Psalter of David and drawn into English meter, with notes to every Psalm in four parts," appeared just before young Edward died. It was then promptly suppressed. The new administration evidently sought to woo Day by awarding him the highly profitable patent to publish the *Abcedarium Anglico-Latinum,* required to be used by every grammar-school pupil in the nation. When it was discovered that while he was Seres's partner Day had printed some "naughty" books of Protestant content, for which Seres had a privilege from Edward, both men were thrown into the Tower of London. Day escaped and made his way to Europe, returning only after Elizabeth was crowned.

A splendid prospect for the business of printed music books loomed after Elizabeth issued her first Book of Injunctions to the Anglican clergy. As head of the established church, she directed that a "modern distinct song . . . an Hymn, or such like, to the praise of Almighty God, in the best sort of melody and music that may be conveniently devised, having respect that the sentence of the Hymn may be understood and perceived," be sung during worship.

The *One Hundred and Fifty Psalms of David in English,* brought back by exiles, an apt model of what the queen had asked for, as well as a vision of the large market waiting, stirred the former partners to action. Seres, his patent to publish the catechism restored by Elizabeth, felt that with it he had secured the patent for Psalms with music and determined to issue such a collection based on Calvinist hymnals. He took a completed manuscript to Day's printing office, which had one of London's few stocks of appropriate music type, as well as qualified workmen and proofreaders. The order was filled, but Day evidently withheld the overrun for surreptitious sale. Seeking relief in the Stationers' Court, Seres got satisfaction when Day was fined twelve shillings for breach of patent and chided for shoddy business practices.

Day then went after and received a royal privilege permitting him, as well as Seres, to print Psalms with appropriate music. Seres's patent included rights to print a pocket-sized *Primer,* a book of daily prayers most families purchased, which included little or no music. Day's patent granted a monopoly to publish "such books as [he] hath imprinted, and henceforth shall imprint," which he took to mean books struck off the music type he owned and had been using. The new privilege was good for seven years, and Day immediately capitalized on it by publishing translations by Thomas Sternhold and others of *The Psalms of David.* There were other translations, but Day's publication of the Sternhold made it the standard and best-selling work for centuries before the advent of hymnbooks. A first edition of several thousand copies sold out quickly and was followed by innumerable others to build the financial base for a major book- and music-publishing business. After initial production costs were recouped, all income went directly into Day's purse, Sternhold being dead and his verse free for the taking.

As a student at Oxford, Sternhold had been noted for his poetizing, and as an officer and groom of the king's robes in the court of Henry VIII, he wrote Psalm translations in the meter of popular ballads and sang them in the royal chapel to organ accompaniment. King Edward enjoyed them, too, and encouraged the courtier-poet, who dedicated to him a book of these verses. By the time of his death in 1549, Sternhold had completed thirty-seven of the Psalms. Schoolmaster and parson John Hopkins wrote an additional seven, which he modestly said could "not be compared with Sternhold's exquisite doings." The remaining 106 were translated by others, but all Psalm books of the time and later were generally referred to as the "Sternhold and Hopkins."

The musical settings were borrowed liberally from Loys Bourgeois. These jolly tunes became so popular with churchgoers that they were denounced by traditionalists as "Geneva jiggs." A strict solemnity was grafted onto them only a few decades after they were first used. Equal value was bestowed upon each note, and the tempos were slowed down to the dirgelike rate Puritan dictators of taste considered appropriate in worship. There is a sorry contrast between the Puritans' accepted musical style and the contemporaneous Anglican and secular music of Byrd, Tallis, Morley, Tye, Weelkes, Gibbons, and others. Most of these remained unaffected by the virus of Calvinism and cherished contemporary European or Catholic musical tradition and innovations.

The fourth edition (1562) contained the first verse of each of the Psalms, translated by a dozen contributors, and music for the sixty-five tunes to which they were to be sung. By the end of the sixteenth century, Day and his successors, now veritably perpetual owners of the privilege, had printed seventy-seven editions, usually three a year, all of which enjoyed excellent sales. Most worshipers had these Psalms bound up with the *Book of Common Prayer*, which accompanied them to church. Day's Psalm books usually included a potpourri of religious miscellany, the Ten Commandments, the Lord's Prayer, the *Te Deum*, the *Nunc Dimitas*, a brief introduction to the rudiments of music, and a treatise on psalmody written in the fifth or sixth century. These books were set in small type of two columns to a page, though more elaborate books of sizes varying from pocket to large folio were also to be had.

During the first half century of British music publishing, more copies of Sternhold and Hopkins were sold than of all other music books, secular and religious. More than 600 editions had appeared by the nineteenth century, for the sun never set on the book as Britons took it around the world, along with their ammunition and rum.

Day experimented with various music-printing techniques to make his psalters more attractive and salable to various social and economic classes. He brought out cheap pocket-sized editions printed from inexpensive wooden blocks, reserving his limited stock of fine music type for more expensive editions. For the musically knowing, he issued part books in large and fancy sizes for special occasions or gifts.

In 1572, he produced an edition using solfège music type, explained in a foreword.

> Thou shalt understand (gentle reader) that I have (for the help of those that are desirous to learn to sing) caused a new Print of Note to be made with letters to be joined by every note, whereby thou mayst know how to call every note by his right name so that with a very little diligence (as thou are taught in the Introduction printed heretofore in the Psalms) thou mayst, the more easily by the viewing of these letters come to the knowledge of perfect Solfyng; whereby thou mayst sing the Psalms more speedily and easily. The letters be these. U for Ut, R for Re, M for MI, F for Fa, S for Sol, L for La. Thus where thou seest any letter joined by the note, you may safely call him by his right name, as by these two examples you may the better perceive.

This simple musical notation, designed to encourage reasonably intelligent singers to improve their skills, came into increasing use as the quality of British and, later, American congregational singing fell into decline. Bourgeois had used the same type in a 1560 Geneva publication, and it was from that city Day imported his characters.

Only once did Day venture into the printing of purely secular music, for whose production the composer paid. England's upper classes had developed an affection for visiting Italian and Flemish vocalists, and their madrigals, Neapolitan vilanellas, and *canzonetta*s. The appearance of Alfonso Ferrabosco at Elizabeth's court further spread the gospel of Italian song. Sales of a pirated 1568 printing from wooden plates of an instruction book for the lute, written by the French guitar virtuoso Adrien Le Roi, and a second edition, six years later, testified to the ascendency of the lute as the country's most popular instrument. Connected by marriage to the great Paris publishing house of Ballard, which enjoyed a complete monopoly of French music printing for 200 years, Le Roi influenced English instrumental styles. Gallard also published the earliest music of Orlando di Lasso and (Roland de Lassus) Philippe de Monte, musicians who had studied in Italy and then taken the rich popular music of that nation to the courts of Europe and England, creating the first public awareness of those foreign love songs doted upon by the British upper classes.

In a nationalistic show of native talent, the English musician Thomas Whythorne put together a cross section of original popular music, including carols, love songs, moral songs, street cries, and Psalms, hoping to remind the nation in which foreign music reigned that Britain had a tradition of its own to remember. Day contracted to print *Songs,* a collection of seventy-six, at the composer's own expense. Having visited Italy and "sundry foreign countries," Whythorne had absorbed the new foreign styles and blended them with his own not inconsiderable talents to create this second printed collection of native popular music issued in England. It contained the first printed solo song with instrumental accompaniment, "Buy new broom," based on a London street cry. Whythorne complained bitterly about Day's failure to merchandise the part books, as he had done for the Singing Psalms, but the fact was that London's musical amateurs looked to better printed and more attractive editions imported from Paris. His efforts did bring Whythorne to the attention of the archbishop of Canterbury, whom he then served as master of music, making settings of his employer's Psalm translations. These were published in a volume containing nine melodies by Tallis, one of which is the theme on which Ralph Vaughan Williams created his "Fantasia for String Orchestra."

When John Day died in 1584, his publishing business, resting on a lucrative base of Singing Psalms and the ABC book and the *Little Catechism,* passed into the hands of his son, Richard. A clerk in holy orders, the youth had no interest in commerce and turned over the firm and its royal patents to a syndicate of seventeen stationers, all of them among the guild's ruling hierarchy. Within a few years, these hard-won privileges were owned by the Stationers' Company itself.

William Seres's patent for a book of devotions, the only other major religious book privilege not owned by the crown, fared little better. Having removed priests as mediators between God and man, depriving mortals of that pantheon of saints who interceded with the Holy Trinity on behalf of supplicants, Protestantism took prayer out of the chapel and into the home. For the first time in Christian memory, religious men turned to God on a one-to-one basis for all favors. In their literature, drama, and the speech of their leaders, Englishmen had discovered the glories of their language and began to believe that the more grandiloquently man spoke to God, the better the prospect for achieving a petition. Hence, a collection of the best supplications for each aspiration would provide those who could afford it an advantage. Seres rose to this challenge and began issuing pocket-sized books of private prayers for "gentlemen, landlords, merchants, rich men, poor men, maidens, wives, single men, households and all Christians," as the 1560 first edition proclaims.

The book was an instant best seller, as it was in many subsequent editions. This attracted others, and Seres was soon before the Stationers' Court complaining once more about breach of patent. His presence bore weight, for he had been one of the founding fathers and five times master. Seventeen publishers were cited for abuse of copyright. Seres won forfeit of a shilling for each impression of prayer books made outside his shop, and enjoyed such extra royalties until his death. Then his patents, too, fell under control of the company, after Day had first purchased them.

## The Byrd-Tallis and Morley Monopolies

When Elizabeth assumed the throne, she issued fifty injunctions before she turned her attention to the Stationers' Company. Having been assured by her advisers that all would go well, the bookmen were patient, but things did not come about as they hoped. In November 1559, the grant from Mary and Philip was confirmed, but the royal injunction pointed to the great "abuse in the printers of books, which for covetousness chiefly regard not what they print, so they may have gain, whereby ariseth great disorder by publication of unfruitful, vain and infamous books and papers." New publications would now be licensed by the queen; a High Commission was created to administer books on religion and politics; and a Commission of Causes Ecclesiastical was charged with licensing plays, pamphlets, and ballads, all of which had been "oftentimes printed, wherein regard would be had that nothing therein should be either heretical, seditious or unseemly, for Christian ears." The function of seeking out and destroying offending materials was put in the hands of government personnel, charged with watching potentially offending printing offices and reporting all untoward actions to their superiors.

Most leading stationers were happy to leave the printing of art music to lesser businessmen, finding little commercial advantage in purchasing complicated music type and employing skilled typesetters and proofreaders for a market that appeared to be satisfied with imported publications. Consequently, they paid little attention to an action by the queen in the middle of 1575.

When Thomas Tallis and William Byrd, the two brightest stars of Elizabethan music, found it impossible to maintain their places as gentlemen of the Chapel Royal on the much reduced daily stipend of seven and a half pence plus a shilling for board, they petitioned the queen for more money. Instead, she gave them the royal privilege of printing and selling secular music and importing ruled music paper, for twenty-one years.

Two less likely stationers did not exist in the whole of England. Tallis was approaching seventy, his greatest work behind him. In an age when it was prudent to parade one's Protestantism, he was a closet Catholic, but he managed to survive rapidly shifting official faiths. After the monasteries were closed, he had lost his post as a country choirmaster and organist. In 1540, he got an appointment to Edward's Chapel Royal and became one of the most notable contributors of new Protestant liturgical music. When Mary Tudor came to power, she kept him in her service, honoring him by a grant of income from country real estate. Byrd was extremely talented, even as a child, becoming senior chorister at St. Paul's at twelve and, at twenty, organist for the newly completed great Lincoln Cathedral. He was recruited for the Chapel Royal, where he continued his brilliant work in virtually every sort of contemporary music and shared the post of state organist with Tallis.

The commercial failure of Whythorne's part books and that of an English edition of Lasso's songbooks a few years earlier had also helped to persuade many publishers that the market for printed art music was not worth their attention. Wealthy amateur British musicians generally bought European lutes, viols, and music books, believing that any foreign master and his music were superior to the home-grown product. Neither Tallis nor Byrd liked Day's work in the Whythorne part books, but had found much to admire in the artistic failure of a reprinted edition of music by Lasso produced by the refugee printer Thomas Vautrollier. He had used handsome type imported from France and was a gifted amateur who understood the responsibility of a music typesetter to be accurate. This was reflected in the careful work of his earlier *Brief Introduction to Music,* probably the first scholarly treatise on music translated and printed in English.

Tallis and Byrd exercised their patent for the first time a few months after it was granted, making arrangements with Vautrollier to print their *Cantiones Sacrae,* a group of motets that were religious counterparts of popular songs. A prefatory tribute to native English music rang in the queen's support of their work.

> British music, preparing for battle, saw that she could pursue her course in safety only if the Queen should declare herself her patron, and promised to equal the nine muses in artistry if she could number as her authors those, whom if they would but compose, would astound the people. Therefore, strengthened by the support of so learned a Ruler, she fears no nation's boundaries or censure. Proclaiming Tallis and Byrd her parents, she advances boldly for every voice to sing.

Neither the music book nor the patent made any great stir. British music buyers continued to favor imported music, and the publishing brotherhood saw it as another ill-fated attempt to promote highfalutin music for which no discernible market existed.

Within two years, Tallis and Byrd were back to Elizabeth with their financial woes, complaining that the music-publishing patent had already cost them in excess of 200 marks. Tallis, who had served the Tudors for some forty years, was about to lose his annual income of ninety pounds from the soon-to-expire land lease Mary had granted, and Byrd had been obliged to give up most of his private students because of the requirement that he be in daily attendance at the Chapel, coming thus into "debt and necessity." Although the queen indicated she would do something to help, Tallis and Byrd never again took advantage of the patent.

The distinguished music scholar D. W. Krummel maintains, in *English Music Printing 1552–1700,* a truly distinguished and scholarly contribution to this and any history, that "the object of the patent was to promote fine music and to suppress inferior music—as they knew it—and indirectly to subsidize the patentees through the sale of copies. Byrd and Tallis were recognized as the finest musicians of their day; only in their hands could such a coercive ploy be acceptable. The patent, in sum, was intended mainly to control not music printing but music itself." Had Elizabeth wished to guarantee some additional income to her composers in this manner, however, an order requiring purchase of the book of motets by cathedrals and churches would have sufficed. The sales of Italian popular music in imported editions were evidently flourishing, and the presumably "inferior music" of street ballads was being bought and sold in London and peddled in smaller cities and throughout the countryside, both of them removed from any control Byrd and Tallis could have effected. Krummel adds:

> Byrd and Tallis probably intended not only to sell the [music] paper but also to suggest a copyist as well as the works to be copied, and finally, the best available musicians to perform them. If a demand for many copies of a certain composition was noticed or anticipated, the text could then be printed. In this light, the "music patent" can be viewed as little more than a formal recognition of Byrd and Tallis as the foremost musicians of their day. The powers over the press vested by the grant were incidental.

Again, however, it failed to provide them with the money they were both after.

Byrd's brilliant Catholic music was written out of his own religious beliefs and could not have been heard in public, or performed by any except recusant worshipers. Tallis had come to the virtual end of his creativity. London's Company of Musicians zealously guarded its opportunities for business from the incursion of amateurs who were leaving their crafts and giving themselves wholly to wandering about, nor did it welcome competition from those Westminster musicians who were most familiar with the pair's compositions. It may be that Elizabeth had in mind merely to soothe the feelings of two favored retainers. She could not press another patent, particularly to household servants, and one of them an undeviating papist, in light of the growing furor over monopolies, which were making a handful of stationers wealthy and depriving less well-situated printers of work and income.

Protests had recently been presented to the lord chamberlain at the behest of 175 printers as well as "glass sellers and cutlers sustained by reason of privileges granted to private persons." Though the Singing Psalms patent was not cited, complaints were made about the monopolies in lawbooks, the Bible and Testaments, almanacs, guides to home medicine, Latin school texts, grammars, primers, Day's publications, and other good sellers. Leading stationers, who looked jealously upon these valuable monopolies, joined the petitioners. The battle went on for ten years, pitting ambitious young stationers against holders of royal patents. The unprofitable Byrd-Tallis license to print music books was occasionally mentioned, though it was usually agreed that most printers would not buy music type even if there were no music privilege. Booksellers engaged in the ballad trade had no problem. The most successful of them, Richard Jones, registered as many as a hundred popular broadsides at a time.

An investigating committee was appointed and reported that the wealthiest booksellers were those who had never invested in equipment and letter type, contracting instead with master printers to do the work. As a result, printers barred from membership in the Stationers' Company continued their surreptitious printing, defying regulations and disregarding statutes.

In 1586, the Privy Council issued a new set of drastic rules affecting printing, on which Stationer's Company officials and government advisers collaborated. The company's power was increased, and it received new authority to search and seize without warrant and the right to enforce extended prison terms for violators. The number of master printers, apprentices, and presses was limited, a most serious interdiction, tending further to freeze out newcomers to the trade. The archbishop of Canterbury's approval was now required in addition to registration. These New Decrees of the Star Chamber for Order in Printing, the last to be issued during Elizabeth's reign, determined the course of both the book and the ballad trade for another century.

Despite their enhanced authority, the stationers could not completely control practices being faced by an expanding industry. Paper, usually of a poor quality, and watered-down ink were sold illegally, within and outside the guild. Competent journeymen were enticed to work for competitors. The regulation that type should be broken up after the mandated initial imprint of 1,500 copies was consistently violated. Piracy flourished, particularly by members with access to the fonts of type and the metal and woodcut illustrations duplicated in best-selling books. Twenty thousand illegal copies of the ABC and 4,000 of the Singing Psalms were uncovered, all infringing on Day's patents, but powerful offenders were merely fined and chastised.

When a "very aged" Tallis, as he wrote to friends about himself, died in 1585, the music patent became Byrd's exclusively. During the previous decade, British music lovers had recognized his talent, but only after foreign publishers included his compositions in new publications did inaccurate manuscript copies of his work begin to circulate. Hoping to profit from this, Byrd decided to use the patent once more. Vautrollier, his old printer, was dead, but his two large music fonts had been purchased by Thomas East, who had been a printer for more than twenty years and had bought Vautrollier's stock to publish a self-instruction music book. This guide for students of plainsong, *A Brief Introduction to the Skill of Music,* was by one of Elizabeth's favorites, the young Irish diplomat William Bathe, who had taught the queen memory improvement. Now East was engaged in preparation of a book of Italian madrigals. He consulted Byrd, whose patent for printing music was still binding. The old composer's interest in issuing his own music proved to be fortuitous for East. Assigning East his patent, Byrd first set the printer to work on a collection, *Psalmes, Sonets and Songs of Sadnes and Pietie,* after hurriedly adding words to purely instrumental music. In this commingling of sacred and popular music, he pointed out in a preface that the songs were "originally made for instruments to express the harmonic, and one voice to pronounce the ditty." His genius was evident in the consummate skill with which he transformed instrumental music to the part-song idiom, using lyrics from the best poets, both foreign and English.

Fourteenth-century Italians had been the first to develop the unaccompanied pastoral song for several voices, using Petrarch's amorous poetry, particularly his *Canzoniere,* love lyrics to an unattainable beauty, the divine Laura. In less than a century, this popular imitation of Christian polyphonic music swept Continental Europe.

Those British gentlemen who could afford to travel for pleasure chanced upon the latest Italian popular music as they basked in Italian culture. A lust for the Italian style of life was nurtured by a handbook that made its appearance in English translation in 1561, Baldassare Castiglione's *The Courtier*. In it, he argued for musical training, pointing out that "in the old days and nowadays [women] have been inclined to musicians and counted this a most acceptable food of the mind." Quite soon, writers of guides to self-improvement were reminding readers that music had many benefits, including the building of the body, since the exercise permitted one "to get the use of the small joints before they have knit, to have them the nimbler." This sort of hint for physical well-being became commonplace in music books once use of Byrd's patent increased.

Though Nicholas Yonge had his hands full providing for nine children, he spent much of his time at his greatest passion, the newest foreign music. His position as lay clerk and musician in London's prestigious St. Paul's Cathedral brought him into contact with amateur singers and a great number of distinguished gentlemen and merchants who often traveled to Europe and brought back the latest music books. His home became a center for these amateurs, and he rendered their favorites into reasonable English, concentrating on simple light lyrics and putting more emphasis on the value of notes than on good poesy.

Fifty-seven songs were published in his *Musica Transalpina,* which appeared in 1588, just as the Spanish Armada was threatening. Included were two by Byrd, which were settings of Italian words by the popular poet Ariosto. Fifteen composers representing the flower of Italian madrigal writing were also included, among them, Palestrina, Lasso, Monte, Marenzio, and Elizabeth's favorite, Ferrabosco, who held four positions at court. By the time a second *Musica Transalpina* was published, by East, nine years later, and after Byrd's patent had expired, the vogue for pure Italian madrigals was subsiding in favor of solo songs with lute accompaniment. The European popular song was at the same time bowing to the pressures of a new form of accompanied vocal music: opera.

In the eight years East used his assignment of the Byrd patent, he brought out eighteen music books: Anglican masses and Catholic services by Byrd, who expected none of the latter to be used in public; Byrd's part books of psalms and "songs of sundry natures, some of gravity and others of mirth"; a book of twenty-eight madrigals, *The First Sett of Italian Madrigals Englished,* by the gentleman-poet Thomas Watson, which contained Byrd's only true Italian-style madrigal, "The Sweet and Merry Month of May"; Thomas Whythorne's second collection of songs; collections of madrigals, ballads, and *canzonettas* by Thomas Morley; songs and psalms arranged for sophisticated musical tastes by John Farmer, William Damon, and John Mundy. His customers were usually upper-class Britons whose appetite for music was shaped in the home and accommodated by native-born and foreign musicians who could not find a place at court or in the retinue of an important political figure or with a major church. Collectively, they taught the nation's adolescents to sing and play, giving them an introduction to contemporary music and the only formal training most would

ever receive on the virginals, lute, and viols. Only a half-dozen schools included music in their curriculum, and there was no true undergraduate instruction in music at the universities or at the Inns of Court. A doctorate in music
was given only to honor some outstanding person and required years of experience and the submission of a written "degree exercise" composed for the occasion and submitted for faculty approval.

Appearing in editions of about a thousand copies, to sell for three to five
shillings a book, music collections included pages of promotional material and
instruction directed to people who did not dwell in or near London and consequently did not have access to those "expert tutors" there available. In the same
way, music by Byrd, Morley, John Dowland, and others gave English gentil-
ity, in the countryside and the capital, its only major access to quality secular
music, which reflected the taste of that most significant patron of British arts
Queen Elizabeth. Once the threat of Spanish victory came to an end, the wealthy
found time to play, and the relaxation of tension gave new impetus to music
making, creating a market for composers as well as makers of musical instruments.

Concerned with only a relatively small market, Thomas East, and the publishers of music books following him, paid little attention to the Singing Psalms
business. Only once did East test the privilege, even though thousands of surreptitious copies were circulating and he owned Britain's only collection of quality
music type. Collecting part settings of psalms by Dowland, Giles Farnaby, and
other well-known composers, he published a psalter in 1592 and another two
years later. But these contained sophisticated music, intended for a quality of
musical training superior to that of the average British churchgoer, and they
thereby incurred no action for this breach of patent.

Byrd's music privilege ended on New Year's Day of 1596, and the composer
made no petition for renewal. He had not published any music of his own for
five years and was then embroiled in litigation involving the crown lease of a
200-acre farm that had been confiscated from a Catholic owner charged with
complicity in treason against the state. On this man's death, survivors had instituted court proceedings to retrieve the property from Byrd. When his patent
expired, anyone could publish printed secular music without fear of liability or
punishment. In order to obtain Stationers' Company protection, East took sets
of his ten best-selling part books for registration.

Clear indication of the lack of profit in the music-book market can be perceived in the general failure of others to rush into production. One who did was
a draper and part-time book and ballad dealer, William Barley, who published
two guides to self-training in music. He first became involved in printing because drapers were entitled to import paper, but he appealed for a transfer from
his own guild to the Stationers' Company, envisioning greater profits owing to
the, for him, ready accessibility of paper. His first publications, *The Pathway
to Music* (1596), reproduced from crude wood-block engravings and containing
no music type to illustrate its "treatise on descant," and *A New Book of Tablature*, a self-help method book for the guitar family of lute, orpharion, and
bandore, demonstrate that neither he nor the job printer he used had any mu-

sical background. The shoddy work of a huckster ready to turn a quick profit, Barley's music books were shot through with printing errors and mismatched words and music.

A system of printed staff notation for the lute family had been introduced by Petrucci as early as 1508, using metal blocks to reproduce the finger board and intricate traditional tablature, with subtleties indicated by specific signs. A special type had been created, the result of improved type-cutting processes, but English publishers continued to rely on the old-fashioned wooden blocks. Not until the mid-sixteenth century was the French system of lute notation introduced generally into music printing on the Continent. It was much admired in Britain. Singers and their accompanists could group around a table and use a single book, in which the lute part was usually printed upside down at the top of the left-hand page, above that of the lead singer. Music for the other voices was printed on the right-hand pages, each instrumental part facing its singer.

Barley's musical incompetence was made most evident in 1597, when a talented printer, Peter Short, who had some music training, issued several sets of part books, among them Morley's *Plaine and Easie Introduction to Practical Musicke,* simultaneously with a work by the most significant songwriter and composer, aside from Byrd, during the last years of Elizabeth's reign, John Dowland. It took a quarter century and the appearance of his *First Book of Songs* for Dowland in 1597 to attain the prestige and popularity in England that his superb lute playing had earned him on the Continent. Attention was at last paid to the British lute song. Very quickly it supplanted the madrigal in popularity as Short printed each of Dowland's songs, both as solos with lute and as four-part airs accompanied by lute, orpharion, and viola da gamba, setting the style that was standard well into the next century.

Morley was already a well-known and admired composer when Short brought out *Plaine and Easie Introduction,* having earlier, between 1593 and 1595, issued four of his music books, all under assignment from Byrd, among them *Madrigals to Four Voices* (1594), the first book of Italian songs by an English songwriter. The most successful music guide written in the sixteenth century, the *Plaine and Easie Introduction* remained in public use for more than 300 years. It was divided into three parts: "the first teacheth to sing with all things necessary for the knowledge of the prickt-song [one written down] The second treateth descant and to sing two parts in one upon a plainsong or ground, with other things necessary for a descanter. The third and last part treateth of composition in three, four, five or more parts with many profitable rules to that effect."

The vogue for part singing set off by the popularity of the Italian madrigal was evident throughout England. Consorts of instrumentalists, amateur and professional, played music for dancing in theaters, taverns, and alehouses. In their homes, singers passed part books to guests at the conclusion of a meal. Morley calculatedly aimed his four-shilling book directly at the middle-class appetite for culture. In the foreword, he posited a situation that could occur only to someone uninstructed in the arts of music. "Supper being ended and the music books, according to the custom being brought to the table, the mistress of the house presented me with a part, earnestly requiring me to sing. But when after many excuses I protested unfeignedly that I could not, everybody began to wonder, some whispered together to others, demanding how I was brought up.'' The book sought to make its readers familiar with all manner of English song, the madrigal and every variation then known, the fashion in which an accomplished singer should perform them, the craft of playing accompanying instruments, and the most popular English singing style. From it, they learned that a proper madrigal was a short poem of six or seven lines, sung to new music or favorite Italian tunes; that singers often also danced the newest steps to the music of "ballatts," with their repeated *fa-la* verse; that, though deceptively simple, the *canzonetta* was really a little madrigal of an odd number of lines for several voices; and that the air printed in large folio books, around which vocalists stood, could also be sung by a single voice to lute or viol accompaniment.

Late sixteenth-century British songs demanded a highly rhythmic vocal style, in the age before the *pian e forte* became the principal accompanying instrument and shaped a more flowing singing line. Both song and singer were hatched out of the percussive elements of the plucked-string family. There was much repetition of words, usually three lines for a phrase. Morley cautioned his readers: "you must in your music be wavering like the wind, sometime wanton, sometime drooping, sometime grave and staid, otherwise effeminate, you may maintain points and revert them, use triplas and show the very uttermost of your variety, and the more variety you show, the better shall you please.''

Elizabethan songwriters understood these conventions, and tailored words and music to the play of voices and the effect desired, subordinating melody to the song. The inherent dance rhythm of their vocal music was occasionally enforced by *fa-la* ornamentation or the addition of a fading *a* sound at the end of rhyming lines.

> The sweet pretty Jinny sat on a hill,
> Where Johnny her swain did see-a:
> He tun'd his quill and sang to her still,
> Whoops! Jinny, come down to me-a.

Enjoying a popularity in late Tudor England like that of the electric guitar in the rock-impacted twentieth century, the lute gave much impetus to production of a British-made instrument, which was quickly esteemed to be the finest in the world. Morley's book taught amateur lutenists how to hold the instrument, where to put their fingers, and how to play, and then provided them with music. The wide appeal of this self-improvement manual caught British music makers of all tastes and ambitions at a time when their national music, was striking out in every direction. Skilled players who had advanced from the tabor and the recorder to the family of stringed instruments, which made its appearance in England much later than it had on the Continent, were also provided for in the book. Morley's airs and ballatts were easily adaptable to the needs of chamber-music consorts.

Morley was by nature and inclination a consummate opportunist, always ready to tailor his talent to commercial gain. Born in 1557, he studied with Byrd, whose teaching made him, as he said, "not only excellent in music, as well as in the theoretical as practical part, but also in the mathematics, in which Byrd was excellent." After earning a degree in music at Oxford in 1588, Morley became organist in one of London's smaller churches, and several years later won a place in St. Paul's Cathedral. Although he had been brought up a Catholic, he permitted himself, in the interests of advancement, to be recruited as an agent in the campaign against papist intriguers. State papers confirm that he helped expose some plotters and "brought divers others into danger." He first came to the queen's attention when some court musicians included a pavane of his during an evening of palace entertainment, and she cheerily danced the night away to the music. Appointment to the Chapel Royal followed, and quick promotion to gentleman.

Byrd made no objection when Morley took his music to Short to be issued in English and Italian editions under the royal patent. Yet Morley did not go with his mentor to ask Elizabeth for a renewal of the privilege. Rather, he intrigued with Sir Robert Cecil, a member of the Privy Council, and obtained a document, effective September 28, 1598, that gave him a renewal of the music privilege for twenty-one years.

Songs and songs in parts, whether "to be played in church, chamber or otherwise," in English, Latin, French, and Italian fell under its scope. The importation, printing, and sale of music paper also belonged exclusively to him. A ten-pound forfeit for every infringement was to be paid to the crown, and Morley was to come into ownership of "all and every such books, quires and papers of songs and songs in parts as aforesaid, and such imprinted paper so ruled as shall be imprinted, ruled, sold, uttered and transported contrary to the true intent and meaning of these presents." The masters and wardens of the Stationers' Company, as well as all "mayors, sheriffs, bailiffs, constables, hedgeborough and all other our officers, ministers and subjects" were called upon to render any assistance Morley needed to enforce the "due expertise and execution of the patent."

Though Short had done a remarkable job printing Morley's thick *Plaine and Easie Introduction,* with its complicated illustrations, musical notation, and diagrams, and East was the first to issue his music, Morley turned to William Barley to serve as middleman in the activation of his new music-printing patent. The Stationers' Company had once again rejected that aspiring publisher's transfer from the drapers' guild, but he continued to publish and sell books, pamphlets, and ballads, from the presses of London's job printers, without license and unhampered by trade codes or practices.

One of the pair, possibly Barley, determined to make another challenge to the Singing Psalms patent, now owned under assignment by a partnership of seventeen highly placed stationers. Two new books were published, one a pocket-sized collection of translations taken without permission from earlier psalmodists, set to a handful of four-line tunes and printed with crude and apparently homemade music type, a typical Barley production, inaccurate and with vocal parts occasionally missing. The other, printed for sale by its compiler and arranger, Richard Allison, was a delight, set in the table-book format first used in Britain for Dowland's *First Book of Songs*. Allison had arranged old church tunes for four voices, with soprano in the lead, to be accompanied by lute, opharion, and cittern or bass viol. This handsome book also contained a fore-word by Dowland.

Five part books of popular songs and instrumental music were issued by Bar-ley during the first year of the patent, two of them collections of chamber dance music assembled by a talented amateur, Anthony Holborne, who recognized the need for some easy-to-play European dance tunes, which he strung together into setts or lessons. These "pavans, galliards, almains and other short airs, both grave and light in five parts" were arranged for full and broken consorts of winds and strings.

Next, Morley formalized the make-up of chamber-music ensembles in the *First Booke of Consort Lessons,* costs of which were borne by a London gentle-man amateur so they could be given as gifts to his friends. Morley arranged his compositions and those of "divers exquisite authors" for a group of six play-ers, the treble lute, bandore, cittern, bass viol, flute, and treble viol.

With many London guilds, trades, and business enterprises loudly proclaim-ing their discontent with the wholesale grant of monopolies, the issue had be-come a subject for debate in the House of Commons. The music patent was occasionally cited, but the problems went far beyond this comparatively small industry. Morley was in poor health, his discomfort increasing when assigns of the Day patent sought to bring action against the two Singing Psalms books Barley had put out. At the direction of Morley's patron, Sir Robert Cecil, the issue was referred for examination to the bishop of London, who found each side arguing for determination by a different authority. The Stationers' Com-pany wished to put the matter into the hands of their old allies, the Privy Coun-cil. Morley, not accountable to the company and its bylaws, held for a hearing in the Court of Common Law. With public opinion against the monopolies, discretion, and perhaps Cecil's advice, prevailed. Morley stayed within the bounds of his patent and never again printed a psalmbook. Further, he began to make the privilege available to other master printers and stationers.

Peter Short secured Morley's assent to reprint Dowland's *First Book of Songs,* its first edition having been exhausted by European sales. The lutenist was an international superstar, more honored abroad than in the land of his birth, even though his tunes were being used for every form of British song, from the psalm to the ballad. The man in the street certainly knew his music, if not his name. When he first applied for a post in the Royal Musick, in 1594, Dowland was thirty-one, but was rejected because of his Catholic faith. European nobles vied for his services, one of them offering, Dowland wrote "a rich chain of gold, twenty-two pounds in money, with velvet and satin and gold lace to make my apparel, with promise that if I would serve him he would give me as much as any prince in the world." Dowland went from court to court, finally turning down a offer to join the pope's household. Only after he dispatched a message to the English government giving information about the "villany of most wicked priests and Jesuits" was permission granted him to return to visit his family.

His songs for lute and voice were being published in Paris, Amsterdam, Rome, Cologne, Nuremberg, Frankfurt, Leipzig. Even Barley had printed some. To put an end to further piracy, Dowland sent a manuscript of the *First Book of Songs* to Short, so that his music would be published correctly, with his knowledge and permission.

Amateurs wishing to learn the secrets of Dowland's legendary technique bought it, as did string players who admired the beauty of his writing. His skill was matchless in suiting his own and words of others to simple, catchy melodies and then setting them to lovely musical accompaniments. Though few Britons heard him perform, many sang and whistled his songs. One of his best known, "Lachrymae," was popular long before Barley pirated it.

Dowland accepted an offer from King Christian IV of Denmark, at a yearly salary equal to that of the monarch's high admiral. It was from Denmark that he sent Short a "newly corrected and amended" copy of the *First Book,* to be brought out in an "authorized" second printing. In late spring of the same year, 1600, Morley gave Thomas East permission to print music books for a term of three years, and he immediately published a *Second Book* of Dowland's songs.

The success of the lute songs, together with the falling off of the madrigals' popularity, impelled Morley to bring out his own book of songs, the 1600 *First Book of Airs,* under Barley's imprint. Once again he proved himself capable of writing excellently in any form he chose and almost the equal of Dowland in duplicating the lute song's range of expression. In the new book was "It was a lover and his lass," written to be sung in *As You Like It,* and still sung.

The effects of continuing inflation, as well as the rising popularity of Dowland''s kind of music, signaled a decline of sales of music books; few appeared in 1601 and 1602. A customer had to buy the entire five or six books of a part-song collection, whereas a single oblong lute book served a group of singers and their accompanist. Dowland's books, among them a third collection, outsold all competitive books.

In an attempt to repair his relations with Elizabeth, which had been jeopardized by the public outburst over monopoly grants, Morley started work on a grand book of madrigals, each one singing the glories of the queen. His inspiration was the 1592 Venetian publication *Il Trionfo di Dori,* in which twenty-nine Italian madrigalists had each written a six-part madrigal ending with the refrain "viva la bella Dori," in celebration of a now forgotten local beauty. Morley hoped that the new book would not only regain the favor of his royal patroness, but also renew interest in the madrigal form. The completed work was entered at Stationers' Hall in 1603, after Elizabeth's death, though the title page of the first printing is dated 1601. A song by Michael East, young son of the printer and a seemingly unlikely name in the glorious roster, appears completely out of the alphabetical order in which the main body of songs is listed. It is quite likely that, with Morley too ill to oversee the final binding, a doting family included the son's composition. In October 1602, Morley's rapidly failing health forced him to give up his duties at court, and within a few days he was dead.

James I, almost immediately after his coronation, in 1603, ended all royal patents. Few music books were published during that confusing year, but one of them was a new edition of the profitable *Plaine and Easie Introduction,* which had become a standard work of reference and instruction.

Himself a book collector and an author whose writings had been pirated, James was concerned about regulation of the trade. He granted a new patent to the Stationers' Company, including in it exclusive rights to publication of all psalters, primers, almanacs, and books of prognostication. The company raised 9,000 pounds to buy off all claims, settling with Richard Day for his family's unexpired and valuable rights to the Singing Psalms and the ABC. The character of English music printing changed dramatically after Peter Short died in late 1603, his widow—then marrying Humphrey Lownes and bringing, through the marriage contract, full ownership of her late husband's shops and equipment—and John Windet, a Stationers' Company official, won the right to publish the psalter. Three or four editions of the book appeared annually, several thousand copies in each, but of poor quality and appearance. Relieved of any competition and secure in its domination of the trade, the company began to cut corners in the production of these money-making books.

In June 1606, Barley finally achieved his long-held desire and was enrolled as a freeman of the Stationers' Company, lending strength to the suit he had instituted against those who had made free use of Morley's patent after the composer's death. A settlement was eventually made, confirming Barley's rights to the privilege, and he was able to collect occasional royalties of twenty shillings a printing from other publishers of part books.

When Thomas East died in 1609, his widow began to sell off the most valuable books he had printed, turning over forty of them printed under the Byrd and Morley patents to a trio of prosperous stationers: John Brown, bookseller; her son-in-law, the music printer Thomas Snodham, and Matthews Lownes, also a printer. Barley did business with these new powers in music publishing, assigning the once best-selling Dowland songs to them. When Barley died in 1613, his wife turned over to Brown, Snodham, and Lownes the Morley patent and other copyrights, giving them ownership of virtually all part books issued since 1588. When the patent expired in 1618, they continued to monopolize a decreasing business in music-book printing and sale. On their deaths, ownership of that music passed into the hands of a minor letterpress printer who had never achieved any recognition as an important stationer.

By then Dowland, too, was dead. He had returned to England in 1603, when there was a new king on the throne, one whose mother was a sainted papist martyr and so would not be bothered by the lutenist's faith. Dowland had been fired by his Danish employer after an argument over expense accounts. Once in London, he published his *Lachrymae, or Seven Tears,* named after his well-known song, registering the work in his own name. He busied himself teaching, performing for admirers and fans, and appearing for fees greater than he had earned in the homes of noblemen and merchants who could then boast that they had been entertained by a king's musician. But the imitators of both his playing style and his songs were to make the fortune that his pride and foolishness had denied him for so long. In his last collection of lute songs, the 1612

*Pilgrim's Solace,* he complained that the new performers had no real training or background, and that the new lute players, though borrowing his style, derided him as being old-fashioned.

When James appointed him a member of the King's Musick, at twenty pence a day, with an allowance of sixteen pounds for the uniform he was obliged to wear, gone were the chains of gold, the velvet, and the satin. His once-popular song settings were now deemed to be too much after the old manner by young composers and musicians. When this sixty-three year-old relict of a glorious past died in 1625, his fame passed with him. Dowland's songs remained only as a reminder of the old-time music, eventually finding an anonymous place in popular music. Only after the twentieth century discovered him was he recognized as one of the half-dozen greatest art-song writers, for what had once been merely popular music was now regarded as work of high quality.

Throughout the sixteenth century, European printers and music publishers had advanced the art beyond the stage then known in Britain. A process using copperplate engraving to duplicate works of art, and capable of reproducing the artificial writing of music, was already a century old, but had not yet been tested by the English. In Europe, political reality had given the engraver's art considerable impetus; the international need for accurate maps of the constantly redefined Continental boundaries and for purposes of navigation, colonization, and peace treaties gave steady employment to master artists. Copperplate printing was first used for music in 1581, by a Florentine publisher, who combined engraving with music type, and a few years later a German printer working in Rome first printed part books with completely engraved musical notation. The Venetian publisher of the *Trionfo di Dori* printed the earliest-known musical score, in 1577, a "study score" of madrigal music. The English did not print music in score for another hundred years. The form of lyric theater eventually known as "opera" was gestating in Italy, and the earliest surviving operatic score, Peri's *Euridice,* appeared in 1600, printed on two lines for solo voices and five for the supporting choruses. The eminent Ballard family continued to control music publishing in Paris, secure with a monopoly continuing until the middle of the eighteenth century, but their minds were unfortunately closed to any technological change until progress and competition forced them into the modern world.

Other than in England, not one European publisher was to devote himself exclusively to the printing, promotion, distribution, and sale of popular music for 150 more years.

The publication and sale of Elizabethan printed music had been a cottage industry in the midst of a thriving business in religious songs and street-ballad music. As in the field of international power, the English came late to it, but they persevered to shape and dominate the business of commercial, popular, and religious music, which in turn moved with colonization into the New World.

# CHAPTER 6

# The Darling Songs
# of the Common People

In *Don Quixote,* Cervantes wrote that barbers of the time were "all players on the guitar and song makers," giving additional authority to the charming notion that a lute hung in every Elizabethan barbershop ready to be used by customers waiting their turn. Britons went to the local barber-chirurgeon not only to have their faces shaved or their hair cut, but also to have blood let or teeth extracted, since barbers also played the role of family doctor and dentist.

Life for the majority of Elizabethans was circumscribed by the requirements of work and a night's rest, leaving little time for even the self-taught to play upon the pipes, tabor, bagpipes, drums, and violins, usually handmade. But no countryman was so isolated that he did not on some occasion hear music. Peasants heard the song of choirs and the music of church instruments. Religion brought even the poorest Briton the earliest musical theater with the miracle play and the pageant. On rare visits to the nearest large community, or a trip to the annual fair, country people heard the music of waits, songs by traveling minstrels, and often stood gape-jawed while the balladmonger and chapbook salesman demonstrated their wares. Many took home the tunes they liked best, passing big-city music into their own major form of self-entertainment, the ballad folk song.

People near hostelries, the earliest centers of entertainment, had frequent opportunity to hear music from London, usually the "three-man's song" sung by travelers relaxing over food and drink. Only a minority of Englishmen ever saw or heard a lap-borne virginals, since most virtuosos on that instrument performed exclusively for admiring audiences in the palaces of the nobility and the wealthy. Had a virginalist appeared in some remote North Country inn, the natives would have regarded his performance in the same way many Americans view a television performance by Vladimir Horowitz, a thing to admire, though the majority of them would have prefered Liberace, who plays tunes they know and gives a better "show." But had sixteenth-century rustics had an opportunity to listen to William Byrd, for example, they would have recognized popular music they knew among the pieces he played.

Byrd, Tallis, Morley, Gibbons, Weelkes, and other composers of genteel art music never hesitated to borrow a likely folk tune or to elaborate upon a street song. The earliest extant manuscript book of music for the virginals, *My Ladye-Nevells Book,* Byrd's compilation of forty-two keyboard pieces, completed in 1591 to be given as a gift from an ambitious courtier to Elizabeth, contained many of the people's favorite songs. This talented composer appropriated many songs of the street: "The Carman's Whistle"; "Fortune My Foe," a ballad tune Londoners sang as they watched men take their places upon the gallows; Henry VIII's favorite song of the chase, "The Hunt Is Up"; "In peascod time"; "Lord Willoughby"; "Sellinger's Round," which J. S. Bach used for a chorale in his *St. John Passion,* known to modern churchgoers as "All glory, laud and honor"; and "Walsingham." The earliest piece of battle music was also in the *Nevell,* Byrd's "The Battle," which concludes with a dance based on the then popular song "Who List to Lead a Soldier's Life." Morley used the lullaby "Baloo," which was well known as early as 1570, and "Go Away from My Window," around which one of the most popular early stage jigs was built, in his *First Booke of Consort Lessons* for chamber-music groups. Dowland, Farnaby, Holborne, and others also adapted the people's music to their higher purpose.

The largest known body of sixteenth—century popular music became known to all classes, in this time before the printing press came to England, through the oral process, transmitted by singers, minstrels, and wandering players. It was first collected from contemporary manuscripts in 1765 by Thomas Percy, bishop of Ireland, in his *Reliques of Ancient English Poetry* and has since been augmented and supplemented by folklorists and collectors of antiquities. Song hunters and musicologists have reconstructed many of the tunes to which this body of lyrics was sung.

These traditional English ballads had a remarkable number of variations among English-speaking people in the centuries after they had first been written down by an educated man. "Lady Isabel and the Elf Knight," for example, has over 160, and a new version can still be heard from a Kentucky balladeer or a Sussex song collector.

The song that most people know as an authentic traditional folk song, "Greensleeves," perhaps the most widely known old British song, entered the commercial process in August 1580, when it was registered at Stationers' Hall. The song had first surfaced in the court of Henry VIII, though there is no truth to the belief that the king wrote this ballad of the lady dressed in green, then the color of lovers and wantonness. Its first publisher called the ballad "A new northern [that is, country] ditty of the Lady Greensleeves."

Such ballads, or one-side-only printings, were regarded as of less value than bound books, and little care was taken to insure their exclusive protection. On the same afternoon, the registry clerk also accepted "A ballad of Lady Greensleeves to Duncan her friend." Both publishers were Stationers' Company members and well-known printers of broadsheet ballads. A "Greensleeves" war appeared to be brewing. Within a fortnight, a third printer received permission to issue "Greensleeves moralized," a moral reflection upon the lady and her light-of-love. Three days after that, the original printer registered a new version, and by the end of the following year four additional "Greensleeves" ballads had been printed and registered. Dowland included the melody in his repertoire. Shakespeare made reference to it, as did other Elizabethan dramatists, and the name became synonymous with that of a woman of the streets. Cavaliers marched to its melody in the struggle between the Stuart family and the Puritans, and seventeenth-century publishers used it for political ballads. A Christmas carol, "What Child Is This," was written to the tune. In the twentieth century, it became best known in an orchestral version by Ralph Vaughan Williams, who made brilliant use of many folk songs.

The career of "Greensleeves" follows a standard popular-music pattern: popular song, a place in the genteel repertory, back to the oral tradition, rediscovery, and, eventually, Muzak.

### The Broadside-Ballad Business

In 1513, Richard Faques, son of the first printer to Henry VII, published a news account of the Battle of Flodden, which resulted in a major British victory and the death of the Scottish king. On the front page, Faques printed a wood-block illustration purporting to be a scene from the conflict, the earliest eyewitness news picture. Those who could not read the words, which included names of both heroes and casualties, contented themselves with looking at the illustration while a better-educated neighbor read the text aloud. This first tabloid newspaper measured five by three and a half inches. In the late nineteenth century, a portion of it was found in the binding of a French romantic novel written shortly before Flodden and later sent to London for repair. News ballads like Faques's battle report passed from hand to hand until they fell apart or were used for waste or wrapping paper. Only some 250 copies of the thousand such books estimated to have been published in Britain during the sixteenth century survive, as prized collectors' copies.

The writer of the 1513 "Ballad of the Scottish King" was John Skelton, self-styled "poet laureate" of England and Henry VIII's tutor from the moment the boy prince was put in his care at the age of eight. Skelton had been admitted to holy orders in 1498, when he was thirty-eight, but was usually found away from his rectory living in sin with a wife and children. The Dutch philosopher Erasmus became a friend of the poet when he visited the British court; he called him the "only light and glory of English letters." Skelton wrote in what he termed a "jagged, tatter'd and ragged" style, but many of his verses were set to music by William Cornyshe.

Many years passed before any printer imitated Faques's news ballad, though collections of ballad poetry were published, only a few of them containing any music. As early as 1505, Wynkyn de Worde had folded a broadsheet of paper to make a pamphlet and on both sides of the leaves he printed *A Little Geste of Robin Hood,* relating the exploits of the greatest hero England knew and about whom men of both high estate and low had been singing for generations. In

1520, John Dorne, an Oxford bookseller, had one of the largest collections of such ballads on sale in that university town, more than 190. With John Gough as printer, John Rastell brought out, around 1525, the first English popular song, words and music printed from a single impression of type and wood block, and an unknown printer issued the first anthology of such music in 1530, the *Twenty Songs*, of which only an incomplete copy rests in the British Museum.

As Englishmen became willing to part with a penny for a single sheet of verse to be sung to a suggested melody, London printers found a new market for their work. By 1540, John Redman, "at the Sign of Our Lady," and John Gough, "at the Sign of the Mermaid," were selling sheets of paper on which story poems were printed on the long or broad side. The printer-publisher's name or initials appeared at the bottom of the text. There was no musical notation, chiefly because printers unable to obtain exclusive patents from the crown could not afford to import music type or to send their work abroad, where printers had access to the new music-duplication technology.

The first broadsheets, known as "black-letter ballads," were printed from the ancient type called "black letter" used to print the Bible and major legal documents in order to give the impression of authority and tradition. This type was used for street ballads until the 1700s, when "white letter" roman type became the standard. Early ballad sheets were from fourteen to sixteen inches long by eight and a half to ten inches wide. The texts were printed in four columns, and when the ballad was very long, in two parts on separate pages. The additional portion was headlined "The second part, to the same tune." Every prospering ballad printer had a stock of woodcut illustrations, which were used at the head of the first sheet, directly under the title and musical suggestion. Some ballads had as many as four of these cuts; others were decorated with scrollwork or arabesque patterns. Many ornamental designs were used again and again at the top of ballads dealing with the same story matter. At the bottom of the sheet, following the final verse, appeared the name and sometimes address of the printer, to comply with the law.

When the ballad served as both a popular song and the advertising for a book on the same subject, such phrases were used as "those which are desirous to see this matter more at large: I refer to the book newly come forth" or "you shall see the full relation in the book newly printed." The London printer who obtained a copy of the prompt book for Shakespeare's 1596 hit show *Romeo and Juliet* from a backstage thief or got it from a shorthand writer who sat in the theater writing down every word issued an unauthorized edition of the play. The ballad on the same subject ordered from a pothouse poet for a drink or some coin told the story of the star-crossed lovers and served to advertise the product of his piracy.

City people bought their ballads at the stationer's stall or from ballad sellers who walked through the streets. In the countryside, ballads were a large part of the itinerant peddler's stock. In many inns, taverns, and homes, broadsides were pasted over drab walls to serve as wallpaper, providing opportunity for word recognition leading to literacy, a tangent benefit never dreamed of by the publisher.

Shakespeare preserved the sales pitch of a transient balladmonger in Act IV, Scene 3 of *The Winter's Tale.* The song salesman, Autolycus, had the same economic motivation as a nineteenth-century piano or song demonstrator in the music department of a large store; as his twentieth-century counterpart, the song plugger seeking to persuade, by friendship and, occasionally, payola, a name bandleader to feature the new tune he is promoting; or, more recently, as the recording-company promotion man, with his ''hottest new wax.''

Every topic was grist for the ballad writer's mill—the miracles of nature, gossip about persons in high society, the doings and plots of England's papist enemies, the venality of priests and friars, which served to make Henry's unpopular rift with the pope more tolerable, or anything to do with the lusty redheaded king and his sex life.

Henry favored any ballad putting him in a kindly light, but once Anne Boleyn was laid in a traitor's grave, those written in her praise and singing of her virtue and not the many lovers preceding the Tudor king, were quickly consigned to the fire. Such ''pestiferous and noisome'' ballads, it was claimed, poured off the presses of alien printers whose allegiance to the nation giving them refuge was suspect.

In point of fact, the first several generations of printers were usually foreigners, craftsmen and typesetters brought over by British stationers who had come into possession of a press but were unable to operate it. Years of patient service, coupled with business acumen, eventually made most of these immigrants their own masters. A number of laws were signed by Henry to curb the activities of these master printers. Certain books were banned; the importation and sale of works printed abroad was forbidden. After he made the final break with Rome, censorship continued, though the state's concerns turned from European Protestantism to papist perversions. Pornographic pamphlets and suggestive ballads about the corruption of monks, priests, and nuns and propaganda demeaning the pope and his followers were encouraged. Troupes of actors on the state payroll toured the nation burlesquing in story and song the conduct of the once-powerful priesthood.

Conservative Britons passed around any new pamphlet or ballad attacking both their king and the statesmen around him who were encouraging his heresy. Spies were planted in Scotland to manufacture and send back purportedly authentic ballads mocking Henry, his sexual appetites and political folly, in an effort to frustrate national unity. This resulted in vituperative correspondence between the two monarchs. James denied any connection with the business, and the matter ended just short of another war. Henry's advisers continued to launch a barrage of propaganda against enemies, native or foreign, using the broadside ballad as a means to mold favorable public opinion. The most effective of the ballad writers was William Gray, well versed in music and author of ''The Hunt Is Up.'' To inspire progovernment ballads ''concerning the suppression of the pope and all popish idolatry,'' Gray compiled a sample book, the fifty-stanza ballad, *The Fantasy of Idolatry.*

In 1543, all previous measures of political and religious censorship were codified in the Act for the Advancement of True Religion. Thirty-three London printers were rounded up, charged with offenses against the new law, a crime carrying three months' imprisonment and a ten-pound fine for the first arrest, life imprisonment and confiscation of all personal property for the second. After being grilled by the Privy Council, their release was eventually ordered, but only on condition that any books and ballads published over the past three years, as well as the names of their authors, be turned over. Because the printing business had by then been established in other towns, Norwich, York, Bristol, and at Oxford and Cambridge under charter from university officials, a provision was added to the new act to include these communities.

Henry died shortly after, and by ancient custom all laws and proclamations made during his reign were no longer effective. His sickly son, Edward, was ten years old, and the men who had educated him and now ran the nation in his behalf began to play their own political games. The issue of Protestantism versus Catholicism was the shoal upon which most foundered.

The ballad war between Protestant and Catholic continued, but it was now only a small part of the music business. Both Londoners and their country cousins had developed an appetite for nonpolitical songs and story poems. Typical of the stock on sale at a stationer's stall was that of the printer Robert Toy, who sold broadsides to street peddlers and traveling balladmongers. His variety of songs included ''I Will Have a Maid If Ever I Marry,'' ''An Epitaph on the Death of King Edward the Sixth,'' ''The Mourning of Edward, Duke of Buckingham,'' a nobleman who had been beheaded on Henry's orders, ''Women Are Best When They Are at Rest,'' ''A Maid That Would Marry with a Serving Man,'' and ''The Day of the Lord Is at Hand.'' The Privy Council continued its watch, even on this innocent repertory, calling in one printer to explain why he had printed a ballad considered treasonous. Released on a bond of £100, he was required to report to the council daily and to turn in not only all copies of his own seditious broadsides, but also all those he could find.

Mary's coronation was six weeks away when she issued the first of many proclamations against Protestant books. But, as her predecessors had learned, it was not easy to police the music trade without assistance from inside. Her reign started on a hopeful note. Ballad writers in the pay of the state wrote new verses anticipating a peaceful reign. Mary not only showed mercy to her enemies and those who had foolishly fallen away from the Church of Rome, but she tempered the speed with which she would restore Catholic worship in London. Not until six months later did a Catholic mass open Parliament, and she continued to keep her own observance of daily mass and confession private and personal.

After a full year passed, she reinstituted all Catholic rites and announced she would marry Philip, the King of Spain. John Heywood saluted the announcement with a ballad, but less admiring poetasters produced ''very evil and lewd songs'' reviling Mary, Philip, the pope, the mass, Catholicism, and other evils of the ''Whore of Babylon,'' as they termed the Roman church. A new Act Against Seditious Words was enacted, calling for the cropping of the ears of both the writer and the printer of such materials, and the cutting off of the right hand for a second offense. "Ballads and other pernicious and hateful devices engendering hatred and discord" were soon turned up.

The most subtle and significant action to control the English-language press took place on May 4, 1557. Though Philip had been off to the fleshpots of Europe for almost two years, his name preceded Mary's in the charter granted that day to ninety-seven "freemen of the mystery or art of stationery." A freeman was a full citizen, who had the right to own property, employ workers, and bind apprentices, to whom he taught his trade, paying them nothing except room, board, and some education. The stationers were delighted with the new charter, which gave them a stature their guild had never enjoyed, having been among the lowest-ranking of London's trade and craft associations.

The politician framers of this document played upon the basic human characteristic that inclines men jealously to guard their property and right to do business. In return for protection, the printers and stationers became a semiofficial policing arm. They were empowered to search "in any place, shop, house, chamber or building, of any printer, binder or bookseller whatever . . . for any books or things printed, or to be printed, and to seize, take, hold, burn, or turn to the proper use of the aforesaid community, all and several those books and things which are or shall be printed contrary to the form of any statute, act or proclamation." Only members of the new Stationers' Company could publish books, and regulations and bylaws were quickly set up to ensure registration of their new books.

All property rights in a printed piece belonged to the publisher. The author might receive payment for delivering a manuscript, and an occasional bonus if it sold well, to ensure access to his future writings. A successful book could go into twenty or thirty editions within a few years, but the author received no more than his first piece of coin. John Stow, a London tailor who went in for writing books, got forty free copies and three pounds for his best-selling *Survey of London,* published in 1598, though, in 1604, the new king, James, rewarded him with a privilege for the right to beg. Writers of broadside ballads rarely got more than a few coppers and all the ale they could drink. Rich amateurs were satisfied to see the finished work and have the opportunity to distribute it among their peers.

Because Stationers' Company masters and wardens were as zealous in the enforcement of their authority while hunting for illicit ballads as for slanderous books, there is less than complete knowledge of ballad history. The record of ballad entries in the official stationers' register, lovingly compiled by Hyder E. Rollins, indicates that some 3,000 were registered. There were countless others, now lost, whose publishers failed to enter them because they were not members or because the verses flouted acts of Parliament and the Privy Council. In addition, some latter-day collectors have regarded many ballads in their possession as so lusty and bawdy that they have confined countless broadsides to private collections or hidden them on locked library shelves.

That iconoclastic folklorist Gershon Legman has written in *The Horn Book:*

"The broadside and ballad collections at Harvard and in the British Museum, at Oxford, Cambridge and a dozen other libraries, which go back to the time of Henry the Eighth and are of the most staggering richness—not to way weight— not a fiftieth nor a hundredth of these ballads have ever been reprinted except for one small corner." This omission of frankly amatory song, the ballads celebrating man's oldest pleasure, Gershon vouchsafes, makes the present the final "time to stop begging for fair play for sexual intercourse, as though it were no worse, really than murder." Because nineteenth- and early-twentieth-century ballad hunters were rooted in a morality different from the present free-swinging liberality, very little of unbuttoned sixteenth- and seventeenth-century Britain can be seen.

The extent of affection for the love song by Elizabethan aristocratic and upper classes was emphasized in one of the first books to be registered at Stationers' Hall. On June 7, 1557, Richard Tottel, the London printer whose office inside the Temple Bar, near Fleet Street, published all lawbooks under a patent from Edward IV, issued one of his few books devoted to literature: *Songs and Sonnets,* now known as *Tottel's Miscellany.* It consisted of 271 poems that had never been printed except in broadside-ballad form or in small private editions for the entertainment of their prominent authors' friends. Many of the verses were by writers unknown, much of the balance by professionals—William Gray, John Heywood, Thomas Churchyard, poet and playwright Nicholas Grimald, and two members of the nation's most prominent families, Thomas Wyatt and Henry Howard.

A dashing courtier and playboy, Wyatt was sent to Europe on diplomatic missions by Henry VIII, failing only to bring back papal permission for the annulment his master so desired. He did, however, import foreign fashions and a taste for Italian music and poetry, which he soon began to emulate, turning the results over to William Cornyshe for editing and performance. Many ladies of the court found themselves unable to say no to the personable newly knighted member of the king's official staff, among them a short, dark, teen-aged lady-in-waiting, Anne Boleyn. Wyatt became her lover, but was soon supplanted by Henry. Before Anne fell to the executioner's ax, condemned for bigamy and adulteries, Wyatt was imprisoned in the Tower. Tortured and then released, he died of a fever at the age of thirty-nine. Among his songs was "Hey Robin, gentle Robin," written with Cornyshe and today a standard feature in recorded anthologies of Tudor court music.

With Wyatt, "Gentle" Henry Howard, Earl of Surrey, introduced British poets to the sonnet form. A dozen years younger than Wyatt and related to him by marriage, Howard was a musician and brilliant, tough soldier, who fought by day and caroused among the lowest elements by night. When the king heard that Howard had boasted he could rule the kingdom better, he ordered him hanged, drawn, and quartered, but relented at the last moment to commute the sentence to mere hanging, the last victim of the royal anger.

The longest lived of Tottel's verses is Lord Vaux's "I Loath That I Did Love," which became popular after its initial appearance and was often borrowed by ballad printers. It was so great a favorite of Shakespeare's, who knew the *Miscellany* well, that he used it in slightly altered form for the show-stopping gravedigger's scene in *Hamlet*.

The pattern of *Tottel's Miscellany* was imitated for the first time in a 1566 songbook, the small-sized collection *A Handful of Pleasant Delights*, issued by Richard Jones, an active ballad printer. Most of it was the work of Clement Robinson, a ballad writer and pamphleteer, some of whose pieces were imitations of songs and sonnets in the Tottel, and others plagiarisms of current street ballads. Similar compilations of profit-making broadsides appeared regularly during the next decade, among them *The Paradise of Dainty Devises* (1576), *Flowers of Epigrams* (1577), *A Gorgeous Gallery of Gallant Inventions* (1578), *The Forest of Fancy* (1579), and a new, enlarged edition of *A Handful of Pleasant Delights* (1584).

It is the measure of a still-prevailing misunderstanding of both the worth and the role of the broadside ballad confronted in these small books by many less than knowledgeable experts and critics that from the first they have marveled that each lyric "has its tune assigned to it by name," that these "are poetical books of the Elizabethan period" and "lyric poems of varied length." As Hyder Rollins observed in a 1928 introduction to *A Handful of Pleasant Delights:* "None of these gentlemen seem to have recognized that the poems . . . are broadside ballads, pure and simple. As such they were collected by a ballad writer for the delectation, not of the literary reader, but of the vulgar, who loved 'a ballad in print a life.' "

Queen Mary's last proclamation urged Parliament to issue additional legislation restraining the press. It resulted in still another injunction against unlicensed printing.

## The First Great Ballad Writers

Though the street-song trade had become a business from which the owner of a printing press might sometimes earn enough to maintain his shop and a few workers, it rarely paid enough to permit full attention exclusively to broadside ballads. Even the most successful ballad publishers issued other popular literature—self-improvement books, popular devotionals, news books, "garlands," which were compilations in pamphlet form of a number of the most popular street songs, and other forerunners of today's mass media's output. Although the broadside enjoyed a great vogue in European countries, it never made the contribution to mass culture there that it did in Britain.

For centuries, customers flocked to the shop or stall looking for the newest pieces, street peddlers and wandering songmongers carried sheets to people outside London and the other major cities, and the wealthy were constantly on the lookout for amatory ballads. Most of this musical ephemera was as transient as the mayfly. But some of it did pass into the oral tradition, remaining in the people's repertory as street songs, play tunes, lullabies, and dance music. Many tunes passed into the hallowed antiquity of folk music, remaining known by the name of the first successful ballads set to their notes and being used again and again for new broadsides long into the second Stuart period. There was always a fondness for the old songs, remembrancers of the old days and the old ways, before music had become so newfangled, before youth had corrupted everything with its tastes for change and the easy way.

All classes and all ages succumbed in 1560 to the great hit song of the day, "The Pangs of Love and Lover's Fits," written by a "notorious tippler and ready writer," William Elderton. The melody was fresh and new, and the lyric form innovative. Both were quickly imitated, but the original enjoyed greater fame and sales. Elderton was an educated man, as references to Latin literature and philosophy in his broadsides indicate, a trained lawyer whose affection for the theater and street life turned him to balladeering and acting after his wife died and ensuing financial difficulties sent him on a lifetime of bohemian excesses. Before he practiced law in London courtrooms, Elderton had been a part-time actor and had once appeared at court in young King Edward's presence. In 1562, his second-best-known love song appeared, "The Gods of Love." Though it, too, enjoyed great popularity, all copies of the broadside have disappeared, only a snatch being quoted in *Much Ado About Nothing*.

The remarkable vogue for Elderton's romantic songs, with their emphasis on worldly love, incurred the anger of the British clergy, who sermonized regularly against his invocations of the ancient Greek and Latin gods. Broadsides supporting the church's crusade to cleanse the ballad trade of its poetic excesses asked:

> What mean the rimes that run this large in every shop to sell
> Tell me, is Christ or Cupid Lord, doth God or Venus dwell?

Elderton eventually found himself involved in a ballad war against the Roman church. The Thirty-nine Articles enacted by Parliament in 1566 to establish the official Anglican creed preserved much of Catholic ritual, but in British garb. Many who adhered to the old religion found their resolve to remain faithful stiffened and continued its worship in open and in secret. Raids began on the homes of persons suspected of such heresy; Catholic literature of all kinds was confiscated and its possessors were punished.

Recognizing their popular appeal, the government recruited the cleverest ballad writers to counter propaganda emanating from the Catholic college in Douai, in the Spanish Netherlands, where saboteurs were being trained and then sent to Britain with rebel priests to do their revolutionary work. These missions included not only intrigue and espionage, but preparation of pro-Roman ballads to be printed surreptitiously and distributed in the streets of London in the dark of night.

Playing the role of loyal Protestant citizens, the ballad writers committed their talents to the government cause. Making its home in the Smithfield district of London, an area of markets, alehouses, and the great annual St. Bartholomew's Fair, the greatest in all England, this confraternity was led by John Awdeley, a freeman of the Stationers' Company. Under his direction, and working out of a printing office in the shadow of St. Bartholomew's Cathedral, Elderton, Stephen Peell, Robert Greene, and others praised the queen, damned the dissenters, gloated over horrible executions, and rejoiced in news ballads celebrating victories over Catholic rebels who had taken the field in the northern counties.

When John Felton was executed for having nailed to the door of London's Episcopalian bishop a copy of the bull issued by Pope Pius V excommunicating Elizabeth, dozens of jubilant ballads hailed the event. Rollins estimates that seventy-five ballads registered in 1569 dealt with rebellion in the north, and most of those registered the following year "were tirades against Felton, the Pope or the Roman Church."

Applauding in verse the gory public executions of priest and saboteur, the ballad writers supported in words and music the national program to unite England under a single state religion. The effectiveness of Elderton's contribution was marked in ballads purporting to be spoken by Pius, cursing and banning all who "speak against my power." However, his impertinent verses angered the Privy Council and the queen, two ballads in particular. The first narrated a supposed assassination attempt against Elizabeth, who had been on the river in her private barge enjoying the evening breezes when "a young fellow in another boat carelessly fired a gun across the river, and the bullet passed within five feet of the Queen, wounding one of her bargemen." The youth was arrested and condemned to death. Within three days he was brought to a gibbet and, after the hangman had placed the noose about his neck, "by the Queen's most gracious pardon delivered from execution." Such was the stuff of which best-selling broadsides were made, and Elderton described the event in "A New Ballad, declaring the dangerous shooting of the gun at the court, to be sung to the tune 'Siche and siche.'" Lest some Spanish hireling or Catholic zealot be reminded of the queen's easy accessibility, the Privy Council determined to suppress all news of the event. The publisher was fined twelvepence and ordered to destroy all remaining copies of the song. Wisely, Elderton had chosen to disappear from public sight. A second offense against public safety effectively exiled him from the street-song trade for a decade. Much to the Privy Council's annoyance, he had found inspiration in the kidnapping of a distinguished Catholic rebel from his place of exile in Europe and his return to England for public execution. The ballad cited not only details of the deed, but also the names of all involved, "tending," as a formal complaint to the Stationers' Company cited, "to the discredit of some princes with whom the Queen's Majesty standeth presently in terms of amity." Once again Elderton's publisher was fined, all copies of the song were destroyed, and the ballad-writing ex-attorney went under cover, serving for the next eight years as master of the boy actors at Eton College and the Westminster Cathedral choir children.

During this period, the Catholic crisis slowly waned, and in its place a new one surfaced. Dissenting Independent Protestants, the Puritans and Separatists who first challenged the structure of the Anglican church in 1570 with an attack by a Cambridge professor of theology, became the chief targets of the keepers of the queen's majesty. On his return to those who loved him best—the wine-beer-, and hippocras-drinking habitués of London's popular taverns—Elderton and his cronies found new fodder for their talents. The colorless Puritans, with their somber clothing, seeming lack of a sense of humor, and hostility to the stage and to secular music, now served as the butt of the comedy and burlesque in which Elderton specialized. More dangerous revolutionaries than the papists, the Independents inspired a witty and satirical body of broadside for the next half century.

Satire and burlesque formed a major portion of the new intimate entertainment Elderton now created. Relying for comedy relief, as did Jimmy Durante, on his "nose maximus," the product of years of drinking, Elderton went from pothouse to tavern performing his old songs and new ones, parodying ballads written by friends, improvising rhymes and japes for a can of wine or a pot of ale. Along the way he won the affection of Deloney, Robert Armin, Philip Stubbs, Richard Tarleton, and other songwriters, as much for the virility and free spirit of his versifying, as for the gluttony, drunkenness, and whoredom they shared.

Elderton, often in jail for debt and being a public nuisance, supported himself also by his news ballads. Among the few extant are those about an earthquake that briefly shook London, an archery shooting bee in the presence of Russian ambassadors and won by stout native archers, and the results of the Parprelate controversy in 1589, during which anonymous Puritan writers attacked Anglican bishops, bringing the Smithfield ballad writers once again into the Privy Council's employ.

Nearly seventy when he died, after spending his last twenty-three years in the ballad trade, Elderton left his name and works sixteen times in the Stationers' Company register, only a small portion of his tremendous creativity. For centuries English-speaking people recited his "Mary Ambree," usually credited to "Anon." Shakespeare knew his songs and quoted from them often, although in time acknowledgment of his authorship disappeared even from the footnotes.

Shortly after World War I, Hyder Rollins, in "William Elderton: Elizabethan Actor and Ballad Writer," provided an insight into the contribution of this significant early songwriter:

> Ballads are written to be judged not as poetry but as songs written to be sung in the streets for the information, edification and amusement of the lowest classes, and, though Elderton shows all the faults of such a form, he always had the merit of tunefulness. It can hardly be disputed that his rhymes are often the equal of those from more exalted pens of the *Tottel's Miscellany* authors . . . [but] his feeling for rhythm, his tunefulness, usually triumphed.

Even as Elderton lay dying, his old associates were going their own way. Philip Stubbs had discovered the merits of Puritanism, and left behind the fleshly and wanton pleasures of Smithfield. As a teen-ager Robert Armin dreamed of the theater while working as a goldsmith's helper, but he took to pamphleteering until he met the famous stage clown and queen's jester Richard Tarleton, who prophesied the lad would one day be his successor and found him a place in an acting company. Immortalized by being named as an actor in the First Folio of Shakespeare, he turned to playwrighting, winning a royal patent from James I, who took a more than personal interest in his well being.

Richard Tarleton had been a highly popular ballad singer and performer before he joined the company sponsored by the Earl of Leicester. In time, he became so celebrated a public idol that publishers often added his name as the author of new ballads, hoping thereby to increase their sales.

Robert Greene, scribbling ringleader of the Smithfield pamphleteers, died shortly after his friend the king of ballads. On the night of September 3, 1592, he lay in a squalid room in the house of a poor cobbler, his head covered with the garland of laurel he had requested for his last minutes, placed there by the family that had housed and fed him in the final days of his poverty. He was only thirty-two, the victim of a fast life and a violent one. His plays, the best of which was *The History of Friar Bacon and Friar Bungay,* were very popular. Though only one of them contained an original song, he made great use of popular ballads in his stage pieces, writing broadsides only for what they added to his purse. An intimate of London's cutpurses, counterfeiters, fences, pimps, prostitutes, and panders, he wrote about his experiences in the underworld, an exposé of local crime whose success lost him his friends among the city's criminals.

His Cambridge friend Christopher Marlowe was dead six months later, possibly the victim of execution by government agents under cover of a tavern brawl over the landlord's bill. As a scholarship boy at college, a beneficence of the bishop of London, this shoemaker's son was recruited for campus espionage and spied upon the political and religious leanings of his classmates. After receiving his degree, he went to Europe on secret business in the employ of a government agency, returning home to start writing the six historical plays and tragedies that brought him rapid fame. His *Jew of Malta* (1580) may have had some influence on Shakespeare's *Merchant of Venice,* and his vivid blank-verse style set a pattern for Shakespeare that can be discerned in *Titus Andronicus* and *King Henry the Sixth.* Marlowe's most famous lyric, "Come live with me, and be my love," from *The Passionate Shepherd to His Love,* has continued to inspire popular songs, as it first did in the broadside ballad, to which a reply was written by Sir Walter Raleigh.

For years before Elderton gave up his crown, the "balladeering song weaver" Thomas Deloney vied for that honor. When the Armada threatened, Britons were heartened by his new ballad written to encourage all who fought "willingly in the cause of the Queen and the defense of the Holy Gospel." Deloney was born in London around 1543, where he learned the weaver's trade and then opened a business in Norwich. The recurrent theme in his novels, histories, and ballads was an admiration of tradesmen, hailing the accomplishments of merchants who raised themselves in society through honest workmanship and pride in their work. This note struck an immediately responsive chord in both the heart and the pocketbook of the newly emerging middle-class business entrepreneur.

Like most ballad writers, Deloney was a man of some education, his first known work being a translation into broadside meter from the Latin. During the 1580s, he was one of the free-lance rhymesters who buoyed morale with news ballads. As the threat of Spanish invasion grew more immediate, he wrote metrical accounts of Elizabeth's visits to camps where troops were preparing to counter the invaders and recounted atrocities the enemy had perpetrated, including such bizarre propaganda as "the strange and most cruel whips which the Spaniards had prepared to whip and torture English men and women."

Deloney's social attitudes, rooted in a middleclass background, filtered through his superior writing skills to mirror those of his faithful readers. He played upon their patriotism, their pride in the small island that had fathered them, and their "loving hearts, obedient minds and perfect faithfulness." Britain's merchant middle class and those who were striving to become part of it were eager for this and ready for education, information, and self-improvement. Deloney wrote collections of popular literature, interspersing prose among sets of ballads in pamphlets known as "garlands," some of which circulated until the early eighteenth century. His *Garland of Good Will* and *The Royal Garland of Love and Delight* were histories of those past glories in which the bourgeosie had played varying but heroic roles. Essentially they both were reworkings of the same collection of historical ballads, first known as *Deloney's Strange Histories,* whose "thirty excellent songs, very pleasant either to be read or sung . . . together with several love lyrics" went through numerous editions.

During one of the periodic wheat shortages, when that British table staple was kept off the market in order to drive up prices, Deloney wrote a very popular ballad of protest against the speculators. These, being men of high position, were able to bring official action against him, and in late 1596, like other balladeers who had offended the establishment, he was forced to flee London. His name surfaced once more, in 1600, when Will Kemp, who had succeeded Tarleton as the most popular comedian, staged a personal publicity stunt. He had been starring in short jiggs, and was best known for the morris dance he performed in them. He proposed to dance from London to Norwich, some 125 miles, betting a sum of money at three to one on his success. Although he spent nine days on the road, the dancing journey took three weeks of personal fatigue and bad weather. Norwich's mayor met him at the city gates and presented him with a lifetime pension of forty shillings a year for having put the city in the national spotlight. Pothouse writers took advantage of the feat, bringing out ballads that considerably embroidered the facts. Kemp's own, official, pamphlet relating the true story failed to compete with a sensational version published by "T. D.—chronicler of honest men."

When Elizabeth breathed her last in 1603, Elderton, Deloney, and the rest of the Smithfield crew were all dead. The wave of Jacobean poets that followed, sophisticated and worldly-wise, looked down on the literature of these pothouse bards, labeling them an "unaccountable rabble of riming ballad makers and compilers of senseless sonnets, who be best busy to stuff every stall full of gross devices and unlearned pamphlets. For though many such can frame an alehouse song of some five or six verses hobbling upon some tune of a *Northern Jig* or *Robin Hood,* or *Lubber La* &c., and perhaps observe just number of syllables eight in one line, six in another, and there withal an 'A' to make a jerk in the end, yet if these might make means to be announced poets . . . we will shortly have whole swarms of poets."

Hyder Rollins saw it more clearly. "Ballads worthy of being called real poetry can almost be counted on the fingers of both hands,'' he wrote in *A Pep-syian Garland*. He cited "Love will find out a Way"; Deloney's "A Farewell to Love,'' which is included in Shakespere's *The Passionate Pilgrim* as by the great dramatist; Elderton's "Mary Ambree" or "The Babes in the Wood,'' which Wordsworth hailed in his preface to *Lyrical Ballads*.

> Ballads were not written for poetry, [Rollins continues]. They were, in the main, the equivalent of modern newspapers, and it cannot be well denied that customarily they performed their function as creditably in verse as the average newspaper does in prose. Journalistic ballads outnumbered all other types. Others were sermons, or romances, or ditties of love and jealousy, or tricks and 'jests' comparable to rag-time or music hall songs of the present (1922) . . . written for the common people by professional rhymsters—journalists of the earth earthy—ballads made no claims to poetry and art. They have always interested educated men, not as poems but as popular songs or as mirrors help us see the life of the people. In them are clearly reflected the life and thoughts, the hopes and fears, the beliefs and amusements of 16th and 17th century Englishmen. In them history becomes animated.

# PART TWO

# 1603 to 1710

# CHAPTER 7

# From James to Anne

James I's mother had been cursed with a loveliness that made her a reigning beauty in the European courts but finally brought her to the executioner's ax her less-favored cousin Elizabeth could have stayed. None of the "snow of her pure face" was evident in the bulb-nosed, weak-kneed, paunchy thirty-seven-year-old who followed Elizabeth to the seat of the English power. Mary, Queen of Scots, had danced, played the lute, and written lyric poetry. Her son was known throughout his Scottish realm as its leading drunkard. However, mother and son shared one thing: both were foolish about men.

Mary was a victim of John Knox's version of Calvinist Puritanism as much as of Elizabeth's dread that she would die and look down to see on her throne the Catholic, French-reared, stunning, ardent, and bonny daughter of a Scottish Stuart king. Mary never ceased to shiver with apprehension in strange, half-savage, half-learned Scotland, which sent witches to the stake and sought salvation by way of the bloody destruction of popish idols.

James knew little of his ostensible father other than his vanity, and he had little of his whispered true parent's, David Rizzio's, cultured charm. That Italian musician had made his way to dour Scotland during Mary's first year of rule, winning a place in her court as director of musical revels, and then as her secretary and adviser. Europe whispered that he was both husband to Mary and wife to the king. In later years, James's enemies laughed and called him "the modern Solomon, for his father was the harpist David."

Mary never saw her boy after he was ten months old and was taken to be educated by Protestants and reared by a succession of regents ruling in his place. At seventeen he pledged his life to defend Calvinist Presbyterianism, insuring his place on Scotland's throne. It was a nation dominated by the clergy and followers of a theology that espoused democracy by insisting on the popular election of its parish ministers, while practicing rigorous control over its communicants' morals.

It was through his mother's bloodline that the English Privy council named

James heir to Britain's throne. In 1603, he became its king, and Scotland and England were united for the first time.

Almost a hundred years earlier, the magic name America had first appeared in one of William Cornyshe and John Heywood's court entertainments, but little attention was paid to the lands across the seas until tangible proof of the continent's treasure of gold and silver poured into the pockets of investors in privateering. Middle-class interest was stimulated further by the stream of travel and exploration pamphlets collected and published by the indefatigable geographer and propagandist for colonization Richard Hakluyt. Readers' brains reeled at the prospect of the income to be had from the importation of "plentie of excellent trees for masts, of goodly timber to build ships and to make great navies, pitch, tar, hemp and all things incident for a royal navy . . . [overseas traffic which] for many years shall change many cheap commodities of these parts for things of high value there not esteemed; and this to the great enrichment of the realm."

Several expeditions visited the New World's coast, and on Roanoke Island a colony was established, first in 1585, and again in 1587. The relief fleet returning over three years later found no sign of habitation, only a tree garlanded with leaves, on which the word CROATOAN had been carved. It is remembered because in August 1587, Virginia Dare was born there, the first child of English parents born in America.

Those gentlemen and merchants who saw the New World as a major profit-making investment quickly harnessed the pamphlet scriveners and ballad writers to pen promotional materials, some of which eventually were shown to the king. Samuel Purchas, who took up Hakluyt's missionary work of promoting and selling Virginia, gave James a number of writings about America, which the king read a reported seven times. The several companies of "knights, gentlemen, merchants and other adventurers" wishing to cash in on the opportunities awaiting them in the New World joined forced and petitioned the king for a royal charter empowering them to begin a colony in Virginia. In 1606, James authorized the establishment of two colonies, not to be within one hundred miles of each other, by the London and the Plymouth companies. These were to propagate the Christian religion among the "infidels and savages living in those parts." As in each of fifteen similar ventures chartered before Elizabeth's death, investment was open to all. Investors were authorized to elect officers of the company, and profits were to be divided on the basis of stock ownership. One-fifth of all gold and silver found was to be crown property.

The most modern sales propaganda methods known to London's financial community were utilized—broadsides, ballads, sermons, pamphlets, and word of mouth. Even as three ships bearing 104 British men and four boys were on their way, poet Michael Drayton's ode *To the Virginian Voyage* was drumming up capital for future voyages. Reports came back of strawberries four times larger than those at home, of "squirrels, conies, black birds with crimson wings, and divers other fowl and birds of divers and sundry colors." The truth, however, was kept from those investors who wanted to hear only about dividends. Within four months of the May 1607 landing at Jamestown, only forty-six of the original 104 were still alive, to be reduced further, to thirty-eight, by the year's end. Losses to the London Company, promoters of the settlement, mounted. Sparse cargoes of sassafras, dyestuffs, and cedar for housing provided little return after the heavy expenses for new supplies being sent westward. Because Britain was slowly running out of wood as its forests were cut down for building materials and the ground thus cleared was converted into farm and pasture land, the cargoes of lumber did make a small profit.

When the owners of the London Company persuaded the king that they needed new financing, James permitted creation of a lottery, with a guaranteed total of £5000 in prizes. Chances, at a crown each, were promoted in extravagantly optimistic pamphlets, hawked around town by balladmongers, reminding men and women of the great wealth the winning ticket holder would come into. The grand prize of 4,000 crowns was delivered to a London tailor, and the company received sufficient income to bargain with the king's advisers to obtain a new charter reorganizing the enterprise. Stocked with fresh funds and a new complement of settlers, the colony soon faced once more diminishing food supplies, mounting Indian attacks, disease, and crop failure.

It was tobacco smoking that saved Virginia. Spaniards had first brought that weed from the West Indies to Europe, where such fashion-setting international gallants as Walter Raleigh popularized the habit. By 1613, over £200,000 were spent annually on this "chopping herb of Hell." Men gathered in alehouses, brothels, and the tobacco shops studding London to enjoy puffing a clay pipe, and many a bawdyhouse sported a tobacco pipe as a sign of both its business and the welcome to be had.

The land around Jamestown proved to be hospitable to tobacco cultivation, and when the settler John Rolfe discovered a method for its curing, growing and exportation of the crop became the colony's chief business. It sold for five shillings a pound in London in 1618, when 60,000 pounds were imported from Virginia. Woman-starved colonists paid 120 pounds of tobacco apiece for ninety young maidens, inspiring new ballads urging more such traffic.

Despite the tobacco profits, investors had not received any return from the London Company. In 1624, James declared its charter null and void, returning Virginia to crown control. By 1640, the colony was shipping home four million pounds of tobacco annually, the principal money crop supporting its population of 8,000 whites, and further enriching James's exchequer.

James's self-esteem had been greatly fortified by the tumultuous welcome London had given him, leading him to believe he could bring about an end to the struggle for control of the Anglican church. Little came of his efforts in the early years except preparations for a new English Bible, which was to become enshrined in literature and history as the "King James Version." Acting on the suggestion of the Oxford College Puritan president, James named a group of fifty-four clergymen to make the new translation. Six committees were formed, each charged with a section of the book, and the members were assigned chapters for translation from the Greek and Hebrew. After reading their work to one another, corrections were accepted and suggestions studied, and the translations were sent to still another committee, for editing and rewriting. After thirty-three months, the first complete draft was ready to be sent to a panel of twelve for approval. The 1,500-page authorized volume appeared in 1611. Few British Protestants were satisfied.

The most fanatically devoted purifiers, the radical Separatists, saw little hope of imposing their rigid Protestantism on a Britain whose ruler was also its religious head, presiding over a state ritual that preserved the "popish mummeries" they despised. New legislation made the Puritan form of worship impossible, driging many of them to Holland, the recently self-liberated Spanish colony. There they found freedom of worship, but within a few years saw their children not only beginning to resemble young Dutch persons in speech and thought, but marrying them as well. After Holland offered land in Guiana, Separatist leaders opened negotiations with some seventy London merchants who were organizing an overseas colony, to whom James had given permission only to sail to Virginia, but no grant to colonize any new area. From the proceeds of shrewd investments and the sale of much of their own property, enough was amassed by the Separatists to buy the boat on which they set sail in the late summer of 1620.

Their 180-ton *Mayflower* carried a mix of two Anglican "strangers" to every Puritan "saint" in its company of 101, dumping them all in late December on a bleak New England coast far north of their expected landfall. The company of middle-class English craftsmen and their families had drunk all the beer and eaten almost all the stores, and found, as one of them later recalled, "no friends to welcome them, nor inns to entertain or refresh their weather-beaten bodies, no houses, nor much less townes to repair to to seek for succor." While these families of Pilgrims, as they now called themselves, subsisted on a diet of salt meat and ships' biscuit, the strongest of them foraged for food.

On December 25, they moved to their final home, the town they had created and named Plymouth. Because celebration of the Lord's birth was a Catholic ceremony, one they had early discarded, together with the singing of carols, they worked as they would have on any day of the week. Although they found corn the Indians, mostly wiped out by plague, had buried against a time of hunger, only fifty of them were alive when spring came. Then, a single Indian showed them how to cultivate corn, assuring continued sustenance. Its production became their chief enterprise, for it often was used in lieu of money. Eventually, Plymouth was able to buy out the London merchants who had invested in their venture, to ship surplus corn home at six shillings a bushel, to import cattle, and to speculate in the fur trade. In twenty years, they numbered 3,000.

From that day in 1609 when James announced to Parliament that "the state of the monarchy is the supremest thing upon earth. . . . For Kings are not only God's lieutenants upon earth and sit upon God's throne, but even by God Himself are called gods. . . . Kings are justly called gods, for they exercise a manner or resemblance of divine power on earth," a battle between the crown and the purifiers of the Anglican church was inevitable. Before he died in 1625, James had offended most of the rising Puritan middle class centering around mercantile London, with its 300,000 inhabitants. He burned two Unitarian radicals, put his lover George Villiers, duke of Buckingham, in control of a foreign policy seeking détente with Spain, married his son off to the Catholic princess of France, and failed to succor or support embattled German Protestant rebels against Spain in their thirty-year war. When he finally did, ending the longest peace England had yet enjoyed, Britons denounced him for the conscription that followed.

The agricultural Catholic north suffered equally with the Protestant south from inflation, which continued to grip the nation, setting off a series of crippling depressions. The Stuart reign had begun on a note of rising hope as a years-long financial crisis came to an end, only to return, from 1619 to 1624 and then five years later, and to last until 1635. When economic troubles did not burden the nation, plagues tormented it and poor harvests starved it.

The new ruler, Charles I, inherited a land and technology upon which the growing merchant class was fattening, and an economy that brought rising unemployment and wages to their lowest point in 400 years. Those who sought to escape religious strife or economic deprivation looked to the lands across the ocean, in which pamphleteers, balladists, and propagandists for joint-stock companies had long promised ''things unknown, erecting towns, peopling countries, informing the ignorant, reforming things unjust, teaching virtue and gain to our Mother Country, a kingdom to attend her and find employment for those who are idle, because they know not what to do.''

Third in the procession of voyagers to the lands where cedar trees touched the skies was a company of 200 members of the newly established Massachusetts Bay Company. Its charter was the usual joint-stock venture, and the first colonists consisted of a small group of merchant leaders dominating a preponderance of persons from the lower classes. Though the real purpose of the leaders was escape from religious persecution, the pursuit of that freedom played no part in the language of the charter. Charles would have no such nonsense. The colony was to engage only in the fish and fur trades, returning a dividend to the company's investors. Having again dissolved Parliament in 1629, hoping to silence the Puritans, who now formed the majority of both London's middle class and the House of Commons, Charles banned Puritan literature and teachings. Puritan ministers were driven out of their churches by the whips of royal troopers.

Led by a Cambridge-educated lawyer, John Winthrop, whose estate and wealth had suffered from the economic crisis, the first of seventeen ships, bearing 2,000 settlers, made its way in 1630 to the new colony. During the following decade, England experienced the greatest exodus in its history. Two hundred thousand pounds was expended to transport 20,000 colonists, only one-fifth of them Puritan. The towns of Boston, Cambridge, Charlestown, Salem, and Watertown were established by newly arrived Britons looking for free land and financial opportunity, and often finding both as the colony prospered from farming, lumbering, and the fishing and fur trades.

Although the Puritan establishment represented only a small proportion of the body politic, it dominated, ruling both religious and secular life. Plymouth Colony was only a few years old when Thomas Wheeler was fined for profane and foolish dancing, singing and wanton speeches, probably being drunk. Another free spirit, Thomas Morton, was expelled from the countryside near Mount Wollaston, to a place he named Merriemount, where "the scum of the earth" soon gathered. Free of Puritan restraints, Morton and his companions thrived. There, he wrote later, "a merry song [was] made, which [to make their revels more fashionable] was sung with a chorus, each man bearing his part; while they performed in a dance, hand in hand about the Maypole, whiles one of the Company sung and filled out the good liquor, like Gammedes and Jupiter."

Indian women were invited to join, a Puritan chronicler wrote, "dancing and frisking together, like so many fairies or furies, rather." Probably the first American to write popular songs, Morton "to show his poetry, composed sundry rimes and verses, more tending to lasciviousness." His maypole, a traditional phallic symbol, disturbed the Puritans, but of more concern to them was the rumor that he was selling firearms to the Indians and that he had trained them in their use. Deported to England in 1630, Morton wrote the earliest exposé of Puritan censorship in America, but new settlers continued to make the voyage west.

Charles, on assuming the problems of governing England, not the least of which was the proliferation of protesting sects, 180 by the time of his execution, faced a seemingly impossible task. Puritan Quakers opposed war, Puritan Independents wanted no king, but, instead, a nation run along the lines of Plato's prescription. Baptists separated and then separated again. Only the Catholics remained ardent in faith and true to dogma, despite new laws and the peril of death. George Calvert, Lord Baltimore, who had returned to the Roman faith of his fathers, applied for a grant of land in America where his coreligionists in Britain and all of Europe might worship freely. He received title to land north of the Potomac River, and in 1634 his son sent the first band of Catholic émigrés to the new proprietary colony.

Not all of Charles's problems removed themselves by going off to America. The middle class of lawyers, doctors, merchants, bankers, and manufacturers was daily becoming a more powerful political and social force. A single factory employed as many as a thousand workers to turn out textiles, leather, and metal goods, brew ale and beer, make candles for home consumption and export. Investors revived and modernized a centuries-old mining industry to meet the demand for more tin, iron, lead, coal, and copper. But British involvement in Continental wars took a toll of these new enterprises, resulting in periods of mass unemployment.

The stammering, art-loving Stuart grandson of Mary, Queen of Scots, ruled, as absolute monarch, from 1629 until 1640, when the now Puritan Parliament returned to wrest control away. By then two percent of all Britons had migrated to the New World; 38,000 of these had made their way to the West Indian colonies of Bermuda, Barbados, Nevis, and St. Kitts. The New England colonies—in Massachusetts, Connecticut, Rhode Island, New Hampshire, and Maine—had a population of more than 17,000 and the Chesapeake colonies had the same, with 15,000 in Virginia and 2,000 in Maryland.

Bloody civil war broke out in England in 1642, pitting royalist supporters of the divine right of kings and its earthly embodiment, Charles Stuart, against Puritans, who refused support. Roundheads, so named because they cropped their hair close to the head, fought against curly-pated Cavalier partisans of the Stuarts over the next several years, until Charles surrendered in 1646. It took three years for the controlling Puritans to summon up enough courage to execute their king and establish the Commonwealth in his place. Four years later, Oliver Cromwell, son of a leading family, Cambridge dropout and one-time brewer, who had been the victorious amateur general of psalm-singing troopers, was named lord protector of the Commonwealth of England, Scotland, and Ireland.

The nation was united in name only. Cavalier aristocrats and gentry who had fought for Charles faced certain bankruptcy after confiscation of much of their property as punishment for misguided loyalty. Many migrated to the American colonies, there to found, among others, the Washington, Madison, Lee, and Randolph families.

Catholic Irish forces allied with the Stuarts fought gallantly against Protectorate forces and lost. Half of Ireland's population of a million and a half died of plague, starvation, and in battle. Catholic children were shipped off to England, and all priests were banished. Hundreds of Irish officers were transported to the Caribbean islands as bond servants. Two-thirds of all Irish lands were ceded to Britons or their Irish collaborators. Immediately after Charles's beheading, Scotland declared its loyalty to his son, welcoming him and crowning him their king. After two years of war, his reign came to an end, and Charles II was driven into European exile.

Under Commonwealth rule the Anglican church was reduced to impotency, its *Book of Common Prayer* banned, its use confined to secret ceremonies. Puritan, Presbyterian, and Baptist clergy alone were permitted to serve the nation's spiritual needs. Only that music recommended in the Sternhold and Hopkins psalters was sanctioned; everything else was proscribed. The cathedral choirs were disbanded, and the great organs were destroyed.

London's theaters had been shuttered at the start of the Civil War, and the new government kept them closed for another fourteen years. The city's favorite spectator sport of bearbaiting was halted, along with all other frivolous pastimes, the animals being destroyed to ensure that the order would be obeyed. Thieves, gamblers, and prostitutes were deported to the colonies as indentured servants, an event celebrated in street songs, whose sale continued in spite of government interdictions. In return for transportation and the promise of food and lodging during the term of service, these white bond servants were auctioned on arrival in America, sold at profits of from fifty to a thousand percent over the initial cost of ten pounds for shipping. In the homes of prospering colonists they joined "trappaned" Britons, usually young women, who had been spirited away from their homes by kidnappers for sale to American buyers.

A temporary reversal of the flow of traffic to the Massachusetts colonies took place when able-bodied Separatists there returned to England to aid in the nation's de-Anglicanizing. In Virginia, political control was veering to ambitious and capable Anglican refugees, Stuart-sympathizing plantation owners whose

Tidewater holdings flourished, giving them economic superiority over some 30,000 white citizens and some 1,000 black servants, slaves, and freedmen, a number that doubled by 1670.

The New England and Southern colonies continued to do business with the New Netherlands settlements though they appeared, to the London government, to be a wedge poised to split its holdings asunder. Starting in 1650, Parliament passed several navigation acts, hoping to put an end to Holland's profitable shipping trade. Conflict resulted, though it became a relatively minor concern when Spain, fearful of plans to establish new British colonies in Cuba and other Spanish-held Caribbean islands, opened hostilities, too. Holland, having gained its independence from Spain, and recognizing that Britain had risen from a small island nation to a position of world power by looting European-bound treasure ships, had adopted the same tactic. Its West India Company, founded in 1621, won for its owners a trade monopoly over all Dutch holdings in the Americas and on the west coast of Africa. Within a few years, Dutch privateering fleets had taken 545 Spanish treasure ships, with cargoes worth hundreds of millions. Holland's claim to North American lands was based on a voyage of discovery by the English-born free-lance navigator Henry Hudson. Sailing under Dutch colors, he traveled by ship from Newfoundland to the Carolinas in the summer of 1609, seeking an ice-free passage to the Far East. After putting into Chesapeake Bay, he sailed up the Hudson River as far north as present-day Albany, finding a land rich in fur-bearing animals and ideal for farming.

Dutch settlers established outposts on the Delaware River and on Manhattan Island, in the center of a broad harbor at the mouth of the Hudson, and at Albany. By 1664, the town of New Amsterdam boasted 1,600 inhabitants, keeping wandering cattle in and marauding Indians out behind a walled street, which became a leading world financial center. The town was a major trading post and market center, where eighteen different languages were common, and business was done in Virginia tobacco and New England produce despite all Parliament's acts forbidding both.

During Cromwell's seeming obsession with control of the Caribbean area, relations with Holland were relatively calm, though officially hostile. On the other hand, the war with Spain, in which France became an unexpected ally, brought about home rule of blood and iron. There was little mourning in August 1658 when the lord protector died, ending a rule that Winston Churchill termed "hated as no government had ever been hated in England before or since." Cromwell's successor, his son, had little of his father's drive or ruthlessness, and soon gave up the office, but not until he had signed a peace with Spain, guaranteeing Britain dominion over the seas and North America.

During the years after he was toppled from the throne of Scotland and forced into exile, Charles II had waited for a call to power, living on borrowed money and royal charity. He responded immediately to an offer from representatives of a Parliament from which Puritans had been ruthlessly purged. As he watched thousands of Englishmen cheering his return to the land of his birth in early summer of 1659, he remarked, "It must surely have been my fault that I did not come before, for I have met no one today who did not protest that he had always wished for my restoration.''

The restored monarch might have been less euphoric had he known that most of that mob looked to him for economic relief and political favor. The royal exchequer contained exactly £11 2s 10p, a sum scarcely sufficient to pay for a day's service of a common foot soldier and the lord general commanding him. Britain was in debt to the tune of two million pounds. Yet Charles was more concerned with the resumption of those royal privileges that had been so long denied him. A Cavalier Parliament at once restored the Anglican church to power. The dissenters—the Presbyterians, Congregationalists, Baptists, Quakers, Unitarians, and even Roman Catholics—found common ground for the first time in history, being equally harassed and threatened with prison and worse. Two thousand Protestant clergy were thrown out of work. The 60,000 members of the Quaker sect, or Society of Friends, who got their name because, it was said, ''they quake and tremble at the word of the Lord,'' were obdurate in their refusal to doff hats to any king or bishop, general or clerk, and worshiped only by giving voice to whatever the Holy Ghost inspired them to utter. Their repression was even more vicious than that accorded the Puritans, since transportation to convict plantations was mandatory when Quakers were caught a third time attending a religious meeting.

New England was no longer deemed the ''poor, cold and useless'' land Cromwell had dubbed it. The colony's continuing illegal trade with the Dutch was costing the exchequer £10,000 annually. So, in mid-1664, a British fleet appeared off New Amsterdam and soon arranged a bloodless surrender of all of New Netherlands. Britain then controlled all of the Atlantic coastline from Maine, into which Massachusetts had spilled over, down to Virginia. Spain governed land to the south.

Opportunity for a man to make his fortune by investing in joint-stock colonization no longer existed, because the head of state wished to enlarge his personal empire and dominion, improving his purse and that of his friends in the process. A territorial grant extending to the Pacific Ocean of all lands between Albemarle Sound almost to the Spanish holdings at St. Mary's River in Florida was given to eight gentlemen proprietors for an annual rental of twenty marks in English money. These privileged courtiers were given authority to build towns, collect taxes, and sell land. Writers of promotional tracts and ballads were again pressed into service to extoll the glories of this new real estate venture.

Some disillusioned Virginians took advantage of the bargain and moved into the isolated Tidewater reaches of northern Carolina, to earn a meager living raising tobacco on small parcels of land. These poor farmers owned few slaves, either black or white, worked their land themselves, worshiped as they pleased, and avoided excise taxes on their crops. The inlet at Charles Town, in the Carolinas, proved ideal for a major settlement. Its first cash crop was rice, and by 1700 growers of that specialty, the best in the world after cross-cultivation with imported Madagascar rice, were producing more than available shipping could handle.

Although some Quakers had begun the migration to the colonies prior to 1653, the imposition of Charles's repressive laws against the sect created a growing exodus by the 1670s. The New World welcome was unfriendly. Massachusetts set a fine of one hundred pounds for harboring a Quaker, and certain whipping and occasional prison faced these intractable and bristly zealots everywhere. Only in western New Jersey, along the Delaware River, formerly held by the Dutch, did Quakers find a grudging welcome and opportunity to pursue their trades of sawmilling, brewing, and cloth making, alongside groups of newly arrived Dutch, Swedes, and Finns.

A home for these schismatically factious people was finally arranged by a recent convert to their cause, Oxford-educated William Penn, son of a British admiral who had had his offspring whipped and then turned out of the family home for his apostasy. There was an eventual reconciliation, on whose strength, following his father's death, Penn presented a bill for £16,000, lent by the family to exiled Charles Stuart. This was apparently wiped off the books in exchange for Penn's Woods, the name proposed by the king, today Pennsylvania. It was the first land grant not bordering the Atlantic Ocean.

A series of advertising ballads and supporting pamphlets, printed to recruit settlers for the new colony, circulated in Ireland, Belgium, and Holland, as well as Germany, where many new dissident sects had surfaced with beliefs closely paralleling Quaker tenets. One hundred pounds purchased 5,000 acres, and smaller parcels could be rented at a penny an acre yearly. Penn's carefully devised advertising and public-relations campaign attracted all sorts—seekers of religious freedom, land speculators, indentured servants, ambitious farmers, and men who believed they could make their mark if provided with opportunity. Philadelphia, the City of Brotherly Love, laid out in 1682, welcomed all newcomers, and soon became a major shipping and business center. Stately brick houses, generally three stories high, after the mode of London, and as many families in each, bordered streets running at right angles to one another, the first in America so laid out, with the cross streets named after trees and the others numbered.

British control extended over more than 1,500 miles of Atlantic seaboard by 1690, stretching from the mouth of Maine's Kennebec River, south to Carolina's Port Royal. Within this area lived adherants of all religious and political beliefs, men of all colors, men not fully satisfied with their place in the British Empire, and most of them suffering from the commercial monopolies imposed upon them by a government 3,000 miles away. That ruling power and its Parliament were dominated by an entente between the church, merchants, landowners, and bankers, all determined to maintain control by the rich over the poor. One-fourth of England's five million people lived in poverty, supporting themselves by charity and begging. Great buildings housed hundreds of workers, ranging in age from five to any oldster who could stay on his feet, to produce finished wares for a shilling a day. Henry Ford's assembly-line system had already been envisioned.

Once Charles had become king, the importation of manufactured goods was regulated and taxed severely, to ensure against competition. Britain wanted only a plenteous supply of raw materials, to be turned quickly into export items and then shipped to the colonies for fast profits. Even the king was a victim of the ruling banking class, so heavily in debt to London financiers—more than a million pounds—that he suspended all interest payments in the nation for a year.

The center of British banking and manufacture, London was the largest city in Europe, doubling its population to 700,000 between 1662 and 1682. Early environmentalists railed against the city's pollution, so incurable that it carried away multitudes by consumption. One-quarter of all children died before reaching sixteen, suffering, as did their parents, from poor nutrition and foul air. Regular epidemics and occasional plagues carried off thousands, since no sewers were available to bear off the effluvia of the city's outhouses, which then spilled into the Thames, the source of drinking water for the poor. One-seventh of the city's people died of plague in 1665, and the following year a new disaster struck, with two-thirds of London going up in flames, leaving 200,000 homeless and resulting in almost a billion dollars in damage.

The city was rebuilt of brick and stone, a fire department was organized, and fire hydrants were installed. Londoners looked to a new future in this rebirth. But there was no bright future in relations between king and state, between Catholic and Protestant. Charles was in the middle of both these interminable battles. On his deathbed, in 1685, he was received into the Roman church. His Catholic brother James became king and head of the Church of England.

From the start, the new monarch affirmed his belief in that same divine right of kings that had led to his father's execution. Within three months, revolt broke out in Presbyterian Scotland and the Puritan strongholds in the southwestern counties. Both were soon and bloodily put down. Catholics were named to high office, and a papal emissary, the first since Bloody Mary's day, attended the king. Yet, on the advice of William Penn, James annulled laws forbidding public worship by dissenting groups and guaranteed freedom of religious choice to all Englishmen. The crown also assumed financial support of the newly named English Catholic bishops.

England's second revolution in a century followed, preserved in memory as the "glorious and bloodless one." Most Britons had been patiently waiting out James's reign; he had no male heir, was in his fifties and not well. Then, in 1688, his first son was born, and in spite of the law mandating that his offspring be baptized as Anglicans, he announced that his son would be brought up in the Catholic faith. Parliament was quick to act; it declared the throne vacant. James II's daughter the Protestant Mary had been married earlier to William III, the Protestant stadtholder of Holland. After secret negotiations with them, to ensure compliance with the wishes of Parliament, power was offered to the Dutch rulers. They accepted it and subscribed to the Declaration of Rights, which ended for all time the divine-rights business, placed Parliament in control, forbid any Catholic from ruling as king, created the constitutional monarchy that has headed England since, and cemented the merchant-capitalist aristocracy's hold on the nation.

It had been one of the fondest hopes of British investors in the New England colonies that the region would produce ample naval stores—tar, pitch, turpentine, and rosin—and other raw materials to make the home country independent of Europe, an aspiration soon dashed. Unlike the southern colonies, which shipped sugar back home, New England turned to local manufacture and did a thriving business with colonial neighbors. In spite of English navigation laws prohibiting trade with other nations, Spanish, French, and Dutch shipping put into New England ports daily, bringing wine, textiles, and fruit, and taking local commodities in exchange, at prices twenty percent less than London rates, thus costing the crown over £60,000 annually in lost taxes, an amount that eventually doubled. Government commissions issued a series of reports and recommendations before the Court of Chancery finally acted, revoking the Massachusetts charter in 1684.

A new governor for the New England colonies was dispatched and quickly brought them, and neighboring colonies, into line. New taxes were levied, redcoated British troops were garrisoned, and the Church of England was imposed on all colonies, regardless of their religious laws.

William and Mary brought only temporary easing of the strained relations between colonies and home government. Although the Dutch rulers stabilized the economic situation by creating the Bank of England, with an exclusive monopoly to lend money to the government, chief attention was to the French threat to Holland. An aggressive foreign policy resulted in direct confrontation with France and wars that were fought in Europe and on the North American mainland for six decades.

Mary's death in 1694 left her sister Anne next in line, and when William died seven years later, this last of Charles's children became ruler of England. Her reign was marked by reconciliation with Scotland, formation of the United Kingdom of Great Britain, under a single ruler, and a national flag, on which were entwined the British Cross of Saint George and the Scots' Cross of Saint Andrew. During this time, England surpassed France in quantity and quality of literary production. The most brilliant writers—Defoe, Steele, Richardson, Swift, Addison, Pope—whose creativity dominated the era, also labored to produce the nation's first recognition of authors: the 1710 Law of Queen Anne, the first copyright law, which provided the basis for protection of intellectual property in the English-speaking world.

# CHAPTER 8

# The Music of God's Englishmen

Within a few months of Elizabeth's death, the printing of Singing Psalms, the catechism, and primers had passed out of the control of individual patent owners and their assigns, often combines of leading Stationers' Company officials, into the hands of the company itself. James had granted a new privilege, differing from all preceding ones, by giving the monopoly in return for an annual contribution of £200 to be used to support the poor. Surreptitious printing of these major works was to be an offense against the entire guild, rather than the individual patent holders, as it had been since the initial charter was given by Philip and Mary in 1557.

The masters, wardens, and communality of the company agreed on joint-stock financing to settle any and all claims, raising the sum of £9,000 by selling 150 shares of "English Stock" at prices scaled according to the three ranks of membership. Those of the top rank were able to get at least a ten percent annual yield on their investment.

Public demand for the psalter was satisfied by new editions, not a year passing without at least two. Secure in their monopoly and brooking no competition, the company relaxed standards of quality, and all other printed books suffered. Paper and ink were of the poorest type, and presses grew more dilapidated and were rarely replaced. The restrictions of 1586, calling for the resetting of type each time 1,200 copies had been printed, were usually bent. Dividends thus increased to an estimated sixty percent, so that shares changed hands rarely.

The first real rival to the standard Sternhold and Hopkins psalter appeared in Amsterdam in 1612, to which Cambridge-trained Bible scholar Henry Ainsworth had gone with fellow Separatists. In the judgment of his brothers in God, "never having his better for the Hebrew tongue in the University nor scarce in Europe," he prepared *The Psalms of David in English* for his coreligionists. It was a small book containing thirty-nine different tunes printed in diamond-shaped notes, half of them borrowed from the standard Sternhold and Hopkins. Most of the rest, Ainsworth noted, "I have taken from the gravest and easiest tunes of the French and Dutch psalms.'' Among these were many of those Genevan jiggs about which conservative Puritans complained. In *The Winter's Tale,* Shakespeare referred to the fondness of some Puritans for these: "but one Puritan amongst them, and he sings psalms to hornpipes." The Ainsworth was reprinted in five editions before it was abandoned near the end of the century by its chief admirers, the Plymouth settlers.

As Puritanism grew more fashionable in London, both politically and socially, the Stationers' Company brought out, in 1621, a new publication, Thomas Ravenscroft's *The Whole Book of Psalms with the Hymns Evangelical and Songs Spiritual.* Twelve years before, at twenty-one, Ravenscroft had edited the first of three printed collections of popular songs for William Barley, and the new book contained forty-eight of its editor's settings, together with music by Tallis, Morley, Dowland, Farnaby, and Thomas Tomkins.

The prolific though second-rate poet George Wither was the first—unlikely but successful—competitor for the psalter trade. He had been enrolled at Oxford at the age of sixteen and by twenty-five was sitting in prison for having written a satire considered libelous. Only the tears of his friend Princess Elizabeth and a new poem honoring her father, King James, won his release, and the monarch's favor. His writings were highly popular, some selling as many as 30,000 printed copies in a few months, with two editions of 300 of each of them having been pirated. He believed that religious songs could do much to gain salvation for sinners, beginning in the cradle with lullabies. Armed with a royal patent, he engaged a now unknown printer to bring out his 1623 *Hymns and Songs of the Church,* the first compilation of his own sentimental church song texts, many of which anticipated the words of nineteenth-century religious songwriters. The music was by Orlando Gibbons, Westminster Abbey's newly named organist, and all of it was original. Hymns for each day of the week, for the seasons, and for special occasions were included. Not yet ready to substitute hymns with words written by man for the Psalms' Holy Writ, the Anglican church simply ignored the collection, even though the patent granted by King James required that a copy, being "worthy and profitable," was to be inserted "in convenient manner and due place" in every psalter printed and sold. The stationers also resisted this, and when James died and his patent was no longer binding, they told Wither to find a ballad-singer to hawk his music. It was an apt suggestion, since Wither's sentimental songs included verses being sung by the people of London and had drawn the admiration of St. Paul's schoolmaster, who likened their author to the Roman poet Juvenal.

Determined to fight the stationers' monopolistic practices, Wither launched an attack on their bookseller members who had refused to stock his work. Fewer and fewer printers, he argued, were publishing books, producing them for book dealers instead. In turn, these merchants fixed prices, stocked only what they owned, "placing all learning in jeopardy," Wither argued in *The Scholars Purgatory, discovered in the Stationers' Commonwealth.* With curiously modern connotations, he charged that

> as it is now [for the most part abused] the bookseller hath not only made the printer, the Binder, and the Clasp-maker, a slave to him, and hath brought Authors, yea, the whole Commonwealth, and all the liberal sciences into bondage. For he makes

all professors of Art labor for his profits, at his own price, and utters it to the Commonwealth in such fashion, and at those rates, which please himself. . . . If the author out of mere necessity, but do procure means to make sale of his own or to prevent combinations of such as be by some royal or lawful privilege; he presently cries it down for monopoly; affirming that men of his profession may go hang themselves if that be suffered.

Authors, Wither said, were usually mistreated, given at best a few shillings for their work, usually printed in execrable editions, and no royalties. For all its nobility of purpose and its logic, this early effort to improve conditions for authors failed, being nearly a century or more before its time.

Despite the state of the business, Wither continued to write, creating many collections of verses and hymns, usually publishing them himself. Occasionally, he condescended to write on order for money. His major work was printed in Holland, the 1641 *Hallelujah or Britain's Second Remembrancer,* which, with its songs "for members of Parliament, for poets, jailors and tailors and others," had a certain success among Puritan members of the rising middle class.

As a loyal supporter of the Stuarts, who had been his patrons, Wither served in the royal cavalry, but he wavered and joined the Roundheads, was captured by his former colleagues and imprisoned in the Tower of London. An impassioned plea by the poet Sir John Denham that, with Wither dead, Denham would then be the worst poet in the nation saved Wither from the gallows. Once out of the Tower, he raised a company of Commonwealth soldiers. At war's end, he emerged with the rank of major-general and became an official propagandist for the new government. When he told Cromwell "some truths which he was not willing to hear," Wither was discharged. On Charles's restoration, Wither was thrown into prison for past sins. He served three years and lived until 1667.

A half century later, people began to worship with secular-hymn poetry written by Isaac Watts and set to sober music. It was another several centuries before the vices of a seller-controlled publishing business were partially eradicated. By then Wither was long forgotten, except for some songs, among them, "Smoke and drink tobacco," a paean, and the poem "Shall I lie wasting in despair?"

The earliest of the viable permanent English settlements in North America, Jamestown, observed its first Church of England services and Holy Communion soon after the initial landing, directed by a minister who carefully observed the official ritual and dogma, the Psalms being sung from Thomas East's 1592 psalter. From the start, Virginia required that "the Almighty God be duly and daily served," and all evaders of this injunction were punished. Services were held twice a day, and the Lord's day was faithfully and unceasingly observed. The first meeting, in 1619, of the colony's ruling House of Burgesses enacted laws compelling services Sunday morning and afternoon, punishing idleness, and promising excommunication for excessive sinning. The earliest Jamestown pioneers hoped to find hoards of gold, like those the Spaniards regularly shipped home, but they coupled that with a requirement of their, and virtually every other, royal charter—the saving of Indian souls. The earliest Burgesses' sessions discussed establishment of a university for the red man's education, to be build on 10,000 acres of land. Little was actually done to keep the first Americans out of the white man's hell, and a massacre of 347 settlers dampened the progress of missionary work among the natives.

When Charles I carved Maryland out of the Virginia grant, to turn it over to a papist court favorite, anti-Catholic sentiment flared. During the Civil War, a Commonwealth fleet was sent to Virginia to stiffen any wavering loyalty and correct any waywardness in observance of Puritan services. The first high-ranking Anglican dignitary came near the century's end, armed with the powers, if not the title, of a bishop. His single lasting contribution was the school named after William and Mary.

By 1710, Virginia was as determinedly Anglican as ever. Quakers were tolerated, but Baptists were banned. The Presbyterian schism had not yet found firm adherents.

The *Mayflower*'s Pilgrims brought little excess baggage, but had a boundless faith in their own impeccable moral rectitude. Each of them went to worship with a copy of the Ainsworth bound into the family Bible. The 300-volume library brought by William Bradford, first governor of Plymouth Colony, contained religious works, but also poetry and travel, philosophical, and historical texts. He also prized Richard Allison's 1599 *Psalms of David in Meter,* printed by Barley.

Massachusetts Bay Puritans arriving in 1630 carried the official Church of England Sternhold and Hopkins *Book of Psalms* and obeyed its command to sing Psalms before and after morning and evening service, before and after the sermon. As in Britain, they followed the Calvinist practice of singing in unison, unaccompanied by any instrument. In the privacy of their homes, some sang the Psalms in harmony, to the accompaniment of instruments, which soon came into the colonies. When New England's clergy expressed their displeasure with the Sternhold and Hopkins renderings of David's words, the principle complaint was, as Cotton Mather wrote a half century later, that although "they blessed God for the religious endeavours of them who had translated the Psalms into the meter usually annexed at the end of the Bible, yet they beheld in the translation, variations of, not only the text but the very sense of the Psalmist, that it was an offence unto God."

A committee of thirty New England divines was appointed to prepare a "more close fitting" translation, each of them being given a portion to render. The major part of the final work was by three clergymen who had been trained at Cambridge. Richard Mather was responsible for the Twenty-third Psalm.

> The Lord to me a Shepherd is,
> Want therefor not shall I,
> He in the folds of tender grass
> Doth cause me down to lie.

The beautiful King James Version of the Bible was little more than twenty years old, yet most Puritans disdained it for having been done under the patronage of Catholic Mary's son.

There was no printing press in English-speaking North America when a grant of £400 by the Massachusetts General Court established America's first college, in 1636. Two years later, as its first classes began, a young minister named John Harvard died and left his library of 300 books and half his estate to the new institution. In gratitude, the college was named for its benefactor and the community housing it rechristened Cambridge, after the English town in which he had been educated.

At about the same time, another clergyman, who was to play a small role in the publication of America's first books, was stricken on board a vessel bound for Boston and died. He was the Reverend Jose Glover, of London, who had invested fifty pounds in the colony's financing, had already crossed the ocean to take a look, and was now returning to be a permanent resident and hoping to be named president of the new college. Toward that end he had actively engaged in fund raising, even then a considerable asset in a professional educator. He was also bringing material to build an iron foundry, as well as a press and a font of type, a stock of paper, and a quantity of books he intended to present to the school.

Glover had signed an employment contract with Stephen Daye, a skilled mechanic well qualified to handle the foundry, and his two teen-age sons, who had some familiarity with typesetting. Once Mrs. Glover, now possessed of a sizable estate, had bought one of Cambridge's finest houses, the Daye family and the printing equipment were housed in a building provided by the Harvard board of governors. Matthew Daye, the older boy, was set to work on the press, and his relatively illiterate father was assigned its mechanical operation. By year's end, the first job-printing order, on one side only, was filled, the 222-word Freeman's Oath, to which every twenty-one-year-old had to subscribe in order to become a citizen of the Bay Colony. The next order was for an *Almanac Calculated for New England,* compiled by Captain Pierce, a skilled mariner, who, having completed the book, carried off a load of local Indians to be traded in the Caribbean for the first cargo of black slaves brought to Boston.

The first book—a bound volume of more than forty-nine pages—printed in North America was next off the Harvard Press, in 1640. Like it, the first book printed in the Western Hemisphere was also a religious work. In 1539, Italian printer Giovanni Paoli had opened a printing office in Mexico City for the leading printer of Seville. He immediately printed and sold a catechism, done from type and dies cast by imported artisans. By the time of his death in 1560, Paoli had published thirty-seven books in the Spanish language, all of them of a religious nature. In all, 204 books were produced by Mexico City's nine printing presses before 1599.

The 1640 New England edition of the *Psalms of David* quickly became known as the *Bay Psalm Book.* Because no music type was available, and no one sufficiently skilled to engrave plates or cut into wood could be found, it contained no music, though the preface did have a few crudely engraved words in Hebrew. Seventeen hundred copies of the 296-page book were struck off, eleven of which survive. The paper had cost 29 pounds, and the printing thirty-three. At twenty pence a copy, the first edition made a profit. The presswork was understandably crude, even poorer than the output of London's now lackluster publishing business. Boston was overwhelmed by the accomplishment and at once rewarded Stephen Daye with a grant of 300 acres of farmland. Later, after quarreling with the press's new owners, Daye worked for Governor John Bradford, prospecting for iron ore with which to feed the Glover foundry.

Almost every Boston church adopted the new book, and churchgoers copied down the five or six tunes called for, pasting them into the back of their new psalter. Detailed instructions accompanying the finished work pointed out that "the verses of these Psalms may be reduced to six kinds, the first whereof may be sung in near forty common tunes; as they are collected out of our chief musicians by Thomas Ravenscroft."

Henry Dunster, Orientalist and minister, Harvard's first president and recently bereft of his wife, the former Mrs. Glover, now owned the press and set to work on a completely revised printing of the *Bay Psalm Book*. In 1651, he published *The Psalms, Hymns and Spiritual Songs of the New and Old Testament*, again without musical notation, containing not only Psalms but Biblical passages, among them the Song of Songs. Several thousand copies were widely distributed, giving young Puritans a rare opportunity to scan, with permission, Solomon's erotic love songs.

Although Dunster soon separated himself from Puritan tenets to become a Baptist, his new book came into use all over New England and as far south as Philadelphia. In Plymouth, however, the Ainsworth remained standard. Thirty-seven editions of Dunster's translations were eventually printed, the last around 1754. Only the rising popularity of Isaac Watts's translations and hymns supplanted it in the British Isles.

In 1698, eight years after the Cambridge press had shut down after issuing over 200 titles, there appeared an edition of the *Psalms, Hymns and Spiritual Songs* containing music. Thirteen melodies, printed from engraved wood plates, with the diamond-shaped notation typical of the time, were bound into the back of the edition. It is surprising that metal plates were not used, Boston then having a number of silversmiths expert in the art of engraving, and the town was the second-largest publishing center in the British Empire.

This tardy appearance of printed music in New England was one symptom of a gradual decline in the quality of church singing and the falling off of skill in note reading and musicianship. The Reverend John Cotton, having been ejected from a British pulpit for the theological severity of his two-hour-long sermons and their subsequent equally lengthy analyses, had arrived in Boston in 1633 and became minister of the First Church. Within a dozen years, he was complaining about this deterioration, and in *Singing of Psalms: A Gospel Ordinance*, he advocated the old practice of lining out. When the Puritan Parliament had abolished the *Book of Common Prayer* in 1644, and with it all church music except that for the Psalms, the minister or some fit person appointed by him read the songs line by line, and the Massachusetts Bay church took up the practice at once. About the same time, the Dutch Reformed church in New Amsterdam also required the presence of a precentor, or *vorzanger*. This method, sometimes called "deaconing," after the church official charged with the duty, was much like the traditional African "call and response," which became a dramatic feature of black gospel music. During the 1950s, young Americans discovered the attraction of lining out when the Weavers, a folk-song group, made their greatest success with the technique in their recordings of the traditional "On Top of Old Smokey" and the convict black singer Leadbelly's "Goodnight Irene."

In spite of the Biblical injunction appearing on the title page of the *Bay Psalm Book* that "if any be afflicted let him pray,/if any be merry, let him sing psalms," which seems to encourage joy in worship, many New Englanders were distressed by the "very extravagant notes" resulting from wandering from tune to tune or the interpolated improvisations of some congregations. Precentors were sometimes at fault, starting in keys too high or permitting worshipers to drift into some secular melody. Boredom often revealed itself in services that lengthened sometimes half again because of lining out.

For decades, the Plymouth church resisted deaconing. It was scarcely needed, since they lived every day with the music of the Ainsworth psalter. But as new generations appeared, and new attractive melodies charmed them, the dozen tunes became more difficult to retain. In 1692, after the colony was annexed to Massachusetts by royal order, the Ainsworth was dropped in favor of more modern publications and lining out became necessary in order to teach the new music.

A few years after that, Boston's fashionable Brattle Square Church finally voted to drop deaconing, the members noting that it was no longer needed by this troublemaking church of Boston merchants. They then issued a manifesto reconstituting themselves along "broad and catholic" lines, beginning with the use of the Lord's Prayer in ritual and the importation of a liberal Presbyterian minister from England. But their iconoclasm was challenged by new directions in church music.

Among this church's members was Thomas Brattle, one of Harvard's most illustrious alumni, a merchant but also a brilliant mathematician, who corresponded with Isaac Newton and numbered among his hobbies study of the microscope and music making on the first organ in Boston. After his death the instrument was delivered from his home to the Brattle Square Church in accordance with provisions of his will. Although they had waged a war of dissent with the Puritans, the congregation was not yet ready for man-made music and refused the gift. The instrument was shipped to King's Chapel, in the first and only Boston parish of the Church of England, on whose porch it remained for months before installation, whereupon it was publicly denounced by Puritan intellectuals as yet another piece of Episcopalian mummery.

## The Advent and Rise of the English Hymn

In an age that resisted the use of any words other than Holy Writ in religious song, those who, like George Wither, set their own spiritual verses to music in the first half of the seventeenth century had to wait for mass acceptance. John Cosin lived the last years of his life as the honored bishop of Durham, where he had served as chaplain in his youth and during that tenure compiled the 1627 *Collection of Private Devotions in the Practice of the Ancient Church*. Driven from his pulpit during the days of the Puritan Long Parliament, he went to France, where he served as chaplain to the royal family and was rewarded for his faithful perseverance with high office.

Twenty-one hymns by Jeremy Taylor were affixed to the end of his *Golden Grove* (1655), a collection of remarkably readable sermons and religious meditations. Like Cosin, Taylor supported the Stuarts, and, as an army chaplain, was taken prisoner. After the Restoration, Charles, in gratitude, named him bishop of Down and Connor.

John Milton's father was a scrivener by profession, earning his living by copying manuscripts and legal documents. He recognized his child's talent early and brought him up deliberately to be a man of genius. Young Milton's precocity was revealed in paraphrases of the Psalms, written when he was fifteen. Of these, "Let us with a gladsome mind" is still current in the Methodist hymnal. Sent to Cambridge to study for the ministry the following year, Milton was temporarily expelled after a quarrel over his singular good looks and upright morality led to fisticuffs. Some of his best verse was written during his studies there, including a group of hymns on the life of Christ. Not intended to be set to music, a task his madrigal-writing father would have relished, these and other of his poetry inspired nineteenth-century Methodist hymnals.

Once called "too Puritan for bishops and too Anglican for the Presbyterians," Richard Baxter was a writer and Anglican minister who served as chaplain in the Roundhead armies, though he resisted Cromwell as lord protector. He found himself among 1,200 clergymen of all faiths who were unable to subscribe to the 1662 Act of Uniformity, which asked for complete loyalty to the Church of England, and went to prison for his resistance. Seven of the eight settings of verse from his 1681 *Poetical Fragments,* in which he eschewed literal transactions in favor of well-written verse, entered the Methodist hymnal in the late nineteenth century.

The author of the Doxology, "Praise God from Whom all blessings flow," probably the most sung words ever written, Thomas Ken, was orphaned at the age of nine, in 1719, and brought up by Izaak Walton, the ironmonger who wrote a classic of British literature about his hobby, *The Compleat Angler.* Ken was educated for the church and served in various posts until his appointment as chaplain to Winchester College, Oxford. There he compiled a *Manual of Prayer* for use by students, which included the famous words. These were not known to the lay public until 1694, when Ken brought them out in pamphlet form because London printers had been selling them in pirated editions. The following year, the pamphlet was appended to the *Manual.* Charles II admired Ken and approved his appointment as chaplain to Princess Mary, the wife of William of Orange. Ken found life difficult at The Hague, where his bluntness sorely tried William, who failed to share his father-in-law's amused tolerance of the minister who was always ready to tell even a king his faults. In 1683, Ken was named chaplain to the fleet and, when Catholic James followed his brother to the throne, was one of seven Anglican bishops who refused to sign the new monarch's 1688 Declaration of Indulgence. Eventually acquitted of all charges of treason, Ken resigned his bishopric to spend his last years writing prose and poetry that reveals the inner feelings of this "good little man," as he was sometimes known.

Though some of the hymns written by Cosin, Taylor, and Baxter did win acceptance during their lifetime, the body of their verse failed to supplant either the revered Sternhold and Hopkins or the Pilgrims' Ainsworth. A few efforts to provide more modern versions of the Psalms of David for church use were made during the Commonwealth; all failed. Francis Rous's 1643 *Psalms of David* and William Barton's *Psalter,* published the next year, gained some approval from Irish and Scottish missionaries, who took them to the colonies in the late seventeenth and early eighteenth centuries. In 1636, George Sandys, an archbishop's son and traveler to America, wrote *A Paraphrase Upon the Psalms of David,* set to new tunes written by Henry Lawes, gentleman of the Chapel Royal. All of these were confounded by the Puritan government's opposition to change.

As quickly as it had outlawed stage presentations, the Puritan Parliament issued a number of ordinances for "speedy demolishment of all organs, images and all matters of superstitious monuments in all Cathedrals, and Collegiate or Parish Churches and Chapels throughout the Kingdom of England and the Dominion of Wales, the better to accomplish the blessed reformation so happily begun and to remove all offences and things illegal in the worship of God." These orders were vigorously enforced. Roundhead soldiers broke down the Westminster organs, pawning the pipes for pots of ale, and in Exeter took two or three hundred pipes from the local cathedral and walked up and down the streets honking on them. Meeting with some members of the cathedral chorus, the soldiers scoffed, telling them, "Boys, we have spoiled your trade, you must go and sing ballads."

Many dismantled organs were sold to private individuals, some to tavern keepers, and others were taken away and hidden by clergy against the time when instrumental music would return to the churches. Makers of church organs were forced to take up other occupations, and became joiners and carpenters. Some owners of alehouses and taverns to whom the Puritan soldiers sold pipes and organs repaired and maintained the instruments, hired musicians, and their places of business became known as "music houses." A visiting Frenchmen bemoaned such use in 1659: "That nothing may be wanting to the height of luxury and impiety of this abomination, they have transplanted the organs out of the Churches to set them up in taverns, chaunting their dithyrambics and bestial bacchanalias to the tune of those instruments which were wont to assist them in celebration of God's praises."

Though he had once commanded soldiers in such destruction, Cromwell, when he became lord protector, indulged his fondness for music. The organ of Magdalen College, Oxford, one of the few places permitted to maintain an instrument, was removed and placed in his suite at Hampton Court, where it remained for six years, and Cromwell performed on it with a certain skill.

By the time of the Restoration, public interest in psalm singing had dwindled, due mostly to its association with the Puritans. With the Anglicans once more in power, it became the duty of the new king's musicians to restore music to the cathedrals and the Chapel Royal, to reestablish ritual, and to remove all vestige of two decades of Puritan aceticism. The new ruler was a man who truly loved music. His taste broadened after he came into contact with modern French music and Italian opera, heard at performances of plays by Molière and operas by Lully. He learned to envy King Louis his orchestra of twenty-four violins that entertained at Versailles with light and melodious dinner music.

Charles wanted to have music to which he could keep time both in church and in his home. During the eleven months preceding his coronation in 1661, his musicians worked furiously to prepare for this occasion of magnificence and display. Charles Coleman, Henry Lawes, Henry Cooke, and Matthew Locke wrote music for processions and parades, and anthems and ceremonial music for the official functions, of such quality that Charles was as proud of them as of his regal raiment. As a result, Locke was appointed composer in ordinary, Lawes was restored to his old post as gentleman of the Chapel Royal, and Cooke was made master of boys of the chapel. Many older musicians who had served the first Charles were named organists at leading cathedrals and were charged with training new choirs, while the old master organ makers were hunted out of their anonymity and put to work.

Captain Henry Cooke found only five trained choristers in the Chapel Royal, all of them elderly. No books of music had escaped the Puritan destruction, and no two organists could agree on music for the order of service. He began to organize a new choir, relying on the experience of command he had gained during the Civil War. When talent hunters found young boys in cathedrals and churches, his men went into action, armed with the ancient rights of kidnapping the office had long enjoyed, and brought them to London. Local churches were often forced to rely on trumpet music and falsetto voices to imitate the sound of boy choristers. While Cooke was training his new chorus, he wrote anthems and introduced instrumental music into the services, evolving a form of religious music that used instruments in combination to accompany trained voices.

During their three years of basic training, Cooke's boys learned to read at sight, sing in Italian and Latin, and to play the organ, lute, violin, and harpsichord. A few learned to compose music. The contemporary diarist John Evelyn noted that "instead of the ancient grave and solemn music accompanying the organ, there was introduced to the royal court a consort of 24 violins, after the French fantastical light way, better suited to a tavern or a playhouse, than a church. This was the first time of change, and now we heard no more the cornet which gave life to the organ, that instrument quite left off in which the English were so skillful."

Charles ordered his Chapel Royal composers to add instrumental music to the anthems, to be played by his private musicians. These new works were used only in his private chapel, to which he repaired on Sunday mornings and on festival days. The ambitious young composers strove mightily to satisfy their sovereign's wishes, writing music in the French and Italian style he admired. Locke maintained his post by producing a steady stream of music, interspersing instrumental music for strings, oboes, and flutes with vocal music for chorus and soloists.

Cooke's work with the Chapel Royal boys bore early fruit. Five of them were turning out original music by 1663. Pelham Humfrey, who came to court as a lutenist at the age of thirteen, was sent to Europe five years later, to learn the musical styles of the Italian-born French master Jean Baptiste Lully. During his absence, he was made a gentleman of the chapel, and then manifested annoying self-importance on his return. Samuel Pepys wrote that he "was full of form, and confidence, and vanity, and disparages everybody's skill but his own." Charles liked Humfrey's style, and the two became friends, a relationship made stronger by the youth's outpouring of music in which he introduced Continental novelties, including an obbligato solo instrument with voices. Charles rewarded the obnoxious young man by naming him to succeed Cooke on the latter's death in 1672.

Humfrey was followed as master by the most important of the new generation of Chapel Royal–trained musicians, John Blow. As soon as his voice broke, Blow had been dismissed from the choir and went to Westminster as organist. In 1674, he returned as gentleman, and among his pupils was young Henry Purcell. Blow rose quickly, holding a series of major positions and finally becoming composer to the chapel in 1699.

The glories of Charles's music came to an end with his death. His brother, a practicing Catholic, had no interest in the Church of England save the prestige of being its governor. The twenty-four-piece orchestra disappeared from religious observances, and opportunity for new music ended. When William and Mary succeeded James, history witnessed another of its major ironies—a Dutch Calvinist now headed the church that had persecuted Calvinists of all persuasions. Neither of the new royal partners used the royal musicians, and Mary ended whatever importance was attached to this ancient tradition when she abolished the singing of prayers and replaced musical worship with Sunday-afternoon sermons.

Traditional British psalmody had fallen out of fashion to a great degree during Charles's reign, replaced by church music of a different kind. This prompted the first full-time English music publisher, John Playford, to attempt a revival of mass interest in the old music by making it appear more contemporary. As a long-time parish clerk to the Temple church, Playford was accustomed to "pitching" or starting off congregational singing. When Charles renewed the Parish Clerks guild charter, the new warrant ordered that every person chosen as a clerk first give sufficient proof of his ability to sing the tunes. However, little attention was paid to the requirement, and illiterates often served the function. To fill what he perceived as a need, Playford began to compile material for a psalter of his own creation. Determined to "add a new string to David's bow," in 1671 he brought out a collection of forty-seven *Psalms and Hymns*, thirty-four of them Sternhold's, one by George Wither, and twelve new pieces, all arranged in counterpoint. In the introduction, he wrote:

For many years this part of divine services was skillfully and devoutly performed, with delight and comfort, by many honest and religious people; and is still continued in our churches, but not with the reverence and estimation as formerly; some not affecting the translation, others not liking the music; both, I must confess, need reforming. These many tunes formerly used by these Psalms, for excellency of form, solemn air and suitableness to the matter of the Psalms are not inferior to any tunes used in foreign churches; but at this day the best, and almost all the choice tunes were lost, and out of use in our churches; nor must we expect it otherwise, when in and about this great city, in above one hundred parishes, there is but few parish clerks to be found that have either ear or understanding to set one of these tunes musically as it ought to be; it having been a custom during the late wars, and since, to choose men into such places, more for their poverty than skill or ability; whereby this part of God's service hath been so ridiculously performed in most places, that it is now brought into scorn and derision by many people.

Playford made some literary repairs to the century-old translations, believing that the "psalms should be judged as ballads for the people, rather than as poetry." The work was not a great success, chiefly, its publisher believed, because it had been printed in large folio size, making it inconvenient to carry to church. Further, the popularity of his best-selling books of popular music, rounds, catches, and airs should have reminded him that the music-buying contemporary Briton preferred three-part harmonizations to the traditional four he used. His acumen in recognizing changing popular taste may have been dulled, or his respect for the duties of parish clerk intimidating, for he repeated the old practice of writing his music in noted of unvarying value, which bored many singers. Seven years later, he brought out a psalter of "the whole of the old tunes" in a smaller, more convenient, size. For the following hundred years, Playford's was the standard work for those who wanted the old settings set down in a style that had become traditional in the conservative churches, one note for each word of text.

Noting that authors of old translations were "certainly both learned and godly men," he added that their piety often exceeded their poetry, even though their work was "valued with the best poesie." During the century, the best British poetry had undergone great changes, from the glory of the works of Shakespeare and his contemporaries, elevated by John Milton's musical use of the language, to the decline into the rhyme-chasing doggerel of the extraordinarily popular Cavalier and Restoration poets. Symbolic of its low estate was the succession of poets laureate preceding Nahum Tate, who was probably named to the post in 1692 as an act of cultural misanthropy by William of Orange, who spoke English only with difficulty.

Tate was born in Ireland, the son of a clergyman, and went to London in 1668 to work in the playhouses, where he became known for his facile adaptations of old works, chiefly a revision of *King Lear,* with a happy ending. William assigned him and the Reverend Nicholas Brady, the royal chaplain, the task of preparing an up-to-date version of the psalter of Sternhold and Hopkins. Brady, too, was an Irishman, who had been educated at Trinity College, Dublin, and was a writer of lyrics for the London stage before he found a place in William and Mary's retinue. In 1696, the Tate and Brady *New Version of the Psalms of David* appeared with great fanfare, and William, as head of the Anglican church, approved it as an official alternative to the old version. A supplement printed in 1700 contained a small number of hymns, among them Tate's

"While shepherds watched their flocks by night," one of six hymns then permitted for use by the Church of England.

In spite of the bishop of London's recommendation of the use of the new version, many conservative Anglican churches hesitated, Brady's own among them, the congregation spiritedly rejecting it. Even Brady's household objected to the work, a servant telling him, "If you must know the plain truth, sir, as long as you sang Jesus Christ's psalms I sung along with ye; but now that you sing psalms of your own invention, ye may sing them by yourselves." Eventually, the Tate and Brady was bound with the *Book of Common Prayer,* and enjoyed wide use and great popularity into Victorian times.

The recommendation of the bishop, as head of the Anglican church, also applied in the New World, where Boston's King's Chapel was the first to vote for using the new version. It was first printed in Boston in 1713, without any music, and most Anglican churches eventually adopted it, though the old version continued in use, particularly among nonconformist sects.

# CHAPTER 9

# Britain's Professional Music Makers

The great and growing company of musicians who flocked to the city on the Thames found it impossible to join the ranks of either the exclusive night watchmen turned municipal musicians, the blue-gowned, red-capped Waits, whose heavy silver chain of office and annual salary of twenty pounds raised them above the ranks of their rivals, or the Company of Musicians, London's guild of music makers. Nothing was left but to join the packs of unlicensed pipers and fiddlers thronging the streets and cajoling passers-by to pay for a penny-worth of dance music. Former tailors, shoemakers, and other would-be players crowded into alehouses, taverns, and public places or intruded upon private parties and municipal functions to sing the old favorite freeman's songs.

The company's control over competing musicians was extended in the first year of James's reign to include supervision of teachers of dancing, many of whom also played musical instruments. Their numbers were reduced quickly by the guild's imposition of rigid tests; all who failed were barred, and a fine of two pounds was levied on anyone who kept his dancing school open on holy days. Having received permission from municipal authorities, the Company of Musicians petitioned James for an extended charter of incorporation, thus bringing into being the Masters, Wardens and Commonality of the Art or Science of the Musicians of London, or Commonality, which now oversaw all minstrels and musicians within the city and for three miles beyond. A code of behavior cautioned against singing "any ribaldry, wanton or lascivious song or ditties"; doing so carried a fine of ten shillings or such imprisonment as thought fit. No fewer than four members could play at weddings, feasts, banquets, revels, or other assemblies, meetings or other functions. Members were cautioned against being seen in public with their instruments uncased or rebuking, striking, or abusing a brother musician, under penalty of heavy fines. From time to time the city added new restrictions, but the Commonality essentially remained supreme over the business of providing music for London's citizenry.

A similar monopolistic situation grew outside the city, where local guilds controlled musical entertainment. Often, these trade associations were headed by waits, and town magistrates, charged with licensing itinerants, maintained that monopoly by withholding permission from occasional visitors in favor of their neighbors. Despite the isolation of distance from London, most local musicians kept in touch with the city's activities and brought their listeners new fashions, new standards, and new pleasures. At the time of Elizabeth's death and until the Civil War, Walter Woodfill wrote in *Musicians in English Society*. "the provinces may have enjoyed more secular music, and particularly more concertized instrumental music, than ever before, and perhaps more than they were to until the coming of modern concert tours and the radio." Those thousands of Britons making their way to New England or Virginia may not have had much room for musical instruments aboard the tiny vessels bearing them, but they did carry an awareness of and familiarity with the music of their homeland that ranged beyond the psalms and the homely simplicities of "hey down derry."

Although the Commonality's jurisdiction over musicians embraced both Westminster Abbey and the royal household at Whitehall Palace, it was usually disregarded by the gentlemen of the King's Music and the Chapel Royal. Charles I's musicians included eleven violins, four viols, one harp, eight players of the hautboy and sackbut, six flutes, six recorders, drummers, fifers, and fifteen singers or teachers. Allowed to supplement their stipends during free time, many moonlighted in London, providing both fine musicianship and courtly manners. They played in the homes of the wealthy, the merchant adventurers, and the nobility, appeared at the public and private theaters to play music during scenes and between acts, and taught the art of lute, viol, and voice to the offspring of the upper classes.

Work opportunities had increased by 1630 in London's 200 or more licensed alehouses, leading to complaints that every building with a back door provided an illegal refuge for those looking "for a song or a tale/or a pot of good ale/to drive the cold winter away." In less than ten years, that number had grown to 2,000 in the western district alone, with another thousand unlicensed places. Authorities strove to end bribery of government licensing officials and to reduce the spread of such establishments, which opened at six in the morning and never closed till after dark. Although the price of malt liquors was fixed by law, and owners could provide each customer with no more than a single hour of tippling, citizens broke the laws with as little compunction as the unlicensed pothouse entertainers.

Prospering Britons, having gained proficiency in the family of viol instruments, the lute, organ, keyboards, and other instruments, now provided the music at home. A wealth of material for keyboards was available on paper, chiefly in manuscript. *My Ladye-Nevells Book,* compiled in 1591, the William Foster and Benjamin Cosyn several virginal books, and the celebrated *Fitzwilliam Virginal Book,* largest and most valuable storehouse of contemporary keyboard music, containing nearly 300 pieces by John Bull, Byrd, Dowland, Morley, Peter Phillips, and Tallis, were all in circulation. Ravenscroft's three collections of material for group singing could be had at stationers' shops, and many families chose to "fiddle at home," Roger North recalled, rather "than to go out and be knocked on the head abroad; and the entertainment was very much courted and made use of, not only in the country but by city families, in which many of the ladies were good consorters and in this state music was daily improving."

The king's gentlemen were learning that their monopoly of quality musicianship was coming to an end. One group of Commonality members, the Blackfriars Music, was "esteemed the best of the common musicians of London," and Sneak's Noise (band of musicians) was so well known that Shakespeare made reference to the group in *The Merry Wives of Windsor*.

In 1634, Nicolas Lanier, master of the King's Music, determined to challenge the powers of the Commonality. Composer, songwriter, scenic designer, and painter, he received £200 annually for his multifarious duties. As the king's art expert, he was often sent to Europe to buy pictures for the royal collection. On behalf of his fellow court musicians he charged that the London group had received its articles of incorporation by an "untrue suggestion," neglecting to tell James that the charter granted almost two centuries earlier, by Edward IV, gave control over musicians to members of the king's household. Charles withdrew the charter and issued a new document, creating the Commonality of the Art and Science of Music in Westminster, with Lanier at its head. Though he was an excellent art master and an adroit court politician he was not very effective as head of the national musicians guild; there is no record of any meeting of its governing body prior to 1661. London musicians took to petitions and counterpetitions, which resulted in some city ordinances and royal promulgations, none with any meaningful effect. When the Puritan majority took control of Parliament, the government paid little attention to the legalistic brawlings of Cavalier gut-scrapers and common bawdy balladeers.

How musicians, or indeed the entire art and science of music fared during Puritan rule is a subject of much contradictory argumentation. One school ascribes to the Commonwealth a hatred of music of all sorts so great that it made the period from 1640 to the Restoration English music's Dark Age. Its enemies found that music was played only in "dens of idling lubbards," that it was used only in "public assemblies and private conventicles as a director to filthy dancing." The musicians who played it ranged over all Britain, they said, "riming and singing songs in taverns, alehouses, inns and other public assemblies, which were fraught with all kinds of lascivious songs, filthy ballads and scurvy rhymes, serving every company and every purpose."

On the other hand, British musicologist Percy Scholes devoted 400 closely packed pages, in *The Puritans and Music in New England,* to put an end to "the long-standing conviction of musical Americans . . . as to the anti-pleasure, anti-art and [especially] anti-musical bias of their New England forefathers and predecessors."

The response to John Playford's first offering of books of popular music and dance tunes gives credence to Scholes's brief. One of Playford's earliest publications, the 1651 *Musical Banquet,* listed the names of eighteen teachers of voice or the viol, and nine keyboard instructors, one of them Cromwell's personal musician, all of whom were engaged actively in business. John Hingston, Cromwell's personal organist and teacher of his daughters, received one-hundred pounds a year for his services, and was permitted to appear before the Council for the Advancement of Music in 1657 with a plan to further that group's purpose. This short-lived body was the first and only official English government body for centuries concerned with the well-being of that art and its practitioners. Hingston had proposed the formation of a corporation to have many of the powers and privileges granted to earlier music guilds. He urged formation of a government-subsidized music-instruction facility for young and gifted people, to replace the schools formerly attached to the great cathedrals and churches, which had been closed by act of parliament. The new group would oversee the musical-instrument manufacturing trade as well, and "suppress the singing of obscene, scandalous and defamatory songs and ballads," presumably thus raising the level of the average Briton's music appreciation. This was all to be funded out of money received from the sale of land confiscated from Anglican authorities who had supported Charles. Little followed Hingston's presentation.

When the lord protector was buried, ten members of his personal music staff followed the body: Hingston, a violinist, and eight boy and men singers who had often entertained Cromwell by singing his favorite Latin and Roman Catholic motets, by Richard Dering. Upward of £60,000 was spent on the little bands of brass and drums that marched here and there among the mourners and the other musicians who provided Cromwell with his last concert.

Many of the gentlemen of the King's Music shared a fall from prestige and financial support during the Commonwealth. A few followed their Stuart master into battle. Those who collaborated with the new government, some becoming members of Cromwell's household, were well paid and much honored. Some cathedral organists and choirmasters were able to maintain their positions and salaries until the last days of the war, and then took to teaching, generally without any hindrance from the authorities, and were kept comfortable by their modest income.

Many church organists found work in taverns. Behind St. Paul's was one where shopkeepers and factory foremen sang in weekly concert while enjoying the ale and tobacco. Ben Wallington, a goldsmith with a deep bass voice, took over direction of these programs, using music chiefly from Playford's *Catch as Catch Can*, compiled by another church organist, John Hilton. Pepys occasionally invited Wallington to his home for an evening of song.

Taverns with organs were known as "musick houses" and were a feature of the resorts along the Thames. In 1663, Pepys traveled by water to such a place in Greenwich, where the master organist provided the company with a splendid improvisation, the voluntary, in which the best musicians were proficient.

After being ejected from his post as an Oxford University chaplain, Edmund Chilmead went to London in 1749 and found employment at the Black Horse Tavern, where he organized a music club that met regularly, drinking ale and smoking tobacco, as was the German custom, and making music.

In his history of British music, written a century later, John Hawkins reported of the era, with a considerable degree of petulance, that "fiddlers and others, hired by the master of the house . . . would scrape 'Sellinger's Round' or 'John come and kiss me' or 'Old Simon the King' with diversions, till themselves and their audience were tired, after which many players on the hautboy would in the most harsh and discordant tones grate forth 'Greensleeves,' 'Yellow Stockings,' 'Gilliam of Croydon' or some common dance tune and the people thought it fine music.''

A small group of such outcasts moved to Oxford, where Charles's former private musician John Wilson recorded their activities. Loving music as he did his late monarch, he larded the journal with many accounts of musical activities. Refugees from the court and unemployed church musicians met each week ''in their chambers . . . playing three, four and five parts with viols and an organ, virginal and harpsicon, joined to them; and they esteemed a violin to be an instrument belonging only to a common player and could not endure that it should be among them, for fears of making these meetings to be vain and frivolous.'' The appearance among them of the German virtuoso Thomas Baltzar was a revelation. After he played at one of their nightly gatherings, Wilson made a search to ascertain whether or not the man's feet were cloven, which would indicate that he'd sold his soul to the devil.

Unlike those in Norwich, Newcastle, and other places, London's waits had been immediately affected by the fall of the House of Stuart. Their salaries stopped, and the weekly Sunday-night public concerts at the Royal Exchange came to an end. But this was temporary; in 1644, seven of them, reduced to poverty, pleaded for redress and so moved municipal authorities that they were restored to the public payroll. The closing of the city's theaters and the curtailing of many other pleasures reduced work opportunities for professional musicians. Where once they got twenty shillings for two hours of playing, groups of Commonality members wandered about the city, their instruments under their cloaks, accosting passers-by with ''Will you have any music, gentlemen?'' Others took on apprentices, out of whose earnings they were entitled to take a share.

Thomas Hosier petitioned for the return of a bass viol, clothing, and other items from his master, Anthony Curtis. Hosier had served three years of apprenticeship before being drafted into the Puritan army and sent to the West Indies. On his return, he resumed his studies with Curtis for another year, during which time he gave his teacher twenty-six pounds out of money he earned as a strolling musician and working for tips in alehouses and taverns. Hosier invoked the act of Parliament that allowed him to credit the four years he had spent in service toward completion of his contract and asked to be released from it. The court agreed, and he got back his instrument.

In general, though the times were not as pleasant for professional music makers as they had been when Charles I ruled, they learned to make do or do without. They often found work in the unlicensed theaters, and when William Davenant began in 1656 to present private musical theatricals, he employed men who later directed the musical renaissance.

Every professional musician and every amateur with an instrument to play was in the line of march or among the spectators greeting Charles II in May 1660. But the hopes they shared were dashed as a flood of French-born musicians, assured of easy pickings in a court where anything not French was deemed to be second-class, contended successfully for places. The liturgical form was changed, taking on the coloration of French court music, and liveried composers were sent off to Paris to learn the new discipline, returning with heads full of Lully, whose intricately rhythmic compositions were becoming Europe's international language.

However, almost at once, Nicholas Lanier was back as master of the King's Music. Though he never summoned the royal musicians of Westminster, whose first marshal he was, into a business session, he began petitioning his master on their behalf for confirmation of their 1635 charter. It was quickly granted, setting off another series of petitions and legal maneuvers by the London musicians, a struggle whose documentation was lost during the great plague and the great fire.

Charles soon fell into debt to his musicians, as to his bankers. One day in 1666, Pepys ran into a new member of the King's Music, John Hingston, and, since Londoners were getting back to normal life after the fire, he invited him into the Dog Tavern for some gossip. After the musician had written out a bass line for some of Pepys's music, the talk got around to life at Whitehall, and Pepys learned that many of the musicians were five years behind in wages. A famous harpist named Evans, who had just died, had been buried in a pauper's grave, without a torch to light the way to the cemetery.

As a government official, Pepys was familiar with the toll inflation and the recent Dutch war had wreaked. The king was penniless, the five million francs received from France in 1662 for the sale of Dunkirk had been spent. To effect economies, the orchestras were halved, and court musicians worked only every second week. A debt of £500,000 incurred by the armed forces and an equal sum owned by his father made the relatively small amount Charles budgeted for music seem trivial. In 1669, £9,400 was appropriated for musical expenses, including salaries, clothing, and other perquisites, repair of old instruments and provision for new ones, and education of the Chapel Royal boys. The sum was insufficient to keep court musicians out of financial embarrassment. And as the king's men looked for work outside Whitehall, the music-loving middle class benefited.

## The First Public Concerts

John Banister is generally credited with producing and performing in the first public concert in London, which took place almost one hundred years before such events were part of Vienna's general musical activities. Though Banister was in better financial shape than other royal music makers, being one of the two or three best paid, money was due him for sums he had advanced for his food and clothing and for violin strings purchased for use by the king's violins.

Born in 1630, the son of a wait who taught him his first music, Banister was a well-known violinist by the age of twenty-six, and served as leader of the orchestra in the first theater productions to take place when the Commonwealth was beginning to pass into history. Once Charles heard him play, Banister was recruited for service at court, and in 1662 was dispatched to France to observe the work of Louis's famous fiddlers and to import their techniques to White-hall. On his return, he selected twenty-four musicians, being promised £600 pounds annually to be divided among them, in addition to their regular stipends.

Banister made no secret of his dislike of the French musicians who had driven English-born men out of royal employment. In return, one of them, Louis Grabu, made an official complaint that Banister was holding out money he had been given to share. He charged further than at least £275 had been withheld in the year 1663 alone. An inquiry followed, and Grabu replaced Banister as leader, though the latter was not dismissed, nor was his stipend reduced, because of his great talent. He continued to be one of the highest-paid court players for many years.

When Banister and eight other musicians were ordered to play in the royal theater orchestra, he learned that large sums were being spent on special scenic effects, music written to order, and uniforms for the musicians. This appealed to him, and he embarked on a song-writing career, becoming composer to the Duke of York's Company. He wrote music for verses by Aphra Behn, John Dryden, Charles Sedley (their song "Ah, Cloris, that you now could," from *The Mulberry Garden,* became so popular that Pepys complained), Thomas Shadwell (whose famous echo song in his opera *The Tempest,* written with Banister, prompted Pepys to request a copy in the composer's own hand), William Wycherley, and William Davenant.

On December 30, 1672, Banister advertised in the *London Gazette.*

> These are to give notice that at Mr. John Banister's house (now called the Musick-School) over against the George Tavern in White Friars, this present Monday, will be music performed by excellent masters, beginning precisely at four of the clock in the afternoon, and every afternoon for the future, precisely at the same hour.

He had redecorated a large downstairs room to look as much as possible like the music room of an inn or tavern, in which, it is believed, he had already conducted similar affairs. The musicians sat on a raised platform in an alcove at one end, hidden from the audience by heavy drapes in which holes were cut to permit the music to be heard. An audience of neighboring merchants and shopkeepers sat at tables and called out requests, to which they were entitled by an admission charge of one shilling. Drinks were fetched from the tavern across the way. Patrons joined in singing their favorite songs, having learned most of the popular music of the day from the series of books John Playford sold. New music was introduced the first day of each month, and when attendance fell off, people were allowed into the big room without charge, but paid half-price for makeshift boxes.

The musicians employed by Banister were often scabs, teachers, chiefly foreigners, and not royal musicians or members of the Commonality. He was breaking a guild stricture by hiring nonmembers to work within the city of London, but he boasted that he procured "the best bands in the town and some voices to come and perform," the musicians playing for a sportula, or share of the proceeds.

In late 1674, the concerts were moved from the disreputable Whitefriars setting to more impressive surroundings outside the city, in Covent Garden, and a few years prior to Banister's death to Lincoln's Inn Fields. Young John Banister took up where his father had left off, producing concerts in a location off The Strand, while also following his parent in the King's Music and the Theatre Royal orchestra.

Once the successful public acceptance of Banister's concerts was obvious, competition started. In 1674, one impresario used newspaper advertisements and handbills, passed out in coffeehouses and taverns and delivered to the homes of wealthy patrons, to promote

> a rare concert of four trumpets marine [six-foot-long stringed monochords played with a bow, named so because it was reportedly used by the navy for signaling] never heard before in England. If any person desires to come and hear it, they may repair to the Fleece Tavern, near St. James' about two of the clock in the afternoon, everyday of the week except Sunday. Every concert will continue one hour and begin again. The best places are now one shilling, and the other sixpence.

Time, length, form, and content of the paid public concert were now fixed.

Amateur players also gave recitals in public, though usually for their own gratification and the pleasure of their friends. Roger North, essayist, wrote:

> [There was] a society of gentlemen of good-esteem, whom I shall not name for some of them as I heard are still living (North probably being among them) that used to meet often for consort after Baptist [Lully]'s manner; and falling into a weekly course, and performing exclusively well, with bass violins, a coarse instrument as it was then, which they used to hire, their friends and acquaintances were admitted, and by degrees as the fame of their meetings spread, so many auditors came that their room was crowded, and to prevent inconvenience, they took a room in [Castle] Tavern and the taverner pretended to make formal seats, and to take money and then the society was disbanded. But the taverner, finding the sweet of vending wine and taking money, hired masters to play and made a pecuniary consort of it, to which for the reputation of the music, numbers of people of good fashion and quality repaired. And the masters observing such a penchant after music, agreed with the taverner and held on the meeting till the crowds were too great for the place and in the meantime the good half-crowns came in fairly, which was not 'bad music.'

This vogue among high society for consorted music received great impetus from the arrival in London of Hortense Mancini, the effervescent niece of France's Cardinal Mazarin. Charles II took one look at the lovely duchess and dismissed his current mistress. Hortense had resided in the French court from infancy and been the familiar of the great Italian singers and actors her uncle invited to Paris to establish opera there. The musical evenings she presented in her London salon attracted the king and the singing stars from his royal theater. Powdered and rouged ladies from the Theatre Royal and the Dorset Garden Theatre flurried about the room, singing their current songs; other beauties, amateurs in their music making only, played the harpsichord, flute, and recently popular guitar. All London copied the duchess's soirees. In 1679, John Evelyn wrote in his diary:

I dined at the Master of the Mint with my wife invited to hear music which was most exquisitely performed by four of the most renowned masters, Du Pru a Frenchman on the lute; Signor Bartolomeo (another in the procession of Italian virtuosi to take London by storm) on the harpsichord; and Nicalao on violin; but above all for its sweetness and novelty the viol d'amore played on with a bow, but being an ordinary violin, played on lyra way by a German, than which I have never heard a sweeter instrument or more surprising. There was also a flute douce, now in much request for accompanying the voice. Mr. Slingsby, master of the house, whose daughter and son played skillfully, being exceedingly excited with this diversion, had these meetings frequently at his house.

Soon after Banister's death, London's first public concert room was built off Villiers Street, in one of the buildings that had replaced burned-out York House, former residence of the duke. Professional musicians, calling themselves the Musick Meeting, took up residence in the new room, where ale and tobacco were forbidden to the beau monde gathering there. The promoters learned quickly the grand secret that the English would spend their money freely to listen to music. Unfortunately, the members of his musicians' cooperative squabbled over the programing and their solo appearances, indicating clearly to the perceptive North that "an absolute dictator" was needed, to "coerce and punish the republican mob of master musicians," thus anticipating the modern autocrat of the conductor's baton. This was the time when one master musician directed performances by keeping time with a roll of music paper, or by pounding a stick on the floor, which usually covered up or deadened the music. In the case of the great Lully, it did more. During the first performance of a Te Deum written for the ailing French king, Lully was thumping his long baton on the floor and struck his foot. An abscess followed, from the effects of which he died. For the next century, less flamboyant directors of instrumental music and the opera sat at the keyboard of a harpsichord or pianoforte and gestured to their players.

In many other sections of the nation, Britons soon had an opportunity to hear the newest and often best in contemporary concert and choral music during special programs marking the birthday of Saint Cecilia, patron of music and musicians. In 1683, a London group first took over the saint's special day to hold a worship service for which new choral music and an anthem were played by an unusually large orchestra made up of the city's finest musicians, followed by a sermon defending cathedral music. After worship, the entire company marched to Stationers' Hall, in whose great room a feast was held and an ode in praise of Saint Cecilia and of music in general was performed, written, as was the service, by Henry Purcell. Nicholas Brady, no longer a struggling playwright, wrote the libretto, the famous "Hail, bright Cecilia!" Except for three years, the day was celebrated regularly for the following two decades, with new music by Purcell, Blow, and others, as well as verse by many of England's greatest, or at least best-known, literary figures, Dryden, Shadwell, Congreve, Thomas D'Urfey, and John Hughes. Oxford followed London's example, commissioning works by Blow, Daniel Purcell, and their friends. Within a few years, Saint Cecilia and music were being similarly honored in Winchester, Gloucester, Wells, and Devizes. In Salisbury, the celebration took place over two days, developing into one of the earliest music festivals, during which sacred music was performed in the morning and concerts of contemporary music in the afternoon.

Edinburgh began celebrating music's patron saint in 1695, with its first public concert. A German musician resident there and known as the city's "Orpheus of the Musical School" organized the festivities. Thirty musicians took part, nineteen of them gentlemen of rank and fashion, and eleven masters. They played orchestral sonatas by Arcangelo Corelli, Giovanni Battista Bassani, Giuseppe Torelli, John Christopher Pepusch, and a native amateur, Hugh Clerk, whose overture was performed. When November weather permitted, the common people had an opportunity to hear the celebratory music through the open cathedral windows and doors, and listened to outstanding musicians who could usually be heard only by paying audiences.

In South Carolina, when colonists became sufficiently wealthy to think of culture and its appreciation and formed a society, in 1762, it was named the St. Cecilia Society.

Once the paid public concert was formalized, the benefit concert was not far behind. In 1678, Charles granted a royal charter of incorporation to the Charity for the Sons of the Clergy. Each year a special cathedral worship featured new music by the most fashionable composers and librettists, and the great feast following in the Merchant Taylors' Hall provided choice popular entertainment. Such democratization of music was greeted with less than enthusiasm by devotees of high culture. Small groups of amateur musicians, music lovers, and part singers formed exclusive clubs dedicated to the private pursuit of music.

Six years after Banister's first afternoon of music and tippling, Thomas Britton, who sold charcoal in the streets, began weekly evening concerts for special friends and acquaintances, which continued for the next thirty-six years. This simple, though greatly enlightened man, was born in London around 1644 and apprenticed at an early age to a coal dealer. After completing his training and basic education, he started his own "small coal," or charcoal, business in Clerkenwell, on London's north side. By the end of the seventeenth century, the district had become a fashionable residential area, but Britton continued to maintain his home and business there until his death in 1714. He eventually became successful enough to amass the autodidact's library, which made him the envied acquaintance of the era's greatest book collectors. He had, in addition to a knowledge of old books and manuscripts, great competence in chemistry and a spirited familiarity with the occult. There is no account of how he gathered his amazing knowledge of both theoretical and practical music.

The venue of the regular Thursday-evening programs was most humble. John Hawkins wrote, in his contemporary five-volume history of music:

[On the ground floor] was a repository for small coals, over that was the concert room, which was very long and narrow and had a ceiling so low that a tall man could just stand upright in it. The stairs to this room were on the outside of the house and could scarce be ascended without crawling. The house itself was very old and low built, and in every respect so poor as to be fit habitation for only a very poor man. Notwithstanding, this mansion, despicable as it may seem, attracted as polite an audience as ever the opera did, and a lady of the first rank in the kingdom, the Duchess of Queensbury, may well remember the pleasure which she manifested at hearing Mr. Britton's concert she seemed to have forgotten the difficulty by which she ascended the steps to it.

The presence of London's wealthiest and most influential musical amateurs evidently brought the newly arrived Handel there one evening in 1711. The most expert players were regulars: Roger L'Estrange, first censor of the press and of popular music during Charles's early years and an ''exquisite'' violist; Obadiah Shuttleworth, a fine violinist who got his hands on Corelli's works in manuscript and introduced them to England; Philip Hart, cathedral organist and composer of fugues; Abiell Wichello, church organist and composer of court and theater songs; the playwright John Hughes, accountant general of the Excise; Henry Needler, an accomplished violin player who established the Academy of Ancient Music and for years was leader of its orchestra of experts; and John Christopher Pepusch, German-born organist and composer to the duke of Chandos. For many years the concerts were free to invited guests and their friends, Britton selling a cup of coffee only, for a penny. In time, he began to ask for an annual subscription of ten shillings and provided the refreshment free of charge.

The strange little man was a customer of the Playford store, buying those bargains in early English music advertised in the shop's various special catalogues. His music library still exists; it embraces all the significant British music beginning with Byrd, Tallis, and Morley, up to the most modern of the early eighteenth century, and his foreign works include those of the best Italian masters of the baroque.

Britton's enthusiasm for mystic phenomena resulted in his death, when a ventriloquist, secreted as a caprice by one of of the small coal man's friends in an abandoned room, frightened him into a faint, from which he never recovered. His funeral was the occasion for great mourning by London's music world, its great and small marching in the procession that followed his body to the Clerkenwell parish church.

# CHAPTER 10

# English Musical Theater

The encounter with the elders of the church in Edinburgh in which an infatuated James of Scotland was involved, when they sought to prevent a return visit by his handsome friend the actor Lawrence Fletcher, provided a foretaste of what the British theater might look forward to. James enjoyed the theater and its actors to a degree one would not have expected, given his austere Scottish upbringing. Shortly after he became king of England, he granted a royal patent to Shakespeare and his partner, the leading actor of the day, Richard Burbage, to form the King's Theatre Company, of which Fletcher was a prominent member. In the next thirteen years, the company gave 177 performances at court, among them Shakespeare's *Othello*, *King Lear*, and *Macbeth*, during which the royal patron often fell asleep, since pure drama bored him.

James was usually lively when masques were presented at court. These costumed spectaculars, with dancing by some of the kingdom's brightest personalities, elaborate scenery, and stage machinery, interrupted by high-flown and occasionally poetical speeches, had been Elizabeth's favorites when she toured her realm. Under James and his son Charles, the masque became the principal form of royal musical theater, falling out of favor only under Cromwell.

The golden age of the masque began in 1604 with the production of Ben Jonson's *Masque of Blackness*, written for James's Danish queen, who had expressed a desire to appear in blackface. Wishing above all things to become poet laureate, and needing the queen's support, Jonson was delighted to accommodate her. He was born around 1573, a month before his minister father's death and was raised by a master-bricklayer stepfather. He learned that trade but ran off to Cambridge rather than pursue it and became a soldier in the Dutch wars. On his return, he joined a company of actors, eventually becoming their director and playwright. One of his first works fell afoul of censorship laws, and he found himself in prison, from which he was released on payment of money borrowed from one of Shakespeare's theatrical partners. As a member of the King's Theatre Company, Jonson continued to write for the stage, but went back to prison after killing a young actor in a duel. His release was effected after he proved he could read, but he had a letter branded on his thumb, and was thus identified for the rest of his life as a felon. For years, he was in and out of jail, charged once with insulting James's Scottish clansmen, later with complicity in the Gunpowder Plot to destroy Parliament and the king, and then for adherence to the Roman faith. His comedies continued to bring him fame if not fortune; he once reckoned that he had earned no more than £200 for all his work.

On Shakespeare's death in 1616, Jonson became "ruler of the poets," and in time Britain's poet laureate, receiving an annual pension equivalent to several thousand dollars a year and a cask of wine. Of the many songs he wrote for his plays and masques, only "Drink to me only with thine eyes" is remembered today.

For the Christmas holidays of 1604, Jonson faced the problem of making the young queen into an acceptable blackamoor and created a work that permitted her and her ladies in waiting to play the twelve daughters of the river Niger who went off with their father to find a place where the sun would no more scorch their faces and bodies into blackness. That happy land was Britain, whose sun was its glorious king, shining down on all without harm. Being made welcome in this land, the painted ladies offered the grand dance traditionally ending all masques, and when the applause was done, the entire company joined in general dancing, audience with performers, in the galliard, courante, pavane.

Since he needed a seascape for his story, Jonson consulted with Inigo Jones, an architect and artist who had studied in Italy and then served the Danish court, from which Queen Anne borrowed him for decorating advice. Jones became the English theater's first scenic designer when he saw Jonson's masque as a vehicle for the exploitation of his innovative ideas about the stage, and an opportunity to present them before an audience more powerful than the nobleman who had sent him abroad to study landscape painting. Under his supervision, the great banqueting hall at Whitehall was fitted with a stage forty feet square, mounted on wheels and raised off the ground to accommodate stage machinery. Once set in motion, wheels and pulleys activated a sea of artificial waves Jones had painted, to give the illusion of distance and an element of realism. For the first time in the court's history, the stage was hidden behind a curtain until the moment the play started. The blackened queen and her ladies were dressed in gold shoes and bright blue gowns, with pearls at the neck and about their wrists to contrast with the stark ebony make-up and wigs.

The queen and her ladies had rehearsed for six weeks, while Jonson worked with Alfonso Ferrabosco and other members of the King's Music and Chapel Royal to create instrumental music for dances and songs, which were performed by professional singers. Little of the music created for the early masques exists today, but from accounts of it and those scores that remain, we know not only that musicians played for the masque, but also that eight of them, dressed in "crimson robes, with chaplets of laurel on their heads," appeared on stage. In his more ambitious later masques, Jonson employed as many as fifty musicians, in both playing and performing roles.

*Masque of Blackness* was a grand success. It cost £3,000 to produce and made Jonson a familiar figure at court, and later, poet laureate, responsible for all royal masques. He wrote almost two dozen of these extravaganzas, collaborating with leading court composers. Ferrabosco was his early favorite, writing the music for some of his best lyrics, including those for his masterpiece, *Volpone* (1605). He also worked with the poet and composer Thomas Campion, the wait William Webb, and Nicholas Lanier, with whom he wrote what might be the first English opera, *Lovers Made Men* (1617).

When Anne died, her son Charles took over responsibilities for production of the masques, continuing to call on the royal poet, but when he became king, he turned his back on Jonson. Though he enjoyed verses the poet laureate had written for his coronation and other galas, it was six years before he called on the now paralytic dramatist to write court entertainment. Jonson then found himself at odds with Inigo Jones, who had become a highly placed court functionary. Their joint production featured Jones's architectural wonders to the detriment of the poetry. Other playwrights, Beaumont, George Chapman, Samuel Daniel, whom Jonson had replaced as court poet in 1604, Thomas Heywood, and Thomas Carew also wrote masques during the poet-dramatist's most glorious days, but their efforts were overshadowed by those of the master. They did, however, gain favor when they abused one of Jonson's innovations, the antimasque, whose interpolated plebeian dances are credited by some historians of the theater as the foundation of modern dramatic ballet. Jonson first used this parody of the masque to precede his *Masque of Queens* in 1609. In the hands of others, this device deteriorated into burlesque low comedy, and near the end of James's reign, the antimasque, utilizing songs, satire, and dancing, and without scenery, was regularly licensed for public performance during the Lenten season, when the major acting companies were barred from appearing and the theaters were let for nondramatic entertainment.

In 1634, James Shirley, a schoolteacher, recent convert to Catholicism, and favorite of Charles I's French wife was nominated by her to write a new masque to be presented before the royal family as an expression of loyalty by the Inns of Court. It was a time when increasingly vitrolic spoken, written, and sung criticism was being aimed at the Stuart family. The most fanatical of the Puritan polemicists, William Prynne, had just been sentenced to a life term and to have his ears cropped for what was regarded as a particularly vicious attack on Queen Henrietta Maria. He had fulminated against the theater, calling the French actresses who were taking the place of young boys in female roles "whores." Overhearing the insult as she was rehearsing a new masque, Henrietta took the word as being aimed at her, and legal action was taken at her insistence.

Demonstrating their support of the crown, London's law schools mounted Shirley's *Triumph of Peace,* at a cost of £21,000, the most expensive production yet known in England. Its music cost £1,000, 200 going for songs written by Simon Ives and William Lawes. The latter, with his brother, Henry, had been trained by the English-born composer John Cooper, who had changed his name to Giovanni Coperario to take advantage of Britons' high regard for anything smacking of Italy. William Lawes eventually succeeded Lanier as chief composer of royal music and as songwriter for the King's Theatre Company. The Lawes brothers were highly esteemed by court poets, many of whose lyrics they set to music for palace entertainments, the theater and, in time, printed collections of songs and airs. Carew, Herrick, Davenant, Lovelace, Waller, Suckling, and others called special attention to their friendship with Henry in published collections, and John Milton wrote:

> Harry, whose tuneful and well measur'd song
> First taught our English music how to span
> Words with just note and accent.

It was to his protégé Milton that Henry Lawes turned in 1634 for a libretto for a new entertainment being prepared for the noble Egerton family. The work was *Comus,* regarded as the best of the Jacobean and Stuart masques. Milton and Lawes were close friends whose first collaboration had taken place the previous year when the Egertons arranged a gala in honor of the family matriarch, presenting a miniature masque, the minor classic *Arcades.* The plot of *Comus* was simply—about a young virgin, with whom a wicked sorcerer wished to have his way, and cast a spell for that purpose, only to be foiled by divine intercession,—but its verse was among the most sublime of the age.

Often boasting that he was Shakespeare's by-blow, William Davenant aspired to the title of the Restoration's leading poet and dramatist, but music history chronicles him chiefly as the man who created the first true opera written by a Briton. His natural mother was the wife of an Oxford vintner and tavern owner often visited by the Bard, who lavished kisses on both mother and child. Leaving Oxford to serve as page to several noble families before he became a hanger-on at court, Davenant began a playwriting career as a prop on which to lean his ambitions. He was given the opportunity to write a royal masque in 1634, *The Temple of Love,* for performance at Whitehall, and then a second, *The Triumph of the Prince of Love,* written to order for the Middle Temple to be presented as a tribute to visiting royal Stuarts. The Lawes brothers wrote a score for this completely musical piece made up of pantomime, songs, and dancing, with none of the masque's traditional speeches or spoken poetry. The queen grew to admire young Davenant and persuaded Charles to name him poet laureate at the age of thirty-two. Occupying himself with official tasks and the pursuit of favor, Davenant turned out verses for social occasions and theatrical diversions and served also as governor of the group now called the Royal Company of Actors. After his *Masque Britannia* was played, Queen Henrietta could refuse him nothing, for in it he had the ancient wizard Merlin conjure up a company of the greatest British poets, all of whom extolled her virtues in the song "Poetic Inspirations from a Queen's Beauty."

Charles rewarded Davenant in 1639 with a patent monopoly for the ownership and operation of a new playhouse and "to act plays in such houses to be by him created and exercise music, musical presentment, scenes, dancing and such like."

Time was running out for the Stuarts and their favorites, however. The Puritans were gaining almost complete control of lawmaking, and the new theater was never built. Davenant was implicated in a Royalist plot, captured, and tried before Parliament. Acquitted, he came down with the prevalent "running disease" and joined the queen in France. She sent him to Britain on several missions, for which he was later knighted for bravery.

The Roundhead Parliament finally won the battle against the theater's depravity by closing them all to the presentation of plays in 1642. Londoners who had found the playhouse cheaper and more rewarding than recourse to the six-penny whores jostling them outside had no place to go. But the city's lower classes had become such devoted theatergoers than no ban could keep them from putting pennies in the box. The managers of the Fortune and the Red Bull, two favorite places of entertainment, kept their doors open, excusing their presentations as being made up of snippets, particularly the bawdier scenes, rather than entire plays. The Red Bull had opened in 1605, instantly becoming the darling of the lower classes, and was enlarged in 1625 to accommodate increasing audiences. Among the mélange of attractions offered were the jigg created by Tarleton and Kemp out of traditional English song, dance, and bawdy comedy, with no pretensions to high culture.

The 1642 ban failed to close down the Bull, and when Cromwell's soldiers occasionally raided its premises, it always opened again, serving as a beacon of robust and unbuttoned delight in a sea of Puritan virtue. Other theaters in the north of London were the traditional home of song and dance, where the audience either got what it wanted or made its desires known; if the players were refractory, a contemporary account had it, "the benches, the tiles, the laths, the stones, orange, apples, nuts flew about most liberally."

The nobility occasionally showed old plays in their homes, but no new pieces were written except for performance in schools, forcing the nation's dramatists to find work in these places. Davenant, now Sir William, was the first of the old guard to return to the city. In 1650, at forty-four, he was put in charge of an expedition of Cavalier refugees bound for Virginia. After a series of mishaps, his vessel grounded in the English Channel and was taken. Sent to the Tower of London to await trial for treason, he took advantage of the solitude to conclude and have printed a heroic poem he had started in France. Only after Milton pleaded for him was he released. Once free, he slipped into the backwaters of London's literary life, surfacing to present a series of musical productions in local private homes. These started with *The First Dayes Entertainment at Rutland House* in May 1656. The public was barred. Music for the evening of "declamations and music after the manner of the ancients" was a joint work, written by Charles Coleman, once a court musician, whose daughter-in-law was the featured female lead; Henry Lawes; that boy chorister who had grown up and won a military title defending king and country, Captain Henry Cooke; and the young composer George Hudson. An aristocratic audience of 150 paid five shillings each to hear this evening of speeches, music, and singing, ended with jibes at the French and their pretensions to supremacy in music.

This occasion was not the first time the Commonwealth had relaxed its restrictions on private showings of this type. The previous year, because Cromwell was courting the Portuguese for support against Spain, James Shirley's masque *Cupid and Death,* with music by Matthew Locke, was played for that country's ambassador by an amateur company.

British refugees and travelers who visited Italy during the Civil War and chanced upon opera were delighted with what they saw and heard. One of them wrote in 1645: "We went to the opera, which are Comedies (and other plays) presented in Recitative music by the most excellent musicians vocal and instrumental, together with a variety of scenes painted and contrived with no less art of perspective and machines for flying in the air and other wonderful notions. So taken, together, it is doubtless one of the most magnificent and expenseful diversions the wit of man can invent." Influenced by the Italian form of musical theater he had enjoyed in Paris, Davenant next presented *The Siege of Rhodes,* England's first true opera, in August 1656. It was not called "opera," a word most Britons would not have understood, but "a representation by the art of perspective in scenes and the story sung in recitative music." Locke, Coleman, Cooke, Henry Lawes, and Hudson again wrote the score, which was sung by a cast including Cooke and young Henry Purcell. Based on the Turkish siege in 1522, the plot concerned a handful of Christian troops holding out against a force of 125,000 enemy soldiers. Davenant called each act an "entry," in order to keep within the law, pointing out further that it was a moral sermon on "the character of virtue in the shape of valor and conjugal love." The music has disappeared, but Davenant's script and some sketches of the scenery are extant.

For some reason persuasive only to Puritan officials, Davenant was next given permission to operate Drury Lane's Cockpit, which had first opened at the start of the century as a fighting place for cocks and then was converted into an enclosed theater. During the Commonwealth it served as an underground playhouse, and its illicit performances were often closed. On one occasion a fine was set, to be paid immediately, and the audience was kept behind locked doors until it was gathered. There Davenant returned to the lecture-recital formula, presenting historical readings, some with music. Public protest mounted against these foreign-influenced presentations, shown to public audiences, and a commission was named by Richard Cromwell. The matter continued unresolved, the new dictator apparently conniving with Davenant for the presentation of an evening of anti-Spanish propaganda, *The Cruelty of the Spaniards in Peru.* A few weeks later, *The History of Sir Francis Drake,* a piece more in the opera tradition and including a number of sea songs of the type upon which British audiences have always doted, was shown.

Shortly before Charles's return to London, a sort of theatrical season was starting, the first in eighteen years, as the Cockpit, the Red Bull, and a sumptuous theater at Salisbury Court opened. On August 21, 1660, a warrant was issued to Davenant and dramatist Thomas Killigrew to assemble two acting companies. Never one to meddle with the souls of women, busying himself instead with an extraordinary number of their bodies, Charles ordered that henceforth only women would be permitted to play female roles. Seeing the theater as a source of supply for his pleasure, he asked for entertainment esteeming "not only harmless delights but useful and instructive representations of human life," which soon became chiefly the spectacle of London actresses dressed in men's breeches.

For a time, the two patentees managed a single company of the city's finest actors, but separated to form the King's Company of Comedians, managed by Killigrew, and the Duke of Yorks Company under Davenant, featuring younger players. Killigrew had been a page in Charles I's court and became a close friend of the future king. Inspired by the things being presented at the Red Bull, he wrote some successful plays for it before the theaters were closed by the Commonwealth. He began operations with his new royal company in an indoor tennis court next to his home; Davenant occupied an old building while a new theater was being built for him. The latter's first production was the old musical success *The Siege of Rhodes,* to which he added a sequel, more play than opera, with women in the leading roles. Tragicomical versions of *Hamlet* and *Romeo and Juliet* followed, giving audiences the happy endings they preferred to the Bard's dramatic resolutions. Davenant's new theater, thirty feet by seventy-five feet, housed Britain's first proscenium arch over a stage thrusting out into the pit, which permitted use of the complicated scenery and stage machinery called for by the musical theater, particularly masques and opera. The fire of 1666 destroyed the building, and a new theater, in Dorset Garden, was under construction when Davenant died in 1668, leaving the patent to his wife and son Charles.

The Theatre Royal, built by Killigrew in Drury Lane on land for which he paid fifty pounds a year rental, held 700 persons, and, like Davenant's, opened only in the afternoon, at half a crown admission. There was no heat in either theater, and the candles serving for light did little to warm the audience or pierce the semigloom. Because Restoration men and women bathed only occasionally, masking body odor with pomades, the atmosphere was fetid by the third act. There were no toilets for the aristocracy and no refreshments except the fruit sold by orange girls, who huckstered themselves and their wares during breaks in stage action. Charles's queen was the first to patronize a public theater, but few other "virtuous" women attended, and then only behind masks. Demimondaine traffic paraded up and down the pit, extravagantly advertising their unveiled delights but hiding their faces. In time, only the most dissolute went to the playhouses, among them men about town who based their manners on those of courtiers. The middle class had lost its habit of theatergoing during the years of Puritan domination. The poor, unable to afford the shilling required, which once had been a penny, also disappeared from the audience.

Both officially licensed companies struggled to attract audiences large enough to support their seasons. Although the command performances Charles occasionally ordered in Whitehall helped to stimulate interest in the theater, they did little for the performers, who had to wait years for their fees. The regular companies of sixteen men and seven women, musicians, scenic designers, painters, stagehands, and supporting personnel drained all the receipts. Except for those dramatists whose work drew crowds, most authors were paid outright for a new work, profiting chiefly from proceeds of the third night, which was often canceled in the interests of economy.

Royal regulations for backstage conduct were regularly issued, but almost everyone sauntered freely into that area, past storerooms in which flats were painted and properties stored. A "woman's shift" was set off from the main dressing room, but few visitors respected its privacy. The opportunity to see actresses undressed to their smocks between costume changes was often as great an attraction as the plays. The Restoration gentleman, who was the theater's chief support, was, in typical Roundhead words, a "fine, whoring, swearing, smutty, atheistical man [to whom the] restraints and pedantry of virtue were unbecoming . . . a man of breeding and figure that burlesques the Bible, swears and talks smut to the ladies, speaks ill of his friend behind his back and betrays his interest."

Recitative opera's appeal waned quickly as audiences grew uncomfortable with the unrealistic drama imposed by the genre's demands. They did, however, want music in the theater, and soon musicians were providing diversion whose appeal was equal to the drama's, and it became necessary to place the music makers where they could be seen. The two or three fiddlers who performed in the first Restoration theaters were soon increased to nine or ten, of the best, and their number grew constantly. By 1675, London orchestras boasted a dozen strings, twice that of Paris playhouses. At the century's end, it was common to see fifty musicians, playing strings, flutes, oboes, drums, and trumpets.

Pepys, for one, had complained about an experiment tried by Killigrew for the opening of his theater, often called the "Drury Lane." The band was placed under the stage, where "there was no hearing of the basses at all, nor very well of the trebles, which sure must be mended." And mended it was, as managers brought the musicians out of the Shakespearean music room hidden from sight in a loft over the stage. A typical dramatist's directions read: "The front of the stage is opened, and and the band of violins, with the harpsicals and theorbo's which accompany the voices, are placed between the pit and the stage. While the overture is playing, the curtain rises and discovers a new frontispiece, joined to the great pilasters, on each side of the stage."

Music was now attracting people to the playhouses in great numbers. A foreign visitor was amazed that "before the comedy begins, that the audience may not be tired with waiting, the most delightful symphonies [instrumental music] are played; on which account many persons come early to enjoy this agreeable amusement."

When news of the British upper-class appetite for European culture and musicianship was noised about, French and Italian performers once again started to migrate in great numbers. Soon, only Vienna matched London as an employer of foreigners, especially after Charles gave a patent to an Italian impresario for the creation of a royal opera company. He occasionally funded the annual £1,700 cost for its musicians from secret-service funds. Among the Italian musician forming the orchestra was the ranking harpsichord virtuoso in England, Giovanni Battista Draghi, well known to songwriters, who called him Mr. Battista out of respect.

Killigrew became involved with the Italian venture, telling Pepys in 1664 that he was planning a new theater to present a six-week season of true opera annually, but he found himself unable to bear the cost and withdrew. Average British playgoers, however, continued to be disturbed because Italian opera was a form in which the whole text, as a skeptic had it, was sung "from one end to the other, as if the persons had ridiculously conspir'd to treat in music both the most common and important affairs in human life. Can any man persuade his imagination that a master calls his servant or sends him on an errand singing? That one friend communicates a secret to another singing? That orders in time or battle are given singing? And that men are melodiously killed with sword, pike and musket?" John Dryden, the poet who mastered the form better than his peers, found himself obliged to cramp his verses, making them "more rugged to the reader that they may be harmonious to the hearer."

When Davenant discerned that an evening of wholly spoken drama was no longer necessary to satisfy his royal patent, he returned to his first love, drama in the form of semiopera, using spoken dialogue between musical selections. Though they had become somewhat old hat, he offered Shakespeare's plays in this form, restoring some of them to their former popularity. *Macbeth* was altered, amended, and modernized, retaining some of the old-fashioned songs written by Robert Johnson a half-century earlier, but with new ones and some incidental music by Matthew Locke. In the last years of his life, Davenant was at work revamping *The Tempest,* with the assistance of Dryden, a newcomer to the theater.

Immediately after Dryden had come to London, during the Commonwealth, leaving the impoverished farm his father had bequeathed to fourteen sons and daughters, he eked out a living by writing verse. His first success came from a tribute to Oliver Cromwell, unfortunately written in the last year of the tyrant's life. When the old order changed, Dryden, ever ready to accommodate, as he was throughout his lifetime, made the necessary political volte-face, welcoming Charles Stuart in similar verse. Since society's enthusiasm for the theater appeared to be making that medium profitable for a writer of his self-perceived talent, Dryden wrote a comedy, called by Pepys "so poor a thing as ever I saw in life almost." This failure did not deter Dryden; he had found a wealthy and aging wife of noble birth, acquiring in the process a brother-in-law of literary bent, Robert Howard. The pair collaborated in 1664 on *The Indian Queen,* a tragedy written in rhymed heroic couplets, rather than the Elizabethans' blank verse. In this semiopera Dryden first established his convention of having normal mortals speak their lines, and the spirits, witches, demons, and priests involved in metaphysical affairs, as well as lovers, whose passion was inspired by extraterrestrial influences, sing their parts.

Paying little attention to either history of geography, the authors made enemies of a Peru and Mexico that did not yet know of one another's existence, but created a success with their battle scenes and processions, exotic chants and fantastical stage machinery. Dryden next attempted another western epic, *The Indian Emperor,* with music by Pelham Humfrey, who was occasionally taking time off from court duties to write for the theater. This second success made

Dryden fashionable, and impelled other playwrights to ape his style. He contracted with Killigrew to provide three plays annually for a slice of profits, guaranteeing him some £350 a year. Among the ten plays written under this arrangement were obscene comedies, one of which was banned after its third performance, but not in time to strip Dryden of his author's night. Included in the twenty-seven tragedies he wrote before his death was a blank-verse version of Antony and Cleopatra's romance, *All for Love* (1678), his most successful, and the only tragedy he wrote without songs. Of it, Dryden said that by imitating Shakespeare he had excelled himself.

Giovanni Draghi was one of London's foreign composers enlisted to write for a series of semioperas in a venture hoping to make a profit from the magnificent Dorset Garden Theatre. This Christopher Wren building, which had cost £9,000, was a financial disaster after only two seasons. Mrs. Davenant and Thomas Betterton, one of the Restoration's best players, had taken over management and expected to be successful with opera in which music served an incidental purpose and actors were asked to sing new, often suggestive, material. Betterton was the son of a cook in Charles I's kitchen, who turned actor when the ban on public plays was lifted after the Stuarts' return, and his wealthy friends had provided most of the Dorset Garden's financing.

The theater's large stage and advanced stage machinery were ideal for these new operas, with their spectacular scenic effects, which brought fame to the house and dividends to its investors. The initial production was a revival of the Locke and Davenant *Macbeth*, followed by a new play by Thomas Shadwell, for which £800 was invested in the scenery alone. Never known for his originality, Shadwell had borrowed from the French playwright Molière for *Psyche*, creating a new concept in British musical theater by experimenting with the *comédie-ballet* born of the Parisian king of comedy's genius. When Molière burst into the French entertainment world in 1659, determined to use the theater to "correct men by entertaining them," he brought fresh air into a stultifying ambience and took his place at the head of the French theatrical world as royal favor saluted his accomplishments while curtailing his budgets.

A command from his master in 1671 to present both a comedy and a ballet demanded that he take stock of his acting company as well as his money. Finding that only a few trained dancers were available, he decided to integrate them into the action of a new play, *Psyché*, with music by Lully. Within a few years, this inspired improvisation developed into a new kind of entertainment, using songs, dances, and choral movements, that became the rage of Paris and the envy of London.

Shadwell lifted this play practically in its entirety, but Lully's score was not to be had, so he commissioned Draghi to write the instrumental music and Locke the songs. Himself a capable composer, Shadwell exercised full control over their work. He had studied with John Jenkins, musician in both Stuart households, and the Italian lutenist Pietro Reggio, who had taken up permanent residence in England. No playwright of the period made as skillful use of contemporary music, nor understood its songwriters so well, as Shadwell. He laid out the order of songs for Locke, indicating which were to to be sung by one or more voices, and "what manner of humour I would have in all the vocal music."

The long-expected opera *Psyche* came forth in all its new ornaments, new scenes, new machines, new clothes, new French dances, in 1673, and enjoyed an eight-day run, something quite unusual. In discussing Shadwell, Edward J. Dent, in *Foundations of the English Opera*, wrote that he "had the makings of a really good librettist. He could imagine an essentially musical situation, and make his play lead up to it as a dramatic climax. It was his misfortune to belong to a generation which produced no musician better than Locke, whose technical accomplishment was decidedly limited. Had he been able to work in actual collaboration with Purcell, he might have profited by Purcell's wonderful command of all musical resources."

The Duke of York's Company immediately went on to its next success, Shadwell's treatment of *The Tempest*, called *The Enchanted Island*, with music by Locke, Draghi, Humfrey, John Banister, staff songwriter for the company, and James Hart, a gentleman bass singer of the Chapel Royal. The production again was an entirely new one, with new scenery and machinery. The orchestra was a large one, of twenty-four strings, harpsichords, and lutes, placed between the pit and the stage. Thirty men and boys of the Chapel Royal, having been granted permission to spend the week in town, served as supplementary singers and ensemble vocalists. Stagecraft was now so developed that Shadwell was able to obtain such scenic effects as "in the midst of the shower of fire the scene changes. The cloudy sky [of the opening shipwreck] rocks and sea vanish, and when the lights return [probably done by raising and lowering the chandeliers and masking footlights, if they were used] to discover the beautiful part of the island, which is the habitation of Prospero.

The continuing acclaim for Dryden's heroic tragedies, embellished with music, and Shadwell's new stagecraft inspired immediate copying. Among those who aped the work of their betters was Elkanah Settle, who had begun his acting career in those short plays known as "drolls," the descendants of the jiggs, performed out of doors, usually at fairs, in order to circumvent the Puritan laws. Settle turned to more serious enterprises after the Restoration, penning several very dull tragedies before his immensely successful *The Empress of Morocco* in 1671, set to music by a number of composers and produced at the Dorset Garden. Fame, fortune, and, most important to Settle, access to the company's most pliant actresses were his. Two years later, his script was printed, decorated with engravings of some of the production's most spectacular scenes. This marked the first such publication known.

The audience's ecstatic response to *The Empress of Morocco* gave the company an opportunity to carve out of the British audience for opera a part for a new form—the musical burlesque parody. Four months after Settle's tragedy opened, a burlesque of it was presented, with one of Shadwell's *Psyche*. Both were the work of Thomas Duffett, a London milliner who wrote for the stage as a hobby. His works satirized the whole business of stage effects and machinery, the splendidly caparisoned royal processions, group dances, and other musical exotica Dryden had introduced and Shadwell had brought to renown. Duffett had not created a new theatrical form, but used those traditional devices that had brought about the jiggs and pre-Restoration drolls, turning them into a satirization of popular semiopera by means of burlesque.

The word *burlesque,* from the French, was first used to denote a literary form protesting the precocity being infused into contemporary French literature. High culturists fought it, one of them, a priest, writing an extraordinarily long tome whose argument was that burlesque was improper because none of the classic writers made use of it. The word entered the English lexicon around 1660, defined as "drollish, merry, pleasant." Davenant was the first to use the word in the theater, in his 1662 production of *The Playhouse to Be Let,* a potpourri of short plays that made pertinent observations on the various directions in which the English musical theater was about to go, which included a burlesque of *Antony and Cleopatra.*

John Wilmot, second earl of Rochester, and the only genius among Charles's court poets, raised burlesque to a high literary form in his play *The Rehearsal,* which attacked contemporaries he did not like and praised only faintly the few he tolerated. Dryden, once a friend, became so annoying that Rochester hired a gang of toughs to beat up the poet laureate. While not disdaining infliction of physical punishment on others, he considered Dryden beneath his sword. This Restoration rakehell, turned vicious writer, was deadly with both sword and pen, as his liege lord learned when Rochester wrote

> Here lies our Sovereign Lord the King,
> Whose word no man relies on,
> Who never said a foolish thing,
> Nor ever did a wise one.

Too much the perfect writer to enjoy the burlesque form of verse, Dryden protested that it appealed only to adolescents, but did stoop to its use, for he took advantage of anything that could turn a coin—for example, writing prologues to other men's plays at two to three guineas each.

Duffett employed burlesque to achieve exactly that "boyish pleasure" Dryden affected to despise. His *Macbeth* lampoon was based on the altered version presented at the Dorset Garden earlier that year. Using the old popular melody "John Dory," sung by spirits to raise the curtain, he had two shades come on stage with a flaming bowl, which was lighted brandy, drink it, and then listen as the three witches sang in praise of London's best-known bawd and then flew off to the music of a popular nursery rhyme. In his *Mock Tempest,* a full five-act stage work, unlike his earlier satires, he used Shadwell's revision exactly as written except for words to the many songs. The final production number burlesqued "Where the bee sucks, there suck I," turning it into "Where good ale is, there suck I."

Duffett's burlesque of Shadwell's *Psyche* was again lifted completely, line for line, and featured lissome actresses playing the men's roles in the new and novel "breeches parts," that were bringing crowds into both royal theaters. About them, the essayist Richard Steele confessed; "I, who know nothing of women but from seeing plays, can give great guesses at the whole structure of the fair sex by being innocently placed in the pit, and insulted by the petticoats of their dancers; the advantage of whose pretty persons are a great help in a dull play. When a Poet flags in writing lusciously, a pretty girl can move lasciviously, and have the same good consequences for the Author.''

Thanks to Charles's edict, no longer did young and pretty lads impersonate women on the London stage. Instead, actresses of all ages and shapes and sizes played male parts, serving as the equivalent of twentieth-century pinups in their appearances in tight knee breeches. Men's attire had become colorful, with ribands and laces, sometimes even effeminate in style. Those better-endowed young women who roused Pepys and his friends in their seats near the stage made no pretense of angelic qualities. That lovely young actress Mary Knep, who sang ''Barbara Allen'' to Pepys's complete enchantment and granted him all ''save the ultimate one'' of the illicit pleasures for which he cajoled her, played one of *Psyche*'s debauched juvenile leads.

Leaving behind two comedies, a masque, and three burlesques, all of which were soon forgotten, Duffett disappeared from the theater's history, though many Britons who never had the opportunity to see his stage pieces continued to sing songs he had written for them, a collection of his *New Poems, Songs, Prologues and Epilogues* appearing in 1676.

No more such burlesques appeared for decades, the two licensed theaters merging sometime between 1682 and 1695 and ending any incentive to satirize rival productions. The seed this milliner-turned-writer had planted burst into being again in 1728, when John Gay felt the need to satirize Italian opera, then dominating the theater. In the mid-nineteenth century, burlesque crossed the Atlantic to the minstrel stage, where Thomas ''Daddy'' Rice, Dan Emmett, and their peers mocked everything from Shakespeare to slavery.

## Popular Music in the Restoration Theater

Novelty continued to save the English theater whenever economic troubles beset it, beginning with the spectacle of female bodies in tight-fitting male clothing. Keenly aware of the Englishman's traditional love songs and music, theater managers relied more and more on their interpolation into every production. Action was interrupted without dramatic reason, with such cues as ''Boy, take your lute, and with a pleasing ayre/Appease my sorrows, and delude my care,'' which delighted theatergoers when a trained singing voice stepped in to take over from the actor. The device was successful, and more and more music was used, as song and dance numbers were programed between the acts in short musical and dancing interludes.

Davenant had been the first to understand and rely on music in the popular theater. Early actresses had only to rely on looks and the very novelty of their presence to draw applause, for audiences forgave anything that came out of a shapely body. But as the songwriters began to write ever more difficult music, responding to the heightened musical knowledge of patrons, the demand grew for virtuoso performers, who could sing as well as act. Roger North wrote: ''Many people came to hear the single voice, who care not for the rest, especially if it be a fair lady: and observing the discourse of quality criticism, I found it runs most upon the point who sings best, and not whether the music be good.''

By the century's end, the favorite star performers usually possessed remarkable ability, being thoroughly trained and able to sing Purcell's or Blow's most difficult music. It was no longer sufficient for a singing actress to be as wantonly provocative as Nell Gwyn, whose talent was self-admittedly for the bed rather than the boards. Only professionally competent performers now dared to appear. Accompanied by lute, guitar, or theorbo, on occasion by a consort of instruments, these singing players brought audiences to their feet whenever they appeared and became public figures who were saluted with cheers of recognition as they went along London's streets. Theater lovers argued the merits of their favorites: Jemmy Bowen, who first appeared as a boy soprano, singing naughty songs, sophisticated even beyond his years of backstage life; William Mountfort, the actor, playwright, and songwriter who had a ''melodious, warbling throat'' and died of the wound given him by an aristocrat jealous of his supposed success with a leading actress; Mrs. Ayliff, who introduced many of Purcell's songs on the stage; Anne Bracegirdle, who began in breeches and died at eighty-five, still active, with a reputation for morality almost equaling that for her singing, but much less deserved; Moll Davies, the young actress who won London's hearts singing ''My love is in the cold ground'' and soon after was raised from the ground to a warm royal bed, where she conceived one of Charles's many illegitimate offspring; and the greatest of them all, the bass singing star Richard Leveridge, who was born around 1670 and excited three generations before his death in 1758. There was little this all-around man of the theater could not do. His deep voice pleased listeners between the acts as well as in parts in major hit plays. He could write either words or music, and his best-known song, ''The Roast Beef of Old England,'' continued to remind its hearers about that time when ''our soldiers were brave and our courtiers were good'' long after he was dead.

Making his debut in 1696 in Thomas D'Urfey's *Don Quixote the Third,* with music by Purcell, Leveridge next took London by storm, singing ''Ye twice ten thousand deities,'' written for him by Purcell in the revival of Dryden's *Indian Queen.* Leveridge's own song-writing career blossomed as quickly as his stage career. By 1699, two books of his songs were on sale, as well as many appearing on single sheets, among the first published British sheet music. He collaborated with many young playwrights, and with D'Urfey on a popular song in praise of fishing, ''Of all the world's enjoyments.'' It was written for the 1699 two-part *History of the Rise and Fall of Massaniello,* and brought new audiences to the theater, who came especially to hear it sung inimitably by its actor composer.

In 1702, Leveridge wrote songs and some music for a revival of a semioperatic *Macbeth,* which owed little to the Bard save its title and some tattered remnants of the original plot. Historians have argued about this score, many attributing it to Purcell, but all agree that it is a fine example of effective theater music. He was also much in demand as a singer in that flurry of English opera in the Italian manner, all sung, that charmed London's elite with its admired "effeminate sing-song," and set new box-office records. A wistful desire by British musicians to equal the international acclaim for Italy's best-known musical form prompted a number of them to offer seasons of locally grown opera. The most successful of these, Thomas Clayton's *Arsinoë, Queen of Cypress,* ran an unprecedented thirty-seven performances, followed by Marc Bononcini's *Camilla,* which ran sixty-four times, with Leveridge doing much to bring in paying customers to both.

When Leveridge had first appeared on a stage, it was in the newly reopened Lincoln's Inn Fields Theatre that Davenant had transformed from a tennis court into the first Restoration playhouse. There he found a home for thirty years, during which he played in masques, pantomimes, burlesques, and plays, for many of which he wrote songs and music. When he was sixty, he was featured between the acts of plays—no longer able physically to play five acts—singing his own ballads and songs by the masters with whom he had grown up. During his last years, he was supported by many old fans, who continued to make annual subscriptions toward his maintenance until his death at eighty-eight, a career spanning the years from Charles to the Hanoverian Georges.

### The Birth Pangs of an English Opera Tradition

The company of Italian musicians that had been licensed by Charles with a monopoly on production of baroque opera departed from England in the late 1670s, its salaries still in arrears. A handful of London productions by a French-directed Royal Academy of Music that followed had also failed to whet the British appetite for Italian opera, even when done in an elegantly lilting Parisian manner. It was not in the Restoration theatergoer's character to sit still for an evening of unrelieved recitative, despite the monarch's admiration for all things Continental.

Perhaps because Dryden believed it was his duty as the nation's poet laureate and royal historiographer, with an annual stipend of £1,000 to indulge his royal master's musical convictions, the era's most feared, and therefore most influential, man of letters felt that the poetic forms in which he excelled might succeed where all others had failed and so enoble British music as they had already done for British drama. He went to work on a national all-singing British opera. He was well aware of that "effeminacy of English pronounciation," with its lack of feminine rhymes making it

> no easy matter in our language to make words so smooth, and numbers so harmonious, that they shall set themselves; and yet there are rules for this in nature; and as great a certainty in our syllables, as either in the Greek or Latin; but let poets and judges understand those first, and then let them begin to study English. The chief secret is in the choice of words, and by this choice I do not here mean elegancy of expression; but propriety of sound, to be varied according to the nature of the subject.

Dryden's three-act *Albion and Albanius,* the first result of his decision, was presented at great expense in 1685 in the Dorset Garden Theatre, and ran for six performances. The title's twin brothers represented Charles and his brother and heir presumptive, James. Originally, Dryden had intended the piece as prologue to a "tragedy mixed with opera, or a drama written in blank verse, adorned with scenes, machines, songs and dances." His principal misjudgment was in the choice of a collaborator. Two of the time's greatest composers were available, John Blow, who never did write for the theater, and Henry Purcell, as well as a number of lesser musicians. It was Dryden's foolishly sycophantic desire to please the king that impelled him instead to choose a favorite, Louis Grabu, a French composer whose "ill accent," both musical and vocal, played havoc with Dryden's customarily lithe verse, turning his hopefully noble phrases into imitation bad French opera. Charles did not live long enough to see Dryden's new national opera or to hear Grabu's music.

With Catholic James king of England, Dryden's usually keen nose for expediency brought him to embrace his new master's faith. Within three years, James was in exile and the dour Dutchman William of Orange and his English wife, Mary, returned Anglicanism to power and fashion. Having made one sharp turn too many, the poet laureate found himself stripped of office and emoluments in favor of Thomas Shadwell, the minor poet and playwright to whom Dryden granted immortality with some nasty verses.

It was without any friend at court that Dryden came nearest to achieving true British opera, in 1691, with *King Arthur, the Worthy Briton,* music by Purcell, from the old libretto to which *Albion and Albanius* was intended as prologue. In common with knowing Englishmen, Dryden considered Purcell the greatest of all British composers, and he was closely allied to the new royal family, to boot. The composer's understanding of opera's requirements in the wedding of English words to Italianate and French music was a source of irritation to the all-knowing poet, and he complained that "the numbers of poetry and vocal music are sometimes so contrary that in many places I have been obliged to cramp my verses, and make them rugged to the reader that they may be harmonious to the hearer; of which I have no reason to repent me, because these sorts of entertainments are principally designed for the ear and the eye, and therefore in reason my art on this occasion ought to be subservient to his."

*King Arthur*'s vaingloriously patriotic plot, originally conceived to delight Charles, was now used to tame the Dutch king. Everything was done on a grand scale to ensure the greatest dramatic impact. The production was so lavish and the fees paid singers and dancers so large that speaking players complained about discrimination. The annoyingly chaste Mrs. Bracegirdle and the sweet-toned Charlotte Butler sang and danced leading female roles, but most of the principal characters did not sing at all in this dramatic work of which music was so integral a part. That was done, as Dryden had so long ago decreed, only by priests and aery and magical spirits, and sung by virtuosic voices that were given ample opportunity to be heard amid the plethora of supernatural elements, written to serve as reason for song. *King Arthur* won an immediate place in the repertoire, and held it until the middle of the nineteenth century.

Stripped of honors and stipend, Dryden spent his last years working as a full-time man of letters, translating Virgil and Boccaccio, urging attention to the unfashionable Chaucer, doing theatrical hackwork, and supervising revivals of his earlier plays, for which Purcell was writing new music—in short, doing anything to put bread on his table. His last years were desperate ones, his health poor and his circumstances wretched. Theater friends arranged a benefit performance, a revival of an Elizabethan play, and Dryden wrote for the occasion *The Secular Masque,* with music by Purcell's younger brother, Daniel. Summoning up his personal vision of the century fast coming to an end, Dryden told of the years he had witnessed, of the hunt-loving first James, Cromwell the warrior, the profligate Charles, of the "old age that was out, and time to begin a new."

Nine months before the century ran its course, Dryden was in a grave in Westminster Abbey, sharing it, in the interest of space, with Chaucer. Though Purcell, and Dryden with him, had created the first nearly national English opera, British theatergoers remained aloof from its uncertain charm, failing to relish that "perpetual" singing. When his ear was satisfied, it was written, "the English gentleman was desirous of having his mind pleased, and music and dancing industriously intermix'd with comedy or tragedy."

## Henry Purcell: Orpheus Britannicus

Henry Purcell died in 1695, at thirty-six and at the height of a genius that, a disciple said, "so far surpassed whatever our country had produced or imported before that all other musical compositions seem to have been instantly consigned to contempt or oblivion." He was six years old when he was admitted to the Chapel Royal as a choirboy, under the disciplinarian Captain Cooke, following the death of his father, who was composer for Charles's Band of Music and master of choristers of Westminster Abbey. Cooke, Humfrey, and Blow were his teachers, and by the time his voice broke, he had already written competent music for worship. Before he was twenty-one, he replaced Locke as official composer for the royal violins and was later appointed organist at Westminster Abbey. Blossoming suddenly, as does the crocus when winter's hold is broken, Purcell began to write music of all sorts, the start of a flow of fantasias for strings, sonatas, "welcome songs" and odes, music for the theater, songs, and instrumental interludes that made him well loved at court and by the music lovers of his land. He wrote for fifty-four play productions, five semioperas, and one opera before he died, as well as scores of those bawdy catches enjoyed by bibulous Britons but offending moralists. The realities of marriage stimulated much of this activity. He married in 1681 and had a son a year later, but his wife reputedly barred the door one cold winter night, keeping him waiting in the chill damp air and thus bringing on his death.

Purcell early wrote theater songs that also proved to be favorites with the ballad-buying public. In his first work, *Theodosius* (1680), a tragedy by Nathaniel Lee, he wrote "Now, now the fight's done," to whose melody two dozen different ballads were written during the next ten years. This sort of piracy was practiced with impunity, there being no copyright law protecting composers; such borrowing continued long after Purcell's death, and more than one ballad "springing from the people" was in truth set to music from the stage. Within a century, Purcell's melodies and those of his contemporaries had become inextricably woven into the popular culture taken to the New World, where they often emerged as pure folk song. The most famous appropriation of a Purcell melody was for "Lillibulero."

When James II assumed power, he attempted to secure a shaky hold on the throne by placing fellow Catholics in strategic places. To Ireland he sent Richard Talbot, earl of Tyrconnel, as lord deputy, giving him full authority over the army and power to reconstitute the civil service with Catholic employees. James enforced his control over London and its Anglican officials by bringing an army of 13,000 troops to Hounslow Heath, a menace to London and Parliament. When the Protestant soldiery refused to enforce orders against the clergy, particularly the Anglican bishops, among whom was the writer of the Doxology, Thomas Ken, James sent the rebellious regiments away and replaced them with Irish Catholic troops recruited by Talbot.

The Protestant soldiers began to sing a recently written ballad entitled "Lillibulero," whose words were by Thomas Wharton, a few years later lord lieutenant. In his old age, he boasted that he had written "a certain Lilli Bullero Song, with which he sung a deluded prince out of Three Kingdoms." A contemporary account details how a "foolish ballad [which] was made at the time, treating with papists, and chiefly the Irish, in a very ridiculous manner, which had a burden [repeated verse] said to be the Irish words lero lero lillibulero, that made an impression on the army, that cannot well be imagined by those who saw it not. The whole army, and at last all the people, both in country and city, were singing it perpetually. And perhaps never had so slight a thing so great an effect." James was plagued night and day by its words and music, to such an extent that he and his followers countered the song with one of their own. When, years later, Charles Burney was tracing the origins of "God Save the King," he spoke with Thomas Arne's mother, whose son had reputedly written the melody. The old lady told him she had heard "Lillibulero" sung "not only in the playhouse, but in the street" during James's time.

Like others, Purcell occasionally borrowed. For centuries British audiences doted on musical mad scenes, in which a soloist exhibited both his voice and his acting ability by delineating the image of a man going mad. Italian opera is replete with this device, the most notable example being the "Mad Scene" from *Lucia*. The most popular singing group of mid-nineteenth-century America, the Hutchinson Family, never failed to bring audiences to a fever pitch with a performance of Henry Russell's "The Maniac," their first success. In earlier times, when the British legal profession found its pleasures in books of law and simpler pastimes than the manipulation of world affairs, the lawyers of London held revels four times a year. During these, stage-struck attorneys entertained their peers with masques, and among the songs written for one of these was the early-seventeenth-century "New ballad of Mad Tom of Bedlam." Seventy-five years later, Purcell made an arrangement of this song, using new words, but he went down in history as its presumed composer.

In another instance, as composer in ordinary to the king, Purcell was summoned to entertain the queen in her chambers. With two singers, he regaled her with a concert of his music. The queen, beginning to grow tired, asked one of the singers if she could not sing the old Scot ballad "Cold and Raw," sometimes known as "Stingo" or "Oil of Barley." As the soprano sang it, Purcell, at the harpsichord, was not a little vexed by the queen's preference for a vulgar ballad to his own music. But, seeing her genuine delight, he determined she should hear the tune again in another context. In 1692, he used it for a soprano solo in a birthday ode for Queen Mary, one of six written during her reign.

During his first decade of work in the theater, Purcell collaborated with the handful of dramatists who contributed all the new plays and revised old ones for presentation by the royal acting company, among them Nathaniel Lee, Thomas D'Urfey, Nahum Tate, psalmist and bowdlerizer of Shakespeare, Edward Ravenscroft, the most popular farce writer of the day, and Charles Davenant, son of the pioneer theatrical manager. After James became king, Purcell increased this activity, because the king had no interest in Chapel Royal services and support of court musicians decreased. Among the work produced was Purcell's only true opera, the three-act *Dido and Aeneas,* to a libretto by Tate of such appeal that it may excuse the barbarities he committed on the glories of Shakespeare. Much of the credit is also due to Purcell's wedding of music to speech. When commercial managers showed no interest in this recitative opera, *Dido and Aeneas* was shown in a school for girls, before a nondiscriminating audience of fond parents eager to see their children take part in a performance of genteel quality. Private schools were the last ground on which theatrical works depending completely on music, rather than on spectacle, could attract an audience. The premiere revealed a composer who had made the Continental mid-baroque opera so British that its viewers went home whistling the new airs. Some of the songs, notably "When I am laid in earth," which was Dido's lament, and "Pursue thy conquest, love," sold in great quantity as sheet music between the acts at public theaters.

Another of Purcell's airs to become a well-known popular song was written for Thomas Betterton's *Diocletian*—"What shall I do to show how much I love her?" Its popularity continued for decades and commanded a place in *The Beggar's Opera* forty years later.

The four years prior to Purcell's death were a frenzy of creativity, his music appearing in forty stage works, ranging from the masterpiece *The Fairy Queen* to throwaway songs interpolated into comedies and farces. His partners included William Congreve; Aphra Behn, the first British woman to earn a living from literary activities, who began her adventurous life spying for Charles II by extracting military secrets from the Dutch through the exercise of her considerable charms; John Crowne, the first English dramatist born in the New World, to a Nova Scotia Puritan family; Elkanah Settle, who wrote *The Fairy Queen;* and many others whose work fed the contemporary theater and then passed into limbo with it.

Purcell was at work on a revival of Dryden's *Indian Queen* when he died, leaving completion of the score to his brother, Daniel. His contemporary Roger North wrote this epitaph for the Orpheus Britannicus, "who unhappily began to show his greatest skill before the reform of music *al' Italiano,* and while he was warm in pursuit of it, died; but a much greater musical genius England never had. He was a match for all sorts of designs in music. Nothing came amiss to him. He imitated the Italian sonata and outdid them. And raised up operas and music in the theaters, to a credit, even of fame as far as Italy, where Signor Purcell was courted no less than at home.'' Marking the debt owed Purcell by Handel and later British composers Edward Dent wrote: ''What Purcell failed to achieve was not to be accomplished by the mediocre talents which survived him. There was just a moment's hope that Handel might have built up an English opera on Purcell's foundations, for it was by reason of his indebtedness to Purcell rather than by mere fact of his residence in this country that we are entitled to claim Handel as in the line of our own composers.''

## The Musical Theater before Handel

As with the court, the character of London theater was changing during a war fought at home against the Irish by both James and William, and that on the Continent against France, which was to last until 1815. These drained the city of its dashing gallants and the brazen lights-of-love they supported. The economy boomed, and the mercantile middle class grew wealthier, from profits realized through loans to the government and ventures into international trade. Taxes, however, increased daily, and inflation ate into profits and dividends. Foreign commerce and domestic manufacture were raising the gross national product, but the theater was strangling from the continued effects of rising costs and a consequent falling off in revenues. By bidding against one another for singers and dancers, and booking expensive ''dancers on ropes, tumblers, vaulters, ladder dancers,'' the two theater companies had, one critic charged, ''debased the Theatre and almost leveled it with Bartholomew Fair.''

Charles's death removed the theater's most prestigious patron, and soon Charles Davenant was obliged to sell the royal monopoly on spoken drama as well as his other assets to lawyer Christopher Rich, for some eighty pounds. Determined to make money out of this investment, Rich treated the players shabbily, giving his leading men but a few pounds a week, signing young actors for pennies and the privilege of appearing on his stage, debauching young actresses, and jobbing the dramatists. The situation grew so intolerable that actor-manager Thomas Betterton organized a strike in 1695, leading his fellow players in a walkout from the Theatre Royal. Taking their grievances to the crown, the troupe received a new patent, which enabled Betterton to offer spoken drama at the venerable theater in Lincoln's Inn Fields, where Davenant had first produced entertainment. The best actors joined, for a decade of showmanship that strove to attract the newly wealthy, many of whom were beginning to regard attendance as an obligation of the refined gentry they believed themselves to be.

Anxious to acquire the luster of the Purcell name, Rich signed Daniel as company composer, a move countered by Betterton, who secured the services of John Eccles, heralding him as the only true and worthy successor to the dead master. For ten years the two houses engaged in a war for audiences, enlisting

every programing trick that could be conjured up, even reviving the Elizabethans in "transmogrified" and prettified versions, staged with a licentiousness
rivaling that of the Romans. The orgy of prurience was capped by Betterton in
1697 with Sir John Vanbrugh's *The Provok'd Wife*, music and songs by Eccles.
Its author was an architect and artist who had occupied himself with playwriting while languishing in the Bastille, rightfully charged with being a British
agent. Years later, he dragged out the old manuscript and handed it over to
Betterton, who produced it with the still toothsome Mrs. Bracegirdle, and the
greatest actress of the Restoration, Elizabeth Barry, who recognized her true
value in a dissolute world, and, according to one who knew, "would not know
you the next morning, unless you had another five pounds for her service."
This production of a play so flagrantly approving of adultery was the veritable
last straw in a battle for public morality that the upper middle class, for the first
time, began to join to shape public taste. Some of the most prominent women
of the day were behind the formation of a Society for the Reformation of Manners, dedicated to putting an end to the wickedness of the London stage. Several new regulations were effected by their efforts, including one that forbade
the wearing of masks in the theater, thus stripping the audience of those virtuous wives and daughters who attended naughty plays secure in the anonymity
of their vizards.

The next year, Jeremy Collier, an Anglican cleric, published *A Short View
of the Immorality and Profaneness of the English Stage,* in which, like critics
in every age, he failed to recognize that the popular arts reflect the times rather
than create them. With this, he launched an attack on the theater from which it
was not to recover for decades. No one was safe from his fulmination, not the
Greek tragedians, Shakespeare, Dryden, or Congreve, nor, in particular, Vanbrugh. In full retreat, that worthy returned to the pursuit of architectural design.
Only Congreve spoke out in his own defense, though half-heartedly. Dryden,
his wet finger ever against the wind, about-faced as always.

The managers donned robes of morality and presented stage pieces heavily
larded with sentiment, hoping to draw back disappearing ticket buyers. A new
generation of stars and supporting players replaced the fading Restoration luminaries. The breeches parts were banished, and no longer could Britons' amorous propensities be excited by the spectacle of a white bosom and silk stockings. Only theater songwriters and composers took the change in stride. Despite
their popularity within the walls of the theaters, their names were known to few
outside. Yet, unaware of their identities, a far greater public knew their tunes,
learned from penny sheet music, and they were poor game for the moralists.

Immediately after Henry Purcell's death, Daniel had left his post as Magdalen College organist to come to London and complete the music for *The Indian
Queen.* Though his music, like that of all his contemporaries, never equaled
Henry's genius, Daniel did write music of good quality, making him much in
demand. During the next years, he wrote several semioperas, as well as songs
for many plays, most notably for George Farquhar's 1707 *the Beaux' Stratagem,* which still occasionally enjoys a spirited revival. With Jeremiah Clarke he
wrote music for one of the earliest British comic operas, Settle's *The World in*

*the Moon* (1697). The pair collaborated once more with Thomas Motteaux on *The Island Princess,* for which Leveridge wrote special songs. Motteaux paid tribute to the songwriters in the printed text:

> I am willing to attribute it [the success of the work] chiefly to the excellency of the musical part. What Mr Daniel Purcell has set is so fine that he seems inspir'd with his brother's wonderful genius. It cannot be but equally admired. The notes of the Interlude by Mr Clarke have air and humor that crown 'em with applause; and the dialogue and enthusiastic song which Mr Leveridge set, are too particularly liked not to engage me to thank him for gracing my words with his composition, as much as for his celebrated singing.

In his later years, Daniel Purcell devoted himself to less frivolous music, concertizing with vocal and instrumental art music, and in 1713 he received an appointment as church organist, which he held until his death four years later.

His chief rival as songwriter and theater composer, John Eccles, was taught music by an eccentric musician father, who in later years, upon embracing Quaker tenets, burned all his musical instruments. Eccles wrote for sixty-six productions, and as Dryden had discovered in Purcell, Congreve found him a congenial partner for his major plays, including the masterpiece *The Way of the World*. Eccles's song "A soldier and a sailor," sometimes known as "Buxom Joan," was written for the 1695 *Love for Love* and appeared in penny single sheets as well as broadside ballads that took this saga of the "half home-bred and half sea-bred" sailor and his Joan and spiced it with further adventures and bawdy details. The music for "O! raree show, O! raree show" was also used for "The Raree Show Ballad, or the English Mississippi," inspired by the bursting of the Mississippi Bubble, a speculative venture to develop trade in the Louisiana Territory.

Becoming director of the King's Band of Music in 1709, Eccles was responsible for birthday odes and other choral works for special occasions. That same year he won second prize in a composition contest sponsored by Lord Halifax, who offered 200 guineas, to be distributed in four awards, the first of one-hundred, the others of fifty, thirty, and twenty. The final competition was held in the Dorset Garden Theatre, which had been specially decorated. The whole fashionable world was in attendance. The usual orchestra section was turned into White's Chocolate House, the entire establishment being moved there for the day, with chocolate, cooled drinks, ratafia, and other refreshments available. In addition to vocalists, eighty-five persons performed. John Weldon, organist at New College, won first prize, Eccles second. Daniel Purcell third, and a German, Gottfried Finger, took the fourth.

Eccles published three volumes of his *Theatre Music* and, in 1710, a collection of one hundred of his popular songs. Soon after, he retired to the country, taking up the full-time pursuit of angling.

Now wealthy from commissions and profits amassed as England's most fashionable architect, John Vanbrugh returned to the theater. He bought a stableyard in the Hay Market district, together with some surrounding property, for £2,000 and persuaded some "persons of quality" to invest an additional £30,000.

Congreve was named manager of the new building erected there, which opened in April 1705 with *The Loves of Ergsto,* a pastoral opera by Giacomo Greber, the first Italian opera sung in its own language in Britain. Neither London's theatrical establishment nor the critics liked the new Queen's Theatre, both arguing that a good theater had been sacrificed to exhibit a piece of architecture in which one could not hear the opera's words. When Vanbrugh offered one of his own plays, the general opinion was that the building was too large for the purely spoken word, too, and was too far out of town for those who did not care to add coach fare to an already high price for admission.

The theater was then rented, for £700 annually, to a group of actors who had walked out on the pinchfist Christopher Rich. Opening with a revival of *The Beaux' Stratagem,* they got into trouble with the licensing authorities. The patent issued by Charles in 1660 gave a monopoly in spoken dramatic presentation exclusively to the licensed royal companies. Many smaller theaters were getting around this restriction by advertising nights of music and variety, but also offering dramatic scenes and even entire plays. Neither Rich nor Betterton held a true patent either. Unable to use the Hay Market theater for spoken plays, the group of actors turned over its lease to some European musicians who intended to bring true Continental opera to London.

Following Purcell's death, few British composers showed any interest in the English Baroque opera he had pioneered. Having lost money in the past because of audience failure to respond favorably to recitative, managers similarly had no interest in true opera. A change was in the wings, however. Several years before, a member of the King's Band of music, Thomas Clayton, had returned from Italy, where he had presumably gone to study music and improve his skills, bringing back a collection of Italian music and operatic arias. He adapted these for use as the original score for a "true, all-sung" English opera based on Motteaux's old play *Arsinoë, Queen of Cyprus,* and auditioned it for the new tenants of Vanbrugh's theater. They were delighted, and Clayton did nothing to disabuse them of the notion that he was its true composer.

Critics did not like *Arsinoë* when it was first performed, but audiences adored it through a long run. Clayton was hailed as Britain's successor to the Orpheus Britannicus. Smelling profits from this sudden new appetite for true opera, the brilliant essayist and poet Joseph Addison submitted his libretto *Rosamund* to the new man of the hour. Having run out of Italian music, that musical fraud, emboldened by his new fame and royalties, ventured to write the music himself. The result was a fiasco, which turned Addison against opera, making him its leading journalist enemy. He observed in the Spectator, a folded sheet of four or six pages, which became the most famous periodical in the history of British letters:

> There is no question that our great grandchildren will be very curious to know the reason why their forefathers used to sit together like an audience of foreigners in their own country, and to hear whole plays acted before them in a tongue which they did not understand. . . . There is nothing that has more startled our English audience than the Italian recitative at its very first entrance upon the stage. People were wonderfully surprised to hear generals singing the word of command, and

ladies delivering messages in music. Our countrymen could not forebear laughing when they heard a lover chanting out a billet-doux, and even the superscription of a letter set to a tune.''

In spite of such criticism, which has had some meaning even in our own time, enough of an audience had developed to make continued production of opera feasible. Italian singers were imported by the boatload to appear at the Queen's Theatre, and the inability of these journeymen artists to sing the English words into which original Italian had been rendered gradually brought about use of the original texts. By 1710, English was rarely used in the Hay Market playhouse.

Time and his monstrous penury finally caught up with Christopher Rich, owner of the theater in Drury Lane and both acting patents. His only rival, Betterton, was in his late seventies and failing in health, but he lived long enough to see Rich stripped of everything and his theater closed. In late 1709, Queen Anne issued a new patent to a favored member of Parliament, as well as an order requiring all royal company actors to return to the Theatre Royal, the only playhouse available since the Lincoln's Inn Fields closed. Rich was a hard man to dispossess. When the theater was finally broken into, the new owner discovered that everything that could be moved and sold had been taken, making the theater unusable. The Queen's, too large for spoken drama, though ideal for Italian opera, whose home it had become, was now the city's only major licensed public playhouse. It seemed to be waiting for the arrival of a young composer named Händel, who had already made his mark in Europe.

The author of England's earliest comic opera was now reduced to working at Bartholomew Fair, to which he brought his old play *The Siege of Troy,* in a version tailored to the taste of that great audience of Englishmen who flocked to this most famous of all outdoor spectacles. Elkanah Settle was near sixty and had spent the past ten months working to strip the play of serious dialogue, substituting crowd-pleasing drolleries for the old high-styled verse. For the first time, the common man had an opportunity to view what his rich betters had been seeing for years—the magnificent scenery and costly machinery that accompanied contemporary theatrical entertainment—as a Trojan horse seventeen feet high and richly decorated, spewed out forty soldiers, swords drawn, to set Troy afire "whilst near forty windows or portholes in the several paintings all appear on fire, the flames catching from house to house, and all performed by illuminations and transparent paintings.''

# CHAPTER 11

# The Business of Music Publishing

Even before James I was on the throne a backstage battle for his favor began as men known to have ready access to his presence suddenly found themselves the recipients of bribes to ensure awards of position, charters, monopolies, and patents. Every post had its price—for example, £25,000 for that of lord treasurer. The stationers' wardens were familiar with the game and played it well, despite the fact that public sentiment against patent monopolies had risen to such a pitch that James was advised to revoke all of them by proclamation. Even after those royal words were announced, his principal courtiers continued to keep themselves accessible to the honeyed words and open purses of seekers after royal patronage. The stationers were almost immediately successful in their lobbying. James soon granted them a perpetual monopoly for the printing of primers, almanacs, and other profitable works, reserving only the Bible and the *Book of Common Prayer* to the crown and the royal printer. In return for this extraordinary grant, the Stationers' Company undertook to pay £200 out of its profits to the poor among its membership who had not found enough work to remain solvent. Despite an increasing rate of literacy, which saw almost half of London's and a third of the home counties' males able to read, conditions for most printers were worse than they had been a few decades earlier, when competition was restricted only by the number of presses in use. Control of every best-selling line of printed works was firmly in the hands of the English Stock, a joint venture of stockholders that issued its wares "for the company of Stationers" but distributed its profits only to shareholders.

There had been no major improvement of the British printing press since Caxton's time. It was still the old wooden press with a screw bearing downward pressure on type forms laid on wooden or stone beds. Though it was a clumsy affair, the press was capable of good work when the pressman worked with care and concern. European printers meanwhile were making some strides. In 1620, an improved press was invented by an Amsterdam printer, W. J. Blaeu; it did not come into English use until the early eighteenth century.

The British were equally slow to adopt use of copperplate-engraving techniques developed early in the fifteenth century. Demands for accurate maps to keep pace with the new age of discovery soon propelled this art form into commercial viability, but by the time European music printers took advantage of the process, engraving was common among most Continental craftsmen. A German artisan known to his Roman neighbors as Verovio arrived in the Eternal City in 1575 and established himself as an engraver and music editor. Some ten years later he issued the first known books of engraved music, collections of three- and four-part short songs in the Italian style. By the time of his death, he had brought out a dozen similar anthologies, beginning the tradition of engraved music printing in which Roman craftsmen excelled. The rise of recitative opera by the opening of the seventeenth century encouraged the development of a new commercial market for full scores of this form. Only engraved copperplates were capable of faithfully reproducing music for this form, as well as for solo keyboard and stringed instruments. British appetite for printed music of the lyric recitative theater was far behind that of Europe, and as a result not a single opera, British or foreign, was among the forty engraved works of music other than the sheet form printed in England prior to 1700.

Some tentative use of engraving was made by the British around 1612, when the first native book containing engraved music appeared. William Hole, a member of the London family who pioneered in the technique, prepared an anthology of music for the virginals to fill an order from a London lady of fashion in connection with a wedding ceremony. *Parthenia* contained music by Byrd, Bull, and Gibbons. Hole and his brother Robert engraved most of the small handful of music books made prior to the Commonwealth, including *Parthenia-in-Violata,* containing dance tunes and songs, published around 1614, and *Fantasias of III Parts* by Orlando Gibbons. In 1639, William Child, composer and organist of the Chapel Royal, published *Psalmes of III Voyces,* which was reprinted in 1650 and 1656, during the Commonwealth. This collection of twenty short anthems for two trebles and a bass was engraved on small copperplates and issued in separate parts.

It is strange that the British sense for business did not extend to the use of copperplate engraving. The less-expensive small sheets of metal were easy to store and to correct. After a sufficient number of copies were struck off for immediate need, they could be placed in reserve against new sales. Their use might have changed the appearance and the character of secular music, as well as its mechanical duplication, had proper thought been given to it. The cost of paper represented about three-fourths of all expenses, and any savings from mechanical operations would have increased profits.

The ruling stationers evidently were happy with the sloppy but profitable products coming off the movable-type presses operated by workers who had little pride in their work. Unprivileged and unemployed printers wanted removal of the official limit on the number of presses established in James's grant. They wished, too, for protection from reprisals by the Stationers' Court, which could "break the petitioners' houses, imprison their bodies, seize their goods and deface their presses and printing instruments without legal proceedings or eviction by information.'' They also wanted to break the monopoly owned by the Stationers' Company, which had boycotted all other books and closed the marketplace to competition. Though these actions were clear violations of the 1692 Queen's Bench Court findings involving the stationers, the government did not wish to end its friendly relationship with its private censoring apparatus. But opportunities did increase when the company compromised, agreeing to an expansion in the number of licensed printing houses to nineteen, fourteen of which could house only two presses, the others five each.

There were occasional efforts by persons outside the trade to fight the organization and its restrictive practices. The lexicographer and grammarian John Minsheu had capitalized on a growing need by British merchants to learn foreign languages in order to engage in international trade. Having written a number of successful simple foreign dictionaries and grammars, in 1611 Minsheu had received a twenty-one-year patent for a new work, a *Guide of Tongues* in eleven languages. Five years later, when the manuscript was completed, he could not find a licensed stationer willing to publish his book and printed it at his own expense. Then he could find no important bookseller willing to stock it. Going to the leading associations of businessmen and merchants, he sold the book by subscription, becoming the first English author to do so. Funding by advance promise to purchase was used by composers, songwriters, and compilers of music for the next two centuries, in both England and America, permitting countless publications that otherwise would never have seen light.

London businessmen who could not buy into joint-stock companies, which were carving up the international mercantile world, began a war against the practice, agitating against the restraint of trade and the price fixing inherent in monopolies. Their vast public-relations campaign enlisted both the unlicensed press and those hack writers whose pens were ever available to the highest bidder to produce a flood of antimonopoly pamphlets and tracts. A majority vote in Parliament issued the 1623 Statute on Monopolies, giving itself exclusive power to grant privileges, except for new products and inventions. The crown was able to reserve monopolies in ''saltpetre, gunpowder, the making or ordnance or shot, and alum mines,'' as well as printing, evidently deeming national defense as important as control of the press, assured only by the existence of a strong Stationers' Company. So the stationers were left more secure than ever and were able to continue the amalgamation of the trade. As their brother stationers were doing with literature, textbooks, and other bound assemblies of the printed word, a small group of music publishers, among whom were stationer officials of the highest level, had accomplished much the same thing. But by 1626, the copyrights of all major late-sixteenth- and early-seventeenth-century music books were in the possession of William Stansby, a London printer and bookseller, and passed thirteen years later to the minor printer Richard Bishop, an indication of the low estate into which music-book printing had fallen.

George Wither's unsuccessful attempt to enforce his fifty-one-year patent for religious songs, granted by James, was foiled by a concerted stationer boycott, forcing him to resort to unlicensed printers and Dutch presses competing for the British market. James had made a number of similar grants: to Ben Jonson when he was named poet laureate; to Minsheu for his multilingual dictionary; to Fynes Moryson for travel books; to the poet Samuel Daniel for his *History of England;* and one for printing briefs on a single sheet of paper granted jointly in 1618 to a handsome young court favorite and the stationer Thomas Symcock, who took it to mean an effective end to the company's 1612 order that five printers were to have all control of broadside ballads. The patent, providing that "all things that are, may be, or shall be Printed upon one side of a sheet, or any part of a sheet; provided one side thereof be white paper," resulted in years of endless litigation by the Stationers' Company in its efforts to foil a daring attempt to undermine its hold. In 1629, even though the patent had been renewed the previous year by Charles I, the courts canceled it, giving Symcock restitution in the form of printing equipment in return for the loss of his investment. During the lengthy litigation, stationers who otherwise held royal patents to be as sacred as Holy Writ had no compunction about violating Symcock's privilege, relying on a company ruling that "the sellers of ballads may print their own copies where they think good."

Another important challenge came in the early 1630s, from a trio of printers, Miles Flesher, John Haviland, and Robert Young, none of whom had yet achieved any high place in the company. Through craft and intrigue they got control of over one-fifth of all licensed presses, the balance belonging to the English Stock. They then bought important copyrights and got the lease of the royal printer's patent for the Bible. Working within a system carefully evolved to prevent such schemes, the trio became wealthy London entrepreneurs, with publishing interests in Scotland and Cambridge as well. Flesher was one of the journeymen printers who had petitioned for relief in 1614. As a boy he had been apprenticed to Thomas East and worked on music books printed under assignment of the Barley patent. While other journeymen were unable to find work, Flesher prospered, by 1617 having enough money to buy a half-interest in one of the fourteen licensed London printing offices and taking over the entire business seven years later, after the death of his partner. Though still a low-ranking liveryman in 1629, he was already one of the city's leading publisher-booksellers, named to the committee seeking to overthrow Symcock's patent, and a partner of both Haviland and Young. Young had been associated with Humphrey Lownes until the printer's death, and then entered into the agreement with Flesher and Haviland.

Near the end of his reign, James gave the universities at Oxford and Cambridge the right to comprint books of which the English Stock had a monopoly. Though they attempted and failed to maintain their exclusive privilege by legal means, the Stationers' Company was forced to stand by while Cambridge printers issued Bibles, prayer books, and the Psalms in meter. Flesher and his partners took advantage of the ambiguous language in the rule, and set up presses in the university town to print works whose copyright otherwise would not have been available.

Acting on behalf of his associates, in 1633 Young got himself named royal printer in Scotland, the poverty-ridden nation that, removed from the stationers' jurisdiction, permitted shoddy duplications of licensed books for shipment to Britain. The trio's major coup came in 1634, when they bought up all outstanding shares in the King's Printing Office in London, together with rights to the Bible and the *Book of Common Prayer*. The king's printer, Robert Barker, from whom they purchased the controlling interest, had just been the defendant in a lengthy suit brought by the king's advocate over "false printing of the Bible in divers places of it, and for printing it on very poor paper." The archbishop of Canterbury was particularly vexed with an error in the Seventh Commandment, reading "Thou shalt commit adultery." All copies of the most recent edition were confiscated and burned, and Barker was put on trial, even though his work was little different from that of the most respected stationers. Actually, Flesher had hired thieves to steal type, ink, and paper from Barker's warehouse, and paid typesetters and proofreaders to corrupt the Bible text in order to get his hands on the privilege.

Controlling production and sale of all Bibles, the *Book of Common Prayer*, grammars, and lawbooks, and earning profits of from £500 to £1,500 over standard returns from each edition, Flesher, Haviland, and Young were frequently called up before the company master for various crimes: exercising questionable title to trade books, exceeding quotas before replacing worn-out type, and printing psalms for sale in Britain on their unlicensed Scottish equipment. All three, however, went to their graves respected men.

Flesher was still active in 1643, having worked his way up in the company hierarchy and served as master for two terms. Seeing portents of an uncertain future for bookselling and publishing in the Puritan Parliament's dislike of the monopoly system, he unloaded his various patents, but exacted full royalties for their duration. Playing the role of friend in need, he shared his fortune with guild members, but lent money only when copyright collateral secured it.

He was one of those stationers whose practices were cited by journeymen printers reduced to carrying plague victims for a livelihood, when they sought relief from the government. They pointed to the multitudes of Bibles and other books being printed in Scotland for shipment to England, and to the conspiracies among ranking stationers to print on poor paper, fix prices, and sell only to each other. Unable to find work or redress, journeymen and even some master printers turned to unlicensed printing. Virtually all the broadsides, whether pro-Stuart or Puritan, came off their presses. Others eked out penny profits from broadside ballads. Small merchants, especially grocers and provisioners, hardware sellers, and dealers in pins, needles, and threads, were the chief outlets for unlicensed books and ballads. Though new laws forbade anyone who had not served a seven-year booksellers-stationers trade apprenticeship, the economic realities of small business and London's appetite for such ephemera made the prohibition difficult to enforce.

Those 500 flowers of the English gentry who formed the Long Parliament in the winter of 1640 put an end to most monopolies and abolished the Star Chamber and all its decrees. Although these actions did not immediately affect the Stationers' Company as a trade guild, they did place in serious jeopardy all grants made to it since 1586. For a while, the company's register remained the official repository for all claims of ownership, and the wardens were still the watchdogs over printing.

One of the first laws touching upon authors' rights appeared in the spate of legislation promulgated by the Long Parliament. Hoping to restrict underground printing, which usually centered on the virtues of the Stuarts and the incompetence of the Puritans, it passed a bill in 1641 requiring that the author's name appear on each printed work, as "an identification of the text's origin and an indication of the writer's consent to publish." It proved ineffective. Whereas 240 titles were registered in 1640, only 71 books were deposited two years later. Despite this apparent drop, the number of printers grew as changes in English political philosophies and reading habits increased demand for cheap books, tracts, and ballads. There was now more work than ever before for printers, and journeymen rushed to open shops.

Among the flood were two editions of *The Doctrine and Discipline of Divorce,* a paperback pamphlet by the thirty-five-year-old poet-turned-Puritan-propagandist John Milton. In 1643, he used the printed word to resolve the problem of a man's relations with a woman, after his seventeen-year-old new wife left him in detestation of that "brutish congress" chaining "two carcasses unnaturally together." Having "hasted too eagerly to light the nuptual torch," Milton used his quill to plead the cause of divorce on a man's petition. Not being registered, the publication brought immediate protest from the Stationers' Company, which cited recent legislation that all books be entered "according to the old custom," the result of strenuous lobbying by members of the company council.

Responding in what is termed the noblest of his prose works, *Areopagitica,* a plea for the liberty of unlicensed printing, Milton argued that "though all the winds of doctrine were let loose to play upon the earth, so Truth be in the field, we do injuriously by licensing and prohibiting, to misdoubt her strength." Parliament appointed a committee to study his violation, but no action was taken. His appeal was limited, however, by his prejudices. With no sympathy for the penny press and the popular ballads with which England was pulsing, he equated such materials with the Catholic church, atheism, and obscenity, all of which he abominated. It remained for lesser men, among them the "penny poets" writing the tracts, pamphlets, news books, and street ballads, to battle for true freedom for the printing press and to war against Puritan repression.

## The Golden Age of Balladry and the Rise of the Newspaper

The seventeenth century, which has correctly been labeled the "golden age of balladry," represented an intellectual turnabout by those educated men who found in their own verse a most felicitous and communicative medium for self-expression. For nearly half a century, Ben Jonson's dictum that "a poet should detest a ballad-maker" reflected the attitude of playwrights and court poets, even though they often referred to both the ballad maker and his songs, well aware of their audiences.

As had Lydgate, Skelton, Heywood, and others of Henry's court poets, the early-seventeenth-century versifiers turned to the tavern poet's meters and soon displaced those brawling, heavy-drinking pothouse bards as creators of the new era's popular songs. Richard Corbett, bishop of Oxford and Norwich, was once Ben Jonson's intimate and held his own among the Mermaid Tavern's habitués, who gathered for conviviality and extemporized versification. Once, on seeing an itinerant peddler unsuccessfully attempt to empty his pack of penny merriments, the doctor of divinity doffed his robe of office and, wearing the song seller's leather jacket, sold all the ballads himself. Having a rare and full voice, Corbett gathered a great crowd, making it a banner day for the wandering Autolycus. Like Corbett, his writer contemporaries Martin Parker, Lawrence Price, John Denham, John Taylor, Alexander Brome, and other Royalist sympathizers used the ballad as well as the sword to capture the hearts of their countrymen during the Civil War. In this time before the newspaper, they recognized the ballad form as the single most effective device with which to win minds. Only one ballad writer of their quality, Andrew Marvell, rallied to the Puritan cause.

Little is known of the early life of the most distinguished professional ballad writer, Martin Parker, successor to Elderton and Deloney. He was probably born in London around 1600, had some education, for his writings contained references not only to contemporary popular literature but also to the classics, and evidently owned a tavern. He threatened to return to that trade after running afoul of Puritan laws and narrowly escaping prison for his "base" ballads. He was familiar with hundreds of ballad tunes and made clever use of them in his broadsides of news, romance, advice, and history. He also wrote chapbooks, works of history, romance, and fancy, and prose tracts, some seventy-five of which have been traced to his pen through official records or allusions in other's works. In an age of unlicensed printing, many others must have been lost from an output labeled, in a petition subscribed to by 15,000 London Puritans, as "lascivious, idle and unprofitable . . . ballads in disgrace of religion, to the increase of all vice." His name never appeared again in the stationers' register, but his most famous ballad, "When the King enjoys his own again," was issued in 1643. The antiquarian ballad collector Joseph Ritson wrote of it in 1790:

> [It was] the most famous and popular air ever heard in this country. Invented to support the declining interest of the Royal Martyr, it served afterwards, with more success, to keep up the spirits of the Cavaliers, and promote the Restoration all over the kingdom. At the Revolution of 1688 it of course became an adherant of the exiled family, whose cause it never deserted . . . upon two memorable occasions, was very near being . . . instrumental in replacing [the crown] on the head of James' son.

Hyder E. Rollins asserted in *Modern Philology:*

> Parker shared the usual fate of ballad-mongers. His songs continued to delight the hearts of the common people and to bring money to publishers, ballad-singers and ballad-revisers, while his own name was rapidly forgotten. It would be impossible to estimate the popularity of his ballads during the hundred years that followed his death. . . . In the technique of balladry and in truthfulness of verse Parker has had no equal among professional ballad-writers before or since his day. Collier's tribute

to him is just: "Surely those who love poetry, and who sometimes unreasonably expect to meet with it in old ballads of a comparatively modern date must be satisfied with this sweet, cheerful pastoral vein of Martin Parker . . . [who] was a much better poet than many give him credit for . . . though he wrote for bread and to please the Vulgar."

Parker and his greatest rival and friend, Lawrence Price, often exchanged answering ballads as well as tributes to each other's talent. Price, a native of London who arrived on the public scene about the same time as Parker, wrote numberless ballads, tracts, and pamphlets before his death in 1680. Possessed of an instinct for survival rivaling that of Dryden, he wore Parliament's ribbon when that body appeared to be winning, but adopted Cavalier ways and costume when restoration seemed a certainty. Surviving Parker by twenty-five years, he continued to write ballads, which daily grew more old-fashioned.

A lawyer whose tragedy *The Sophy* was applauded just as Puritans were shutting down London's theaters, John Denham fought for the king during the Civil War, at home and abroad. He was knighted by Charles and received land grants for his loyalty. As royal surveyor of works, he built Burlington House and Greenwich Palace, and improved London's streets.

Known as the "Water Poet," John Taylor was a Thames River boatman in the last years of Elizabeth's reign who published his first book in 1612. He continued to bring out pamphlets at his own expense, foundering temporarily on the rocks of Stationers' Company monopolies, but then succeeded with a number of gossipy little booklets about his adventures. One detailed a visit to Scotland made without a penny in his purse; another, his attempt to sail the Thames in a brown-paper boat. He plumped for Charles in 1640 and then went off to Oxford, riding out the Long Parliament by operating a tavern and writing verse lampoons against the Roundheads. He returned to London to watch the king's execution and remained to await the inevitable warrant for his arrest, which arrived later that year. His books and papers were seized. He was released four years later to die in peace.

Hailed as the English Anacreon, Alexander Brome was a feisty young lawyer-turned-songwriter-and-poet, whose songs were sung so often his friends were certain he was headed for immortality. During the grim times from 1648 until the Restoration, he was an editor of antigovernment news books, to which all the Cavalier ballad writers contributed. When the king did come into his own again, eight volumes of Brome's songs and prose were printed in London, with laudatory verses by Izaak Walton, ballad lover and fishing devotee.

None of the youthful poetry written by Andrew Marvell, including his best-known stanzas, "To his coy mistress," was printed during his lifetime, though much of it was very popular and often repeated. He was better known for his dedication to the Puritan cause, and he played the role of a Martin Parker for Oliver Cromwell, though of a more inflexible character. Although often expressing admiration of the Stuart king and the poets who rallied to his banner, Marvell allied himself with the Puritans following his meeting with John Milton. After graduating from Cambridge at the age of eighteen, he had traveled extensively in Europe, returning an accomplished linguist, and became tutor to children of wealthy country families. Under Milton's influence he succumbed to Cromwell's personal magnetism and wrote a number of poetical works in his praise, including one in 1650 in which he hailed the dictator as a modern Julius Caesar. Even though a single stanza in that work praised the manner in which Charles had gone to his death under the headsman's blade, Cromwell hired him to tutor a ward, and in 1657 employed him as assistant to his Latin secretary, the now blind Milton. When the Long Parliament was dissolved, Marvell was elected to the body replacing it, remaining a member until his death eighteen years later. One of his first votes approved digging up Cromwell's body and its beheading, but he did fight to save Milton, in the name of English letters, from reprisal for past political activities. For many years, he wrote ballad satires against the excesses, corruption, and decadence of Charles's court and his officials, wisely choosing to confine his work to one-side-only broadsides. The first collection of Marvell's work appeared in 1680.

In 1649, the Long Parliament, then completely dominated by the military, passed a printing act, hoping with it to end the activities of pro-Stuart balladeers, tract writers, and contributors to news books. This most drastic act against the book trade since the decree of 1637, as well as against other productions of London printers, at least 250 of whom were engaged in printing broadside ballads prior to 1648, put policing back into the stationers' hands. Most of the previous regulations were reinstated, among them the limit of two on the number of presses outside London, and the reinstitution of searchers to seek out "disorderly" printing. However, recognition of a burgeoning hunger for popular literature of all sorts stimulated in the authorities an awareness of the need for sufficient presses on which to print counterpropaganda against the pro-Royalist materials being disseminated. Limits on London master printers were ended, and within a week thirty-six of them put up security for their good behavior and joined the Stationers' Company. Most of these were already engaged in periodical publication, the new and profitable field of journalism that had emerged after the fall of the Stuarts and to which the ballad writers were devoting most of their attention.

The printing of news accounts was already an old tradition. Those early printers who were unable to obtain a valued privilege from the Tudors, or were not equipped for book printing, had to look to job printing, on one side only, of advertisements, handbills, proclamations, and those ever-ready sources of income, the broadside ballads, none of which needed official permission. The first published ballad known, John Skelton's report on a battle between England and Scotland, issued in 1513, is also the first known example of British journalism.

Spurred by the mass duplication of books following Caxton's importation of a printing press and type, literacy had increased among the business and upper classes, but few people had any access to the state's political news-gathering facilities. By the mid-sixteenth century, staffs of intelligencers, early foreign correspondents who also served as secret agents, sent back reports detailing affairs in Europe. The rise of mercantilism and foreign trade developed a further demand for information, which was supplied in time by enterprising printer-stationers, who created the "news book." Cut and folded into sixteen sheets, four by five inches in size, to sell for a penny each, the news books, like most printed publications, had a title page, the actual news starting on page three. In them readers found items about wars, treaties, royal marriages, and other matters affecting the balance of power or influencing current events. However, as a subservient ally of the Privy Council, the Stationers' Company frequently suppressed printed material that might lead to domestic controversy, and major commercial interests were forced to create their own newsletters for circulation among international bankers, merchants, and statesmen. Nearly 500 English news books were issued from 1590 to 1610 alone, though only 200 of them ever entered the stationers' register, the balance being withheld to avoid censorship.

With little interest in matters across the Channel before they were made a public issue by the state-controlled propaganda apparatus, the average Briton got his local news by way of the broadside ballad, sung to a new or familiar tune. These accounts of scandal, gossip, fantastical events, weather phenomena, murder and other crime were hawked through the streets for a penny each.

The major publisher of a late-sixteenth-century newspaper was John Wolfe, son of a wealthy fishmonger who learned the printing trade from John Day and became a freeman of the Stationers' Company in 1584. After completing his apprenticeship, he traveled on the Continent for a few years, learning new printing techniques in Holland and Italy, where he saw his first newsletters. On his return, he invaded the Bible-printing monopoly first, then that of the psalms, grammar books, and William Seres's prayer guide, while leading a secret combination of printers, typesetters, table makers, bookbinders, and booksellers who believed in the right of any Englishman to print whatever he chose, regardless of "any commandment Her Majesty gave to the contrary." When the stationers' masters sought to force adherence to the bylaws and regulations, Wolfe answered, "Tush, Luther was but one man and reformed all the world for religion, and I am that one man who must and will reform the government of this trade."

Obdurate in this resolve, Wolfe eventually forced Day, under a secret agreement, to print copies of the Singing Psalms, which he sold to the patent holder for twopence halfpenny, and Day sold for sixpence. Wolfe rose to high company office in time and eventually set up his business in Stationers' Hall itself. By purchasing every press offered for sale, he came to own more than any other single stationer. During the five years he printed news books, 1589 to 1593, he pioneered in developing the newspaper, creating typographical innovations later adopted by news publishers, one of which was the earliest known printed solicitation for subscriptions to a periodical, his *Journal of Advertisements,* in 1591. Appointed City of London printer in 1593, he abandoned the news business to specialize in printing official proclamations, circulars, registers, and other municipal documents.

Early in James's reign, additional prohibitions and edicts affecting the newsbook trade were issued. Under increasing state controls and the selfish vigilance of the stationers, more repressive than it had been under either Mary or Elizabeth, news books went into decline. Armed with Blaeu's new press, and helped by regulations limiting the number of presses in England, Amsterdam printers bought English type and began to issue a regular news sheet in 1620, intended for distribution in London. Their advantage was short-lived. Late the following year, English printers imitated them and issued a few single sheets of news items. And in 1622, Nathaniel Butter, a leading stationer, joined with two fellow booksellers to issue the first coranto, or news book that appeared at weekly intervals. Butter had been at the game for many years; a 1609 Privy Council order had forbid further publication of his *News from the Sea of Piracies by the Turks*. His new front pages bore the date and number of the issue, each of which was twenty to forty pages, printed on paper seven and one-half by three and three-quarters inches. Its foreign correspondents reported "divers particulars concerning the news out of Italy, Spain, Turkey, Persia, Bohemia, Sweden, Poland, Austria, the Pallatinates, and divers places of Higher and Lower Germany" in a folksy and friendly style. There were no editorials, but the Privy Council, regarding any compilation of foreign current events as "so ill, as the Lords would not have it known," usually confiscated the issues. A complaint by the Spanish ambassador regarding coverage given his government brought about the 1632 Star Chamber decree forbidding any more printing of foreign news, thus closing off such information for the next six years and leaving the public to learn it from penny broadside ballads.

Charles I restored the news press in 1638, granting Butter and his partners a twenty-one-year monopoly on publication of foreign news, an event celebrated that year in a special ninety-six-page edition, *An abstract of some special foreign occurences brought down to weekly news of December 29,* capsulating all the events of the previous 2,200 days not permitted by the government to appear in print at the time. Now, news books of four pages began to appear at infrequent intervals, selling for a penny.

One of the first Puritan Parliament's actions in 1641 was the revocation of Butter's patent. Stripped of his monopoly, he was unable to cope with the printing trade's changing nature. The 1648 edict ending limitation of the number of master printers was a final blow, and Butter fell into obscurity. He was buried as an act of company charity.

Other printers fared better, issuing some 200 news publications during the Commonwealth. The best known and longest lasting was the quasi-official *Mercurius Civicus,* which took the first half of its name from Butter's *Mercurius Britannicus,* and whose title page boasted a dedication to "truth impartially related to prevent mis-information." Like most of the licensed news books, the *Civicus* had a page size of eight by six inches, and appeared regularly, to sell for a penny. It carried advertising, randomly placed throughout each issue, at sixpence per insertion, but as inflation raged, space rates were driven up.

Most of the news books were written by Grub Street pamphleteers who had learned their trade by writing popular literature for London's mass market. The most brilliant of these songwriter authors, Parker, Taylor, Samuel Sheppard, and John Cleveland, wrote, edited, and published surreptitiously printed newspapers espousing the Cavalier cause. Puritan editors railed against these publications.

The merchandising, distribution, and advertising techniques used in selling broadsides were employed by the news-book printers on both sides of the political controversy. Printers supplied vendors, and vendors employed hawkers, who were Everyman's only contact with the newspaper and its writers. For several years, the Long Parliament employed the Stationers' Company in its age-old role as semiofficial overseer of the press. In 1643, Henry Walley, who served as company clerk from 1630 until 1652, was named official licenser of such "small pamphlets" as news books and broadsides. Despite his not inconsiderable powers, virtually all of the enormous number of ballads written during the Civil War and the Commonwealth never entered the official register. After 1656, and until the Restoration, ballads carried the phrase "licensed according to Order," with the name or initials of each publisher underneath.

Oliver Cromwell's record in the matter of a free press was as bad as that of the most despotic modern dictator. Shortly after the army-dominated Parliament named him lord protector, the music-loving Cromwell ordered the closing of all but the two official sixteen-page newspapers. After his death and with the certainty that a Stuart king would soon be recalled, a third paper appeared, edited by a young schoolteacher, Henry Muddiman, who had written and published a number of weekly news books. The era of modern journalism began in 1665 when Muddiman was granted free postage for his new weekly newsletter, the *London Gazette*, which is still printed. He was allowed to use the mails without charge, and anyone in Britain who cared to had a similar privilege in sending information and news to the editor, whose paper was sold for an annual subscription of five pounds.

## John Playford, the First Full-Service Music Publisher

Out of the confused welter of government decrees, shoddy printing-trade practices, and official interdiction against most popular culture, there rose the first Englishman to devote all his energies and professional activities to the business of music publishing and promotion. He was John Playford, born in 1623 to a bookseller residing in Norwich, home of one of the oldest and most important guilds of professional musicians. For nearly a century, the town waits had been playing outdoor Sunday-evening concerts. When young Playford was six, these gay evenings were drawing such vast and boisterous crowds that the town court bowed to Puritan protest and ruled that the musicians could no longer disturb the Sabbath air with secular music. With these concerts and the daily music of street musicians, Playford's interest in popular music apparently developed early. His dedication to religious music was stimulated by access to Norwich Cathedral, whose organist and chorus master were well paid to provide music and train a special choir of eight boys.

In his mid-teens, Playford was apprenticed to a London bookseller and grew to manhood in the great city of 350,000, developing rarely disguised Royalist sympathies. His apprenticeship was completed prior to 1648, and his name first appeared in the Stationers' register the same year, as vendor of some pamphlets printed for him.

It was the most chancy of times for a young man to try his fortune in the book trade, particularly for one with Royalist leanings. Ten days after the execution, on January 31, 1649, of Charles Stuart, Theodore Jennings, into whose hands all licensing of news books, pamphlets, and ballads had been placed, issued permission to Francis Grove to print a new ballad, "The King's last farewell," which was quickly peddled through the streets by mongers, who were promptly roughed up by the military and arrested. Jennings did not repeat his error, nor did any other law-abiding printer. No ballads dealing with the late ruler appeared until 1656. There were many pamphlets purporting to be true accounts of the late monarch in his last days of imprisonment and suffering, forty-seven editions of one within the year. Among these highly varnished portraits of the amiable and inept monarch as an Anglican saint was a three-part narrative sold by Playford.

After nine months of hoping by severe martial laws to purge the press and the publishers of their sins, Parliament issued the Printing and Licensing Act of 1649. Penalties were increased for all infractions, and anyone who wished could engage in the business, but only after putting up a bond of one hundred pounds against publication of any material deemed seditious. Those failing to do so faced a fine of ten pounds and destruction of their press and type. Ballad hawkers were no longer permitted, and when taken were conveyed to the House of Correction to be whipped as common rogues and dismissed. Punishment was not confined to Londoners. A wandering singer, whose pack included a stock of new ballads, was seized one Sunday after prayers. He had been singing to some townspeople, and was locked in an "ugly hole under a bridge, where by extreme dampness and closeness of the place, he was suffocated within a few hours later."

An immediate result of the new law was a warrant for the arrest of Playford and two printers who had run off another edition of the pamphlets dealing with Charles's trial, last speech, and execution. There is some mystery as to what happened next, but it is fair to believe that having also printed and sold Commonwealth documents and pamphlets, he was forgiven his breach of the law. Yet his name did not appear in the register for almost a year.

Undaunted by these proscriptions, the underground Royalist press lashed out at these acts. Streetwise ballad sellers learned to avoid arrest by changing the traditional prayer for the king's well-being, with which they usually closed all demonstrations of their wares, and now blessing Parliament. But when a sympathetic audience gathered, one sang:

> And now I would gladly conclude my song
> With a prayer as ballads used to do,
> But yet I'll forbear, for I think er't be long
> We shall have a King and a Parliament too.

Many historians have hailed Playford's first venture in publication of popular music as an act of courage, pointing to the Puritans' hatred of all things popular—music, dancing, sports, and the theater. Through its acts of censorship and control of the press and public entertainment, the Puritan government did make the period of the Civil War a dark time in man's struggle for freedom of

expression. There were, however, many cases of personal liberty. The Britons'
traditional love of music could not be legislated into oblivion. Though the great
theaters were closed, the Red Bull, the Fortune, and other theaters of the people pulsated with the music of jiggs and drolls and songwriters supporting the
Commonwealth used both traditional tunes and recently popular music for their
ballads. In view of this and the continual daring shown by many London printers, pamphleteers, news-book and ballad writers, Playford's decision to print
and sell a collection of popular music for the violin in 1650 represented his
keen anticipation of its sales potential, rather than any gallant defiance of authority. For much of his life he displayed an innate awareness of public taste,
commercial appeal, and a precognition of new trends—the faculty of knowing
a good tune when he heard it—which characterizes all the towering figures in
popular music's history.

Playford found in Thomas Harper, of Little Britain, London, a craftsman who
had worked with music type almost twenty years before, when, in 1632, he had
been reduced to bootlegging psalters and incurred the Stationers' Company's
wrath. He was eventually forgiven and taken into membership. The first Playford issue, *The English Dancing Master, or Plain and Easy Rules for the Dancing of Country Dances, with the tune to each dance* was entered in the register
on November 7, 1649, and put on sale in his shop near the Inner Temple church
door early the following year. This compilation of 104 ballad tunes, most of
which had never appeared in print before, was crudely reproduced in old-style
diamond-shaped notation. Its melody lines were neither barred nor harmonized,
but it was a success. Known best as *The Dancing Master,* the next edition,
which was enlarged and more carefully edited, appeared some twenty months
later. Playford's first child went through eighteen editions in all, between the
initial printing and 1728, and grew to 900 tunes in three thick volumes.

Playford, having successfully taken bead on a carefully selected segment of
London's affluent and respectable, aimed at the social pretensions of his customers in *The Dancing Master*'s preface, while neglecting to point out that most
of the tunes he was peddling were the very ones the vulgar ballad trade used
for its rhymes. Many of the most outspoken anti-Commonwealth ballads were
being written to the very melodies the publisher claimed would make "the body
active and strong . . . graceful in deportment" simply by treading country dances
to the music of a fiddle.

Recognizing that Britain's propensity for group singing had never abated,
Playford next issued a series of best-selling compilations of those old tunes he
felt "were in danger of being forgot." These included rounds, the earliest of
which was "Sumer is icumen in," and their modern variants, ribald, pun-ridden,
and bawdy catches, as well as the "freemen's songs" of Henry's day, inter-
larded with new part songs by the best-known masters in London.

John Benson, the London printer to whom he had been apprenticed, became
the first of several publishers with whom Playford entered into partnership to
issue music and song books. *The Dancing Master* was followed by *A Musical
Banquet* and *Musick and Mirth,* the latter appearing under various names. No
similar books of popular music had been printed in England since Ravenscroft's

trio from 1609 to 1611. *A Musical Banquet* demonstrated Playford's uncanny anticipation of changing tastes and the needs of his customers, for it included a section of how-to lessons for the lyra-viol, a small bass on which one played chords, employing much plucking of strings. Its tuning was much easier, and the use of letters rather than notation made it possible for amateurs to be adept rather quickly.

Playford engaged John Hilton, the songwriter, composer, and parish clerk of St. Margaret's Church, Westminster, to edit the first of his *Musick and Mirth* series, *Catch as Catch Can.* Thrown out of work when Puritan soldiers tore down church organs, Hilton eked out a living as church clerk and worked whenever possible as a purveyor of whatever music provided employment.

The catch book appeared in 1652, its title page showing three male singers sitting around a table on which an open music book rests. The catch, as Ian Spink explains in *English Song Dowland to Purcell,* was written on all subjects—

> religious, serious, humorous, bibulous, amorous or scurrilous. Conviviality is the prevailing mood and drinking catches outnumber all the others. . . . The *double entendre* was the favored device in the bawdy catch. The aim was for one or two lines to come together during the course of the song, so that by means of judiciously placed rests in the several parts, indelicate obscene phrases otherwise unsuspected would emerge. William Cranford's "Here dwells a pretty maid" (from *Catch as Catch Can*) provides an example, and again it depends on the conjuction of the second and third lines.

| Here dwells a | pretty maid | whose name | is |
|---|---|---|---|
| whole | her whole | her whole life | her |
| you may kiss | you may kiss | | you may kiss |
| Sis | You may come in and kiss | | Her |
| whole estate is sev'nteen pence a year; | Yet | | |
| you may kiss her if you come but near. | | | Here |

New editions of *Catch as Catch Can* appeared regularly, full of bawdy ballads to catch the shilling or so the books cost. Dialogues, glees, airs, and ballads were gradually added to the series, which grew from 143 songs in the initial printing to 255 in 1673, and even more in the tenth, and last, edition (1746) of *The Pleasant Musical Companion,* to which its name was changed in 1686.

*A Musical Banquet*'s "rules to sing and play on the viol" was the first of many similar Playford publications to appear with expanded text and musical illustrations. The most significant was the 1654 *Introduction to the Skill of Music,* very soon the most popular rival of Morley's 1597 *Plaine and Easie Introduction.* It went through more than two dozen numbered editions in a century. Its second, published in 1655, was enlarged and in two parts: the first contained instructions for playing the viol and singing; the second was *The Art of Setting or Composing Music in Parts,* a revision of Thomas Campion's 1613 treatise made for Playford by the viola da gamba virtuoso Christopher Simpson. The tenth edition, 1683, dropped the old-fashioned manual for one by young Henry Purcell.

Regularly issued catalogues of the Playford stock included similar instruction books for the cittern and gittern, the division viol, flageolet, the virginals and harpsichord, appearing as each instrument became popular and remaining in print long after the publisher's death.

More advanced music, catering to the educated tastes of Britons who had been exposed to modern European music, also found a place in the Playford stock. He had got hold of the original engraved copperplates for Gibbons's 1620 *Fantasias* and Child's 1639 *Psalmes,* and reprinted both. These and ten other publications represent all the Playford music books printed from engravings, the remainder being from movable type, which brought him into argument with composers, who thought them not accurately reproduced.

During the initial period of preparing music books that appealed to various tastes, Playford issued the first of a series of *Select Airs and Dialogues,* printed for one or two voices to sing to the theorbo, lute, or bass viol. Sixty-seven songs by ten writers were included. Some of them were refugees on the Continent, but not even those living around London were aware of the book until it appeared. Sales were brisk. Another edition appeared two years later, with eighty songs, and the third in 1659, with 125, some by Playford himself. He was ready to reveal his own talents by then, placing his work alongside that of well-known writers who had become his customers and friends. All modesty disappeared when Pepys haunted his store, constantly in search of complimentary copies of the newest music, and great composers vied for his attention.

One not so impressed was Henry Lawes, twenty of whose songs had been printed without his knowledge or permission in the first *Select Airs*. He made little secret of his displeasure. A previous dealing with a publisher, Humphrey Moseley, had been totally unsatisfactory; to lend a cachet of authenticity to an edition of Edmund Waller's verse, brought out without approval, the poet being in exile in Europe, the title page carried Lawes's name as having set all the poems to music, making the edition presumably an accurate duplication of Waller's words as written out for the composer. An edition of Milton's poetry followed, again mentioning Lawes, even though he had not proofread and approved the printing. Lawes's work on a projected collection of songs for publication by Moseley was temporarily halted by the death in action of William Lawes. A collection of psalms, set to music by the brothers, came out under Moseley's imprint in 1648, with a laudatory poem by Milton, hailing Lawes, "who taught our English music how to/span words with just notes and accent." Unfortunately, when the book did appear, in four small volumes, music by "servants to His Majesty" was no longer commercially viable, despite Milton's imprimatur. No lover of the Stuarts, the master of verse had great affection for Henry Lawes, "the friend of poets," who had been named a gentleman of the Chapel Royal in 1626 at the age of thirty. Lawes was an expert lutenist with a gift for writing music that was said to resemble the rhythmic and tonal effects of speech. That talent and his respect for their words were highly valued by those gallant poets who hoped to gain the Stuart court's attention and did so with his exquisite settings of their verses, heard for the first time during royal entertainments. Herrick's "Gather ye rosebuds while ye may," Waller's "Go, lovely rose!," Lovelace's "To Lucasta: Going Beyond the Seas," Milton's

*Comus,* and scores of other poems, by Suckling, Carew, and other Cavalier poets won the nobility's admiration through Lawes's music.

With such credentials, Lawes persuaded Playford to bring out the first of three books of his *Select Airs and Dialogues,* with an engraved portrait of the composer on its title page, a distinct honor. Lawes complained in the preface that Playford "had made bold to print in one book about twenty of my songs whereof I had no knowledge till the book was in the press, and it seems he found these so acceptable that he is ready for more. Therefore the question is not whether or no my compositions shall be public, but whether they shall come first from me or from some other hand; and which is likeliest to afford the true correct copies I leave others to judge." Lawes believed he could write out his own songs with more accuracy than they could be set in type, a complaint evidently made by others, who kept their songs from mechanical duplication, relying instead on manuscript in their own hand. In the 1659 edition of *Select Airs,* Playford challenged them.

> My cares, pains and charge hath not been small, by procuring true and exact copies and daily attending to the oversight of the press, as no prejudice might redound either to the Authors or Buyer; and Herein I resolve to meet with those Mistakers, who have taken up a new (but very fine) opinion, That Music cannot as truely be printed as Prickd [written by hand] that no Choice Airs or Songs are permitted to come in print, though 'tis well known that our best Musical Compositions, either of our own or of Strangers, have been and are tendered to the World by the Printer's hand; To convince the former and to testify my gratitude to these Excellent Masters, from whose own hands I received most of these compositions, do I say this much, that this is my present endeavor, and care in the true and exact publishing this Book will redound to Public Benefit, and the Authors Reputation.

England had long lagged behind the Italians in regard for the violin, the instrument usually played for dancing to *The Dancing Master*'s tunes. Attitudes changed dramatically after the German-Swedish virtuoso Thomas Baltzar arrived in England in 1655. Recognizing the future in Baltzar's skill and popularity, and anticipating that gentleman amateurs would soon be taking up the violin in preference to the lute, Playford published instrumental music for viol and violin by Matthew Locke. *Apollo's Banquet,* issued in 1657, contained instructions and a "wide variety of new tunes for the treble violin." Its popularity never abated, and it went into a tenth edition in 1720.

The variety of English music advertised for sale at Playford's in 1653, only three years after he had gone into business, included "all the music-books that have been printed in England, either for voice or instruments," and virtually all publications since Elizabeth's reign. Eleven "lately printed" volumes ran the gamut from the philosopher Descartes's *Compendium Musicae* (1650), translated into English, to *The Dancing Master*'s vulgar music. His shop was a gathering place for amateurs of all musical tastes, as well as for collectors of old and rare books. The Playford home served as a branch store.

In 1655, Playford married the mistress of a boarding school for young gentlewomen, located in the rustic and pond-bejeweled suburb of Islington, where she instructed her young charges in reading, writing, musick, dancing and the

French tongue. Perhaps the young teacher came into the Playford shop in search of music one day, and the two fell in love over a copy of his *Introduction to the Skill of Music,* with which she proposed to improve her pupils' skills.

Playford's fortunes continued to rise. His customers and the musicians with whom he dealt took to calling him "Honest John," for his friendliness in business dealings. A respected church layman, he served the Temple Church, lining out the psalms for hesitant singers. In 1662, he left the rooms above the store and moved his wife, Hannah, and son, Henry, into a spacious house in Islington, reflecting both his business progress and his rising place in society.

In that storehouse of information and trivia about Restoration England, Samuel Pepys's *Diary,* the author reveals various details about Playford's store and its stock. Playford had soon established a price schedule that remained constant during much of his life. A bound volume of the *Introduction to the Skill of Music* went for two shillings; a bound set of the three volumes of Henry Lawes's *Airs and Dialogues,* known as *The Treasury of Music,* ten shillings; *The Musical Companion,* including Hilton's *Catch as Catch Can,* with a book of other songs, three shillings sixpence; *The Dancing Master,* bound, two shillings sixpence. On November 22, 1662, Pepys bought a copy of the country-dance-music collection for his "wife's woman Gosnell, who dances finely, and there meeting Mr. Playford, he did give me his Latin songs of Mr. [Richard] Dering which he had lately printed." Pepys noted on May 23, 1663, that he took his lyra-viol instruction book to the shop to be "bound up with new paper for new lessons," since the publisher also performed the several functions of a stationer, of which bookbinding was a chief source of income.

In 1666, almost three months after the Great Fire, Pepys went shopping for music bargains, though he received much merchandise gratis from Playford. Although public halls, the Exchange, churches, hospitals, and some 10,000 homes had gone, Playford's was not damaged, and Londoners continued to buy music there. Pepys saw barges and boats laden with whatever possessions were saved crossing to the Thames's south side and remarked in his diary that one of every three salvage craft carried a virginals. The conflagration did take some toll of the London printing business, for Pepys learned that the new edition of *Catch as Catch Can* was not ready, "the fire having hindered it." The following spring, when Pepys took home a copy, he found "a great many new fooleries in it."

Playford's also served its customers a variety of other wares, sometimes medicinal, advertised in the back pages of music books.

> At Mr. Playford's shop is sold all sorts of ruled paper for music and books of all sizes ready bound for music. Also the excellent cordial called the Elixir Properties, a few drops of which drank in a glass of sack or other liquors is admirable for all coughs, consumption of the lungs, and inward distempers of the body; a book of the manner of taking it is given to those who buy the same. Also, if a person desired to be furnished with good new Virginals, and Harpsicons, if they send to Mr. Playford's shop they may be furnished at reasonable rates to their content.

When Charles Stuart returned on May 30, 1660, Playford watched as 20,000 militiamen escorted him through decorated streets resounding to the music of bells and horns, drums and trumpets. The day after, the nation learned that it would be a time of gaming, whoring, and drinking. Playford's enthusiasm for the Stuarts and the kingdom never wavered, however, and, shrewd business-man that he was, he soon saw a new market for Catholic music, Charles mak-ing no secret of his tolerance of Roman worship and its music, which he had heard during his exile. In 1662, Playford demonstrated his affection for the old Catholic music by printing *Cantica Sacra,* a collection of Richard Dering's mu-sic, which had been dedicated in 1626 to the queen dowager, Henrietta Maria, Charles's mother, whom Dering had served as organist during the first year of her marriage. Born the illegitimate child of an English country gentleman, Der-ing was educated in Italy, where he embraced Catholicism. As Richard Di-ringo, he made a great European reputation, and collections of his music were published in Antwerp as early as 1597. In 1610, after returning to Britain, he earned a bachelor of music degree at Oxford, but his faith made professional activities difficult, and he returned to the Continent, serving in 1617 as organist to a convent of English nuns in Brussels. Shortly after the first Charles's mar-riage, Dering was named to Her Majesty's Chapel and made a member of the King's Musicians. He died in 1630, openly professing his Catholic beliefs.

Pepys was among the first owners of Dering's *Latin Songs,* receiving a com-plimentary copy in late November 1662. Despite its title, the volume included secular music, two volumes of Dering's Italian canzonets, published in Ant-werp in 1720, being bound with the religious music. Playford's enthusiasm for Dering had been shared by Cromwell, who was very taken with the composer's Latin motets.

Unfortunately, the Dering collection, with its royal connection, did not have the sales Playford expected, and in 1666 he complained that it and "all solemn music was much laid aside being esteemed too heavy and dull for the light heels and brains of this nimble and wanton age." Fortunately, there were customers aplenty for the popular dance music with which he had started his business and the instruction books that taught Britons how to play their new instruments. The nine-stringed lute of Elizabethan times had become an unwieldy monster with twenty-four strings, taking so much time to tune that many never had a chance to play it. If a lutenist lived to be eighty, people joked, he probably had spent sixty years tuning and fixing his broken strings. The guitar had taken its place. With its six single strings and simple tuning, it was easy to learn, pleas-ant to listen to, and had none of the inconveniences of the lute.

Both Charles and Louis of France were enamored of the instrument. Early in his reign, Charles stole the Italian virtuoso Francesco Corbetta from the French court, where the guitarist had taught its king one of the only two things he learned. The other, all Europe mocked, was how to dance, and that Louis learned from his court ladies. Corbetta was installed in the royal palace as a member of the queen's household and provided with a young British wife against the winter's cold. The court quickly learned that the Italian was a true master of the guitar, with a style so full of grace and tenderness that he gave harmony to the most discordant instrument. Charles's passion for Corbetta's music brought the instrument into such vogue that everyone took it up. It could be found on a lady's dressing table as often as beauty patches and rouge.

Unlike Pepys, who preferred the old-fashioned lute for music making, and thought the new-fangled guitar "but a bauble," and was much troubled that such pains "should have been taken on so bad an instrument," most Britons found the guitar convenient for all home entertainment.

Playford was quickly ready for this market, reissuing instruction books for stringed instruments printed a decade earlier, and now brought up to date. In a preface to one of these, he took note of the craze:

> Not a city dame, though a tap wife, but is anxious to have her daughter taught by Monsieur La Novo Kickshawibus on the Gittar, which instrument is but a new old one, used in London in the time of Queen Mary as appears by a book printed in English of instructions and lessons for the same about the beginning of Queen Elizabeth's reign [Adrien Le Roy's *Première Livre de Tabliture de Guiterre* (1551)] . . . but being not different from the Cithern only was strung with gut strings, this with wire which was in more esteem (till of late years) than the gittar. Therefore to revive and restore this harmonious instrument I have adventured to publish this little book of instructions and lessons.

The musical renaissance effected among the boys and men of the Chapel Royal by Captain Cooke stimulated British interest in the new instrumental, vocal, and liturgical music the king ordered, and the newly licensed theatrical companies soon learned of the potency of vocal music, adding new wings to flights of poetry and bringing customers into the royal playhouses. Playford maintained his contacts with musicians in both venues, and it was members of the King's Music who first told him about a nine-year-old Chapel Royal boy whose precocity and smoldering genius impressed the publisher sufficiently to slip a three-part song written by the youngster into the 1667 edition of *The Musical Companion*. So began a lifelong friendship with Henry Purcell, whose music he published for many years. Court musicians also provided him with access to music they wrote for the theater, where they were permitted to moonlight by a monarch who was constantly behind in paying members of his household. In 1673, Playford began a new series, which continued until 1684, containing "most of the Newest SONGS sung at Court and at the Publick THEATRES." The 383 songs issued in these five books collected play song lyrics by the best and the worst of contemporary dramatists: John Crowne, Natt Lee, Wycherley, Dryden, Behn, Thomas Southerne, D'Urfey, and Thomas Ottway. The words were married and sometimes well to music by the company of professional theater songwriters preceding Purcell: John Banister, Humfrey, Alfonso March, Robert Smith, and Nicholas Staggins. Their tunes were in that style Charles loved, the toe-tapping, triple-time melodies of France and Italy. Roger North remembered that "for songs he approved only the soft vein, such as might be called a *step tripla* and that made a fashion among the masters, and for the stage, as may be seen in the printed books of the songs of that time."

Charles was highly pleased with the first book, *Choice Songs and Airs*. It contained Pelham Humfrey's most popular song, "I pass all my hours in a shady old grove," whose words the king had penned. Exercising royal prerogative a few months earlier, Charles had judged a competition among German, Spanish, French, and English singers. When the Whitehall Palace program ended, the king pondered and then chose Humfrey's song as the best of all he heard that evening, modestly refraining from a confession that the words were his.

In *Choice Songs and Airs,* the last of a series, an ailing and unhappy John Playford made his farewells to those music buyers, "lovers and understanders of music," whose tastes he had catered to for thirty-five years.

This fifth book of new songs and airs has come sooner [by three months] to your hands but the last dreadful frost put an embargo upon the press for more than ten weeks, and to say the truth there was a great unwillingness in me to undertake the pains of publishing any more collections of this nature. But at the request of friends, and especially Mr. Carr who assisted me in procuring some of these songs from the authors, I was prevailed with. Yet indeed the greatest motive was to prevent my friends and countrymen from being cheated with such false work as is daily published by ignorant and mercenary persons, who put musical notes over their songs, neither minding tune nor right places, turn harmony into discord. Such publications being a scandal and abuse to the science of music and all ingenious artists and professors thereof. This I conceive I was bound to let my reader understand and that in what I hitherto have made public of this nature my pains and care has ever been not only to procure perfect copies but also to see them true and well printed. But now I find my age and the infirmities of nature will not allow me the strength to undergo my former labors again. I shall leave it to two young men, my own son, and Mr. Carr's son, who is one of his Majesty's Music, and an ingenious person whom you may rely upon that what they publish of this nature shall be carefully corrected and well done, myself engaging to be assisting to them the overseeing of the press for the future, that what songs they make shall be good and true music both for the credit of the authors and to the content and satisfaction of the buyers and that they may never be otherwise is the desire of your most faithful servant JOHN PLAYFORD

Playford had left Islington and moved back to London, to Arundel Street, off The Strand. John Benson, his first master, had ended their association a few years after it began, and for a short time in the mid-1660s Playford had shared the shop with the bookseller and publisher Zachariah Watkins. Since then no other name had graced the shop's sign. In 1681, Charles had finally rewarded Playford for his loyalty and contribution to the science of music by directing that he be elected to office in the Stationers' Company, but action by some members against him took away this honor. Upset by this outcome, tired and unwell, Playford felt it was time for his son, Henry, born in 1667, and having Henry Lawes as his godfather, to try his own wings. Now twenty-seven, Henry had learned music publishing and selling during a prolonged apprenticeship in the Temple Court store, serving the parade of illustrious figures who bought from its stock. Henry was not to be the giant his father had become, the times and changing technology eventually combining to bring the family business to its inevitable end.

One key to that prospect lay in the talents of a young craftsman named Thomas Cross, the son of an engraver who did title pages and portraits for Playford publications. Purcell used him to engrave his 1683 *Three Part Sonatas for vi-*

*olins and harpsichord or organ,* which was sold by public subscription. Left
with most of the edition unsold, Purcell offered the remainder to the Playfords
for disposal and, realizing that he was not cut out for music publishing, gave
his new work, later known as *Ode on Saint Cecilia's Day,* to his old friends to
print. As was usual with the Playfords, it was set in movable music type, and
stood out in wretched contrast to Cross's beautiful handiwork. Purcell had to
look to others, those who used the improved engraving techniques, to assure
greater accuracy and clarity.

Too old to change, John Playford continued to put his trust in music type
until his death, using copperplate engravings only for frontispiece illustrations
or title pages. Neither Playford was a printer, and in the early days John used
Thomas Harper, and after 1658 William Godbid, owner of rare and unusual
fonts of type, who specialized in books of mathematics, navigation, Greek, and
Latin. When Playford's nephew John, son of his rector brother, Matthew, was
ready for apprenticeship, he got him a place in Godbid's Little Britain shop,
where the youth remained until his master's death in 1679. He then went into
partnership with the widow, Anne Godbid. Following her death, in 1682, he
took over the business. His uncle sent him all his printing work, and never hesitated to recommend him and the "ancient and only printing house in England
for variety of music, with workmen who understood it very well" in spite of
their sloppy work on Purcell's *Ode.*

The elder John Playford died in November 1686, his passing evoking a flood
of musical elegies, principally that by Purcell, with words by Nahum Tate.
Britain's Orpheus and Dr. John Blow, the country's two greatest musicians,
walked in the procession of dignitaries that followed their friend, mentor, and
publisher to his grave.

## Charles and the Stationers

Playford's complaint in the preface to his *Choice Songs and Airs* about the bad
quality of certain music issued by "ignorant and mercenary persons," stemmed
from recent developments in the ballad trade, and the crown's strained relations
with the printing and bookselling business.

When Charles returned, booksellers controlled the English Stock, and therefore the Stationers' Company, and used every political ally to regain the power
they had enjoyed before the Commonwealth finally abrogated the last of their
privileges. Having witnessed the printed word's effectiveness in toppling the
Puritans and securing Charles's restoration, the new regime did not intend to
alienate them. Because the Stationers' Company had long served as a semiofficial censoring and policing body, Charles's advisers played along for a time.
Thus, despite the fact that the printers were threatening to form their own guild,
the company hierarchy was optimistic about the future, even though the English
Stock had become less profitable an investment, never rendering more than a
six percent dividend to its limited partnership.

A committee was named to prepare new regulatory legislation. At its head
was the recalcitrant Puritan William Prynne, who had been a victim of the com-

pany in 1633, being sentenced to perpetual imprisonment, having his ears cropped, and a fine of £5,000. He served as counsel to the Stationers' Company during the Commonwealth. In the complex political situation following the downfall of the Cromwell government, Prynne had been elected to Parliament. The legislation he and his committee now proposed was a mixed bag of regulations that pleased neither the publishers nor the printers. The number of the latter would be reduced, by age and attrition, to twenty, and limited to two presses and two apprentices each. This effectively put an end to the solidarity needed to form a new organization. Though rights of registration and copyright were reinstated, and all printed work was required to publish that fact facing the title page, the traditional power of supervision over the unlicensed press was removed.

A newly created post of press surveyor was given to Roger L'Estrange, a writer and a leading pamphleteer for Charles's cause, whose almost fanatical devotion to the Stuart family rendered him above suspicion. Soon the company and L'Estrange were at one another's throats, which continued until he relinquished the position in 1688. He raided printers, paid bribes to informers, and censored manuscripts. At least twenty rebellious printers were put on trial, and the stationers cried that he intended to destroy their ancient guild as well. Competition increased from hundreds of unlicensed printers and booksellers, who produced thousands of unlicensed works despite L'Estrange's efforts. New blows came in the form of plague and fire. The plague of 1665 killed more than eighty printers and many booksellers and dealers; the conflagration the following year burned down warehouses, bookstores, printing offices, melted type and machinery, and destroyed finished books and stocks of paper.

It required all the surviving stationers' energies to sustain the company during this dark period, which came to an end with the great demand for new books to replace those in libraries that had been burned or in collections being rebuilt after total destruction.

An additional responsibility given L'Estrange in 1663, which would seriously affect the book and street-ballad trade, was a monopoly of "all narratives not exceeding two sheets of paper, mercuries, diurnals, playbills, etc.," which encompassed all periodicals except Henry Muddiman's pioneering newspaper. Around 1655, after the appearance of thousands of unlicensed ballads inspired by the emotional and intellectual conflict between supporters of the Commonwealth and those longing for the king to come into his own again, a small group of stationers formed what became in effect the Ballad Stock, which shared ownership, production costs, and profits from new editions of traditional ballads as well as publication of new street songs. As soon as L'Estrange extended implementation of his monopoly to cover ballads, the group was forced to do business with him and print the phrase "with allowance Roger L'Estrange" and the date of issue at the end of each ballad. The same phrase also appeared on all small books, pamphlets, and tracts issued by stationer members, whose meetings L'Estrange generally attended.

After the fire of 1666 burned out the Ballad Stock partners, the cooperative Ballad Warehouse was established by the survivors, initially at Pye Corner in the Smithfield district, to which booksellers, chapmen, and balladmongers came to buy at wholesale. The stock included not only old ballads, old broadsides, and new street songs, but all kinds of chapbooks, whose popularity eventually displaced the black-letter ballads in which the Ballad Stock had specialized. This trade in street literature eventually moved to warehouses in the Cheapside district.

Around 1670, broadside ballads with musical notation, often inaccurate, began to appear for sale on London streets and in stores. D. W. Krummel writes in *English Music Printing 1533–1700:*

> [In its musical complexity] the broadside ballad cannot be compared with the later song sheets. The melodies are simple and unaccompanied. Most are traditional tunes (indeed, the ballads with no printed musical notation at all often mention the very same tunes, in a note below the caption title which reads 'To be sung to the tune of. . . .'). A number of sheets have printed musical notation which amounts to nothing more than a random sequence of music type. Chappell thought 'such mere claptrap jumble' . . . was intended mostly 'to take in the countryman' and . . . Chappell was quite right in believing that much of the printed music was not intended to be taken seriously. The music may have been intended as a clever attempt to deceive the deceiver—a cruel huckster's trick performed on the ignorant tolt who wished to show his friends that he really could read music when in fact he could not. Even when the musical quotation make some sense, the intrinsic interest of the ballads is very slight. The tunes, whether notated or merely named, are mostly the standard ones which would have been known from the oral tradition.

It was against such work that Playford railed in print, and probably to his customers as well, as did the composers and songwriters whose pieces often were pirated in that fashion.

As a stationer and an official, for a time at least, Playford heard many complaints about the manner in which L'Estrange's monopoly reduced the scope of most printer-publisher-bookseller's catalogues. The Licensing Act of 1662 was renewed until 1679, when it expired, not to be renewed again for six years, but the press surveyor remained a force with which the company rarely could cope, unless it complied with his privilege. Having lost its original charter and Book of Ordinances, the Stationers' Company printed its bylaws, for the first time, in 1678. One of the most significant clauses sought to keep all internal business practices out of the government courts and inside the guild. But mismanagement of the licensing procedures and malpractice by major members brought about a number of new ordinances seeking to put an end to reprinting bestselling works without permission or license. The process of registration was tightened, but within a few months abuses were resumed.

From the time the Licensing Act expired until 1700, five successive unsuccessful attempts were made to achieve protection of property rights in printed works for the publisher. The role of the author was beginning to change. No longer would he, as had Milton with *Paradise Lost,* sell a work for a small sum of money, which amounted to giving away his property. Instead, writers looked to Dryden, who had struck a bargain with Jacob Tonson, a major bookseller, giving him all new works, and becoming a man of property and means as a result. Realizing that registration in the company records no longer had any meaning to them, and abandoning the practice—only three titles being deposited in 1701—booksellers initiated a public-relations campaign, making use of the dismal situation facing authors and their families. Tonson proclaimed:

> It has been the constant usage for the writers of books to sell their copies to booksellers, or printers, to the end they might hold these copies as their property, and enjoy the profit of making, and vending impressions of them; yet divers persons have of late invaded the properties of others by reprinting several books, without the consent and to the great injury of the proprietors, even to their utter ruin, and the discouragement of all writers in any useful part of learning.

It appeared that the time had come for a new law, one enforcing ownership of printed books, and music as well, and, in doing that, putting an end to the patent power of the Stationers' Company.

## The Invention of Sheet Music and the Fall of the House of Playford

In 1682, Henry Playford opened his own store near Temple Bar, not far from his father's shop, and adjacent to the concentration of city lawyers, many of whom were ardent lovers of music. Henry's first commercial venture was *Wit and Mirth, or an Antidote Against Melancholy,* a book of verse without music, long thought a drollery, but the forerunner of D'Urfey's immortal *Wit and Mirth or Pills to Purge Melancholy,* a similar miscellany but having the music to which each lyric was sung. Henry's collection of bawdy art poems and their parodies was one of the last original publications bearing the Playford name. The principal Playford store proudly displayed its heir's new publication, as did that of an old family friend and business associate, the bookseller and music dealer John Carr. A company freeman, Carr published some music books, the most important of which was Matthew Locke's *Melothesia,* a keyboard instruction manual, printed in the composer's last year and said to be the first of its kind in England. In it Carr advertised his stock, which was typical of that being carried in the late 1670s, two decades after Playford had brought the trade into being. Available were "songs and airs, vocal and instrumental, already prick't; lutes, viols, violins, guitars, flageolets, castinets, strings and all sorts of musical instruments." Carr was also the selling agent for *Musick's Monument,* a labor of love by the amazing Thomas Mace, a Cambridge clerk who devoted his life to music in spite of physical infirmities inflicted on him by Roundhead troopers, who had tortured him and broken both his arms. Unable to handle a lute, Mace fashioned a "table organ" for the instrument, and when his lute's soft tones became inaudible, he invented a double lute, or dyphone, an instrument of fifty strings, which augmented and increased its sound and gave a fullness to the bases.

Carr's son Richard was a violinist in the king's private orchestra and Henry's best friend. When Honest John Playford determined that age and the rigors of ill health were too pressing, he placed his store in the hands of the two young men. He continued to remain in close contact with the business, however, working on special collections and generally supervising printing and publishing, so that his successors would sell "good and true music."

Henry Playford was admitted to full Stationers' Company membership in March 1686, and his name appeared on the firm's publications until the early eighteenth century. Under his supervision, new editions of the best-selling standard instruction books and collections of popular vocal and instrumental music appeared regularly. In some cases he merely altered the titles. The 1685 *Theatre of Music* was previously *Choice Songs and Airs;* it still employed the familiar "newest and best songs sung at Court and Public Theatres" and solicited material for future printings, promising, if songwriters brought correct manuscripts to the store personally, "faithfully to print from such copies, whereby they may be assured to have them exact and perfect." No compensation was mentioned or discussed, the act of printing them being considered a service which "would prevent such as daily abuse them by publishing their songs lame and imperfect, and singing them about the streets like ordinary ballads." Playford and Carr did not intend to sell those "common ballads sung about the streets by footboys and linkboys." So great was the demand for their kind of music that the *Theatre of Music* ran through four books in two years, with Carr's name on all but the last, since he had left to go into business for himself.

Though Playford collections dominated the trade for many years, there were periodic publications of the same type of music, few truly competitive. The Bowman family of Oxford booksellers issued a compilation of "songs for one, two and three voices" with musical accompaniments in 1677, 1678, and 1679, and John Banister, with Thomas Low, printed his own *New Airs and Dialogues* in 1678. Pietro Reggio, the Italian lutenist whom Pepys found "slovenly and ugly," though he loved the man's singing, issued an engraved book of his own songs in 1680, dedicated to the king and containing music he had written for the London stage. The bookstore near the Royal Exchange owned by Joseph Hindmarsh brought out three volumes of *New Songs,* ballads and lyrics for the theater, by Thomas D'Urfey, set to music by London's best-known composers. Out of that bastion of unlicensed Scottish printing, Aberdeen, came three editions of John Forbes's *Songs and Fancies.* All of these were available at Playford's, contrasting sharply with the house's quality production.

The character of published English popular music was undergoing change, though less subtle than that of the new technology that would bring it to an even larger market. Those triple-time songs Charles fancied were losing out to more tuneful ones set in common time. Most of the songs in John Playford's last books conformed to the new taste, whereas in earlier editions they had been a decided minority. Theater songs were becoming more flamboyant, more appropriate to the action, and asked so much musicality of the actors that a handsome face or well-formed bosom was no longer enough for a leading place in the acting companies. These songs and their highly trained singers were liberating one another from the influence of Italian opera, and even when removed from their original source, the songs took on a life of their own. Authors consciously placed "their lyrics in natural relationship to the context of the play, and the content of the songs [was] intimately related to the situation which it accompanied,'' according to R. C. Noyes in *Conventions of Songs in Restoration Tragedy.*

Although Henry Playford incorporated changing musical styles into his theater collections, he did not come to appreciate the changing technology being imposed by the process of engraving until late in his career. His experience with Purcell's beautifully engraved *Sonatas* did not persuade him of the indisputable merits of the new method. He chose to put his trust in the typesetter's hand and the proofreader's eye, and accepted their inevitable mistakes and carelessness.

Thomas Cross, the engraver, signed his name to his first known work, the Purcell violin and keyboard sonatas, adding to it "Sculpt," designating his trade, "one who cuts, carves or scratches." Working on copper initially, Cross introduced pages of neat and clearly cut music, and almost at once had nearly the whole of London's engraved music-printing business. Composers were delighted with his accuracy, and printers began to look to the quality of their own work. Because copper was an expensive medium, Cross experimented with zinc and pewter plates, using the etcher's needle and acid, to turn out the first individual pages of sheet music. It was no longer necessary to buy an entire book of songs to get a particular favorite; Cross's engraved single-sheet songs, printed in large quantities on half-sheets of thin paper, sold for a few pennies a copy. Flute-playing customers soon had a special incentive to purchase, when, in addition to the melody and harmony lines, a treble melody line for the flute was engraved at the bottom of each sheet. His work was displayed everywhere. Though Cross did not confine his work to sheet music, he always boasted that he engraved everything "exactly" and "truly," whether penny ballads, collections of songs by Eccles, Purcell, or Leveridge, or such an instruction book as *Military Music* (1697) for the hautboy.

Some London printers had sought to improve the old-fashioned fonts of music type still being used after a century, among them Frances Clarke, Thomas Moore, and John Hepinstall. In 1678, the three printed *Vinculum Societatis or the Tie of Good Company,* (for John Carr) from a new font that marked the first radical change in the design of movable music type since the earliest days of the Byrd and Tallis patent. Notation was changed from the traditional diamond shape to oval, and the tied note was introduced to England. Europeans had first viewed tied notes in 1532, when they were introduced in France, but, like the British, they continued to utilize the old lozenge shapes. The tieing of notes by the tails of quavers and semiquavers, then unknown to music type, came to compete with Cross's artistically and correctly cut notation as the oval shapes began to appeal to music buyers. Many music printers and publishers took to using the new type, but the compositor's careless and uncertain hand continued to plague them. Purcell ran into the problem in 1691, on the publication of his vocal and instrumental music for *The Prophetess,* better known as *Diocletian,* which he offered for sale by subscription. The music, scored for first, second, and tenor violins, bass viols, flutes, oboes, a bassoon, and two trumpets, with solo vocal parts and many choruses, proved to be a printer's nightmare. To ensure accuracy, Purcell corrected all the printed copies in his own hand, advising his clients that he had employed two separate printing offices, one of which was not up to the job, and that the production costs had eaten up all the money advanced by subscribers. Even the Orpheus Britannicus, the most admired and popular composer of his day, found subscription publication an uncertain business and eventually had to rely on London publishers to bear the cost of his increasingly complicated music.

Despite continuing interest in legislation to protect property rights in all printed works, the very popularity of Purcell's music brought about continued robbery of his compositions. In the last years of his life, his songs for the revival of Dryden's *Indian Queen,* with the hits "Ye twice ten thousand deities" and "I attempt from love's sickness to fly," were issued without his permission or knowledge. John May and John Hudgebutt, music dealers who published the *Queen*'s complete music and libretto in one volume explained their larceny most adroitly:

> The publishers to Mr Henry Purcell
> Sir, having the good fortune to meet with the Score or Original Draught of your Incomparable Essay of Music compos'd for the Play call'd *The Indian Queen:* it soon appear'd that we had found a Jewel of very great Value; on which account we were unwilling that so rich a Treasure should any longer lie bury'd in Oblivion; and that the Commonwealth of Musick should be depriv'd of so considerable a Benefit. Indeed we well know your innate Modesty to be such, as not to be easily prevail'd upon to set forth anything in Print, much less to Patronize your own works, although in some respects inimitable. But in regard that [the Press being now open] any one might print an imperfect copy of these admirable songs, or publish them in the nature of a Common Ballad, we were so much the more emboldened to make this attempt, even without acquainting you with our Design; not doubting but your accustomed Candour and Generosity will induce you to pardon this Presumption. As for our parts, if you shall think fit to condescend so far, we shall endeavor to approve ourselves
> Your obediant servants . . .

Purcell had no recourse in the confusion at Stationers' Hall and became used to piracy of this kind. Cross and other sheet-music engravers rushed out his theater music almost immediately after it was first heard, often converting his tunes into penny ballads for the street trade.

Though he found that setting lyrics for D'Urfey's song "The Parson among the peas" caused him more trouble than writing a Te Deum, Purcell rarely turned down an opportunity to collaborate. The last song he wrote was the favorite "From rosey bowers," in the third act of D'Urfey's *Don Quixote.*

After Purcell's death, his widow, Frances, turned to Henry Playford for help in supporting a brood of three small sons. He acted as selling agent for her publishing venture. Six works were issued, including a harpsichord instruction book that went into three editions, and the great *Te Deum and Jubilate* for Saint Cecilia's Day, 1694. With her approval, Playford released a collection of Purcell's vocal music in 1698, the *Orpheus Britannicus,* "a collection of all the choicest songs for One, Two and Three voices, composed by Mr. Henry Purcell, together with such symphonies for violins or flutes as were by him designed for any of them, and a Thorough-bass to each song figured for the Organ, Harpsichord or Theorbo-lute.'' Even though the streets of London sounded to ballads set to Purcell's music for a century more, except for this volume only a relative handful of music by him remained in print after his death.

As interest in the old and traditional English music waned, except among collectors, Henry stored much of this stock in the house near the Thames that had been left him. Three Playford catalogues exist in the British Museum, from which an impression can be gathered of the merchandising problems facing the nation's once most prestigious music dealer. The first, a four-page affair, listed 130 items, printed after a scheduled auction failed to take place because bidders outside London could not attend. Dowland's *Introduction for Singing* was available at two shillings, and Ravenscroft's *Parthenia* for a half-shilling more. Job lots of remaindered music were also available; fifty sets of the five-year-old edition of Thomas Farmer's *First Consort of Music* could be had for two shillings a set. In 1691, there was even more shelf-purging in the sixteen-page offering of ''ancient and modern music books,'' over one hundred books of ''divinity, physic, law, etc.,'' and 338 other music items. Among these was the first complete opera, written in 1600, Peri and Caccini's musical setting of Ottavio Rinuccini's *Euridice*. A 1697 catalogue offered ''all the choicest music books . . . from these thirty years past, to the present time.''

The mounting demand for inexpensive single-sheet music, printed overnight and capturing opera and theater songs just heard for the first time, was a fact of life Henry Playford generally failed to accept, though he did begin to use the ''new London character,'' the tied note, in 1698, twenty years after it had been introduced. His heart and spirit were locked in affection for the music books that built the house of Playford, and he made several attempts to restore the business to its former eminence. Hiring a room in a centrally located London coffeehouse, he arranged demonstrations of his stock and held concerts three times a week, during which browsers could have musicians perform selections they were considering for purchase. In 1701, he sought to harness the growing interest in singing clubs, offering the *Catch as Catch Can* collection as an official songbook and arranging with his co-publishers and distributors around the country to provide singing teachers for the weekly meetings. Two years later, he tried to offset the selling of songs at a penny by advancing a scheme for book merchandising that offered something like a music book-of-the-month scheme. All of these failed, and the demise of his business seemed imminent. Even his only venture into the penny single-sheet world did not save him. As the century was ending, he issued a new edition of D'Urfey's 1682 *Wit and Mirth,* containing popular songs and verse he believed would challenge the appeal of the penny songs. The new collection which added to its title *or Pills to Purge Melancholy,* was finally expanded to six volumes and contained hundreds of the favorite songs of the sheet-music variety. It never achieved meaningful sales in Henry's lifetime, nor did his father's old system of musical notation, employing letters in place of notes with which to play psalm tunes. This was advertised with an instrument of John Playford's invention, supplementing the instruction book and selling for fifteen shillings. It, like so much of the Playford stock of the last years, disappeared, except for occasional mention in auction catalogues.

In the early 1700s, Henry Playford disposed of his shop, good will, plates, and standing sheets to the music dealer and publisher John Cullen, whose business was located near Fleet Street. Henry left the music trade and busied himself selling engraved prints, paintings, and "other adornments" from his home. He died a few years later—the records do not indicate exactly when—and with him came to an end the Playfords, who had created the modern English music-publishing trade.

## The New Music Business, 1700

Cross's development of inexpensive engraved music plates resulted, as always with new devices, in an increase in the number of printed songs. A poet complained:

> Duely each day, our young composers bait us
> With most insipid songs, and sad Sonnatos.
> Well were it, if the world would lay embargos
> On all such Allegros and Poco Largos;
> And would enact it, those presume not any
> To tease Corelli, or burlesque Bassani;
> Nor with division, and ungainly graces
> Eclipse good sense, as weighty wigs do faces.
> Then honest Cross might copper cut in vain
> And half our sonnet-sellers starve again.

Sonnet sellers were not starving, nor were the printers and publishers of music, since a change was occurring in upper-class British homes. The harpsichord or spinet had taken the place of the old-fashioned virginals and the guitar. A keyboard instrument from the famous London maker Charles Haward had cost five pounds in 1688; the current price had quadrupled. Haward improved the harpsichord's quality with a pedal, which modified the tone and reduced the work of shifting jacks and pedals, making late-seventeenth-century keyboards a far cry from the virginals that once rested on player's laps. The new instrument stood on its own legs, permitting feminine players to sit at it in comfort. This restored-to-popularity instrument was also ideal for the single-page theater and court songs that had become popular. London's music stores carried lines of harpsichords and spinets, on whose music racks rested the latest engraved songs and operatic arias in the Italian manner. Gentlemen of the house could participate by accompanying on the German, or transverse, flute, which had supplanted the old flageolet and recorder.

By the early 1700s, much of the city's music business clustered in the area west of Temple Bar, at the junction of contemporary Fleet Street and The Strand. Christopher Wren was just completing his new gateway into the City, and, nearby, St. Paul's Cathedral was being rebuilt after the Great Fire. The churchyard offered a resting place for those who came to browse and buy in the music stores bordering its greenery, since they could stretch on the grass and listen to the music of worship or the sound of Jeremiah Clarke, St. Paul's organist and a theater songwriter.

Music publishers were using either or both of the standard printing techniques, Cross's engraving process or traditional movable type, but with improvements of a sort. A young printer, William Pearson, made some additional contributions to the tied-note fonts and, as a result, dominated music printing until his death in 1735. His first music book, *Twelve New Songs,* issued principally to demonstrate his new music type, had impressed the trade at once and stimulated Henry Playford to hire him to reprint all of the firm's publications set in the old type. Most of the psalters issued during the early eighteenth century used Pearson's type, its high quality competing effectively with engraved products. Cross continued to monopolize that market, despite the presence of a handful of young engravers, whose second-rate work appeared from time to time. Some of these newcomers used punches, a European innovation dating back to 1660, combining their use with engraving. These short steel rods, shaped at one end into the different musical characters and letters of the alphabet, were used for the heads of notes, and later for clefs, time signatures, and other symbols, as well as for the words of a song; the stems of notes, ties, slurs, and staves were done with the etcher's tools.

Only after John Walsh began publishing in 1695 had the use of music punches developed in England. When pewter became generally available around 1700, this softer material easier to work, replaced more expensive copperplate as music plates' chief medium. The Golden Harp and Hautboy in Catherine Street was, until Walsh's death in 1736, his chief base. There he changed the character of music merchandising.

Walsh began his publishing business with a series of inexpensive engraved instruction books for flute, violin, and other instruments, advertising them in the *London Gazette.* He used standardized title pages and filled in type through a passe-partout, the cut-out central portion of an expensive engraving, but produced an individual and apparently lavish appearance. He also issued many single-sheet songs, using inferior engravers to turn out the work. He was probably an engraver himself, because he devised many of the new methods in which his business pioneered.

It was his royal privilege that contributed the major portion of his income, however, his Protestant faith having won him the favor of the dour and devout William of Orange. His exclusive trade with the British Army in military band instruments came about just when the forces were growing in strength, securing the throne for William and Mary and bringing Marlborough to glory on the Europe's battlefields, and thus providing substantial profits to the patent holder. The use of music for military signals was only a few centuries old. As the size of armies increased and the use of gunpowder in cannon and muskets muffled the spoken command, the fife and drum and bagpipe, the trumpet and trombone sent men moving and into battle. Military musicians also provided open-air concerts, played for officers during meals, and supplied personal entertainment, in addition to marking cadence for men on parade.

Nicola Matteis, another in a long line of Italian violin virtuosos who period-
ically astounded Britons with their seemingly diabolic skill, had been dead only
a short time when Walsh brought out a collection of his music in 1696. The
Italian influence on British concert music was at a zenith, Matteis having played
a chief role in making it felt. Arriving about 1670, after traveling on foot from
his homeland through Europe, his proud arrogance when he was first taken to
Whitehall Palace in the hope that he might be placed on the royal household
staff cost him Charles's favor. He continued, nevertheless, to flout all convention by insisting on complete silence when he played before English concert-
goers, who were just beginning to learn to listen. Despite his seeming pretensions, he trained many of London's leading musicians, and the wealthiest of
them arranged a very elaborate publication of four books of music lessons, of
which Matteis made presents to his favored pupils, and for which they left two
to four guineas a copy, considerably more than Playford was charging for similar publications. The Matteis lessons were among the most beautiful music books
of their time. They were engraved by (Thomas) Greenhill and serving as an
inspiration to Thomas Cross to work with musical notation. In his last years,
Matteis enjoyed such financial success that he lived luxuriously in a large house.
When he died, he was mourned by pupils and audiences as the greatest violinist
in the world, greater even than the Cremona master, Arcangelo Corelli.

Matteis's influence on the course of English music was not recognized by
many contemporaries, though Roger North paid him special tribute:

> As a grateful legacy to the English nation he left them a general favor for the Italian
> manner of harmony, and after him the French (which Charles had imported with
> the Restoration) was wholly laid aside, and nothing in town had a relish without a
> spice of Italy. And the masters here began to imitate them, witness Mr. Henry Pur-
> cell in his noble set of sonatas, which however clog'd somewhat of the English
> vein, for which they were unworthily despis'd, are very good music.

Inspired to love for the fiddle by Matteis, many Britons traveling in Italy sought
out Corelli and returned with a new appetite for Italian violin music. To this
Walsh wished to cater, and having come into possession of the Greenhill plates
made for the lessons, he extracted from them songs the Italian master had written for the violin and also the guitar, on which instrument he was also a performer of virtuosic caliber.

Ever anxious to increase profits and cut costs, Walsh, who had tried other
and cheaper metals, settled on pewter, or "tin," plates made from an alloy of
lead, tin, and antimony, which was easier to work and less likely to break than
zinc, and far less costly than copper.

European printers working with punches had replaced movable type on a limited
basis for several decades before Walsh recognized the economies implicit in
their use. He then increased their scope until the entire process could be completed by a single workman with a hammer. The results were not always of
good quality, but the cost-cutting practice enabled Walsh to smother most of
his competitors. He was able to issue new songs on a weekly basis and advertised them as a regular special Thursday feature in the shop he owned with his

agent-partner John Hare at St. Paul's and in one on The Strand operated by his son-in-law, Peter Randall.

The commercially successful, although often crudely printed, music coming out of Walsh's pressroom included collections of theater music, instruction books, half-sheet music, and many pirated publications. These were less expensive than a distinguished stock of music by the Italian baroque masters Vitali, Veracini, Bassani, Torelli, and that master of masters Corelli being sold by London agents of the Amsterdam printer and publisher Estienne Roger. North was so impressed with Roger's work that he proposed a statue be erected in his honor in London, but did admit that Walsh's piracy had resulted "in all the music any amateur could want for either practice or diversion." Walsh had organized a highly competent operation of European agents, who sent the latest Roger publications as quickly as they came off press, so that bootleg editions were on sale in London at considerably lower prices before the Dutch publisher's agents, two French book and music dealers on The Strand, could offer authentic editions.

Walsh was also cutting into Cross's profits, since the latter could not lower himself to use music punches and, with zinc plates, produced work of less delicacy. Cross warned music buyers against the new methods, engraving on his song sheets "Beware of ye nonsensical puncht ones" or "Engraved by T. Cross in Crompton Street Clerkenwell, near the Pound who is arriv'd to such perfection in Music that Gent. may have their Works fairly engraved, as cheap as Puncht and Sooner; he having good hands to assist him, Covenanted for a term of years; He can cut Miniture, without having it writ with ungum'd ink, to take upon the Plate, as they do for other People." He eventually triumphed in this war of quality against quantity, and T. Cross, Sculpt., fell victim to the advanced technology he had done so much to shape. Walsh was in virtual control of London's music-publishing business and grew more powerful and prosperous. Competition from the St. Paul's area or from dealers along The Strand was of little consequence, and the Walsh family remained on its throne of monopoly for half a century.

In 1703, the Walsh catalogue boasted ninety-two items, and increased dramatically through the years. Series of song collections sold throughout that period for one shilling sixpence. *Harmonium Anglicana* eventually became the profitable *Monthly Mask of Vocal Music, or The Newest Songs Made for the Theatres and other occasions* and sold for sixpence. The sporadically released series of new music for harpsichord, *The Ladies Banquet,* cost from two to three shillings. The most illustrious item was the *Italian Opera Series,* which did much to make Handel England's favorite opera composer. These long upright folio scores started with Clayton's 1705 hodgepodge of plagiarized Italian music *Arsinoë, Queen of Cypress.* Containing only the overture and principal songs, the books gave Walsh a corner in music from the Italianate operas. Plates from the series were also used to issue single sheets of every production's hit songs, saving production costs and introducing the music to people who did not attend the playhouses. Walsh was convinced early that he should never place the time of issue on his music, and he continued to operate on the principle that women and music should never be dated, a practice that obtained in British and American music publishing until legal requirements made it necessary to print the date of first issue.

Walsh's publications, most of which were printed without permission of their creators, were temporarily legitimized by the 1710 Law of Queen Anne, the first "Act for the Encouragement of Learning by Vesting the Copies of Printed Books in the Authors, or Purchasers, of Such Copies." Under its terms, he and all other purchasers, that is, publishers, had exclusive rights to their publications for another twenty-one years. His international pilfering was also blessed by the new law, the statute exempting "Books in Greek, Latin or any other Foreign language beyond the sea."

While none of them yet knew it, Walsh, the operators of the Queen's Theatre, operagoers, and, indeed, British music itself were all ready for the appearance of a most distinguished composer and songwriter, G. F. Händel. Within a few years, Walsh and the young German would engage in one of music history's most celebrated composer-publisher relationships, which would bring about yet another change in the character of English popular music.

# CHAPTER 12

# Music Making in America

The Virginia colony was barely twelve years old when the first professional musician in English-speaking America sailed up the James River in search of the fabled land London's ballad makers were promoting, where they hoped to find the "long-lived peace and plenty" that sat "smiling on her brow." John Utie was a fiddler who paid for part of his passage by playing the viol to amuse his fellow travelers. He learned quickly that Virginia was a place where men died daily from the bite of a snake, swamp fever, or the arrows and war clubs of hostile red men, a land offering little opportunity for a musician to practice his trade. As a new arrival, Utie was entitled to at least fifty acres of land for himself and the same for each member of his family over age fifteen. He began raising tobacco along the river. Later, he moved north to the banks of the York, to a plantation he named Utiemaria. A person of some consequence by 1625, he was in a position to misappropriate company tobacco, with which he was charged, in a written complaint, by a neighbor, who labeled him "a fiddling rogue and rascal." As a member of the twenty elected burgesses governing Virginia in the New World's first legislative assembly, Utie had the sympathy of the Jamestown court, and his accuser found himself at the bar of justice instead, charged with slandering the defendant by referring to him as a "fiddler" and was made to pay damages and utter an apology. Having learned that power lay in landholding rather than music making, Utie confined his viol playing to the entertainment of his family and friends and amassed more land.

Although fiddlers and other musicians were held to be second-class citizens by many colonists, seventeenth-century British settlers, in general, including many Puritans, loved music with the same passion that had made the land of their birth the musical nation of the day. Rich and poor alike shared the common legacy of a repertoire that made no differentiation between popular and serious music. Only melody mattered. In time, while the poor enjoyed such tunes as "The Carman's Whistle," "Sillinger's Round," "Fortune, My Foe," and "Go from My Window" in the streets, wealthy music lovers listened to variations on them written by eminent musicians and performed on lutes and keyboard instruments by their properly brought-up children or by excellent professional musicians whose services were always available to prosperous patrons.

The first mention of the word *America* was in a song in William Cornyshe's play with music the *Interlude of the Four Elements*. In the era before newspaper advertising, joint-stock company managers exploited their charters to colonize, manage, and direct Britain's new possessions, well aware of how potent cheap music and literature were and utilizing both in promoting their ventures. Pamphlets rhapsodized over the glories of Virginia, and broadside ballad writers rhymed "Florida" with "stolida" and "sordida" to the tune of "Sillinger's Round," seeking to recruit investors and participants, or to solace losers in the state lotteries financing voyages to America with the prospect of major returns from small investments in a ticket. The Puritans, supposedly most antipathetic to popular songs, promoted travel to a land where a "church unspotted" by papist heresy could grow in peace with "proper new ballads," one of them urging migration to a New England where

> you never need to sow or plough
> there's plenty of all things enough;
> wine sweet and wholesome drops from trees
> as clear as crystal and without lees.

One-fifth of the 20,000 Englishmen who took ship to New England were steadfast Puritans, became disenchanted with the way of life they were required to follow, and returned home. The relative absence of popular entertainment was only a small factor in this, for even the most devout Calvinist grew up in a society prizing music of all sorts, and his taste for it ranged widely. Robert Brown, one of the founders of the Puritan discipline, was esteemed as "a singular good lutenist," and the first shipload aboard the *Mayflower* sailed to the songs of family and friends left behind, among them many who were expert in music. The tiny ship on which the Pilgrims sailed had little room for such luxuries as large musical instruments, but within ten years even settlements along the New Hampshire frontier numbered hautboys and recorders in their inventories of possessions. Wills, diaries, and other documents reveal that a considerable quantity of musical wares was imported after the basic necessities were supplied. Until church bells were shipped and hung, the drum and trumpet called the faithful to worship and the militia to duty. The second, more affluent, tide of colonists imported viols and basses along with smaller instruments, so that by the turn of the century one diarist would lament about the quality of repairs made to his wife's virginals.

That ancient and universal gadget known to Britons as a "jew's-harp" or "Jew's trump," possibly because Jewish traders introduced it into England, was also available in large supply, because of the ease with which it could be shipped and learned. Colonists using it excited the curiosity of Indians with whom they traded and bought priceless pelts for a single instrument. That Native-American music of which William Woods wrote with admiration in 1634, the "lullabies to quiet their children, who generally are as quiet as if they had neither spleen or lungs . . . [and] a good ear might easily mistake their untaught voice with the warbling of a well-tuned instrument,'' was often displaced by the twang of a jew's-harp.

The vast majority of the Northeast's earliest settlers were poor country people, who first lived solitary lives in rural areas where, until their small communities could support a communal tavern, they had little opportunity to hear or make music in the company of others. In singing to themselves and their families, they recalled the long ballads of home, performing them usually without any accompaniment. Alan Lomax, in *Ballads of North America,* writes of these as being

> slow lyric pieces with highly decorated melodies, or lilting dance tunes, often to a high-pitched sometimes ''womanish'' nasal tone. A tense throat allowed little variation in vocal color, but great delicacy in ornamentation. The effect was a mournful, wailing sound, like an oriental oboe suitable to the inner melancholy and conflict of the songs. The fiddle was the most widely used instrument, and as played, it was another high pitched, reedy, wailing voice, seconding and matching the singer or the lilting dance tunes.

In their isolated, rigorous pioneer life the first English settlers had little time for any but solitary amusements and personal entertainment. Their small outpost farms and settlements edged against a black forest peopled with menacing Indians and wild animals. Fever thinned their ranks, and starvation often took an additional toll. Their spiritual overseers labored to instill a notion that their sole purpose in life was to work, that work alone could bring them that heavenly blessing which would enable them to survive in the face of an unknown lying behind the farthest ridge. This severe ethic was observed initially in both the Virginia and the Massachusetts colonies. When Sir Thomas Dale found starving Jamestowners playing at bowls in 1611, he promptly forbade the sport, ordering ''the galley for three years'' for anyone who failed to fill his work quota. The Virginia settlements and Plymouth existed first as communistic experiments in living, where no idle drone was permitted.

After the initial demands of colonization were satisfied and people had time for themselves, government control over leisure grew even stronger. New England's constables were directed to search after all manner of gaming, singing, and dancing, even in the privacy of homes, and dancing was forbidden at weddings. Connecticut ended public use of tobacco, and Virginia, where the weed was enriching local planters, matched that grim ascetisicm. In 1619, the Virginia General Assembly officially enforced Sunday observance, banned gambling at cards and dice, set regulations to avoid sartorial excess, and dealt severely with infractions. Only after the work load was spread, through the importation of white bond servants and exiled thieves and the rounding up of gamblers and prostitutes, did plantation owners and middle-class freemen find time to enjoy the slower pace of life enforced by the climate.

For many years, the Sabbath was the most inviolable of days in the Massachusetts Bay Colony, where even unnecessary walking in the streets and fields was outlawed, though only for those above the age of seven. One New London couple was hailed before the court for sitting under an apple tree on the Lord's Day.

Puritans everywhere never forgave James I his rhetorical "when shall the common people have leave to exercise if not upon Sundays and holidays" and had the public hangman burn his 1618 declaration that "after the end of divine service, our good people be not disturbed, letted or discouraged from any lawful recreation, such as dancing, either men or women, or from having of May-games, Whitsun-ales and Morris dances, and the setting up of Maypoles and other sports therewith used," in spite of the fact that he banned bearbaiting, musical plays, and bowling. Holidays were observed with solemnity in New England, but on Christmas Day of 1621, most of Plymouth did not observe the birth of Christ, busying itself instead with regular chores. When a small group of newly arrived non-Nonconformists celebrated in the streets, pitching the bar, playing stool ball and the like, town magistrates confiscated their playthings, declaring it against the municipal conscience to celebrate a Catholic holy day. The Long Parliament had wiped Christmas off the calendar and clapped all carolers in jail. Soon, singing of such songs of joy gradually disappeared except in remote country areas. Not until Charles Dickens's *Christmas Carol* did yuletide singing and other seasonal customs come back to the cities.

Authorities could not completely suppress days of public celebration, in either New England or the middle colonies. New Year's Day, Easter, Pentecost or Whitsunday, Guy Fawkes Day, Thanksgiving, and Christmas continued to be observed outside Puritan colonies. Later in the seventeenth century, special days celebrated annual fairs, where people of all stations were amused by wandering ballad singers and other entertainers. Military events and the birthdays of local aristocracy or British royalty, among those loyal to the crown, provided reasons for assemblies, formal dances, and special diversions. Militia Day, or Muster or Training Day, brought crowds to watch all adult males, including servants, both Indian and black, learn military exercises in preparation for Indian attacks or raids by the French and Catholics, who fenced the British in along the Atlantic Coast, and march to the music of a fifer or trumpeter and a drummer.

Despite official sanctions against most displays of public celebration, many New Englanders had transplanted traditional pastimes that had provided communal pleasures for centuries. They gathered for church- and house-raisings, apple parings, quilting bees, shooting matches, husking bees, and, on occasion, unabashed displays of affection. The simple pleasures were generally accompanied by music for singing and dancing, provided by the fiddle, mouth harp, or homemade flute. Evenings called "kitchen junkets" were usual along the New England frontier, a farmhouse being cleaned out and swept, the floors sprinkled with corn meal, and a jug of cider placed outside the door. On a Saturday night young people danced there until midnight, took time out for food and refreshment, and then carried on till dawn.

The arrest on complaint of Boston's clergy in 1685 of Thomas Stepney, a recently arrived dancing master, signaled the invasion of public social dancing. Stepney was ordered to post a fifty-pound bond against resuming his classes, temporarily saving Boston from the devil of terpsichorean displays and their attendant sins. It is wrong, however, to gaze upon the somber portraits of seventeenth-century Puritans and think them all the strait-laced, prim, teetotaling men with few of the juices of conviviality that their oil-painted replications might indicate. The pleasures of the ale mug and wine glass were among their chief joys. Like most of Europe, seventeenth-century Englishmen had a basic distrust of water, for either drinking or bathing. There were few who were ever wet all over at one time during their entire lifetimes, a hygienic tenet that traveled to the New World. The water taken from wells or from lead and wooden pipes laid in the streets of some British towns as early as 1600 was for household use only, to nourish family pets and farm animals, and to flush away the trash indiscriminately hurled out of windows. Settlers took to the New World that notion of cleanliness, together with the chamber pot and the privy, or "house of office."

In Britain and America alike, the lower classes drank beer or ale, and their economic betters wine and also spiritous liquors, which were beginning to make an appearance in England just as colonization got under way. Fermented drinks were served as dietary necessities, to prevent scurvy and typhoid. The first doctor known to have been in Boston was fined in 1630 for attempting to cure scurvy with a potion made chiefly of water. His patient went back to unpasteurized homemade beer. The Pilgrims on the *Mayflower* ran out of that gift of the gods just before the winter coast of New England was sighted. The wealthier settlers who followed them a decade later were accustomed to better food and finer liquors, but had in common an aversion to water.

Under the management of merchants who had fled Commonwealth terror and come ashore with capital sufficient to fund new industry, the resources of virgin forests and a well-stocked sea were harnessed. Fish was salted and shipped to England, Spain, and Portugal, and shingles, timber, and cooperage to Britain. Once Boston businessmen discovered the immense profits to be made in the sugar trade, new international shipping traffic ensued, and America found its own mother's milk in the West Indies, particularly Barbados and Jamaica, New England's chief customers for salted codfish, pork and beef, barrel staves, and native crafts. Massachusetts farmers raised horses to provide the islands with animal power to haul cane sugar and to drive grinding mills. When the sale of black flesh was added to the mix, there evolved the triangular shipping trade that made New England wealthy in the late seventeenth and early eighteenth centuries. Cargoes of whale oil, minerals, iron, wood, and naval stores were dispatched to the West Indies, whose single-crop industry, the manufacture of sugar, made the planters wealthy but dependent on foreign commerce for both necessities and luxuries. Boston sea captains traded cargoes of foreign merchandise for molasses, one of sugar's by-products. New Englanders developed a distilling process that converted molasses into rum, and made Boston the largest producer in the world of that inexpensive and plentiful spiritous fluid. It sold locally for two shillings a gallon, supplanting hard cider and beer. The trade raised the colony's standard above that of England by as much as a hundred percent.

Once New York, Philadelphia, and the Southern colonies learned the pleasures of New England rum and native hard cider, most late-seventeenth-century men, women, children, and even otherwise abstemious white Americans drank both, slightly cut with water, during every meal of the day. The clergy was no stranger to this national enthusiasm for alcohol, many a church deacon wobbling home in a stupor after a night of religious business.

Increased prosperity and the growing use of nature's own highways, the inland waterways, as the chief and most comfortable means of transportation confirmed the national fondness for fortified liquors, and led to the establishments of taverns, alehouses, and inns to provide drink, food, and lodging in a convivial atmosphere. For the first time, there was a place other than the meeting house and church where one could meet old friends, make new acquaintances, and witness the newly burgeoning entertainment business. Popular music had found its first public forum, and the phenomenon was national. By mid-century, one-fourth of the buildings in Dutch New Amsterdam sold ale and tobacco. Almost every Southern ferry crossing or county seat had at least one public house, compelling Virginians to enact laws to curb public drunkenness. In 1676, the Virginia Assembly suspended the licenses of all taverns except those in the capital city, Jamestown, and on two ferries crossing the York River, a main traffic artery, and limited these to cider and beer.

Excessive drinking in public grew in spite of laws passed to curb it. Fines, confinement in the stocks, public whipping, being made to wear a red letter *D* about the neck, all failed in their purpose. Besotted Americans grew in number. As the eighteenth century dawned, a civilized man began his day, before coffee was a commonplace, with a good portion of straight rum or corn whiskey. Workers and apprentices got a serving of hard cider or rum during regular work breaks, as part of contractual agreements with employers. Wealthy families started the large midday meals with a forerunner of the predinner martini, good rum toddies, and served good strong beer throughout the meal. Boston's taverns were permitted to sell no more than a single quart of beer to a customer, but no limit was placed on what one could buy with food, and many customers downed eight to ten quarts a day.

Only ten years after it was founded, Boston found it necessary to issue an ordinance calling for the appointment of fit men to sell spiritous liquors, and licensed the city's first tavern in 1634. Three decades later, widow Alice Thompson was charged with selling liquor without a license, receiving stolen goods, selling drink to minors and servants, and providing "frequent secret and unreasonable entertainment in her house to lewd, lascivious and notorious persons of both sexes, giving them opportunity to commit carnal wickedness, and that by common fame, she is a common bawd." She was convicted, whipped with thirty-nine stripes, fined fifty pounds, and placed in prison. A few years later, her privileges as a citizen were restored, following her contribution of enough money to build thirty feet of the great new harbor sea wall.

As the number of establishments supplying conviviality to New Englanders multiplied, competition for patronage grew, and shrewd barkeeps recognized the value of a bit of free food and some simple entertainment to lure clients away from competitors. The same enterprise that had prompted London tavern owners to gather up church organs, outlawed by the Long Parliament, to provide popular music led their American peers to draw upon native talent, both white and black, for entertainment. By the end of the seventeenth century, the colonial tavern was a social center, in which one could hear the latest news and gossip before the appearance of the first American newspaper. London newspapers were available in hostelries drawing affluent trade only when brought by sea captains.

In larger communities, licenses to operate inns or taverns were doled out with care, but in rural places only the capital and some local prestige were needed to engage in the business. By 1690, Boston, English-speaking America's largest city, with 7,000 inhabitants, had fifty-four places where one could eat, drink, and hear some form of secular music. These were licensed taverns, alehouses, and retail shops. An unknown number of dives and speak-easies, operating without a license, were along the waterfront and catered to seamen.

Philadelphia, second in population, with 4,000, was the national center for vice and debauchery. In 1700, a law was passed regulating tavern licensing and the sale of liquor after hours, which also affected those illicit drinking places usually situated in caves along the Delaware River. Intoxication in the Quaker City was measured by a rhyme.

> Not drunk is he who from the floor
> Can rise again and still drink more.
> But drunk is he who prostrate lies
> Without the power to drink or rise.

License fees provided the royal governor, whose perquisite they were, with so rich a source of extra income that he granted them wholesale to any who were willing to pay the asking rate.

The earliest report of fraternization between whites and both free and slave blacks in public places came in 1690 from Newport, the fifth-largest community in the colonies, where 2,600 persons lived. That Rhode Island seaport, situated on a cape jutting out into the Atlantic, appointed men to inspect all its tippling houses for such breaches of order. Although one alehouse owner was warned to stop entertaining blacks at unreasonable hours of the night, the practice generally continued to plague municipal authorities for years.

Soon after Boston banned shuffleboard, bowling, and gambling in 1647, these pastimes resumed in illicit hostelries, to which young people went to meet, much to the disturbance of nearby neighbors. Action was rarely taken, because of the miscreants' connections with the town's best families. When the Castle Tavern's proprietor decorated a room in which to present to his lower-class patrons exhibitions by a wandering performer, he was visited by a delegation of city fathers and persuaded to abandon the plan.

Among the first buildings erected by the Dutch West India Company on Manhattan Island was a brewery, and soon the business in beer was second only to the fur traffic. The settlement, behind a wooden wall to keep out red men, quickly filled with houses turned into taverns, to which laborers and tradesmen flocked for brandy, beer, and tobacco; burghers and town leaders enjoyed their evenings of food, music, and dancing in private clubs.

South of Pennsylvania, plantations had sprung up along the rivers and creeks. Ships from London unloaded their cargoes on the planters' private docks and took on board tobacco and other exports. The development of small communities was frustrated by these great landholdings and vast tracts of crown land, making communal gathering places, taverns and inns, few and far between. Social events took place in the great houses, whose owners looked forward to the visits of friends equally anxious for gossip and political news or to the sudden appearance of a presentable traveler from Europe. The dancing that followed was done to music from Playford's *Dancing Master,* men, women, and children all capering through its patterns of jigs, reels, and square dances. Occasionally, blacks performed on crude banjos or homemade fiddles, playing music they had learned by eavesdropping on the music of their white owners. It was a cross-fertilization; visitors from Europe and the north were amused to see Virginia and Carolina gentry performing dances much influenced by slave-quarters celebrations rarely seen by strangers. One described this abandoned dancing as "without method or regularity. A gentleman and lady stand up and dance about the room, one of them retiring and the other pursuing, then perhaps meeting in an irregular fantastical manner. After some time another lady gets up, and then the first lady must sit down, she being, as they term it, cut out. The second lady acts the same part which the first did, till somebody cuts her out. The gentlemen perform in the same manner."

In the early 1700s, New Englanders trod the measures of sophisticated minuets, gavottes, and rigaudons to the music of small combinations of flute, viols, and keyboard. Public social dancing was relatively recent in the Bay Colony, dating to that time in 1658 when the game of football, regularly played in the streets, was outlawed because of injuries to innocent bystanders. Many of Boston's young men turned to dancing as an outlet for their energy and shared its pleasures with their sisters and friends. Upper-class young people went from town to town to sing and dance in taverns and ordinaries that stayed open until early morning. The Reverend Cotton Mather dealt with this growing cancer on the public body in *An Arrow Against Profane and Promiscuous Dancing,* the reprint of a sermon. The troublesome dancing master Stepney, who arrived in 1685, in the midst of Mather's crusade, flippantly boasted that a single lesson from him taught more divinity than the entire Old Testement, leading another Mather, Increase, to distribute a new edition of his earlier attack on "gynaecandrical, impleaded and petulant" dancing, with its "unchaste touches and gesticulations." It did little better than Cotton's diatribe. Both lived to see their young parishioners enjoy Christmas week with dancing, feasting, and frolicking, and some eight-year-old daughters of the congregation give dancing parties to celebrate their birthdays.

Lewdness was triumphing by 1713, when George Brownell openly advertised lessons in dancing, violin, flute, and spinet, as well as quilting, and no delegations came to complain and no effort was made to drive him out of town. Dancing schools flourished, and New England's drinking places served as regular way stations for those new itinerant vendors of household necessities, the Yankee peddlers, who had begun their traffic along the Baypath Trail, linking Plymouth to Boston, and then extended it into a road along which they reached the most remote settlements of the central colonies, the far South, and the western frontier. Like balladmongers of old England, they carried popular street songs in the packful of notions they bore on their backs or on their horses, causing another Mather to lament: "I am informed that the minds and manners of many people about the country are being corrupted by foolish songs and ballads which the hawkers and peddlers carry into all parts of the country." As in England, the broadsheet was serving Americans as their earliest tabloid newspaper. Among the supplies carried by the peddlers were some British ballads and broadsides that were regularly shipped overseas as wrapping paper and stuffing in boxes of imported goods. However, the majority of the ballad stock was purchased in quantity from journeymen and apprentices, who, like young Ben Franklin, thus supplemented their small wages through this early manifestation of the business of popular music in America.

# CHAPTER 13

# The Business of Music Publishing in the Colonies

The Massachusetts Bay Colony continued to dominate the American printing and book trade until just before the Revolution. Boston, where hundreds of books, pamphlets, and broadsides were issued before the end of the century by a company of thirty booksellers, became the second-most-important publishing center in the British Empire. This eminence came to a temporary end in 1711, when the most destructive fire the colony had yet known destroyed more than a hundred buildings, nineteen bookstores among them. Even the gallant efforts of the city's engine companies, with volunteer firemen manning buckets and two water-pumping engines, failed to contain a conflagration that was touched off by a drunken woman servant.

From the early days, the men who governed the British New World viewed the printing press as a source of civil danger, as had the ruling powers of England. In 1671, Sir William Berkeley, royal governor of Virginia, reported to the home government the happy news that the colony had no free education or printing, and therefore no civil disobedience or discontent. On ascending the throne some fifteen years later, James II sent colonial authorities notice that they were to remain responsible for the licensing of any printing press and its products.

Those ministers, lawyers, and intellectuals who constituted New England's major power bloc were children of immigrants who themselves had been denied access to the printing press because of nonconforming and anti-Anglican Puritan views. When the first printing press in English-speaking America was set up in Cambridge, it was supervised by the church authorities governing Harvard College, who exercised the same control over freedom of the press that had frustrated their Puritan forebears.

For half a century, anyone with a manuscript viewed as unsatisfactorily uplifting sent his work back home for printing, usually at his own expense. Virtually all of the several hundred pieces rolling off the Harvard press before 1690 were first approved as essential to the salvation of those already saved. Anne Bradstreet, the first American versifier of significance, had to send her collection *The Tenth Muse* to London in 1650, despite its approval by some of the Massachusetts clergy and her own connection with one of the colony's leading families. Its second edition, some twenty-eight years later, and six years after the poet's death, came off a new Boston press that had been imported to break Cambridge's monopoly and the rule of Boston's clergy. The first best seller by an American author to be printed in America, Michael Wigglesworth's *Day of Doom,* was printed in Cambridge in 1662. This popularization of Calvinist tenets was written in doggeral verse, easy to recite or sing, and became a favorite, next only to the Bible. One in every three New Englanders bought its first edition, of 1,800 copies, and within fifty years it went through four more printings and four British editions.

The 25,000 Bay Colony settlers included nearly one hundred Oxford and Cambridge graduates in 1640, and there were also many self-educated men of impressive learning and knowledge. In 1637, a bookseller first offered his skill to repair volumes damaged in passage from Europe, and ten years later, the city's first bookseller, Hezekiah Usher, started to build private libraries of new editions imported from London. Usher and the other book dealers in Boston amassed some of the most imposing collections in the English world for their customers. Cotton Mather, with his father, Increase, who wrote 564 books, owned one of the largest private libraries in the world, containing more than 3,000 volumes.

Most of the Cambridge press output prior to 1700 has been lost, and is known only by its titles, and if Stephen and Matthew Day, the first tenders of the machine, printed any broadside ballads to pick up money from the penny trade, they, too, have vanished.

Only after the Massachusetts General Court tempered some of its adverse rulings was Marmaduke Johnson permitted to operate the first privately owned American printing press, starting in 1674. A London-trained typographer and printer, he had arrived in Boston around 1660, bound for a period of three years to the New England Company for the Propagation of the Gospel, the principal investor in the colony. He was paid £140 annually, as well as sufficient meat, drink, washing, and lodging, for a twelve-hour, six-day week. After producing some sixty books and countless pamphlets and broadsides under his articles of service, Johnson went into business for himself. He eventually bought his own press and types, and in the six months before his death he brought out a single book, the first privately printed in the colonies.

Johnson's printing office was purchased by one of those singularly universal men who seemed to abound in the fresh air of North America. Son of a brewer, member of Harvard's class of 1667, watcher of comets, printer, engraver, and guitar player, John Foster was the first independent publisher of native American literature. During his six years of activity, he carved a woodcut illustration for the frontispiece of one of his publications and made the first map of New England for another. He printed a number of secular broadsides, among them funeral verses and memorials, and the first American medical advice, dealing with smallpox and measles. Given his affection for music and the guitar, as well as his woodcutting ability, it seems natural to guess that he also cut and printed music for himself and his friends.

Foster's publications were sold by Boston book dealers and distributed around New England by peddlers. At the turn of the century, colonial mail service was still in a backward state, though there were routes for it between Virginia, Philadelphia, New York, and Boston, usually based in taverns. Some colonies began to keep post roads and bridges in good repair, and to improve ferriage over the main trade avenues, the rivers and other waterways.

British efforts to control commerce between the colonies by passage of the Navigation Acts limited trade in specific items and stipulated that certain products be purchased only through London brokers and carried only in British ships. To keep a lid on colonial competition, a series of acts restricted the iron, woolen, and hat trades, among others, which had a lasting effect on commercial expansion. By the eighteenth century's first decade, New England imported almost twice as much as was shipped out, whereas the Southern colonies, with a booming trade in tobacco, rice, indigo, and naval stores, imported items worth £150,000 and exported £219,000 worth of goods, putting their landowners and merchants in the excellent financial condition that permitted early importation and support of those cultural luxuries theatrical entertainment and professional musicians.

As economic underdog, New England learned early to create its local business with little reliance on Britain. Hezekiah Usher, performed the stationer's traditional functions and was the first commercial vendor of the *Bay Psalm Book,* whose fourth edition was printed specifically for him. Many almanacs, books, and other printed materials off the Cambridge press bore his imprint, and Harvard relied on his judgment of public demand to fix the number of copies to be printed and for supplies of paper and ink. Usher's son John took over the business in 1676, receiving its ownership and a sizable legacy from Hezekiah's investments in real estate. Young Usher continued working with Cambridge, stocked London's newest books, and used Foster for some of his own publications. His political connections led to his being named treasurer for Massachusetts and an envoy to England to negotiate the purchase of Maine. He also prevailed on the General Court to grant him the first printing privilege in American history. Generally, he was paid by the colony to print new editions of its General Laws and Liberties, but in 1671 he offered to bring out the most up-to-date volume at his own expense. Fearful that the printer doing the work for him might bring out a bootleg edition, Usher applied for and received an official order, effective for seven years, giving him exclusive rights in the edition, and setting a triple-cost penalty for any copies made without his consent.

Among Boston's company of booksellers in the 1690s were some recent arrivals who had experience as professional stationers. Because their baggage sometimes included stocks of printed materials, which they offered for sale at reduced prices or auctioned off to the local trade, they were most unwelcome to booksellers. The most enterprising was Benjamin Harris, who introduced a number of modern British merchandising techniques and became the foremost book dealer in Boston. He had published anti-Quaker and anti-Catholic books in London and been involved in the gigantic hoax of trying to persuade people of a Catholic conspiracy to kill all Protestants in a single vast massacre. He had escaped from prison and fled to Massachusetts with false papers. In a shop located near seven other bookselling establishments, he installed a counter, and tables to attract feminine trade, and sold chocolate, tea, and coffee. It was one of the first coffeehouses in the colonies.

In 1690, he employed printer Richard Pierce to issue the first newspaper in America, *Publick Occurrences Both Foreign and Domestick*. Containing one blank page and three of print, about six by ten inches in size, it was dedicated to "the curing, or at least the charming, of the spirit of lying, which is much amongst us." Because it was unlicensed, the authorities suppressed it after its first issue, which contained a story libeling the French king for his morals and an exposé of corrupt dealings with the Narragansett Indians, contents that did little to win official approbation.

Harris also published, and probably compiled, *The New England Primer*, the "little Bible," which became the best-selling primary-school textbook in a region that had mandated compulsory education in 1649. It is estimated that between six and eight million copies in many editions, were sold between its first appearance, in 1690, and 1840. Like many of his innovations, this, too, was probably borrowed from English creators. The London printer John Gaines had already registered *New England Primer or Milk for Babies* at Stationers' Hall in 1683. The first edition sold out so quickly that orders from Boston booksellers could not have been filled, and it was unknown locally before Harris revised the copy he had brought with him, filling it with local references, and published it as his own in two editions in the first year.

For generations, New England's youngsters learned their alphabet, spelling, prayers, and formed their play songs from its contents. Later editions taught them to end each day with "Now I lay me down to sleep,/ I pray the Lord my soul to keep" and instilled them as well, through repetition, with certainty that only education would lead to temporal success.

> He who ne'er learns his A.B.C.
> Forever will a blockhead be.
> But he who learns his letters fair
> Shall have a coach to take the air.

Nine of Boston's fifteen books printed in 1690 came from Harris's store, and when he returned to England in 1695, he was assured of a place in history as a leading American bookman.

When, in 1710, Queen Anne's law putting an end to Stationers' Company control over competitive printing in Britain and extending protection to new publications took effect, the situation in the colonies was centuries behind. Only John Usher's monopoly of publication of the Bay Colony's laws provided ownership in any single printed American work. Only one paper mill existed, and the cost of important paper was steadily escalating. Except for Boston's flourishing publishing trade, only a handful of printing presses were operative, in New York, Maryland, and Pennsylvania, and their owners did business only with their local governments. With limited stocks of type, most of them were unable to set, run off, and sell anything but the legal forms, broadsides, pamphlets, doggerel memorials, and quick-selling broadside accounts that were the trade's mainstay.

American talent did find expression in print, but the work was usually produced in England. Publisher-booksellers who could afford to gamble on uncertain native products were more interested in the profits flowing from the importation or unrestrained reprinting of best-selling fashionable London items, made viable by the ocean's vastness and inadequate copyright protection.

The next century witnessed yet another of history's repetitions. As the broadside ballad turned men in a direction the state found inimical, pressures were applied and the dogs of censorship turned loose. The true power of the broadside ballad was not to be foiled, as the Scottish political writer Andrew Fletcher noted in his 1703 allegorical piece *Account of a Conversation Concerning a Right Regulation of Government for the Common Good of Mankind*. In an often misquoted portion of the dialogue, to which the strains of "Yankee Doodle" could serve as accompaniment, he said:

> Even the poorer sort of both sexes are daily, tempted to all manner of lewdness by infamous ballads sung in every corner of the streets. One would think, said the Earl, this last were of no great consequence.
>
> I said, I knew a very wise man so much of Sir Christopher's sentiment, that he believed if a man were permitted to make all the ballads, he need not care who should make the laws of a nation. And we find, that most of the ancient legislators thought they could not well reform the manners of any city without the help of a lyric, and sometimes of a dramatic, poet.

# CHAPTER 14

# Black Music Comes to English America

As Europe emerged into the light of the Renaissance from the intellectual stagnation of its Dark Ages, an association of twelve northern Italian islands lifted itself to international prominence and became Christianity's richest city-state, Venice the Golden. "We are Venetians first, then Christians," it boasted. Attracting bankers, traders, and sailors from all over the world to do business along the Rialto, Venice became Europe's world trade center. Venetian galleys plowed the Mediterranean Sea, transporting all manner of merchandise. Occasionally, a cargo of Christian men and women, captured along the Dalmatian coast, was consigned to Muslim harems and the labor force, and from this trade in young white Slavs the word *slave* followed.

Rising expectations of profits from international trade, together with the series of military adventures called the "Crusades" into the Middle East, ostensibly to retrieve the holy land upon which Jesus had walked, brought an ever-expanding awareness of the world as it really was. But fifteenth-century investors still prayed that, should some vessel fall into the eternal blackness surrounding mankind on all sides, it would be at a point far beyond the uttermost profitable port of call.

Venice was the first to refind a way overland to fabled India and storied Cathay, and entered into treaties that gave it monopolistic access to those markets. When Constantinople fell in 1453 to the Ottoman Turks, passage to the Black Sea and the profitable markets beyond was barred to all Christians. Venice paid an annual toll of 100,00 ducats for the right to trade in Turkish ports. Denied access to the Mediterranean until they bought the right from Venice and engaged in war with the Muslim dominions controlling North Africa to the Atlantic, other Europeans turned southward in search of new trade routes to the silks and spices of the Indies. The Portuguese began to work their way along Africa's western coast, astounded to discover lush tropical greenery where Aristotle had long promised burning wasteland, and simple, sturdy black men free for the taking. Ship captains started to carry them from their African homes, baptize them into the glories of Christianity, and then sell them to work in the fields of the wealthy or the lands of the clergy. Black slavery was not new to Africa; it was a centuries-old practice that was modernized after Muslim military and cultural conquest swept the Western world.

By 1448, more than 900 African slaves had been imported into Portugal, a rising nation carving an empire out of lands discovered by its explorer-navigator captains. A perverse democracy existed in the Portuguese slave markets, since refugee Spanish Jews were offered for sale alongside Africans. Limitless supplies of blacks were tapped by ships returning from the southern Atlantic and dumped alongside cargoes of gold and ivory traded from African chiefs in exchange for the surplus slaves the ships could not carry.

Even as Columbus was engaged in his several voyages of exploration of the Caribbean islands, looking for India, Portugal's fleets were rounding the Cape of Good Hope and making their way toward the main Asian trade terminal, Calcutta. There they picked up ginger, nutmeg, pepper, cinnamon, cloves, and other treasured spices. More far-ranging voyages of discovery and conquest followed along eastern Africa, from India to the Red Sea, where Portugal became the first western nation to plunder the riches left behind by Alexander the Great.

Transporting horses, metalware, fabrics, and other trade items, Portuguese ships made increasingly regular runs along Africa, encouraging the transplantation or creation of African states to serve as suppliers for the slave trade. The Spaniards were quick to take advantage of the new cheap-labor market. Slaves were used in the conquest of Mexico and the seizure of Peru. Although Philip II condemned the trade, black slavery flourished in the West Indies, sometimes in slave pens owned by British joint-stock enterprises.

When it was learned that the indigenous American Indian was not sufficiently sturdy to cultivate Spain's Caribbean sugar fields, the Spanish began to use Africans in large numbers. Ten thousand slaves were shipped there annually by 1550, and by the end of the century, some 900,000 Africans had been moved in.

Around 1513, one Portuguese commander who had sailed into the region suggested to Abyssinia's Christian king that he dig a canal to connect the Nile to the Red Sea. Had this been accomplished centuries before the Suez Canal effected a shortcut to the Far East, the character and culture of the African slave trade would have have brought a more Near Eastern influence to bear on Afro-American music and tradition and changed dramatically the character of modern popular music.

Senegambia, the western area between the Senegal and Gambia rivers, was the first African region to engage in the slave trade with western Europeans. As demand increased, making the business more lucrative, rulers there punished all crimes with enslavement and took to intertribal war to meet the quotas imposed by the whites' hunger for free labor.

The pattern was repeated. After the Portuguese, the Spanish, English, French, Dutch, and Genoese arrived to offer bargains in European wares to local rulers in return for trade and diplomatic relations. Once established, the foreigners bargained for prisoners of war and criminals. The business grew slowly until firearms were added to the barter pot. Insidiously, the slave traffic became so profitable that only the most noble-spirited men could resist, and they usually were soon disposed of. The trade became completely ingrained in Africa's economy.

Ever a continent of diverse cultures, many of which had no written language before the white man's coming, much of Africa's history was oral, preserved in art and music. Traditional historiography until recent years held to the theory that black Africans were transplanted from an environment of questionable personal culture and hurled into a social isolation that was soon blurred by encroachment of the Anglo-Saxon presence, which effectively stripped all the past. Contemporary scholarship continues to provide knowledge of the culture existing in the west coast slave pens and developed on American plantations and farms and in settlements. There is vast documentation to demonstrate that the language of the Wolof Senegambians, from lands around the Senegal River, contributed most to the black American dialect. Though few in number, Wolofs were the first to arrive on mainland America, where they translated local languages into a patois in which to communicate with whites. As Samuel Charters has noted, in *African Journey,* it is from Senegambian roots that Afro-American dance, song, and music spring. Like much of Africa, Senegambia was a land where music was a daily ritual, involving every man, woman, and child; where people without a written language preserved in music the occurrences of the day and their history.

Of west African music making, Alan Lomax, in *Folk Songs of North America,* has said:

[It was] largely a group activity, the creation of a many-voiced, dancing throng. Typically, a leader raised the song and was answered by a chorus of blended voices often singing in simple chords, the whole accompanied in polyrhythm by an orchestra of drums, shakers, handclapping, etc.

Few African instruments survived in North America, but African musical habits did. The slaves continued to sing in leader-chorus style, with a more relaxed throat than the whites, and in deeper-pitched, mellower voices, which blended richly. The faces of the singers were animated and expressive; the voices playful. They used simple European chords to create harmony of a distinctive color. If not actually dancing as they sang, they patted their feet, swayed their bodies, and clapped out the subtle rhythms of their songs. A strong surging beat underlay most of their American creations, and this was accompanied in an increasingly complex manner as they improvised or acquired instruments. Words and music were intimately and playfully united, and "sense" was often subordinated to the demands of rhythm and melody. Community songs of labor and worship and dance steps far outnumbered narrative pieces, and the emotion of the songs was, on the whole, joyfully erotic, deeply tragic, allusive, playful, or ironic rather than nostalgic, withdrawn, factual or aggressively comic—as among white folk singers.

For more than two hundred years these two contrasting musical cultures dwelt side by side in America in a state of continually stimulating exchange and competition. Song material passed back and forth across the racial line so that it becomes increasingly difficult to say which group had contributed most to a song. As in the West Indies and parts of South America, true Afro-European songs, and especially dances, developed, which gained continental, then world-wide popularity. Ineed, it seems very likely that one day all American music will be *cafe-au-lait* in color.

Black slavery reached the American mainland in 1619, as recorded in John Smith's *Generall Historie of Virginia, New-England, and the Summer Isles,* when "about the last of August came a Dutch man-of-war that sold us twenty Negros." Details are sketchy, but it appears that these blacks were treated exactly the same as indentured white servants; they contracted to work for a specified number of years, had no political or civil rights during indenture, but eventually became freemen. Those who achieved their liberty received a gift of land, and then often owned slaves themselves. Traffic in black lives was at a minimum initially, with only about 300 Afro-Americans in the colony of Virginia by 1650.

Eleven indentured blacks arrived in New Amsterdam in 1626, and after nineteen years of service were given grants of farmland. The largest grant was forty-five acres, the average thirteen. Black farmers owned property in some of today's most fashionable sections of Manhattan before 1660. Then chattel slavery was introduced by British authorities and restrictions against ownership of property by blacks were imposed. During the late seventeenth century, the New York colony had a greater proportion of black slaves than any northern area, due mainly to the demand for cheap labor by owners of the great Hudson River Valley estates.

Captain William Pierce, compiler of New England's first almanac, exchanged a shipload of Pequot Indian prisoners of war for West Indian black slaves in 1638, fetching them home in his ship *Desire*. Such trade continued with Barbados planters, blessed by the church and made legal by an amendment of the colony's Body of Liberties that promised bond slavery would not exist unless it involved prisoners or war or those who "willingly sell themselves or are sold to us." Those colonists who could afford slaves preferred whites, chiefly because blacks cost more. As a result, New England's black population rarely exceeded two percent of the whole.

After failing to produce viable crops of grapes, silk, oranges, olives, sugar, and cotton, planted in desperate turn, the first several generations of Virginia landholders faced disaster, and only an astonishing British passion for Tidewater tobacco saved them as the weed's price went skyrocketing. By the time of the Restoration, the colony shipped home so much tobacco that customs duties were four times greater than for any other export. White Virginia and Maryland farmers who owned small holdings, usually worked by a scant half-dozen black, white, or red servants or slaves, failed to cope with tobacco's ruinous effects on the land. The owners of large estates, who used their profits to add land and increase production, could counter the damage by rotating crops. As the black presence increased and the niceties of Christian teaching were abandoned in the interests of plantation economy, stiffer controls, to avoid real or imagined threats to civil order, were incorporated into Maryland and Virginia laws by passage of hereditary slavery statutes. Slavery was a legal institution in all the mainland colonies by 1700, and the status of black Americans seemed fixed. Then the slave business grew still larger, with the introduction of Madagascar rice into the Carolinas late in the seventeenth century.

From the earliest encounters, Europeans had remarked on the innate enthusiasm for dancing and singing in the settlements and villages of western Africa. The black man's lamentations in song had impressed the Portuguese looking at slaves for sale in the Lisbon market in 1445. The British and Spaniards, initially locked out of Africa by the papal Line of Demarcation, had had to force their way into the continent. By 1620–21, a British captain, Richard Jobson, had explored the Gambia River area. In his account, *The Golden Trade or a Discovery of the River Gambia and the Golden Trade of the Aethiopians,* were these comments on the music:

> There is without doubt no people on earth more naturally affected to the sound of music than these people; which the principal persons do hold as an ornament of their state . . . at any time the Kings or principal persons come unto us trading in the River, they will have their music playing before them, and will follow in order after their manner, presenting a show of state . . . both night and day the people continue dancing, until he that plays be quite tired out; the most desirous of dancing are the women, who dance without men . . . while the standers-by seem to grace the dance by clapping their hands together after the manner of keeping time.

In 1647, after seven years of civil war, during which he lost position and fortune supporting the Stuart cause, Richard Ligon, age fifty, made his way to the Caribbean. He had an amateur's knowledge of music, having served in earlier years as executor for his friend the court composer John Coprario. Among the things he saw was an improvised ballards, similar to an instrument Jobson had seen twenty-five years earlier, an African wooden xylophone, also known as a "bafalo." Macow, chief musician and keeper of a plantation grove, watched Ligon play a theorbo and, after hearing the difference in notes made by shortening or lengthening a string, assembled six round sticks of different size, on which he could play a scale. Ligon showed Macow the difference between sharps and flats, which he understood, thus persuading the Englishman that many blacks were capable of learning the arts.

Almost a half century later, the famous British naturalist Hans Sloane, while still a young doctor, accompanied some officials on a tour of inspection of royal Caribbean possessions. He was thereafter responsible for one of the earliest printed notations of a European's perception of the music played in Jamaica then. "Upon one of their festivals," he wrote in a published reminiscence of that journey, "when a great many of the Negro musicians were gathered, I desired Mr. Baptiste the best musician there to make the words they sang and set them to music," which was done, and it appeared in Sloane's book.

Profiting from their observations of the place of music in the African's daily routine, slave traders often ordered their human cargoes to sing and dance to reduce tension, raise spirits, and, in general, make their valued property more presentable to buyers. Because there was a mortality rate of twenty to thirty percent, often by suicide, some captains regularly let the slaves come on deck into the sun and made them jump and dance to bagpipes, harp and fiddle.

Much of the seventeenth-century African musical tradition was preserved only in the West Indian islands, where the proportion of blacks to whites ranged from five to one to as high as twenty-five to one in an average population of more than 40,000. In the Chesapeake and New England colonies, blacks were scattered among a white population that usually treated them as it did white servants. White labor was scarce, and the demand for black slaves increased until there was hardly a house in 1687 Boston, no matter how small, that did not have one or two in service. In 1690, more than 400 black servants lived there, half of them native-born and several generations removed from their African roots. Living among whites, they had little opportunity to hear or see and small interest in black music or black culture. In colonies where the ratio of blacks to whites was greater, dancing after Sunday services was permitted. The Reverend Morgan Godwyn, who arrived in Virginia in 1665, found this laxity "barbarous and contrary to Christianity. . . . That I may not be thought too rashly to impute idolatry to their dances, my conjecture is raised upon this ground . . . they use their dances as a means to procure rain.

A book of "friendly advice to gentlemen planters" published in London in 1684, recommended black singing and dancing to white audiences. In a dialogue between Master and Slave, the writer included the wistful, though accurate—even if couched in language more Whitehall than Africa—statement by an Afro-American slave: "Amongst ourselves we endeavor to forget our slavery, and skip about, as if our heels were our own, so long sometimes, till our limbs are almost as weary with that as with working."

Only New England's government pressed for the religious education of slaves. In 1650, as they were revising the Massachusetts Body of Liberties, the authorities first showed concern for their chattels' souls and required that "all masters of families do once a week catechize their children and servants in the grounds of religion." This extended to the singing of psalms, an early introduction to black people of this ingredient of Puritan culture. A black woman belonging to its minister had been baptized and received into the Dorchester church in 1641, though the church did segregate those blacks permitted to share worship into pews marked "BM" for black men and "BW" for their women. Much more attention was paid to New England Indians, who often shared bondage with Africans. John Eliot, one of the committee of three who rendered the *Bay Psalm Book*'s translations, dedicated his life to missionary work among them, something that was not being done among black people. By 1675, he had converted and baptized 4,000 and had organized twenty-four congregations, some of them with native ministers. He translated and published primers, psalters, and catechisms in native languages after completing the first Bible of any sort published in America, the 1663 Indian-language Old and New Testament. Only after believing that he had saved every red man within view did Eliot extend his ministry to blacks, in 1674.

Others took up this ministry, including Cotton Mather. He spoke out in 1689 against his fellow citizens who kept slaves, and four years later he organized a Society of Negroes to meet on Sunday evenings in his home at the city's Second Church for instruction in music and religious texts. Much of Boston's reluctance to provide any religious training or education to blacks stemmed from the crusade among them by the Society of Friends, followers of George Fox, who preached that Christ had died for "the tawnies and the blacks, as well as for you that are called whites." To keep this heresy out of Massachusetts, any ship captain who brought in a Quaker was fined one hundred pounds, and a fine of five pounds was levied for possession of any Quaker text. Blacks welcomed to Quaker meetings heard no joyous worship, the Friends having contempt for ornate liturgy and avoiding any sort of music.

Throughout the seventeenth century, the Anglican church was a meaningful presence only in the Carolinas, Maryland, and Virginia, in the last of which half the parishes lacked ministers in 1700. Any attempt to introduce the church in the northeast was answered with "purification," and though Anglican parishes were organized in New York, Pennsylvania, New Jersey, and Delaware in the 1690s, their strength never equaled that of New England's brand of Calvinism. Expressing a belief in 1701 that many Americans had become "abandoned to atheism and infidelity," British Anglican church councils supported formation of the Society for the Propagation of the Gospel in Foreign Parts. For the next eighty years, America was the only "foreign part." Missionary teachers were recruited and sent to work among white and black heathen, minister schoolmasters were assigned to existing American pulpits, and great efforts were dedicated to the evangelization of black slaves and Indians. The last, and very minor, mission marked the first serious effort to recruit blacks into the Anglican church, by instructing them to Scripture and religious music and teaching the fundamentals of reading and writing necessary to achieve confirmation. Incredulous slaveholders were told by these missionaries that their blacks were brothers under God, entitled to an equal place in His grace.

Elias Neau, a society missionary assigned to New York's Trinity Church, went to work at once to save the city's black people. Located at one end of Wall Street, Trinity was built on a large tract of land donated by the royal governor and known as "the king's farm," which finally made it the wealthiest Anglican parish in America. Trinity attracted wealthy merchants and powerful city fathers, most of whom owned slaves. New York blacks increased in number after 1700, going from 750 to over 1,600 in twenty years and forming a fifth of the population. There were freemen among them, who had bought or won liberty and were engaged in various trades. In 1704, Neau opened a school for the city's blacks in an upper room at Trinity, where by 1726 more than a hundred English and Negro servants studied the catechism and sang the obligatory psalms and verses.

The SPG's most significant work was done in the Carolinas, where there were slightly more than 1,000 slaves by 1700, 800 of whom spoke English. Many Carolinians scorned missionary work, but some planters did lend support, building chapels on their plantations and encouraging conversion, baptism, and the marriage ceremony. London supplied Bibles and the *Book of Common Prayer* for distribution to the blacks and Indians, but denied them the glories of a minister and choir in embroidered vestments and the music of organ and instruments. Though the SPG won many small skirmishes, succeeding in baptizing slaves with their masters' approval, it did lose the major battle, that of persuading Americans that blacks were truly a part of the nation. And, in spite of Neau's pioneering missionary work and religious education in New York, there, in 1712, America was shocked by the first major slave uprising. Some two dozen blacks set fire to a house and killed or wounded eighteen whites. In the terror that followed, nineteen slaves were executed, some of them in a particularly horrible fashion.

The future held an even more serious challenge. The English new World was on the threshold of a trade and commercial explosion that would increase the number of black Africans in America to 150,000 and slow down their acculteration.

# PART THREE

# 1710 to 1790

# CHAPTER 15

# England, America, and the World

In the early summer of 1714, Queen Anne lay in her bed, a victim of depression caused by the conflicts about her successor raging around her. Her last child was dead, and Britain was divided between the Catholic-supported Stuart pretender and the English-born Protestant dowager electress of Hanover. The most recent war with France had not been of Anne's choosing, but her American colonials called it after her and cheered its victorious conclusion, which added Newfoundland, Nova Scotia, and the Hudson Bay region to her empire. Americans had been reluctant allies, going into combat only when danger loomed from Indian depredations, and they invented the business of paid substitutes to serve in place of men rich enough to avoid service. At the war's conclusion, Spain still held Florida, and France and its Indian allies controlled Canada and all of the rest of North America from roughly 500 miles inland.

Anne died in August 1714, and the elector of Hanover, whose mother, the dowager electress, had also just died, was invited to become king of England. The new monarch, George I, spoke no English, and his chief British advisers no German, so state business was conducted, as his political apponents said, on "a diet of bad Latin and good punch," enabling the fifty-four-year-old plain, blunt man to devote himself to wine, two mistresses brought from Germany, and the new British conquests he could make in love's fields. George never did learn English, and soon gave up meeting with his official cabinet, leaving Britain's most powerful man, Robert Walpole, to serve as England's prime minister. The empire was in the hands of Whig politicians, who gave it almost thirty years of peace and prosperity, and corruption. Only some 150,000 property owners were qualified to vote for members of Parliament in 1715, and they saw to it that their interests were England's interests and that Whigs remained in control. The struggle continued, however, between them and the Tories, between those who spoke for the gentry and the mercantilist autocracy and those representing the nobility and the Church of England.

Early Georgian England was predominantly self-sufficient and rural. Most of the forests had been cut down, and the price of imported American lumber was rising. The exploitation of the vastly cheaper fuel bloating British coal fields, and then the development of cooked coal, or coke, made possible the rolling mill, which produced purer iron and, in time, high-grade steel. These and even tougher materials were used for the steam engine, and, with that machine, technology was created that could harness rivers and waterways. Factories followed, taking over the spinning and weaving trades, which had for centuries been done in the home. The Puritan and Whig merchant classes grew wealthier each day, trading in textiles, sugar, tobacco, iron, shipping, and coal, their interests determining England's foreign and domestic ambitions and policies.

With 700,000 inhabitants by 1740, London was the largest city on the globe, ten times bigger than Bristol, Britain's second city. Poorly lighted, partially paved, and sewerless, London was filled with the clatter of horse-drawn carriages, wagons, and carts and the cries of peddlers, who supplied most daily necessities, against a counterpoint of street singers and barrel-organ players. Taverns, inns, grogshops, public gardens, and theaters offered entertainment and liquor, whose production had risen to over seven million gallons annually. A man could get drunk on gin for a penny and then find a night's free sleep in the city jail. Public executions in every district continued to be a spectator sport, and criminals still swung to their death to the strains of ''Fortune, my foe.'' A lecherous society that had returned woman to the twelfth century, from which Elizabeth had temporarily extricated her, was served by 50,000 prostitutes. Decent women were barred from most of the city's 3,000 coffee and chocolate shops, as they also were from divorce except by a special act of Parliament. Soap was expensive and water scarce, and those eccentrics who wished to bathe stood in a tub. Indoor plumbing was a century away.

George died of a fit in 1727, on one of his regular visits to Germany. He was succeeded by his son George, who spoke English and, like his father, relied on Whig support, knowing that a Tory regime would immediately restore the Stuarts.

Britain maintained a protectionist trade policy toward the American colonies, passing a series of acts intended to put restrictions on local manufacture, measures a corrupt civil service never could enforce. When British hat makers discovered the colonies were producing 10,000 hats annually, an act was passed requiring Americans to export beaver pelts to England and then buy the finished product, with duties and double transportation charges added. Another act forbade construction of mills in America, though by 1776 factories in New Jersey, Pennsylvania, Virginia, and Maryland were producing one-seventh of the world's supply of iron. Violation of repressive acts became a game, enabling the colonial well-to-do to enjoy continual prosperity until the Revolution.

George II had a war named after him, too, the third in the series between France and England, from 1740 to 1748. Britain's military might was concentrated on the Continent, alongside German allies, leaving home forces to beat off a Scottish-supported invasion by the Cavalier adherents of Bonnie Prince Charlie, last of the Stuart pretenders. The peace treaty of 1748 required the return to France of a fortress guarding the mouth of the St. Lawrence River, in

Canada, the only significant spoil of war in that conflict. Except for frontier skirmishes with the French and attacks by their Indian partisans, the colonies had been unaffected militarily, but a continued French menace along the northern and western borders of the British colonies was a nagging issue.

By 1750, the American population had grown to a million persons, 300,000 of them in New England, a similar number in the Middle Colonies, and the balance scattered through the South. Restless Yankee souls, feeling themselves stiffled by the nation's growth, established new homes in the back country. The Germans, first of the non-Britons to immigrate, started arriving in the seventeenth century, and by 1776 more than 100,000 of them had found homes from Maine to Georgia. Three hundred thousand misnamed Scotch-Irish, many of them Lowland Scots who had been transplanted to Ulster, came to "wild Amerikay." Poverty-stricken, many were redemptionists, having indentured themselves for a period of years. Later arrivals eventually moved into the back country of the Middle Colonies, where new lawmakers taxed and ruled them. Highland Scots who had supported Bonnie Prince Charlie in his ill-fated venture to gain the British crown joined their fellow countrymen's migration to North Carolina. After George II offered a pardon and transportation to America to all Scots who would pledge allegiance to the House of Hanover, "Going to seek a fortune in North Carolina" became a favorite Scottish song and dance.

Only one new colony was planted during this period. Having been shocked by conditions in a London debtors' prison and concerned about pauperism, James Edward Oglethorpe, a member of Parliament, envisioned a new land where people might find a "calm retreat from undeserved distress," no absentee ownership of vast landholdings, no slavery, and no liquor. He would bar only Catholics and Jews from that utopian dream. With support from wealthy friends and a crown land grant, he went to America in 1732 as the first governor of what became Georgia. Among the usual promotional ballads and pamphlets for the venture was one conjured up by an imaginative writer about a Florida Indian now grown to the age of 300, and his father fifty years more, both products of a salubrious climate. Georgia attracted people of many faiths and nationalities, but never did truly realize its founder's dream, and by mid-century, the deed of rights was returned and royal rule reinstituted. Oglethorpe's monument was the community of Savannah, America's largest city by 1776.

In the 150 years after Samuel de Champlain established a trading post at Quebec in 1608, French explorers, traders, and fur trappers probed and explored New France, and Catholic missionary priests cemented alliances with countless native tribes by the impressive ritual of Holy Baptism. The Bourbon kings' lily banners flew over a thousand settlements, missions, trading posts, and forts, west from the Appalachians, south of the St. Lawrence and its parent Great Lakes, and down the Mississippi to New Orleans. The 1713 Treaty of Utrecht, which served as George I's coronation present, had effectively stripped France of many American holdings and gave the English a monopoly of the slave trade. As the ancient rivals fought yet again, profits, and the taxes on them, from the rich triangular trade in sugar, slaves, and rum, built British naval superiority to two to one in ships of the line. In America, meanwhile, the French went about

the business of securing the Ohio Valley, and unleashed their Indian coreligionists for a war of terror on colonial border settlements. Investors sought to
preserve their frontier holdings with an exuberant but amateur soldiery, which
was quickly sent home in defeat by the professionally trained French. By the
summer of 1754, France was more than ever in control of the west.

A Plan of Union, for all the colonies but Georgia and Nova Scotia, was proposed, to carry on a fully supported effort against their old enemies. But colonial assemblies, unable to arrive at any determination of a common political
objective, rejected the proposal, as did the British government. Although the
odds of fifteen colonists to every monsieur indicated otherwise, the conflict in
the west went the other way. A force of British regulars and colonial militia
was devastatingly and shamefully beaten near Pittsburgh in 1755, and London
understood that time had come for the main battle to resume.

This world conflict is known to history as the Seven Years' War; in America,
the French and Indian War. At its conclusion, the French were driven out of
India, their Spanish allies were defeated in the Philippines, and Prussia emerged
as a significant European power. The Treaty of Paris, signed in 1763, changed
ownership of half the North American continent. Except for two small islands
in the St. Lawrence and New Orleans, France gave up to England all land east
of the Mississippi and Canada.

At the war's end, a new king sat in Whitehall, George III, the first of the
Hanovers to be born in England. He thought of himself as an Englishman, a
Christian, and a gentleman. Historians have a mixed judgment of him: some
concede that he possessed a pure and generous love of science and mankind;
others think he was more often mad than sane. His excesses eventually inspired
the rebellion in America.

During the French war, almost every American seaport had engaged in illegal trade with the enemy. In the main shipping lanes from New York and Philadelphia to the Caribbean, provisions of all kinds, food, and lumber were exchanged for French wines, sugar, and molasses. Middle Colony merchants made
extraordinary profits, particularly in New York, where British troops were concentrated. Customs duties on legally imported spiritous waters doubled in a year,
the English soldiers being addicted to strong waters. How many gallons of bootleg
rum they also consumed is lost in time, but contraband molasses had become,
as John Adams put it, "an essential ingredient of American independence."

The burden of supporting a war on three continents and financing the infla-
tionary peace that followed taxed the British economy severely. The national
debt had doubled, and the cost of governing America rose to £350,000 in 1763,
and by 500 percent in the next few years, and then doubled again in the following ten. Yet those engaged in the West Indian slave trade returned home with
fortunes sufficient to buy them election to Parliament, and the wealthy continued to grow richer by both continents.

The Industrial Revolution was in full motion, catering to new markets created by a growing population that threatened to burst national boundaries. Colonies around the world sent raw materials to the motherland and got manufactured goods in return. Practical, rather than visionary, English men of science

endeared themselves to merchants by regularly providing a parade of new mechanical marvels.

Unable to fund colonial defense by taxing these wealthy citizens, the British government taxed the colonists. The Sugar Act, passed in 1764, placed heavy levies on sugar, coffee, wines, and many other imported products. Boston needed £100,000 worth of molasses annually to keep its distilleries operating, and the new taxation caused many of them to fail.

In 1765, Parliament enacted a stamp tax to raise additional revenues, a form of fund-gathering that raised substantial sums annually in England. All printed matter, including newspapers, licenses, legal documents, books, and playing cards, was subject to a new levy. Foreign-language newspapers and documents required a double fee. A newspaper advertisement needed a two-shilling stamp, a liquor license one that cost twenty shillings. With their operation in jeopardy, newspaper owners and printers undertook to shape public opinion. Pamphlets of protest, revolutionary broadsides and handbills, and patriotic ballads rolled off the presses in quantity. Although government representatives sought to silence them, nineteen of the forty-one papers published in America remained in business in 1775.

Called thus into action, a group called the "Sons of Liberty" appeared. Hard times, high prices, and inflated money helped to band colonists at every economic level into such militant protest groups. Out-of-work mechanics and unskilled workmen marched side by side with college graduates and merchants. The unscrupulous among them looted and razed homes of American-born customs officials, burned their effigies, and caused conservatives to question the probity of the newspaper editors who had inflamed them.

Boycotts were organized against use of the tax stamps locally, and extended to any British import carrying the hated stickers. The Stamp Act was repealed after four months of agitation, but Parliament declared its right to tax the colonists and called for more troops to pacify the protesters. Then, the Quartering Act made Americans responsible for the bed and board of their unbidden watchdogs, who were to be provided with "fire, candles, vinegar and salt, bedding, utensils for dressing their victuals, and small beer or cider, not exceeding five pints, or half a pint of rum mixed with water to each man," though they were not yet quartered in private homes.

His chancellor of the exchequer, another in a procession of advisers and cabinet ministers with whom George III waged a fruitless power struggle, next levied duties on glass, paper, painters' colors, lead, and tea, the last at threepence a pound. Americans, who used tea as a substitute for plain water, lacing it with molasses or sugar, resented this particularly. Although the East India Company had a monopoly on its shipment to America, tea from Holland's East Indian possessions was often smuggled into Boston and New York.

The new increase in the price of paper set printers off on another drive to rouse citizen resistance to the latest levies. Boston led the way. With a major share of the colonies' printing presses and newspapers, it became the source of most published propaganda, and was responsible for establishing a commercial policy that called for nonimportation of any goods affected by the new taxes.

The daily presence of red-coated troops on Boston streets affronted people, and the papers regularly reported accounts of fighting between peaceful citizens and drunken soldiers, and made references to the supercilious insolence of British officers. Liberty trees, or poles, symbols of protest, were set up, and then cheerfully cut down by British soldiers. On Sundays, groups of redcoats gathered in front of churches and sang bawdy songs or their new favorite, "Yankee Doodle." It became dangerous for troopers to walk along the streets, since they were often pelted with oyster shells, eggs, snowballs, or refuse. The mounting tension between citizens and soldiery culminated in the final horror of the March 1770 Boston Massacre. Five Americans were killed when troops fired into a crowd. Among them was a black sailor, Crispus Attucks, one of many Afro-Americans active in the Sons of Liberty.

It was a dramatic decrease in overseas trade, in less than a year, resulting from the boycott that led to repeal of all duties except that on tea. Parliament gave up taxation without representation for the moment. Three years later, in an attempt to rescue the financially ailing East India Company, surplus stocks of tea were dumped on the colonial market, at prices fixed lower than ever, but payment of the tax was vigorously enforced. A dramatic act of resistance to British authority followed: the Boston Tea Party, of December 16, 1773, when a band of Sons of Liberty dumped £15,000 worth of tea into Boston Harbor. It took two months for news of this gesture of criminal defiance to reach London and another month before Parliament drafted legislative reprisal. Both innocent and guilty suffered when Boston Harbor was closed to all traffic until the destroyed tea was paid for. In addition, the Massachusetts charter was almost annulled and the Quartering Act was strengthened.

Then, for the first time, colonial Americans joined together in a cause of mutual concern. The 1770 massacre had received little attention outside the north, but the new measures were deemed a common injustice. Food and money poured in overland to assist Boston, cut off from all supplies by a reinforced military presence and a fleet of warships in the harbor.

In September 1774, the first Continental Congress met in Philadelphia. After seven weeks of deliberation, a declaration of grievances condemning England's actions emerged, asserting the people's rights, among others, to take up arms in defense of their honor. The Continental Association, to coordinate a "non-importation, non-consumption and non-exportation agreement," was formed, local committees being called upon "to observe the conduct of all persons touching this Association," and to discourage "every species of extravagance and dissipation, especially horse-racing, and all kinds of gaming, cock fighting, exhibition of shows, plays and other diversions and entertainments."

Moderates sought to reverse the home government's policies, proferring conciliatory measures for Parliament's consideration. Though one such plan passed, further restrictions led to crisis. When King George heard of the action fought by "embattled farmers" at Lexington and on Concord's rude bridge, he wrote: "America must be a colony of England or treated as an enemy." For once, the majority of his government supported his judgment.

On the eve of a conflict that would confirm their destiny and shake a world from its authoritarian royalist roots, the colonies contained two and a half million people, of whom about fifteen percent were staunchly loyal to the crown. Twenty percent were black, half of whom were under fifteen years of age. The head of each family, which averaged six members, had a life expectancy of thirty-eight years. A man's wife was his property, as she had been of her father before her marriage, and she and her offspring labored from sunup to sundown. Few understood fully the perils ahead, but many were prepared to lick the red-coats and topple ''crazy George'' from his seat of power. Others continued to yearn for reconciliation.

Meanwhile, a navy was commissioned, the Second Continental Congress met in Philadelphia, fortifications were started, a commander in chief was named, and companies of riflemen and militia were formed in all the colonies.

Events during the winter of 1775–76 inexorably drove the loose combination of colonies toward an assertion of complete independence. George had taken over full charge of the war effort and bargained with distant German relatives for the purchase of troops. Half a million pounds was exchanged during the war for the loan of 30,000 trained Hessian soldiers, nearly half of whom never returned home. Americans were shocked by this human sale, although a ball discharged from a Scot's musket or a bayonet in the hands of a West Country yokel was as effective as a smartly delivered German fusillade.

One particularly effective event during this troubled period was the appearance of a collection of essays called *Common Sense*, written by a recently arrived corset maker, author, editor, and sometime ballad writer named Thomas Paine, who had migrated to change his luck. A facile and fertile writer, who usually worked with a decanter of brandy nearby, he produced copy ready for the press even after the third glass. His paperback book of some sixty pages came off a Philadelphia printer's press during a severe scarcity of paper. The publisher had to scrounge in local warehouses for enough stock to produce the first edition. It contained these daring words:

> A government of our own is our natural right, and when a man seriously reflects on the precariousness of human affairs, he will become convinced that it is infinitely wiser and saner to form a Constitution of our own in a cool deliberate manner, while we have it in our power than to trust such an interesting event to time and chance.

*Common Sense* struck home. Despite the paper shortage, editions appeared throughout the colonies. By midyear, some 150,000 copies were sold, a distribution of ten million in terms of today's population.

In March 1776, the British suddenly withdrew from Boston, sailing north to Nova Scotia, and for the first time in years the colonies were free of military occupation. Buoyed by this and other gains, the several colonies argued for union and confederation, a drive for liberty culminating in the appointment of a committee of five—Thomas Jefferson, Benjamin Franklin, John Adams, Roger Sherman, and Robert Livingston—to frame a statement of purpose and prin-

ciple. The resulting Declaration of Independence, part lawyers' brief, part catalogue of crimes and perfidies for which George III, and not Parliament, was
blamed, sounded a cry for the right of man to take up arms against oppression.

Even as the Congress pondered approval of the new document, 32,000 British troops appeared off New York City, ready to pacify the rebel colonials.
During the next six years, war dragged on, scarring each of the embattled new
states. Still smarting from the defeat suffered during the Seven Years' War,
France took advantage of Britain's distress and went to the aid of the colonists,
though they, reluctant to become involved in any more foreign entanglements,
accepted help only after it was evident they could not win alone.

In 1781, having been given access to the best gunpowder in Europe, and
with the support of a French fleet, troops battle-hardened in fighting in New
York, Pennsylvania, Virginia, and the Carolinas bottled up a British force at
Yorktown. Standing at full attention as 7,000 redcoats laid down their arms in
surrender, marching to a tune that had been admired by street ballad makers
even before the Restoration, the Americans watched a war ending and a world
turn upside down.

George preferred to abdicate rather than sign his name to a peace that would
take much of his empire, but he never signed the letter of resignation prepared
for him. The price of defeat was indeed high. The "damned Yankees" won
their independence and all land between the Mississippi and the Alleghenies,
plus access to the Newfoundland fishing grounds. Spain, a secret ally reluctantly won to the American cause, got Florida and control of New Orleans.
France, bankrupt and exhausted militarily, took Senegal and Gorée in Africa,
a few Caribbean islands, and some East Indian possessions. Revolution followed, and the execution of King Louis and most of his government. And out
of those bloody horrors came Napoleon.

America's struggle had exacted a tremendous economic toll. The Continental
Congress's creation of paper currency set off runaway inflation, which depre-
ciated money issued in 1776 by a thousand percent in four years. Unavailing
efforts were made to enforce wage and price controls, setting initial ceilings of
seventy cents a day for a carpenter and forty-two cents for a tailor. A shave
was fixed at three and a half cents, milk at nine cents a gallon, rum at sixty-
three for the same quantity, and a night's lodging at five cents. Yet shoes rose
to twenty dollars a pair and milk to a dollar a quart.

Operating under the Articles of Confederation, ratified in 1781, the new nation faced many problems in its struggle for viability. The new charter gave the
Congress authority only to supervise the operation of a "league of friendship,"
each state retaining its sovereignty. British politicians, determined on revenge
for the humiliation of the successful rebellion, reduced imports to half their pre-
war peaks. In the Mediterranean, American diplomats found it impossible to
end harassment of their shipping by Algiers, Morocco, Tripoli, and Tunis without payment of protection money. Several states imposed excessive taxes on
interstate commerce. Unable to effect redress of their grievances, some bankrupt merchants and small farmers turned to the violence that had made them a

nation. A rebellion led by Daniel Shays in 1786–87 was stopped only after confrontation by federal troops.

There were bright moments. American ships, manned by officers and men who had beaten the formidable British, sailed all over the world. They touched China, to exchange many trade items, including the North American ginseng root, so esteemed by the Chinese for medicinal purposes, for tea, silks, and other Oriental commodities. The production of wool, glass, furniture, shoes, nails, and iron items increased, and experiments with silk culture in the South went on. More paper mills were erected, and the domestic manufacture of letter and music type and presses aided an energetic book trade, so that by 1800 the importation of foreign printing materials virtually ended.

A convention of men from seven states, initially, came to order in the Philadelphia State House on May 25, 1787, and elected George Washington president of the meeting, which sat for four months of deliberations. It ended on September 17, after the Constitution of the United States of America was drafted and approved by its creators. Not until May of 1790 did Rhode Island, last of the original thirteen colonies to do so, ratify the new document. By that date, there had already been a sufficient number of approvals to put the new government into being. George Washington, the only logical choice, was unanimously chosen by electors to serve a four-year term as president of the new republic. Having won the esteem and affection of men he led through years of war and the nation's adoration as its father figure, the Virginian proved to be an inspired selection.

# CHAPTER 16

# The Business of Music Publishing

## Music Publishing in England

The Act for the Encouragement of Learning by Vesting Copies of Printed Books in the Authors, or Purchasers, of Such Copies, the 1710 statute of Anne, for which sixteen book publishers had zealously lobbied, became the law of England and its possessions after April 10, 1710. It had resulted from a battle of self-interest, innocently abetted by contemporary authors, preeminent among whom were Addison, Defoe, Steele, Pope, Richardson, and Swift. Their purported friends, a group of booksellers headed by Jacob Tonson, the greatest publisher of his day, used the writing skills and social prestige of these fine writers to effect protection of published writings. Like many subsequent laws, this one was of benefit chiefly to users, rather than creators, of intellectual property.

Reportedly, some authors had composed the act, which began by saying that "printers, booksellers and other persons have of late frequently taken the liberty of printing, reprinting and publishing or causing to be printed, reprinted and republished without the consent of the authors or proprietors or such books and writings, too often to their very detriment, and too often to the ruin of them and their families."

Initially, the publishers had proclaimed concern for those "learned men" who "spent much time and [had] been at great charges in composing books, who used to dispose of their copies upon valuable considerations, to be printed by the purchasers." But, they also pointed out, "of late such properties have been much invaded by other persons printing the same books either here in England or beyond the seas, and importing then hither, to the great discouragement of persons from writing matter that might be of great use to the public, *and to the great damage of the proprietors.*"

When it became evident that the House of Commons was at long last of a mood to pass legislation to enforce property rights, the publishers were almost solely motivated by their concern for the continued use of the recently devised scheme known as a "conger." This was a pool of fewer than twenty booksellers, combined to participate in profits from mutual ownership of valuable publications. The name came from the eel that swallowed up all small underwater life within its reach, usually far beyond its seven- or eight-foot length. Like that marine creature, such combines fattened and grew off their neighbors, picking up copyrights for very little at trade sales and auctions from which nonmembers were barred. Production costs were then prorated among the members, each participant taking his quota of the finished edition of printed sheets and binding them himself. Such a partnership had its own peculiar trade benefits. Benjamin Tooke, one of three stationers who had petitioned the crown for a copyright law in 1707, was the warehouse keeper of the company's supplies and was several times found guilty of buying paper and paying for it out of guild money, but withholding parts of the shipment for a conger's use. Members of a conger got finished sheets at a special rate, well below that charged others, and as a result the book trade had fallen into conger control. In 1704 alone, one such group distributed 47,000 books, considerably in excess of the stationers' Company's own English Stock monopoly of almanacs and psalters.

In effect, congers had become smaller and more efficient monopolies, excluding printers from participation. The most farseeing realized that they would benefit most from new laws that appeared to democratize the Stationers' Company's regulatory powers. The new act was their personal victory, reducing the stationers to ineffectiveness. Under the act, protection was no longer reserved to company freemen, and registration in Stationers' Hall records was open to all; if refused, it could be secured by advertising in the official register. The statute also required that nine copies of each new publication be sent to the Royal Library, and other copies to the colleges, within ten days of publication. To avoid the pirating of editions printed in sets, the congers usually chose not to enter them, or, at most, only a single volume.

Though authors now presumably owned "the sole liberty of printing or reprinting" their work for an additional fourteen years after first publication, providing they were still alive, the new act extended far more important privileges to the bookseller publishers. Works registered by them prior to enactment of the new statute were protected for an additional twenty-one years before going into the public domain. New work was also protected for fourteen years. Violation in any form entailed seizure and forfeiture of all printed materials, and payment of a penny-a-page fine for each work issued, half going to the crown, the balance to the injured owner. However, the law did not apply to Ireland, where pirates flourished, competing vigorously for the London trade with European bootleg printers.

The 1710 statute has been hailed as the first affirmation of authorial rights, which it really was not. The bookseller stationers' long right to exclusive printing was extended; the authors had to wait another sixty years for clarification of their rights. When they did determine to hold their copyrights, little attention was paid to their writing. They soon learned that outright sale alone resulted in the advertising and promotion that sold books.

Several hundred English bookseller publishers, half of them in London, competed with one another, but the author was at their mercy. Writers sold their manuscripts outright, sometimes receiving extra payment when their books sold well. One well-known author, who generally got from £100 to £200 per book, initiated the subscription system, publishing his own work after receiving half-payment in advance from his customers; the balance was due on delivery. It proved to be a merchandising technique publishers soon adopted on behalf of their stables of writers. Handel offered his 1720 success *Radamisto* in a vocal edition of some one hundred copies at the time when John Gay sold his own *Poems on Several Occasions* by subscription, making about £1,000. Profits like those were made possible by the poet's friends, two of them paying for fifty copies each, and even Handel, a friend and sometimes collaborator, bought a single copy.

The prior year, Jacob Tonson, a leading conger organizer, ventured into the street-song market and published a multivolume edition of Thomas D'Urfey's anthology of popular music, begun by Henry Playford in 1699. Sold by subscription, the collection appeared first as *Songs Compleat Pleasant and Divertive.* In 1720, demand prompted a new edition, and a sixth volume was added, the work being renamed *Wit and Mirth or Pills to Purge Melancholy,* under which title it continues to be adored by lovers of early popular music and bawdy songs. Its more than 2,000 pages contain almost a hundred of Henry Purcell's songs, some by Handel, and others by D'Urfey, Blow, Eccles, Clarke, Leveridge, and other British masters who had turned to the London playhouses in order to augment their incomes.

There was never sufficient profit in early sheet-music publishing to attract conger interest, because when demand arose for a particular item, engraved plates could be purchased or rented. Songs were usually omitted from conger-published London playhouse works, and, profits from even the most popular penny song sheet being considered trivial, the trade remained the music publishers' and printers' province. Only after the growing popularity of single-sheet songs intended for performance in the home by amateur spinet and recorder players and singers did booksellers look to the business. Occasionally, songs from a particular stage success were bound together and advertised as the complete vocal score, but because production costs were high, these rarely contained any orchestral music or parts. However, elaborately engraved and handsomely bound editions of the full music of a popular masque did appear, intended for the wealthy music-loving collector.

## John Walsh and the Dance-Book Business

By 1720, John Walsh was the leading English music publisher, his printed catalogue of more than 600 contemporary editions and pirated publications rivaling that of his most illustrious predecessor, Playford, and dwarfing that of his competitors. He had prospered from the introduction of production economies and shortcuts, using punches in place of the more expensive copper engravings for single-sheet music. His work had an appearance of quality, which was achieved by the outright theft of stylish, elaborately engraved title pages from foreign publications. The portion bearing the author and composer credits and the publisher's imprint was sawn out, and the blank spaces were filled with newly punched lines, a passe-partout device much used in both England and America in later years.

Most London music publishers continued to do business in the streets and alleys around St. Paul's, but Walsh was still on Catherine Street, off The Strand, a location more convenient to the government offices with which he did business as royal music seller to the first two Georges. With a keen sense of public taste, like that of John Playford's, Walsh kept in touch with new trends that might affect the business, particularly the rebirth of interest in social dancing. Playford's *Dancing Master* had gone through more than a dozen editions since its 1650 debut, with hundreds of new steps added regularly as "country" dancing moved from the village green to London's plush salons. Sometime in 1706, Walsh took over printing of the popular dance instruction books, issuing annual supplements of two dozen of the latest figures. By the time of his death, in 1736, he had in stock over 1,000 old and new dances, their figures illustrated by engravings showing the variety of "capers and cross-capers of all kinds, the pirouettes, batteries and all steps from the ground." These new exuberant dances grew increasingly complex as social dancing moved in new directions in imitation of the professional dancers who were joining the royal acting companies. By mid-century, one-third of Covent Garden's roster of eighty-eight performers were signed for their dancing abilities alone, since box-office figures soared whenever it was announced that a particular dancing star was to do one of his famous specialties.

Most of the dancing personalities were foreign, but it was an Englishman, John Weaver, who created and then developed that particularly British theatrical form the pantomime. His use of dance, acting, and voiceless motion had made the "panto" into a national rage by 1720, taking it far beyond the dancing discipline on which he had based the original productions. Beginning as an entr'acte performer, by 1702 Weaver was offering a personal interpretation of the classic European commedia dell'arte, combining acrobatic dancing with his own ballet steps to depict a mythological anecdote to the music of a street song. His earliest pantomimes generally took place between the fourth and fifth acts of the featured drama, the time when admission prices were reduced to attract shopkeepers and clerks who had worked long past the time when the performance began. His dancing skits—they were little else at first—and those of his imitators drew a new and enthusiastic audience, and permitted management to raise prices for late admission. The plots grew longer and more involved, and original music became increasingly important to the pantomime's appeal. Bookseller publishers printed small booklets carrying a "description" of the plots and the words of any accompanying song. On cheap paper, these early "programmes" were usually thrown away, but a few survive in museums. They contain many of the traditional French names for ballroom dances employed in the pantomimes, making audiences aware of the *sarabande, entrée, chaconne, gigue, menuet, bourrée* and others, linking as they did the name with the step involved.

Public demand for novelty and new variations did much to stimulate the most talented stage dancers, and soon many types of figures and steps were embodied in the pantomimes, creating a new challenge to playhouse composers. Traditional and classic figure dances, eccentric dances, game dances, acrobatic dances, and national dances provided grist for the choreographic mill. The Irish jogs and trots, Highland flings and lilts, sailors' hornpipes and reels became standard in British and then American variety entertainment, maintaining their hold on audiences for the succeeding two centuries, after they had first made their way onto the stage in the pantos.

Unlicensed London theaters, forbidden to use spoken dialogue, resorted immediately to the pantomime, which permitted full evenings of musical theater, replete with dancing, singing, pageantry, and material borrowed from and burlesquing Italian opera, all without interference from the lord chamberlain. Because their audiences were being lured away, managers of the Drury Lane and the Queen's Theatre in the Haymarket offered similar hours-long evenings, filling not only the boxes and pit, where the quality displayed itself, but those gallery benches that held the mob.

The music for Walsh's 1728 edition of the *Dancing Master* was not markedly different from that of its 1650 progenitor, but the steps accompanying it had become extravagantly sophisticated. The once bucolic country dance was now high society's contredanse. The middle class followed fashion, buying these teaching books in order to remain *au courant* with the newest fads, providing Walsh and the music business a profitable shelf item as the dance-lesson book became a standard best seller.

When the 1701 *Island Princess,* music by Jeremiah Clarke, with contributions by Daniel Purcell and Leveridge, scored its initial success, Walsh immediately assembled a group of engraved songs and duets from it and issued them in book form as a "vocal score," a companion to the printed playscript, thus creating a viable piece of musical merchandise by correctly anticipating public taste. This first vocal score and similar collections of penny sheet music in fancy bindings were important symbols of the success of a new play.

For London's largest music-business enterprise, Walsh sought out and bound as apprentices talented young printers and engravers, among them several who became leading mid-century music merchants. In addition to a stock of musical instruments and assorted items, Walsh's main inventory was music books, teaching pieces, and a schedule of monthly publications, including regular song collections. Sonata and violin concerto publications cost from four to six shillings a copy and were usually pirated from Estienne Rogers's Amsterdam editions. The most expensive items were larger instrumental works in sets, for nine to fifteen shillings. Prices continued to remain stable, even after Walsh's death, when the general British economy did not.

## Handel and Music Publishers

When Clayton's *Arsinoë*, the first full-length, all-sung, Italian-style English opera was premiered in 1705, it was a financial failure, even though it created an
immediate sensation among certain theatergoers. Throughout the several decades during which English opera continued to emulate the Italian form, only
well-to-do box and pit patrons turned out in any meaningful number for opera
productions offered occasionally throughout the regular season. When the cost
of imported Italian singers mounted and sets grew more costly, opera acquired
the financial support of wealthy aficionados and climbing social pretenders for
its subsistence.

The first to publish the "full" score of an English opera, John Cullen, a stationer and music dealer dedicated to quality production, used copper engravings, rather than the pewter plates John Walsh had adopted. Binding together
thirty-seven songs from *Arsinoë*, printed on one side only, Cullen added some
sketchy instrumental music, an overture, and a minuet. Recognizing in the result a source of new sales, Walsh jumped feet first into the new vogue, as had
theater managers who saw in the all-sung opera a possible solution to box-office
problems. He brought out folio vocal editions of each new work, and sold in
penny sheet form individual songs that had gained public acceptability.

The quality of Walsh's operatic output increased dramatically with the appearance in London in 1710 of the twenty-four-year-old German composer Georg
Frideric Händel, recently employed as music master to the elector of Hanover.
Desirous of visiting London, where people actually paid money to go to concerts and the success of second-rate composers of Italianate opera was the talk
of European music circles, he obtained leave of absence from the Hanover court.

Many Londoners, willing to risk life and purse in the crime-ridden streets
around the Queen's Theatre, where Italian opera ruled supreme, went to see the
artificially created male sopranos who sang the leading heroic roles, a traditional convention of that baroque music play. As early as 1668, Pepys reported
that Italian "eunuchs" were being imported by the royal playhouse for treble
singing, and at the end of the century, two were still on the payroll, receiving
twenty pounds per performance. Their unique musical abilities resulted from
sex operations performed while they were children, which prevented the lengthening of their vocal chords and foiled any subsequent lowering of vocal pitch.
Falsetto singing had always been important in British music. Men singing boys'
parts helped restore the Chapel Royal to glory, but many Britons thought the
castrato style just another symbol of the wicked foreign influences corrupting
the nation. Yet the virtuosity of the art's best masters intrigued sufficient ticket
buyers to raise Italian opera to a position of social dominance.

The first true castrato to sing in a London production was an indifferently
talented Italian who starred in the 1707 *Thomyris, Queen of Scythia*, a mélange
of crowd-pleasing arias and duets, chiefly by Scarlatti, put together by John
Christopher Pepusch. The Italian sang in his native tongue, the balance of the
cast in English. In late 1708, opera lovers had their first opportunity to hear a

male soprano star of the first magnitude, the Cavalieri Nicholini Grimaldi, fresh from triumphs in major Italian houses. Following the smell of English gold to its London source, Grimaldi won the city's affection as a singer and actor.

Although they worked only a few evenings a week, in contrast to the four or five demanded of English actors, Italian opera singers earned hundreds of pounds annually. Reigning native actors were rarely paid more than £200 to £300 for a full season. Grimaldi's first Queen's Theatre contract was for 800 guineas a year, with an additional £150 for each new opera he introduced. He and his company of singers had become such an expensive commodity by 1710 that London opera once again was in serious financial trouble. Ticket prices were raised to make up part of the deficit, the management explaining it as an assurance of the presence of "the greatest star of the times." When a season of twenty-three nights returned only two-thirds of the £4,000 expended on salaries, production costs, promotion and other charges, Grimaldi suggested that the Venetian funding system be used. Recognizing that a mass audience would never fully subsidize opera, that city's authorities provided a huge subsidy, and all further deficits were met by increased admission charges and an annual subscription drive for support from the wealthy and socially aspiring.

Händel's name had become well known throughout Europe by 1709, following the brilliant success of his fifth opera, *Agrippina,* at its premiere in Venice, where it had a run of twenty-seven successive performances. An accomplished organist and harpsichordist, he had become the intimate of leading Italian musicians, among them the Scarlatti brothers, and other writers of popular contemporary concert music. In addition to his native German, he spoke fluent Italian, which stood him in good stead with the temperamental stars he dealt with later. He had little English, thought later he spoke it fluently, but always with a music-hall German accent.

When he arrived in England in 1710, business matters at the Queen's Theatre were as desperate as ever, even under the management of Aaron Hill and Johann Jakob Heidegger, an unlikely pair. The former, a young man Händel's age, was a minor writer and world traveler, who had some interesting notions about a return to those elaborate machines and decorations that had enchanted audiences in Purcell's time, and was then at work making improvements in the house's storerooms. Heidegger, a charming Swiss adventurer, was known as the ugliest man in the nation until an even more hideous old woman was found to claim the honor from him. The pair took Handel, as his name was soon spoiled, in hand, introducing him to London society and to Queen Anne. He was given unlimited access to the theater in the Haymarket, where he indulged himself at its concert organ and and renewed acquaintance with some singers who had been members of *Agrippina*'s original cast. One of them featured, in English, an aria from that work, and brought Handel even more fame.

Hill had already dashed off an English libretto, taking it from Tasso, and had it rendered into Italian for Handel to set to music. The work was done in two weeks, and *Rinaldo* opened in late February 1711. As was the custom, ticket subscribers received both admission and a printed text in English and Italian, an early form of theater program that also contained the names of the characters. To sing the hero, Hill and Heidigger selected their major box-office draw, the great Nicholini Grimaldi. The supporting cast was of almost equal popularity. No expense was spared in providing the machinery and decoration Hill had promised. Sparrows and chaffinches provided a sensation upon being released during the "Bird Song." In addition to a fire-spitting dragon, miraculous vistas of storm-tossed seas, singing mermaids, and airborne chariots, as the *Spectator* reported, the opera was replete with "thunder and lightning, illuminations and fireworks; which the audience may look upon without catching cold, and indeed, without much danger of being burnt; for there were several engines filled with water, and ready to play at a minute's warning, in case any such accident should happen."

Fire was a constant danger in London theaters, which were illuminated far in excess of Continental playhouses. About eight dozen candles were consumed every evening. In addition to hand-drawn fire engines, water cisterns on the roof and around the theater were ready for instant use. An inspector general lit the lamps and candles and remained available to take charge of carpenters, stagehands, and servants should any flame appear. Perhaps because of such precautions, London had no major theater fire for more than half a century.

Handel's amazing speed in producing an entire evening's score in less than fourteen days was due to considerable borrowing from his own earlier work. Half the score was pillaged from the recent past, most of it melodies lately performed in Hamburg or Italy. He received about £600 from the theater for his services as composer and music director for each of fifteen performances during the next several months. The success not only solidified the Queen's Theatre's position as opera's true home in London, but also accounted for so great a number of captured sparrows that the *Spectator* feared "the House would never get rid of them; and that in other Plays they may make their entrance in very wrong and improper scenes . . . besides the inconvenience which the Heads of the Audience may continue to suffer."

Seated at the harpsichord, directing both players and musicians, Handel did a considerable amount of musical improvisation, filling in places for which he had not written music and accompanying singers in their vocal decoration of da capo arias. Walsh rushed out a collection of *The Songs in the Opera of Rinaldo, Compos'd by Mr. Haendel,* at nine shillings a copy, which had run through several editions by summertime. A pit-band violist duplicated the original music, receiving twenty-six pounds from Walsh for copying it during performances. The harpsicord improvisations, with which audiences were lured night after night, remained locked in the composer's head. Aware of the potential market for these, but despairing of ever getting them, Walsh employed William Babbell, a member of the royal band and famed for his phenomenal memory and keyboard talent, to attend the opera regularly. After each performance, Babbell reconstructed the improvisations from memory, until all were set down on paper, and *The Symphonies or Instrumental Music for Rinaldo,* in three instrumental parts, was published. This was followed by an edition of Favorite songs from the opera, arranged for the flute. Handel did not receive a penny for any of these printings. In an excess of self-esteem, Walsh let it be known that he had made £15,000 from *Rinaldo*'s music, prompting the composer's rejoinder, "Next time I will publish the opera and Walsh can write the music."

Many of *Rinaldo*'s easily sung tunes became the ballad writers' property, and penny sheet music with English words soon appeared on the streets. One of these, an aria for the hero, had a long career as the drinking song "Let the waiter bring clean glasses."

Now the lion of the spring's music season, Handel was invited to many of the best homes and was among the select few who climbed a rickety London stairway to listen to and play music in the home of the charcoal dealer Thomas Britton.

As summer began, Handel realized that his leave of absence had now been almost nine months, so he returned to the elector's court. In the interests of economy, Georg Ludwig had closed the Hanover Opera House, one of Europe's finest, a 1,300-seat theater, and Handel had no outlet for his creativity. After a tedious year of writing music to be played by members of the royal family and the court, Handel returned to London, promising to return as quickly as possible. He never returned to the post, and though he spent much time on the Continent, he renewed his service to Georg Ludwig only when that minor German noble became George I of England.

Handel's return was a confirmation of London's leading place in European music. A wealthy family provided him with an apartment in Burlington Palace, on Piccadilly, where he resumed work on a new opera. He spent part of each day in the district around St. Paul's, where publishers, instrument dealers, and musicians abounded, gathering in the churchyard and in nearby taverns. He took every opportunity to use the church's great organ and, to the delight of its patrons, Queen Anne's Tavern's harpsichord. Once, as he was drinking with friends, a choir singer rushed in to tell him that an edition of keyboard music by an old German friend was on sale in a nearby music store. Handel sent out for a copy, and, never moving from the instrument, ran through two volumes of music, amazing his hearers with his facility.

Two of his hastily collated operas were rushed into rehearsal. But after two cheaply mounted performances, played to packed houses, the theater's new manager skipped the country with all the receipts. Evidently Walsh believed he had printed all the Handel he could sell, or else he recognized the slapdash quality of the new pieces, because he did not issue any of the German master's work for several years. Another reason may have been Handel's new association with Queen Anne. As financial dealings throughout his life indicate, Handel was no starry-eyed dreamer in fiscal matters; he kept his eyes open for the prospect of gain. With no legal way to collect his share of royalties from Walsh, he realized that only royal favor could provide the income he needed to live in the style he desired. The post of royal composer had not been filled since John Eccles left it to become master of the royal band. Seeing an opportunity there, Handel wrote a birthday ode for the Queen, something he had never done for his Hanoverian master. Delighted by this apparently gratuitous show of affection from the servant of a distant German relative she detested, Anne assented to the suggestion that the Te Deum Handel had most conveniently just dashed off be used to mark the Peace of Utrecht, which ended the war between France and the British coalition. Events of such national significance had always been marked by Henry Purcell's *Te Deum* for Saint Cecelia's Day, written in 1694, and use of the young German's music signaled his place in line to be the royal composer. This was soon confirmed by the settlement of an annual pension of £200 on him, despite the unequivocality of the English law that no foreigner could receive a crown grant or hold civil or military office.

Following Anne's death, in August 1714, Handel's German lord was named king of England. The sound of a German voice amid the clatter of his English-speaking subjects tempered George's anger, and he forgave Handel. The king attended a performance of the Utrecht Te Deum, and later, incognito, a revival of *Rinaldo*. Anne's pension was confirmed, George matching it with one of his own, and Handel's former pupil Caroline, now princess of Wales, added another £200 for services as music tutor to her daughters. For the first time since his arrival, English newspapers began to spell his name properly.

After being warned by management not to take any encores, no matter how much the audiences cried for one, Grimaldi, in 1715, starred in Handel's new *Amadeus of Gaul,* another audience pleaser, its new scenery and awe-inspiring stage fountain bathed in lights rivaling anything Britons had seen. It alternated with *Rinaldo*. Handel rewrote parts to suit the capabilities of new performers, providing occasional "new symphonies," interludes, and dances, among which are the concertos for various instruments so beloved by present-day record buyers. The season came to an abrupt close when supporters of Scotland's Catholic James III attempted a short-lived revolt there, frightening London Whigs into visits abroad. The king was absent in Hanover, having gone there for the sound of German, the taste of its foods, and the embraces of mistresses who understood his language.

Handel had been invited to speculate in a scheme that was making his wealthy patrons and friends even wealthier. He invested £500 in the South Sea Company, a trade monopoly in the southern hemisphere, and applied his dividends toward a trip to Germany. When king and composer returned in early 1717, the latter found a new and more liberal patron in James Brydges, the earl of Carnarvon, later the duke of Chandos. This magnificent swindler made his first fortune as paymaster-general of the British armed forces during Queen Anne's War, increasing it considerably by manipulation of South Sea Company stock. Once Handel accepted the post of composer-in-residence, Chandos ordered new music for his considerable staff of musicians and singers under direction of Pepusch. Income from these works was augmented by keyboard lessons for the royal princesses and other high-born students, music and theory lessons for illustrious amateurs and a few promising, hopeful professionals, and the creation of music to order.

The first of Handel's compositions to find a regular place in the concert repertoire, *The Water Music,* resulted from a commission. George ordered a summer's evening of music on the river, to be funded by subscriptions from courtiers eager to share the king's company. A member of the royal household, who was, incidentally, married to one of George's two German mistresses, offered to finance the entire evening himself and asked Handel to write appropriate music. On July 17, 1717, barges left Whitehall, one of them bearing fifty musicians, hired at some £150, for the evening. George enjoyed Handel's music so much he ordered it played more than three times, before and after the splendid late-night banquet waiting at the end of the royal progress.

The public did get to know many opera tunes from single-sheet songs and music books, and paying customers represented only a minor expression of British taste for the form. Yet manager after manager learned that opera did not pay, that high-priced castrati might bring in audiences, but never in sufficient number to create real profits. Heidegger began producing evenings of more commercial appeal—public balls, subscription masquerades and concerts, and, in 1718, a season of comedy in French, which proved even more popular than opera. The masquerades, however, were the most profitable, clearing 300 to 400 guineas for a night of food, gambling, and the music of two orchestras. Public concerts were more popular than ever, particularly those in Hickford's Room, situated near the Haymarket in a remodeled dance room and then in the York Building Concert Rooms, on Villiers Street. These drew business away from the immense Stationers' Hall, which was traditionally rented for that purpose. After 1713, Londoners were regularly offered benefits, concerts, and recitals by the greatest opera stars and foremost instrumentalists, and English premiers of new works by many of Europe's most famous composers. Audiences were especially responsive to the performances of children. Early in 1716, the twelve-year-old son of a stage dancer, destined to become master of Her Majesty's Band of Music, Matthew Dubourg, appeared there as "The Boy." He had first come to public attention at one of Britton's evenings, standing on a stool to play a Corelli concerto. A half-century later, in Hickford's Room, then on Brewer Street, eight-year-old Wolfgang Amadeus Mozart and his thirteen-year-old sister performed a benefit concert, playing the young boy's own music.

Some of Handel's vocal and instrumental music was heard at Hickford's and other such rooms, but new music written for the duke of Chandos was performed only at his patron's parties and social gatherings, safe from Walsh and his stenographer agents. This specially commissioned music, scores and parts, was the property of Chandos and was placed in his private library. In 1719, fearful of the possible scandal facing him from collapse of the South Sea Company, Chandos asked for an inventory of his belongings, against the day he might become bankrupt. Several dozen Handel scores, as well as the original manuscripts of his earlier works, were listed. One result of such a patron-composer relationship was that only Handel's works from abroad and collections of music written for public performance in England were published. The very popular *Water Music* did not get into Walsh's hands until 1733, and then only after agreement between composer and publisher.

Many new popular songs were coming out of the tragicomic-pastoral farce, a stage entertainment introduced by John Gay to burlesque Italian opera. Almost from its start, in 1715, this theater form drew heavily on popular music for its scores, evolving finally into *The Beggar's Opera,* in 1728, which drove

Handel out of the opera business and changed the form of British musical theater. Gay's inspired operatic parodies made no rift in his friendship with Handel, who was flourishing among those of London's artistic and literary geniuses who swam into the gilded nets of Burlington House of Candos' Cannons. Critics felt that Gay had created "the best dramatic libretto Handel ever had," for *Acis and Galatea,* the first stage work to come out of the composer's English experience. It promptly disappeared into the Chandos library until Thomas Arne brought it out for a public concert in 1731, without Handel's permission. Chandos's patronage had certain short-term benefits for Handel, but long-range consequences for the English-language musical theater. Roger Fiske points out, in *English Theatre Music in the Eighteenth Century:* "It is sad that this masterpiece was not taken up by either playhouse [Covent Garden or Drury Lane] until many years later, for it is as actable as any English masque, and its production might have encouraged English opera and interested Handel in its problems."

### Opera Financing in London, 1720 to 1726

While many, like Gay, derided opera and countless others called for its gilded return to a London stage that could not support it, the practical Handel got down to the brass tacks of business to participate in a scheme to ensure its reappearance. With sixty-two rich and nobly situated, though not always born to the purple, British gentlemen, he guided the creation of a new financial endowment, for the Royal Academy of Music. During an era in which such blue-sky operations as the South Seas Company brought new fortunes to speculators, aristocratic investors were usually positive they possessed business acumen far superior to that of baseborn merchants. Fifty shares, at £200 each, were offered to a relatively closed circle and were promptly bought out. The sixty-two supporters got two lifetime passes for each purchase; George was put down for five.

The venture represented a radical departure from the manner in which high culture had traditionally been financed in England. No longer would opera flourish only at the sufferance and pleasure of its aristocratic patrons. Now it was to be a public commodity, its stock listed on the Royal Exchange, from which its shareholders hoped to profit. A king's warrant named the lord chamberlain to be governor of the academy, and Handel as master of its music, commissioning him to go abroad and sign the best singers available, specifically the new reigning male soprano, Francesco Barnardi, of Siena, who took his stage name, Senesino, from the city of his birth. Handel immediately went to Dresden, where the castrato was starring, but failed to lure him to London. He did sign others.

Shortly after Handel completed a brief visit to his mother's home in Germany and was on his way back to Britain, Johann Sebastian Bach turned up in search of him, having walked twenty-five miles for the purpose. The two most significant composers of their time were destined never to meet. Handel had probably not yet heard of the village organist-composer.

The Swiss highbinder Heidegger had been reappointed manager of the opera company and was setting up the first season, starring singers contracted for by Handel and hiring others, in preparation for a grand opening. That evening's glory was taken away from Handel. Among the shareholders was a considerable faction from great houses—Rutland, Queensberry, Sunderland, Marlborough—all social and political opponents of the House of Hanover. Recognizing Handel's obligation to his one-time German prince, they hired their own men as staff composers, Giovanni Porta and Giovanni Bononcini, whose works had been played long before Handel's arrival. Bononcini was given every possible privilege and guaranteed an income of £500 and a home at Marlborough Palace, and a Porta opera opened the season, with the king absent.

The pro-Handel party was of sufficient strength, however, to install him as master of the orchestra at an annual salary of £800 in addition to fees for each original opera. His *Radamisto,* the academy's second production, premiered on April 21, 1720, an evening of glittering social and musical success. Scalpers asked forty shillings for a place in the gallery. The king and his ladies, his German mistress and their daughter, also a Handel pupil, and the prince of Wales sat in the royal stage box, with a crowd so great that people fainted from the excessive heat cheering the new opera. Every Italian operatic convention was observed, except that the title role was sung by a woman, a plumply pregnant soprano Handel had signed for £1,600, in place of the reluctant Senesino. Again Handel was king of the London opera, and after *Radamisto* had played nine performances, George affirmed his royal predisposition to Handel by issuing him a privilege of copyright. For the next fourteen years, Handel had the exclusive right to print and publish his music, and by the king's command all British subjects were forbidden to infringe upon that right.

Armed with this patent, Handel chose to go to the music printer and publisher Richard Meares, Jr., who operated a shop on St. Paul's north side. Walsh was still the official music servant of the crown, but Handel preferred Meares's accurate and artistic work, produced from expensive copperplates. A notice in London papers informed the public that Meares had entered into an understanding with the composer, hoping by this to dissuade Walsh from his usual piracy.

When the South Sea Company bubble burst in the summer of 1720, the value of its stock dropped overnight by more than seventy percent. Many investors lost money, Handel among them, although such insiders as Chandos rode out the storm with little loss. Many academy directors who had speculated in this joint-stock flotation were beginning to lose their taste for hazarding any more money on the opera and made a call for additional public financing.

Handel ventured to recoup his lost capital by arranging with John Cluer to print a ninety-four-page edition of his harpsichord music, already issued as *Pièces a un & deux clavecins* by Estienne Roger, in Amsterdam. Taking newspaper space to announce that the Roger publication was "surreptitious and incorrect," Handel proposed to issue a proper edition, including some new compositions, and promised that if the reception was favorable, there would be more.

Beginning in 1715 by making shopkeepers' signs and printing labels for distillers, apothecaries, and perfumers in gold, silver, and other colors, the house of Cluer had expanded within a few years, taking over some of the cheap-book printing that had long been the Ballad Warehouse's monopoly, to become a leading supplier to chapmen sellers of ephemeral literature. A line of home remedies and patent medicines like those nostrums John Playford advertised was added next, including Hungry Waters, Dr. Bateman's Pectoral Drops, the True Elixir Against Bugs, amd Daffey's Elixir Salutis, all manufactured by Cluer. The printing office's work was generally regarded as more than adequate, and its terms were most favorable to the composer.

Handel's *Harpsichord Lessons* went on sale in November 1720 at the sign of the Hand and Music Book in the Haymarket, owned by a recent German immigrant who had Anglicized his name to Christopher Smith. Born Johann Christoph Schmidt and a university friend of Handel's, he was persuaded to leave the wool trade and come to England with his two sons and go into the music business as the composer's exclusive sales agent. Selling for a guinea, the *Harpsichord Lessons* was an expensive book; Walsh sold similar publications for two to nine shillings. The volume contained eight suites, and became the most popular work for harpsichord ever printed. British method books continued to carry snippets, and European printers pirated them completely in bootleg editions that outdid sales of Rameau, Bach, and Couperin.

Handel and Meares were justifiably proud of the work turned out by an aging Thomas Cross and his apprentice assistants in the vocal score of *Radamisto* and hailed its "elegancies" in newspaper advertising. The book was a true gem, with only one hundred numbered copies printed and all final corrections made by the composer himself.

Persuaded by Handel's rivals and the guarantee of £2,000 a season, Senesino finally arrived in England and immediately joined the cabal intriguing against "the Alpine faun," as enemies called Handel. Even the royal family and its adherents became involved in these machinations, the king and the Whigs supporting the composer, whereas the prince of Wales, who fought his father on every possible issue, and other Tory noblemen were for the Italian house composers led by Bononcini. One result of these intrigues was the success of Bononcini's publication of chamber duets, *Cantate a duetti*, whose subscription list, at two guineas a copy, produced the largest amount ever amassed in London by a composer.

Things turned around once more with Handel's new *Ottone, King of Germany*, co-starring Senesino and a new Italian prima donna. Francesca Cuzzoni's singing was superior to that of her partner, performing, as she did, according to a gallery spectator's shout, "with a nest of nightingales in her belly." Exercising his 1719 commission, Handel had secretly brought Cuzzoni to London by means of a financial arrangement that shocked the city when it was revealed. She was guaranteed £250 for her mere appearance, a total of £2,000 for the season, and proceeds from a benefit performance to which tickets went for as much as fifty guineas. Aware of her reputation as a "veritable devil," possessed of a temperament surpassing that of the pompous Senesino, who was past his singing prime, Handel welcomed Cuzzoni by announcing himself as "Beelzebub, chief of the devils," and when she sang an aria contrary to his direction, he grabbed her and threatened to throw her, temperament and all, out the window. Virtually every tune in *Ottone* was a hit, one aria becoming the favorite of gentlemen who had taken up the newly fashionable German flute, and another serving as the final melody of the overture and a fixture on English music racks for a decade. London society now was, as John Gay wrote to his friend Jonathan Swift, "a world where music reigned, real fiddles, bass-viola and hautboys, not poetical harps, lyres and reeds . . . folks that could not distinguish one tune from another, now daily dispute about the different styles of Handel, Bononcini and Attilio. People have forgot Homer and Virgil and Cicero, or, at least, they have lost their ranks: for, in London and Westminster, in all polite conversations, Senesino is daily voted to be the greatest man that ever lived."

Despite the academy's expenses, which were, as skeptics had promised, often twice receipts, stockholders, management, and staff thrived on the sudden and unprecedented social acceptance of opera. A seven percent dividend was declared. In the 1721–22 season, a subscription ticket system was introduced, offering fifty performances for twenty guineas, half to be paid in advance and the balance in easy installments. Spectators were admitted to rehearsals for a guinea a head, and revenue was further supplemented by evenings during which stars sang the most popular arias and duets, followed by an onstage public ball.

The backstage wars went on as Handel's supposed collaborators combed Greek, Roman, Spanish, and English literature for heroes a fading and plumpening Senesino could play: Julius Caesar, Alexander and his father, a Tartar warlord, Richard I. Cuzzoni's leading European rival, Faustina Bordoni, came to the King's Theatre in early 1726 and set off a feud that waxed hotter with each new role played by either. Where Cuzzoni was fat and unkempt, Bordoni was small, shapely, and beautiful. She perfected a new kind of singing, it was said, employing her voice with "a neatness and velocity which astonished all who heard her," contrasting exquisitely with Cuzzoni's sweet and clear high notes. In *Alessandro,* Handel carefully doled out arias to the two, writing, for every crowd pleaser Bordoni warbled as a Persian princess in love with the conqueror, an equally magnificent one for Cuzzoni, her rival for the Greek's affection and bed. *Alessandro* played eleven times in May 1726, an unheard-of run for London opera. Each performance was watched with apprehension while Cuzzoni's claque dominated the applause one evening and, the next, Bordoni's silenced all opponents with its bravos.

After two decades of varying popularity, that "exotic and irrational entertainment" as Samuel Johnson dubbed it, had seemingly reached a zenith. Secure in the favor it appeared to enjoy from an adoring audience, the management disregarded Addison's worthwhile admonition that "a composer should fit his music to the genius of the people, and consider that the delicacy of hearing and the taste of harmony, has been founded upon those sounds which every country abounds with; in short, that music is of a relative nature."

As a knowing Italian counseled an aspiring Roman composer, London wanted "few recitatives and many arias."

It did not matter whether one was High Church or Low, Whig or Tory, for George or the pretender. High society was engaged only in devotion to Handel or Bononcini, Bordoni or Cuzzoni. One evening, when Crown Princess Caroline attended, the performance was interrupted by hissing from one faction, clapping from the other; there were catcalls and a fight in the pit. Almost immediately, goaded by their supporters, the prima donnas began tearing at one another's hair, while Handel accompanied the fight with beats on the tympani. Before the house was fully cleared, spectators scrambled onstage to tear down the scenery. In spite of George's death a few days later, the scandal continued to excite London, and it inspired a brief farce in a licensed playhouse, as well as grumbling among the masses, who saw the opera house as a nursery for lewdness, extravagance, and immorality.

## Handel and Music for the Hanovers

There was something in Hanover genes that prompted its eldest males in each generation to loathe one another. Each of the three Georges despised both progenitor and his own issue. When word came to George Augustus that his father was dead and that he now ruled as George II, little sorrow was expressed. Had it not been for the good offices of the new queen, Caroline, Handel would have been one of the first casualties of this mutual aversion. But she supported him boldly, as did the intellectuals in her circle—Gay, Pope, Newton, Berkeley, and their peers. Handel had taught her music, and her daughters were still his pupils. So she played a major role in getting him a commission to write anthems for George's coronation, on October 14, 1727.

The composer directed forty voices, an organ newly installed behind the Westminster Abbey altar (which went to America in time), and an orchestra of 160 strings, trumpets, oboes, and kettledrums, in the performance of four new anthems. These, like those written for Chandos, eventually influenced the course of High Church liturgy. New minuets written for the occasion were played a few weeks later at a court ball marking the new ruler's first birthday as king.

Performances of Handel's music were not confined to the London opera stage and royal functions. The Utrecht Te Deum was played outside the city for the first time on Saint Cecilia's Day, 1727, at Bristol Cathedral. The traditional banquet afterward was almost an all-Handel program of vocal and instrumental music. Concerts like those in Hickford's Room were spreading to the provinces, and music clubs had sprung up in York, Lincoln, Lichfield, and Norwich. Handel's concertos and overtures fell as pleasantly on country ears as on those of patrons of London concert rooms. After he introduced an inexpensive, modernized form of Italian and German sacred cantata, which he labeled "oratorio," in 1728, singing societies formed throughout the nation to sing his romanticized musical re-creations of Bible stories.

Secure as king's composer, musical director of the opera house in the Haymarket, instructor of the royal children, Handel was the prototype of a Georgian gentlemen, walking London streets in a scarlet velvet suit and holding a gold-headed cane. He had more than £10,000 in savings, the British citizenship granted him in one of George I's last acts, and a house near Grosvenor Square, where he spent the remainder of his life. He was often preoccupied with trading in South Sea stock, that company having been brought into a semblance of fiscal responsibility by an act of Commons that confiscated over one and a half million pounds from its directors for the relief of investors. Growing increasingly autocratic as his reputation blossomed, Handel vented the same spleen on audiences paying to observe rehearsals as he did on musicians and Italian vocalists. He was becoming stout, as well, a portent of the corpulence that contributed to the miserable health of his last years.

Only publishing income failed to keep pace with this progress, though that, too, seemed about to be corrected. He continued exclusively with Meares for a short time in 1721, and then made a temporary peace with John Walsh, who paid seventy-two pounds for the music of *Floridante,* issuing it in full score, vocal score, and arrangements for one and two flutes. Relations between them flourished for the next two years, although Walsh began reducing his advances for new music. The successful *Ottone* (1723) went for forty-two pounds, and *Flavio,* shortly after, for sixteen less. Meares continued to issue the old publications, now printed from copperplates, still under assignment from Handel.

In 1723, Walsh brought out the first of a new series of *Overtures for Violins in 4 parts, for Concert,* editions for harpsichord, two violins or oboes, tenor violin and bass, as well as full parts for two oboes, bassoon, first and second violins, viol, violone, and bass. In all, he published sixty-five of such Handel music in parts and thirty-three in score. He made instrumental arrangements of opera music available in the provinces and played a major part in encouraging the formation of local music clubs. At first, he had used the music of other King's Theatre composers in this series, but recognizing the German composer's sales appeal, he concentrated on his music thereafter.

Handel's lifelong passion for accurate musical notation brought about another break with Walsh in 1724, and he went back to Cluer, who was not in business with Bezeleel Creake, a bookseller. Cluer's experience in the cheap-book trade suggested to him that small-sized music publications would have certain sales appeal, and he tested this new type, advertising, for sale by subscription, *The Fine Book of Music,* an engraved, pocket-sized work containing eighty-one songs, among them, twenty Handel arias. Volume I, retitled *A Pocket Companion for Gentlemen and Ladies,* came out the following year, and sold more than 1,000 copies, to 466 subscribers, and unprecedented sale for the time. Its buyers included music lovers and patrons, some of whom purchased as many as fifty copies. The second volume of these accurately engraved and beautifully produced music books was issued in late 1725. Of these, 950 were immediately distributed to subscribers, among them was, as he was to be on all future lists for Handel's music, a mysterious John Hare, Jr., who was usually down for a number of copies. John Hare, Walsh's long-time associate, died in September 1725, but the business was carried on by his son Joseph. When Walsh pirated each new Handel work printed by Cluer for sale by subscription, it may have been done with Hare's connivance. No longer having access to music existing only in Handel's possession, Walsh was thus able to offer early arias that had never appeared in print before the Cluer edition, even in spurious publications, almost immediately after *The Fine Book,* appearance and that of its successors.

Because customers for the publication included many to whom the opera's Italian was not a familiar language, Cluer employed a songwriter and composer of burlesques, Henry Carey, to write English words for some of the arias. Carey's "Sally in our alley," published in 1715, continued to be an English-speaking-world favorite for centuries, and other Carey street songs and playhouse ballads were issued by Cluer on packs of playing cards, each one containing words and music of a different piece transposed for flute.

Handel learned to his sorrow that Walsh's over-the-counter sales were greater than Cluer's subscription merchandising in the shrinking market for printed Italian opera music. Fewer than one hundred subscribers signed for the vocal scores of his 1726 and 1727 operas. Among them was the usual John Hare, Jr., who bought at least a single copy of each work, as well as William Neale, of Dublin, down for six copies. It was from these that Neale pirated Handel's music, free to do so because Ireland was not included in the 1710 statute or in George's privilege issued to Handel.

In the spring of 1728, the Royal Academy of Music was in its ninth and final season. *The Beggar's Opera,* John Gay's masterful burlesque of Italian opera, was playing to sold-out houses nightly. Handel made one last effort to publish his own music and, using Cluer's Printing Office, now managed by Thomas Cobb, newly married to the widow owner, printed *Richard the First* himself. Walsh proved to be unbeatable, however, selling new printings of the opera almost immediately after Handel put them out, meanwhile also pirating dances, arias, and instrumental music by Handel, all taken from manuscript or privately issued books, or obtained by bribery of musicians. In late 1729, Handel capitulated to the inevitable; he sold all rights in a new opera to Walsh for twenty-six pounds. Mrs. Cluer also sold all her Handel material to Walsh, who had finally abandoned stamping music on pewter for use of the copper-engraving method of quality printing long employed by Cluer.


## Resurrection of the Old Ballad Business

The old and honored chapbook-publishing business received its greatest new impetus from the decline in popularity, among large-city purchasers, of black-letter ballads with the advent of single-sheet songs. Printers who specialized in the old broadside-ballad business turned now to a promising market for chapbooks. Old ballads were set as prose, and Elizabethan jest books were edited to fit the twenty-four pages of a chapbook. The handful of former ballad printers clustered around Bow Churchyard in London continued to dominate the chapbook market, under the Cluer, Dicey, and Marshall families, who modernized the trade by using new production methods and reduced costs by large-scale printing, to become giants of the business.

Shortly after 1730, Cluer's dropped out of music-book printing to bring out novelty items and participate in production of Doctor Bateman's Pectoral Drops and other nostrums. A patent had been obtained in 1726 for the Bateman remedy, and with the guidance of an enterprising promoter, Cluer and other dealers in chapbooks and old ballads prospered from a growing national reliance on medicines approved by royal charter.

In 1736, Cluer's printing business was purchased by a relative, William Dicey. As William and Cluer Dicey, later Dicey & Co., it printed ballads, trade cards, signs, and chapbooks. By mid-century, in association with Richard Marshall, the enterprise had a virtual monopoly, like that of the last century's Ballad Warehouse, of the wholesale supply and distribution of inexpensive reading material—the penny histories, romances, almanacs, and popular ballads that were sold for twopence to sixpence by traveling chapmen, whose packs included pins, combs, garters, shoelaces, and other small commodities. A Dicey and Marshall catalogue issued in 1764 offered 150 classic chapbooks, the only form of printed literature known to lower-class Britons other than the religious tracts attacking such street literature distributed by the Society for Promoting Christian Knowledge. Parents were admonished by the society for preferring "Tom Thumb," "Guy of Warwick," or some other "foolish book before the Book of Life," and were urged to keep their children from the old romances, profane ballads, and filthy chapman's songs, all of which "fill the heads of children with silly and idle imaginations."

In addition to the *Penny History Books, Small Histories,* and *Book of Amusement for Children on Various Subjects,* all adorned with a variety of engravings, Dicey and Marshall carried a stock of nearly 3,000 different ballads, most of them with "woodcut illustrated horrors, hangings and other marvels," which Gershon Legman, in *The Horn Book,* call "the combined murder mysteries and comic books of their time." The London market for them had dried up, but the provinces doted on these old stories and songs. Mid-eighteenth-century rural British and Scottish ballad buyers learned and made part of their folk tradition many broadside songs that had entered the commercial process by way of registration at Stationers' Hall some one or two centuries before. The publishing house whose founder first printed operatic scores for Handel was now offering "Captain Ward and the Rainbow," the ballad of an Elizabethan pirate, sung to Handel's tune for " 'Twas when the seas were roaring"; "Chevy Chase," first registered in 1624; "The Great Boobee," sung to "Sellinger's Round"; "Patient Grissel," written by the silk weaver and songwriter Thomas Deloney as a broadside; and hundreds of songs now counted among our musical tradition's jewels, authors and original publishers long forgotten.

## Handel's Oratorios, Opera for the Middle Class

Before the summer of 1728, the Royal Academy of Music's leading singers, recognizing a sinking ship, found new places with Venetian opera houses. Debts mounted; money was owed to tradesmen, performers, musicians, and others who had helped mount the King's Theatre productions. A new board of directors could not be assembled, and the academy passed into history, having presented 500 performances of opera, almost half of them by Handel. The theater's lease now belonged to Heidegger, with whom Handel went into partnership, putting up £20,000 of his own money, to which the new king promised an additional

£1,000 annually. Handel again went off to Europe in search of singers, and on his return presented two operas in late 1729, neither of which found favor with an audience that had been trained by Gay's opera, it was said, to love nothing but minuets and ballads.

Ballad-opera writers were busy hunting down Handel's most appealing tunes, choosing a minuet for Charles Johnson's *Village Opera;* an aria for *The Fashionable Lady,* by Benjamin Franklin's American friend James Ralph; a hornpipe and gavotte for Charles Coffey's *Beau in the Suds,* which was played with great success on the first tour of professional actors in the colonies, some twenty years later.

Hoping that Senesino, once a sure-fire box-office attraction, might reverse the trend, Handel brought back the castrato at £1,400 for the season. Their ancient animosity went on, but the Italian did bring in crowds, until a rival company, stole away the best singers and effectively drained box-office receipts. This was still another way for the new prince of Wales to strike back as his hated father, through Handel, but the plot proved that opera could not support even a single theater, and both foundered.

Handel was then involved in a new form of inexpensive theater, best known as the "oratorio," which in his time "bore two almost contradictory meanings at once . . . anything from a secular cantata to a biblical opera," according to the *Britannica Book of Music,* and for which mass enthusiasm existed on a scale previously unknown in England. His involvement began back when he was enjoying the duke of Chandos's patronage and wrote a sacred masque based on the story of Esther, called *Haman and Mordecai.* In 1732, seeking some music with which to surprise Handel on his birthday, the master of the Chapel Royal children found the original score and presented it privately in his home for Handel, sung by the boys and soloists, accompanied by a small orchestra of amateur musicians. A second performance, by the Academy of Ancient Music, took place in the York Building's Great Room. Both offerings were without Handel's permission, as was a third, part of a series sponsored by Thomas Arne's upholsterer father to show off the talents of his son and daughter. Handel's immediate reaction to this show of interest in an almost forgotten work was a production under his own direction at the King's Theatre. Changing the title to *Esther* and supplementing the original text, by Alexander Pope, with additions by the dramatist and poet Samuel Humphreys, he revised the score. The orchestra was increased in size, and solo parts were sung by members of the King's Theatre Company. To placate the bishop of London, who opposed presentation of a "sacred story" on a playhouse stage, advertisements noted that there would be "no acting." *Esther* was an unqualified success; it was repeated five times that month and effectively replaced a York Building presentation.

As always, Handel had a number of irons in the fire. He was also writing songs and incidental music for Covent Garden and an instrumental-music series for Walsh, who was now issuing engraved scores and parts, including the *Water Music.* A word book of *Esther* appeared after its full text was printed in the *London Magazine,* with neither Handel's permission nor any royalties.

Aaron Hill, Handel's former collaborator, who had translated *Rinaldo*'s libretto in 1711, wrote, after seeing the new kind of stage presentation, urging Handel to "deliver us from our Italian bondage" by the further creation of music on a foundation of English poetry. Handel needed little such encouragement, because he was pleased with *Esther*'s success and at work on another oratorio, though he had not yet fully given up Italian opera. When the new sacred work failed, rather than lower admission to bring in audiences, Handel instituted organ recitals between the acts. His trip that summer to Oxford, ostensibly to receive the university's honorary degree of doctor of music, clearly showed that audiences outside London were also eager to see him and hear his music. Because the season in London was over for the summer, Handel took along almost a hundred theater musicians and singers for a series of concerts of old and new music in the college churches and its new theater. For the occasion he wrote a third oratorio, *Athalia*, which was sung before an audience of 4,000. It was reported that he cleared some £2,000, much of it going toward the keep and pay of his musicians and singers. However, he did refuse the degree, perhaps because it was customary to pay the school in return for the honor, and he had other needs for the money.

The King's Theatre now filled only for oratorios, the premieres of new works when the royal family was in attendance, and the revival of his most popular operas, and it became increasingly clear even to Handel that London audiences had truly lost any taste for Italianate opera. Heidegger left the management, and Handel entered into partnership with young John Rich and the syndicate of investors that had built a new royal theater at Covent Garden, which possessed the finest acoustics in London because of its wooden structure, flat ceilings, and decorative draperies. In the autumn of 1734, Handel produced his operas, oratorios, and concerts of instrumental music there, alternating with Rich's regular presentation of musical plays, ballet, drama, and pantomimes starring the actor-manager. For the next three years, British-born and British-trained singers joined Italians and Germans in productions of old and new Handel. Their most successful offering was *The Feast of Alexander*, written in six weeks to Dryden's ode for the 1736 season of Handel oratorios. Covent Garden's pit was covered over for this work, leaving room for an audience of 1,300 who left £450 at the box office.

On March 13, 1736, John Walsh, Sr., died, leaving the family music-publishing and instrument-making business to his son, together with an estate believed to be about £30,000. The sum was a testament both to this major publisher's taste and judgment and to a business acumen greater than that of his contemporaries. Having learned that he was better off working with Walsh than being robbed by him, Handel made no change in his arrangements with the family. Young Walsh assumed publication of the Handel scores, beginning with *Atalanta*, a new opera written to celebrate the prince of Wales's nuptial rites. He published six Handel operas in the next four years, usually selling fewer than 200 copies of each. The name John Webber, "organist of Boston," appeared on one of these subscription lists, but that of Mr. Cooke of New York, who regularly bought a single copy of each Handel opera, was missing.

Frederick, the heir apparent, had evidently made peace with Handel, prompting the king to withdraw his support of the opera company. The following season, 1737, proved to be disastrous despite the success of Lenten oratorio offerings. When Handel's flawed opera *Giustino* became the unexpected inspiration for the John Frederick Lampe–Henry Carey *Dragon of Wantley,* John Rich enjoyed a hit show comparable to *The Beggar's Opera,* being performed seven times more than the earlier favorite. *Wantley's* stage dragon was as awkward and ridiculous as the monster Handel had called for in *Rinaldo* and did much to drive nails into Italianate opera's coffin.

Handel was out of the opera wars temporarily, having run through the £10,000 with which he had started his own company. Rheumatism racked his frame, and a stroke had paralyzed his right side and arm. England's curative waters did little to relieve the pain, and he was taken to Germany to bathe at Aix-la-Chapelle. His absence from the opera house was little noticed by British audiences.

## Copyright in Mid-Century

Concern over Handel's health and the probability that, should he not regain use of his right hand, "the publick will be depriv'd" of his fine compositions had nothing to do with a bill for "more effectual securing sole rights of Printed Books to Authors &c." introduced into the House of Lords in April 1737 by Henry, Viscount Cornbury. Among its proposed provisions was copyright protection for twenty-one years for all books whose authors were dead, life plus eleven years for those still living, twenty-one years should the author die within ten years of publication. The 1710 Bill for the Encouragement of Learning was approaching its demise, and even those works written by authors still alive and renewed after fourteen years were in danger of going into the public domain. In Handel's case, the special grant from George I had expired.

In 1735, the newly formed Society for the Encouragement of Learning had begun efforts to reduce the congers' power. The 1710 Law of Queen Anne had placed in their hands control of the works of Shakespeare, Milton, Dryden, and other best-selling authors, also removing them from copyright in 1731. At that time, these monopolists entered into a gentleman's agreement to ignore the lapse. The elder Jacob Tonson, one of the 1710 legislation's prime movers, was nearly eighty, but his son and nephew helped to maintain his firm as the leading London bookseller and publisher. Starting in business with the purchase of Dryden's *Troilus and Cressida* in 1679, using a borrowed twenty pounds, Tonson had continued to purchase equally profitable works for similar small amounts. The poet-playwright was eventually put on a small weekly stipend, in return for which he translated Virgil and compiled works of poetry in a relationship that was marked by Dryden's eternal complaints about his employer's meanness and penury. The old man's shrewd acquisitions through participation in the major congers created an outstanding catalogue, which included such music-connected items as *The Beggar's Opera* and others of Gay's stage works, librettos for various operas, and exclusive rights to the Dryden ode used in Handel's *Feast of Alexander.*

Leading lovers of literature joined against what was regarded as the "Gothic barbarity" toward authors displayed by Tonson, and proposed corrective copyright legislation. Conger members, meanwhile, petitioned the House of Commons for new laws that would make Queen Anne's law even more effective against "surreptitious editions and impressions," pleading once more "the great expenses" sustained by their piracy. Viscount Percival, one of Handel's most ardent fans, joined the Society for the Encouragement of Learning, which was headed by Lord John Carteret, lord lieutenant of Ireland and related to some of the composer's prize pupils and patrons. The group proposed to serve as publisher of suitable works, and to turn over all profits after expenses to the authors. Members of the House of Lords were twice able, in 1735 and 1738, to bottle up and then effectively defeat these proposals, the second of which, Lord Cornbury's bill, might have changed the future course of copyright. It sought, among other things, to limit any author's assignment of works to a term of ten years, "except in his last will and testament," Cornbury arguing that "the true worth of books and writing is in many cases not found out till a considerable time after publication thereof; and authors who are in necessity may often be tempted to sell and alienate their right which they will hereby have to the original copies of books before the value thereof is known."

Booksellers did succeed in amending the law in 1739 by a measure directed against importation of books and putting an end to the government's power to fix the price of books.

### The Oratorio Triumphs

After unusually large doses of Aix-la-Chapelle's cure, including sitting over vapor baths three times longer than prescribed, Handel regained use of his affected parts and returned to London, in time to write a funeral anthem to mark Queen Caroline's death. Performed by some 180 musicians and singers, the work persuaded skeptics that the master was as good as ever. Handel once more essayed the publisher's role, bringing out a 193-page folio edition of *Alexander's Feast,* to sell for two guineas a copy because of the great amount of engraving entailed by the vocal choruses. Considerable sympathy for Handel's serious financial state, of which he made little secret, brought about excellent sales, and the packed house of 1,300 at a benefit concert netted him another £1,000. A large statue of him was erected in Vauxhall Gardens' Great Grove, and the sympathetic management included his music in all its public concerts.

In spite of his problems, Handel was quick to join with fellow composers and a group of leading musicians to form the Fund for the Support of Decayed [Dead] Musicians and Their Families, later the Royal Society of Musicians of Great Britain. This charity came about following the chance meeting by two musicians of the orphaned sons of an oboeist, who were eking out a living selling asses' milk on the London streets. The fund was initiated to lend the boys support, and was then extended to be a permanent assistance establishment. Handel frequently appeared in benefit concerts for the fund, writing new concertos for the occasion, and he left a considerable sum to this charity in his will. One fund-raising event, in March 1739, featured a revival of *Alexander's Feast,* which had become a national favorite in the three years since its first performance, and was considered among the best of Handel's works for its instrumental and choral music. The latter struck a specially responsive chord in the British, with their zest for singing, particularly in its use of English words in place of the usual Italian Jabberwocky the composer employed. Church authorities' objection to Handel's religious oratorios was confounded by his use of Dryden's poem, narrating the destruction by Alexander of a Persian city at the urging of the Greek courtesan Thaïs. Handel's scoring of trumpets and cellos as featured instruments and the popular organ concerto interlude found favor with people of all tastes throughout the nation.

In October 1739, George II issued a new grant of copyright privilege to Handel, affirming as well young Walsh's exclusive rights to all the composer's works for fourteen years. A notice of this royal license and protection was affixed to the last Handel work sold by subscription, the *Twelve Grand Concerts,* known today as "Opus 6," which was delivered to its one hundred subscribers in April 1740.

Handel was still sufficiently infatuated with Italian opera to involve himself in the unsuccessful production of several new works in that genre during 1739–40, but he was about to devote most of his time and effort to the form that brought his greatest success, the religious oratorio, reaching its zenith of accomplishment with *Messiah.* Credit for much of this new direction was due to his friendship with a wealthy amateur poet and patron of the arts, Charles Jennens, who collected Handel and regularly subscribed for multiple copies of new publications. After making it a point to meet Handel, Jennens frequently invited him to the palatial mansion that earned the banker his nickname, Suliman the Magnificent. In 1735, he had written to Handel, offering a libretto, presumably based on the Bible story of Saul and David, but not until Handel contracted for the King's Theatre in 1739 to present Lenten religious music did he get to work on the text. The resulting three-act *Saul* was introduced in January 1739, before a large and splendid audience, one particularly excited by the "Hallelujah Chorus" and the "Dead March," featuring a pair of artillery kettledrums borrowed from the Tower of London, where they had been placed as part of Marlborough's booty from the 1709 Battle of Malplaquet. A word book for *Saul* was off the presses in time for the third performance, followed by Walsh's edition, in two books, of its "celebrated airs in score." The "Dead March" was even then enjoying a popularity that extended into the twentieth century.

London went through its worst winter in men's memory that year, and Handel, for the convenience of customers, covered the walkway from the road to the Lincoln's Inn Fields theater entrance, the place he had rented for a season of his music. His hope was to revive enthusiasm for opera by playing it during evenings of oratorio, but his audiences were determined to enjoy entertainment in English only, attested to by the popularity of *L'Allegro, Il Penseroso ed il Moderato,* bowdlerized by Jennens from Milton's poems. Even after thirty years of eternal hope and diminishing response, Handel insisted on giving Italian opera one more, its final, chance. His last two productions had such poor response that Walsh could not find sufficient subscribers to buy their arias and music. On the other hand, performances of his music for voice in English increased steadily.

Those London working-class audiences who went to Cuper's Gardens, along the Thames, for music, dancing, food, and fireworks were regaled, as were visitors to Vauxhall and Marylebone, with music by Handel and a growing band of imitators. On Saturday nights during the summer of 1741, amid the noise of fire wheels, fountains, and skyrockets could be heard music from *Saul,* organ concertos from Handel's Opus 5, and, as advertised, on July 4 "a grand new piece of music, an original composition by Mr. Handel, called Porto Bello." Though not by Handel, the song celebrating Admiral Edward Vernon's victory in the Caribbean was a single-sheet hit and continued to be credited to the German composer for years. As "Hosier's Ghost," it served many a patriotic American balladeer as a rousing good tune for his verses of protest. Admittedly, Handel addressed his music to the aristocrats and wealthy Britons who attended the royal theaters, but he was also known among the masses as the creator of some of their favorite popular music. Since 1736, sheet-music buyers had been collecting fortnightly issues of music printed from copperplates, and decorated at the head with elegant and delicately engraved vignettes of contemporary life made by George Bickham. Each number of four pages was dedicated to a leading English political or social figure and included songs by Arne, Purcell, Lampe, Carey, Leveridge, Boyce, and other songwriters and royal playhouse composers, as well as Handel arias. Some of his music was printed with its original Italian words, and some, including " 'Twas then the seas were roaring" and "The submissive admirer," was in English. The engraver-publisher George Bickham gathered up the copperplates in 1740, in excess of 200 and brought them out in two volumes of a hundred plates each. Subsequent editions appeared, continuing Handel's presence alongside the most famous popular songsmiths of the period.

Music and songs of a different sort came out of Handel's next trip away from London. Writing on behalf of three Dublin charitable organizations, the duke of Devonshire, lord lieutenant of Ireland, invited Handel to come to that city and conduct fund-raising concerts of his own music. Working with a text supplied by Jennens, during the summer of 1741 Handel completed a three-part nondramatic oratorio based on the life of Christ, which he titled *Messiah.* Immediately after arriving in Dublin, late that year, he appeared in a service of music "in the cathedral manner," for support of a local hospital, and then announced the sale of tickets for six musical entertainments in a theater he had rented. The venue was a new music hall on Fishamble Street, owned by the Dublin music publishers John and William Neale, who regularly subscribed for Handel's opera books in order to pirate them. A second season of sold-out performances began in February 1742, after Handel had received a royal extension of permission to be away from London. Importing singers from London and using the best local talent, often forcing Dublin theaters to close for the evening as a result, he began preparation of a gala concert, in which his "grand new oratorio' would be offered to raise funds for Dublin's jail prisoners, a local hospital, and an infirmary, the prime reason for his presence in Ireland. In order to accommodate an additional hundred persons, ladies were urged to remove the hoops supporting their wide skirts, a plea they cheerfully obeyed for an evening that promised to be the season's social highlight. It was an occasion for which critics did find, as one put it, words "wanting to express the delight it afforded to the admiring crowded audience. The sublime, the grand and the tender, adapted to the most elevated, majestic and moving words, conspired to transport and charm the ravished heart and ear." The three local charities received £127 from the proceeds, and, freed of his commitment, Handel undertook a presentation of *Messiah* for his own benefit. The top panes of glass in each of the music hall's windows were removed for the comfort of spectators during the warm June evening on which the second performance brought Handel honor, profit, and pleasure.

Little was heard of Handel after his return to London until the first of 1743, when he and John Rich, as patent holder of Covent Garden, importuned city authorities for permission to produce a new work, *Samson,* written to another of Jennens's recastings of Milton's words. Complaints began almost at once that Handel had hired all the goddesses from farces and singers from other theaters. Kitty Clive, a popular comedienne, was signed to sing Dalilah, the temptress courtesan. More crowded audiences than ever attended, and more people were turned away from the 1,850-seat house, during the eight nights the Israelite hero's story was played. Handel stretched the season into twelve nights, on the ninth announcing a new sacred oratorio, his *Messiah.* The news was given abruptly, for fear of an angry reaction to the use of a New Testament text for a work of clearly theatrical nature, this being the composer's only oratorio to employ words from the Gospels of the Apostles.

Handel had correctly perceived a response chord in the British id with his *Esther* and continued to work the same magic ever after, enchanting Englishmen with continued use of Old Testament stories. The British saw the history of the Jews and their heroes and heroines as a national saga much like their own, finding in the Israelites a people with whom they could easily identify. Like storied Israel, they were a small nation that had won a place among the world's leading powers by obeying the Old Testament God's commandments. Unlike European denominations that had parted from Rome in protest, the Anglicans were more firmly rooted in the Old Testament than in the New. The most important texts in their worship were by David the Psalmist, who rejoiced in the triumph of his election to eternal grace. The New Testament, on the other hand, depicted a supreme being with whom the English were less comfortable than with the Old Testament's Jehovah. The apolitical Messiah was not of this earth and an infinitely more complicated persona, whom they relegated to the confines of church buildings. They found Him difficult to cope with as Handel depicted Him, and their reluctance to deal with *Messiah* resulted in its withdrawal after three performances.

A true child of his father, young John Walsh understood their problem and rushed out an edition of songs in score from the successful *Samson,* a second collection soon after with the overture in score, and by autumn 1742 a complete edition of the work in score. *Messiah* enjoyed a different fate in print. Walsh set aside the copperplate engravings of the full score after they were completed in 1749 and never touched them again, even to issue a collection of the leading songs, only an overture to the "Sacred Oratorio," as he named it. After his death, in 1766, his successor, William Randall, who had been left the business and the Catherine Street shop, printed a complete edition of *Messiah,* using the seventeen-year-old plates.

During its three solitary English performances, *Messiah* earned the tribute that is traditionally paid its "Hallelujah Chorus": the now mandatory custom of "all standing." Only the "Dead March" from *Saul* enjoyed such a gesture before the evening of March 23, 1743, when George II rose to his feet when the chorus started, prompting the entire audience to do the same. It was two more years before an English audience stood for "God Save the King," and then only as a sign of patriotism, for Bonnie Prince Charlie threatened the kingdom from the north and the French were poised on their side of the Channel with a force of 15,000 men ready to invade.

Problems of health returned, and Handel was obviously failing when he returned to work in the summer of 1743 to write new oratorios for the next Lenten season. *Messiah*'s mixed reception had made him apprehensive, and he used a libretto revised by William Congreve for *The Story of Semele,* labeled as "in the manner of an oratorio" but, in truth, an English opera disguised. It dealt with the ancient Greek gods' amorous escapades, a factor in its eventual failure. *Joseph and His Brothers* was patently sanctimonious, and the most ardent Handelian still scorns both plot and music. He doctored its score by adding the popular Te Deum written earlier that year to celebrate George's victory over the French at Dettingen. Only by raising admission prices and increasing the number of presentations did Handel's income from the theater increase. For the first time since 1738's debacle, he was able to draw against profits to invest £1,300 in three percent annuities.

The 1745 season was a minor disaster, the faithful failing to come and hear one of his notable accomplishments, *Hercules,* like *Semele* a musical drama posing as an oratorio. Its libretto, based on Greek legend, was by another of the clever literary clergymen of the time, the Reverend Thomas Broughton, who was, fortunately for Handel, a cut above most of his peers and contributed a text that matched the music's quality. Theatergoers' minds continued to be intent on Prince Charles's military threat to London, and the house never quite filled for the undisputed glories of his second work, *Belshazzar,* one of his major triumphs, with a libretto by Jennens that had twice as much text as Handel could use. A tiring sixty-year-old Handel next offered *Messiah* as an inducement, hoping to repeat the Irish success, but it failed once more, and those who knew him well whispered that he was suffering from "a disorder in the head."

He had wit enough, however, to pay off his singers and raise additional funds by selling two organs he had installed in the Haymarket theater. This done, he went off to Tunbridge Wells for the waters, to return in August as the Scottish revolt was prospering and sane Londoners were contemplating the removal of funds from the Bank of England in preparation for a sudden departure. There being no one more patriotic than an honorary Englishman, Handel rose to the challenge of the day and wrote patriotic songs, including one for the company of Drury Lane volunteers to be sung against an onslaught of pro–Bonnie Prince Charlie ditties.

Using the form he had developed to stir faint hearts with such mastery, he next composed another of his major masterpieces, *Judas Maccabaeus*, based on the Maccabean story preserved in the Apocrypha. He started work immediately after the decisive Battle of Culloden, in April 1746, when William, a son of the king, put an end to the rebellion by butchering those defeated Scotsmen who did not take their own lives. "Billy the Butcher" was enveloped in the victorious Jewish folk hero's warrior robes by the Reverend Thomas Morrell, suggested to Handel as a collaborator by the prince of Wales. The completed work was a glorious success, playing to audiences not only of traditional aristrocratic playhouse-goers, but also of a new public of middle-class merchants and their families. These bourgeois newcomers found it simpler to attend the theater because Handel had discarded the subscription-ticket system for a first-come, first-served selling scheme. *Judas Maccabaeus* and its creator became these Britons' notion of what their own music and their own composer should be, settling him more firmly than ever as the country's major voice for its political and military aspiration of being the victorious custodian of a world empire.

The Peace of Aix-la-Chapelle, marking England's victory over European rivals, provided Handel a golden opportunity to put into music the spirit of triumphant celebration engulfing the nation. A vast fireworks display was planned for April 26, 1749, coincident with the performance of outdoor music commissioned by the crown. A rehearsal at Vauxhall Gardens four days earlier caused one of the city's major traffic jams, as 12,000 people stopped up London Bridge on their way to the pleasure garden to see Handel at work teaching his musicians the "Royal Fireworks Music."

The last decade of Handel's life was a time of artistic and financial triumphs. *Messiah* became an annual musical event after he conducted a benefit performance for the Foundling Hospital in 1750 in front of a crowd so great that the work had to be repeated for the benefit of those who had purchased tickets but could not get into the theater. Despite near-blindness, Handel continued to compose, dictating music to young John Christopher Smith, the son of his old friend and music sales agent. Virtually all of his music except *Messiah* was available in printed score as well as in arrangements for harpsichord, violin, or flute. Five bound books of his opera and oratorio songs, some 400 in all, were on sale in vocal score and instrumental parts, as were eleven sets of overtures. Their sale and that of Walsh's publications added to his income, but in no measure as significantly as profits from public performance of his oratorios presented under his own auspices. His profits were invested in annuities, eventually producing an estate of £20,000.

Walsh's ownership of Handel works continued after the composer's death, in 1759, a royal privilege in 1760 extending protection for fourteen years to a publication of *Six Organ Concertos,* Opus 7, and to music "never before Collected or Published together." For much of his life, Handel had sought to confound piracy by publishing his work himself or authorizing publication only of favorite songs and their accompanying instrumental music. This he did for business reasons rather than for protection of intellectual property, a concept whose time had not yet arrived. As were those Elizabethan theater managers who forbid printed reproduction of their hit plays in order to frustrate rival productions, Handel was well aware that possession of a true and complete score of any work made it possible for others to challenge him at the box office, his chief means of income from music. A genius he certainly was, but he was also a businessman, and never hesitated to borrow from others, picking up a good melody from wherever it came. He justified this practice once by remarking, "Well, it's much too good for him; he did not know what to do with it." What Handel did with borrowed things did indeed make them live long after their true composers had been forgotten. The list of composers, mostly Italian, whose bars of music he lifted is long and grows longer as musicologists focus with increasing intensity on the eighteenth century. In creating his oratorios, he also occasionally borrowed from himself, usually duets he had written or appropriated for his operas. Twentieth-century composers, protected by international recognition of their property rights, look askance at Handel's time, when borrowing was the general custom. Even those royal patents provided to Handel and to Walsh failed to achieve exclusivity, and if the most prestigious and well-connected composer of his day was the victim of seemingly larcenous publishing practices, how could those less fortunately situated composers and songwriters hope to enjoy the fruits of their creativity?

### Some Mid-Georgian Music Publishers and Their Songwriters

Thomas Cross's death, in 1733, took away the "father of sheet music," but left behind many entrepreneurs who carried on, improving the innovation for which he was responsible. Hundreds of these music merchants are catalogued in that indispensable chronicle *Music Publishing in the British Isles . . . ,* compiled by Charles Humphries and William C. Smith. The contributions of only some of these directly affected the character of American popular music or the songwriters whose work they printed.

In 1740, John Johnson went into business directly across from Bow Church, in Cheapside, using plates he purchased from the Cooke and Wright families. The former had been in business for only some eight years, beginning with publication of songs from Thomas Arne's burlesque opera *Tom Thumb,* written with Henry Carey. The Wrights had made and sold musical instruments and supplies from about 1710, in vigorous competition with John Walsh. Their catalogue included popular songs and country dances, often the same and looking the same as their rival's. Wright was without prejudice in piracy, stealing from native-born and foreigners alike. Young Daniel Wright had his shop in St. Paul's Churchyard, under the sign of the Flute and Violin. He specialized in teaching books for those instruments, but issued music as well.

Johnson was the first to break John Walsh's unwritten law that music should be printed without a date, to preserve the fiction of its newness. Johnson publications often carried the year of issue, among these the harpsichord-and-voice edition of Arne's ground-breaking *Artaxerxes* and Geminiani's *Harmonical Miscellanies,* both printed in the early 1760s for their writers. Only the best-known composer could expect the cost of publishing to be borne by the publisher, and he was obliged to pay for all work—engraving, printing, binding—and paper, as well as giving a twenty percent commission to the publisher. Like others, Arne sold out of his home once initial demand for his publications subsided, and advertised the availability of his music in friendly shops where little or no commission was paid. This practice continued for decades in spite of the copyright law of 1774, which was intended to improve authors' rights. As late as 1781, as Humphries and Smith pointed out, an oppressed songwriter complained in London's *Morning Herald:*

> The Composers of music, in London, most respectfully acquaint the nobility and gentry, that henceforth their new music will be sold at their own dwelling houses; the reason for this is, the music-shop keepers take so much advantage over the composers, viz. 1st when a set of music sells for 10s 6d the music shop takes half a crown of their trouble of selling it. I think sixpence or a shilling profit is sufficient for a copy, as the only trouble is to sell it to the person who asks for it in the shop as is customary with the booksellers. 2ndly, the music-shop keepers take the seventh copy for their profits which they call allowance; consequently their remains only 6s 3d out of the half-guinea to the composer for printing, paper and other expenses. The composers of music will refer to the impartial judgement of a generous public, if it is just, that when a good composition appears, and is accepted by the public, that the music-shop keepers, take the money, and for the composer remains only the honour, by which he is to live. Consequently the shop keepers live by the sweat and labour of the composers, and are, into the bargain, very insolent and impertinent towards them.
>
> Thus muchly from
>
> APPOLO.

It was in the Johnson shop that young Charles Dibdin, fresh from the country, found employment in 1760 as a harpsichord tuner and handy boy of all work, which provided the aspiring tunesmith with a valuable insight into popular music's latest trends. In that same year, Johnson published what Roger Fiske calls "the only publication of its kind," an overture and the accompaniments composed by William Bates for a modernized comic-opera version of the 1731 ballad opera based on Richard Bromes's *Jovial Crew.* Upon Johnson's death, in 1763, his widow carried on the business for more than a decade, then sold most of the stock and valuable engraved plates to the Scottish music publisher Robert Bremner.

This important London music merchant arrived in London in 1762 to open a branch on The Strand of his Edinburgh store. His first publication was a British edition of his own instruction book, *The Rudiments of Music,* followed by collections of songs and country dances, reels and tunes, of his native land. The melody known today as "Auld Lang Syne" appeared as the strathspey "The

Miller's Daughter'' in Bremner's 1765 *Collection of Scots Reels*. Britons used the word *overture* for both the opening music of operas and musical plays and the sonata-form instrumental music known today as a "symphony." Regular issues of the *Periodical Overtures,* begun by Bremner in 1763 with one of Johann Christian Bach's symphonies in score, did much to make Englishmen and Americans familiar with the most modern concert music. Recognizing the changes taking place on the Continent, Bremner was the first London publisher to issue Johann Stamitz's symphonies. This Bohemian composer and violinist had organized and shaped the best orchestra in Europe, made up of virtuoso musician-composers. Based in Mannheim and supported by the ruling duke, it was a source of wonder to Europeans for the dynamic contrasts of its playing, the result of Stamitz's training and a challenge imposed on its contributing players. The Mannheim School did much to shape the transition of concert music from Bach's and Handel's polyphonic style to the homophonic school of Haydn, Mozart, and the early Beethoven, bringing about the orchestra's standardization into basic strings, woodwinds and horns. The school's influence was also felt in London, where musical-theater composers began to use its fast-slow-fast pattern, with attention to contrasts in sound.

Bremner introduced Haydn's music to England, being the first to publish his chamber music and early symphonies, usually taking them from French publications, which were pirated from the composer's original scores and parts, obtained surreptitiously. In his early 1730s, Joseph Haydn was already recognized by European publishers as a valuable commodity, and they did all they could to obtain his music, leading to his international reputation. There were many unauthorized editions like those of Bremner, which led to the suppression of some of his music, since Haydn, too, wished to maintain control over it. Only now is it being rediscovered, by musicologists.

Bremner also published Karl Friedrich Abel, boyhood friend of Johann Christian Bach, and his London roommate after the great master's youngest son arrived in London in 1762. A resident musician to Queen Charlotte, Abel was the last great virtuoso of the viola da gamba, that bass viol on which Jacobean amateurs doted. Together, Bach and Abel presented public concerts of contemporary music in Hanover Square's new hall. In the 1775 season, profits of £3,595 were realized. The programs served to bring Bremner's catalogue to the attention of amateur musicians, who then presented their own "Gentlemen's Concerts" to private audiences.

Among the gentlemen with whom Bremner did business were some from the colonies, for whom he generally selected music and shipped it on consignment. One of his American customers, Francis Hopkinson, first came into his London shop during a visit in 1766–67, referred to the music merchant by John Bremner, a relative in Philadelphia who taught music. After the Revolutionary War was over, Hopkinson, a signer of the Declaration of Independence, resumed business with the London store. In 1785, he returned a case of music, complaining that it contained "too great a proportion of expensive Concert music and unknown authors," prompting a flurry of mail revealing the extremely personal relationship between the two. "That my catalog is the most substantial one in the world cannot be denied," Bremner wrote, "and for that reason its contents ought to be seen in the New World."

Employing skilled engravers, using high-quality letterpress work, and printing on strong, thick paper that accommodated itself to constant use, Bremner enjoyed an excellent reputation as a publisher who gave good value, not only in concert music but also in folios of the most popular playhouse musicals. He was a wealthy man at the time of his death, in 1789, owner of freehold property in the country and by the sea, as well as the house in The Strand, on whose ground floor he conducted his business.

The Bremner stock in trade and engraved plates were purchased at auction by John Preston, musical-instrument maker and dealer, a neighbor who specialized in musical-theater song folios, sheet music, and books of Irish, Scottish, and Welsh songs and dance music until the 1830s. In 1803, Thomas Preston bought the entire stock of Harman Wright, who had come into possession of the old John Walsh plates and advertised himself as "Successor to Mr. Walsh." In the acquisition were the opera, oratorio, and instrumental engravings Handel had scrupulously supervised. Preston's also published that very important series of Scottish, Irish, and Welsh song collections edited by George Thomson, who employed Pleyel, Haydn, Beethoven, Kozeluh, and Weber to make instrumental accompaniments and Robert Burns as chief source of the highland songs' words. The Preston catalogue was purchased in 1850 by Novello & Co.

In the last quarter of the century, most English music publishers relied on engraved plates, usually of high-quality metal, although wooden plates were also in evidence. During Handel's life, the quality of printed music was generally poor, often a mixture of engraving and punched notation, despite such outstanding artistic achievements as the Bickhams' *Musical Entertainer,* in 1738–39, and Benjamin Cole's work. He was a publisher and engraver who cut *Songs and Duettos in the Burlesque Opera, call'd The Dragon of Wantley* and issued *British Melody or the Musical Magazine.* This collection of English and Scottish songs, one-quarter of them set to music by Lampe, was issued in parts in 1738–39. Cole also did a craftsmanlike job on the engraved music of *The New Universal Magazine, or Gentlemen and Lady's Polite Instructor,* which appeared between 1751 and 1759.

One reason for the falling off in quality was the growing importance of the newspaper as a medium for advertising and promotion of musical publications. In 1733, there were seventeen London papers, one of them, the *Daily Advertiser,* beginning as a journal that justified its name, but gradually it added news items and essays to increase circulation and its space rates. By mid-century, the London press approached the hundredth anniversary of its transition from sixteen-page penny news books to four-page dailies. During the late 1600s, Playford and other publishers used open spaces in their publications to list works for sale or to call attention to new editions or their sidelines of medicines. Now, the press, including a flood of magazines, gave space to the world of music. Publishers advertised their new editions regularly in the papers, promotion that evidently produced sales, since it continued throughout the century. Moreover, program listings of the royal playhouses usually heralded performance of new songs or orchestral works by popular composers, which also assisted music stores and publishers.

With demand for music wares increasing after the 1760s, much of it stimulated by the press and advertising, newcomers joined the trade, most of them caring little for quality work. Not much attention had been paid to significant innovations created around 1750 by the German music publisher Johann Gotlob Breitkopf, of Leipzig, or that in 1765 of a London music store owner named Henry Fought. Both dealt with movable music type, a technology neglected for more than a century except for Caslon's work.

Breitkopf was twenty-six when, in 1745, he took over the family printing business, established a quarter of a century earlier by his father. Out of it flowed works of history, theology, and philosophy, beginning with a Hebrew Bible. Young Breitkopf was well educated and maintained relationships with leading German literary figures and philosophers. After ten years of experimentation, he introduced a new body of music type, one that abandoned traditional prototypes. Rather than cast each note, stem, and stave as a single unit, he broke the symbols down into components, separating the various parts of what formerly were single pieces of type. This led to reduction of casts and brought mass production of mechanically duplicated music nearer to practical reality. Though far less expensive than contemporary engraving, the very number of separate units and their complexity kept Breitkopf's fonts from universal use. His business competitor the French type founder Pierre Fournier had been at work along similar lines and introduced his results around the same time. His type was larger and not as suited to the requirements of increasingly complicated scores resulting from the influence of Stamitz and the Mannheim School. The 200-year stranglehold on music publishing in France by the Ballard family mitigated against any use of either new type, even if both were advanced and less expensive. In Italy, Breitkopf's type was used only on a minor scale. He was determined to make immediate and practical use of his invention, so he began to publish scores by Leopold Mozart, Karl Philipp Bach, Johann Adam Hiller, and other popular composers, amassing a warehouse stock of music in both print and manuscript, drawing on scores from Paris, London, Amsterdam, and other major music-printing centers. He advertised internationally in a series of catalogues distributed chiefly to connoisseurs, collectors of handwritten music manuscripts, and wealthy amateurs. His series of *Thematic Catalogues* of music in manuscript, distributed in five parts and sixteen supplements between 1762 and 1787, was a misnomer, for it duplicated opening passages rather than themes.

In this age when international copyright laws did not exist and composers relied on royal favor for highly doubtful protection, a lively trade existed in hand-copied instrumental and vocal music. This generally came from the workshops of professional music copyists, who produced music on demand, much as had their pre-Gutenberg predecessors. Many composers who had situations with princes of the church, major or minor royalty, or wealthy private individuals were obliged to make their music available only to their patrons, who sometimes caused certain pieces to be duplicated by hand for distribution as

valuable gifts to friends or elegant tokens of their respect. As a result, Breitkopf, Walsh, or any other enterprising music publisher had only to obtain printed
copies, usually pirated, or to buy or borrow manuscript copies, often duplicated
surreptitiously by the composer's own copyist, and then print and distribute the
work.

Breitkopf complained in the original *Thematic Catalogue* that composers were
loath to send him their music, adding that he proposed to "take steps to acquire" music for which he saw a demand. By whatever means, he built up a
major stock of the most popular concert music, putting his profits into the highly
valuable manufacture of colored paper and playing cards and establishing bookselling establishments in Germany. His two sons were taught the printing trade.
The older, however, became a musician and moved to Russia, where he remained until his death; the second proved to be an amiable dilettante with no
head for business. Fortunately, he had as his best friend G. C. Haertel, a shrewd
entrepreneur, to whom he turned over the family business after his father's death,
in 1794. It became known as Breitkopf and Haertel, still a major German music-
publishing enterprise.

During the 1760s, the senior Breitkopf had distributed specimen sheets of his
new music type internationally with little success. Probably inspired by those
sheets, Henry Fought, variously described as a native of Lapland or Germany,
who did business as a music publisher from 1765 until 1770 in a shop in St.
Martin's Lane, London, took out a patent in 1767 for the exclusive right to
manufacture, use and sell "certain new and curious types by me invented for
the printing of music as neatly and well in every respect as hath been usually
done by engraving." He divided each note into five separate pieces of metal
type, creating a font of 166 different characters, which included markings, numerals, accents, and all else needed. He submitted specimens of his work to
the Society for the Encouragement of Art, Manufacture and Commerce, founded
in 1754 to stimulate artists and inventors by granting subsidies, and received
from it a commendation, finding his new method an answer to all purposes of
engraving on wood, tin, or copper and at much less expense. London's music
merchants paid no attention, though Fought did produce sheet music printed
from his type at a penny a page, or eighteen pages for a shilling, cheaper than
the usual rate of sixpence for an engraved sheet. In 1770, he sold his entire
stock and plant to Robert Falkener and left England. The new proprietor worked
with Fought's font for the next decade, offering "Overtures, Cantatas and the
Choicest Songs" at a penny a page, with little marked success.

Had they taken advantage of either Fought's type or Breitkopf's fonts, English music publishers would have increased profits substantially during the last
decades of the eighteenth century. Despite the rapid growth of middle-class
Britons' interest in music making on the piano, production costs rose, due chiefly
to the new complexity of printed publications. The number of sheets required
for full score and parts increased far beyond the capabilities of London engravers to meet the demand, but publishers persisted in ignoring the more productive technology easily available to them. This resulted, Roger Fiske has pointed
out, in the publication of only one full musical-theater score between 1775 and

1800, *The Lord of the Manor,* music by William Jackson and libretto and lyrics by General John Burgoyne. The production and sale of individual songs, however, grew steadily, attracting purchasers who often first heard these new compositions at Vauxhall, Ranelagh, and the other pleasure gardens.

In 1783, James Harrison, of Paternoster Row, enlarged his bookselling business—reprinted editions of popular novels—by publishing the fortnightly *New Musical Magazine,* the first periodical aimed at the sheet-music-buying public. It was followed, in 1788, by the *Lady's Musical Magazine* and the *Gentlemen's Musical Magazine,* and seven years later by the *Monthly Magazine,* among others. In America, aware of the success of these publications, the earliest music publishers, particularly Isaiah Thomas and Benjamin Carr, issued similar magazines. Selling for one shilling sixpence an issue, the *New Musical Magazine* regularly offered printed keyboard arrangements of theater songs by Samuel Arnold, Maurice Greene, and other playhouse favorites, sections of Handel oratorios, and such old music as the vocal score for Purcell's *Tempest.* By purchasing five consecutive issues, one could own a complete vocal edition of *Messiah* for seven shillings sixpence. A bound volume of it, printed from plates Handel had personally corrected, were available for two guineas, an indication of the economic reality implicit in Harrison's magazine. As a bonus, each subscriber received a four-page installment of *An Universal Dictionary and General History of Music,* printed on a sheet of letterpress paper that could be folded, cut, and preserved to complete the book.

Using the same plates as those that produced his magazine, Harrison issued theater-song collections, which included many pieces no longer available in any other form. Samuel Arnold served as Harrison's adviser, music editor, and proofreader, and used the store's printing and binding facilities for the uniform edition, for sale by subscription only, of all Handel's music. One of Harrison's best-selling items was *The Battle of Prague,* printed in *New Musical Magazine* in the early 1790s. Franz Kotzwara, a King's Theatre violist, who brought the original manuscript to Harrison, never dreamed of the world-wide craze for his composition, which continued through much of the following century. He originally wrote the piece for piano, with violin, cello, and drum accompaniment to depict the sounds of war heard during an attack by Prussian troops on his birthplace some thirty years earlier. Its popularity crossed the Atlantic almost at once. In 1793, after Carr introduced it in a Philadelphia concert, that city's first music publisher, John Moller, issued it in a seven-page version, and in less than two decades thirty-one other Americans had copyrighted and printed the music. Kotzwara never knew of the fame of his piece; he hung himself the summer before it was introduced to London audiences.

Harrison introduced another piece of music merchandising in 1792, where he offered "100 guineas worth of Music" in the proposed 250 issues of *Piano Forte Magazine,* to sell for two and a half shillings a copy. An inducement to subscribe was the publisher's signed "note of promise," in each issue, to give to those who purchased all 250, "an exquisite brilliant-toned and elegant pianoforte, far superior to many instruments sold for Twenty-five guineas each." The complete 250 issues were never produced, however, and the pianos never presented. In its pages, the magazine provided a wide range of English vocal and instrumental music arranged for keyboard, from 1743's *Comus* to work written at least fourteen years before. Changes in the copyright law in 1774, restoring protection to creators of literature and music, led Harrison to restrict his use of music to works that were clearly in the public domain. Though the new law provided for a renewal period of fourteen years if the author was still alive, many composers, unlike writers, failed to take advantage of the provision.

Music publishers who survived into the next century were hard-headed pragmatists who saw the trade as a venture-capital business. Napoleon derisively labeled England a "nation of shopkeepers," and although this was not entirely true, income from investments in domestic enterprise and foreign commerce did provide aristocratic industrial capitalists and the rising bourgeoisie with the income that kept the music publisher and instrument dealer in business. England had become the wealthiest Western nation, and the cost of its music reflected that status. Prices of sheet music, scores, and parts and of pianofortes and other genteel music-making devices were higher there than elsewhere. Within a period of twenty-five years, John Bland became a major music merchant, owing 12,000 plates at the time of his death in 1795. The circulating library of literature, long a main source of income for the Stationers' Company, was transformed into the Musical Circulating Library, from which one could borrow, for a small fee, virtually any printed work, even those of Elizabethan times. The stock of more than 20,000 printed music items owned by Samuel Babb in 1778 grew to over 100,000 within ten years.

Successful music merchants had a capitalist's regard for the value of a pound and an eye for the opportunity presented by a competitor's failure. The fall of the free-spending house of Longman's, agents for leading European music publishers and distributors of Haydn's music in London, was as much an indication of things to come as was George Walker's seemingly overnight success. A bookseller who opened a music store on Great Portland Street in the 1790s, Walker introduced yet another form of dubious merchandising. Advertising sale at "half price" of his stock of popular sheet music, ranging from Handel's songs to the most recent Vauxhall favorite, he printed on each copy a price double what he now asked, having introduced tinted paper to explain the higher cost. Bargain buyers poured into his shop.

## Haydn and the Music Business

After replacing Italy as the Western world's music center, Austria produced no printed music until the mid-1770s, when a major publishing enterprise was begun by the Artaria family of Lake Como. Ten years earlier, the family had been granted a royal privilege to operate an art business in Vienna, and in 1776 brought in its first music printing press. Artaria & Co. issued its first catalogue in 1778, and within a decade was an internationally famous house, with agents in London, the firm of Longman & Broderip. The fall of Longman's was an example of vainglorious overextension and the abandonment of traditional judgment, which produced such curious excesses as payment of top price to composers and songwriters whose music the company wished to own. The firm sometimes went as high as a thousand guineas for the rights to a popular Covent Garden musical.

The family business had been opened in 1767 by James Longman and had gone through a series of mergers and a program of expansion during the 1780s under direction of the founder's son John. A new entity, Longman & Broderip then extended the range of its publications, catering chiefly to the amateur keyboard player and drawing-room vocalist. Branch stores were opened in the Haymarket and, during the season, at Margate and Brighton. By 1790, the firm carried the largest stock of printed music in London and went heavily into the musical-instrument market, manufacturing spinets and pianos as well as strings, reeds, and winds. A horse-drawn wagon, emblazoned with the words *Music Sellers to His Royal Highness the Prince of Wales,* made deliveries to customers. Long before Haydn's first trip to London, in 1791, Longman's was carrying his most famous instrumental music in score and parts.

A few years after Longman opened his store near St. Paul's, the Breitkopf *Thematic Catalogue* made its first reference to symphonies written by Franz Joseph Haydn. Haydn was then twenty-five, the son of an Austrian cook and a Croatian master wagon maker who played the harp and sang the Slavonic music that is reflected in his son's work. The boy's talent was recognized early, and he received his first training in St. Stephen's choir school, where he learned the violin, reading, writing, arithmetic, Latin, and religion. When his voice began to break, it was suggested by his Viennese teacher that he undergo castration to preserve its youthful sound. He refused and was dismissed, at the age of sixteen. For the next decade, he taught voice and piano, wrote some music, and served as valet and accompanist to the vocal pupils of Nicola Porpora, the greatest singing master in Europe. One of Haydn's keyboard sonatas attracted the attention of a music-loving minor nobleman, who hired him, at 200 gulden and keep, to write music for a small resident orchestra of eight pieces and any number of amateur musicians who occasionally joined it. During the winter, when the weather in Bohemia grew too severe, the entire household went to Vienna.

There, Prince Paul Esterházy hired Haydn away to serve as Kapellmeister for a staff of musicians and singers maintained at the family seat. When Prince Paul died, in 1762, his brother Nikolaus assumed his place and immediately chided Haydn, asking him to apply himself more diligently to his duties and to send him the first copy of each new composition, cleanly and carefully written, as an example of attention to his post. When Haydn wished to give a gift of his music to friends whose kind offices had helped him, he used the services of Vienna music copyists to write out correct duplicates. Now, his master's injunction required him to continue using their services. Yet neither knew that some of them were making extra copies to fill orders for Haydn's music. Shut away in the country, Haydn had little idea of what was happening in the fast-growing world of the music business or of the increasing reputation of those purloined copies.

When printed copies of music he believed he owned exclusively were shown to the prince, he suspected collusion between Haydn and the publishers. Haydn was able to dissuade him, and finally received permission to sell copies of juvenile works, authorized sales of which did even more to make his music available to collectors in Venice and northern Italy, wealthy monasteries, and powerful members of the German nobility. Nowhere, however, did he become more popular than in France, where his first string quartet was printed, without his knowledge, in 1764. This was followed by some of the eighty symphonies written for the Esterházys, which were brought out by Parisian publishers who had obtained the materials from Viennese connections. Copies of the French publications got to London, where Robert Bremner then issued his own editions of the quartet.

Even before 1770, Haydn was in such demand that publishers issued anything written by a composer with a suitable Austrian name, but credited the works to "Giuseppe Haydn." Among such counterfeits was instrumental music by his brother Johann Michael, who was himself a successful Kapellmeister. Breitkopf advertised Haydn symphonies in manuscript before 1776, and in 1768 the leading Haydn pirate, J. J. Hummel, of Amsterdam and later of Berlin, began the appropriation of the music master's work that came to an end only after Haydn entered into working agreements that permitted authorized publication.

Haydn was named official director of all Esterházy musical activities, now held in a new and magnificent palace, modeled after Versailles and built at great cost in an isolated region of northern Hungary. The prince loved the new residence and stayed there during most of each year, to the discomfort of both conductor and musicians. In 1772, Haydn reminded his patron of that frustration in the forty-fifth symphony, the "Farewell." During its performance, each musician blew out the candle over his music stand when his part of the final movement came to an end and retired from the hall, until only Haydn remained.

Esterházy was a competent musical amateur, performer on a sort of viola da gamba, the baryton, and an absolute fanatic for the Italian opera buffa of Cimarosa, Paisiello, and their followers. For his pleasure and that of hundreds of visiting guests, he added an opera house to his estate in 1768, and staged professional productions that Vienna envied. Haydn wrote almost all of his sixteen stage works for this house and a second theater, where large marionettes appeared in musical plays. Among the companies of Italian singers hired on contract for these productions, Haydn discovered the raven-haired Luigia Polzelli, whose aging but compliant husband shrugged when she displaced in bed the composer's childless, drunken, and unpassionate wife of some ten years. An illegitimate child was born.

Most of Haydn's music was written prior to Nikolaus's death, in 1790—the fifty string quartets, a number of masses, eighty symphonies, pieces for the piano and harpsichord, and songs. Other works still keep turning up in middle-European treasure-troves, where they have been gathering dust since being acquired in authentic manuscript. The fame of Esterházy's house musician was reaching even the outermost great courts of Europe, whose princes sent expensive presents, hoping to persuade Haydn to write something especially for them. He had become more sophisticated about the ways of publishers, having opened lines of communication with Parisian music merchants through the services of one of the Esterházy staff on a trip to France. In spite of arrangements he made, more counterfeit music ascribed to him was sold in France during the next twenty years than the real thing. Hoping to frustrate pirating of his newest music, Haydn began to spread copying work among several scribes, so that no one possessed the complete version.

In 1779, Haydn entered into a first-refusal agreement with the house of Artaria, beginning with publication of the keyboard sonatas, some chamber music, and six symphonies, and he personally corrected engraved plates. To demonstrate his independence, he sold three symphonies to other publishers, and he took three years to send Artaria the complete autographed set of parts for his *Prussian Quartets,* Opus 50, for which the publisher had advanced 300 gulden.

Britain's ambassador to Austria served as intermediary to arrange an agreement between Haydn and William Forster. Forster had arrived in London in 1758, driving cattle to pay his way. He found work as a violin maker, then opened his own store, gaining royal patronage in the process. In 1780, when the Haydn negotiations began, he was one of the city's most important music dealers, and the subsequent understanding with the composer made him even more prominent, leading to his publication of more than one hundred of Haydn's works, including eighty-two symphonies under an exclusive arrangement. Forster first published Symphony No. 74, ''a favorite overture in all Parts composed by Giuseppe Hayden of Vienna and Published with his Authority,'' which sold for two shillings sixpence. It was printed on paper for which the composer paid, as was the custom.

Fully aware now of the importance of his name on the title page of a piece of music, Haydn began to engage in shrewd dealings. He reminded Artaria, who had been publishing almost all of his available music, that Parisian publishers offered to engrave all future compositions ''on terms most favorable to myself,'' and opened negotiations with publishers in other countries. The promoter of a concert series sponsored by a Parisian Masonic lodge wrote in 1785, offering twenty-seven louis d'or for each of six symphonies, and another five for their publication rights. Haydn sent six works to Paris in 1787, the ''Paris'' symphonies, Number 82 to 87, and immediately sold them to Artaria as well, then to Forster, receiving seventy pounds, for which he threw in *Seven Words from the Saviour on the Cross,* originally for four strings and then arranged for orchestra. Having learned that any work with the name Haydn or Mozart on its cover had guaranteed sales, music publishers began to issue their concert music in sets of three or more works at premium prices.

### The First Haydn Concerts in London

Music-loving Englishmen took Haydn to their hearts the moment pirated Paris editions of his music appeared on the shelves of London's music and book stores, and eagerly awaited an opportunity to see the master in the flesh. Haydn had intended to go there in 1782, in response to Charles Burney's invitation to present some operatic works, and he wrote a set of three symphonies for the visit, but the journey did not materialize. Then Wilhelm Cramer, violist trained at Mannheim under Stamitz, and director of the King's Theatre music, wrote to Haydn offering any sum he wished for an appearance. Other impresarios and managers did the same, all without success. In 1787, the London music publisher John Bland was sent to Europe by a group of investors headed by John Peter Salomon with instructions to return with a signed contract binding Haydn to a series of concerts. Salomon was a German-born violinist who had played Haydn's music at every opportunity when he served as music director for Prince Henry of Prussia. In 1780, he had moved to London, worked for a time in the Covent Garden orchestra, and then become involved in presentation of the Professional Concerts, which had replaced the Bach-Abel series at the Hanover Concert Rooms. Though Bland did not collar the lion, he returned with some new Haydn music, including a string quartet for which he gave his best razor, after hearing the composer say, "I would give my best quartet for a razor." Undaunted, Salomon kept up a barrage of mail to Haydn, hoping to wear down his resistance to travel abroad.

The tide turned when Prince Esterházy died, leaving Haydn an annual pension of 1,000 florins, to which the new prince added another 400 after disbanding the orchestra and singers Haydn had patiently built into an extraordinary musical group. Hopeful of an ample living from the pension and his music, Haydn moved to Vienna, with his wife, his mistress, and his son. Salomon was returning to London after hiring some European singers for another of the eternal efforts to restore opera in England when he heard of Esterházy's death and determined on another attempt to persuade the composer. The new offer was irresistible, despite Haydn's fear that he might never see Vienna again and Mozart's pointed reminder that the maestro knew no English. Salomon offered a total of £1,200, almost five times Haydn's annual pension, three hundred more for six new symphonies, 200 for a series of twenty concerts, and a guaranteed 200 from a benefit concert.

Impresario and star arrived in England on New Year's Day 1791, and made their way to Salomon's London house. A private room with piano waited at Broadwood's, the leading piano emporium, a custom that was carried on afterward whenever a great musician visited the city. Haydn was an overnight sensation, the new social lion. Members of the royal family visited him, ambassadors paid court, and old and new friends danced attendance. London's major musical organizations asked for his support. The press carried news of his every coming and going.

The first scheduled concert took place on March 11, 1791, Salomon directing his own orchestra of thirty-five to forty musicians. Haydn had the pleasure of witnessing public demand for an encore of his Symphony No. 92's adagio, with its reminder of the old ballad "Lord Randall." Such a rare occurrence caused a morning paper to write, "We cannot suppress our very anxious hope that the first musical genius of the age may be induced by our liberal welcome to take up his residence in England."

Wealthy ladies, believing that Haydn's coaching would lend their playing a touch of his genius, fought to study with him, offering exorbitant fees, which he usually refused except in the cases of royalty and the very rich. He was amazed by the sum of money eminent leading masters made by teaching off-spring of the wealthy. "If a singing, dancing or pianoforte master charges half a guinea a lesson," he wrote, "he demands six guineas entrance fee, payable at the first lesson, because during the course of the winter many Scotch and Irish people engage the best masters for their children as a matter of pride. . . . The entrance fee is waived when the master charges a guinea. It must be paid at each lesson." Haydn had been paid only twenty-five shillings a month only a few decades earlier.

During this visit, Haydn introduced the six new symphonies ordered by Sal-omon, half of the glorious fourteen "London" group considered by many to be his most significant and inspired instrumental creations, and also offered Numbers 90 to 92, written for the Paris Masons, among other instrumental, vocal, and religious music. The symphonies should have been Artaria's under the 1780 agreement, but Haydn had also sold them to a Paris music house, which issued them in 1790. As Artaria's London agents, Longman & Broderip considered the British rights their own and did not bother to engrave new plates, but, instead, slapped an imprint over the imported French edition.

Number 92 was the most popular of Haydn's works commissioned by Salo-mon, and it won new plaudits when Burney arranged with Oxford to give the visiting master an honorary music doctorate. Haydn, unlike Handel, was will-ing to pay for the honor. Three concerts were presented during Commemora-tion Week, in early July, Haydn setting tempos from the school's organ and scoring his greatest triumph with Number 92, which was ever afterward inex-tricably linked to the scene of that occasion, though it had been programed to substitute for a work written for the ceremony that could not be properly re-hearsed. Every occasion on which Haydn's music was presented became a cel-ebration of his genius and a showering of idolization upon him. When he vis-ited the royal palaces and the mansions of the mighty, no music but his was performed, with the prince of Wales sometimes playing the cello in duets. Eve-nings always came to an end after Haydn sat at the piano to sing for his hosts and guests, a few of whose female members resumed their ardent admiration in the privacy of boudoirs or bedrooms.

Haydn's euphoria was somewhat ruptured when he found himself in the mid-dle of a continuing lawsuit brought by Longman & Broderip against Forster, charging violation of their property rights in Haydn's music through the con-nection with Artaria. The quarrel had begun in the early 1780s, after Forster issued some music under "authority" of the composer, believing he had exclu-sive rights in England by virtue of the contract between them. Haydn had re-sponded to Artaria's earlier query about the arrangement by saying that he had not been paid properly by the Viennese company, had had to look elsewhere, and had found Forster. When requested by Forster to appear as a witness, since he was in England, Haydn wrote that he was ready to do business with anyone who paid him more than twenty guineas a work.

In six months, however, he was again dickering with Artaria, asking for sev-eral times the twenty four ducats he had been offered for a piano fantasia. Because his international reputation as the greatest composer made it possible for him to take such a tack with music publishers, the litigants made their peace in the interest of business. Longman & Broderip was making substantial profits from a piano-and-violin arrangement of the Oxford symphony, printed with two pieces by Jan Dussek, handsome thirty-year-old pianist who had also been brought to London by Salomon for a concert series. Haydn was an old friend of Dussek's father, a well-known Bohemian musician and composer, and extended his friendship to the young pianist, who was the first instrumentalist to sit on a London stage with his right side to the audience, the better to expose his handsome profile to female audiences. Gossip about his exploits among highly placed European ladies, including a supposed intimacy with Marie Antoinette, did as much to fill halls as his pianism. When he married the daughter of Domenico Corri, owner of a small London music store, he went into business with his father-in-law, and Haydn sold them his "Six Original Canzonettas," with poems by Anne Hone Hunter, the wife of a leading surgeon. Among the songs was "My mother bids me bind my hair," which was printed as sheet music in America before the end of the century. This was not the first piece by Haydn to be pirated in the New World. Alexander Reinagle did him that honor in 1788 by printing "Haydn's Celebrated Andante for the piano forte" in his twenty-page folio *Twelve Favorite Pieces,* issued in Philadelphia.

Spending the summer of 1791 in England preparing twelve concerts and two benefits, with an opportunity to "study the English taste," Haydn felt that the new works "should both amuse and please the musical public and rivet them" in his favor. His complaint the following winter, that "never in my life have I written so much in one year as during the past, and it has entirely exhausted me," was justified, particularly for a man of sixty, in an age when life expectancy was far less. He wrote more than the called-for six symphonies, Numbers 93 to 98. Learning of the continual financial problems facing William Napier, a music publisher who entered the business after gout made it impossible for him to continue as a player in King George's household band, Haydn resolved to do something for him. Earlier, Napier was forced to sell copyrights in such successful musicals as *The Flitch of Bacon, Rosina, and The Maid of the Mill* for £540, and, having run through that sum, was in danger of being locked in debtors' prison. Haydn agreed to arrange the second volume of Napier's series *A Selection of Original Scots Songs* for piano, violin and/or cello. The success of Haydn's settings of such songs as the old popular Elizabethan "Love will find a way," so old it was considered Scottish, "Green grow the rushes, o," "John Anderson, my Jo," and "Duncan Gray" was so great that Napier found himself in a position to pay Haydn fifty pounds for the work and offer one hundred for another volume.

Haydn made new friends and found old ones. The Storaces, Stephen and his sister Nancy, and Michael Kelly, a stage personality and composer of comic operas, invited him to their homes, where he played chamber music with his hosts and recalled the days in Vienna when Nancy had appeared in the first performance of *Figaro* and the maestro had played in a quartet with Mozart, Dittersdorf, and Vanhall, at the Storaces.

After attempting to woo Haydn away from Salomon with larger fees, managers of Professional Concerts brought over one of his European pupils, Ignaz Pleyel, for concerts of his own music. Despite a "murderous harmonious war," confined to the London press, in which some argued that Pleyel's music was superior to Haydn's, the teacher and his pupil, the future founder of a piano company bearing his name, remained friends and attended one another's performances.

There was no doubt, after the last of fourteen Salomon concerts, that the old master had "kept the upper hand," according to a newspaper. His new works were a series of triumphs. Even movements from the symphonies were encored in response to spontaneous demand, and innovation that first took place at the premiere performance of his Symphony Number 93. Audiences took to cheering his musical jokes, particularly the second movement of Number 94 and the surprise that give the work its name.

His influence on theater music grew. New roles for trumpets and drums enlivened playhouse scoring as house composers began to write in the Haydn style that was the rage of the town. Samuel Arnold, for one, lifted music from the "Surprise" Symphony for a scene in his blackface musical *Obi,* and others did him honor by borrowing song tunes and dance music.

Publishers rushed out editions for piano trios of his latest symphonies, versions that sold better than the parts, and small private orchestras performed arrangements of the same music for flute, two violins, viola, cello, and piano, published jointly by Salomon and the new firm of Dussek & Corri. Demand was so great for these that the engravers' plates soon showed definite signs of wear.

The master's head next reeled from a series of parties given to celebrate his return to Europe, where he was confronted by a series of changes in his stature when he finally arrived in Vienna, in late July 1792. His stopover in Bonn had been pleasant, and there he completed arrangements to take young Beethoven on as a pupil. The new Prince Esterházy, however, regarded Haydn as a servant, highly placed, of course, but still a servant, even though he had returned with a doctorate from one of Europe's most important universities and had conquered a world power with his music, both accomplishments redounding to the credit of the Esterházys. Mozart's death, at the end of 1791, struck him with its full impact now, and the poor reception of his six English symphonies distressed him more. Finding little demand, Artaria delayed their printing for years. Only the statue erected at his birthplace by a group of admirers helped to mollify the hurts.

Salomon once more wrote, asking for a return tour and six new symphonies, on the same terms as before. Haydn returned to London in early 1794. He had hoped to bring Beethoven along, but that budding genius was exhibiting strange behavior. Finding Haydn a careless instructor, he was secretly taking lessons from others, more strict, and had showed little enthusiasm for the trip. Haydn's long-time and presumably faithful copyist, Jacob Elssler, father-to-be of the great dancer Fanny, accompanied him instead.

For the following eighteen months, this newly anointed God of musical science, as he was now often hailed, enjoyed another series of triumphs. Only in England, he wrote, did a benefit performance bring in £400. The troubled political situation in France played its own part in filling concert halls, as aristocrats and merchants devoted to Haydn's music and now refugees from the Terror competed for tickets with the British. The French were, if anything, an Austrian journalist reported, even more enthusiastic than the English, so that in the midst of the "finest passages in soft adagios they clap their hands in loud applause and thus mar the effect. In each symphony of Haydn the adagio or andante is sure to be repeated each time, after the most vehement encores."

Once again the Dussek & Corri piano-trio versions of themes from the new symphonies were great sellers. The slow movement of the new tour's most successful piece, Number 100, the "Military," with its martial instrumentation, also achieved a success. Its finale made its way into the world of popular music as "Lord Cathcart's Welcome," appearing in a number of collections as a country dance. Very quickly this symphony became the most famous work of its kind the Western world had yet known, hailed as the finest Haydn, or indeed anyone, had written.

Ominous events followed Haydn's rejection of an invitation to join the royal household during its summer vacation and the pointed suggestion that he take up permanent residence in England. His concerts were boycotted by the Hanovers. A bill for twenty-six performances at parties given by the prince of Wales went unpaid, and suddenly Haydn's press coverage ceased. Few noted his departure in the early autumn of 1795, the 768 pages of music he had written for England apparently forgotten.

## Haydn's Last Years

His new prince, another Nikolaus, cared little for his house composer's music, preferring that of his imitators, and an increase of his annual retainer to 2,300 florins, or £200, far less than the returns from a single London benefit concert, muddied the situation further. As the shadow of Napoleon and his armies loomed over the Austrian Empire, a loyal Haydn was inspired to write a national anthem that would elicit the same nationalistic response he had witnessed whenever Britons rose to the strains of "God Save the King." A poem was commissioned and set to music, a Croat melody remembered from childhood. The new song was first heard on the emperor's birthday in 1797, performed, by decree, in all the nation's theaters and music halls. It remained the Austrian national anthem until Hitler outdid Napoleon and overwhelmed the nation, but was reestablished after peace came.

Haydn took time out to write the piece while he was at work on his masterpiece for massed voices, *The Creation,* an oratorio inspired by his British visits. In 1791, he had attended Westminster Abbey's annual Handel Festival and wept when more than a thousand musicians and singers performed *Messiah.* He had remarked after the occasion, "I want to write a work which will give permanent fame to my name in the world," but he set to work to fulfill such an ambition only after twelve Austrian nobles promised a purse of 300 florins to ensure its completion. His text was the German translation of material compiled for Salomon from Milton's *Paradise Lost*. Working more slowly than usual, Haydn completed the oratorio in early 1798, for a performance on April 29. An elegant audience of Poles, Viennese, Britons, and the flower of Austrian musical and literary society filled the royal palace, and a vast crowd listened outside. With a second performance the following season, the work netted Haydn a total of £300. *The Creation* was played for the first time in England in 1799, from a score of 120 pages hurriedly turned out by a copyist in six days, exactly the same time God took for his His own Creation.

Longman's had been of no assistance in obtaining the complete score and parts, having fallen on hard times. Its painted delivery wagon was constantly on London streets, to persuade the public that trade was thriving, even when the shop was often empty. The firm had run short of cash, and while looking for new investors found a silent partner in Muzio Clementi, the first composer to write specifically for the pianoforte and a brilliant keyboard virtuoso, whose influence can be heard in the Beethoven concertos. Clementi had been bought, for fourteen years, from his parents by a British music lover who promised to give him a proper music education. This proved to be exceedingly effective, because when he completed his term of service and made his debut, at the age of twenty-one, he was already the most brilliant pianist England had yet heard. After touring Europe, he settled in London in 1782 and won new fame as a conductor. However, the demand for his instruction was so great that he devoted his time to pupils at a guinea a lesson, eventually amassing the fortune that permitted him to invest in Longman & Broderip. By 1798, chiefly due to soaring production costs and business expenses, the firm was bankrupt and the original partnership dissolved, to be reorganized as Longman, Clementi & Co. Eventually, John Longman was ousted and a new firm created, headed by Clementi and financed by a group of businessmen, to engage in production of an improved pianoforte, built under his direction and containing mechanical devices he had perfected. With the Clementi name as a symbol of its perfection, the instrument became the best-selling one of its day. For ten years, beginning in 1802, Clementi traveled through Europe demonstrating the piano and opening national sales agencies. He made arrangements with Breitkopf & Haertel to serve as their London representative. But after withholding royalty payments for two years, he stole the English rights to the major new Beethoven compositions. When he died, at the age of eighty, in 1832, Clementi was buried in Westminster Abbey.

The Longman name appeared on signboards of London music shops until the 1830s, when it was absorbed into the first Chappell family enterprise, the beginning of a popular music dynasty that is still known in England and the United States as a major publishing force.

Clementi had controlled the Longman catalogue when *The Creation* was first performed in London, but his relations with Artaria were strained. Moreover, his success as a music publisher had determined, in part, Haydn's intention to be his own master and print and sell copies of his new oratorio to the Austrian and British empires' ruling families. Only after the first edition did he turn over printing and distribution rights to Artaria, which, in turn, sold them, with the plates and remaining copies, to Breitkopf & Haertel. Their publication of *The Creation,* with both the original English and German words, was probably the first multilingual edition of any score and parts. Its success in Europe equaled *Messiah*'s. Choral societies were formed for the specific purpose of performing it. The first American publication was in 1818, by Thomas Badger, of Boston, on the occasion of an extraordinary performance by the local Handel and Haydn Society over three evenings, one part on each night.

Haydn expected to repeat that triumph with *The Seasons,* his oratorio based on James Thomson's poem. It proved to be his last major work; as he said when completing the score, it "has finished me." *The Seasons'* initial success was much like that of *The Creation,* but, unlike that work, it lost its popularity over the years.

In 1800, after first asking the composer's permission, Breitkopf & Haertel issued the first of twelve volumes of Haydn's *Complete Works,* his piano music, songs with keyboard accompaniment, and the piano trios. Haydn did not respond to the request, but the firm kept trying for his approval, sending gifts, and did not resolve the matter until a young Saxon public servant based in Vienna took over the negotiations. In 1806, he visited the "cheerful and well preserved man," charming him and winning permission for the Leipzig firm.

In 1800, Britain's Vienna legation did the same for George Thomson, the Scottish civil servant who was collecting folk songs of the British Isles for publication. He had been surprised when Napier's volume of Scottish songs arranged by Haydn appeared, believing that the revered Austrian was above such work. But it became apparent that Haydn was interested in making money. The British commercial attaché arranged an agreement with Haydn, and the diplomatic pouch was used for correspondence and manuscripts delivery. Haydn's 230 arrangements of Scottish and Welsh folk songs were sold to Thomson for two florins each, nearly £291. The composer was proud of the work, proclaiming that he "would live in Scotland for many years" after his death because of the songs. Actually, Haydn found many of the melodies repellent and unattractive, but he believed his individual touches and revisions "made these relics of old national songs most palatable."

Thomson did not send the verses to Haydn or his regular composers, offering only the melodies, and expecting piano variations as well as accompaniments. Even if one of the Europeans had any meaningful command of the English language, he would have been hard put to create the proper marriage of various dialects and colloquialisms, often bawdy, or their sentiments to the authentic music.

Even though the Continent was in the midst of a war, virtually all of Haydn's string quartets were available in print there. Young Pleyel brought out a French edition, having continued a good relationship with his teacher, who was regarded in France as an international cultural asset. Though he was an enemy national, French authorities permitted a Paris performance of his *Creation* in 1800, and French music lovers visited him to pay their respect during the occupation of Vienna in 1805 and 1809. As the seventy-seven-year-old composer lay near death, a French colonel sang from *The Creation* at his bedside. Afterward, Haydn recovered sufficiently to be taken to his piano, where he played the Austrian national anthem three times before collapsing. Periods of unconsciousness came and went, and on May 31, 1809, he died.

Haydn's body, buried near his suburban Vienna home, was removed eleven years later from the neglected grave, with its simple tombstone, and taken to the Esterházy estate in Hungary. The coffin was opened, and it was discovered that Haydn's head had been removed. Some years later, old colleagues confessed they had removed it to protect it from desecration. In 1895, a wooden box with glass windows, in which the skull reposed on a pillow, was sent to the museum of the Society of Friends of Music in Vienna, where it continues to repose on public display.

A decade after his death, his symphonies, particularly the London pieces, had been played almost to death. The fantastic catalogue of nine symphonies by his pupil Beethoven had taken their place in the public's affection and dominated the concerts halls that once had pulsed to music of a more genteel and kindly time. It was more than a century before musicologists, chief among them H. C. Robbins Landon, began the work of restoration to ancient glory, removing from Haydn's music the inevitable transcribing and printing errors and editorial "improvements" made in publishers' back rooms. Not until this was completed could Haydn's symphonies sound as they had when he directed them from a harpsichord.

## Copyright Later in the Century

Little legal action involving the piracy of musical works took place during the middle third of the eighteenth century. The market was a small one, and major publishers had little true competition. On the other hand, bookselling and publishing were major enterprises because of increasing literacy and the consequent wide interest in works of science, philosophy, and religion as well as trade in works of fiction and popular poetry.

Powerful booksellers, secure in monopolies obtained by their participation in various congers, began to appear in the courts with increasing frequency, to argue that an author's exclusive right in his work was implicit in common law, beginning with the act of creation. They won a series of victories, and it was the general understanding in the trade that the publisher had a perpetual right in any work legally obtained from its author and that this right was transferred whenever a copyright was purchased from its previous owner. Unable to get such a provision written into law, the largest booksellers applied regularly to the Chancery Court, the highest legal body next to Parliament, for injunctions to stop others from publishing books that had been sold by their authors, even though the works might no longer be protected by the 1710 statute. John Bunyan's *Pilgrim's Progress from This World to That Which Is to Come* (1684) had gone through ten editions within a year and innumerable ones after that. A provincial printer, believing the book was no longer protected and anxious to tap the continuing market for this desperate allegory of man's fate, issued his own printing and was immediately enjoined. A major London stationer pleaded that he had purchased Bunyan's work from the stock of a retiring bookseller and that consequently he owned the right to its publication. The injunction was reaffirmed. Through similar court actions, the theory of perpetual copyright ownership grew as a just and proper bookselling concept.

Both John Milton's 1667 poem of the rebel angel Satan's fall from grace and his *Paradise Regained* enjoyed a new vogue with the growth of Wesleyan Methodism and the resulting individual concern for man's soul and original sin. A London bookman reissued the works in 1738 and was promptly served with an injunction after the Tonsons demonstrated in Chancery Court that they owned the original assignment given by Milton for five pounds down and an additional thirteen from the sale of 3,000 copies by the time of his death, in 1674. The Tonsons' rights were reaffirmed, and then once more in 1752, when they were permitted to restrain publication, not only of the original verses, but also of newly written annotations and a biography of Milton in which the text was cited.

Fearful that their luck might run out, major London booksellers created a cash fund of more than £3,000 to finance lawsuits against printers and publishers infringing on perpetual copyrights. The old 1693 restriction on the number of printers had been lifted, and there was an increase in the provinces. Because the conditions of the statute of Anne did not extend to Ireland, the printing industry there was a particular problem. Booksellers outside London who refused to contribute to the fund for litigation were barred from dealings with the major London houses as "enemies of the trade."

Opportunities to make significant use of the fund came in 1763 and again in 1774, both involving a work by Scottish poet James Thomson, who arrived in London in 1726 near starvation and almost shoeless, having been robbed on the road. He got a pair of new shoes for his poem "Winter" and a purse of twenty guineas for dedicating the work to a man of wealth. Other patrons subsidized the indolence for which he became notorious while he completed a poetic cycle of the year, which finally appeared in book form as *The Seasons*. Its publisher, Andrew Millar, a crony of the Tonsons, paid the poet £242 and 10 shillings, and received a perpetual assignment in return. He registered the book at Stationers' Hall. A flippancy dashed off in the presence of Frederick, the prince of Wales, won royal favor for Thomson and some irregularly distributed allowances. In 1740, charged by Frederick with the preparation of a birthday entertainment, Thomas Arne used a Thomson libretto for *The Masque of Alfred,* writing some appropriate dance music and a few songs, including music for Thomson's "Rule Britannia," which won the poet eternal fame.

James Thomson was dead some twenty-five years, and *The Seasons* was thirty-four years old, when Millar instituted court action in 1763 against Robert Taylor, a newcomer to publishing, for issuing a new edition of the by then classic poem. Millar's claim to perpetual ownership was based on an interpretation of common law in affect long before the foolishness of Anne's statute, and his claim was upheld. Chancery judges had been sufficiently persuaded that the ancient common-law property right had not been affected by the 1710 act.

Thomson's ghost and that of Millar, who had died in 1769, visited the Chancery Court again in 1774. At the sale of Millar's estate, a conger of fifteen books publishers headed by Thomas Beckett purchased *The Seasons'* copyright for £550. Following that, Alexander Donaldson, who operated a London bookstore in which he sold cheap reprints of popular books, all manufactured outside British jurisdiction, in Edinburgh, made an inexpensive reprint of *The Seasons*. Its great popularity brought Beckett and his conger partners charging into court for an injunction, a proper accounting of sales, and prompt payment of all profits. All were ordered. Donaldson took his appeal to the House of Lords, the only body allowed to overturn a chancery finding. When the final count was made, twenty-two lords had voted for the Scottish defendant and eleven for Beckett, effectively ending the principal of publishers' perpetual ownership.

The booksellers made a final effort to halt the sunrise. A committee of the House of Lords listened as witnesses stated their case against the recent reversal. One testified that he had entered the trade as an investor, buying the stock of a deceased publisher for £2,000, half of it for the transfer of copyrights. From time to time he had acquired additional copyrights, spending more than £10,000 and now, with his conger partners, he enjoyed a monopoly of most English books. These had all been purchased, he admitted, purely as a profit-making venture, with no determination of quality, only of sales potential. Counterpetitions were filed by booksellers in Scotland, London, and Westminster, by many printers, and even by Americans. Following their hearings, the Lords castigated this "set of impudent and monopolizing men who combined together and raised a fund of upwards of £3000 in order to file bills in Chancery," and the attempt to get a bill through Parliament that would extend periods of protection was thrown out.

An equally significant challenge was made shortly after to the bookseller-dominated Stationers' Company's reliance on ancient perpetual privileges, this one involving the printing of almanacs. Half a million of these highly profitable chapbooks, which served as a calendar and source of other information necessary to daily life, and into which a diary was usually placed, were sold during the last two months of each year from the warehouses of the English Stock. The company relied for its exclusive control of such publications as the almanac and the psalter on James's 1603 royal grant and letters patent. The most vigorous incursion into this privilege came from a journeyman printer, Thomas Carnon, after his application for admission as a full freeman was rejected. Using experience gained working in his father-in-law's, John Newbery's, chapbook and patent-medicine business, Carnon printed and sold annual diaries containing the same information as the almanacs, but he called his product "memorandum books" or "daily journals."

An injunction was issued in late 1773, to which Carnon's attorneys responded by insisting that James had no right to grant such an exclusive monopoly. Carnan's position was upheld, and the injunction dissolved. Thus, a few months after the concept of perpetual ownership was struck down, the Stationers' Company lost another of James's grants that "they and none others shall imprint the Books of private prayers, primers, psalters and psalms in English and Latin, Almanacs and Prognostications within this Realm."

The inevitable result of these great decisions, which chiefly affected the pocketbooks of bookseller investors, was a change in the character of the Stationers' Company. The number of London booksellers increased greatly throughout the remainder of the century, but fewer apprentices applied for admission, and there was a notable influx of printer candidates. Many musically qualified individuals went into music publishing only on the basis of their training and personal interests, rather than through preparation as apprentices and journeymen. Others, choosing not to go through the full ritual in order to attain freedom and complete status in the company, merely purchased redemption from the articles of indenture. A process of relative democratization evolved, one that saw small tradesmen who sold paper and ink sharing the prestige of membership with large investors in all aspects of the business.

## The Darling Songs of the Common People

Pre-Industrial Revolution Britain was a land of marked divisions in both economic and social terms between city and countryside. The stout peasantry lived as it had for ten centuries, self-sufficient and self-contained, resisting for as long as it could change in traditional pleasures. As forests disappeared and the nation looked to America for timber, wood shakes, masts, and other raw materials to be processed in home or factory, things began to change. Businessmen sent their own native laborers out to claw at green hills and their rich beds of fossil fuel, until by mid-century the skies over London were weighted with pollution from coal. Two million acres of vegetation disappeared in a hundred years, to be replaced by farms, hamlets, and mines, which became in turn villages, towns, and urban blight.

London, the largest city in England and the world, with a population of 700,000, one-tenth that of the nation, had become an overgrown seaport into which sailed exports from colonial possessions that formed the yet undeclared empire. Filthy slums contrasted sharply with handsome mansions, gaming houses, rising cathedrals, pleasure gardens, powerful banking houses, brothels, and shops, all catering to the varied tastes of a rising mercantile middle class or those of an ostentatious aristocracy. Whereas a solitary balladmonger enlivened the summer day in the country, hundreds of the trade walked London's streets, and those of Bristol, Norwich, and other cities, hawking printed songs by demonstrating them.

The music of illiterate clodhopping rustics was viewed with contempt by city dwellers, except for those songs whose ancient tunes were wed to sophisticated bawdry by hack writers, mediocre poetasters, and occasionally by men of ability, or those darling songs of the common people that were sometimes perceived as art.

Throughout the century, the broadside ballad, usually issued with words only and no musical notation, but with mention of the old tune to which it was to be sung, sold more individual copies than the engraved song sheet. Most Britons, having little or no musical training, satisfied their love of secular song with the broadside ballad or the chapbook. When the playhouses and pleasure gardens increased their use of new popular music, two markets developed to satisfy disparate audiences, one for those capable of understanding musical notation and a far greater one for the printed ballad.

Country people and villagers, denied the outpourings of sheet music produced by Thomas Cross and without access to a newspaper, relied for their supply of favorite old ballad stories and new broadside verses, as well as chapbooks of old and contemporary history, on the Ballad Warehouse's stock, distributed among them by wandering chapmen. As the price of paper rose, economy dictated a reduction in size to four and a half by sixteen inches, called a "slip" and about half a standard folio sheet. Chapbooks preserved an almost forgotten past and played a role, as once had the Elizabethan broadside ballad, in extending a meager literacy, teaching reading by recognition of printed words that told an already familiar story. In their few pages chapbooks kept alive such stories as *The Pleasant and Delightful History of Jack and the Giants, The Unhappy Birth, Wicked Life and Miserable Death of that Vile Traitor and Apostle Judas Iscariot,* and *The History of Doctor John Faust,* provided almanacs for the poor, and preserved the old jokes, funny stories, and riddles of *Joe Miller's Jests,* which appeared first in 1739, and then in new editions and imitations for the next several centuries.

As the Industrial Revolution, eternally hungry for manpower, moved people from countryside to centers of population, where raw materials and modern transportation concentrated, uneducated Englishmen acquired a smattering of learning. Much of it came from newspapers, from illustrated chapbooks, which recounted, much as do the twentieth century's comic books, traditional literature or fiction oriented to the less educated, from sheet songs from opera, and from political broadsides. The spread of printing offices to smaller cities and towns produced cheap literature and broadsides appealing to tastes more naïve than those of London, and also increased literacy.

Urban Englishmen heard popular music not only in pleasure gardens, taverns, and municipal concerts, but also in the worship of dissenting flocks, into whose fervent hymns popular secular melodies were being introduced. The Society for Promoting Christian Knowledge and the Society for the Propagation of the Gospel in Foreign Parts, both founded by the Anglican church, and sects seeking reformation of that church, all adopted those sinful and corrupt ballad melodies for their purposes. They were the first to print and distribute small pamphlets and chapbooklike tracts, as religious propaganda and as a means of fund raising. Royal soldiers and sailors and London's hackney drivers were the original targets for appeals for moderation in drinking, stealing, and swearing during the early 1700s. By the time of Napoleon's wars, this library had grown to awesome proportions.

Hannah More, a bluestocking who brought about an early type of sexual equality, at least in the discussion of literature, did much to raise the writing and production of religious tracts to levels approaching those of such professional chapbook publishers as the Diceys and the Marshalls. An intimate of Samuel Johnson, More wrote several plays, one of which packed Covent Garden in the 1770s, before she turned to dramatic works based on subjects from the Bible, intended for use by the new Sunday-school movement. In 1780, an English philanthropist, Robert Raikes, sponsored the creation of a Sabbath-day school for the religious education of his factory workers, to which was soon added a Saturday school where they were taught reading and writing. The movement spread quickly; the Sunday School Society was organized in 1803, reaching the United States soon after. A suggestion by the bishop of London prompted More to write a tract, interspersed with ballads, denouncing the ideas of liberty, equality, and fraternity delineated by Thomas Paine. Like Charles Dibdin, she used her pen to sell patriotism to those who would have to do the dying, preaching the glories of an England that had "as much liberty as can make us happy and more trade and riches than allows us to be good." The success of that political chapbook persuaded her and a group of London evangelists to write pamphlets, for those "vast numbers who have now learned to read," selling for a penny of less and serving as

> antidote to the poison continually flowing through the channel of vulgar and licentious publications. These by their cheapness, as well as by their being, unhappily congenial to a depraved taste, obtain a mischievious popularity among the lower ranks. It is not the impure novel or romance which attracts the common labourer's ear, or defiles his cottage, but his gross and polluted phrases which may often be traced to those profane and indecent songs and penny papers, which are vended about our cities, towns and villages, by hawkers, of whom it is a low statement to say that more than 20,000 are employed in this traffic.

The business of street literature, darling songs of the common people and all, had truly become a substantial industry.

# CHAPTER 17

# The Days of
# Watts and the Wesleys

Queen Mary's introduction, late in the seventeenth century, of Sunday-afternoon sermons at court and the founding of a Lutheran chapel in 1700 by Queen Anne and her Danish consort, Prince George, put an effective end to the Chapel Royal's ancient eminence. Musicians assembled for King Charles were disbanded for lack of interest by either William and Mary or Anne. The Anglican church had fallen upon evil times in London, although outside the city it was still popular with the masses despite a universal belief that its clergy were lazy and usually held in contempt. Daily services were discontinued in the great churches, holy days disregarded, and Communion scheduled irregularly. Though attendance was small, music by the late Henry Purcell and his ailing mentor John Blow could be heard in Westminster Abbey, St. Paul's, St. James's, and St. George's. Parish churches still suffered from the decades-old order of council mandating the speedy demolishment of all organs, images, and "superstitious" monuments. Country people clung to the songs of David and, usually led by a parish clerk who lined out each phrase, bleated out Sternhold and Hopkins's metrical translations or the recently published Tate and Brady *New Version*. For those who felt comfortable only with the old three-part harmonization stemming from freemen's songs, with each note of equal value, John Playford's settings were available.

Late in the century, the small country churches began to go their own musical way, organizing groups of amateur instrumentalists and singers to provide music at morning prayers or evensong. The British clergyman K. H. McDermott collected accounts of 111 such groups throughout Britain during the following century, employing twenty-four different musical instruments, among them flutes, bassoons, oboes, trombones, recorders, violins, viols, and basses. Few churches outside the major cities owned an organ until the nineteenth century. In 1770, a contemporary wrote, the Sheffield Parish Church had no organ, but an immense box was suspended by chains high over the west gallery. Into it musicians and singers, both men and women, climbed by means of a ladder, bearing oboes, fiddles, and other instruments, including the bum-bass, a one-stringed tub-and-stick contrivance used by novelty music-making groups. Accompanying "shrill and stentorian voices, they contrived to make as loud a noise as heart could wish." In the 1760s, church singers and musicians in Suffolk formed themselves into a ring, their backs to the congregation, and, he added sang "improper psalms to all kinds of new jiggish tunes," and when they left their own church, strolled six or seven miles to another, there to display their talents.

In the fifth century, Saint Augustine had given definition to the hymn: "for it to be a hymn, it is needful for it to have three things, praise, praise of God and these sung." George Wither waged and lost his fight with the Stationers' Company over a royal patent allowing the binding up of his *Hymns and Songs* into the *Book of Common Prayer,* but popular religious songs like his made their way into the common people's awareness and were sung throughout the week rather than in church on Sundays. It was a minister of one of the most rigid nonconformist persuasions, the Baptist Benjamin Keach, who can rightfully be termed the "Father of Hymn Singing." He was the first to ask his congregation to praise God by singing words of "human composure." As early as 1608, Baptist Separatists had broken with the Church of England over the matter of baptism of infants, finding no Biblical substantiation for the act. Despite great persecution, by mid-century 20,000 Baptists worshiped in churches scattered throughout England, and from them came some of the earliest Bay Colony settlers. When Massachusetts passed laws banning them and whipping and imprisoning Baptist ministers, a group led by Roger Williams moved to Rhode Island to set up the first Baptist church in America. By 1700, they thrived in most colonies.

Benjamin Keach was fifteen when he joined the sect, and several years later he became a preacher, and went to London in 1668 to serve a small suburban pastorate. His congregation grew, drawn to meetings by his forceful ability, and possibly by his introduction of rousing music. Although the Baptists had banned singing in worship, Keach, in 1675, called for a hymn after Communion, pointing out that the Apostles had done the same after the Last Supper. Some years later, his flock voted to include a hymn after each sermon as well, drawing on verses composed by their pastor. In 1691, he published a collection of 300 of these, *Scriptural Melodies,* most of which were set to traditional tunes, but some to appealing ballad music.

The first hymnbook, as the term is known today, appeared in 1707: Isaac Watts's *Hymns and Spiritual Songs.* It broke for all time the Psalm-singing tradition by "giving voice to the religious thought and emotion of the average believer," according to Millar Patrick in *The Story of the Church's Song.* Born in 1674, Watts was the oldest of nine children of a Puritan deacon. His talent for making rhymes and verses, and the Latin, Greek, and Hebrew he learned in a local grammar school before he was ten, brought an offer to prepare for the Anglican priesthood. He went instead to a noncomformist school. On his return, complaining to his father about the solemn and ungrateful music bawled out in the local church, he was challenged to do better and began to write hymn poetry. His verses, 110 hymns written by 1696, were instantly popular, among them his most famous:

> When I survey the wondrous cross,
> On which the Prince of glory died,
> My richest gain I count but loss,
> And pour contempt on all my pride.

In 1698, Watts was named assistant pastor to a London Congregationalist Independent church and three years later became its full leader. In continual ill health, small and uncomely, he offered his heart to a young woman, who refused him, remembering years later that "I loved the jewel, but I did not admire the casket." He never spoke of love again, except in his hymns and sermons.

Britain's Congregational church and other nonconformist groups adopted *Hymns and Spiritual Songs,* but the Church of England, committed to the traditional and conservative, would have nothing to do with the book. The approval of Puritan Massachusetts was tentative. Watts sent a copy to Cotton Mather, who wrote in his diary, "I receive them as a recruit and a supply sent from Heaven *for the devotions of my family. There I will sing them* and endeavour to bring my family in love with them. I would also procure our booksellers to send for a number of them, and persuade my well disposed neighbors to furnish themselves with them."

Benjamin Colman, a British-trained Presbyterian who served as first pastor to the liberal Brattle Square Church, in Boston, took to imitating Watts's poetry. To him, the Londoner was "a great master . . . and a burning light and ornament of the age," but the Wattsian hymn remained unwelcome to Coleman's presumably enlightened flock.

A second British edition of the *Hymns* appeared in 1709, as Watts was going into physical decline. Becoming seriously ill in 1712, he went to a wealthy friend's country home and remained there for the rest of his life, serving as tutor to the children and family chaplain. His free hours were given to creating 600 hymns. His 1715 *Divine Songs for Children,* later enlarged as *Divine and Moral Songs for Children,* was the first hymnbook written for the young. In its pages a child could find comfort in the dark

> Now I lay me down to sleep,
> I pray the Lord my soul to keep.
> If I should die before I wake,
> I pray the Lord my soul to take;

learn practical virtues

> In works of labor, or of skill,
> I would be busy too;
> For Satan finds some mischief still
> For idle hands to do;

or prejudice

> Lord, I ascribe it to Thy grace,
> And not to chance, as others do,
> That I was born of Christian grace
> And not a heathen or a jew.

Before his death, in 1748, at the age of seventy-four, Watts produced more than sixty books, collections of hymns as well as works of theology and philosophy, among them some that were used as university textbooks.

It was years before his hymns supplanted the *Bay Psalm Book* in New England, where Cotton Mather came to despise what he regarded as the hymnist's "disqualified and shallow" theology. However, there were contemporaries of Mather who sang from imported copies in the privacy of their homes, repeating verses that were already household poetic homilies. In 1728, Benjamin Franklin issued one of the earliest American editions of Watts's *Psalms of David* (1719), but complained that it did not prove the best seller he had expected. Once the hymns burst upon Americans as part of the Great Awakening of the early 1740s demand swelled, and editions were issued in New York, Boston, and Philadelphia, and the songs came into general use in all but the most conservative Calvinist churches.

Watts became a sovereign inspiration to those hymn compilers and writers whose songbooks provided great impetus to the eighteenth-century American music-printing trade. His influence is more subtle in twentieth-century popular music. The "old Doctor Watts songs," as they were called, affected black gospel music and its singers. Mahalia Jackson, for one, grew up on them. "You should hear those choirs in South Carolina and Georgia," she told Tony Heilbut, as he reported in *The Gospel Sound,* "they sing those hymns and tears run from my eyes. I just want to jump up and shout. Looks like I find myself when I hear them." Other black artists remember them as having shaped their own musical consciousness, leading Heilbut to believe that

by an obscure twist of cultural history that dour [Watts] hymn

> Father I stretch my hand to Thee
> No other help I know.
> If Thou withdraw Thyself from me
> Wither shall I go?

became an ancestor of the modern blues. Its mood of desolation and loss, of having tried the world and found it wanting, is in itself a kind of cosmic lament, while its simple metrical structure anticipates the 16-bar-blues, a form so common in gospel [music] that I call it the Gospel Blues.

Although his music was in the anthem tradition flowing from Byrd, Tallis, and Gibbons to court composers of the late Restoration and the new vitality of Handel's church music, William Tans'ur possessed little of Watts's genius for those after-sermon hymns that had become so appealing to English-speaking churchgoers. Yet he was the most reprinted British anthem writer to appear in late-eighteenth-century New England collections, as well as a singularly unrecognized contributor to American white gospel music. Born Tanser, in 1706, to a poor English laboring-class family, he varied the family name often, calling himself William le Tansur before finally settling on the spelling that adorned his best-known hymns. As a young man, he taught music, organized singing groups, played the organ, and published and sold a number of theoretical volumes that enjoyed numerous reprintings. America's first true songwriter–music publisher, William Billings, learned his music from Tans'ur, whose *Royal Melody Compleat,* in a Boston reprint edition, was the up-to-date instruction book of this ambitious twenty-two-year-old ready to make his mark on the world.

Watts's influence was most important to other British hymn writers, inspiring, among others, Philip Doddridge, Anne Steele, the first woman hymn writer, Stephen Stennett, and the Wesleys. Like his mentor, Doddridge refused assistance to prepare for the Anglican priesthood and received his education at a nonconformist academy. His writing was voluminous, including about 400 hymns published after his death. An invalid from childhood, Steele shunned all contact with the world after her fiancé died a day before their scheduled marriage. She wrote 144 hymns, 34 psalms, and 30 religious poems, which appeared first in 1760 under the pseudonym Theodosia. They found an immediate place in English and American hymnals. Stennett, a third-generation Baptist preacher, was one of the most influential pulpit speakers of his day. Londoners flocked to hear his sermons, and George III was a particular friend. Stennett's hymns in time became so inextricably woven into the pattern of Protestant church music in America that they eventually appeared in nineteenth-century Southern "shape note" collections, believed to be of true folk origin.

### The Wesleys and Their Followers

The first attempt to provide more felicitous musical literature for American worshippers came to an end with a grand-jury presentment against its compiler. John Wesley had been recruited by the Society for the Propagation of the Gospel in Foreign Parts to take the place of a recently deceased Georgia chaplain. As had his father, John studied for the ministry at Oxford, where with his younger brother Charles he became troubled by the state of the English church, particularly the lack of fervor demonstrated by its clergy. With others of similar sentiment, they formed Oxford's first Holy Club, dedicated to regular and frequent prayer and fasting, programed Bible study, and weekly Communion. They found themselves regarded with skeptical amusement by their teachers and more worldly fellow students, who called them "Bible moths" and "methodists" because of the disciplined religious program they followed.

In the late autumn of 1735, on board ship for America, the brothers discovered the intellectual appeal and emotional pull of church music performed by a group of twenty-six hymn-singing Moravian colonists, also bound for Georgia and hoping to establish a school for Creek and Cherokee Indians. The Moravians, descended from Bohemian followers of the revolutionary Jan Hus, were the latest group of Middle European Germans to seek religious freedom and economic opportunity in English America, a migration that had begun in 1608 with the recruiting of German and Polish glass blowers for Jamestown's first glass factory. Among the earliest to protest against Roman Catholic dogma and rule, the Moravians had been sustained through years of bloody persecution by a hymn tradition founded on secular music. The Wesleys were especially moved one evening when a storm threatened their vessel and they found comfort in the hymns of their new friends. The collection of music books John had brought to be used by his flock was increased by the gift from one Moravian of the newly published collection of 999 Moravian church songs, the *Gesangbuch der Gemeine in Herrnhut.*

The Wesleys' father, Samuel, was a hymn-writing cleric who often expressed his disdain for the "scandalous doggerel" of most Psalm translations, a judgment shared by his offspring. John brought to America the new Tate and Brady, Isaac Watts's *Hymns* and *Paraphrases of the Psalms of David,* and London's newest song collections, but the Moravian hymnal proved to be a revelation, firming John's belief that religious songs of human composure could and should be a principal arrow in his quiver. Almost at once be began to translate from the German, producing what the late-nineteenth-century hymnist W. Garrett Horder called "the finest translations in the English language, whilst they have the high honor of having opened to us the rich treasures of sacred song which Germany possesses."

Easygoing Georgians quickly recognized John and Charles Wesley as troublemakers when they sought to restrict admission to Holy Communion, insisted on the Baptist practice of adult baptism by full immersion, and argued that blacks, even though slaves, should be allowed to share in the church's blessings. Charles lasted only four months before returning to England, But John continued his ministry to Savannah's only church, finding time to become romantically attracted to the niece of the colony's chief magistrate and bailiff, who had higher ambitions for his ward and soon married her off to a more suitable colonist.

Late in 1736, John Wesley sent a collection of seventy hymns to Charles Town, South Carolina, for printing, using the services of Louis Timothy, a French Huguenot who had learned the trade in Franklin's Philadelphia shop, where he had exhibited such proficiency that the printer put up the money for Timothy's Carolina printing business for a half-share of profits. An educated man, Timothy also served as the first librarian of the lending library founded by Franklin and other young Philadelphia intellectuals. When Charles Town's previous printers died of the coastal fevers, Timothy moved his family and took over the abandoned press. He published the colony's first newspaper and did the sort of job printing Wesley required.

Half the hymns in Wesley's seventy-four-page octavo *Collection of Psalms and Hymns* were by Isaac Watts, five were translated from the Moravian by John, five were by his father, five by a younger brother, but none by Charles. Six of the songs were adapted from the early-seventeenth-century poet, musician, and rector George Herbert, who died while accompanying himself on the lute, singing his own hymns and anthems.

Having continued his suit of the now married Savannah belle, Wesley found himself being investigated by the colony's grand jury, an action instigated by the furious chief magistrate. He was charged with, among other things, having introduced "into the church and services of the Altar compositions and hymns not inspected or authorized by any proper judicature." Before any further action was taken, Wesley departed the New World. Only two copies of his hymnal exist today.

Once again in London, he pursued acquaintance with local Moravians, experiencing among them that "spiritual conversion" which shaped his future, an enlightenment Charles had undergone only a few days earlier. John spent the rest of his life in evangelistic work, preaching more than 40,000 sermons and traveling 200,000 miles, mostly on horseback. "Once in seven years I burn all my sermons," he wrote, "for it is a shame if I cannot write better sermons now than I did seven years ago." In fifty years of militant ministry among the poor, the dispossessed, and the downtrodden, John built British Methodism into an established church with over 70,000 members. Wesleyan Methodism brought about the nineteenth-century American evangelical revival, with its camp meetings and gospel songs, and led to the next century's white gospel music. Though he produced only twenty-seven original hymns and translations, John Wesley published sixty-four hymnbooks in fifty-three years of association with a remarkably prolific brother, author of 6,000 hymn texts.

"With that wonderful instinct for gauging the popular mind which was one element of his success," John Julian wrote in *A Dictionary of Hymnology,* Charles Wesley "saw at once that hymns might be utilized not only for raising the devotion, but also for instruction and establishing the faith of his disciples. He intended the hymns to be not only a constituent part of public worship, but they were also a kind of creed in verse."

Charles still lives in

> Jesu, lover of my soul,
> Let me to Thy bosom fly,
> While the nearer waters roll,
> While the tempest still is nigh;
> Hide me, O my Saviour, hide,
> Till the storm of life is past;
> Safe into the haven guide,
> O receive my soul at last

and the Christmas hymn

> Hark! all the welkin rings,
> 'Glory to the King of Kings.'
> Peace on earth and mercy mild
> God and sinners reconciled,

which his colleague George Whitefield altered to"Hark! the Herald Angels sing/'Glory to the new born King!' "
and

> 'Christ, the Lord, is risen today,'
> Son of man and angels say,

Raise your joys and triumph high,
Sing Ye Heavens, and earth reply.

Charles became a field missionary, preaching to all who would listen the militant message his brother also taught, but he never separated from the Anglican church and long regretted that John had done so. The pair worked together in compilation, editing, and the publication of a body of Protestant hymnody whose impact equaled that of Watts's works. Though the Watts songs won the devotion of nonconformist audiences almost at once, the Wesleys' work never achieved full acceptance among non-Methodist Americans until after 1794, the year "Jesus, lover of my soul" appeared for the first time in an American book, *Divine Hymns or Spiritual Songs,* by a Baptist minister of Brentwood, New Hampshire, Joshua Smith, whose compilation went through eleven editions before 1803. By that year, Methodist circuit-riding preachers were at work along the southern and western frontiers, joining Baptist and Presbyterian ministers in the vast revival movement, during which Charles Wesley's often anonymous but highly popular revivalistic songs rang out in wilderness clearings and rustic churches.

The Wesleys had an ear and a taste for good tunes that people liked, and they tied their messages of faith to them. Charles had many friends among the London theaters' musicians. The music for his *Twenty Four Hymns on the Great Festivals* (1764) was written by a German-born pit-band bassoonist, playhouse songwriter, opera composer, and Methodist convert, Johann Friedrich (later John Frederick) Lampe, who came to London in 1725 and found employment in theater orchestras, often playing for Handel. He married the soubrette Isabella Young, and was introduced to Wesley by the wife of Covent Garden's owner-manager, John Rich. Wesley borrowed one of Lampe's successful sheet-song tunes, "He comes! he comes! the hero comes!," written in 1739 to salute Admiral Vernon, fresh from his triumphs over the Spaniards, and made it "He comes! He comes! the Judge severe!" When this hymn entered frontier camp-meeting literature during the early nineteenth century, the evangelistic phrase "Roll, Jordan, roll" was added after each line, and it remained a Southern favorite, its secular roots and creator forgotten, as the white spiritual "Roll, Jordan, roll." On Lampe's death in 1751, Wesley was moved to write the mourning hymn "Tis done, the Sovereign's will's obeyed."

Wesley often found music for his hymns in melodies written for the musical theater and operatic arias, borrowing freely from Handel, Felice di Giardini, and other Europeans who came to London to provide Italian opera.

Only dimly recognized as a reminder of the influence Wesleyan Methodism exerted on the people of its time, the hymn "Amazing Grace" has found a place in American popular music far more important than that of any of the Watts or Wesley creations. Its writer, in the words he prepared for his graveyard marker:

John Newton, clerk,
Once an infidel and libertine,

A servant of slaves in Africa;
Was by the rich mercy of our Lord and Saviour
Preserved, restored and pardoned,
And appointed to preach the Faith
He labored long to destroy.

Eleven when his ship-captain father first took him to sea, in 1736, Newton served aboard a ship of the line after being impressed into the naval service. He deserted, was recaptured, flogged, and locked in prison, but he escaped to join the crew of an African slave trader. Eventually, he became captain of his own slave ship, and when death seemed near in 1748 after his waterlogged craft threatened to sink, he was reportedly inspired to write the words

Amazing grace, how sweet the sound,
That saved a wretch like me!
I once was lost, but now am found,
Was blind but now I see.

The experience brought him into contact with John Wesley, and with his encouragement he left the slave trade and began to preach, being ordained in the Episcopalian church. He served as curate in the small village of Olney in 1779, where the troubled poet William Cowper found relief from the turmoil of the asylum to which he had been temporarily committed. The two became friendly and worked on a collection of 348 hymns, which appeared in 1779 as *The Olney Hymns,* in three volumes and including ''Amazing Grace.'' Cowper's mental state worsened, and he contributed only sixty-seven of the hymns, Newton writing the remainder, some of which still remain in Methodist, Episcopalian, Baptist, and Congregational hymnals. The ''old African blasphemer,'' as Newton described himself, spent the last twenty-seven years of his life in London, preaching regularly until he was eighty and long blind.

George Pullen Jackson, in *White and Negro Spirituals,* described John Cennick as ''the real founder of folksy religious song in the rebellious 18th century movement,'' the Great Awakening of the 1740s. Leaving his work as a surveyor, Cennick joined John Wesley to study for the ministry. After a quarrel with the evangelist, Cennick joined those London Moravians who had inspired Wesley's conversion but were now his antagonists in matters of doctrinal interpretation. In the three volumes of hymn collections he published before 1755 was ''My Jesus all to Heaven is gone,'' according to Jackson ''one of the most widely sung religious lyrics among the country folks of America during the entire 200 years which have passed since it appeared.''

Others in the Wesley circle whose work continues in use include Augustus Montague Toplady, writer of ''Rock of Ages,'' and Edward Perronet, author of ''All hail the power of Jesus' name,'' both of whom broke with John Wesley to become bitter theological enemies. Toplady was converted to Methodism while a Trinity College, Dublin, student and was ordained in the Anglican church with Wesley's blessings. In his thirties he became an outspoken critic of Wesleyan Methodism, and wrote many tracts against it, including a piece in which he argued the statistical impossibility of man's debt to God ever being paid, except by the blood of the Crucifixion, which was anathema to the Wesleys. The Perronet family went to England from Switzerland as Huguenot refugees in 1680, and Edward's father was an Anglican vicar and a close friend of the Wesleys. Incurring John's wrath because of a poetic satire of the established church, young Perronet was removed from his post as leader of the Huntingdon Chapel in Canterbury and, like Toplady, ostracized. "All hail the power of Jesus' name" first appeared in the November 1779 issue of *Gospel Magazine,* edited by Toplady, and went through numerous revisions before it found its present form. Several musical settings have been used, the best known is by Perronet's close friend William Shrubsole.

## America's First Great and General Awakening

While New Englanders were getting their first taste of hellfire-raising evangelism from George Whitefield, the region's religious leaders were in the continuing throes of an agonizing theological ferment. The Puritan power structure that had shaped secular life for nearly a century had lost its dominance over most churchgoers, and narrow and old-style Calvinists like Cotton Mather watched their conservative hold being shaken. Salem's witchcraft hysteria in the 1690s, for which many blamed the Mather family, had eroded their popularity and "broad and catholick" Boston liberals installed the broad-minded Benjamin Colman, an admirer of Isaac Watts, in their Brattle Square Church. A Mather was deposed from the family's traditional post as Harvard's president, replaced by a Brattle Square Church layman. Conservatives now looked to the newly formed Yale College as the training place for new clerisy to support them against the liberal assault. Although the Brattle Square congregation's enlightenment did not extend to Watts hymns or the use of a church organ, it was in the forefront of the progressives' battle to change the quality of worship by the introduction of the "new way" of singing, since even in those places where Watts had been grudgingly accepted his hymns were lined out.

In 1728, Yale graduate Jonathan Edwards left the New York Scotch Presbyterian flock that had called him at the age of eighteen and joined his grandfather in ministry to a western Massachusetts congregation. Eighty-four-year-old Solomon Stoddard was seemingly ageless in his fervid determination to save the foundering church by innovative preaching and order of worship. Dedicated to the new way in church singing, he trained his parishioners to read musical notation, leaving behind the "rote," which relied on precentors' failing memories.

When his grandfather died, Edwards took over the church and became the Massachusetts frontier's leading clergyman. Following the pattern Stoddard had set, his services "abounded in singing," and worship at the Northhampton church became "greatly enlivened," he wrote, as people sang "with unusual elevation of heart and voice." Rarely leaving his church except for special invitations to Boston, Edwards delivered sermons that denounced the new philosophies offering man that easier way to salvation, the gift given through Christ's death for man's sins, soon to be propounded by the Wesleys. Beginning with the young, he offered the familiar Puritan doctrine of redemption only for the predestined select new England saints, but he declaimed it in a manner that personalized it for each of his listeners. The new generation flocked to Northampton, ready to be castigated for its failings and then admitted to a conversion that guaranteed salvation. So great were the processions of the penitent that the church fathers financed a new edifice, twice the size of the old. Ministers as far south as the Middle Colonies marveled at the wonders performed by Edwards, and a pamphlet recounting "the surprising work of God in the conversion of many hundred souls in Northampton" startled Boston's clerisy and inspired Colman, who hoped for a a similar local counterattack on the devil, to write to the famous British evangelist George Whitefield, who was then in Georgia on a fund-raising tour on behalf of an orphanage he had established there.

Whereas Edwards was a dignified theologian who committed his themes to paper and delivered them politely but firmly to his listeners, Whitefield was an improvising actor who roared out the terrors of hell and then spoke of Christ's grace in a lover's whisper. Lord Chesterfield said that men would weep when he spoke the name Mesopotamia, and actor David Garrick envied the preacher his declamatory art. A tavern keeper's son who once served spirituous liquors to his parent's customers, Whitefield made his way to Oxford, to receive the education that never got in his way. At the university he became one of the Wesleys' crowd, joining their Holy Club and in time following them to Georgia, where he arrived just after John's hurried departure. Methodism's seeming intractability—Wesley had forbidden women to come to church in expensive clothing and persuaded Oglethorpe to ban Sunday fishing and hunting—had cooled Georgians to the Wesleyan brand of Anglicanism, and Whitefield returned to England to be ordained a Church of England priest. The cathedral pulpit he would have enjoyed was not available, and a small parish church offered an uninspiring prospect. So Whitefield began to preach in open fields to great gatherings of coal miners and other economically depressed groups. His voice boomed out over thousands as he talked of private conversations with God, watching "white gutters made by their tears" appear on the cheeks of his unwashed audiences, or prayed over the "mad shoutings and tearings off of garments" that characterized his evangelizing revivals until his death.

Whitefield was twenty-six in the late summer of 1740 when he arrived in Boston, on Colman's invitation, ready to start a "great and general awakening." In his baggage were Watts's *Hymns* and the Wesleys' *Hymns and Sacred Songs,* recently published in England, both of which were passed out to the New England clergy, who soon came to marvel as their hidebound parishioners were won over. During the previous year, Whitefield, who spoke no German, converted Germans who spoke no English. Later, he was able to move Franklin, who preached the gospel "a penny saved is a penny earned," to empty his pockets into the collection plate when he had intended to drop only a small coin.

The visiting spellbinder's weekly schedule of forty hours of preaching was set aside as he prayed, spoke, and sermonized in and outside Boston churches: on the Common to 5,000, to a crowded First Church and then afterward outside to the 8,000 who could not gain admittance. When he returned from a brief trip to the back country, 30,000 Bostonians welcomed him. "The reason congregations have been so dead," he stated pompously before his final departure, "is because dead men preach to them," a nose-tweaking that gained him little friendship from the intellectual Boston Congregationalists and Anglicans, who found his posturing excessive.

When he left for home, by way of New York, Whitefield sent Edwards a farewell present of some "man made" hymns by Isaac Watts. Northampton promptly took them to its heart and "sang nothing else, and neglected the Psalms wholly," said Edwards. Though he "disliked not their making some use of the hymns," he "liked not their setting aside of the Psalms." He established a compromise. Watts's texts were permitted only at the end of the afternoon service, the Psalms being sung during the rest of each Sunday's worship.

Annoyed with his presumption, Yale blamed its alumnus for the Whitefield vogue, leading Edwards to accept a call from the new Scotch Presbyterian College of New Jersey, later Princeton, and become its president, but complications following a smallpox infection carried him off before he could assume office.

A band of lesser religious spellbinders soon appeared, some of them later judged to be mentally disturbed, and the enthusiasm for revival preaching subsided. In 1744, Harvard rescinded the enthusiastic welcome it had accorded Whitefield by coming out in public opposition to his ministry.

That magnetic preacher was now above such petty annoyances, and he made five more tours of American cities before a final one in 1770, during which he died in Newburyport. His visits gave churchgoing America "its first taste of the theatre under the flag of salvation," according to Ola Elizabeth Winslow in her biography of Edwards. The Watts and Wesley hymnals he distributed promoted their popularity among worshipers who had grown dissatisfied with the solemnity of metrical Psalms and hoped to see Jesus through eyes more sophisticated than those of their forebears. In 1753, Whitefield had compiled his own hymnal, for use in the London Tabernacle, built for him, and introduced it to the colonies on one of his visits.

Many Presbyterians continued to resist these man-made hymns. This, and other differences, led to a split that divided the denomination into "old side" and "new side" members. The old preferred to stay with the traditional Singing Psalms; the new placed their faith in the Tate and Brady and the Watts. It was not until 1831 that an official Presbyterian hymnal satisfactory to both sides appeared. Until then, an observer wrote, the imitation of the "braying of asses, rather than the divine melody so often recommended in Scripture" characterized most old Presbyterian flocks.

The Scottish Ulstermen who settled in the Middle Colonies back country during the 1740s had twice been transplanted from traditional Presbyterianism's somber environment. Their recently settled communities, stretching down to the Georgia hills and into the Alleghenies, presented a nagging challenge to some progressive churchmen, who determined to create their own great awakening. Many native-born missionaries now dispatched to work among the new Amer-

icans were graduates of the "Log College" at Neshaminy, Pennsylvania, begun about 1726 to train revivalist preachers and teachers. Samuel Davies, one
of the new breed, was dispatched to Virginia's western counties and rapidly
attracted communicants because of his talent for verse making and special gift
for pulpit oratory, upon which Patrick Henry modeled his own not inconse-
quential abilities. Following Davies's discovery that amiable religious songs attracted more celebrants than the old liturgy, he introduced Watts hymnals to
both white and black worshipers. From the start, he had extended his ministry
to blacks, recommending to slaveowners the Christian's obligation "to propagate religion among the Heathen." Though they were segregated in Virginia's
churches, blacks held their own in singing the Watts songs from hymnals provided by affluent northern Presbyterians in response to Davies's pleas. Shortly
after he left Virginia, in 1753, at the age of thirty, to succeed Edwards as president of Princeton, Davies wrote: "I can hardly express the pleasure it affords
me to turn to that part of the gallery where they sit and see so many of them
with the Psalm or Hymn Books, assisting their fellows who are beginners, to
find the place, and then breaking all away out in a torrent of sacred harmony,
enough to bear the whole congregation to Heaven."

Other denominations also extended their missionary work to the frontier, attending to the salvation of both white and black. SPG Anglicans attempted to
bring both races "speedily to offer praise to God" by the introduction of hymn
singing.

The first changes in American Anglican music came about more than 200
years after Henry VIII's war with Rome. As had the Puritans who separated
from them, American Anglicans continued to sing from printed psalters. Until
the Revolution, the American branch of the Church of England was supervised
by the bishop of London, who never troubled to appoint an American bishop
to assist him in that duty. For eighty years, the SPG was the church's sole missionary arm, seeking to attract and convert colonials to a faith that, as the symbol of a ruler responsible for their economic and social discontent, daily grew
less attractive. Only a relatively small number of Americans subscribed to the
sect, among them George Washington and at least two-thirds of the Declaration
of Independence's signers, a breach of taste forgiven them, in the interests of
the public good, by the vast majority. Fashionable churches, supported by prosperous and influential Anglicans, were among the first to use church organs and
steeple bells. In 1727, St. Philip's, in Charles Town in the Carolinas, imported
the organ used in the coronation ceremonies for George II. Christ Church, in
Philadelphia, purchased its first organ in 1728; New York's Trinity commissioned the building of one in 1738. Bruton Parish Church, in Williamsburg,
used a chamber organ during the late 1740s and installed a permanent one fourteen years later. The first chime of bells was installed in Boston's Christ Church
in 1745, Paul Revere being among those hired to ring the changes. St. Michael's in Charles Town installed a heavier peal of bells some twenty years
later; it was taken from the colonies by Loyalist Anglicans who accompanied
evacuating British troops in 1782. Only after Boston's Congregational churches
finally accepted the organ did the city's oldest church, the Old Brick, where

once Cotton Mather preached, decide to install one, in spite of the resistance of its minister, Dr. Nathaniel Chauncey. He was the enlightened liberal cleric who had, a half-century earlier, chided conservatives for fighting the trend to "regular singing." In May 1785, he preached a farewell sermon and told the church members that it would not be long before he was in his grave and that he knew an organ would be installed before his head was cold.

American Anglicans played a major part in the development of the nation's musical life, beginning with their employment of skilled Europeans to provide suitable music for worship. One of the earliest was Charles Theodore Pachelbel, distant relative of J. S. Bach and son of the Nuremberg organist-composer Johann Pachelbel, whose "Canon" was taken to heart by middle-of-the-road radio programers in the late 1970s. He arrived in Boston in 1732, aged forty-three, soon after the mezzotint engraver and music and dance instructor Peter Pelham presented one of that city's early concerts in the great room of his residence. The German music master struck up a friendship with Pelham's talented eleven-year-old son, and began teaching him and other Boston children the harpsichord, guitar, and other simple instruments.

Between 1729 and 1731, the Anglican cleric and philosopher George Berkeley lived in Rhode Island, raising funds and planning for the construction of an Indian school on the island of Bermuda. His sermons were popular with worshipers at Newport's Trinity Church, attracting people from distant points every Sunday. The new town of Berkeley named itself in his honor, and, on his return to London, the now Bishop Berkeley sent them a new church organ, the largest imported during the eighteenth century. Berkeley's residents would have nothing to do with the popish device, begging the bishop to send it elsewhere. He gave it to Trinity, whose wardens hired Pachelbel to supervise the installation. Young Peter Pelham went with the musician, and the pair gave music lessons while the organ was being set up. Newport was not a place for a musician of Pachelbel's temperament to earn a living, as his successor, a British organist, learned. "The want of instruments," he wrote, "together with the nigardliness of people of this place, and their not having a taste for music render it impossible for anyone of my profession to get a competent maintainance here . . . it is no better than burying one's self alive."

Eventually, Pachelbel and young Pelham moved to New York, giving a concert there in January 1736 in the home of a local wine dealer, charging four shillings for a program of songs and instrumental music. The following year, Pachelbel turned up in Charles Town, drawn there by reports of the community's enlightened interest in the arts and music. He introduced the traditional European observance of St. Cecilia's Day on November 22, 1737, with a benefit concert in the city's new theater, and, following custom, composed a cantata in honor of music's patron saint. Until his death, and despite increasing rheumatism of the hands, Pachelbel remained St. Peter's organist, even though lightning twice seriously damaged the imported instrument.

Peter Pelham, Jr., turned up in Boston in early 1743 and announced his services as a music teacher, having "served nine years under the tuition of an accomplished professor of the art of music." His father had married the widow of an Irish tobacco dealer named Copley, whose six-year-old son, John Single-ton, was already surprising his London-trained artist stepfather with signs of budding genius. Young Pelham's credentials impressed the wardens of Bos-ton's new Trinity Church sufficiently to engage him as music master and first organist. Sometime after 1759, he left for Virginia, where he became regular organist at Williamsburg's Bruton, playing on its portable chamber organ in lieu of the great instruments he had known. For four decades, he served Bru-ton, supplementing an annual salary that ranged from sixty to seventy-five pounds by taking on all the odd chores available to the era's music masters. As an important figure in the region's cultural life, he taught music, sold instruments, concertized, wrote music for religious and social occasions, and, when wan-dering troupes of British actors passed through, conducted the pit orchestras in performances of London musicals. As prices rose, Williamsburg authorities, rather than raise his salary, increased his duties. Pelham was committee clerk in the House of Burgesses, director of currency printing, and, during the Revolution, keeper of the local jail, a post that came to an abrupt end when some British prisoners of war escaped while in his charge. Pelham died in 1802, blind and forgotten, in his daughter's Richmond home. However, during the forty-five years he had performed as organist in Virginia's capital city, he was the com-munity's chief professional musician and introduced many of the Founding Fa-thers, among them Washington and Jefferson, to the delights of music by Han-del, Boyce, Greene, Corelli, Arnold, Vivaldi, Purcell, and his teacher and friend, Charles Theodore Pachelbel.

The tradition of Chapel Royal boys was introduced in American Anglican, or Episcopal, churches by immigrant musicians who organized and taught such choirs. The first was in New York's Trinity Church, early in the century; the second, at Philadelphia's Christ Church, sometime in the early 1760s. In 1764, the choir sang from a new hymnal, *A Collection of Psalm Tunes,* compiled by Francis Hopkinson, later secretary of the Navy, vestryman and church warden, and self-proclaimed "first native of the United States who produced a musical composition." The collection contained some original pieces by him, which were usually performed whenever he substituted for the official church organist.

After Britain's loss of the colonies, the Anglican church in America was re-garded as "a church in ruins," a fact its generally highly placed members rarely bothered to acknowledge. Sophisticated foreign visitors marveled at the Sunday-morning church spectacle, the Marquis de Chastellux writing of a 1781 visit to Philadelphia:

> the services of the English church appeared to me a sort of *opera,* as well for the music as the decorations, a handsome pulpit, placed before a handsome organ; a handsome minister in that pulpit, reading, speaking and singing with a grace en-tirely threatrical; a soft and agreeable vocal music, with excellent sonatas, played alternately on the organ; all this, compared to the Quakers, the Anabaptists, the Presbyterians, etc., appeared to me rather like a little paradise itself, than as the road to it.

In 1786, an assembly of Episcopalian clerics and laymen made the first meaningful effort to get the church back to its business of salvation with the formation of the Protestant Episcopal church of the United States, effectively removing from its name any English connection. A committee assembled a proposed *Book of Common Prayer,* edited by Hopkinson, which waited until the next century for acceptance, a period during which organizational and missionary skills restored the denomination to much of its former glory.

The eighteenth century ended with the United States on the eve of another great awakening, one profoundly rooted in the verses of Watts, the Wesleys, and other British and American hymnists. Their man-made hymns had become the first true American popular song, the music of the people, sung at work and play and rendered unto God of a Sunday. As had its British predecessor, America's first true music business grew from an ingrained desire on men's part to sing praise to their God in a language they could comprehend and from the determination of their teachers to improve the way in which that music was sung.

# CHAPTER 18

# The Business of Music Publishing

### The Americans Learn to Sing

The first *Bay Psalm Book,* with thirteen melodies in printed notation harmonized for two voices and based on John Playford's *Introduction to the Skill of Music,* was available to Bostonians in Michael Perry's bookstore, where in 1698 could also be found imported psalters and music books printed from metal type or engraved plates, with which the crude wood-block publications of the Cambridge press contrasted poorly. Four generations had grown since the 1620 landfall off Plymouth, during which time many vaguely remembered French and Dutch Ainsworth tunes had almost disappeared, moved into limbo by more singable popular tunes. Such encroachment of those "darling songs" into the liturgy was not an American phenomenon, nor did it stem, as often deplored by the Puritan clerisy, from a new generation's predilection for "idle, yea, foolish and pernicious songs." There reposes in the British Museum a copy of the 1642 edition of William Slayter's *Psalmes, or Songs of Sion,* in whose margins an unknown owner indicated suitable and favorite ballad substitute tunes for the several psalms, at least one of them, "Walsingham," from a bawdy stage jigg.

American traditionalists were disturbed not only by these trespassing melodies, but by the very quality of church singing, which jarred on the ears of trained singers. Congregations had not yet assembled the choirs that were a nineteenth-century American glory. Harvard, the New England ministry's earliest incubator, did provide musical training of a sort some years after its founding. In 1700, the college library still housed graduate theses, some of which contained "tunes with directions for singing by note." All of them were soon after destroyed in a fire.

Two Boston bookstores, Perry's and that owned by Samuel Gerrish, stocked Morley's and Playford's instruction books, and the latter's *Whole Book of Psalms,* the best known and most popular work of its kind at the time. All three could be found in many private libraries. One of these was owned by Samuel Sewall, a wealthy mackerel shipper and money lender, and future chief justice of Massachusetts. He was fond of music and occasionally wrote a broadside ballad to celebrate some special event. That interest qualified him to serve for twenty-four years as the South Church's lining-out deacon, but even he found himself often intending one melody but falling into another, going into a "key much too high," or setting one melody but carrying on "irresistably" into another.

For a decade, Cotton Mather complained that the psalmody in his newly built all-brick First Church, just west of the State House, was "of a variety and regularity inferior," making a note in his diary in 1721 to do something about it. Consistently, he was against any change in worship, being one of the group of clergymen who opposed installation of an organ in the Brattle Square King's Chapel and making no secret of his pleasure when the instrument failed to attract new converts. Though he enjoyed Watts's hymns in the home, he insisted that they had no place in church.

A few months after his resolution to do something, Mather released *The Accomplished Singer,* a pamphlet intended to "preserve Regular Singing in the assemblies of the faithful." This brochure served as a promotional device for Samuel Gerrish, who published it and was about to issue some others dealing with the same subject written by three Harvard-trained ministers. Whether it was orchestrated or not, Gerrish's advertising and promotional campaign was as effective as any contemporary music-merchandising program.

Gerrish's shop, near Brick Church, was a favorite meeting place for bibliophiles. He was also extremely well placed in local society, having married Samuel Sewall's daughter after his first wife was killed in an Indian raid. He had published all of Cotton Mather's works, as well as those of Thomas Prince and other Bay Colony intellectuals. An astute merchandiser, he introduced book auctions to America, holding them in the Long Wharf's coffeehouse.

Soon after Harvard-trained Reverend Thomas Symmes preached a sermon dealing with A.R.S.es, or Anti-Regular Singers, at his rural church north of the city, with such success that he was invited to deliver it from urban pulpits, Gerrish brought out *The Reasonableness of Regular Singing or Singing by Note.* It had been written by Symmes under the pseudonym Philomusicus and reminded its readers that New England psalm singing had so deteriorated that it would soon dissappear if the old proficiencies were not restored.

In January of 1721, Gerrish advertised an anonymously written "small book containing 20 Psalm Tunes, with directions how to sing them, contrived in the most easy method ever yet invented, for the ease of listeners, whereby even children or people of the meanest capacities, may come to sing them by rule, may serve as an introduction to a more Compleat Treatise of Singing, which will speedily be published." This first American music instruction book, which led to the revival of singing and the training of many eighteenth-century Americans, was the work of the second of a trio of Harvard ministers who were determined to do that "something" contemplated by Mather. He was John Tufts, pastor of the Newbury church from the age of twenty-five, in 1714. His "new and easie" method used letters instead of notes: *F S L M* for *fa sol la mi,* printed on a staff, with rhythm indicated by dots. Tufts borrowed the notation from the

1698 *Bay Psalm Book,* where it was printed under the appropriate notes, and had been used by John Day in his late-sixteenth-century editions of the Singing Psalms. Symmes regarded it as far more comprehensible than the solmization serving Western man since Guido d'Arezzo devised it in the eleventh century. The book sold out, and within four months Gerrish was advertising a new edition, with eight more psalm tunes, selling for sixpence a copy and five shillings per dozen. Tufts's name as compiler was still not indicated.

The name of Cotton Mather's well-known nephew Thomas Walter, Harvard 1713, assistant pastor in Roxbury, and the last of the trio engaged in promoting "the new way," was prominent in the subscription list being circulated around Boston in early 1721 for the "more compleat Treatise of Singing" promised in Gerrish's advertising. John Franklin's printing shop turned out the work, *Grounds and Rules for Music Explained,* with the help of young Benjamin his apprentice. Walter's book was printed from engraved plates, among the earliest known to have been made and used in Boston, and almost certainly cut by the London engraver Francis Dewing, who had arrived in 1717 equipped with a copperplate printing press. Far more expensive than Symmes's pamphlet, Walter's *Grounds and Rules* went for four shillings a copy. Its Recommendatory Preface was signed by the Mathers and a dozen other prestigious clergymen, followed by a text explaining note reading. The final section contained a number of well-known psalm tunes, printed for the first time in America in three-part settings, in the typical British lozenge-shaped notation, with bar lines, another American first.

Walter's new settings won great popularity, and a Society for Promoting Regular Singing was formed. In March 1722, Walter was the featured speaker at a Thursday-afternoon concert by a chorus of ninety persons. His pulpit talk was immediately published by Gerrish, and was joined on the shelves in October by a second edition, printed "in a fold suitable to bind with Psalm-books." In all, his manual went through eight editions, the last in 1764, long after the author's untimely death in 1724, mourned as the passing of a "true New England genius."

## The Singing-School Movement Is Born

Despite complaints from "guardians of the past," a singing-school movement was soon fully under way. Beginning at Boston's Brick Church, the movement spread around the Bay area, its primers either the Tufts or the Walter. Two or three evenings a week, from half past five until after seven, young people met for instruction by some talented musician and singer, engaged by church officials. Tufts and Walter appeared frequently at such sessions, arguing the case for regular singing and ridiculing its opponents. In early 1723, Gerrish added to the attack with *Utile Dolci* by Philomusicus, now identified as Thomas Symmes, a "Joco-Serious Dialogue concerning regular singing." In it the writer enumerated the charges against the new method, which had been labeled "Quakerish . . . popish . . . bawdy, yea, blasphemous," and a scheme to make money for Samuel Gerrish, which it certainly had accomplished. Symmes called attention to those "comical objections" that stated that Puritan ancestors had got to heaven without knowing how to read music and that predicted that the singing-school movement would encourage the young to stay out late at night, which they did, and so fall into the company of "lewd and loose" persons. To demolish these arguments, Symmes concluded, in a witty exposition of his cause, that "music is as real and lawful and ingenious an art" as reading, writing, or cyphering, and predicted that musical training "would divert young people . . . from learning idle, foolish, yea, pernicious songs and ballads."

The rote versus note controversy daily grew more heated, sermons and pamphlets appearing in quantity both pro and con. The Braintree church, built where Thomas Morton had danced and frisked "and worse" with Indian women a hundred years earlier, suspended members until they promised to behave and sing by rote rather than the new way. Cotton Mather lamented to an English friend that the back-country Puritans were calling innovations in music training the bringing in of popery and the worshiping of the devil. The public argument was, as differences over quality and taste have ever been, of most value to the publishers and book and newspaper dealers. With the Reverend Tufts now a public personality, Gerrish brought out new editions of the singing book, featuring his name and increasing the number of tunes written in letters instead of notes, printed from engraved copperplates and selling at a higher price. Because he had come into open conflict in the pages of his newspaper with members of the Boston intellectual and clerical establishment, John Franklin was no longer favored with Gerrish's printing work. As evidence of the strides already made by singing-school scholars, the later editions were printed by others with music in three parts. Irving Lowens writes in *Music and Musicians in Early America:* "Just how good a judge of music [Tufts] was is evident from the fact that no less than 18 of the 37 selections (appearing in the last six editions 1728–1744) have remained in common use until contemporary times. The musical influence exerted by the tunes in the *Introduction* until later 18th-century American collections has not been fully appreciated; there is no tune supplement published before the Revolutionary War which does not bear, to some degree, the impress of Tufts' musical tastes." Lowens also concludes that Tufts "may well have a valid claim to be considered the first American composer, as well as the author of the first American music textbook" because "no English publication of [some of the] . . . tune[s], either before or after the appearance of the *Introduction,* is known."

Despite the scorn of their elders, young people in rural areas met two or three evenings a week at some central location, usually a tavern, with a portable writing desk that could hold a candle, one of Gerrish's music textbooks, and manuscript paper, also available at his store. After studying music from either the Tufts or Walter manual, demonstrated for them by a singing master, they often ended the evening with a sermon delivered by an enlightened minister who favored regular singing. The Reverend Nathanial Chauncey, of New London, once praised this pursuit of education in words that twentieth-century arbiters of taste might take to heart: "As old men are not always wise, so young men are not always fools. They are generally more free from prejudices than elderly people, their present age disposes them to mirth, and it should be a very joyful and acceptable thing unto elderly people to see them forward to improve their mirth according to scripture directions.''

There had been a singing school of sorts in Boston prior to 1714, some years before Gerrish began publishing music, but Virginians had been learning their music from itinerant masters as early as 1710. William Byrd II, son of a slave-trading land speculator who acquired vast holdings and helped to build William and Mary College, got his business training in London, where he discovered the pleasures of the musical playhouse. One afternoon before Christmas 1710, he bought two music training manuals from a traveling musician and began to teach himself, his wife, and their two sons the new way of singing psalms, probably from a later edition of the Playford psalter. Other Virginia planters and their families learned two-, three-, and four-part singing as a social grace, benefiting whenever they could from the temporary presence of traveling musicians.

Because of smaller distances, the spread of community singing schools was more easily accomplished in New England. There, pupils learned to copy music and words from printed books, or sometimes from a piece written by a master or an advanced fellow student. The music was not always religious in nature, nor the evening always on a high plane. Though it was written later in the century, a Yale student's letter to a friend at home reported the temptations existing: "At present I have no inclination for anything for I am almost sick of the world & were it not for the hopes of going to a singing meeting tonight and indulging myself a little in some of the carnal pleasures of the flesh, such as kissing & squeezing, I would be willing to leave it now.''

On the season's last evening, the master sold music books and supplies to the graduates, and directed them in a "singing lecture," a concert for friends and families. Having learned all they could be taught, the best singers banded into singing groups, eventually earning a place in the first seats of the church gallery to lead the psalm singing. In time, they formed themselves into America's first church choirs, spelling the final doom of lining out.

Tufts and Walter ruled supreme in the American singing school until mid-century, when the church anthem, a sacred choral composition that had become an essential part of Anglican worship, was made known to American musicians and singing teachers by imported British music books. The most accomplished singing-school graduates found the anthems exceedingly rewarding music to learn and perform. During the 1750s, several American publications designed for singing schools went on sale that contained references to "anthem" pieces, though no true anthems were included. The most gifted music engraver to appear before the Revolution, James A. Turner, of Boston, cut a sixteen-page tune supplement and a page of music instruction to be attached to the reprinted edition of John Barnard's British 1641 collection of *Selected Church Musick*. Sometime prior to 1760, the writing schoolmaster William Dawson collected tunes used in Philadelphia churches and published *Youth's Entertaining Amusement or a Plain Guide to Psalmody*. Boston's first professional organ builder, Thomas Johnston, engraved a similar instruction book and tune collection. A skilled etcher and ornamental painter, Johnston was a paid soloist in the King's Chapel, where he built and installed an organ whose echo was the envy of most other Boston churches. South Carolina woodworker Jonathan Badger, who was in love with music, compiled and issued, from engraved copperplates, the 1752 *Collection of Best Psalm and Hymn Tunes,* the first of its kind in the South. After assembling a chamber organ for his own amusement, he began to build instruments for others, advertising their sale in local newspapers, and in 1755 he opened a singing school for "plain psalmody."

The same small group of seventy-four melodies was constantly duplicated in these collections, to which were soon added ones influenced by the more ornate modern anthems inspired by Italian opera music and Handel's religious works. But it was William Tans'ur's *Royal Melody Compleat* (1755) and the 1763 *Universal Psalmodist* by Aaron Williams that were the most influential books of their kind in America and the most frequently plundered by subsequent New England compilers and music publishers.

In New York, interested young musicians finally heard Handel's *Messiah* in 1770, when William Tuckey introduced its overture and some fifteen excerpts, two years before the work was performed in Germany. Leaving his post as Bath Cathedral's director of choral music, Tuckey came to America and found employment in Trinity Church as a clerk in 1753. He taught singing to the church's Charity School pupils and added to a small income by giving lessons in adult evening classes. Until his death in 1781, he subsisted on income from playing the organ, teaching the harpsichord, organizing church choirs, composing music to order, and producing concerts of his own works and those of colleagues. Because booksellers would not publish his music, he issued his own sacred anthems and choral music, financing the printing by subscription and selling it through local dealers and agents in Baltimore, Annapolis, and Charles Town.

For the majority of its students, the singing school had become the common man's social club, his amateur theater, and the only place where one could mix a seeming pursuit of religious obligation with personal pleasure, a benefaction usually reserved to the rich. Boston tradesmen had their own club, complete with officers and regular dues, which met weekly for instruction. A Philadelphia school had to limit attendance to students and family in order to keep away curiosity seekers looking for free entertainment. For the first time, aspiring soloists performed for the delight of friends and neighbors, and then graduated to a place near the pulpit in the first church choirs. Hopeful composers and songwriters learned in these schools how to copy music and how to put down on paper their own notes, and were able to offer them for performance. With no other place in which an American could receive basic music training, other than from the itinerant professors affordable only to the wealthy, virtually every tunebook compiler of the late eighteenth century was a singing-school graduate, became a professional singing master to earn a living, and then became a music publisher to promote his own music. There were exceptions, but they came late in the century.

There were also many, more pragmatic, Americans who, in this era of rising political ambitions, used the singing school as the arena in which they learned how to move men. A widely proclaimed "master in vocal music," Samuel Adams used his splendid singing voice to further a political career. A failure by middle age, having been church deacon, garbage collector, tax collector, and bankrupt brewer, Adams harnessed communal singing and became a principal architect of New England's revolt against George III. He organized singing schools for Boston's workingmen, there embracing "such opportunities for inculcating sedition, till it had ripened into rebellion. His power over weak minds was surprising," a bitter political rival said on leaving Boston in 1776 for exile.

Others saw profit to be made in the full-time operation of big-city singing schools as commercial ventures, their major support and articles of conduct subscribed to by parents and pupils before admission. Unlike church-supported training for the improvement of singing, or those transient rural academies organized by musician teachers that drew locals to the only place of public entertainment available, the urban singing school served as a social center for the young, providing them with an occasionally annoying but necessary cultural asset.

Some forty years after Samuel Gerrish flooded the New England market with instruction books and psalmody, a singing-school graduate and divinity student named James Lyon, assembled and published the first significant American collection of new Protestant church music to contain native music, including six works by its editor. In its 198 pages of music and 12 of instruction, *Urania, or a Choice Collection of Psalm-tunes, Anthems and Hymns* (1762) provided modern music of the kind with which British composers were changing hymnody in the Church of England. The volume also contained the first American printing of the melody for "America," or "My country, 'tis of thee," which had been used for one of Whitefield's own evangelistic songs, "Come, Thou almighty King." The British national anthem, "God Save the King," was not heard in the colonies until 1769, when William Tuckey ended a benefit concert with the song, as was the practice in London's concert rooms and theaters.

Lyon was born in Newark, New Jersey, in 1735, and attended the College of New Jersey at Princeton, where his classmate Francis Hopkinson, of Philadelphia, was something of a rarity, having been taught music by a private tutor. Formal music training was unknown at Princeton or in the handful of similar institutions in existence by 1760. Even as late as 1783, Yale students had only flute accompaniment when they sang in chapel. In spite of the differences between them, Lyon and Hopkinson wrote and performed music for school activities, including commencement odes, musical entertainments, and a production of Thomas Arne's London hit *Alfred,* to which "Rule Britannia" was the rousing musical finale. While still at Princeton, Lyon was already at work on his giant *Urania,* writing "the plainest and most necessary rules of psalmody," and arranging music by British writers John Arnold, William Knapp, James Green, and the recently arrived Tuckey, as well as some by his classmate Hopkinson. When no Philadelphia book dealer would finance a work of the size and proportions Lyon proposed, the young student was obliged to pay for the printing by soliciting subscriptions, one dollar in advance and another on delivery. He called on affluent Philadelphians, wrote to clergymen detailing his scheme to improve and spread "the Art of Psalmody in its Perfection" throughout the colonies, and advertised a proposal to finance the venture.

William Bradford, grandson of Pennsylvania's first printer and an active bookseller, binder, and stationer, would not put Lyon's manuscript on press before he was paid. With almost $200 on hand from subscribers, Lyon placed a public notice, advising that engraver and printer had now begun work. In late 1761, subscribers got their copies of the compilation. A second edition appeared in 1767, and the third in 1773, when Lyon was in Machias, Maine, eking out a living as minister to the local Presbyterian flock. Ordained in 1764, he had first been sent to Nova Scotia and some years later moved his family to Maine, where he died, still owed his annual salary of forty-eight pounds. At one time, his pay was almost ten years in arrears, and he was forced to subsist on fish he caught in the local bay's icy waters.

The formula used in *Urania,* patching and pasting from British tune books, becoming easily available in American bookshops, and then raisining them with native American music, appealed to Josiah Flagg, boyhood friend and close neighbor of Paul Revere. As teen-agers they had been bell-ringers at Christ Church. Although Revere never had a true ear for music, Flagg was a more than competent amateur. The two spent the last half of 1763 working on a music book after their families were stricken during one of the smallpox epidemics that plagued Boston regularly. Times were bad, and Revere had taken up copperplate engraving, in which he was never brilliant, to increase his income. The plague had almost put an end to trade in Flagg's jewelry store and reduced the sale of Revere's silverwork, so they spent their considerable free time on the music book, Flagg setting the tunes and including a few of his own, Revere engraving the music plates. The following February, their *Collection of the Best Psalm Tunes* went on sale, an eighty-page book, the largest yet issued in New England and containing hymns and anthems, "the greatest part of which never before printed in America." Lyon's *Urania* was cited as one of the compilation's important sources. Flagg also made much of the fact that New England–made paper, from one of Massachusetts' few mills, was used. In an appeal to "buy American" during a period when the stamp taxes were plaguing native manufacture, the publishers hoped that people would purchase the book for that reason alone, even though most of the music was of English make. There was also light, catchy music of a sort Bostonians were not yet used to. A psalm tune by Flagg was made available on a modern recording by the Colonial Band of Boston, from which may be discerned the work's immediate appeal. Revere also engraved Flagg's second compilation, *Anthems Collected from Tans'ur* (1766), which included a song from Handel's *Saul.* The relationship came to an end as a less than profitable one for Revere, his ledger still containing an entry for £150 due from Flagg for a half-share of production costs.

The unusual spectacle of two regiments of British redcoats marching into Boston on October 1, 1768, with muskets charged, bayonets fixed, colours flying, drums beating, fifes and drums playing, created a madness in Flagg that persisted until his death. The British had brought in instruments many Bostonians had never heard, though some knew of their existence from printed concert music. The sound of bassoons, oboes, French horns, and other exotic instruments induced Flagg to form the First Band of Boston, recruiting its members from the city militia. He trained and drilled his musicians into Boston's favorite music making group, and within a short time presented them at the Concert Hall on Queen Street in a program of music by the London Bach, Handel, Stamitz, and other British luminaries, interspersed with songs from the London theater.

In association with Trinity Church's organist, David Propert, Flagg next offered a subscription season, combining the First Boston Band with the British 64th Regiment's musicians, the band that had marched into Boston and inspired him. Trinity's boys choir, trained by Propert, performed portions of Handel oratorios during the evening programs.

By 1777, Flagg's preoccupation with music brought about a separation from his wife, a public brawl with his son, who was left to care for his mother and two sisters. On October 23, Flagg presented another benefit concert in Faneuil Hall, the city's trade market, whose large meeting room served as the "cradle of liberty" for many gatherings of New England patriots assembled to unite against British abuse. During that evening, fifty singers performed excerpts from *Messiah,* and the evening ended with a rendition by Flagg of "The Liberty Song," the Sons of Liberty's marching hymn, certain to bring any Yankee crowd to its feet. Realizing enough money from the concert to take him to Providence, Flagg remained there and served as a colonel of a Rhode Island regiment during the Revolution.

## William Billings

The curious mixture of autodidact music masters, spawn of the singing school, and a rising tide of musical awareness resulting from the influx of musicians trained in Europe, many of them failures in their own land, produced William Billings. New England's most illustrious eighteenth-century musical son bears a more lively resemblance to popular-song composers of the late nineteenth and twentieth centuries than he does to contemporaries like Hopkinson, who was the product of a cultural elitism dedicated to emulating the genteel music of his European idols. Had he lived a century earlier, Billings would have been an object of the religious establishment's scorn, because he believed his own religious music was "twenty times more powerful as the old slow tunes." His lifelong ardor for music was so intense that he became the first American composer to devote all his time to music and music alone, writing it, performing it, and hoping to persuade his fellow Americans that it was his property.

Contemporary accounts described him as "a singular man, of moderate size, short of one leg, without any address, and an uncommon negligence of person." He also suffered a permanently broken shoulder, one eye, and a withered arm. Disgustingly addicted to snuff, he carried a supply in a leather-lined jacket and rather than take it in the manner in fashion, between thumb and finger, sniffed from a handful between his thumb and clenched fists. "Still he spake and sang and thought as a man above the common abilities."

Billings was born in Boston on October 7, 1746. His physical misfortunes came from the genes of his father, who left him a single shilling on his death, effectively cutting off the fourteen-year-old from any claim to an insignificant estate. Self-taught, except for a few years in public school and in singing schools, Billings found his first job in a tannery, soaking and rinsing, liming and curing, animal skins. It was smelly work and mean. Hampered by his crippled body, he never mastered a musical instrument, though his stentorian voice carried all before it. His true music abilities were first perceived by John Barry, his only known instructor, ten years his senior and teacher in the niceties of music of the parishioners of New South Church. Billings learned music from a small handful of how-to books, writing out his lessons in chalk on the tannery walls, copying from Aaron Williams or Tans'ur, to whom Barry introduced him.

When Barry and Billings opened their own singing school in 1769, the latter was already well on the way to completion of his *Rueben,* his first born, an original songbook for singing schools and church use. The last section was completed on his twenty-fourth birthday, when he took it to the printing offices of Edes and Gill, on Queen Street. There the rest of the book had been waiting eighteen months, so that it could be printed on American-made paper. The printer-publishers of Boston's major supporter of the patriot cause, the *Gazette,* Benjamin Edes and John Gill would not soil their hands with goods of British manufacture. Among the hundred or so pages of closely printed type and music in *The New England Psalm-singer,* which came off press at the end of 1770, was a frontispiece engraved by Paul Revere, who usually did such work for Edes and Gill, publishers of his own cartoons and engravings. The crudely cut music was by another, and not in the style of the work done for Flagg's collections. This first tune book of completely original music written by a native-born American was advertised in the *Gazette* fifteen times during the following winter and spring, announcing its availability through a group of book dealers in Boston and its environs.

As the work was going on press, Billings had applied to the Massachusetts General Court for the exclusive privilege of selling and distributing it. The petition was delivered November 7, 1770, and six days later a bill was brought up and effectively pigeonholed until the next session, one legislator questioning that one so young could be ''the real Author of the book.'' In the absence of protection, printers pirated the book, notably Daniel Bayley, of Newburyport, one of the most successful of the New England stationers, a talented engraver and organist in his town's St. Paul's Church. Six years earlier, he had issued *A New and Complete Introduction to the Grounds and Rules of Music,* combining Thomas Walter's title and introduction to his successful 1720 music book with Tans'ur's *Royal Melody,* which had been published in London in 1754. Just as Billings completed his *Psalm-singer,* Bayley was reprinting Williams's *Royal Harmony.* Such piracy had become increasingly profitable. Various repressive import and stamp taxes had increased the price of imported literature, and with the demand from singing-school students for new music, such items as the Williams and the Billings collections were an attractive item to men like Bayley.

During the next several years, Billings worked as an itinerant music master, teaching the art and selling his books to pupils in many New England communities. In Stoughton, Massachusetts, he married Lucy Swan, one of his pupils, who died in 1795 after giving him five children. Though his book enjoyed popularity and its songs were often sung in churches, it had not sold sufficiently to warrant a second printing. After completing a new work, Billings hesitated to print it without legal protection. In a preface to one of his pirate reprintings, Bayley made reference to "some masterly hands who have not yet permitted any of their work to be made public," possibly referring to Billings.

In late 1772, Billings petitioned Royal Governor Thomas Hutchinson and the Massachusetts legislature for some meaningful protection for both his first book and the new work, reminding them that his earlier plea had been lost or misplaced and renewing his request for the sole right to print and merchandise his own compositions for any number of years the body saw fit to establish. An old friend from New South Church, Samuel Adams, was a power in the House and speeded passage of Billings's privilege through both bodies of the government. The William Billings Copyright Act gave him exclusive rights in his music for a period of seven years and fixed a penalty of ten pounds for each and every "printing, vending or bartering" without the author's permission in writing. Never having forgiven Adams his role in fomenting the Boston Massacre of 1770, stolidly loyal Governor Hutchinson was delighted to refuse approval of this legislation. Denied his rights, Billings withheld publication of the second book, though he worked strenuously to secure public performances of the new music.

In the face of Hutchinson's intractability, Billings, more devoted than ever in his zeal for the cause of freedom, became an active Son of Liberty. When needed, he served as a volunteer transport worker, his physical condition precluding any more active service, and he saw duty as far from Boston as the hills of upper New York during the first years of the war for independence.

Adams had learned early the power of popular songs and made effective use of music in molding the minds and spirits of Boston's common folk. In Billings he had a songwriter whose thoroughly American music appealed to both the fighting man and those on the home front in the war against George's tyranny. "Chester" which first appeared in the *Psalm-singer* was soon one of the struggling nation's favorite marching and patriotic tunes. It lent itself to group singing in spirited rhythms, and when played slowly to muffled drums, served as a moving funeral dirge. Four new verses by Billings, more than equal to the music, invoked God's assistance against a foe who had come with "haughty stride," commanded by those red-coated generals Howe, Burgoyne, Clinton, and the rest "in one infernal league combin'd."

Once the British had cleared out of Boston, Billings resumed teaching music, directing the Brattle Square Church choir and conducting classes in a young people's club at old South Church. Edes and Gill had been forced to suspend publication of the *Gazette* during the occupation, and although Gill remained in Boston, Edes had taken the press and fonts of type across the harbor in a rowboat to set up a newspaper in Watertown. When the enemy departed, Edes returned, dissolved the partnership, and took his share of the equipment, effectively putting the old firm out of business. Billings took his new book to Edward Draper and John Folsom, publishers of the *Independent Ledger,* a weekly that had become popular after suspension of the *Gazette.* In early 1778, the first printing of a leather-bound *Singing Master's Assistant,* "an abridgement from the *New England Psalm-singer;* together with several other Tunes, never before published," came off the press, its plates engraved by Benjamin Pierpont, of Roxbury, and a considerable improvement over the sloppy anonymous work in the first collection.

Yet another effort was made by Billings to obtain protection, this time from a government he hoped would recognize his contribution to the patriot cause. He submitted a petition to the Massachusetts General Assembly on June 12, 1778. Apprehensive that "some avaricious person, or persons, will, in a piratical manner, intercept and copy . . . to the great prejudice of your petitioner," Billings asked for a ten-year vending and printing privilege. Once more he was disappointed, and the way was again open for the mass pirating of his songs that followed, forty-four of the *Singing Master's Assistant's* being printed in various compilations during his lifetime.

This first tune book to appear after hostilities had begun was an immediate success, filling the void that resulted from paper and materials shortages in the war's first years. Only after the Massachusetts legislature appointed local vigilance committees to conduct linen and rag collections did the shortages abate somewhat, and permit production of Billings's new book. The problem was never completely solved, however, and music printing was seriously affected by the vast demand for paper to be used in the making of currency, newspapers, government proclamations, broadsides and documents, and even to wrap every bullet fired.

Because many of the songs in his first book were now, he wrote, "not worth my printing," Billings selected and corrected the most popular of them as the core of a new collection, "an abridgement of the *New England Psalm-singer*" with forty-seven new pieces. Many of these were already well known—"Chester" in its new wartime version and "Lamentation over Boston," written with Samuel Adams to remind Boston of the British occupation. The new book, *Billings Best,* was carried by soldiers and used for singing around the campfire and on the march. It went through five editions before 1790. With his music well known throughout the colonies, even though often from pirated editions, Billings's fortunes had improved. Old South Church paid him £150 for two months of summer classes alone. Other well-paying assignments came up, and with profits growing from the sale of his music from his own home, Billings purchased a new house for £6,000 of inflated currency. The 1779 *Music in Miniature,* a small oblong book intended to be attached at the rear of a psalter, was the first and only collection he published containing some music he did not write.

With the war over, Billings was ready to take down his harp from the willow tree upon which he had hung it in 1776 and write "frivolously popular" music "of modern invention." He brought out a 1781 *Psalm Singers Assistant.* It contained twenty-four fairly difficult pieces of music for four voices in its 104 pages and the warning that these were not for beginners, but for well-trained singers who wished "to tickle the ears" of audiences. Because copper was scarce and paper extravagantly high in price, he could afford to issue only a portion of the new modern music he had completed. The engravings were by British-born illustrator John Norman, who arrived in the colonies just before the Revolution and rode out the war years in Philadelphia as a successful commercial artist. There he cut the engravings for one of the earliest music instruction books produced in the new nation, *The Compleat Instructor for Violin,* by the London music teacher H. B. Victor, who had migrated in 1774. Born in Germany, Victor had served the princess of Wales and played the organ in St. George's Church after reaching England in 1759. He brought two exotic musical instruments of his own invention to America, a tromba doppio con tympana, consisting of two trumpets and a pair of drums fastened to the feet to be played by a single performer, and a cymbaline damour, resembling the musical glasses perfected by Franklin. In Philadelphia, he taught piano, violin, German flute and gave lessons in theory to local pupils, for whom he prepared a series of teaching books, the first, for violin, published in 1778.

In 1781, Norman moved to Boston, opening a music printing and publishing business with production of the Billings plates. He engraved almost every sacred tune book released in Boston during the following decade, publishing some of them himself. In 1783, he hired Billings to edit a new monthly periodical, *Boston Magazine,* intended to "be as useful and entertaining as possible." Its October issue contained the first popular song printed from movable type cast in the United States. It was made by William Norman, the engraver's brother, from punches he cut and with tools of his own making. Though novel, the results were irregular and poor. The type was used only once in the *Boston Magazine,* but, undaunted, William Norman published music during the 1790s, presumably also from type he made.

Never an easy man to work with, Billings was soon ousted from the editor's job, and returned to teaching in Boston churches and producing concerts of his music. In 1785, he issued *The Suffolk Harmony,* the last book of his own music to be published by him. Again John Norman made the plates, for thirty-two compositions, printed over fifty-six pages. Despite Billings's national fame, the small book never went into any more editions, though for the first time he enjoyed legal protection in his new work. Massachusetts had at last enacted protection for intellectual property. Prodded by Noah Webster, the legislature led the way to a national copyright law by passing "An Act for the Purpose of Securing to Authors the exclusive Right and Benefit of publishing their Literary Production for Twenty-One Years." Violators were liable to a "sum not exceeding Three Thousand Pounds, nor less than Five Pounds." As the law required, Billings deposited two copies of *The Suffolk Harmony* in the Harvard Library to secure his copyright, which was good for Massachusetts only. Elsewhere he was in the public domain.

Billings had been, in 1782, at the zenith of his reputation, the best-known American composer and songwriter, creator of more than eighty percent of about

280 American tunes being printed in domestically produced music books. Almost every new compilation contained some of his work. Four years later, at age forty, his eminence was challenged by young newcomers. Although the preface to the important *Worcester Collection,* issued by the new printing and publishing firm of Thomas and Andrews, credited him with pioneering efforts—"For the progress of Psalmody in this Country, the Publick are in a great measure indebted to the musical abilities of Mr. William Billings of Boston"— it pointed to the threat facing him: "The New England States can now boast of many authors of Church Musick, whose compositions do them justice."

Boston selectmen made Billings one of four inspectors of police, at a salary of twelve pounds annually, with duties including "seizing and securing all baskets for measuring coal that are not of the dimensions . . . the law directs." Through social and political connections, he secured other minor municipal offices—street scavenger, hog catcher, and inspector of leather—all of which assisted in feeding and clothing a family of three daughters and a newly born son.

The new nation was in its second year of financial depression, and what money was being spent on such luxuries as printed music went for more modern publications, like the *Worcester Collection,* which was to go through eight revised editions by the end of the century. Nineteen of Billings's songs were in the first edition, and the book's very popularity effectively cut into the sale of his own publications.

The advent of new tunesmiths Andrew Law, Daniel Read, and other New Englanders reduced public interest in the former leather tanner's music. After he mortgaged his house to a neighbor for forty pounds in 1790, friends and former students organized a benefit concert to ensure food for the family.

Billings became friendly with a recent arrival from Europe, the Dane Hans Gram, Brattle Square Church's organist, whose art songs appeared regularly in the *Massachusetts Magazine,* published by Thomas and Andrews. Its March 1791 issue carried the first orchestral score to be published in the United States, an arrangement by Gram of his own "Death Song of an Indian Chief," written for tenor, strings, two clarinets, and two E-flat horns. Isaiah Thomas, senior partner in the Worcester and Boston publishing enterprise, was the first to import music from England after the Revolution, thus becoming the major music publisher in New England, if not the nation. His first big-selling music item was the *Worcester Collection.*

In desperate need of money, Billings asked Gram to discuss with Ebenezer Andrews, Thomas's associate, the sale of all his unpublished music and reprint rights in the published works. A memorandum from Andrews to Thomas, in Worcester, stated the issue:

> Billings, through Gram, wishes us to purchase his music of him. He has got 200 pages by him, that never was published, 9 or 10 tunes of which Gram had played on his harpsichord, and thinks very good. Gram supposes he would ask 30 to 40 pounds for all his music (what he has in manuscript and what he has published) but thinks he would take less, and it might be worth our while to purchase, as they would serve occasionally to introduce into the *Collection.* If you have any inclination to purchase, at any rate, I will ask Gram to get Billings' lowest terms.

Thomas showed no such inclination.

The following spring some of Billings's friends presented a proposition to Andrews, offering to underwrite by subscription a new Billings book, and by midsummer arrangements had been made. When only about 500 or 600 copies had been subscribed for by October, not enough to pay production costs, the committee proposed that a mortgage on the house in which the family now lived be taken as security.

The last Billings tune book, *The Continental Harmony* "containing a number of ANTHEMS, FUGUES AND CHORUSES in several parts, NEVER BEFORE PUBLISHED," appeared in 1794. Except for four revised older pieces, all of the music was new. Many of the texts were from Watts, but only a few of the songs from the composer's last years, indicating his faltering interest in music.

Lucy Billings died in 1795, leaving her husband with the upbringing of the five children, the eldest seventeen. In the next years, he published only a few single songs and taught in singing schools around Boston. In early autumn 1800, William Billings, "the celebrated music composer" died, for the last few years a resident of his newly married eldest daughter's household. He was buried in an unmarked grave somewhere in Boston. After his house was sold and all debts paid, his estate was worth $836.25.

Within a few decades, Billings's music had disappeared from the new books of "correct" music that sought to reform such "general and most deplorable corruption of taste" as he had wrought. Only in collections intended for Southern buyers or the far frontier were his tunes still available, and even there his name was soon forgotten and his melodies were believed to be old folk songs.

It remained for the twentieth century to restore William Billings to the place he deserves.

### Andrew Law

The chief missionary for the late eighteenth century's drive to improve music, Andrew Law, was much like Billings in his concern for property rights in music, although he was far more litigious and a sharper businessman. Better born and better educated, citizen of an era that saw the development of a national copyright law, improved printing technology, a favorable economy, increasing access to the new markets created by an expanding frontier, Law sought to establish a business in music for the singing school and the church singer that he could control completely.

His grandfather was a Connecticut governor, in which colony Law was born, in 1748, and where he resided for most of his life, though he did attend the Baptist-sponsored Rhode Island College (now Brown University) in Providence from 1771 to 1775, graduating with a master's degree. Because the school provided no training for the ministry, Law studied privately with a Congregational preacher. Any youth of his musical inclinations was certainly the product of a singing school, and he may have attended one conducted in Providence by Billings in 1774.

Law, his kin, and neighbors were active around Boston in June 1775, some

of them taking part in the Battle of Bunker Hill, where Connecticut troops engaged in sharp and bloody combat. In the furor after that defeat, a flood of
militant poetry appeared, usually printed in broadside for the widest circulation.
One of the most dramatic pieces was "The American Hero," written by the
Reverend Nathaniel Niles, who lived some thirty miles from the Law home in
Cheshire. Law set the words to a tune of his own, called it "Bunker Hill," and
gave New England a war hymn almost equaling the popularity of "Chester."

Licensed to preach the gospel, Law went to a small rural town in 1776 and
embarked on a lifelong musical career by beginning to compile his first collection of the "best and approved tunes." He had learned the printing trade from
a brother, William, a Cheshire businessman, and in June 1777, having purchased copper, "firewood to boil ink," and paper, he advertised in nearby New
London a proposal to print the work. The book was to contain about 200 pages
"neatly engraved on plate," but the "fluctuating state of our public affairs"
made it impossible to ascertain an accurate price. *Select Harmony* went on sale
in early 1779, containing only half the promised pages. Law had purchased
thirteen of the tunes from their American composers, used nineteen English tunes
never before printed in America, and the remainder came from available books,
among them Billings's first two.

In 1781, as he was at work on a revised edition, Law learned that Daniel
Bayley was bringing out his own edition of *Select Harmony,* and he petitioned
the Connecticut legislature to restrain Bayley from the piracy, though not naming the printer specifically. Within the month, the Assembly granted Law a sole
license for his music for a term of five years from October 1781, with a £500
liability for illegal printing, plus court costs, but valid only in Connecticut. Where
Billings had failed, Law triumphed, receiving the first legal copyright granted
to a citizen of the five-year-old United States.

As a resident of Massachusetts, Bayley was unaffected by the Connecticut
grant and issued several printings of Law's tune book, even after the revised
edition went on sale. Despite this competition, Law's book was a success, selling more than 5,000 copies before 1790, while a Law-Bayley name-calling feud
went on in the pages of the Connecticut press. A small psalm tune supplement
by Law, much like Billings's own *Music in Miniature,* intended to be bound
into the back of the family psalmbook, appeared in 1781, an inexpensive piece,
which sold 3,000 copies in a ten-year period.

With three books in print and several more in preparation, Law began a decade of travel around the country, organizing singing schools, training traveling
music teachers, who peddled his growing catalogue, and establishing distribution and sales agencies outside New England. In late 1782, he was in Philadelphia, the nation's capital city and hub of political and cultural life, where he
opened the School for the Instruction of Ladies and Gentlemen in Vocal Music.
His Philadelphia distributor was Robert Aitken, who had just completed production of the first Bible in English printed in America. The following spring,
Law presented a graduation concert and left the city, placing his school in the
hands of a bright young Philadelphian, Andrew Adgate.

Once again in Cheshire, Law completed two new books by year's end, *A*

*Collection of Hymn Tunes* and *The Rudiments of Music,* depositing both in the Harvard Library in order to get a Massachusetts copyright and thus foil Bayley, his old antagonist. *Rudiments* was a conscious imitation of a similarly titled work published in Scotland twenty years earlier, with which he had recently become familiar. To it, he merely added a singing-school method and some Anglican chants, hoping to move into the Episcopalian church music-book trade. Several editions appeared, published in varying lengths to meet prospective customers' desires, sheets being added when necessary, or removed to reduce the price.

Trouble with local sales agents proved to be a problem that vexed him until his death. Although he had outlets as far south as the Carolinas, none of his dealers ever did the job he expected, and most were usually behind in payments as well. Even Noah Webster proved to be a delinquent account. That Yale graduate, author of the *Blue-Backed Speller,* as it was later known, was on his crusade to persuade state governing bodies to do something about temporary copyright while the Constitution was being written and ratified. Webster financed his mission by teaching, often setting up a singing school, at which he promoted Law's tune books. Occasionally, the two met in New York, Philadelphia, or Baltimore, but their friendship deteriorated as bills continued to be overdue.

After two unhappy years in New York, where he had moved in late 1784 to open a music school and improve sales and distribution, Law faced an uncertain future. Bayley was still at work, borrowing without permission or payment. Isaiah Thomas, of Worcester, had become another source of frustration. Whereas that canny publisher observed Massachusetts' copyright protection, he had no compunction about dipping into material that enjoyed only Connecticut's restrictions, and fifty-four of Law's tunes were personally chosen by Thomas for the first (1786) edition of the *Worcester Collection.*

Webster recommended that Law go south to study the markets there, and he went to Charleston, where Anne Timothy, granddaughter-in-law of John Wesley's 1737 printer, was official supplier of printing, operated the local bookstore, and carried Law's catalogue. Regularly supplied by overwater delivery, she had been apprised of the composer's presence and advertised it widely, to his great pleasure. However, this most musically receptive of eighteenth-century American cities appeared to have little interest in or need for teachers of sacred singing, and Law departed an unhappy man.

After ten disappointing years in the music business, he returned to the church, and was ordained in September 1787 by a council of Congregational pastors to work in the gospel ministry. His assignment to the South provided another disappointing experience. During this season of his discontent, he devised a new merchandising scheme; he put together a group of itinerant singing-master salesmen, who, under exclusive contract to use his publications, were to organize local academies in rural areas of the middle states. For one free book for every half-dozen sold, these traveling music drummers pledged "to use Mr. Law's Collections of Sacred Music and no other in my schools, nor be influential of introducing any other book or books for the term of five years."

Law traveled throughout western Pennsylvania, Maryland, and Virginia to set up schools, recruit salesmen, and supervise their activities. One of his men went into the field with a load of his works: seventy *Select Number,* thirty-five *Select Harmony,* fifty-six *Rudiments of Music,* and fifteen *Hymns and Tunes,* and within a few months opened three schools and was establishing a fourth.

Although Law hoped to be the first New England music-book compiler and publisher to venture into the frontier market, he found that his one-time Philadelphia assistant, Andrew Adgate, was there before him, and with a half-dozen tune books of his own.

Two years after having gotten his start with Law in 1783, Adgate, a former mechanic, opened his own singing academy, which was quickly turned into Philadelphia's most advanced public lyceum, Mr. Adgate's Institution for Diffusing More Generally the Knowledge of Vocal Music. A group of Philadelphia dignitaries and intellectuals served as trustees and raised funds by the sale of annual subscriptions of eight dollars for twelve student concerts, "public singings" that became one of the city's leading occasions. Adgate's universal musical taste manifested itself in singing books he issued in collaboration with Philadelphia bookseller John McCulloch, a Scottish printer. One of the compilations was a slim sixteen-page volume of popular songs, *The Philadelphia Songster* (1789), pseudonymously edited by Absalom Aimwell. It contained catches, glees, tunes from the London theater, and a pair of American love songs. Adgate's other collections were of a purely religious character.

The grandest of the institution's concerts was given in 1786. American music by Billings, Lyon, and Tuckey, all written prior to 1780, was programed alongside that of Handel and other European masters. As many as 300 performers appeared, including a 230-voice chorus made up of pupils. Among the innovative techniques introduced in the school by Adgate was the use of a seven-note system to replace the centuries-old English solmization, standard in America: the syllables *fa, sol, la, mi,* the first three repeated to complete the scale. The addition of *ba, do,* and *na* provided a teaching and learning aid on which his pupils evidently flourished.

Having been informed that Adgate's books were competing favorably with his publications in western Pennsylvania, and jealous of the national reputation of the Uranian Academy, as Adgate's school was later known, Law embarked on a campaign of ghostwritten vilification of "Mr. Adgate's New Plan," which ended only when his own complicated business affairs occupied him fully and Adgate was dead of yellow fever, in 1793.

Andrew Law next was to venture forth to do battle with the music world during a time when the nation had its own new copyright law, and Americans who had learned to sing during the eighteenth century were spreading their wings to embark on the exciting musical prospect before them.

# CHAPTER 19

# English Musical Theater

Queen Anne's death in 1714 brought about great changes, one of the least of which was the renaming of the theater in the Haymarket. This newest of London's playhouses was now known as the King's Theatre, though it had no need for a royal theater patent, since it offered only musical works and little or no spoken drama. Throughout the century, only two of London's major scenes of entertainment—the Drury Lane and Covent Garden—were patent houses, featuring words-only fare. All others garlanded every performance with dancing, music, and songs, employing every conceivable form of popular entertainment dependent on music in order to obey the law and attract audiences. Out of this public exposure of theater music grew a publishing business, first the family enterprise on The Strand begun by John Walsh, then those of the Welckers, opposite the opera house and later on Gerrard Street, William Smith, John Johnston, Robert Bremner, Harrison & Co., William Napier, the Corris, George Walker, and John Longman. It was from these and lesser music publishers and stores that visiting Americans bought vocal scores and sheet music of the great hit presentations and took the sound of the English musical theater to their colonial homes.

Sir John Vanbrugh's triumphal piece of architecture, as it was called, built in the Haymarket in 1704, immediately proved to be infelicitous to spoken drama but startlingly favorable for Italian opera. Once Handel had unveiled his original operas and captured the fancy of London's *haut monde,* this house, built in a then shabby part of the city, removed from the center of activities and a good coach fare from its competition, rivaled that of Venice in the glitter and sparkle of its audiences. The importation of European opera stars, all at enormous salaries, restored attendance after interest had fallen off, and opera again became, as John Gay wrote, "the reigning amusement of the town . . . real fiddles, bass viols, and hautboys, not poetical harps, lyres and reeds. There's nobody allowed to say *I sing* but an eunuch, or an Italian woman. Everybody is grown now as great a judge of music as they were of poetry, and folks that could not distinguish one tune from another now daily dispute about the different styles of Handel, Bononcini and Ariosti.''

This upper-class interest dwindled in the mid-1720s, following disclosure of the mishandling of public investment in the Royal Academy of Music, which presented opera, and after an onstage brawl in the presence of royalty between the two leading Italian sopranos, egged on by their claques.

John Rich, manager of the unlicensed theater in Lincoln's Inn Fields, rebuilt in 1714 over the remains of the tennis court on which the Restoration stage was spawned, learned a curious thing about lower-class audiences. When he sought to capitalize on the vogue for opera by giving English-language presentations, as well as full-length plays, the better-paying box and pit seats were filled but the galleries usually were empty. When he offered pantomimes, plays, and afterpieces, the reverse was true. Logically, he proceeded to combine the two, offering pantomime and ''grotesque dancing,'' farces, processions, rope dancing, acrobatics, animal acts, recitatives and choruses borrowed from opera to nightly audiences of more than a thousand. Regularly, they flocked to these offerings of commedia dell'arte farces with spoken dialogue, which developed into pantomimed versions of such old stage staples as Faustus, Harlequin, the Greek gods and their forays among mortals, and plots lifted from Molière's stage hits. For decades, in Britain and later in the colonies, *Harlequin Dr. Faustus or the Necromancer, Harlequin Sorcerer, Apollo and Daphne or the Burgomaster Trick'd,* and similar pantomimes were sure-fire attractions. Among Rich's players in these was Anthony Aston, the first professional actor to have appeared in the colonies, some twenty years earlier; he also wrote songs for the Lincoln's Inn Fields Theatre.

John Ernst Galliard, a German composer and oboe player, writer of music for St. Paul's and the Chapel Royal, was promoted by Rich from a place in the theater orchestra to write vocal and instrumental music for the pantos. When the Drury lane discovered that its opera presentations did not attract upper-class audiences from the Haymarket, it, too, added pantomime to the programs, usually with songs and dance music written by Henry Carey and the theater's orchestra director, Richard Jones. The instrumental pieces became known as ''comic tunes'' and were brought out annually, first by Walsh, in collections of *Comic Tunes &c. to Celebrated Opera and Theatre Dances,* arranged for harpsichord, violin, or German flute. Pantomime songs appeared as single sheets and afterward in bound collections. John Gay's ''Newgate Calendar,'' written to the melody ''Packington's Pound,'' was interpolated into *Harlequin Sheppard,* inspired by the exploits of the famous highwayman Jack Sheppard, whose escape from the famous London prison was the talk of the town. Gay wrote the song after a notorious mulatto highwayman, Blueskin, assaulted a rival thief with a knife during a courtroom appearance.

Theater designers and carpenters made a contribution that also added immensely to the pantomime's attraction. Whenever new scenery and special stage machinery were advertised, prices doubled and the houses still filled. Jupiter was transformed into a bull within the audience's sight; dragons appeared in flames, spewing out grotesque demons; Harlequin, Punch, Pierrot, and Scaramouch rode on spirits in the air; sheaves of wheat danced; flasks and oranges flew through the air, and when *Harlequin Sheppard* was played, newspaper advertising hailed the accuracy of the scenery as "painted from the real place of the action."


## "It made Rich gay and Gay rich . . ."

On January 29, 1728, John Rich sounded the death knell for Italian opera in England when he offered a new work by John Gay, *The Beggar's Opera,* at his Lincoln's Inn Fields Theatre. The script had been offered to Drury Lane and rejected before Rich got his hands on this new form of musical theater, the ballad opera, so known because all of the sixty-nine tunes were familiar ballad songs, melodies the audience knew well enough to whistle while the actors sang.

None of Gay's earlier stage works had been particularly successful, although his poetry and popular songs, some of them written with Handel, were well known and loved, as were others written for that form of "tragi-comi-pastoral farce," a kind of stage entertainment burlesquing Italian opera, that Gay had introduced to the stage as early as 1715. The success of his "Newgate Calendar" undoubtedly moved him to deal with London's underworld in the new play. The cast of characters was made up almost entirely of malefactors: the highwayman Macheath; his two "wives," who would steal or kill for him; Peachum, receiver of stolen property; a corrupt prison keeper; and a supporting ensemble of felons, cutpurses, prostitutes, and other riffraff. Part of the work's truly fantastic success can also be attributed to the fact that some saw it as an attack on the Whig party, then in power, as well as a parody of the Italian opera to which high society flocked. It had been Gay's original intention to have his players sing each song without accompaniment, but Rich convinced him that an orchestra would enhance the production. John Christopher Pepusch, the Lincoln's Inn Fields musical director, wrote a special overture and the orchestrations. Pepusch had arrived in England in 1700, at the age of thirty-three, and immediately found work in the Drury Lane orchestra, where his training in theory and composition helped to refine the scores for early productions of British-written Italian-influenced operas. The powerful duke of Chandos employed him as house composer and musical director until Handel became the nobleman's darling. Pepusch then took up Rich's offer and became his staff composer. In 1724, his friendship with Bishop Berkeley, then actively engaged in organizing a college in Bermuda, where the composer would serve as professor of music, led to a proposed trip to the New World. When the boat in which he was to sail sank, Pepusch returned to the theater. His arrangements of *The Beggar's Opera*'s disdained "wild, rude and often vulgar melodies," which he disliked, and brought him greater acclaim than all his previous work.

Gay had dipped into both Playford's various editions of *The Dancing Master* and D'Urfey's *Wit and Mirth, or Pills to Purge Melancholy* for his music, selecting such old favorites as "Greensleeves," "Chevy Chase," "To Old Sir Simon the King," "Packington's Pound," "A lovely lass to a friar came," and "Lillibulero," to which Pepusch's arrangements gave a modern quality. In addition to his own two hit songs, " 'Twas when the seas were roaring'' and "Black-ey'd Susan,'' Gay borrowed music from Henry Purcell, Eccles, Jeremiah Clarke, and Handel, whose march from *Rinaldo* proved to be the show's outstanding hit.

*The Beggar's Opera* became the most successful theatrical presentation in London's memory, playing sixty-two performances before the season ended for the summer. When it was evident that the play was a success, John Watts printed the libretto, in a small book with single-line engraved tunes in the back. A second edition followed, containing Pepusch's overture, and then a third with the overture in score and all of the songs with added bass accompaniment.

The opera soon spread to theaters in all the great towns of England, playing as many as thirty or forty performances in many, and then in Scotland, Wales, and Ireland. In Dublin, it was played by a troupe of child actors, none of them yet adolescent. The American colonies were introduced to its charms in 1751. It remained a favorite for the next two centuries, enjoying regular revivals, one of the most successful that in London during the late 1920s, which had a run of 1,463 performances.

Londoners enjoyed a catch that said the production "made Gay rich and Rich gay,'' a fact, for the production cleared over £4,000 after expenses. The author received nearly £700 from four benefit performances, his only source of income from the work, and another ninety guineas from Watts for the copyright.

Throughout his life, Gay's friends, and they were many and in high places, remarked on the extraordinary good fortune that was his when he needed it most. Orphaned as a boy, he was brought up by an uncle and educated in a country school whose master had a penchant for rhyme, recognized a superior talent in young Gay, and encouraged him to write verse plays. Finding little to excite him in the dry-goods trade to which he was apprenticed, Gay made his way to London, where his wit and keen mind were quickly appreciated. In his early twenties, he was secretary to Aaron Hill, who had just become one of the Drury Lane's managers.

Living in eternal pursuit of the rich life his birth had denied him, and dedicated to achieving his goal through an ingenious facility with words and smooth skill in bowing profoundly and speaking deliberately in the presence of anyone who could aid him, Gay won early fame for his verses. An appointment in 1712 as secretary to the duchess of Monmouth proved to be more substantial than literature had. With such a patroness to support him, Gay issued several collections of verse and became the talk of the town. He was recognized as a major literary light, together with Addison, Steele, Defoe, and Pope. His next move upward was assisted by the earl of Clarendon, whom he accompanied to the court of Elector George of Hanover, which, as his friend Handel had warned, was a dullish place. During the stay, however, he won the friendship of young Prince George and his wife, Caroline. When his third play, *The What Do You Call It,* opened in 1715, the royal pair, now the prince and princess of Wales, came to watch. It was an entertainment Samuel Johnson called "a kind of mock-tragedy, in which the images are comic, and the action grave,'' baffling that friend, who could not reconcile the audience's laughter with the drama's apparent gravity. It baffled most other playgoers, too. As soon as it was discerned that Gay had written something to be laughed at, the play enjoyed great success, as did one of its songs, performed by the inimitable Leveridge, " 'Twas when the seas were roaring," set to music attributed to Handel. A few years later, Leveridge collaborated with Gay on another extraordinarily popular ballad, the first of the Jolly Jack Tar songs, "All in the downs," or "Sweet Williams farewell to black ey'd Susan," which concludes with the phrase that became the standard cliché about men who sail before the mast; having "in ev'ry port a mistress."

John Gay's uncanny talent for wedding a good tune to smashing words manifested itself in even his earliest stage works. He was a regular visitor to the annual festivals of the Commonwealth of Ballad Singers and Mongers, held in the St. Giles district, for which, with Swift, Steele, and others, he wrote new material. His poetry contained sufficient allusions to the most popular darling songs of the common people to show that he was a true aficionado of the genre.

Another indication of Gay's wide knowledge of popular music was the use of songs in *The Beggar's Opera* taken from an anthology of Scottish song lyrics, *The Tea-Table Miscellany*, compiled by the Edinburgh wigmaker and poet Allan Ramsay and issued in 1724. In 1718, Ramsay had compiled *Scots Songs*, music English-speaking people had been enjoying for centuries and which they usually called "Northern" or "country" songs. Though no book of native secular music had been published in Scotland until John Forbes's *Cantus* in 1666, containing some native tunes, popular music from that neighboring nation had already inspired such British hits as "John come and kiss me," "Sawney was a dawndy lad," and "Within a furlong of Edinburgh town," all of them the work of London's theater songwriters and written in the Scottish manner. Playford's various editions of *The Dancing Master* and *Wit and Mirth* contained similar songs, as well as some truly authentic music, creating a taste for northern music. Henry Playford issued *Original Scottish Tunes* in 1701, and John Walsh included Scottish music in the 1717 and later editions of *The Merry Musicians or a Cure for the Spleen*, a collection of "the most diverting Songs & Pleasant Ballads set to music." Among them were some by James I and David Rizzio, Mary Queen of Scots' musician and secretary.

Ramsay's collections did not contain any music, and in 1726 the Scottish singer William Thompson compiled and had printed *Orpheus Caledonius*, "fifty of the best Scotch songs set to music," many of which were in the Ramsay, but for which he had set the basses. The book was a great success, and with it as a repertoire, Thompson became London's favorite Scottish vocalist.

Charles Burney named the new element infusing highland music during the period from 1720 to 1750 "Scottish snap." It reversed the traditional dotted note so that the short note in the beat was followed by a tied long one. The use of Scottish snap rhythm in popular dancing, chiefly in the strathspey, which became popular with English dancers, did much to promote its use in British music. Italian composers, too, fell upon the device with so much relish that critics complained about the "cutting short of the first of two notes in a melody," which was constantly used at the opera.

Furious because he considered that Thompson had stolen his material, Ramsay collaborated with Alexander Stuart, a trained musician, and brought out, in 1726, *Musick for Allan Ramsay's Collection of Scots Songs,* arranged for the harpsichord, to whose later editions other Scottish writers contributed. Both volumes, lyrics and music, went through innumerable editions as the British grew more addicted to northern songs. It was from both the Ramsay and the Thompson that Gay selected five melodies for his ballad opera, but without any credit to the originals, a practice continued by many others until the end of the century, when the poet Robert Burns applied his genius to an anthology of native songs with "words and music done by Scotchmen."

*The Beggar's Opera*'s success demanded a sequel. At its conclusion, Macheath, soon to be transported to the West Indies as a bondsman, advised Polly to go to America, where she would have a fair opportunity to get a husband. Following him to the Caribbean area in the ballad opera sequel, *Polly,* the young woman, through mishap, is sold into slavery. After escaping captivity, Macheath disguises himself as a black and joins a band of pirates, quickly becoming its leader. During a raid, Polly, disguised as a boy, is captured by Macheath's band. Neither recognizes the other. An attempt by Macheath's current mistress to seduce the unwilling handsome lad fails, and, like Joseph in Egypt, the youth is accused of rape. Polly eventually finds meaningful love with the son of an American Indian king. Gay again selected most of his tunes from the popular repertoire, three by Handel, including minuets from the *Water Music,* the same number from the Italian composer Ariosti, some French melodies, and tunes from the Ramsay collections. Pepusch again made the orchestrations, a little less condescending to the "vulgar" task in the face of the success and esteem his earlier effort had brought him.

Remembering pointed references to the crown and the government in *The Beggar's Opera,* officials arranged with the lord chamberlain, whose option it was, to ban *Polly.* Rather than hurt Gay's purse, this action added to his fortune. With the connivance of his good friend the duchess of Queensberry, wife of a Scottish noble, *Polly* was printed for sale by subscription, one copy going for £400, Gay's book royalties were far greater than they would have been from a theatrical production. The printed edition of *Polly, an opera, being the second part of The Beggar's Opera* contained its music in a supplement. The first important Irish music publishers, John and William Neale, who also pirated Handel's music, issued an illicit "corrected edition, set with bases proper for the violin, harpsichord or spinet."

A production of *Polly* some forty years later proved that it was no *Beggar's Opera.*

Although the new form he created continued to dominate the British musical theater for most of the next ten years, Gay never came near equaling his initial success, and not for lack of effort. Ballad opera was recognized as good box office, and London producers set to work building or improvising new theaters in which to cash in on the new craze. Though profits from ballad opera enabled John Rich to build a new theater on Bow Street, with a capacity of nearly 2,000, for some reason he showed little interest in the type of stage work he had introduced. In 1732, the Drury Lane's royal monopoly was renewed, further strengthening its control of spoken drama in England, even though most comedy and tragedy had been evicted from its boards by the success of Gay's ballad opera and those in unlicensed theaters whose experience with musical presentations enabled them successfully to cater to the rich new market. Nearly 200 one-, two-, and three-act ballad operas appeared in print, many of which were produced on stage. Initially, they depicted London's low life, upon which Gay had drawn. The settings soon changed to pastoral glens and the quiet streets of country villages, and then to sophisticated drawing rooms in the city, where intrigue resulted from the attraction of men to women. Contemporary politics, with its scandal and excesses, next offered a background, and, last, mythological tales of the lives of Greek and Roman gods. Indeed, as one early ballad opera sang:

> Since songs to plays are now-a-days
> Like to your meals a salad,
> Permit us, then, kind gentlemen,
> To try our skills by ballad.

## The Licensing Act and Popular Music

Even as ballad opera was coming to the conclusion of its first decade of importance, new theaters were being erected—one in Goodman's Fields and another in the music room of a wooden house at Sadler's Wells to which Londoners flocked in good weather to partake of the curative waters and be entertained in the process. The Whig government engaged in a calculated effort to restrict theatrical entertainment, hoping to limit all plays to the royal theaters. There, control could be maintained over the contents of scripts and such expressions of political opposition as Gay's ballad operas, and satirical stage pieces on the order of Henry Fielding's *Tom Thumb* (1730) could be repressed. Throughout the 1730s laws were offered to Parliament seeking to regulate the theater. Actors from the nonpatent houses were particularly subjected to harassment and arrest under provisions of a 1713 act of Queen Anne, similar to the old vagrancy laws, that classified "players of interludes" as rogues and vagabonds. The Licensing Act was finally made law in 1737, officially limiting presentation of spoken drama to the two licensed theaters and putting control of all entertainment into the hands of the lord chamberlain of the royal household. Any person wishing to perform in public "for gain, hire or reward" was obliged to obtain a license to do so from him, and any new play or adaptation of an old one was to be sent to him for rejection or approval.

The effect of this legislation was felt at once as theaters and music rooms closed their doors. Suddenly deprived of a venue in which to offer presentations, London theater managers resorted to ingenious means in order to skirt or completely evade the act. Wooden puppets, requiring no license, proved to be one viable substitute for breathing actors in successful productions of Shakespeare's plays, ballad operas, and farces. The art of representing humans by manipulated inanimate objects had advanced far beyond the crude efforts of the hand- and stick-puppet masters who entertained sixteenth-century lower-class watchers in town and country with religious dramas that soon took on ribald secular connotations. With the promise of new freedom following the Restoration, Italian puppeteers returned to Britain, where they had been offering their own form of public diversions since the earliest days of Elizabeth's reign and from which they were forced to flee when Puritans closed down most entertainment. British puppet masters had learned advanced European techniques and marionette construction in the interim, and their productions of the genre's literature became major attractions at London's Bartholomew, Southwark, Tottenham Court, and Welsh fairs. Sometime after 1660, Punch, a British variation of Italian comedy's Punchinello, with his wife, Judy, their squalling child, and the Devil became major players in the hand-puppet shows to which English people of all ages and sexes became devoted, with a passion foreigners found difficult to comprehend. The artificial actors used in Hanoverian times were about five feet high, the size of *Sesame Street*'s characters, made of wax rather than heavier wood, and operated by strings, sticks, and clockwork. Four American Indians, chiefs of the Iroquois tribe, visiting London in 1710 as part of a public-relations campaign intended to persuade these British allies of the nation's might and prestige, were among audiences coming to the Punch Theatre to see an "incomparable entertainment call'd THE LAST YEARS CAMPAIGNE," a battle fought by the duke of Marlborough and the French, in which manufactured wax actors played all roles.

The famous crippled dwarf master Martin Powell, manager of the Puppet Theatre, began demonstrating his mastery of the art in a Bartholomew Fair booth, offering a modern version of the old morality play *The Creation of the New World*, "newly revised with the addition of Noah's Flood." Richard Steele became a devotee of Powell's theater, giving it frequent publicity in his *Spectator* essays. When the Haymarket offered Handel's *Rinaldo*, with its flights of chaffinches and sparrows, Steele expressed his preference for Powell's concurrent production of *Whittington and His Cat*, whose animals, he believed, were better trained, among them a pig dancing a minuet with Punch. During the five years Powell operated his Puppet Theatre, he was said to have made so much money that he could buy all the poets of England ten times over.

Performers who found it difficult to obtain licenses, and who could not easily substitute puppets for themselves, looked for various platforms upon which to ply their craft. America's first professional actor, Tony Aston, in his fifties, advertised performances in taverns and public houses of "his most learned, serious, comic and whimsical entire rhapsodical declamation" as well as his specialty act "The Drunken Man" and his "learned comic demonstrative oratory on the face, with English, Scotch, Irish and Negro Songs," in appropriate costume. The last of these were, presumably, picked up from American and West Indian blacks during his tour of the colonies in the early 1700s.

An unemployed actor, James Lacy, found himself in prison after presenting a one-man show without the lord chamberlain's permission. Undaunted, after release he carried on in a public hall, offering lectures on a text from St. Matthew and charging spectators two shillings a seat. This device was often used by actors who went to the new United States a half-century later, when theaters were closed by official order.

### David Garrick and the Royal Playhouse Composers

The Licensing Act was three years old in 1740 when the government showed more concern for censoring plays than licensing theaters. The Goodman's Fields company was reorganized and moved back to its old home in the East End, far from the fashionable part of the city. There they began to offer "concerts of Vocal and Instrumental Music, divided into Two Parts," a subterfuge intended to permit presentation of a play during the intermission at no charge, purely for the actors' "diversion." It went unchallenged, and the concert format was imitated by other managers. The Goodman's Fields company was in its second season without official hindrance when it discovered among its members a slightly built wine salesman in his middle twenties who was possessed of superior acting powers. He was David Garrick, to many the greatest actor of his day.

Born to an army family, Garrick first demonstrated his ability at the age of ten in an amateur production of *The Recruiting Officer.* Most of his formal education had come from Samuel Johnson, seven years his senior, in the boarding academy operated by that as-yet-unheralded poet and lexicographer. When the school closed, Johnson and his pupil went off to London, one horse between them, taking turns in the saddle as they made their way to the cultural center of England. Johnson soon found employment as a hack writer, and Garrick joined his brother in the wine business, but also wrote poetry and a play and acted in amateur theatricals.

His first work, *Lethe,* a satirical afterpiece, was accepted in 1741 for production at the Drury Lane, where the musical accompaniment to his lyrics was composed by the staff arranger and composer, Thomas Augustine Arne, then thirty-one years old. During the course of peddling his brother's wine, Garrick struck up friendships with actors from the Goodman's Fields troupe, who perceived in him a source of spirits at discounted prices and took him into the company. His genius was soon apparent, and Garrick was cast as the lead in Shakespeare's *Richard the Third* as adulterated by Colley Cibber, making his debut "for the actors' diversion" between the halves of a "concert of music." A shortish man, Garrick was physically as well as mentally suited to the role of the evil humpbacked monarch, and his intense characterization and others that followed brought a new element of acting to the British stage. In a short time, fashionable and titled London made nightly pilgrimages to the seedy part of London to see Garrick. During the first season, he played eighteen roles, in comedy, tragedy, farce, ballad opera, and Harlequin in pantomime, packing the house on those evenings when advertisements reminded patrons that he would be on stage. Affected by the sudden rush to view the East End's new star, the licensed theaters complained to the lord chamberlain, who promptly shut down the Goodman's Fields. Out of work, but having found center stage most agreeable, Garrick accepted a record offer of £500 a season from the Drury Lane.

During the next five years, he came to rule the English theatrical world with a new style of acting, conquering all with a voice that was, a partisan argued, "sweet and harmonious, easy in its transitions, natural in its cadence, and beautiful in its elocution." An actor who saw in him an end to his own popularity scoffed, "Garrick is a new religion. Whitefield was followed for a time, but they all come to church again." They never did. Dr. Johnson, angered by his former student's success, grumbled, "David looks much older than he is, for his face has had double the business of any other man's; it is never at rest."

James Lacy, who had first tested the Licensing Act and won a prison term for that presumption, was the Drury Lane's new manager. He feared that his star would be lured away to Covent Garden, because Garrick had become an economic keystone of the British theater during the period when many wealthy Londoners fled the city in fear that Bonnie Prince Charlie would seize the city and topple the new German dynasty from the throne. Actors learned that when Garrick was ill or absent it was wise to cancel a benefit evening, since the house would be bare. In 1747, Lacy offered the British theater's new superstar a partnership in the Drury Lane's management, and thus began twenty-nine glorious years for the royal patent theater. A company of nearly 150 actors, singers, dancers, and entertainers was supported by a budget usually exceeding £25,000. Audiences filled the small Drury Lane, where they had unlimited vision of every facial nuance in the demonstrations of a national ensemble acting technique in which Garrick constantly drilled the players down to the least important performer.

Twenty-four of Shakespeare's plays were offered in new versions, usually provided with happy endings, tailored to the actor-manager's specifications by England's most facile poets and versifiers, enhanced by new background music and songs, a tradition Garrick revived. Under his direction, English operas were written to compete with Covent Garden, a much larger house, accommodating more than a thousand persons. Garrick also increased the Drury Lane's presentations of stage dancing and ballet, enlarging the theater orchestra for such occasions.

The director of the Drury Lane's band and music master of the house was Thomas Arne, then England's most highly regarded native composer. He made his first significant impact on music lovers in 1738, at the age of twenty-eight, when he wrote the score for a Drury Lane production of a new three-act version of Milton's *Comus,* the masque written a century before. London buzzed with the happy prospect that an English composer who might fill Purcell's shoes had finally arrived.

Arne was born in 1710 to a London upholsterer, who placed him in a lawyer's office as a teen-ager, only to discover that the lad preferred to play violin in an amateur chamber orchestra. Young Arne had begun music studies on his own, after smuggling a small harpsichord into his upstairs bedroom and muffling the string in order not to be heard practicing. He then took lessons in secret from a colleague of Handel's. After discovering Italian opera, he often attended, dressed in servant's livery, taking his place upstairs in the Haymarket gallery, which was free to domestics. Finally reconciling himself to Thomas's musical aspirations, the elder Arne sent him to Francesco Geminiani, the Italian who taught Britons how to play in the authentic Continental fashion.

In 1732, the father financed a series of English opera productions, with young Thomas conducting and Susanna Maria, his sister, singing leads in works by Lampe, John Christopher Smith, Handel's friend and music agent, and Thomas's own new version of the ill-fated *Rosamund* libretto by Addison. The performances attracted theatergoers who had been deprived of their favorite Italian operas by the success of Gay's *Beggar's Opera* and Handel's resultant defection in favor of English-language oratorios. The Arnes' music series came to an end with Thomas's burlesque of Fielding's *Tragedy of Tragedies, or the Life and Death of Tom Thumb,* with the youngest Arne, five years old, in the title role, a score young John Walsh promptly issued in sheet music and tune book.

Arne continued to write for the stage, the best known of his compositions being the frequently revived *Comus* and songs for *As You Like It.* The settings of "Under the greenwood tree" and "Blow, blow thou winter wind" immediately found a place in the standard concert repertoire. In the summer of 1740, Arne's reputation was considerably enhanced by a performance of the patriotic masque *Alfred,* played before a relatively small group of the prince of Wales's friends. The work was one result of the poor relations between George II and his heir, Frederick, who had been thrown out of St. James's Palace and took up residence at Clivedon, an imposing Thames-side estate. To mark the anniversary of the House of Hanover's ascendancy to England's throne and his daughter's third birthday, two masques were commissioned, Congreve's *Judgement of Paris* and a work based on a libretto by James Thomson, the prince's Scottish pensioner and author of the famous long poetic work *The Seasons.* Though the latter, *Alfred,* dealt with England's Saxon king and his Danish wars, it also called for appearances of other British rulers, Elizabeth among them. Accompanied by trumpets, winds, and strings, the masque ended with a chorus singing the last of ten Arne songs, "Rule, Britannia." Since France was once more threatening to involve the country in a continental war, the song swept England almost at once. Song sheets were printed, but the words and music were first published under a royal grant assuring Arne of a fourteen-year copyright, appended to the score of another of his masques. "Rule, Britannia" took on the character of a national anthem.

During this time, the theater was suffering a serious economic crisis, and after Susanna Arne, now wed to the actor son of poet laureate and theater manager Colley Cibber, sang one of the lead roles in the Dublin world premiere of Handel's *Messiah* and intrigued her brother with reports of the city's vital musical life, Arne moved to Ireland with his wife of six years. He remained several years, returning in 1745 as the Drury Lane's musical director and beginning a long connection with London's pleasure gardens. As conductor of music at Vauxhall and later at Marylebone and Ranelagh and writer of popular songs first offered there, Arne became a well-known figure. In these formal gardens, where all vegetation was carefully trimmed and kept neat, and classical statuary of nymphs and satyrs or contemporary figures dotted the winding paths, whispering lovers assuaged their passions in well-hidden dells and wanton baggages were available in plenty for the city's gallants. After a five o'clock opening, a shilling entry fee bought access to all manner of alfresco joys: food; entertainment; trompe l'oiel pictures painted on transparent materials and lighted from behind to create a stunning effect; waterfalls, fountains, canals, and artificial ruins; fireworks, and the sudden burst of illumination as the long summer day ended and night fell. Bands and pipe organs entertained in large amphitheaters, the balconies of which contained "little ale-house" boxes, accommodating seven or eight people. The ladies, in evening dress and occasionally masked, ate and drank while listening to concerts of vocal and instrumental music. Innovations were often presented, such as two grand bassoons, the greatness of whose sound was said to surpass that of any other bass instrument whatever. There were rehearsals, such as that of Handel's *Royal Fireworks,* for which 12,000 tickets were purchased, creating so vast a traffic jam that no carriage could pass on London Bridge for three hours; vaudeville exhibitions; pantomimes; rope walkers; equilibrists, and the best-known popular singers of the day, including Tommy Lowe, of the Drury Lane, who played Macheath, introduced "Rule, Britannia," and was a Vauxhall attraction for twenty years before he laid aside enough money to buy Marylebone, its competitor; Charles Bannister, the imitator of castrati; the Covent Garden prima donna Nan Catley; J. C. Bach's pupil Mrs. Weichsel, who sang her teacher's songs. Handel often went as a paying customer to hear his own cantatas, passing by his statue, placed in Vauxhall by the management as a signal honor to the world's greatest living composer.

Arne wrote an immense number of songs for the three major gardens, publishing twenty books of them. The first two, in 1745, *Lyric Harmony,* were sold by subscription from his home. He received twenty guineas for each of his collections, which became an annual affair under the general title *Vocal Melody,* with occasional others, *The Agreeable Musical Choice, Summer Amusement, The Winter's Amusement, The Vocal Grove,* and the last, in 1777, *Syren,* most of which were also available at his home after the stores had run through the books' first splash of popularity. They were usually printed for voice with keyboard accompaniment and music for the flute, but Arne also published full engraved scores of his most successful theater pieces.

When David Garrick assumed control of all Drury Lane offerings, Arne was already reckoned one of the nation's cultural glories, a judgment in which the actor did not concur, and he brought in the slightly deaf organist and composer William Boyce. A St. Paul's choirboy, the son of a cabinetmaker, and taught by Maurice Greene, master of the King's band, Boyce had written the songs for Vauxhall prior to Arne's arrival. For the following decade, Arne was in constant rivalry with a series of composers hired by Garrick in his search for a musician to his taste. The master of the Drury Lane took to calling Arne the Rapscallion and a good-for-nothing behind his back, epithets he brought on himself in part by a sour nature and flagrant womanizing, from which his natural son Michael was born in 1740. The boy inherited much of his parent's talent, exhibiting his precocity at the age of ten with publication of *The Flow'ret,* a collection of popular songs including the public favorite "The Highland Laddie."

To Arne's considerable chagrin, Boyce, who was almost exactly his age, received a doctor of music degree from Cambridge at a four-day festival of his music. During the event, Boyce left his place at the harpsichord to conduct the orchestra, standing before it, the first Englishman to do so in public. When Garrick staged a virtual competition between Arne and Boyce, ordering an all-sung afterpiece from each, it was Boyce who won, with the two-act *The Chaplet* (1749), played more than one hundred times in the next year and often in the colonies. The piece's overture is the third of Boyce's *Eight Symphonies,* all of them overtures to stage works, published in 1760 by the young John Walsh. They were discovered in the twentieth century by an English conductor and properly identified as to their source by Roger Fiske, in his brilliant *English Theatre Music in the Eighteenth Century.* Boyce's *The Shepherd's Lottery* (1751) was, as Fiske points out, the first English musical stage work "to have a finale of the type later known as 'vaudeville' because of its prevalence in popular French opera. This consisted of a song, usually strophic, with ensemble or choral refrains in which each of the main characters was allowed one verse. It may be presumed that vaudevilles were always sung with the company lined up across the stage and facing the audience."

Immediately after Boyce's success with *The Chaplet,* Arne stalked out of the Drury Lane to join John Rich at Covent Garden, where he was never completely happy either, although he did write several works that brought him great acclaim. He found far more satisfaction as a teacher of singing, one secret of his success being his great concern for clarity of enunciation. The most brilliant of his many pupils was Charlotte Brent, who became one of Covent Garden's stellar soloists during the 1760s. Arne wrote many songs to display her remarkable voice and powers of bravura execution, which added to his reputation as a vocal coach. His place at the Drury Lane was filled in part by James Oswald, a Scotsman who had approached Garrick to confide that his music store and publishing office had become the meeting place for a group of amateur and professional musicians calling themselves the Society of the Temple of Apollo and who wished to keep their activities from public knowledge. However, Oswald did offer Garrick the group's composing and arranging services, which were promptly accepted to fill the void created by Arne's departure. Only a quarter-century later did the eminent British music historian Charles Burney reveal that he was a member of the society. He had been apprenticed to Arne at the age of seventeen for a period of seven years, under the usual terms that obliged him to give his master any money he earned. He did very well playing at Vauxhall and the Drury Lane and accompanying Mrs. Arne, who was a highly regarded professional singer and did extend tenders of affection to the young musician because of her husband's constant philandering. After a few years, a wealthy friend bought Burney's freedom from Arne, paying £200 for the privilege, and he began to write for Oswald. The Society of the Temple of Apollo was created as a device to keep news of Burney's profitable activities from his former teacher. When Burney wrote an expanded version of *Alfred,* in which Garrick strutted as England's Saxon king, only two of the original songs were preserved, "Rule, Britannia" being one of them. A petulant Arne took out newspaper advertising to remind Londoners that he was the hit song's true composer.

In 1755, Boyce was named master of the King's Music and had no more time for the theater, devoting himself instead to the volumes of *Cathedral Music* upon which much of his renown is based. When the Seven Years' War was three years old and a flotilla of barges and 18,000 French regulars were braced to invade England, the threat prompted Garrick's *Harlequin's Invasion,* with music by a number of composers. The score included Arne's setting of Garrick's

> Hearts of oak are our ships,
> Jolly tars are our men;
> We are always ready,
> Steady, boys, steady,
> We'll fight and we'll conquer again and again

to a melody he lifted from Boyce's music for an earlier pantomine. The song and the music were to be heard again and again in America.

Arne returned to the Drury Lane in 1755, to find a new rival for the post of principal composer, John Christopher Smith, the son of Handel's old friend and a stepson of Mrs. Cluer, the music publisher. Smith had come to England at the age of eight with his father, at Handel's urging, studied with the German master, and was now regarded as a most promising musician. With Garrick as librettist, he wrote several full-length, all-sung versions of Shakespeare's plays, which did not do well at the box office. The lyrics were borrowed from many sources, both old and recently printed, comic scenes were deleted as being old-fashioned, and plots were changed to give Garrick and his players opportunity to appear as more modern characters. Finally, Garrick and Smith did produce a hit, *The Enchanter* (1760), a "Turkish tale," for which a national appetite was beginning. By then Arne had finished with the dictatorial Drury Lane manager and been welcomed at Covent Garden. Things were taking a turn for the better for him, Oxford at last giving him the music doctorate he so desired.

During the years after John Rich built the new Covent Garden, in 1731, the playhouse had become best known for its musical presentations. Large numbers of dancers were maintained, and when stage dancing became fashionable, foreign masters were imported to create new choreography. Covent Garden's splendid orchestra played the latest popular music between acts, Handel's *Water Music* being the most demanded, as well as works by other Europeans residing in London. Newspaper advertising listed the music to be played during the intervals, a practice that ended in the 1740s. Though its singing cast was talented, Covent Garden had no woman as popular as the town's favorite comedienne, the delectable Kitty Clive, who was a fixture at the Drury Lane for some forty years. She was its star when Garrick made his debut in London, and Doctor Johnson continued to label her "the best player I ever saw" when she retired at the age of fifty-eight, in 1769. Clive was among the first to introduce Irish songs in the patent theaters, singing in Gaelic the "Ellin A Roon" that became an American hit, and she was never allowed, by either pit or gallery to leave the stage until she had sung at least one of the songs written for her by Handel, or an aria from his oratorios. Handel wrote the part of Dalilah in *Samson* with her in mind, and she also appeared in many of his productions of *Messiah*. The song for which she was best known was "The Life of a Beau," words by James Miller and music by Henry Carey, which she first sang in 1738. Although she was self-taught, Mrs. Clive, like other featured performers, used her own funds, not only for vocal coaching by the house music master, but also for songs that were exclusively her's. In a 1744 contract dispute, she complained that her out-of-pocket expenses included large sums to the Drury Lane's master of singing, over and above the 6 pounds paid him weekly by the management.

During the 1760s, Covent Garden took the palm from the Drury Lane as London's favorite musical playhouse. This was owing to many factors: better facilities in which to see and hear music, a larger and more comfortable seating capacity—2,100 against the Drury Lane's tightly packed 500 less, and a new interest in musical productions sparked by John Rich's new son-in-law, James Beard, the most popular singing star on the stage, who actively solicited new vehicles suited to his talent and perception of the audience's taste for things relating to modern contemporary themes. Within a few years, Covent Garden was all the fashion, its audiences surrendering their affections to a new style of comic opera despite a detractors' claim that "very indifferent poetry was set to old tunes, without character and scarcely with any sentiment." This may have been true in part, but Covent Garden's string of new musicals brought increased attendance and a group of new hit songs that soon appeared both in sheet music and in publications patterned after Walsh's *Comic Tunes*.

At Beard's urging, Rich hired Arne as house composer and at once set him to work writing what turned out to be his most successful stage works, beginning with the short, twenty-three minutes exactly, afterpiece *Thomas and Sally,* starring Beard and Charlotte Brent. It opened in November 1760, accompanied by an orchestra in which clarinets appeared for the first time in an English theater. The piece remained in the London and American repertory for the next four decades, and *The American Musical Miscellany,* an excellent guide to the musical tastes of the new nation, published in Massachusetts in 1798, included its opening song. The libretto went on sale opening night, and a printed edition of the full musical score—overture, songs, dialogues, duets, and dance tunes—was published by Arne in 1761 and reissued by an assignment of copyright to John Walsh, Jr., who had inherited his parent's nose for commercial stage works. This short pastoral opera was the first successful Jolly Jack Tar stage musical, dealing with the much admired British seamen presented first on stage in Congreve's *Love for Love* (1695) and continuing to Gilbert and Sullivan's *H. M. S. Pinafore*. *Thomas and Sally's* lustful country squire made determined advances on the virginity of a country maiden whose swain was away at sea. Barely managing to preserve that jewel, she greeted her returned lover for a happy ending. Persistent record collectors may find, in dusty bins, the Intimate Opera Society of Great Britain's full version of this historic musical.

The success of Arne's first Covent Garden production was due most to his new collaborator, Isaac Bickerstaffe, a young Irishman who began his social and sexual career at the age of ten, while serving as a page to the lord lieutenant of Ireland. He picked up additional "unnatural appetites" as a marine officer, a service from which he was dismissed under discreditable circumstances, and he ended his life in exile on the Continent after committing "an unmentionable" sexual offense. Bickerstaffe counted the most illustrious literary figures among his friends, if not his lovers—Johnson, Garrick, Gainsborough, Joshua Reynolds, and Oliver Goldsmith—and lived the life of a successful playwright, whose chief income came from the sale of printed librettos and the proceeds of the third, sixth, and ninth performance of each play, taking all receipts after the players and his composer and the musicians were paid. The composer, on the other hand, made his income from sales of his printed scores, usually sold from his home by subscription after initial sale at music stores, his weekly theater salary of 6 pounds, the charity of his collaborator, lessons in singing and music, and work outside the theater in such places as Vauxhall. Critics rarely considered the instrumental music, even though it and the hit songs did as much to bring in audiences as the plot and dialogue.

When Rich died in 1761, Beard took over complete artistic control, giving Arne his head in the process. After a dull beginning, Arne wrote the ploddingly successful *Artaxerxes,* produced in 1762 complete with castrati and providing Beard with a bravura role as the villainous Persian general and a major hit song, "Water parted from the sea," its words written by Arne, who had learned that working alone greatly increased his profits. With it and other hit songs, such as "The soldier tir'd with war's alarms," also from *Artaxerxes,* and "Thou like the glorious sun," from his oratorio *Judith,* he wrote some of the best-known pieces of theater music in England and America in the second half of the eighteenth century. Though *Artaxerxes* was never produced in America until the following century, its two songs were available in sheet music, songbooks, and hand-drawn manuscript. Mrs. John Johnson, widow of the London publisher, issued the full score after its premiere, adding further circulation to the songs. Jefferson's library at Monticello contained both, and a barrel organ imported from England for sale in Philadelphia in 1771 with twenty rolls of music contained another of the *Artaxerxes* songs, "In infancy," which eventually became the music for the nursery song "The Queen of Hearts she baked some tarts."

With *Artaxerxes* a thoroughgoing success, its songs were reprinted in monthly periodicals, thus gaining additional currency around the English-speaking world. Garrick staged several unsuccessful imitations, adding to Arne's self-satisfaction. He was less pleased by the sudden enthusiasm being showered on Bach's recently arrived twenty-seven-year-old son John Christopher, who had been named master of music to the new young queen, Charlotte. Pining for the Germany she had so recently departed, she was happy to share the guttural glories of their mother tongue with Bach. Although Arne had introduced clarinets to the theater, young Bach was being credited with that innovation, and his partisans condemned Arne's translation of *Artaxerxes,* pointing out that Bach had done far better with Metastasio's original story in an opera produced in Turin concurrently with Arne's in London. Supporters of Italian opera lobbied successfully for Bach's appointment as the Haymarket's musical director, expecting him to restore the theater to its days of glory under Handel. Once again, Arne's claim to the title of Britain's best composer was being challenged by a German. The success of his new works, however, was to move English opera into new directions and add new luster to an already splendid record of achievement.

Among the imitations stemming from *The Beggar's Opera*'s success were stage works dealing with village virtue and pastoral innocence, rather than the whores, highwaymen, and street people of Gay's masterpiece. The first and best of these, *The Village Opera,* (1729) by Charles Johnson, also used well-known ballad melodies. The plot dealt with a wealthy young man masquerading as a servant in order to win the heart of a lady's maid, only to learn after a series of misadventures, coincidences, and impersonations that she is, like him, highborn and wealthy. Many others used it before Johnson did, and before Bickerstaffe settled upon it for his next venture with Arne. The result was *Love in a Village,* (1762), a ballad opera but with a difference, because, as Bickerstaffe wrote in his dedication of the work to Beard, who played a role written expressly for him, the tunes were not the old familiar ballad melodies. Nor was the music written in the old-fashioned manner prevalant when Pepusch reluctantly set Gay's libretto to music. Arne wrote nineteen of the forty-three songs, six of them new. The remainder were lifted from Italian opera, contemporary instrumental music, songs from Vauxhall and Ranelagh, from the pens of Boyce, Handel, Galuppi, Giardini, Geminiani, and nine others, as well as a few new popular tunes to which Bickerstaffe wrote new words. For the between-the-acts dances, performed by a young actress whose scanty dress occasionally permitted her bosom to be bared, Arne chose "Nancy Dawson" and Leveridge's "Roast beef of England," among others. Influenced by Handel, the quality of British musicianship had improved greatly since 1728, and Arne was well aware of the progress of music from Purcell's and Pepusch's simpler orchestrations; so he scored the music for an orchestra of nineteen, doubling on strings, winds, and horns in postludes, rather than *The Beggar's Opera*'s traditional harpsichord introductions.

As was the custom, the *Love in a Village* libretto was on sale opening night, December 2, 1762, and an engraved full score was published by Robert Bremner a few months later. Many editions of the songs, arranged for keyboard and voice, appeared, and within a few years, libretto, music, and songs were on sale in leading American cities. One of the oddities of the score was the song "In love should there meet a fond pair," credited to Mr. Bernard, a pseudonym for George III, who was, according to contemporaries, "qualified to compose," having been taught to play the harpsichord by Handel.

Four years after its London opening, *Love in a Village* was introduced to American audiences, who quickly declared their fondness for this new type of stage musical, the "pastiche," from *pasticcio,* lyric drama with music "compiled from the most eminent masters." Unlike Gay, Arne had not truly created a new form; he had merely borrowed a device used in Italian opera for many years, particularly on the Haymarket stage, where most of the past seasons' operas were made up of music "from the best masters."

After more than thirty years and forty-four operas, Handel turned his attention in 1741 to other and more lucrative musical forms, that year completing *Messiah.* He had tried to get the man in the street into his theater by abandoning the subscription system that funded opera in England for years, and sold tickets to anyone coming to the box office with money. His last opera, *Deidama,* a comic musicalization of the Greek military hero Achilles's adventures among palace ladies while disguised as a young girl in order to avoid going off to the Trojan War, was full of genuinely popular tunes. Walsh, however, was unable to sell the printed score, so much had London theatergoers lost their taste for the German's English-language operas, which dealt mostly with foreign subjects in which they had little interest.

When Handel's programs of opera, pastorales, odes, and his popular instrumental music were abandoned, the opera house in the Haymarket, where they were given, was taken over by an Italian opera company, sponsored by a wealthy British patron. A series of European composers was imported to write new works for upper-class audiences, to restore the house to its former glory. Among these were Baldassare Galuppi, whose toccatta was much admired by Victorians, including Robert Browning, who wrote a poem about it; the Florentine Francesco Veracini; and Christoph Gluck, whose best-known work, *Orfeo, ed Euridice,* was some twenty years in the future. Most Englishmen had, as Burney wrote in his *General History of Music* (1789), lost their taste for the "hasty, light and flimsy" style reigning in Europe at the time, "which Handel's solidity and science had taught the English to despise." The introduction of full-length Italian opera by these visiting masters did improve attendance for a time, but reduced it when serious foreign opera was offered. Walsh's regular publication of *Favorite Songs from the Opera* and his *Delizie Del Opera* failed to stimulate patronage.

The advent of more demanding and talented conductors, more glamorous prima donnas, the introduction of operatic pasticcios, and the return of comic opera eventually made an evening at the Haymarket once again a pleasant experience. Many of the new operas were by Galuppi, who was winning fame for comic pieces written after he returned to his native Italy. His chief collaborator in most of them was Carlo Goldoni, the great Italian playwright, who had turned his national theater around by creating new comic works to replace the timeworn comedia dell'arte.

There was, therefore, little new in the pastiche or medley. Gay's ballad opera was exactly that, made up of borrowed tunes arranged for orchestra and sung to new words. Pastiche operas were extremely popular in European houses during the eighteenth century, and Arne, recognizing their appeal, had turned to the device for *Artaxerxes.* His next works for Covent Garden, including his

solitary attempt to write an all-Italian opera, hooted off the stage after two performances, were usually disasters. Five years were to pass before he again wrote
music of any kind, an absence regretted by few.

## Enter Samuel Arnold

Riding high on his success with *Love in a Village,* Isaac Bickerstaffe found
ready and willing collaborators in two young musicians, Samuel Arnold and
Charles Dibdin, both of them in their early twenties. A Chapel Royal boy hired
by Beard after Arne's self-imposed exile from the theater, Arnold was immediately put to work on Bickerstaffe's *The Maid of the Mill,* an adaptation of
Samuel Richardson's *Pamela,* the tale of many attempted seductions of a reluctant virgin, whose virtue was rewarded by marriage, the only price she ever
placed on it. In the new and narrow morality of George III's court, most of the
juices of Richardson's lusty thousand pages were drained and little of the original plot was retained by Bickerstaffe. As had Arne, Arnold prepared a splendid pastiche for the comic opera, writing only two of the thirty-eight songs,
taking the remainder from French and Italian opera, but including some songs
written for the production by J. C. Bach and an overture composed by the amateur music lover Thomas, sixth earl of Kelley, who had been taught by Stamitz and wrote so much like his master that his work is often mistaken for that
of the man who trained him. In light of his noble station, the earl had been
given an automatic copyright on anything he wrote, good for nineteen years,
and he assigned that in the new stage work to Robert Bremner, recently arrived
from Scotland. The entire score of *The Maid of the Mill* proved to be so popular that the music was kept in manuscript to prevent the overfamiliarity that
would harm ticket sales. When Bremner finally published an authorized edition
for voice, harpsichord, or violin in 1765, it carried the warning that "who-
soever presumed to print or write out for sale any song in this opera will be
prosecuted by the author and proprietors with the utmost rigor of the law."
Arnold made little profit out of the success, received only twelve pounds for
his share from Bickerstaffe, while the dramatisti enjoyed an income from benefit performances and sales of the printed libretto, an eighth share in which he
sold for twenty pounds to the Fleet Street publisher Thomas Lowndes.

The popular organist and songwriter James Hook's departure from Marylebone Gardens for Vauxhall in 1774 was a sign of Marylebone's downward decline, as clerks, nursemaids, and the lower middle class poured into what had
long been a gathering place for the gentry. The display there of fireworks and
other spectacles arranged by the management to lure in this new clientele turned
away the music-loving patrons, who followed Hook to Vauxhall. Using money
from the dowry provided by his new parents-in-law, Arnold took over Marylebone, where he staged a number of popular musical comedies, known as
"burlettas," something between the ballad and the comic opera in content and
musical complexity. The most successful was a revival of Pergolesi's *La Serva
Padrona,* called *The Maid the Mistress* in its English translation, a light, me-

lodious short opera that influenced the theater in Britain much as Goldoni had done in Italy.

In 1772, a French pyrotechnician was employed to create an outdoor fireworks show that continued to be Marylebone's chief attraction, despite neighbors' complains about the noise and smell, when Arnold discovered a new outlet for his talents, to replace summertime activities at the pleasure garden, where the cupidity of staff and partners was bilking him of profits, he sold the money-losing real estate to a builder. His friend George Colman had resigned from Covent Garden's management and taken over the third royal playhouse, the Little Theatre in the Haymarket. Arnold, extremely busy during the winter months with lessons and other musical duties, found that this theater, whose season ran only from late spring until early autumn, offered him the stage he needed. He wrote most of his theater music for it until his death. One of the earliest projects was the 1777 first staging of Gay's *Polly,* known only from the printed versions, and no such success as its predecessor, but Arnold's *Spanish Barber,* based on the Beaumarchais play *The Barber of Seville,* was constantly revived until the end of the century.

In 1779, Arnold began to collaborate with the Irish playwright John O'Keeffe, who, because his eyesight was failing, required the services of an amanuensis to put his hit plays down on paper. The most profitable of their works was the 1781 *Agreeable Surprise;* it had more than 200 performances at the Little Theatre. O'Keeffe had been a child actor in Dublin. He wrote a well-received play at the age of fifteen and headed for London. His knowledge of Irish songs, which he constantly sang, provided the ingredient that made his stage works not only highly individual but also extremely popular. For the first time in his career, Arnold found himself making more money than his playwright partner, due chiefly to the relationship he had developed with a new music publisher, John Harrison, who produced a forty-volume "complete" Handel, full of editorial errors, which recent musicology is correcting, thus permitting the German's music to be heard as it was intended. Among other duties, Arnold served as consultant for the *New Musical Magazine,* which contained sixteen-page supplements of piano arrangements of old theater vocal scores. He also organized the Glee Club, a group of London music teachers who met regularly at London taverns to sing old songs and some new ones; took up compilation of *Cathedral Music,* a project halted by Boyce's death, which became Arnold's most important contribution to concert music; and found time to write full-length musicals for performance during the summer at the Little Theatre. The most important of these was *Inkle and Yariko,* written with George Colman, Jr., in 1787, and popular for fifty years, a highly controversial work based on London's treatment of its blacks and the whole question of slavery.

London's black population of 15,000 had increased after the American Revolution through the influx of colonial slaves who had served with the British Army and were being distributed on a virtual aliquot basis around the world. With no work for them in London, they were soon reduced to begging, winning the name "St. Giles' blackbirds" from the slum district to which they were confined by their economic condition. A Committee for the Relieving of the

Black Poor, formed in 1786, offered a plan to send the overflow to a newly established colony at Sierra Leone, on Africa's west coast. The effort failed, few wishing to leave Britain, and the fifty white prostitutes who took advantage of the proposal did not make ideal pioneers. Despite efforts by liberal young members of Parliament, no effective legislation was passed to deal with the problem. In 1787, the stalemate provided Colman with a powerful theme. His play was based on the reportedly true account of a British trader in Barbados who was saved from death at the hands of natives by a young black woman. After reaching safety together, he sold his rescuer into slavery, despite the child she bore him. London magazines picked up the story, christening the man Inkle and the woman Yariko. Colman added a second romance, between a white London Cockney and a black woman, and treated all the characters most sentimentally, leading to the marriage of Inkle and Yariko.

The work proved so successful during its summer run that Covent Garden acquired its rights for the regular season. For years, it played in major theaters, and, like the Union Jack, was carried by British actors abroad to Calcutta, Jamaica, and the United States. Obviously, even though white Englishmen were aroused by the black man's plight as depicted so dramatically in *Inkle and Yariko,* the perception of whiteness as the ideal continued to be paramount. Charles Dibdin, in particular, usually treated blacks as either comic figures or pathetic images and victims of white man's greed.

## Charles Dibdin, "Tyrtaeus of the British Navy"

Isaac Bickerstaffe chose well when he asked Charles Dibdin in 1767 to contribute music to the pasticcio he was at work on, *Love in the City.* Only in his early twenties, Dibdin already had some impressive theater experience, having worked with Michael Arne on Garrick's version of *A Mid-summer Night's Dream,* written songs and some moderately successful plays for Covent Garden, been a smashing success when he stepped in to take a leading role in *The Maid of the Mill,* and was the first major figure to write theater music who had some understanding of the responsibilities and requirements of a working actor. Before his day in the sun ended, Dibdin wrote enough songs to fill 600 pages of small print, and though his name may not have been known there, his music was loved by Americans, as witness the *American Musical Miscellany,* half of whose theater songs, words and music, were by Charles Dibdin.

He was born in 1745 to a silversmith–parish clerk in Hampshire, the twelfth of fourteen children, and had little formal education. Before his teens, he turned up regularly in nearby Winchester, singing at the college, the race track, the local concert rooms, and for hangers-on at the courthouse. The cathedral's organist took a liking to him and taught him enough of that instrument's rudiments to persuade the youth that he was capable of filling a vacancy in the organ loft of a nearby church, only to be turned down on account of his age. In 1760, his brother Tom was in England, between tours of duty overseas for the West India Company, and sent for Charles to join him in London. The city's musical delights astounded the boy. He visited not only places of religious worship and music, but also coffeehouses and pleasure gardens, where the newest songs were played and sold. Tom Dibdin apprenticed him to music publisher and instrument dealer John Johnson, who was located in Cheapside, opposite Bow Church. Learning that Charles was familiar with keyboards, Johnson immediately put him to work tuning harpsichords. It was there he learned how to handle songs like "Moll Peatley," "Bobbin Joan," and "Lillibulero," and took up extempore playing, first improvising melody lines, then setting them down in songs, which his master promptly rejected. From the vocal and piano music published in the shop, Dibdin was able to learn the basics of committing music to paper. When Tom was captured at sea by a French man-of-war and placed in a naval jail, Charles was left to make his own way and took some of his songs to a popular singer in one of the smaller outdoor gardens. These proved so acceptable that the Thompson brothers, last of the St. Paul's district publishers, bought his music outright for six guineas, selling it for one and a half pence a copy. This experience set Dibdin off on a lifelong hatred of the publishing craft, unaware that the publishers' treatment was generous. Unknowns were usually asked to pay for paper and printing as well as a twenty percent commission on all sales.

In the Thompsons' stock, he discovered collections of Corelli concertos and Rameau's books of theory, and studied them to complete his minimally basic music education. Helped by a new friend, who introduced him to the theatre's magical world, Dibdin got work as a chorus boy at Covent Garden, and promptly amazed everyone by his ability to write out complete vocal scores from memory. John Rich saw a future Leveridge in him and gave encouragement, but the eccentric theater owner's sudden death dashed that prospect. Dibdin then worked to hone his singing actor's tools at Covent Garden during the season and in provincial companies in the summer.

His big opportunity came when he, nearly twenty, was selected to replace an ailing performer cast as Ralph, the second singing lead, in the Bickerstaffe-Arnold *Maid of the Mill*. The production was an enormous hit, and Dibdin became one of its most talked-about players, called back to encore each of his singing numbers. The Ralph hankerchief he wore onstage was adopted by the city's smart young men, and he was signed for three years as a permanent Covent Garden company member, at three pounds a week the first year, with a pound increase each year after. The opportunity to work with Bickerstaffe came, and he not only wrote some of the piece's best songs but also played one of the Cockney leads in a story about London's working classes.

It was evident to all that a new and exciting songwriting talent had appeared. Arne sought him out and won the young man's friendship when he helped him out of a serious argument with the orchestra musicians, who had threatened to drive him out of Covent Garden. The arrogant composer and bumptious actor had much in common, not the least of it their skirt-chasing. As a teen-ager, Dibdin had married a woman of no particular beauty for her money, through which he went quickly. He abandoned her then to begin an affair with one of

Covent Garden's pretty dancers. The relationship continued for eight years, producing two illegitimate sons, both of whom also became theater songwriters.

Because he played the harpsichord, Dibdin was often assigned to the theater orchestra, and on May 15, 1767, he made history by playing—to accompany a singing actress between the acts—a pianoforte for the first time on a stage. Driven from their homeland by the seemingly interminable Seven Years' War, German refugees had built square hammer harpsichords, the kind he used. These eventually put an end to a century of British affection for the true harpsichord.

After a relatively unsuccessful script dealing with London life, Bickerstaffe returned to pastoral subjects, winning success with *Lionel and Clarissa,* half of whose score Dibdin wrote for forty-five pounds. Although he told friends that the dramatist was after music "as cheap as possible," he continued to work with Bickerstaffe, on what would become one of their most successful works, *The Padlock.*

Having grown weary of backstage bickering, and deaf as well, John Beard had sold his share of the Covent Garden's patent, for £60,000 to a group of investors headed by the elder George Colman, a playwright who had quarreled with Garrick over royalties and was determined to best his former friend at the box office. Bickerstaffe found Colman intolerable, and the new proprietor was making Dibdin's final year of his three-year contract a living hell. Only their joint work on a short comic opera made life worthwhile for them. The plot was a short story, "The Jealous Husband," by Cervantes. It concerned the efforts of an old miser to protect both his gold and his young wife by placing a padlock on his front door. Although, as Samuel Johnson wrote, "there was as much fornication amongst farmers as amongst gentlemen," in deference to convention, Bickerstaffe changed the wife to a young ward and extended the part of a black servant to suit the talents of a leading actor who had learned the local dialect in the West Indies.

Unlike Americans, Britons used poor whites for the cheapest sort of manual labor, and the Industrial Revolution was devouring white men, women, and even small children at a tremendous rate. London investors in the triangular slave trade, meanwhile, made millions annually. Black slaves were found in most large cities, some 14,000 of them in the years just before the American Revolution. Small black children were often purchased to serve as pages in wealthy households or as pets for indolent women. Older blacks were generally treated as in America, being bought and receiving no salary for their domestic services. Many enlightened Britons saw the slave trade as a blot on the national honor and, like Doctor Johnson, who had educated and freed his black servant, agitated for the change that finally resulted from a 1772 court decision that freed any black man the moment he stepped on British soil.

Most blacks, in America and Britain, had had in common their introduction to their new masters' language in a West Indian slave pen. Though many African influences remained in the resultant black English, white men perceived it as a very limited vocabulary, made up of words that usually changed the final syllable into *ee,* or pronouns that chose *we* for *us, he* for *his, me* for *I,* and a *d* or *t* for *th.*

Mungo, the slave owned by *The Padlock*'s miser, was a black counterpart of the mid-eighteenth-century white servant stereotype, cowardly and shiftless, devoted to those who treated him well, impertinent and disloyal to those who did not, fond of drink, always ready to accept a bribe, given to considerable fancification of the language in a hopeful attempt to speak as did his master, and determined to provide the play's happy ending.

Blackness had often intrigued English dramatists. Shakespeare's Othello was a well-educated Moor; in 1695, Thomas Southerne made a five-act play of Aphra Behn's novel about an African prince, *Oronooko.* James I's Danish queen commissioned Ben Jonson to write his first masque so that she and her ladies could appear in blackface. Polly, heroine of Gay's suppressed second ballad opera, did not recognize her missing lover Macheath when he passed in black make-up as a local pirate. And just the previous year, one of *Love in the City*'s cast was a black servant. Although Tony Aston had advertised a program of Negro songs at Goodman's Fields some twenty years before, there had never been a leading black character in the British musical theater before the night Charles Dibdin appeared, in appropriate costume and make-up, as Mungo. Once more fortune was playing a role in the composer's life.

Earlier that spring, Garrick's ballet dancer wife had persuaded Dibdin to audition for the Drury Lane company, and then recommended to her husband that he listen to the new short opera she had just heard. Recognizing that at last he had access to the best theater composer he had yet found, Garrick hired Dibdin and agreed to Bickerstaffe's transfer to the Drury Lane. The curtain went up on *The Padlock* on October 3, 1768. Dibdin had come to covet the part of Mungo so much that he wrote music much too taxing for the actor cast, who finally resigned. The evening's main attraction was Garrick as Hamlet, but after seeing Dibdin as a black slave, it was he audiences came to see for the next fifty-three nights. The songs Dibdin wrote for Mungo, including the hit "Dear heart, what a terrible life I lead," were not true black music, only a white man's perception of what such exotica should sound like, but they set the pattern for all future such characterization and were in demand for years. Dibdin estimated that over 10,000 copies of the vocal score, published by John Johnson, were sold during the next two decades, wearing out three different sets of printing plates. A year after its London opening, *The Padlock* was staged in America, with the young actor Lewis Hallam, Jr., playing Mungo, and soon after, the words to one of the songs were first reprinted in the Poet's Corner of an American newspaper. Once more Bickerstaffe made more money from the play than Dibdin, who complained that whereas the author realized some £1,700 from sale of the libretto, he got only forty-five for writing all the music. Still, his first child, born out of wedlock, was named Charles Isaac Mungo, for its father, his collaborator, and the role in which Dibdin became the toast of London.

Only because his next work, *Damon and Phillida* (1768), was not much liked did Dibdin sell rights to the original libretto and score for fifteen pounds. His brother Tom had been released from a French prison and faced large debts built up during his incarceration. A contract with Ranelagh's owners to be house composer and singer for one hundred pounds a summer helped with the financial problems, too, and out of this connection came the earliest of Dibdin's popular street songs, which were often written with Bickerstaffe.

Relations with Garrick began to founder during preparation for the 1769 Shakespeare Jubilee celebration at Stratford-upon-Avon. The actor had written a new entertainment, composed of songs, odes, and choruses, which contained not a single word by the Bard. As he had often done, Garrick designed a competition, unbeknownst to its participants, assigning several composers, including Arne, to write music for his lyrics. Furious when he learned of the trick, even though it was his score that was chosen, Dibdin complained loudly about the writing and rewriting he had endured before Garrick was satisfied, and for which he had not yet received payment.

The greatest actor of his day rose in a foul temper on the day of jubilee to find a driving rainstorm threatening to bring the celebration to a stop. He was quickly mollified when Dibdin appeared with musicians to serenade Garrick with the song of which he was most proud, "Let beauty with the sun arise to Shakespeare, Shakespeare, Shakespeare!" The entertainment itself was a vast success, for Garrick had learned that it was best to present Shakespeare in music, dance, or pantomime. Delighted with Dibdin's work, he presented the songwriter with twenty guineas, even though the trip to Stratford and return cost twenty-six. Garrick brought the successful production back to London as *The Pageant of Shakespeares Jubilee,* with Dibdin's music as well as that of other competitors in the secret contest. The only tangible evidence of the Bard's plays was in seven floats drawn across the Drury Lane stage depicting tableaux from *Romeo and Juliet, Hamlet, Richard the Third,* and other plays. Londoners crowded the theater during a run of one hundred performances, and Johnson published *Shakespeare's Garland,* a collection of Dibdin songs written for the jubilee.

Dibdin worked out the balance of his Drury Lane contract under great tension. At the start of their relationship, Garrick was enthusiastic about his music, but that initial approval wore off as Dibdin, constantly in debt, drew against his salary and steadily increased his obligation. The borrowing was started to pay off Tom Dibdin's debts, to which was added the cost of an East India Company commission, and was then made a necessity by the songwriter's foolish habits and expensive way of living, leading to further strained relations with the theater manager. When Bickerstaffe ran off to France following a homosexual encounter with a soldier, a scurrilous pamphlet appeared raising the issue of immorality between Garrick and the dramatist. Though Dibdin was among the first to leap to the actor's defense, Garrick was far from grateful. He still had to tolerate tardiness, absence from rehearsals, failure to meet deadlines, music he considered inferior, and all because Dibdin wrote new works that drew in customers.

The situation changed abruptly with the success of *The Waterman,* an afterpiece first offered to the Drury Lane, as contract required. When it was rejected, the Little Theatre management produced it. The work had grown out of all-sung special material known as "dialogues," written, beginning in 1772, for the Sadler's Wells Theatre, an unlicensed house that could offer only musical works without spoken dialogue. The new brick building erected in 1764 elevated the character of entertainment presented there, to draw in a more affluent, better-behaved audience of shopkeepers, middle-class merchants, and their families. The new manager, Thomas King, knew Dibdin and began to commission dialogues from him dealing with life among London's Cockney lower class. The people in these short singing pieces evolved into *The Waterman*'s characters, self-reliant, honest, and hard-working. Their leader was Tom, owner of a small boat on which he ferried people on the Thames. The song "Waterman's Delight" was the show's hit, enjoying popularity in revivals that continued until Queen Victoria's death.

Angry because Dibdin had enjoyed such success outside the Drury Lane, Garrick commissioned a new Cockney musical, *The Cobbler* (1774). Despite its leading song's popularity, the afterpiece was withdrawn when a claque of the songwriter's enemies, all friends of the stage-dancer mistress he was about to desert, children and all, forced it off the stage. Determined to rid himself of the troublesome composer by any means possible, Garrick posted a notice that he was withholding Dibdin's salary until a debt of £200 was paid in full. Fearful of bailiffs in search of his assets, Dibdin avoided the Drury Lane, even when his last work there, *The Blackamour Wash'd White,* was announced, but seen by very few. The librettist, a modern and very muscular clergyman, Henry Dudley Bate, had incurred the enmity of a London man about town when he thrashed the man in public for an insult to a woman Bate knew. A professional prize fighter sent to punish Bate was knocked unconscious. In final revenge, a group of paid rowdies made such an uproar each time the piece was played that it was taken off the stage after four attempts to present it. The script does not exist, and the music is rare, but it did deal with blacks, one a leading character.

Harassed by collectors, unable to get employment at either of the two patent theaters, Dibdin fled to France, "to expand my ideas and store myself with theatrical materials," he said. The thirteen-hour Channel crossing was most unpleasant, though it did inspire "Blow high, blow low," the first of many songs with a nautical flavor that, in time, brought him great fame, the affection of a nation engaged in extended wars with France, and government pensions in recognition of their propaganda and morale value. Dibdin had only pity and contempt for the French. He detested the runaway lovers, smugglers, exiled duelists, and riffraff of English bankrupts, of which he was one, who thronged to France, particularly to Calais. Only the landlord of a local inn who assisted in clearing Dibdin's piano through customs won his regard. A new woman was with him, another Drury Lane actress, who stayed until he was free to marry, after the first Mrs. Dibdin died. The pair moved to Nancy, a stop on the touring circuit of professional opera companies. Attending every performance, Dibdin found plots enough for seven new works, one of them a full-length musical,

against his return to London, which was daily growing inevitable as tension
grew between France and England over the former's support of the American
rebels.

A Covent Garden contract binding him for one year at ten pounds a week
took him home. He provided the required three short works, but the success of
the past was not his again. Desperate over his continuing financial straits, Dibdin decided to take up his brother's invitation and go to the Orient, where Tom
had grown wealthy in the East India Company's service. Fate stepped in again,
however, dealing him another tragic blow. Tom was struck by lightning, losing
the use of one side of his body, and on his way back to England with wife and
child died and was buried at sea. In his grief, Dibdin wrote "Poor Tom Bowling," a song that remained in the British popular song literature until recently.

His Covent Garden contract was renewed for the 1780–81 season, but it was
evident that the end was near for him in the royal theaters. Composers were
obliged to be more compliant to theatrical managers' wishes, more in tune with
the times, more in favor with theatergoers, so he turned to the unlicensed houses,
to the puppet shows, and to that early form of circus the equestrian theater.

In the early eighteenth century, riding-school owners learned that the best
way to attract clients was to display their own skills in public demonstrations
at fairs or in open fields near their stables. Having witnessed their success, an
innkeeper in the London suburb of Islington hired Thomas Price, one of the
town's best riders, to lure customers to his out-of-the-way place of business.
Rivals soon appeared to challenge Price's most popular stunt, riding three horses
at full tilt. The most spectacular of them was William Sampson, a cavalry veteran who jumped a pair over fences, did handstands on their backs, crossed
under their bellies from one side to the other, and fired pistols as he galloped
full speed toward the spectators. Another rival added a swarm of bees to his
act, letting them settle about his face as he did his stunts.

As public enthusiasm for horses and riders took on a hysteria like that for
present-day rock stars, it remained for an astute business-minded equestrian to
bring the demonstrations into a controlled area to which admission could be
charged. He was Philip Astley, a former sergeant-major of His Majesty's Light
Dragoons, who enlisted at the age of seventeen and got his first stripe two years
later by leading a company of conscript shopkeepers and tradesmen in a charge
against French lines, winning for them the nickname Regiment of Tailors. Astley's skills eventually won him the highest noncommissioned rank, and he bought
himself out of the service when he was twenty-seven and ready to launch a
career entertaining people. He started in a field near Westminster Bridge, with
his wife, another fine rider, taking shillings at the gate and providing music on
a bass drum. Before performances, the hopeful impresario rode through London on a white stallion presented by a grateful cavalry commander, handing out
bills announcing them. Soon he began to sing as he rode around the arena. Crowds
poured in, and he found it necessary to surround the field with a paling fence.
George III rode by one day, took Astley to the palace for a command performance, and gave him a royal patent for the riding field. The stallion added many
tricks to the program, counting up to twenty, taking handkerchiefs out of spec-

tators' pockets, playing dead. When Astley's savings grew enough, in 1770, he opened a wooden theater, with sheltered seats around an open area in a former lumberyard near Westminster Bridge. Following a royal princess's death, he purchased timbers from the scaffolding erected for the funeral ceremonies and roofed over his building. Other attractions were added: a strong man, rope dancers, dancing horses, acrobats, a crocodile, and then his son, "a five-year wonder, the greatest equestrian performer of tender years in the world." Receipts averaged forty pounds a day.

In order that all ticket buyers could see the entertainment, Astley eventually installed a wooden ring forty-six feet in diameter in the center of his house and built a stage at one end. An orchestra sat between these two centers of attraction, providing music for the "grant equestrian dramatic spectacles" depicting national events. In early 1782, he advertised programs combining "all the splendours of Theatre and Fair" in a now magnificent amphitheater illuminated by candlelight, and the new production of *Mazeppa,* imported from Europe, where he had just toured and performed before the crowned heads of France and Austria and their courts.

During this visit to the Continent, Dibdin persuaded a group of businessmen to put up £15,000 to finance the Royal Circus Equestrian Philharmonic Academy, near Blackfriars Bridge, just outside the lord chamberlain's jurisdiction, to evade licensing problems, they hoped. An employee of Astley's, Charles Hughes, was hired to arrange equestrian spectacles. Dibdin was to manage the enterprise and stage musical programs of short pieces featuring singing and dancing. Their building was ready in 1782, but was closed immediately for want of a permit, as was Astley's for the same reason. Only after Astley pointed out to the lord chamberlain that the patent presented by George III also included control of the playing in public of trumpets by any but the royal musicians, and that he was also entitled to a penny each time the instrument was sounded at a fair, a playhouse, or a music room, did the lord chamberlain capitulate to his request for permission to operate as in the past.

Merely ignoring the order to cease activities, the Royal Circus also opened its doors, and London had two equestrian shows bidding for public favor. During the clamor over licensing, Dibdin built up a company of actors, dancers, and singers, all of whom, like members of similar Parisian "nurseries" for the stage, were children. The Genoese pantomimist Giuseppe Grimaldi, Covent Garden's ballet master for the past thirty years, was assigned to train twenty of these minors. He promptly bound them to himself as apprentices, thus entitling him to any money made as the result of his lessons. There was nothing unusual about this practice in the London theater. Most playhouse composers had similar arrangements with their pupils, receiving all fees for public performances during the contract term. Arne, Arnold, Dibdin, and many others profited every time their students were paid. But Grimaldi took to abusing the child dancers, as he did his own small son, Joseph, who later became Victorian England's greatest clown. Parents complained to Dibdin, but he chose not to change a long tradition.

Conspiring together, the Italian and Charles Hughes waited for the proper time to oust Dibdin, who still owed hundreds of pounds to creditors and was continually harassed by bill collectors. The theater was very successful during its first season, grossing almost £10,000 from programs of musical plays, ensemble and solo dancing, and horsemanship. Hughes's wife, a trick rider, topped Philip Astley's famous turn—riding with his head balanced on a small pot—by doing the same and then adding pot to pot; she was followed by an eight-year-old girl of the ballet company who was trained to ride two horses at full gallop.

During the next season Dibdin wrote many all-singing pieces for the Royal Circus children and players, "two or three pantomimes, four or five other intermezzos or a more trifling kind, at least fifteen ballets, each taking 12 to 14 airs, and an overture; and a variety of things more inconsiderable . . . for this strange, and to me, very unfortunate place" as he wrote in his memoirs. After attempting to bully his investors into paying him more, he was discharged and then imprisoned for debt. He used this time to write a book about his experiences with the Royal Circus, producing an exposure of backstage life and child-performer abuse that attracted little interest.

This period marked the lowest point of Dibdin's career, a life that was studded with many crises, usually of his own making. One legal document from this period turns over the sole right of printing, publishing, and vending five songs from Royal Circus productions for the sum of five pounds five shillings, about half the weekly payment from Covent Garden. One bright spot was the ten performances at the Drury Lane in 1785 of his *Liberty Hall,* out of which came his songs "The High Mettled Racer," "Jack Ratlin was the ablest seaman," and "The bells of Aberdovey." That success persuaded Hughes, now the Royal Circus's licensee-owner, to buy new material from Dibdin. But a plan to open a new theater financed by a wealthy merchant met with disaster when a storm tore down the framework, and with it went Dibdin's own investment of several hundred pounds of profit from his newest songs. Part of the scheme was the diversion of water from a nearby stream in order to stage "the greatest spectacles through the medium of hydraulics," a project he shelved only temporarily.

Production of some of his new works by the London playhouses enabled Dibdin to take a place in the country, giving him the privacy he desired to write music and complete a few long-contemplated projects. In the summer of 1786, he started a weekly magazine of satire, the *Devil,* with mostly original material. It folded by year's end, even though it had sold as many as 4,000 copies in a single day.

The Royal Circus continued to be second in popularity to Astley's, which was renamed the Royal Grove for the painted foliage adorning its interior. The new productions, virtually none of them Dibdin's, which were advertised as "more magical, pantomimical, farcical, tragical, comical," featured such exotica as German and Cossack horsemen, "Ethiopian Festivals" demonstrating the "whimsical actions and attitudes made use of by the Negroes," war entertainments, dumb shows, and the latest popular songs. While its owner was back in the cavalry during the 1794 military crisis involving France, the Royal Grove burned to the ground. It was rebuilt as the Royal Ampitheatre under the prince of Wales's patronage. There and in buildings succeeding it, the Astley family

and their successors presented glorious evenings—music, burlettas and pantomimes, beautiful girls, clowns, trick riders, and horses, horses, horses—until
the late Victorian period.

Though Tom was dead, Dibdin still looked to the East, as the place a once-
important London playwright and composer could make a fortune, as his brother
had. He was determined to go to India as soon as enough money could be raised.
His grand plan was a tour of England, to bid "adieu to a generous public who
have afforded me a long and liberal patronage," and with his profits be off to
where streets were paved with gold, particularly for Englishmen. Beginning in
late May 1787, he traveled through the provinces for fourteen months, giving
one-man shows, playing to audiences who knew and loved his songs and came
to see the man who had played Ralph in love in *Maid of the Mill* and *The Padlock*'s Mungo. Though the latter was often revived, no one had yet matched
him in the role, so he gave them its songs and dialect, and they enjoyed every
minute of his performance. Those provincial Britons who had never seen Dibdin or *The Padlock* got a taste and liking for blackface performers during this
trip, one that persisted through the century and into the present, with radio and
television performers.

In *The Musical Tour,* a book about his adventures in the hinterlands, Dibdin
published some of his monologues and songs, among them ones dealing with
West Indian slaves as he portrayed them onstage, as well as a variant on "Yankee Doodle," which pleased his audiences as a good joke on the American rebels who were engaged in setting up their own government. To add to his funds,
he sold the rights to more new songs, receiving two guineas for one and a half-
guinea for another, learning later that the publisher netted £200 from the latter,
which served only to confirm his contempt for music merchants.

With *The Musical Tour* safely in a publisher's hands and the police at his
heels, Dibdin packed wife and family aboard a ship bound for India. The Channel weather was foul, as it seemed always to be for this bard of the bounding
main, but it inspired no new "Blow high, blow low." Instead, he quarreled
with the master, cheered on near-mutinous sailors, and suddenly found himself
back in England, forced there by the weather. There was nothing for it now but
to begin paying off his debts. In lieu of going once again to Fleet Prison, he
rented an auction room in Covent Garden, where he began his own special form
of musical theater, Table Entertainment, which was to sustain him in the lean
years ahead.

These one-man shows were little more than evenings of song and story with
accompaniment performed on an instrument of his own devising and having all
the properties of a pianoforte and chamber organ. Near it stood a side drum, a
set of bells, a gong, and a tambourine, on which he varied the musical background. More like a person entertaining friends in his own drawing room than
a public performer, Dibden bent his near-sighted eyes close to the manuscript,
studied the notes for a moment, and then sat back on his chair to deliver songs
in a sweet and mellow baritone. His first presentation, in 1789, *The Whim of
the Moment,* contained another of his great hits, "Poor Jack." Though the first-
night audience was only sixteen persons, word of the entertainment got around,

and soon people crowded the room, always demanding encores of that song. In his memoirs, Dibdin complained that he could never get "Poor Jack" published and was finally forced to sell it and eleven other songs for sixty pounds, from which the publisher cleared £500. Others, however, remember that he himself printed the song and set up a street stall, to which crowds scrambled to buy "Poor Jack" in sheet music still wet with printer's ink. The success evidently persuaded him to become his own publisher and distributor, for in 1790 he set up business in a room on The Strand, which he christened Sans Souci, where he sold song sheets of his new table-entertainment material and old pieces from the musicals written for Covent Garden, Drury Lane, and Sadler's Wells. The sale of each song was completed with the signing of his autograph on the cover.

In 1796, he moved to a little house on Leicester Place, and in this second Sans Souci sold music by day and gave one-man shows by night in a room whose walls were decorated with his drawings, usually landscapes, for which he had a certain small talent.

The time of his greatest success as a writer of popular songs followed, the most acclaimed of them dealing with the men who sailed the seas in the navy. Believing that the typical punishment meted out to seamen was more severe than that given black slaves in America—since slaves were worth money, whereas seamen could be replaced by the press gang—Dibdin wrote in *The Musical Tour* of a flogging he had witnessed. At the end of 650 lashes out of the 1,000 ordered for attempted desertion, the bleeding youth was removed to the guardhouse, where he died the following morning. Such punishment was not unique, and Dibdin understood the need for discipline, because "depredators who have gone to church to pick pockets have converted into good citizens in the forecastle of a man-of-war." But, he complained, "foremastmen are generally punished with rigour, and the crimes of officers were too often palliated and softened into errors."

His heart was always with Jack Tar, an affection running through much of his music, reaching its most touching in the song written for his brother, "Poor Tom Bowling." In it and such pieces as "The sailor's consolation," "Saturday night at sea," "Tom Tackle," "Nancy," "The Lucky Escape," "Death or victory," and "The flowing can," runs a chord of sympathy, concern, and admiration. It echoed in the hearts of Britons, who sang, loved, and purchased his music and the heartfelt ditties that impelled thousands to enlist in the naval service as the French war grew more desperate. The songs won for him the honored title "Tyrtaeus of the British Navy," after the Greek poet commissioned by the Spartan council to write verses that would inspire men to join the struggle against Athens. In gratitude, the British government granted Dibdin an annual pension of £200 in 1803. Three years later, a new ministry, forgetting his contributions and mindful of economy, canceled the grant.

Dibdin should not be remembered only for his songs of seamen, most of them written for several dozen table entertainments between 1790 and 1809. There were other, equally popular, songs: those of the hunt, "To Batchelor's Hall" and "The Hare Hunt"; those about common people, such as "The Lamplighter," and those dealing with the black man.

Though he bought a London license each year from 1792 until 1808 "for recitative, singing and music by himself only," three times a week except on high holidays, Dibdin also ventured outside London, traveling thousands of miles through England and Scotland, and wrote a book of observations illustrated with his own pencil drawings. He was near sixty when the nineteenth century started, but his energy and interest in writing never abated. A five-volume *History of the English Stage* appeared in 1800, and his last book, a novel, in 1807. Tired of the music business, when the government pension was granted he sold his entire stock of music and 360 of his copyrights to the Oxford Street music dealers Ann Bland and E. Weller for £1,800, prepared to live on the proceeds and his government grant. When the latter was annulled, he was forced to increase his public appearances. His voice had deteriorated, and the public taste was uncertain. He was no longer a box-office attraction, and theatrical managers cared little for his new music. His two illegitimate sons, Charles and Thomas John, were making their own mark in the music world, but he ignored them, as he always had, even though they took his name.

The proceeds of a public dinner given in 1810 by the leading theater composers and writers were invested in annuities to make secure his future and that of his wife and daughters, and his ego was further restored when a once-again grateful government restored his pension. He died in 1813, at sixty-nine, victim of a paralysis. Over his grave was placed a slab bearing lines from the song he had written so long ago for his brother Tom:

> His form was of the manliest beauty:
> His heart was kind and soft,
> Faithful below he did his duty,
> And now he's gone aloft.

Charles Dibdin left behind a body of popular music unmatched by contemporaries, some 900 songs in all, of which at least 200 were known throughout the English-speaking world. Of all the twentieth-century's tunesmiths, perhaps Irving Berlin parallels him best in quantity, quality, and the affection of those who sang his music. "My songs," Dibdin once wrote, "have been the solace in long voyages, in storms, in battle; and they have been quoted in mutinies to the restoration of order and discipline," so great was their hold on those who knew and loved them.

## The New London Songwriters

The eighteenth century's last decades witnessed an increase in the printed duplication of vocal scores from the theaters and the appearance of a new group of composers and lyricist-playwrights, working in the new styles evolving from Italian comic opera—the Arnes, Dibdin, Stephen Storace, William Shield, Arnold, the Linleys, James Hook, William Jackson, Michael Kelley, and others whose songs in time formed a partial base for federal America's first full-time music publishers. Their songs appeared in hundreds of American pocket songsters, and in the choice collections of fashionable songs published in the United States until the mid-nineteenth century.

The occasional appearance of one of the hundred or so musical plays and operas printed in full score, engraved single-song sheets, and the compilation of these into a sort of vocal score did much to alleviate theatrical production difficulties prior to the early 1760s, providing musicians with suitable materials. The three-lined printed sheet music, with voice at the top, appeared only near the end of the century. With little access to printed music, musicians outside London relied on orchestra scores borrowed or rented from London producers or composers, and sometimes used bootlegged scores, copied without permission in the royal playhouses, or bought reconstructions of the full vocal and instrumental scores made by musical stenographers who sat in the pit or gallery. If none of these was available, a single instrumentalist, playing harpsichord or violin, provided accompaniment in provincial playhouses.

The bustling quality of the music written for the playhouses in the 1760s, with its increased use of wind instruments, presented an economic problem to music publishers, which they solved by simply abandoning publication of full scores, a decision enforced by production increases of upward of 300 percent. Vocal scores of musical plays sold for from three to ten shillings, much less than the two guineas asked for a Handel vocal score, but they did provide theater composers with a principal source of income. It was the introduction and successful promotion of the pianoforte that spurred sale of theater songs and simple instrumental music and made music publishing a more viable profession when many London music houses turned to instrument making and merchandising. These changes also introduced theater music to the lower classes to a degree greater than ever. Household servants learned the newest songs, much as did blacks in America, by the acculturative process of eavesdropping. "The love of music is now descended from the Opera House in the Haymarket to the little Public houses about this Metropolis," an aristocrat complained in 1775, "and common servants may now be met who pretend to as much judgement as my Lady Duchess."

The people's darling songs took on a new character after the success of *Love in a Village, The Padlock, The Maid of the Mill,* and other stage works in the *style galant* of Scarlatti, young J. C. Bach, Haydn, and Mozart, and were taken to their hearts by upper-class Englishmen after hearing that modern music in the symphonies and concertos introduced by Bach and Carl Abel in their London concert room. Comic operas with spoken dialogue reigned in most theaters, influencing in turn the pleasure gardens' music and that of other places where the lower orders met. The most popular plays included popular songs, many of them old melodies dressed with new lyrics, and scored in the modern style.

It was the success of Richard Brinsley Sheridan's comic operetta *The Duenna,* after its first showing in late 1775 at Covent Garden, that brought to the fore the Linley family, of Bath, into which the playwright had only recently been accepted as son-in-law. Father, daughters, and son made an impact on the British music world with their comeliness and their talents. Smitten by the beauty of seventeen-year-old Elizabeth Linley, singing at one of the concerts regularly produced by her father, Thomas, composer, singing master, and musical impresario during Bath's social season, the young Irishman wooed and won her, but not her parent. Once the success of his comedy *The Rivals* made Sheridan a national celebrity, Linley relented. In that piece Sheriden introduced Mrs. Malaprop, whose "as headstrong as an allegory on the Nile" and other blunders of the tongue soon had London creating "malapropisms" of its own. Sheriden succeeded in restoring Restoration comedy in *The Duenna,* but without the obscenity in which Charles and his court reveled, and it ran for seventy-five nights that season, making its author so wealthy he could not bear the thought of his wife, the most beautiful woman in England, continuing to sing in public. Its success also supplied part of the £35,000 the senior Linley paid for a half-share in the Drury Lane's management, where he named himself musical director at once.

Thomas Linley, Jr., shared the same year of birth, 1754, and considerable precocity and future promise with Wolfgang Amadeus Mozart, who became his friend after the pair met in Italy as teen-agers. Linley as a child prodigy had studied with Boyce. He performed publicly on the violin at the age of eight and made his first appearance as a dancer and instrumental performer at Covent Garden two years later. While still in his teens, he conducted his father's Bath Promenade concerts. He left Britain in 1766 to study with Pietro Nardini, the great violinist and master, returning to London at nineteen to conduct the Drury Lane house orchestra and appear as solo instrumentalist between the acts there. When Linley, Sr., worked on *The Duenna*'s score, his son assisted in compiling and arranging it and wrote most of the truly original music in this extraordinarily popular comic pastiche. His arrangements of the Scottish and Irish airs to which Sheridan wrote the lyrics were among the day's most popular songs. This young man, called by Roger Fiske "the most promising [English] composer between Purcell and Elgar," died at the age of twenty-two, dragged to the bottom of a small lake into which he fell by the weight of water filling his boots. He left behind enough vocal and instrumental music to fill two volumes.

Greatly shaken by his son's death, Linley threw himself into his duties at Covent Garden, writing music and coaching new singers. One of them, Dorothy Jordan, the fruit of an illicit backstage romance, became an overnight sensation in the winter of 1785 after singing a new song written by Linley for James Cobb's *The Stranger's at Home.* The melody he used was at least a century old, and it had won a second round of popularity at Covent Garden in the 1750s. It was later to become the music for an American hit song, "The Hunters of Kentucky." The original was called "The golden days of good Queen Bess," then "Alley Croaker" in the 1750s, and when sung by Mrs. Jordan, "When first I began, sir, to ogle the ladies." After being signed as second actress to the incomparable Mrs. Sarah Siddons, Jordan achieved her fame in London, as she had in the provinces, playing breeches parts, for which she was neatly endowed. Her offstage life was colorful, and her liaisons led to frequent absences from the stage for "the call of maternity." The duke of Clarence, subsequently William IV, fathered ten of her children during a period when she earned thirty pounds a week at the theater, which he supplemented with £1,000 annually. When, on the advice of George III, Clarence wished to reduce that sum by exactly half, she responded, on the bottom part of a playbill, "No money returned after the rising of the curtain." The best known of her offspring is the song "The Blue Bells of Scotland," which she is said to have written, although it may have been bought from a playhouse songwriter. She introduced it in one of the plays in which she starred. It became her trademark, and audiences never let her offstage until she responded to their shouts for "The Blue Bells!"

The provocative Jordan shared the attention of Drury Lane backstage habitués with a company of the city's finest and prettiest singing actresses, among them Mrs. Elizabeth Wrighten, brought to the ensemble by Garrick in 1769. When she ran off to America in the early 1790s, she lived the last pages of a fascinating career as a singing actress and one of the first American women songwriters. Among the roles Wrighten played were many musical farces and entertainments created by James Hook, perhaps the best writer of catchy theater songs and second only to Dibdin as the creator of popular hits.

There was little pertaining to music other than a broken-down harpsichord in the parlor of Hook's cutler father's residence in Norwich with which to entertain the young boy, who had been born crippled. Even after an early operation, he remained clubfooted, walking with the marked limp that kept him from childhood sports and games. Instead, he learned music quickly from a Norwich Cathedral organist and was performing in public at six. At eight he wrote music for a ballad opera, and when his father died three years later, he sought to support his mother and the other children as a musician, advertising lessons on the keyboards, guitar, flute, and violin and offering to tune instruments or copy music. Around 1763, he went to London and played the organ in a teahouse, where hot loaves, tea, coffee, and liquor were available, as well as "milk from cows who eat no grain," drawn from the animals by a pretty dairymaid. Hook won fame quickly as writer of prize-winning music, which was included in his first publication, *A Collection of English Songs*. He came to Samuel Arnold's attention in 1768, when Arnold had just purchased Marylebone Gardens, and was employed as resident organist and composer, appearing onstage just before Arnold's comic operas and burlettas. With his employer's encouragement Hook tried his hand at the musical theater with some success, prompting Arnold to increase his duties and reduce his chance to write anything but the vast number of new songs, cantatas, and instrumental music needed to entertain Marylebone's patrons.

The new popularity enjoyed by the pianoforte stimulated Hook, and off season, when Arnold was not constantly after him for new music, he began to instruct pupils on that instrument, earning as much as £600 a year. In 1774, he moved to the more fashionable Vauxhall Gardens, remaining there for some fifty years and writing more than 2,000 songs for it, most of which appeared in annual collections of his music published by the last St. Paul's music house, that of the Thomas family.

The speed and glibness with which Hook wrote for the gardens probably kept him from gaining the public stature of his musical-theater contemporaries. During winters, however, until he was seventy, he turned out stage works with regularity for all three licensed theaters. Although none of his work was outstandingly distinguished, it generally contained popular songs written for the gardens, which enjoyed great popularity with theater audiences.

Americans knew James Hook almost as well as did the English. Hundreds of his songs were published by them, usually appearing with the phrase "by Mr. Hook" after their titles, an indication of his fame. The most popular, as in England, were those seemingly authentic folk songs, so authoritatively did he write in the British and Scottish folk idiom. Benjamin Carr's ten-page *Favorite Songs Sung at Vauxhall Gardens,* published in Philadelphia in 1794, was purchased by Jefferson. It included "The Caledonian laddie," one of Hook's famous "Scottish" songs.

After the great success of its John Burgoyne–William Jackson *Lord of the Manor* production, the Drury Lane was again regarded as the most important city playhouse, a reputation that changed in 1782, when Covent Garden produced a new full-length musical by Samuel Arnold, *The Castle of Andalusia.* When he first presented it to them, the management was unimpressed, forcing him to stage the work with his own money. It was at once hissed off the stage by a claque employed by Arnold's enemies, and he found it necessary to turn it over to Covent Garden for £200. He complained later to Haydn that it made over £20,000 for the new copyright owner. The libretto was by John O'Keeffe, who, as was his custom, sang to Arnold the Irish melodies he wished included in the score, among them the song folklorists know today as "The Poacher."

In December of the same year, Covent Garden added a new hit to its repertoire, *Rosina,* an afterpiece by William Shield. Its plot was naïve, dealing with an attempted seduction, sudden contrition on the part of the would-be seducer, and a happy ending in which everyone found a true mate, but it continued to be revived for almost a century. Shield's selection of original music and popular street-ballad tunes pleased from the start, in both London and America, where it was so popular that the first English-speaking company to play in New Orleans performed *Rosina* during an initial 1818–19 season.

Shield was a singing teacher's son, born in London in 1748, and his parent's best pupil. Orphaned at nine, he was sent to a boat-building relation, who allowed the boy to continue his violin lessons. Shield later studied counterpoint with Charles Avison, the British organist, composer, and aesthetician, and once Geminiani's pupil in Italy. After two years with a touring company, Shield, in 1772, took a viola chair in the King's Theatre orchestra, eventually becoming section leader. His success with *The Flitch of Bacon* at the Little Theatre in 1778 led to the post of Covent Garden staff composer, in which capacity he remained until 1807. For ten years prior to his death, in 1827, Shield was master of the King's music.

Shield wrote a number of major afterpieces following *Rosina.* The most popular was *The Poor Soldier* (1783), about a former Irish grenadier who had served in America and retired to the Irish village from which he came to live among "pipers and fairies, football players and gay hurlers." Once more O'Keeffe sang from his great store of Irish tunes remembered from childhood to provide a score that remained popular long after the work was retired from the boards. "How happy the soldier," George Washington's favorite song from his favorite musical play, was, with "The heaving of the lead," "The wolf," "Old Towler," and "The frolicsome fellow," among the Victorians' favorite ballads, their creator by then forgotten.

While the hundred-year-old Drury Lane fell into disrepair, Covent Garden was assuming its position as London's most important musical playhouse. In 1780, the Drury Lane had become a victim of the rising tide of public antagonism to an effort to restore Catholics to the personal freedom from which they had been barred by law since the late sixteenth century. Catholics could not hold public office, practice law, inherit land, or join the armed forces, but they did all these things and more, evading laws as officials smiled. The Act for Catholic Relief, passed by the House of Lords to repeal most of the restrictive legislation, immediately prompted a flood of public discontent, particularly among the lower classes, who were stirred up by opponents of religious and political freedom for Catholics. During riots in 1780, hundreds were killed by militia or in fires set after unrestrained looting, and the Drury Lane was seriously damaged. A troop of soldiers was posted against further depredation, a custom that continued for a century. The mob had struck against the theater because its owner-manager, Richard Sheridan, was one of Parliament's liberal members who advocated reform of the old anti-Catholic laws.

In 1789, the King's Theatre, home of Italian opera from the lush days of Handel's first successes through dark years when British comic opera took away its audiences, was burned. The loss was more than £70,000. Within a year, 3,600 could sit in a rebuilt edifice ideally suited for singing and music. With the Drury Lane still closed after the rioting, Sheridan, looking for a new building in which to present his next season, took over the King's Theatre. Because of a conflict over restoration of a full license, however, a new style of singing and dancing was in order, bringing about the presentation of vast spectacles. This resulted in the almost immediate demise of singers whose style and vocal projection were insufficient to the cavernous building's demands.

The problem created a marvelous proving ground for the Drury Lane company's new house composer, Stephen Storace, who had learned the trends in modern musical drama from Mozart. Storace was born in 1763, the son of an Italian bass player who was leader of Marylebone's orchestra. The father trained him, and by the age of ten Stephen performed Tartini's and Giardini's complicated music with a skill beyond that of many of his elders. At twelve he was sent to Naples Conservatory to study harpsichord, violin, and composition. Throughout his life, Storace was torn between the violin and composition. In 1778, his sister Ann Selina joined him in Italy. Three years his junior and already possessed of a magnificent voice and the beauty that would later attract Mozart, the Austrian emperor, and many others into her bed, Ann studied voice in Venice, and at the age of fifteen began a series of engagements in major

Italian opera houses, culminating in 1783, when she was signed to be the prima donna of Vienna's Imperial Opera House.

Storace accompanied her to Austria and joined a circle of young British musicians, among them Michael Kelly, an actor who had appeared in Dublin musicals and was under contract to the Royal Court Theatre. The group's artistic mentor was Mozart, at work on a new opera, *The Marriage of Figaro,* to a libretto by the court poet Lorenzo da Ponte. Storace struck up a close intimacy with Mozart, who found time not only to assist him in the preparation of two operas to be staged in Vienna, but also lent him da Ponte for the book of the second, an adaptation of Shakespeare's *Comedy of Errors.*

*Figaro* was performed for the first time in May 1786, with Kelly singing two roles and Ann Storace as Susanna. The complexities of her romantic affairs and the demands of her husband, a theater musician, had completely disarranged her life. The problem was solved when the emperor sent her husband out of the country and took his place in Ann's bedroom. Finding himself in prison after striking an aristocratic army officer in defense of his sister's honor, Storace traded life in Austria for immediate departure from the country. With Kelly, the Storaces returned to London, where they made an immediate impression with stage technique learned in Europe. For example, rather than stand in the traditional single place downstage near the footlights in comic operas, they moved about the stage while singing, which gave life and bustle to musical plays. Kelly joined the Drury Lane, and Ann, now known as Nancy, was signed by the King's Theatre. Upon completing a new opera for his sister, Storace busied himself with publication of a series of *Storace's Collection of Harpsichord Music,* issued between 1787 and 1789, containing his and Mozart's music for piano and strings. Mozart had planned to join Nancy in London, but his father's health and ensuing death kept him in Europe, denying her a lover and the English musical theater those musical miracles Mozart would probably have produced.

Backstage intrigue by the predominantly all-Italian company drove Nancy to the Drury Lane, and the reality of providing for a new wife led Storace to accept the post of composer there. At twelve he had lost his respect for singers when he was hired to copy music for an Italian prima donna and learned later that the one hundred pounds she received for a single song netted her nine shillings a note. Nancy filled the decaying playhouse with her glorious voice in European works adapted by Storace without compunction and in original pieces heavily influenced by Mozart and the modern Italians. Their first joint success was the full-length *Haunted Tower,* set in William the Conqueror's time and involving ghosts and other terrors, anticipating the Gothic novel introduced shortly after by Ann Radcliffe. *The Haunted Tower* was performed sixty times in its first season, remaining a favorite in Britain and America for half a century. Its vocal score, published by Longman and Broderip, contained an engraving of the scenery, a mysterious tower and the coastline on which the drama took place, an innovative decoration that was followed in similar publications. Storace was hailed for a score that told the story entirely in music, in place of the usual single songs set between dialogue. Brother and sister continued to work their magic on audiences, with *The Siege of Belgrade* (1791), *The Pirates* (1792), and *Lodoiska* and *The Cherokees* (1794), all full-length, all-sung plays in which Storace's original scores usually contained music heard during his Viennese days and extracts from the Mozart works he was publishing, among it the first waltz ever heard on the English stage.

*The Cherokees,* the first British musical with such an American theme, had for its subject the tribe of North American red men most familiar to Londoners. Ever since 1763, a Fleet Street waxworks had displayed the Cherokee king with two of his chiefs in their "country dress." That was the year tribal representatives from the Tennessee–North Carolina mountains came to London to see "their father" the king. They were frequently drunk in public from the variety of punch, syllabub, and Frontinac pressed on them by Englishmen, who followed them in large crowds, 10,000 one evening at Vauxhall Gardens. James Cobb, who wrote *The Cherokees,* knew them no better than viewers at the wax museum and proceeded to create the cliché of the American Indian, still obtaining in the Anglo-Saxon consciousness, as drunken, silly, and evil men. He gave them stuffy speeches to sing, setting these to some of Storace's finest music.

His health failing rapidly from gout, Storage took to the use of opium to reduce the pain, which seriously affected his string of successes. He died in 1796, at thirty-three, leaving behind some of the musical theater's most impressive work.

Ann Storace left Britain and lived for some years on the Continent, where she had an affair with a young English tenor, John Braham, who scored a personal success in Storace's last work, *Mahmoud.* After her return to Covent Garden, she bade the stage farewell in 1808 and died a decade later, after accumulating a great fortune as one of the most sought-after concert stars.

Michael Kelly, signed as manager and actor by the King's Theatre after Storace's death, wrote more than sixty stage pieces and many popular songs. He opened a music-publishing office next to the theater and also took a flyer in wine importing, failing in both. It was often said that none of his music was original, but borrowed from Europeans, and Sheridan once threatened to have a sign made saying, "Michael Kelly, Composer of Wines, Importer of Music."

The creative challenge posed by Stephen Storace went mostly unheeded after his death, the musical stage reaching a low point in the quality of its productions. After a ten-year sabbatical, Hook made an inconspicuous return in 1795 and continued to produce second-rate work for the next twenty years. Shield, reengaged by Covent Garden in 1792, left five years later and gave up the stage completely in 1807 to devote full time to concert music. Men like William Reeve, who rose from the singing chorus to become Covent Garden's musical director for a short time and part owner of Sadler's Wells, produced little of true worth, though much of it was published in the United States.

There were a few bright moments, among them Samuel Arnold's *Babes in the Woods, The Mountaineers,* and his last important work, the 1801 ballet *Obi, or Three Finger'd Jack.* Set on a Jamaican sugar plantation, *Obi* was replete with voodoo, runaway slaves, murder, and kidnapping.

Despite the decline of theater music's quality, songs by Dibdin, Reeve, Hook, Arnold, and others afforded the new American music-publishing business free music on which to found much of its early economic viability. Many of the sheet-music imprints coming off presses in New York, Boston, and Philadelphia were merely pirated editions of British stage music. The theatrical companies moving west and south from large northern cities to follow the moving frontier took both the best and the worst of the English theater with them, singing this popular music to people who had never heard of Covent Garden or the Drury Lane.

A number of factors appear to be responsible for the musical anemia of much late-eighteenth-century English music. Not the least of these was the threat of French republicanism and an increasing awareness that Napoleon was dedicated not only to the destruction of the empire on which the sun had not yet set, but to world domination as well. Britain's most promising composers were either dead or soon to be, but few of them could have matched the genius and talent of a handful of Europeans who were winning the admiration of musicians and audiences alike with what Dibdin termed "floods of German nonsense."

Ever since Handel's arrival, Britons had looked upon Germany as the fount of musical genius, and the triumph of Haydn's symphonies enhanced that notion. The production of low-priced pianofortes and an expanding catalogue of music for them did much to take music making out of the theater and music room and into the parlor. The growth of Wesleyan hymnody, infused as it was becoming with popular elements, made happy vocalists out of congregations who found solace and inspiration in the new religious denominations. With the subsequent broadening of participation in the music process came an inevitable change in standards of acceptance and the opportunity for both British and American entrepreneurs to satisfy this new public taste.

# CHAPTER 20

# America's Musical Theater

A little more than eighty years after the first professional musician arrived in Virginia, a strolling actor made his appearance, young Tony Aston, a jack-of-all-trades who had worked on the Drury Lane's stage before going off to the American colonies in search of his fortune. With some Carolina adventurers, he sailed from Charles Town to sack the Spanish settlement at St. Augustine, on Florida's east coast, but returned empty-handed in January 1703, as he remembered, "full of lie, shame, poverty, nakedness and hunger." Aston boasted, thirty years after, that he then took to entertaining in New York, the Jerseys, Virginia, and Maryland before going back home.

The 2,000 rice and indigo planters who made up America's first aristocracy of the rich indulged themselves in emulation of London's upper-class social pleasures, and there quickly grew in Charles Town an environment in which the traditional servants of the wealthy—professional hairdressers, tailors, restaurateurs, dancing masters, actors, keepers of luxury shops, and musicians—found regular gainful employment, decades earlier than elsewhere in British America. By 1737, benefit concerts were supplanted by a subscription season, and the balls that once had been a bonus to attract audiences were now full-fledged occasions attracting the cream of planter society. George Whitefield's exhortations put a quietus to most popular entertainment during the 1740s, and Carolinians continued to endure the sermonizing of evangelists, but traditional conviviality continued. In a single year, locals consumed the contents of 3,000 dozen glass bottles, which were regularly refilled with imported Jamaican rum. What evangelism could not accomplish was finally done by the great hurricane of 1752, which leveled 500 buildings and the city's first theater. This was reconstructed in time for the arrival of the first professional acting company in 1754. There had been actors before, playing in theaters dating back to the first one in 1736, but Lewis Hallam, Sr.'s troupe was made up of Covent Garden, Goodman's Fields, and Drury Lane veterans. The resident musicians they found in Charles Town rivaled in ability the playhouse instrumentalists back home.

Charles Town's musical theater had started in January 1735, when Louis Timothy's *South Carolina Gazette* recorded the first theatrical attraction since Tony Aston had entertained. A troupe of players, origin unknown, offered several evenings of entertainment, presenting on February 18, the first American performance on record of a ballad opera. *Flora, or Hob in the Well,* a London favorite usually known as *Hob's Opera,* was written by John Hippisley, a low comic who tailored the work to his own particular talents. The airs for this bawdy farce of deception and sexual intrigue were culled from D'Urfey's *Wit and Mirth,* Playford's *Dancing Master,* recently printed Scottish song collections, and some theater presentations.

The following year, a new theater was built near the city's burying ground, and in it Charles Town theatergoers saw for the first time in America the spectacle of a young woman clad in men's tight breeches. The production was George Farquhar's *Recruiting Officer,* with the popular song "Over the hills and far away," regularly sung as part of their ritual by American Masons, the first true patrons and financial supporters of the colonial theater and all music. Throughout the eighteenth century, the good relations between stage people, musicians, and the Antient and Honorable Society of Freemasons provided a marketplace for composers and songwriters, gave actors offstage recognition they had long been denied in England, and led to a social alliance with purveyors of popular entertainment. Masonic processions inevitably marched behind bands of musicians, and actors who had been received into the secret order enjoyed even greater income from special benefit performances as fellow Masons filled the house, having paraded there en masse. Local lodges made public appearances, regularly buying out the pit for a performance of some special play, enjoying an evening punctuated by onstage renditions of Masonic songs and instrumental music, as well as the declamation of prologues, odes, and epilogues honoring the fraternity.

Such an audience usually included the most distinguished local citizens. From the moment the secret movement crossed the Atlantic in 1730, when the first lodge was established in Philadelphia, Freemasonry attracted the most prominent middle-class gentry and officials through its camaraderie, prestige, elaborate ceremony, and secret ritual. Franklin was a leading member and printed the first American Masonic book in 1734. Washington used a Masonic Bible at his first inauguration. Paul Revere was a major functionary of the Massachusetts lodge. Masonic symbols, the truncated pyramid and fiery eye, which decorate the great seal of the republic and the back of the dollar bill, bear testament to Masonry's influence among the Founding Fathers.

The formation of Charles Town's St. Cecilia Society in 1762 formalized the community's arts and music programs, attracting the finest musicians in response to advertisements in northern newspapers and magazines. A French first violinist got 500 guineas a year, and "one of the finest" French hornists was paid 50 guineas for a single season. Assisted by amateur musicians, the society's orchestra offered contemporary music by Handel, the blind Charles Stanley, Johann Hasse, Vivaldi, Corelli, Boccherini, Arne, and other living composers, whose music was ordered from northern book dealers. One hundred and fifty St. Cecelia members signed an annual pledge of twenty-five pounds for the regular season and made up any deficit on demand. Before the Revolution, the cream of immigrant instrumentalists worked there, adding to their salaries income from teaching and the sale of manuscript copies of their own music and that of European masters. Peter Valton came from London, where he had studied with Boyce in the king's chapel, and played organ in the local Anglican church, sold spinets and other instruments, wrote music for sale locally, and advertised it in New York and Philadelphia papers. The Dutch organist and former student of Geminiani, Peter Albrecht van Hagen tried his luck in America for the first time in 1774, introducing himself and his bride to Charles Town with a benefit concert, but when prospects of armed conflict grew, he left, to return with his family in the late 1780s, taking up residence in the north.

During hot Carolina summers in the 1760s, when the wealthiest families made an annual trip north to Newport, those musicians who remained worked in one of America's first pleasure gardens, the New Vauxhall, just a short ride into the countryside, where the management offered free tea and coffee. It could not survive, however, without the patronage of the wealthy.

Benefit concerts for local musicians were given during the British military occupation, and when peace came, St. Cecilia concerts returned to the city that now was known as Charleston. Its proximity to the West Indies offered a sanctuary to French musicians and singers fleeing their own revolution. The music and operas of Pleyel, Grétry, Gossec, Dussek, and Haydn were performed by these refugees before they appeared in the north.

Though not Anglican, the Mathers of Boston agreed fervently with that church's interdiction against players and providers of other "foolish and vain" pastimes. They were in the forefront of a movement to drive French and English dancing masters and their "promiscuous couplings" out of the Bay Colony, although they assented when the politically well-connected owner of the Castle Tavern, Captain John Wing, offered magic shows and displays of swordsmanship for the delectation of his patrons. The promising young Harvard student Benjamin Colman, who was preparing for the ministry, was merely reprimanded after the first performance in a college building of his tragic drama *Gustavus Vasa,* but he was asked never to repeat that blasphemy.

Boston was able to resist the eighteenth century's secular inroads only as long as the city fathers remained in control. Cotton Mather needed no Great Awakening to drive him to action, and in 1702 he formed the Society for the Supression of Disorders. It grew so quickly that ancillary groups spun off to carry on a war against vice. Lists of young men who frequented "wicked houses" were prepared, and these wayward gentlemen were visited and prayed back to predestined salvation. Because the city was a major seaport, the presence of foreign seafarers had stimulated the growth of bawdyhouses, to which lawyers, officers, gentlemen, merchants, journeymen, and apprentices were finally admitted, in spite of Mather and his watch and warders.

A bowling green was opened in 1713, and horse races were run in Cambridge. Dance instruction flourished only after an English organist, imported to man the King's Chapel organ but unable to survive on the thirty pounds paid him, began with impunity to teach the terpsichorean arts, and sell musical instruments, instruction books, and ruled music paper.

A strolling entrepreneur exhibited *The Italian Matchean,* moving pictures of wind and water mills, ships sailing the sea, and other curious figures, at twelve pence per viewer. Martha Adams, one of hundreds of that surname in 1730s Boston, showed "the king of beasts and the only one of his kind in America" at her house in the city's South End. A dozen years later, a great white bear competed for Bostonians' pennies with a nearby waxworks show, whose chief attraction was a figure of that Dutch lady, heralded in London broadsides, who bore 365 children at one time, "most strangely punished by God." In time, displays of trained dogs and of horses, bears, moose, and a caged lion, who had been drawn through the northern colonies by oxen, were all shown without any action taken by the authorities. There were even periodic bouts of bear-baiting, that age-old British spectator sport that appealed to people of all social classes.

Lovers of the drama went to John Mein's Bookstore on King Street in the mid-1760s, where a circulating library contained a thousand books, available to members for one pound eight shillings a year, and providing many volumes of playscripts. The *New England Weekly Journal* published the most popular London stage works in installments. Yet the professional theater was not destined to flourish in this city until the end of the century, because a series of legislative acts was passed against those "great mischiefs which arise from public stage plays." A riot ensued outside a State Street coffeehouse in mid-century when it was announced that all places inside had been filled to view a neighborhood production of Otway's *Orphan.* Twenty pounds was levied against the sponsors, and each player and spectator was fined five pounds. Using the same subterfuge employed by London stage managers to evade the Licensing Act, public readings then provided the only substitute for the true thing, except for some occasional and clandestine presentations.

When Boston became the major assembly point for British armed forces fighting the French and their Indian allies, gentlemen officers complained about the absence of true theatrical entertainment. They did find brothels in profusion, and every other house was a tavern, but there was nothing resembling the playhouses back home.

Less than a hundred miles to the south, Newport had become a veritable Gomorrah. Its first public house had opened in 1643, and within fifty years the town was noted for its liquor and food, the elegance of those who found the climate salubrious, the beauty of its women, and some twenty rum distilleries. Early in the century, merchants and planters from Charles Town and the British West Indies had discovered the invigorating breezes that came in off the Atlantic during the summer season. This small city, which already had a substantial and cultivated population, became America's first vacation watering hole for wealthy Southerners. Local taverns offered billiards, ninepins, and an occasional declaimer of the drama even before the influx of summer visitors. But with their arrival, social clubs, card games, balls, and assemblies flourished, drawing musicians and entertainers to serve the vacationers' pleasure. Serious musicians found that Newport provided little "competent maintenance" for persons of their attainment, but players of music for dancing were much in demand.

Philadelphia was second only to Boston in its long resistance to the theater, dominated as it was by the Society of Friends, which hoped to enshroud all the inhabitants in the plain clothing and simple manners the sect had adopted. The riots, gambling, races, and entertainment regularly accompanying fairs that took place from 1688 were countenanced, but only in the name of commerce. Country people used the occasion to display their wares and make shopping trips into the big city. Within the city, laws were passed regularly to curb "rude and riotous" sports, forbid plays, interludes, and other licentious displays, and control the unlicensed groggeries that were housed in caves along the Delaware River.

The Quaker Yearly Meeting constantly warned the young against "going or being in any way concerned in plays, games, lotteries, music and dancing," but dancing masters plied their trade, lotteries served to sell newly built houses and subdivisions of building lots, and the city had a problem with transvestism. An innkeeper was hailed before a court, accused of permitting two men to display themselves before his customers "being mask't, or disguised in women's apparel."

The suspension of horse racing was the last straw for Philadelphia's gamblers, sportsmen, and popular entertainers, who moved to Society Hill, just outside the city's southern limits. There, in 1724, was advertised a "New Booth," with stage, pit, and gallery, offering a rope walker and a pantomimist.

Samuel Pierpont advertised lessons in "the art of dancing" with evenings of country dancing every Thursday, and dance masters from London taught the latest steps, promising to endow their students with "the most graceful carriage in dancing and gentle behaviour in company." The City Dance Assembly, which attracted Anglican high society to evenings of dance and drink, was shut down immediately after George Whitefield stormed into town and spoke his mind. He affected all social levels, and religion became the only subject of conversation. Instead of singing ballads, people entertained themselves with psalms, hymns, and spiritual songs. Philadelphia erected the first evangelistic tabernacle in America for that visiting exhorter of souls.

In 1742, control of the city passed out of Quaker hands into those of politicians supported by local merchants and businessmen, who generally were by disposition inclined to enjoy popular entertainment. Four years later, a visitor lamented that there was no "gay diversion" available, but had he chanced on the Coach and Tavern near the State House, he would have seen puppet shows with "changeable figures two feet high," and in Lockwood's, nearby, heard the Musical clock that played sonatas, concertos, marches, minuets, jiggs, and Scotch songs from the pens of Corelli, Alberoni, Handel, and "other great and eminent Masters of Musick." There was also a clandestine theater operating behind high society's closed doors, where young men and women read and acted out new London plays, easily procurable from local bookstalls. One of these stage-struck young ladies left home to go on the road with a company of actors after seeing them perform in a makeshift theater set up in a warehouse in the autumn of 1749. Making his Water Street building available to the Murray and Kean Company of London Comedians had given Mayor William Plumstead an opportunity to flaunt his authority in the face of the Quaker Meeting that had castigated him when he left it to come a member of Christ Church. The old war-horse Addison's *Cato* was the first presentation. The company's repertoire entertained audiences in New York and Virginia a few years later.

These London comedians were mostly amateur players, third-rate performers, stage-struck working-class people determined to make their way in a new world, doing badly what they loved best. They did, however, bring America the first performances of works destined to make up a standard repertory for decades: *Richard the Third* in Colley Cibber's "improved version"—all that Americans knew of this play until the nineteenth century; George Lillo's *George Barnwell,* a drama of passion and murder, written in English middle-class language and confirming many of its social aspirations; Congreve's *Love for Love;* Dryden's *Amphytryon* and *Spanish Friar;* and *The Beggar's Opera.* Most of the plays contained songs, interpolated years earlier to accommodate the British appetite for a bold ballad, lustily sung, but to bypass the royal patents. In the London tradition, the Murray-Kean troupe offered musical farces on the same bill with tragedy and comedy, their repertoire including old and new Drury Lane, Haymarket, and Covent Garden fare, complete with songs.

The Quaker establishment struck back at Mayor Plumstead, getting corporation officials to require a bond from the players against any breach of morality, and the Comedians left town in the dead of night to go north to New York.

The time's moral climate and the English Puritan church's influence on contemporary society were obvious in all the northern colonies except on the slender island at the mouth of the Hudson, making it inevitable that the theater would take permanent root in the one city that was already the most cosmopolitan habitation on mainland North America. When it surrendered to the British in 1664, eighteen different languages were heard on its streets, and its official documents were written in Dutch, French, and English. Philadelphia had a similar mix of nationalities, but the Quakers' iron fist dominated development of local culture long after New York was famed for the elegance and style of its upper classes. The English merchant aristocracy there possessed a breeding that surprised sophisticated travelers, and a liberal attitude toward intellectual and religious freedom continued to attract not only wealthy and educated immigrants from Continental Europe, but also the artisans, craftsmen, laborers, and servants who made it function. By 1700, New York's taverns and coffeehouses provided an excellent international cuisine to all classes of townspeople, and a convivial meeting place in which to conduct business and enjoy London newspapers, French food, Spanish madeira, Indian tea, and African coffee.

Free-spending royal governors dedicated themselves to the re-creation of London's court life, marking the monarchs' birthday and celebrating military and naval victories and national days of commemoration with outdoor displays, bonfires, receptions, and the provision of ample spirits with which to drink their majesties' health. Gotham gentry and their wealthier peers living on estates up the river vied with one another in such exhibitions. Public balls were in vogue by 1735, with the latest in French dances and country figures, and sumptuous entertainment afterward.

Actor Richard Hunter had petitioned the colony's governor in 1699 for leave to present theatrical entertainment, but no record survives that he was success-ful. Tony Aston passed through a few years later with his declamations, dance, and song. In 1714, Governor Robert Hunter, who was an intimate of London playwrights, satirized local political opponents in his farce comedy *Androboros (Maneater)*, the first original play written and printed in America. The perfor-mance by amateurs in 1730 of *Romeo and Juliet* in a Manhattan tavern was the first presentation of Shakespeare in America, even if it was a bowdlerized ver-sion with the obligatory happy ending that saw the lovers alive and in each other's arms. The next year the city boasted the New Theatre, in the loft of a Broadway warehouse, near Beaver Street, owned by local merchant and polit-ical figure Rip Van Dam. There, a local barber and wig dresser who numbered the transvestite royal governor among his clients starred in *The Recruiting Of-ficer*. The response was so pleasing that he offered the room's 400 spectators three other plays: *Cato, The Beaux' Stratagem,* and Susannah Centlivre's *The Busy Body*.

Concerts did take place before mixed audiences, but William Bradford did not report them in his newspaper, the city's first. Music was not a news item until Peter Zenger began the competing *Weekly Journal* in 1733, and even then it got short shrift. The latest Goodman's Fields and John Rich pantomimes were shown by Henry Holt in a dancing and concert room he opened in lower New York in 1739. A London dancer and choreographer, Holt made his way across the Atlantic after the Licensing Act reduced opportunities for players and stage directors, and presented theater dances and painted perspectives of Europe's and America's most noted places in his studio.

Musicians who could not find work in England came first to New York. Among them were organists, who manned the city's newly installed church organs, Trinity Church's new instrument, built by John Klemm, and the one at the Garden Street Dutch Reformed Church, given by Governor William Cosby while he was wooing a beautiful Dutch heiress. Others supported themselves by concertizing in local taverns, and a singing master announced in 1740 his readiness to teach the complexities of sight reading with the Walter and Tufts instruction books.

The prospering community had become a regular stop for traveling exhibi-tions, among them the camel brought with great difficulty from the deserts of Arabia and German Hans, the educated horse which presumably understood arithmetic, could distinguish colors, drink wine, and was assisted by an eques-trian clown. Only after George Whitefield departed was a "curious musical ma-chine" displayed. Performed entirely by clockwork, it produced the pealing of St. Bride's bells in London and a magic lantern revealed Friar Bacon, Doctor Faustus, the blind Beggar of Bednal Green, a jigg-dancing piper, a fencing master, Italian mountebanks, Dutch skaters, and other figures, all larger than man or woman.

There were public demonstrations of a camera obscura, which magnified the circulation of blood in a frog's foot and a fish's tail, and displays of electricity, with fire darting from all parts of the body. Puppet shows and waxworks were transplanted to Manhattan's public rooms, where Punch and his company showed the tragedy of Elizabeth and Mary Queen of Scots, and the rise of Dick Whittington from poor kitchen boy to lord mayor of London. Peg Woffington, the Drury Lane actress considered the most beautiful woman in the world, was displayed in a waxworks, alongside the English royal family, Hungarian nobility, and other replicated attractions. After a decade of such minor fare, the theater proper arrived, in February 1750. The Murray-Kean company came to town, and with them Nancy George, the young Philadelphia miss who had run off to pursue Thespis. Permission was secured from the governor to play in Van Dam's Nassau Street Theatre, and two seasons followed, ending when Kean left the stage for a literary career, and a financially strapped company went to Virginia, where audiences were apparently less demanding and new theaters and remodeled barns awaited. The Comedians wandered through the Southern colonies for the next several seasons.

## The Hallam Companies of American Comedians

Among the actors who sought to circumvent provisions of the 1737 Licensing Act with presentations in nonpatent theaters were members of the Hallam family. Adam operated a booth at Bartholomew Fair. Many of his children appeared there, and one took over a theater attached to the pump house and well in the Goodman's Fields section of London for six seasons of pantomime before beginning production of unlicensed spoken drama. Action was brought in 1747, and the lengthy legal problems persuaded Lewis Hallam that more favorable circumstances awaited in the colonies. In 1752, Lewis, his wife, twelve-year-old son, Lewis, Jr., with a small stock of wardrobe and scenery and ten actors, sailed for America. After several years of barnstorming in the Carolinas, Virginia, Pennsylvania, and New York, they went to Jamaica, where Lewis Hallam, Sr., died. His wife married David Douglass, manager of an acting company from London whose ranks had been thinned by malaria, dysentery, and yellow jack. The best players from each troupe were merged into a company that set sail for New York in 1758 with a repertoire of twenty-four plays and fifteen afterpieces, virtually all of them containing music and songs that spanned nearly a century of British theater music. With a handful of new material, these "best plays, operas, farces, pantomimes exhibited in any of the London theatres these ten years past," as Douglass advertised them, were seen in New York, Philadelphia, Newport, Annapolis, Charles Town, and small communities nearby.

As at home, these evenings began with the playing of traditional opening music by musician members of the company, with local amateurs sometimes joining in. A prologue, spoken or sung, and revised to fit special local situations or audiences, followed. Then came the main piece, three to five acts— Shakespeare, a historical drama revised to lessen its realities of life and death, a standard work from the British repertory, or a recent London success—and the farce, ballad opera, or pantomime afterpiece, more dependent on music. Intermissions were given over to the individual talents of company members or local performers or singers, who provided a wide variety of entertainment.

The enthusiasm with which vacationing Carolinians greeted the company in Newport took Douglass to Charles Town, where the company remained for much of the next four years. The theater built for them was elegant, and an average of £375 a week came into the box office. Travelers from England told of the new kind of comic opera being presented in London, and Douglass went to see for himself, returning with new players, including some experienced pupils of Arne. Bickerstaffe's *Thomas and Sally* and Arne's full-length *Love in a Village* were added to the repertory. Nancy Hallam, America's first female stage star, played a leading role in the latter.

In 1766, Douglass moved, with many of his players, to a new building outside Philadelphia, the Southwark, the first American theater erected to be permanent. He and his newly named American Company looked about for appropriate vehicles of American authorship, as much for social and political advantage as with any expectation of finding a worthwhile play. In April 1767, he announced a new production, *The Disappointment,* whose libretto had just been published. The author of this first American ballad opera was Andrew Barton, the pseudonym of a local citizen who wished to caricature Philadelphians' enthusiasm for hunting pirate treasure presumably hidden in the vicinity by Blackbeard. Within two days, Douglass bowed to pressure, and the new work was canceled, being unfit for the stage because of its personal reflections. This so-called significant landmark in the history of the American musical theater proved to be its own disappointment. Irving Lowens, in reviewing a recording of it for *High Fidelity/Musical America,* said, "I would submit that there is one simple reason why it never reached the stage in the eighteenth century, which has been overlooked, and that is merely that it is an awful show and an impossible bore." It does, however, use as one of its ballad tunes "Yankee Doodle," one of the earliest references to what was obviously then a popular and well-known song.

Douglass salvaged some political advantage by immediately offering another American work, Thomas Godfrey's *The Prince of Parthia,* the first native play produced on the American stage by professional actors. With Francis Hopkinson, the painter Benjamin West, and other recent graduates of the College of Philadelphia, Godfrey was determined to make the city an intellectual and cultural oasis like upper-class London. The group's forum was the *American Magazine,* issued first in 1758 to a subscription list of 850 persons in the colonies, the West Indies, and London. *The Prince of Parthia* was completed and offered to Douglass that same year, when the company made its initial appearance in Philadelphia. After the playwright's death in the Carolinas from heat prostration, his friends published a posthumous collection of his poetry and this play. Containing elements of *Othello, Romeo and Juliet, King Lear,* and some more modern dramas, the play was set in Parthia just before the time of Christ and included incidents of incest, rape, suicide, murder, and brutality. It played once and never again, and never again did Douglass venture into American dramaturgy.

After the erection of his third New York playhouse, the John Street Theatre, west of Broadway and seating 900, Douglass opened in December 1767 with *The Beaux' Strategem*. For the thirty years of its life, the John Street was Manhattan's only theater and provided the stage for both professional and amateur actors in a variety of plays, concerts, social dances, the early circus, and displays of strength and fencing skills.

During summers, when the John Street closed because of the stifling heat, actors and musicians found work at the New Vauxhall Gardens, a pleasant rural retreat near the city on Chambers and Greenwich Streets. The owner, "Black Sam" Francis, a Haitian mulatto, provided refreshments and entertainment within view of the Hudson River, whose shoreline has since been moved blocks away by the magic of modern land reclamation. For eight shillings, a lady and gentleman could stroll through the upper and lower gardens and the grotto, view waxworks, marvel at Italian fireworks, and refresh themselves with pastries, tea, coffee, or stronger drink. When the theater closed, Francis presented concerts, weather permitting, every Monday and Thursday. Out-of-work players and musicians offered songs from the London stage, Handel arias, and instrumental music.

Francis had come to the colonies as a free man in the 1750s and was soon known as an honest innkeeper and caterer of quality food and drink. He abandoned Vauxhall in 1773 to open his elegant Queen's Head Tavern, in the former Delancey mansion near the Merchant Exchange on Broad Street. New York's leading patriots gathered there to hatch plots against the royal government and sing songs of liberty. When war broke out, Francis left its management to his wife and pretty daughter and volunteered for service. During the British occupation, he aided American prisoners and engaged in espionage, for which he was rewarded in 1782, an act of Congress granting him £200 "in consequence of his generous advances and kindness." He had changed the spelling of his name to Fraunces, and it was in his hostelry that Washington made his Farewell Address to his favorite officers. When the general moved to New York in 1789 as first president of the United States, he selected Sam Fraunces as the steward of his official kitchen. They parted only after an argument over the price of a bit of Hudson River shad.

In the early 1770s came the tax levies on glass, lead, paints, tea, and many necessities obtainable only from abroad, as well as enforced quartering of British troops in civilian households. Paper money was disappearing, and the ranks of the poor grew daily. Massachusetts had already reinforced its suppression of popular entertainment, and the £300 gathered weekly at the John Street's box office, the pomp and parade, the decoration of the scenes, the novelty and splendor of the dress, the music there threatened similar legislation in New York. Douglass increased his newspaper advertising, expecting sympathetic treatment on the editorial pages. He also created stunts to attract audiences, one time staging an authentic Indian war dance, performed by visiting Cherokees.

The situation was little better in Philadelphia, where the company traveled for the 1768–69 season. Douglass added novelties, including the first appearance in America of two Italian brothers who displayed pinwheels, sparkling fountains, and other fireworks onstage between acts. Francis Hopkinson made an appearance, speaking an original prologue that pleaded for toleration of the theater. At the New York end of his two-city circuit, Douglass offered the first American production of the recent London smash hit *The Padlock,* with Lewis Hallam, Jr., as Mungo, using an accent learned in the West Indies. Hallam was esteemed as a better player in the blackface role than Charles Dibdin, who had created it in London.

The following summer, Douglass tried his luck in Albany, New York, playing for a month in a converted hospital. Any foray into Boston was clearly inadvisable, as Douglass learned when he performed three evenings of "lectures" there to an audience consisting mainly of British soldiers. From Charles Town came the news that patriotic Carolinians would no longer support theatrical entertainment.

From mid-1770 until the Revolution, the American Company also visited Virginia and Maryland, playing in both large communities and smaller settlements to audiences long starved for any reasonable facsimile of the London theater. George Washington went to a new brick theater Douglass erected in Annapolis, to indulge a taste for the stage that continued all his life. New actors brought scripts and music from the latest hits, many of which the American Company introduced only a few months after London first saw them, furthering the illusion that Americans were *au courant* with the latest London culture. Infatuation with company members Nancy Hallam and Maria Storer on the part of colonial dandies made both a considerable box-office asset, as much for the breeches parts Nancy played as for the music of her voice and her admirable figure, and Maria's enchanting singing voice and her beauty, depicted in the frontispiece engraving of a songbook printed in Williamsburg, *The Syren,* dedicated to her.

Despite such niceties, the American professional theater's end was inevitable, and in the summer of 1774, the Continental Congress, meeting in Philadelphia, pounded a last nail into the coffin when it resolved that "we will, in our several stations, encourage frugality, economy, and industry, promote agriculture, arts and the manufacture of this country, especially that of wool; and will discontenance and discourage every species of extravagance and dissipation, especially all horse-racing, and all kinds of gaming, cock-fighting, exhibitions of shows, plays and other expensive diversions and entertainments."

In February 1775, Douglass, his family, Nancy Hallam and a few others sailed for Jamaica. Lewis Hallam played in London for a short time and then joined the others in the Caribbean. Until the War for Independence ended, this troupe of professionals, regularly augmented as their children grew and other actors came to the West Indies in search of opportunity, pursued the pledge made when first they presented their talents in the New World:

> Our faithful mirror shall reflect to view
> Those blooming virtues which reside in you:—
> Long may they flourish—long in vigour bloom,
> 'Till fair Jamaica rival Greece and Rome!

## Musical Theater during the Revolution

Once hostilities began, professional actors were well advised to play the role of patriots or make their exit from the rebelling colonies as gracefully as possible. The best had already gone off to the West Indies, maintaining in that oasis of peace the American Company's quality until the times and social climate permitted a return.

Of those who stayed, none served his adopted country with the zeal and brilliance of the Dutch pantomimist and dancer Francis Mentges, who, as William Francis, was featured in the Douglass company. After Congress outlawed the theater, he remained in Philadelphia, and when war began joined the army and eventually won the rank of colonel. For many years after the war, except for a visit to England in 1788, he taught social dancing, and was among the distinguished citizens who welcomed his old friend Washington when the wartime hero entered the nation's capital as president. Actors were recruited for a revived American theater in Philadelphia during the early 1790s, and he was signed on at a salary of forty dollars a week, far more than the usual five dollars paid to most players, to work as a choreographer and featured dancer. When he was too old to continue with his usual skill, he became a character actor, and enjoyed a national reputation as the finest of his kind.

The theater was effectively closed down by Congressional fiat when the fighting started, and this was enforced by local Sons of Liberty, who were determined to suppress this form of British aristocratic taste as well as any other trappings of a tyranny they fought. Americans who had enjoyed the playhouse found themselves acting out their favorite works in the company of friends, reading from published playscripts. For many years this interest had made publication of old and new works a profitable business for Yankee printers and booksellers. The demand was now increased, and the price of printed librettos, stage comedies, and English tragedies vaulted with the inflation. The theater was partially restored under British aegis, in the form of benefit seasons, all profits going toward support of widows and orphans of fallen soldiers and sailors in the service of England. Colonial printers brought out reprintings of favorite plays and new plays by patriotic Americans who took to this form for propaganda purposes. Mercy Otis Warren, wife of a leading Massachusetts rebel, had never seen a live performance when she wrote several plays in support of the American cause, intended chiefly to be read aloud. None of these was ever produced, but their published editions served to add fuel to the spark that burst into flame at Lexington.

British officers, accustomed to the pleasures of London's patent theaters and the pursuit of amiable soubrettes, hoped to relieve the tedium of occupation life in wild America with amateur theatricals, using daughters of Loyalist supporters in feminine roles. General John Burgoyne, friend of David Garrick and certainly the best playwright then living in the colonies, provided an arena for these activities. The Boston that had passed a law in 1750 far more drastic than Congress's 1774 resolution was shocked when he commandeered the "cradle of liberty" for use by his soldier players. In the autumn of 1775, he authorized use of the commodious Great Hall above the central marketplace, built by Peter Faneuil to be used for public entertainment. Box and pit seats sold for one dollar that winter for programs of comedy and tragedy and a performance in January 1776 of Burgoyne's *Blockade of Boston,* a ballad farce whose songs were printed on a broadsheet as a souvenir of the performance. Mrs. Warren responded quickly to the effrontery with her *The Blockheads,* which mocked the blockading English soldiery's vaunted bravery as well as that of its American supporters. When the English sailed from Boston the next March, the theater went, too.

New York then became the major British stronghold, after an army of 20,000 under General William Howe threw out Washington's untrained militia and small army cadre. The English commander was knighted for the triumph and entered a smoldering city to the strains of Lampe's "He comes, the conquering hero comes," played by one of the many military bands attached to the occupying regiments. Almost 500 buildings had been destroyed in a fire that leveled most of lower Manhattan, an area that became known as Canvas Town for its collection of tents, huts, and temporary buildings, in which an unbridled night life of crime, drunkenness, and prostitution reigned. The area around Trinity Church became an open-air mall, complete with military musicians playing for strolling officers, their imported camp followers, and the sons and daughters of returned Loyalist families. The John Street was renamed the Theatre Royal, and in it a company of army and navy amateur actors offered eighteen performances during the winter. The theater was always packed, with the ladies making their usual brilliant appearance.

In the summer of 1777, Howe took to the field and made his way ever closer to Philadelphia, finally occupying it in September and then settling down for the winter while Washington established camp at Valley Forge, some thirty miles away. Howe's "strolling company" made ready for a second season, in Douglass's Southwark Theatre. Because printed scripts of the new plays were scarce, and the officer performers had to copy out their parts in longhand, advertisements in the reestablished Loyalist press called upon the citizenry for assistance. Robert Bell, who had published Thomas Paine's *Common Sense,* came forth and provided local editions of the needed plays. The season, from January to May 1778, was made up of farce plays, staples by Farquhar and Shakespeare, and John Home's extraordinarily popular *Douglas,* believed by many Scots to be the work of a new Bard of Avon.

Despite Congressional objection, theater made its appearance at Valley Forge at the same time the enemy was enjoying a comfortable and warm playhouse nearby. A much admired band of six musicians was directed by Colonel Proctor of the Pennsylvania militia, who bought the music and instruments and paid each person who played out of his own purse. In addition to this group, who doubled on wind and strings to play accompaniments for a Valley Forge production of *The Padlock,* the camp was full of fifers and drummers attached to each company of soldiers. Musicians sometimes played during dinners Washington gave for visiting foreign dignitaries. After Burgoyne had been defeated at Saratoga the previous summer, France became an open ally, and the Spaniards were making overtures of friendship. Representatives of each were frequent visitors to the winter camp. Many soldiers brought their own instruments along to war, entertaining their comrades with music or playing for camp shows created by Colonel Mentges. Officers and their ladies appeared at Valley Forge in *The Recruiting Officer* and Addison's *Cato,* which was performed in May 1777 before a large and receptive audience that found the scenery excellent and applauded the performances.

The lavish *Mischianza* of water music, jousting, and a banquet held on the Delaware's banks to send General Lord Howe off to England at the end of the Philadelphia theatrical season in May 1778, as well as reports of the violations at Valley Forge of the edict against popular entertainment, impelled the Continental Congress to restate its antagonistic attitude toward the theater in particular. Because of the order, Washington refused an invitation from a favorite officer, Lafayette, to attend a performance at the Southwark, where an acting company made up of American soldiers performed following Philadelphia's liberation in the summer of 1778. It is highly unlikely that Congress would have dismissed the nation's most beloved leader, but there was sufficient agitation against him among the highest ranks that he wisely chose to avoid any problem.

Howe was succeeded as commander by Sir Henry Clinton. This sybaritic and music-mad officer returned to the security and comfort of New York.

Officer actors returning from Philadelphia joined with the resident troupe, which had been presenting a second season in New York of military theatricals, to form the talented company that added to the city's pleasure during the next five years. Acting "By Permission of His Excellency Sir Henry Clinton, Knight of Bath," the Royal Theatre players presented nearly 150 performances. A pit orchestra of fourteen soldiers included Hessian Corporal Philip Pfeil, who as "Phile" wrote the music for one of his adopted nation's first hit songs, the 1798 "Hail! Columbia." Occasionally, displays of fireworks were provided, interrupted often by squibs thrown into the audience by rebel sympathizers.

New Yorkers had access to other forms of entertainment as well. Bullbaiting was revived, a stout and vicious animal providing satisfactory diversion. Music of all kinds—popular songs, instrumental concerts, and works from London concert rooms—was performed in the Royal Theatre and at other large halls in Manhattan. The sports-minded watched cricket matches in the Brooklyn and Greenwich suburbs. Subscription balls were advertised regularly, attendance limited to 200, drawn from the ranks of the military, civil servants, and gentlemen residing in town. Opera glasses were available for rental, and when the vagaries of New York's weather proved difficult to curb, the theater management advertised its intention to use "every method to keep the house as cool as possible." Box ticket holders sent their servants several hours in advance of curtain time with a note giving the number of places to be held. Often, their mission accomplished, they slipped into pit or gallery seats, much to the management's consternation and ticket holders' complaint.

The New Musical Theater

When the war ended, repatriation of British servicemen went slowly, and the presence of uniformed officers was a common sight in many large cities for more than a year. These bored gentlemen provided a ready audience for the emerging American theater. Maryland was the first state to violate Congress's resolution; it permitted erection of Baltimore's first theater in 1781. The manager and impresario for this venture was a former singing, dancing member of the old Douglass company, Thomas Wall, under whose direction a group of professional and amateur actors, singers, and musicians, some of them trained in London and veterans of the American Company, offered a season of British hits. Because musicians of good character were difficult to locate, performances often had to make do with a handful of instrumentalists, or only a harpsichord, as in the old days. Summer, Wall took his players to Annapolis, where the brick theater built by Douglass still stood, and to smaller Maryland communities.

After Wall's death, the management was inherited by Dennis Ryan, who was aware of popular music's potency and made greater use of the actors' singing and dancing talents. During a lengthy southern tour, a singing trumpet player, a virtuoso bagpiper, and an eccentric dancer attracted large audiences. Ryan's death led to the immediate demise of a theatrical venture that was gaining ticket buyers, and left the field to the returned Lewis Hallam, Jr.

America's first fine actor and manager made his postwar appearance in late 1783. Provided with a power of attorney, Hallam hoped to restore his right to the theaters erected and still owned by his stepfather and to receive permission to appear on stage. Few of Philadelphia's town fathers looked with favor on a growing sentiment in the land that American artistic and cultural pursuits should be available to all. The only positive response on their part had been the civic pride with which they looked upon native son Francis Hopkinson and his all-sung ballad opera *America Independent or The Temple of Minerva,* the 1781 ''oratorical entertainment'' hailed as ''America's first grand opera.'' In actuality, it was a pastiche of well-known melodies from the London musical-theater repertory, including music by Handel, Lampe, John Weldon, Niccolò, Jommelli, and others. None of the work was original except Hopkinson's text and his selection of the tunes to which the words were sung.

The opera had been written at a most appropriate time, for the French and Americans had not yet devised the strategy that would pen Cornwallis on the Yorktown peninsula and end the struggle. After the British surrender, Washington attended the first of two performances of Hopkinson's opus in the Philadelphia home of the French ambassador, joining, on December 11, 1781, a circle of American leaders, all of whom found the entertainment a stirring call for national unity.

Hallam, arriving in Philadelphia in response to an invitation that promised recompense for his banishment, petitioned the General Assembly for repeal of the statute against ''shows, plays and other expensive diversions,'' sweetening his appeal with a proposal that the theater should be taxed. Favorable legislation was framed, prompting a flood of petitions for and against, as the Quaker establishment harnessed its forces in opposition to the bill and brought about its defeat. At once, Hallam fell back on many of the devices his great-grandparent and others had used to fight the Licensing Act of 1737. The Southwark was cleaned and reopened as an "opera-house."

His "representations and harmony" included a vocal "Monody" to the memory of leaders fallen in the recent war, with newly composed music, some Shakespeare, "a serious investigation of his morality, illustrated by speeches," a farce afterpiece, and usually a bit of flag-waving calculated to strike home in patriot hearts. Tickets for these performances were usually available at local bookstores, as were printed playscripts of all words to the special pieces of music and songs. Although Hallam had not yet gotten official permission to perform, he recognized the state's power with a semiofficial VIVAT RESPUBLICA on all his advertising.

Because of his failing health, Hallam took on a partner, the notorious womanizer but fine actor John Henry, a London player who had been with the old Douglass company and was competent to take the actor-manager's place in many leading roles. Henry's wife, the actress and concert singer Maria Storer, returned to the occasional breeches parts for which she was famous, playing in "lectures" that included *Hamlet* as an illustration of "filial piety," the "pernicious vice of scandal" typified in *The School for Scandal, Richard the Third* as an object lesson in the "fate of tyranny," and "improper education" demonstrated by *She Stoops to Conquer.*

The young dancer John Durang performed during intermissions. He was born in England and came to Philadelphia with his family just at the end of the British occupation. He received his training from local émigré European ballet dancers. His peasant dance, "alemande," pantomimes, and, particularly, "hornpipe," a forerunner of modern tap dancing, aroused the devotion of admirers, who hailed him as the first American dancing star. The music for "Durang's hornpipe," which was published many times during the next century and inspired dancers to imitation, was written for him by an extraordinary German musician named Hoffmeister, who was only three feet tall. One of the roles in which Durang was most popular was that of Friday in the pantomime *Robinson Crusoe,* done in blackface. Before he retired from the stage in 1811, Durang trained many of his children in the steps for which he was famous. His complicated hornpipe, beginning with a great leap onstage from a hidden trampoline, was preserved in choreographed illustration, detailing the constant shuffles, pigeon wings, cooper shuffles, and traditional ballet postures.

The combined Hallam-Henry troupe, calling itself the Old American Company in order to dispel any British connotation, moved to New York in 1785, and found it far more hospitable than Philadelphia had been. Beginning with "lectures," a declaimed and sung version of the Garrick-Dibdin *Shakespeare's Jubilee,* pantomimes by Durang, and the obligatory monodies and patriotic rondelays, Hallam slowly introduced works from the patent playhouses that had been offered prior to the Revolution. A novelty, the Eidophusikon, was somehow acquired from London, where the Drury Lane's staff scenic designer, Phillipe Loutherbourg, had invented it in 1781 for viewing in his home by select audiences for a fee of five shillings. With pivoting screens, exotic paintings, transparent shades, three-dimensional models made of clay and varnished wood, the machine used advanced mechanical techniques to create a series of motion pictures, shown inside a box ten feet wide, six feet high, and eight feet deep, lit by lamps in front of which slips of stained colored glass were placed. The Eidophusikon program included moving scenes of the mighty falls of Niagara, sunrise over a fog-shrouded Italian seaport, and Satan reviewing his armies of devils as depicted in Milton's *Paradise Lost,* to musical accompaniment.

Durang's considerable talent included a facility with brush and pen, and he was responsible for the "superb and pantomimical fete," as Hallam advertised the magic-lantern show, combining "the powers of music, machinery and painting" in the storms and shipwreck viewed by a packed house from the safety of wooden benches. The music was provided from the pit by a small group of mostly European players. In the band were the Hessian soldier-violinist Philip Phile, who, with many of his comrade mercenaries, had remained in America, and Henri Capron, a French cellist, who doubled on reeds. Phile served as leader, setting the time and rhythms, and the Briton John Bentley sat at his harpsichord, playing the chords, cuing actors as they broke into song, sometimes joining them in the chorus, and occasionally also playing minor stage roles. Bentley was responsible for the selection and composition of new music for Old American Company productions, including Hallam as Mungo in *The Padlock.* Durang danced to Bentley's music in *Robinson Crusoe,* which had, as advertised, a "dance of the natives" as well as other "pantimimical mummeries at which common sense stood aghast and idiots wondered."

Other groups of actors were beginning to make their way around the new nation—Ryan's American Company of Comedians, the New American Company, the Real American Company—but none had the drawing power of the Hallam-Henry players and were without access to big-city theaters. They played as far south as Savannah and Charleston, north to Albany, New York. Hallam and Henry had worked in Richmond and Baltimore in 1786, but afterward limited their activities to the large cities.

Wherever actors appeared, a spate of reaction from press and pulpit followed, much of it stemming from the theater's traditional association with London, where many of the actors had received their early training, and the repertoire of virtually all-British offerings. Many Americans were troubled by the presentation of such lascivious comedies as *The Recruiting Officer,* with Congreve's ancient but smutty wit, and the pernicious *School for Scandal.*

Much of the audiences' affirmatively enthusiastic response to Old American Company offerings was for Thomas Wignell, the best comic actor of the day, who learned his craft from Garrick and came to America in 1774. His appearance as the blundering Irish veteran and the Irish songs he performed in *The Poor Soldier* made an American hit out of the Shield-O'Keeffe success. As a New England bumpkin servant in Royall Tyler's first play, *The Contrast,* Wignell played a major part in getting acceptance for the Old American Company by the nation's cultural jingoists and intellectuals. Tyler's five-act comedy, with two interpolated songs, came at a time when many Americans were seeking to establish their country's place in a growing art form. Wignell gave many who avoided the theater for religious or moral reasons an excuse to attend as a manifestation of their patriotism.

Tyler, a Harvard-trained attorney, had never seen a play until five weeks before his comedy was first shown in New York, on April 16, 1787. Born in New England, he served honorably during the war. When it was over, he courted John Adams's teen-aged daughter, drawing from that Savonarola of the popular arts the comment that Tyler was too much the poet for any possible union with an Adams. In New York on business in 1787, he had his first opportunity to see the professional theater. His only previous contact had been parlor readings, from which he had learned the requisite character stereotypes employed by Wycherley, Farquhar, O'Keeffe, and Dibdin: a manly, sentimental, and courageous hero, a likable and less than thoroughly villainous villain, a coquettish young lady, a fop to play opposite her, a chaste heroine, and two comic servants as contrast to one another.

Tyler's contribution to these theater clichés was the genuinely American quality of the attitudes, national perceptions, and high-mindedness of his good types in contrast with their antagonists, who were the embodiment of what Yankee America found wrong with aristocratic England and corrupt France. His major creation was the Yankee Jonathan, whose judgments mirrored those of the Bostonians who fought and helped win the Revolution. Jonathan's song was the national American anthem of the time, "Yankee Doodle," which the common man had been singing with pride and challenge in the face of the ridicule the tune had originally been put to by British officers. He sang it to a cook who had been paid to seduce him, in response to the request for "a song to please the ladies, such as 'Roslin Castle' or 'The maid of the mill' " both from London plays. After announcing that he "can't but sing a hundred and ninety verses," Jonathan sang the best-known four and then leaped on the woman, expecting a warm embrace as reward. The other popular song used by Tyler was "Song of the Indian Chief, Alknamook," which had not yet been printed in America, though it was already well known. The melody was declared by its London publisher to be "an original air, brought from America by a gentleman long conversant with the Indian tribes, and particularly with the Nation of the Cherokees." Words were written by Anne Hone Hunter, Haydn's hostess and collaborator while he was in London for the Salomon concerts.

A few days after seeing *The School for Scandal*, Tyler completed his comedy, which was an immediate success in New York and then in Philadelphia, where it was presented by Hallam just as the Constitutional Convention was assembling. Washington was among the subscribers to a printed edition of the "first dramatic production by a citizen of the United States in which the characters and scenes are entirely American." Because Philadelphia's ruling class still opposed theatrical presentations, a "reading" was arranged to lure convention delegates. Wignell's performance failed to persuade the authorities, and the Old American Company continued evading the law by the old sophistries, and then gradually offered the same repertoire that had succeeded in New York.

In early 1789, the city in which the Liberty Bell first tolled became the second major American community to license the professional theater, after the campaign of a newly organized Dramatic Association had obtained repeal of the ten-year-old Act of Prohibitions, and the Southwark was reopened. There the Old American Company began to operate "under authority," as it soon did along a circuit that included theaters in New York, Baltimore, and Richmond.

Those distinguished and powerful Philadelphians who had lobbied for repeal of the antitheater laws found much to be desired not only in the Old American Company's performances, but also in the condition of their theater. Like most playhouses, it was nearly forty years old and located in an unfashionable section of the city with muddy and poorly lighted streets.

Admission ranged from fifty cents to a dollar fifty, but one could buy a season ticket for fourteen dollars. The John Street in New York was typical. The audience sat on wooden benches, although the boxes were sometimes furnished with cushions and had bolts inside "to prevent any interruption." Their doors were locked by a screw key, used by a doorkeeper after proper tickets were presented. A stove in the lobby offered the only source of heat, and on a cold winter night many crowded around it for comfort. Printed librettos of musical plays and scripts of dramas were sold in the lobby for twelve and a half cents. French brandy, Holland gin, oranges, apples, raisins, peanuts, mince pies, and custards were sold, though many theaters barred sale of intoxicating drinks until the conclusion of the featured play. Fire hazards lurked in the foot warmers brought in during cold weather and in the incessant tobacco smoking.

Hissing, thumping, and stamping in the gallery usually brought on the orchestra, whose entrance was announced by the sounding of a bell. Once they were seated, another bell introduced the overture. As many as twenty musicians, among them America's most talented professionals, responded to the first violin's nod and began to play. They were fairly compensated, fourteen dollars to the director-conductor, perched behind a harpsichord or square pianoforte, and ten dollars a week to the two or three first violins, viola, cello, and bass, and, when the score called for them, reeds and winds, brass instruments, and side drums. Whenever the orchestra struck up a Jommelli chaconne or a Haydn symphony, cries of "Give us Bonypart crossing the Rhine" or "Washington's March" or "Yankee Doodle" came down from the gallery gods, to convince the perspiring conductor that a change was in order. If he failed to obey, violence usually ensued, as many a Briton or European, unfamiliar with American taste, learned to his sorrow.

Tyler's success with *The Contrast* encouraged another young American, William Dunlap, a facile if not greatly talented painter. At the age of seventeen he had finished a portrait of Washington, then fresh from victory at Yorktown, and was overwhelmed by the conqueror's praise. He went off to London to study, but spent most of his time at the royal theaters. After two years with Benjamin West, he returned, just as *The Contrast* made its success. As a young boy in New York, Dunlap had seen Clinton's thespians, and then wrote heavy dramas, with no success. He began work on a repertoire for the Old American Company, but when John Henry rejected the first offering because it had no role for his current mistress, Dunlap announced that he was ready to rewrite, willing to do anything to secure a place in the arena in which he felt he would have the power to do much good. In the following eight years, America's first professional playwright turned out a half-dozen moderately successful pieces, usually revising British war horses by setting them in America, people with Yankee types. The farce *Darby's Return* brought him true acclaim. It was a spin-off from Shield's *Poor Soldier*, with a fat part for Wignell. Dunlap, who played the flute and enjoyed singing in taverns, provided Washington's favorite actor with a number of songs, filled with sure laughs. The publication of this comic interlude led to performances of it by other professional groups and amateur players.

When Thomas Wignell suddenly announced his exit from the Old American Company, Hallam and Henry realized that, despite their success with new plays by American writers, fresh new faces, well trained in the newest acting techniques and familiar with the best of London's playscripts were required. Henry went to London to sign singing performers. His prime catch was John Hodgkinson, the self-styled "Provincial Garrick," who was earning a certain reputation outside London singing and acting roles made famous by the great Drury Lane actor-manager. Hodgkinson was born to a farmer who eventually bought a Manchester public house, in which the youth served as potboy. His pleasing voice won a place in the cathedral choir, and he learned to play the violin from musicians who entertained his father's customers. While still an apprentice to a merchant, John took up with some amateur actors, who recognized his fine voice and gave him leading roles in back-alley productions of such fare as *The Padlock*. Thrashed by his master for this breach of contract, young Hodgkinson ran off to join an acting company in the spa town of Bath and played the Midland circuit, several times in support of Mrs. Siddons.

In 1791, to rid himself of the theater manager's wife with whom he had run off, Hodgkinson wrote to Hallam in New York, offering America the services of the "principal player in the kingdom." Henry found him in Bath and signed the twenty-six-year-old actor and a young singing actress Hodgkinson was determined to take to the United States with him, Arabella Brett, who, the daughter of a Drury Lane actor, had grown up backstage. Mrs. Hodgkinson, as she became known, was regarded as "an amiable woman and a good wife," but was also a dipsomaniac, who created problems for a generation of American theater managers.

The vessel that took the Hodgkinsons to New York in September 1792 carried ten other performers signed by Henry, among them an again pregnant Mrs. Wrighten of the Drury Lane, now married to a Mr. Pownall and with two grown daughters, and Alexander Placide, who would, in time, displace Durang as the country's leading dancer.

Mary-Ann Wrighten Pownall was forty-one and hopeful that the American theater would treat her as royalty as had the Drury Lane. She had been seventeen when Garrick found her, pretty and with a very fine voice, but "clumsy of figure." Others failed to share his judgment, and she became one of the company's leading performers, playing saucy chambermaids and forward heroines in works by Dibdin and Linley, and scoring a great success in Burgoyne's *Lord of the Manor,* a part she got through her husband, a prompter and minor official at the theater. In 1787, she ran away from husband and children to find bliss in the arms of a dealer of spirits, until she left him to return to the stage. Mrs. Wrighten made her last London appearance at Covent Garden in 1792.

Walking New York's streets in breeches and stockings and wearing an old-fashioned powdered wig with a braided hair twist, John Hodgkinson was an immediate public spectacle, getting attention that served his new employers well. He triumphed as Petruchio, Othello, Richard, Captain Macheath, and in other roles, replacing John Henry in many of them, to Hallam's great personal pleasure, because relations between the managers had reached open hostility. When, in a moment of pique, Henry placed his share of the partnership on the block for $10,000 Hodgkinson promptly grabbed the offer. From early 1794 until 1796, when William Dunlap bought a part interest and became manager, the company appeared under a Hallam and Hodgkinson banner.

Now well entrenched in New York social life, the company presented the first American comic opera, *Tammany,* in the early spring of 1794. The libretto was by Anne Kemble Hatton, the score by James Hewitt, the new musical director, and Hodgkinson starred. Mrs. Hatton, a sister of the young and sensational British tragic actress Sarah Siddons, had arrived in New York with a husband whom Dunlap thought a "vulgar man." Having considerable social ambitions, she drew on her theater background to write a play about the patron saint of the benevolent and fraternal association of pro–French Republic anti-Federalists called the Tammany Society. On the first day of each May, they celebrated the feast of the "titular saint of America in their wigwam on the banks of the Hudson." Flourishing in the late 1680s, the Delaware chief Tamenen had done business with William Penn, and was facetiously canonized as patron saint in 1770. His name became associated with those staunchly patriotic, anti-British politicians who referred to themselves as Columbians rather than Americans.

The Hattons proclaimed their Columbian sympathies and brought the new playscript to Tammany officials, who were delighted and persuaded Hodgkinson to produce the work with the society's financial support. Hewitt was assigned to write the music, which, with the libretto, has disappeared. Only copies of the lyrics survive, in small books that were sold at the theater just before every performance. Opening-day advertising announced that two songs had been removed at rehearsals, though they were included in the printed pamphlet, making this first American musical the first to have songs deleted from the score before opening night. Hewitt later published a few of *Tammany*'s songs individually.

As expected, reaction was mixed. Having paid for the production, Tammany loved this tribute to its patron saint. The Federalists deemed it "a wretched thing, literally a melange of bombast." While conducting the orchestra, Hewitt was attacked by members of the audience because he would not respond to repeated shouts for "Yankee Doodle."

The scenery, designed and executed by an Italian mechanist and scenic artist, Charles Ciceri, came in for particular praise. Until his fortuitous arrival, fleeing from Philadelphia's yellow fever plague, New Yorkers had become accustomed to shabby old sets fast becoming black from age and the city's pollution. Ciceri's near-genius, nurtured in London and Paris opera houses and theaters, created spectacles that astounded ticket buyers during the 1790s. For the first time, they saw practicable doors, windows, Gothic halls, and mountain torrents, devised by Ciceri for the Eidophusikon's transparent scenery, one of the John Street's objects of wonder.

The artist's realistic settings of Switzerland were a prime factor in the excited response, in April 1796, following the first professionally produced all-American musical production still extant, *The Archers or the Mountaineers of Switzerland,* written by Dunlap, with a score by Benjamin Carr. The composer owned a Philadelphia music and publishing office, with a branch in New York, and was a well-known singing actor and concert soloist.

For his subject, Dunlap chose the Swiss mountaineers' revolt, led by the master bowman William Tell, against Austrian occupiers, doing so thirty years before Rossini wrote his better-known opera on the same theme. Except for a song, and perhaps a march published by Carr, none of the score remains. On the basis of the few pieces of *The Archers'* score remaining, and the five other musical plays, many songs and afterpieces, and other work by Carr still extant, some historians believe this William Tell musical to be work of a talented composer, one greatly influenced by Handel. *The Archers* was staged a number of times during the years following its premiere, but gradually disappeared.

Most music written for the Old American Company was the work of James Hewitt, with occasional assistance from Victor Pelissier, one of the few composers and arrangers who did such work during the federal period. Short of stature and astigmatic to the point of near-blindness, Pelissier had arrived in Philadelphia from France in 1792 and moved to New York the next year to join the John Street orchestra as first French hornist and composer-arranger. He wrote music for eighteen productions and his own musicals, many of them in collaboration with Dunlap. His score for physician Elihu Hubbard Smith's *Edwin and Angelina,* a musical version of a Goldsmith novel, enjoyed small success, an indication of the little general interest in original American musical plays.

During rehearsal for *The Archers*, Hodgkinson succeeded in ousting Hallam, from both artistic control and a starring role the Englishman coveted, by guaranteeing Dunlap that buying into the ownership would enable the playwright to present any work of his own he chose to. After swallowing the bait, Dunlap learned that his talents did not extend to successful theatrical management. His regular mix of old favorites with new works, many of them his or by friends, failed to keep him from bankruptcy. He was never silent in condemning "mercenary managers" who satisfied audiences with exhibitions of a man "who could whirl around on his head with crackers and other fireworks attached to his heels," rather than presentations that could correct social ills and help bring about a perfect society.

The new, "remarkably commodious" 2,000-seat Park Theatre, on Park Row near the Poorhouse, built in 1797 at a cost of $130,000, and Ciceri's increasing skill afforded Dunlap a stage on which to produce more elaborate parades, grand marches, and processions, employ larger singing and dancing choruses, and present patriotic spectacles for which Hewitt and Pelissier arranged old music or created new scores. Some of these were successful, but they all provided new material for the music-publishing businesses opened by Benjamin Carr and Hewitt. Dunlap's production of a play by that "European Shakespeare" Augustus von Kotzebue brought playgoers into the theater during the yellow fever scare of 1798, when nothing else could, and kept the Old American Company in business. Such "dutch stuff," written by the imperial Austrian court dramatist, in Vienna and later in St. Petersburg, freely translated and often much altered by Dunlap, annoyed the actors but delighted spectators. The best known was *Pizarro in Peru,* with music by Hewitt, which became the most performed American drama for the succeeding three decades, playing in New York, Philadelphia, Charleston, and New Orleans, only *Richard the Third* enjoying more popularity. A high point in the tragedy detailing the Incas' destruction by gold-hungry Spaniards was the leap over a chasm by a mortally wounded Hodgkinson, child in arms, a moment made magic by Ciceri's stagecraft. Hewitt's music accompanied scenes in which the libretto called for a "sacrifice offered by the Inca consumed by fire from above" a procession of priests and priestesses "to the sacrifice with hymns and invocations" and a "triumphant march and procession of the warriors returning from battle with their prisoners."

Pelissier wrote music for Dunlap's version of *The Virgin of the Sun,* adapted from Kotzebue, which was performed an unheard-of five times in a row due to public demand for another sight of the grand procession of native worshipers to the Temple of the Sun. Several very popular songs came from the revision of Dunlap's best play, the failed *André,* a sentimental retelling of the British spy's last days, that became a success as the musical play *The Glory of Columbia—Her Yeomen.* The heroes of this patriotic stage work were "the three glorious Columbian yeomen whose incorruptible honesty preserved West Point and the American Army." Performances of the piece were a feature of Fourth of July celebrations.

Despite most favorable public reaction to these presentations, the syndicate that built the Park Theatre was forced to sell it to John Jacob Astor in one of the real estate transactions that enabled the one-time music dealer to take over title to most of lower Manhattan. The leaseholders had been unable to make the $450 annual profit required for solvency, owing in some part, to a growing presence of the "professional beauties and beautiful professionals," ladies of the evening who used the theater to conduct business. Boxes were set aside for them, and regulations issued that "no persons of notorious illfame will be suffered to occupy any seat in a box where the places are already taken," to avoid intrusion on liaisons in progress. Righteous people would not attend the Park.

In 1805, after another autumnal visitation of yellow fever forced him to close the doors, Dunlap retired from the Park Theatre's management. He had lost his taste for a national theater that depended for success on money and had become, in New York at least, a playground for the gallery, whose occupants rained apples, nuts and gingerbread on the heads of the audience in the pit, many of whom also had to dodge drippings of wax from overhead chandeliers, the theater's principal lighting, and a meeting place for the "fashionables" in the boxes, with noise, ostentation, and bad manners. After 1812, Dunlap devoted himself almost entirely to writing and painting, wandering the northeast in good weather as an itinerant portrait artist. His series of books about the arts culminated in the *History of the American Theatre*. Only once did he return to the stage, in 1828, with his most profitable venture, *A Trip to Niagara,* written, he confessed, chiefly to exhibit its painted scenery. With music by Charles Gilfert, one of a Slovak family of music publishers, the piece showed some 50,000 feet of scenery depicting a journey from the New York wharves up the Hudson River, through rain, fog, and moonlight, past Albany, along the newly built Erie Canal, and finally to Niagara's majestic falls. The players, a group of American tourists and visitors, stood on the deck of a stationary steamboat as the scenery was dragged past them.

Until his death, in 1839, Dunlap was a leading figure in New York's literary and art circles, the intimate of a group of Americans who brought the new nation its first internationally recognized culture, among them the writers Washington Irving and James Fenimore Cooper, painters John Trumbull, Gilbert Stuart, and young Samuel Morse, inventor of the telegraph machine.

## Musical Theater in Federal Philadelphia

The Old American Company's monopoly of Philadelphia's top-flight professional stage entertainment was broken in April 1794 when a stock company, recruited chiefly in England by Thomas Wignell, presented the O'Keeffe-Arnold *Castle of Andalusia.* The evening was three years in the making, dating from the day a group of civic-minded citizens met with the comedian, who had just severed his ties with Hallam and Henry, to discuss building a playhouse in the nation's capital city. Wignell, esteemed as one of America's finest actors, was to be responsible for all presentations, but the stockholders set up their own system of checks and balances by naming a local favorite, Alexander Reinagle, as musical director. Considerable prestige had been added to the nation's musical life from the day in 1786 that this fine pianist, a musician and conductor of top rank, arrived in the United States. His first public appearance took place in June 1787, when he played before Washington and delegates to the Constitutional Convention, with such success that he was later engaged to give music lessons to the great Virginian's adopted daughter.

Reinagle was born in London in 1756, the son of an émigré Austrian trumpet player, studied in Scotland with Raynor Taylor, and became an intimate of Johann Christian Bach. The death of a beloved brother, whom he had supported with income from music lessons and concertizing in such exotic places as the Portuguese royal court, moved Reinagle to try new opportunities in new places. Prospects for European musicians in the New World were reputed to be excellent, and he sailed there. In New York, he advertised himself as a "member of a Company of Musicians" of London, presumably the centuries-old musicians' guild, and played in the John Street orchestra during the Old American Company's second season. When the players moved to Philadelphia, he took up residence there. After reorganizing the city concerts, Reinagle introduced four-hand piano music with a recent Haydn sonata, and then, with Washington in the audience, performed his piano concerto, an overture, and that popular Scottish dance the strathspey. A few months later, as the number of his students grew, he published the first book of music issued in Philadelphia, *A Selection of the Most Favored Scots Tunes.*

Reinagle's full-time involvement with the theater began when many of his Philadelphia friends and pupils arranged for his appointment as the new theater's musical director. Because most English-born theater people were reluctant to reside in Philadelphia, where resentment still smoldered over the Hallam-Douglass company's apparent desertion of the nation just as war was beginning, Wignell was sent to England to recruit performers. He left Reinagle to supervise construction of the new playhouse. The theater, on Chestnut Street, was modeled after the royal theater in Bath, surpassing in style and beauty anything yet built in America. It accommodated 2,000 on its backless benches and in boxes lined with pink paper behind cushioned seats. The house was decorated with crimson curtains and glass chandeliers, and over the stage an emblematic representation of ''America encouraging the drama'' bore the motto ''The Eagle suffers little birds to sing.''

As a master Mason, Reinagle turned out city leaders for the cornerstone laying, opened the theater in midwinter 1793 with three concerts, and promptly shut the doors until Wignell's return. Among the players the latter had signed was the Drury Lane veteran Mrs. Oldmixion, who gave the company the finest trained woman's voice in America, Elizabeth Kemble Whitlock, one of the Siddons sisters, and Susanna Rowson and her husband.

The Chestnut Street Theatre opened after a delay of thirteen months, with Reinagle presiding at the pianoforte and George Willingham, an old friend from England, conducting the orchestra. The house was crowded to its full capacity. A farce afterpiece by Mrs. Hannah Cowley, a successful comedy writer, served to introduce Mrs. Rowson, who was herself the author of a best-selling book. She became a valuable addition to the company, not because she was an outstanding actress, but because she provided new songs and musical plays. Her naughty novel *Charlotte Temple* (1791) was still selling astonishing quantities, and until publication of *Uncle Tom's Cabin,* also written by a woman, was one of the nineteenth century's most successful works of fiction. Susanna Haswell Rowson was born in England in 1762 and taken as a young child to the American colonies by her British naval officer father, who was stationed in Massachusetts. After the shots at Lexington, the family was interned until 1778, when an exchange was made and they returned home. Susanna showed her literary bent at an early age, and her first novel was published in 1786, under patronage of the duchess of Devonshire. Six other books followed, and then came the sensational *Charlotte Temple,* the story of a young woman seduced by a British officer and taken by him to the colonies during the American Revolution.

She married William Rowson, a trumpet player and leader of the band attached to the Royal Guards. After Rowson bought himself out of the service with his wife's money, he joined an acting company. Although publication of her novel in 1791 brought Mrs. Rowson international fame, the copyright laws failed to provide the fortune that should have accompanied it. Her husband was declared a bankrupt in 1792, while the couple was working in the Edinburgh theater where Wignell saw and signed them.

Mrs. Rowson took advantage of Philadelphia's booming publishing business to arrange with Matthew Carey for publication of *Charlotte Temple,* which was an immediate success, selling 50,000 copies in the first twenty-five years. She wrote a number of songs, one of which, to Reinagle's music, a Dibdinesque ballad imbued with a vision of America as a maritime power, "America, Commerce and Freedom," from the pantomime *The Sailor's Landlady,* sold well throughout the country. She next wrote her first musical play, *Slaves in Algiers.* Congress's determination to counter growing threats from the Barbary States— Algiers, Morocco, Tripoli, and Tunis—provided the plot. People of both political parties grew ever more furious over the actions of Barbary pirates, who had taken fifteen American ships and made slaves of 180 officers and men. As did most European nations, the United States paid tribute for protection against attacks of this nature, and in 1793 a naval force sailed against the boldest of the pirate cities, Algiers. Nothing came of this action, but early in the following century, a naval force smashed the pirates in their strongholds and cleared the western Mediterranean for American shipping.

Possibly because of the scorn of one of America's first theater critics, the unpopular William Cobbett, who doubted the author's sudden conversion to patriotism and questioned her self-expressed title of Poetess Laureate of the Sovereign People of the United States, *Slaves in Algiers* played in Philadelphia and Boston a number of times in the next several years. The Reinagle score was duly acknowledged by Rowson in the printed libretto, which thanked him for "the attention he manifested and the taste and genius he displayed in the composition of the music."

The next Rowson play, *The Volunteers* (1795), again to Reinagle's music, was inspired by the Whiskey Rebellion, which had taken place the previous year in western Pennsylvania. After the federal government placed an excise tax on homemade spirituous liquors, the Scotch-Irish frontier Pennsylvanians resisted all efforts to collect it for the moonshine products of their pot stills, tarring and feathering revenue agents, until a force of volunteer militia was marched into the district. Only a twenty-page pamphlet, printed for Rowson to sell at the theater and in stores, containing words and music is left; it has fourteen songs, one of them borrowed from Charles Dibdin.

In *The American Tar* (1796), "founded on a recent fact at Liverpool," Rowson collaborated with Raynor Taylor, another expatriate British musician and composer. Its song "Independent and Free" was printed at the authors' expense for sale to theater audiences.

Later that year, the couple joined the Boston Theatre Company, whose audiences were fervently Federalist in their sentiments and appreciated Rowson's literary work. She was nearly forty and was tiring of the stage, having appeared in over seventy parts, among them Katherine in Garrick's reworking of *The Taming of the Shrew,* Mistress Quickly in *The Merry Wives of Windsor,* and one of the two female leads in *The Padlock*. She retired the next year to open a select school for young ladies. Her husband continued to work as an actor, prompter, and theater musician before he was appointed clerk of Boston's Clearing House. The caliber of instructors at Rowson's academy was of the highest and included émigré European musicians. Susanna Rowson remained a prolific literary figure until her death, at the age of sixty-two, with a weekly magazine, textbooks, poems, and occasional popular music to her credit.

The Philadelphia company built theaters in Baltimore and Washington, its first, before 1795 and worked this three-city circuit, including some seventy-five musical plays as part of its standard repertoire. After Wignell's death, in 1803, Reinagle worked in partnership with Wignell's widow. Friction between them led to his departure to take up residence in Baltimore, where he managed a new theater and worked on his music, setting Milton's *Paradise Lost* to orchestral accompaniment. He died in 1809. Most of his music was destroyed in a fire, with his personal effects and the harpsichord on which he had entertained presidents and audiences for more than twenty years.

## Musical Theater in Federal Boston

In 1790, when Lewis Hallam and John Henry sought permission to open a theater, the forty-year-old anti-popular-entertainment laws, the result of an attempted presentation of Otway's blank verse *Orphan*, were once more invoked. Great agitation for their repeal followed, and when Samuel Adams fulminated in Faneuil Hall against the stage, he learned that he could no longer move Bostonians as he had once done in that great room.

Once again actors took to speaking the moral lectures and acting in the exhibitions that had broken the ice in New York and Philadelphia. A new Exhibition Hall seating 500 was constructed, and handsome Alexandre Placide came from New York, where he had landed earlier that year, one of the new actors brought to America by John Henry. With him was a beautiful, kittenish ballet dancer, Martine, thought to be his wife. The two were featured in pantomimic ballets that closed each evening at the Exhibition Hall, following the introductory addresses, "musical entertainments," tumblers, slack-wire dancers, and other variety performances, which were preparing the city for the delights to come. Placide, the first great colorful figure in the annals of American dancing, was an extraordinary rope dancer. Stemming from an ancient rustic sport, and the forerunner of modern wire walking, the rope dance became a sophisticated form about 1740 and continued as an important variety ingredient until the decline of vaudeville. Placide's style, developed at Astley's Circus and the Sadler's Wells Theatre, his grace and magnetism did much to attract female audiences to the theater in these early days of the struggle for public acceptance. Dressed in a light silk Spanish costume, with silk stockings, pumps, and two watch chains, he offered something new to Americans, who had been exposed only to English dance techniques, in presentations that were little more than London pantomimes about Robinson Crusoe and commedia dell'arte figures. Alexander

Reinagle, waiting for his Philadelphia theater to be completed, served as leader of the orchestra during the three months of unabashedly true musical theater and dramatic performances in late 1792.

This all came to an end at the instance of Massachusetts' attorney-general, who served a warrant for the arrest of the Exhibition Hall's manager. All scheduled performances were canceled, and manager and players departed.

A group of Bostonians offered stock in 1793 for the construction of a new theater, limited to 120 shares at fifty dollars each, with no more than two shares available to a single investor. The Federal Street Theatre, completed the next year, was hailed by theatregoers as "far superior in taste, elegance and convenience" to any building in Britain. A large and ornate dancing room was built at one end, and a projecting arcade enabled carriages to deliver theater-goers under cover, a real courtesy in this era when the streets were still un-paved and any random sidewalks were made of wood. Card and tea rooms were available to ticketholders bored with the entertainment, and a complete kitchen fed the hungry. A master of ceremonies was installed to keep the audience off the stage and out of the orchestra area and persuade the gallery "mob-ility" to refrain from raining a flood of eggs, peanuts, vegetables, apples, stones, nuts, and gingerbread onto those in the pit and Boston's aristocracy and its befeath-ered companions in the boxes.

Both the Old American Company and Wignell and Reinagle's troupe drove local performing groups out of the Federal Street Theatre by launching an in-vasion of New England, starting in Boston. The conservative townspeople didn't care for the novelties with which the two companies had been winning audi-ences elsewhere and preferred the old traditional London fare. This may have been due in part to the lack of outstanding singers during the first several sea-sons, or the absence of creative presences like Hewitt, Pelissier, Taylor, Rein-agle, and Carr. Trille laBarre, Federal Street's first conductor, did write music for revivals of old plays, but his successor, Robert Lemont, was far more in-terested in concert music. The van Hagens, in America for the second time in 1798, were lured by the prospect of work in the city's new playhouse, the Hay-market, the second to be built in one year. The senior van Hagen was eventu-ally hired to lead the Federal Street orchestra. He wrote only one original work, music for a London afterpiece, and some of the mandatory overtures for which the gallery clamored.

Representing stockholders whose political sentiments ran counter to the Fed-eralist owners of its rival, the Haymarket brought onstage new works that would appeal, it was hoped, to Jeffersonian democrats. The five-act *Battle of Bunker Hill,* complete with currently popular patriotic ballads and dedicated to Aaron Burr, was such a success that it enjoyed nine consecutive performances. Its au-thor was the recently arrived Irish revolutionary John Burk, who boasted there was an English price on his head. After a $2,000 profit, he offered a manu-script of the play to other managers around the nation for $500 a copy, prom-ising they would make eight times that at the box office. Federalists everywhere agreed with one opinion that it was "the most execrable of the Grub Street kind,'' but *The Battle of Bunker Hill* played to packed houses. The Haymarket's *West Point Preserved,* the re-creation by poet William Brown of Benedict Arnold's treachery and Major André's sad fall, was equally successful.

Having been relegated to secondary roles because of John Hodgkinson's anxious desire to keep his new wife, the former Miss Brett, in the spotlight, Mary-Ann Wrighten Pownall left the Old American Company for Boston in 1795. During her several seasons in New York, she had written with the company's musical director, James Hewitt, who may have known her in England. They appeared together in concerts, and in the winter months of 1793 she joined him in six programs offered by members of the John Street orchestra, during which she sang from the *Book of Songs* she and Hewitt had published and advertised for sale. She also traveled to Philadelphia soon after for similar concerts and advertised a since-lost thirty-page booklet containing ''some pastoral songs, written by herself at an early period of life,'' and the speech she made to concert audiences on behalf of recently arrived French musicians.

Her songs were popular features of her personal appearances and between the acts at the theater, and she had a stock of them for sale in her dressing room. In September 1793, she broke her leg, but when Anne Hatton, her *Tammany* not yet written, put together the outline of a ''musical trifle,'' Mrs. Pownall wrote the dialogue, added songs, and made a triumphant appearance on crutches. When her leg mended and the season came to an end with Hodgkinson's announcement that her annual salary would be cut, she went to Boston for a concert and interviews with the local theater management. There was no work available, and the concert audience was so small that she called on their charity and netted $200. She had returned to Boston with twin daughters, who had joined her on their father's death, and son Felix, age four, who made his stage debut singing one of his mother's songs. Her daughter Mary played the crowd-pleasing ''Battle of Prague'' on the pianoforte and joined mother and sisters in trios.

Realizing that her daughters were exposed to the continuing blandishments of Manhattan's young men, who viewed them as fair game when they visited her backstage, and with no offer of work in Boston, she signed with a new theatrical company being formed by Charleston's second theater. During Holy Week, with the theater available to her for the customary benefit performance enjoyed by all actors, Mrs. Pownall sang ''A Grand Concert Spirituale'' of songs from Handel oratorios, and provided a printed pamphlet containing the words of the anthems and songs she presented. On the theater stage she continued to be hailed for performances ''far superior,'' one said, ''to anything ever heard in this city before.'' In April 1796, this woman, in her mid-forties, and liberated before her time, gave birth to a daughter. Soon after, she resumed her place on the theater and concert stage.

The recital she planned for August was canceled when word reached her that her sixteen-year-old daughter Caroline had run off with an acrobat. Eight days later Mary-Ann Wrighten Pownall was dead of a broken heart. In Caroline, Alexandre Placide found both beauty and talent. The couple settled in Charleston, where he trained her in dancing and ropewalking. The former Mrs. Placide had disappeared, victim of an attractive man who never offered her a wedding ring. Caroline Placide became one of America's best dancers and actresses, and her handsome children and grandchildren starred in the pre-Civil War theater.

Fire put the Federal Street Theatre out of business in 1798, the first of a series of conflagrations that destroyed many of the country's original playhouses, but a second Federal Street was ready for the public at the end of 1799.

## The Circus and Popular Music

Shortly after Philip Astley opened his first amphitheater riding house in London, some colonial horsemen advertised their equestrian skills, including playing a musical instrument at full gallop. In 1773, John Bates, fresh from appearances in Europe, performed in an indoor arena off the Bowery. Others toured the colonies, riding before men of wealth and Southern gentlemen farmers whose own abilities were imposing. Many of these wandering riders copied Astley's now classic comedy routine, the "Regiment of Tailors" off full tilt against a French army. Only Congress's 1774 edict put an end to these early circus tours.

Demonstrations of the art of manège, accompanied by three drums, fife, and trumpet, were shown three times a week in Philadelphia, Boston, or New York during the 1780s by the Yankee rider Thomas Pool. His three trained horses played dead, bowed, and sat "like a lady's lap dog"; Pool flip-flopped and somersaulted on horseback, and an assistant clown did comic exercises.

John Bill Ricketts, the first great American circus showman, once a pupil of Astley's London rival Charles Hughes, came from England in 1792. At last open to show business, Philadelphia welcomed his riding academy and circus. Audiences grew, and he opened a larger building, directly across from the Chestnut Street Theatre, evoking that management's complaints about such a vulgar intrusion. His friend George Washington, who shared a common enthusiasm for superior horsemanship, came to Ricketts's aid, and his riding theater received exclusive rights to Saturday-night performances in the city. When Washington's favorite charger became too old to ride, Ricketts bought the animal and exhibited Old Jack in a side show. That autumn the rider-manager took his troupe to New York for a short season of "greater variety of Equestrian Exercises than has yet been exhibited," which now included clowns and acrobats, a fireworks artist, and the great dancer Durang.

Ricketts's permanent Manhattan amphitheater was built two years later, and, like those he built afterward in Boston, Philadelphia, and other places, was wooden, domed, and circular in form, and lighted by candles that set off the extravagant decorations he believed essential to his patrons' pleasure. Painters created landscapes and portraits, and the boxes were decorated with the coats of arms of the sixteen states then comprising the union. Flags were everywhere. Durang created a repertoire of ballet and comic dances, with music written and arranged by Monsieur Rochforte, the production's musical director. Durang's ballet *Dermot and Kathleen,* based on *The Poor Soldier,* caused a scandal with the leading actress's revealing costume, and she was hissed off the stage. Pantos based on incidents from the American past included *The Battle of the Kegs,* with Francis Hopkinson's popular song, *The Whiskey Rebellion,* and *The Battle of Trenton* to James Hewitt's concert piece. Thirty-two such presentations were offered in a single season.

Ricketts strongly contested the Old American Company's New York monopoly during the off-season of 1796, when he came north with these spoken and sung pantomimes, performed by actors on leave from the Charleston theater, where Placide was training dancers in his own style. Among these were Spinacuta, a ropedancer, acrobat, scenic designer and painter, and choreographer, and Matthew Sully (whose son Thomas became a major painter), who quickly supplanted Wignell as the city's favorite singing comedian. On nights when his patent did not permit theatrical presentations, Ricketts offered concert music programs. With the profits from this successful summer, he built New York's 1,500-seat New Circus, lavishly decorated and furnished, from which the odor of horses never disappeared after the first season.

Formidable competition came in 1797 from a French immigrant, Philip Lailson, who successfully introduced the circus-with-music in Charleston and built his Pantheon across from the New Circus in Manhattan. Lailson opened with grand displays of horsemanship, concluding each evening's performance with pantomimes starring Sully, whom he had lured away from Ricketts. His presentations grew so lavish that within a half-year he went into bankruptcy and sold off stage furnishings, sets, costumes, and all movable equipment. The items for sale included scenery for twelve elaborate afterpieces, among them Gluck's *Richard the Lion-Hearted* and Monsigny's *Deserter*.

In March 1798, Lailson challenged Ricketts on his own ground in Philadelphia, and the two circus companies gave the Chestnut Street players a run for their money. Alexandre Placide was imported to produce ballets with music from the pastoral dramas of Lully, Monsigny, Philodor, and other French composers. It was a war Lailson again lost but which eventually brought down Ricketts. Having drawn full houses with elaborate musicals, Ricketts devoted more time to music than to the displays of equestrianism that first brought him fame. In December 1799, the pantomime *Don Juan,* freely based on the Gluck opera and starring John Durang was announced. In the final scene, Don Juan was to leap into the mouth of hell, where the furies, receiving him on the points of burning spears, were to hurl him into the bottomless pit. A short time before the spectacle, some fire pots used for stage effects burst into flames, and the amphitheater burned to the ground, a $20,000 loss.

Gone were the white columns, stage, rings, and weathervane in the shape of Mercury, who was, among other things, the god of commerce and gain. Ricketts found work with his Chestnut Street Theatre competitors until he set aside enough money to take ship to England, resolved to be done with America. The vessel on which he sailed sank at sea; all were lost.

### The Dawn of a New Century

American entertainment, relying heavily on music, dance, and variety turns, was, at the end of the century, flourishing along the seaboard. There was no need, as there continued to be in England, to evade the provisions of a licensing system that permitted all-spoken drama only to certain playhouses. American managers continued to present musical plays exactly as British actors were doing in the motherland, and used the wide net of entertainment rooted in the people's music to draw the diverse audience necessary to fund the theater. All-spoken entertainment awaited the late nineteenth century.

By 1795, New York, Philadelphia, and even staid Boston troupes were familiar visitors to smaller communities, like Hartford, Albany, Newport. In the South, where ballad opera was sung and danced within a decade of John Gay's imaginative *Beggar's Opera,* professional groups continually criss-crossed the land, building theaters, visiting state capitals and centers of both great and small population. Their performances inspired imitation by amateurs on the campuses of recently constituted institutions of learning, just as they did in the drawing rooms of the nation's wealthy, where lovers of the theater read to one another from playscripts.

Thespians of more or less talent had crossed the mountains by 1790, to offer entertainment in Pittsburgh. In 1797, Washington, Kentucky, a settlement of about 500 souls, watched an amateur production of *The Padlock,* with a local Mungo bewailing:

> Whate'er's to be done
> Poor black man must run.
> Mungo here, Mungo dere,
> Mungo everywere.

This was an omen of things to come in the development of blackface popular music and the theater it sustained.

# CHAPTER 21

# The Business of Music Publishing

### American Popular Music: Technology and Copyright

Queen Anne's 1710 statute had little impact on American printing and publishing. It was a logistical impossibility for a colonial bookseller-publisher to register his work, within ten days after publication, at Stationers' Hall or deposit copies in the royal and college libraries in Britain. Those native authors whose writings were printed in America often sent manuscripts or copies off to London, hoping for the supreme compliment of having their work go on sale in that book-publishing capital of the English-speaking world.

Fourteen years passed after Benjamin Harris's short-lived *Publick Occurrences* appeared in Boston, the first publication of its kind in the New World, before printer Benjamin Green was hired to produce the *Boston News-letter* for the town's postmaster, John Campbell. A bookseller by trade, Campbell had been issuing hand-copied newsletters based on reports by his postrider mailmen and the sea captains who brought overseas mail and packages to his shop. It also borrowed freely from London magazines, to which Campbell had first access. Only with government subsidy and free use of the colonial postal system could any such newsletter survive until Americans of all social classes learned to care about news in a medium other than the broadside ballad.

Until the Revolution changed the political status quo, one printer in each colony had enjoyed a guaranteed income from his undeviating support of the crown, the royal governor, and the legislature. Newspapers issued under official patent were mouthpieces for government policy and public notice, and their monopolistic privileges extended to printing of all legal forms, notices, proclamations, laws, and other government business. When paper money was authorized, these printers were trusted to issue the new currency, a most profitable business in an America whose continuing problem with inflation was often caused by unrestricted issuance of legal tender. The oldest extant American broadside ballads, "The dying speech of Old Tenor [Tender]" and "Billy Broke Locks," deal with the issuance of paper money to replace the hard cash of Spanish pieces of eight.

The majority of master printers doing business prior to the 1750s were trained in England and came to the New World when opportunity for their work was severely decreased by government edict and Stationers machinations. Their independent newspapers competed with the officially supported press, making them ready allies of the radicals working to foment change. The magazines they printed imitated British periodicals and provided verse makers with a place for their ballads, laments, love songs, and memorials, the "Poet's Corner" featured in virtually every publication. Economic interests, not the least of which were the stamp taxes raising the cost of paper, put these printer-journalists into the forefront of the colonial struggle that ended with independence.

Despite pressures and scarcities, the colonial printers' output was greater than can be known. Time and the transitory nature of their products has destroyed or caused to disappear into private collections nearly three-quarters of the estimated 86,000 newspapers, broadsides, ballads, and books printed between 1639 and the new republic's first year, 1783. Many house walls were covered with printed paper, which served as insulation or decoration and eventually crumbled into dust.

American presses issued a veritable sea of theological words, chiefly sermons, 444 of them by Cotton Mather alone. These sermons were often the equivalent of contemporary magazine articles hoping to assist readers to spiritual peace of mind and acceptance of life as it is. The Boston divine's sermons on the efficacy of inoculation as a preventive against the spread of the smallpox regularly besetting Boston did much to bring about public acceptance of the procedure, and printed sermons in favor of singing by note instead of rote helped Samuel Gerrish promote sales of his singing-instruction books.

## The State of the Printer's Art

No matter where he worked, the eighteenth-century printer had a hard, if sometimes enjoyable, life, working long hours, carrying great weights of metal type and forms, and manipulating a press that was changed little from the improvement of Gutenberg's equipment made a hundred years earlier by a Dutch printer. In 1727, according to Rollo Silver, in *Publishing in Boston, 1726–1757*, Worcester printers charged fifty to sixty shillings for a standard sheet of four finished book pages. In less than twenty years, the charge more than doubled, though in Philadelphia such work was done for half the cost, nearly approximating London prices. Most early American printing was done through the barter system, the publisher providing type, ink, paper, and even food in exchange for completed and dried sheets, which he then had bound. When several booksellers joined in publication, costs were shared, and the title page usually listed all the partners' names.

The paper used was imported chiefly from England, but the finest and most expensive came from Holland, where an improved shredding machine gave that nation worldwide supremacy in the quality of paper. America's first paper mill, the Rittenhouse factory, built in 1690 in a suburb along the Wissahickon River known as "German-town," was followed by a second in 1713. Other mills sprouted up in the region around Philadelphia, and by the republic's first year, half of the ninety papermaking plants were within six hours' travel of that city.

American publishing, indeed the Revolution itself, could not have developed without women's castoff undergarments and other rags, an ingredient necessary to paper manufacture and a military requirement of the highest priority. Every order, proclamation, memorandum, recruiting poster, and map was on paper, and that staple was used for the counterfeit British currency that financed part of the struggle. Paper wadding was driven home into the barrel of all weapons as part of the priming. Throughout the century, appeals for rags were constant.

Quick to notice any competition that might intrude on their crown-granted monopolies, London merchants took their complaints to the House of Lords, which oversaw the business and economy of all colonies. The growth of American papermaking did increase dramatically, but it was never able to end the shortage, and the home government never took steps to curb its growth.

Until 1769, one had to send to England or Holland for a printing press and then wait more than three months for delivery. In that year, a Connecticut clock and watchmaker, Isaac Doolittle, successfully duplicated the iron screw at the heart of the printing press, which created sufficient force to bring paper against inked type. His first machine was sold to a Philadelphia printer. A few years later, that city's master cabinetmaker joined with a whitesmith and blacksmith to produce forms, frames, cases, and other allied equipment. When the war was over, machinists and inventors experimented with innovations and borrowed them from English patents. In 1796, a New Jersey machinist advertised the first good-quality, locally produced press, for seventy-five dollars.

Type casting was available in Pennsylvania in 1730, but it was of German letters only, produced for the active religious and music-book business established there. Good-quality English-language type came from Holland, whose foundries supplied most such requirements until William Caslon cut punches and made fonts of letters and numerals for London printers. Before that, English type founding was in a state of decline, dating back to the 1637 Star Chamber order fixing the number of type founders at four, supervised by the Stationers' Company. Unable to replace deteriorating book type needed for documents, licenses, burial notices, advertising cards, and handbills, British job printers turned to engravers and calligraphers to produce and decorate their work. For the first time since Gutenberg revolutionized the technology, the scribe was once again a presence. Rolling presses costing only a sixth of the thirty-pound hand press reduced the cost of engraved title pages and interior book illustrations, and job printers, needing less overhead, equipment, and manpower than their more prestigious peers, flourished as never before.

When England entered an age of elegance to match its undisputed financial sway, job printers strove to match the development of general decoration. Banknotes, stock certificates, theater tickets, and other beautifully engraved pieces came off London's rolling presses. Since city streets were not yet numbered, store owners relied on trade cards bearing a picture of their shop signs as their major form of advertising, and these, too, became more artistic.

Letter type retained the same uninspired mechanical form it had been for more than a century, but engraved printing took on an artistic quality and technological excellence that made it a thing of beauty. The writing master brought his ornate curlicued calligraphy to job printing, creating whole bodies of alphabet lettering. The most brilliant of specimen books produced by these artist-craftsmen was *The Universal Penman,* compiled and published between 1733 and 1741 by George Bickham, Sr., an engraver, book illustrator, and political cartoonist, to demonstrate his work and that of twenty-five other London writing masters.

Bickham and his son George engraved and published highly individual sheet music, considerably advancing the art Thomas Cross brought to English music publishing. It was their work that decorated the indecent farce *Flora, or Hob in the Well,* the first ballad opera heard in the American colonies. Young Bickham's masterpiece was the luxurious collection *The Musical Entertainer,* which first appeared every two weeks from 1736 until 1739 as a regular publication of four pages of popular songs and sold for sixpence. Working with an etcher's graver and scorer for staves, ties, clefs, and signatures and with punches to stamp the heads of notes, Bickham incised the words, illustrations, decorations, and vignettes that are a brilliant example of the calligrapher-engraver's art.

*The Musical Entertainer* fostered innumerable imitations, *Calliope* (1739), *Clio and Euterpe* (1748), *Amaryllis* (1746) among others. All of them found their way into American libraries and introduced people remote from the playhouses to songs by Purcell, Handel, and Corelli, by theater songwriters Leveridge, Green, Lampe, Boyce, and Thomas Arne. Each song was set for solo voice and a figured bass, with an appropriate single-line arrangement for the flute at the bottom of each page.

A handful of type foundries did exist in London around 1700, but there were few qualified letter cutters to make the punches from which the type was cast. Bickham's work and that of others did much to inspire England's first master letter cutter to improve the rude design of his country's typography. William Caslon was apprenticed in 1706 at the age of thirteen to learn the lorimer's trade, engraving designs and decorations on musket and pistol locks and decorating gun barrels. After completing his education, he began making tools for the London publishing business, cutting punches and engraving letters. The Society for the Propagation of Christian Knowledge, the Anglicans' chief missionary arm in places other than the American colonies, published the Bible in various languages. When a New Testament and the Psalms in Arabic for use by Christians in the Near East was contemplated, the society turned to Caslon for a font of appropriate type. A grant of twenty guineas funded his first foundry, a building near the engraving shop financed for him by three leading London booksellers, who had recognized his unique talent.

Assisted and supported by them and the society, Caslon created many new type fonts, his first specimen book, issued in 1734, displaying thirty-five of his design. By 1739, he dominated English printing. The king's printer used only Caslon type, and most books were set in Caslon, the type known today as "colonial." American printers purchased brevier fonts of Caslon type, whose letters heralded the coming of a war for freedom when they were used for the Declaration of Independence.

Caslon was one of a fanatically dedicated group of music lovers who made London a center of amateur music making. He installed an organ in his home and often attended concerts at the Castle Tavern on Paternoster Row, along which booksellers clustered. Performances in his home were usually of Corelli's music, with some English and Italian opera overtures and Handel's more modern ones. An evening's entertainment always concluded with one or two Purcell songs or a few catches.

When Isaiah Thomas boasted in the 1786 first edition of his *Worcester Collection* that it was printed from imported music type, it was Caslon's work that enabled the first great American book and music publisher to "print any kind of Church, or other music, in a neat and elegant manner, and . . . cheaper than such work has heretofore been done in this country."

The use of locally cast music type was long in coming to both England and America because it was expensive to produce and only a large edition warranted its use. There was no significant American market until the end of the century. Type was cast in bulky forms that did not lend themselves to convenient storage, and because most music sales continued to be on demand, engraved plates could be more conveniently maintained, taken out when demand warranted, and then returned to the shelves. Moreover, engravings lent themselves admirably to the publication of popular music, providing an easily stored catalogue that offered additional revenue with little promotion.


## The Franklins

The careers of the Franklin brothers, James and Benjamin, illustrate the two courses an eighteenth-century American printer could pursue, each with its own rewards and deprivations, one suiting a maverick in a social structure that enforced conformity and the other affording recognition and success by working within the system, though occasionally seeking to change it.

Like many provincial Britons who left their native land in the 1680s, Josiah Franklin was driven to do so by economic reality. The annual minimal cost of living was twenty-six pounds, which only five of every thirteen families could expect to earn. There was little left, except to that three percent of families owning thirty percent of the income, for purchase of the silks Franklin dyed to support his family. So he took his wife and small children to Boston, where, promotional ballads and brochures assured him, the standard of living was three times greater than at home and opportunity abounded for a willing worker. Franklin took up the candlemaker's trade, and by 1715 was his own master, a property owner, and the father of seventeen children, two of whom, James and Benjamin, became printers.

James served a teen-age apprenticeship in his father's hometown of Eccton's printing offices and went to London to find work when he was set free of the articles. At the age of twenty-one, he had saved enough money to buy a press and type and returned to Boston. As a visiting Englishman wrote, the city's exchange was "surrounded with Booksellers' shops, which have a good trade," and whose custom was essential to the success of three local printing offices. Two of these were owned by descendants of the Green family, which had ruled Massachusetts printing since the Cambridge press was established. They had the colony's official business and printed the only newspaper and most of the books published locally. James found a house across the street from Boston Prison, set up his old-fashioned press and type, stored his paper supply, and was ready for business. Fortunately, his father was well situated among Boston's ruling order as a member of Old South Church, serving as precentor when Samuel Sewall was indisposed. Consequently, orders dribbled in from a church friend, Samuel Gerrish, which supplemented James's small income from job printing for lawyers and shopkeepers.

His twelve-year-old brother, Benjamin, signed articles of indenture for a term of nine years, during which James was obliged to teach him the "art and mystery of printing" and provide lodging, food, clothing, and laundry. Young Benjamin proved to be an unsuspected asset. James had learned in London how readily extra coins were made by writing, printing, and selling penny ballads. The long hours during the night that Ben had spent reading had sharpened his gift for rhyming, and he now tried his hand at ballad writing. Inspiration first came in November 1718, after five people drowned while attempting to land a rowboat at Boston's lighthouse in an autumn gale. The event shocked Boston, giving the Reverend Cotton Mather a sermon and sending Ben to his quill and ink. The virgin effort was, as he remembered in the *Autobiography*, "wretched stuff, in the Grub-street ballad style [but] sold wonderfully, the event being recent, having made a great noise." His vanity was flattered by the ballad's reception, and he would have been further pleased had he known that it was translated and sold in France as *La tragédie du phare*. A second ballad was born in the spring of 1719, after the British pirate Edward Teach was tracked down and killed by a force of Virginians. Josiah Franklin ridiculed both ballads, despite their great success, and told his son that "verse makers were generally beggars." Franklin said later, "So I escaped being a poet, most probably a very bad one."

Boston's ballad trade was almost exclusively in the hands of its most successful stationer, thirty-five-year-old English printer Thomas Fleet, who had fled religious persecution and arrived in Boston in 1712, with a press and letter type. He began to do work for booksellers, but also printed and sold ballads and small books for children. He was a competent rhyme maker, as may be seen from his ballads opposing imposition of the stamp tax on paper in the 1750s, but his broadsides rarely were original, being mostly imported British street songs. He became wealthy and owned slaves, training one of them to set type and work the hand press. This forgotten black man was also a skilled woodcutter, who engraved ballad and nursery-book illustrations. In 1719, Fleet issued *Songs from the Nursery, or Mother Gooses's Melodies for Children,* a small book made from wooden plates carved by his black slave. No copy of his first collection in America of children's popular songs has ever been found. The first English edition of Mother Goose songs appeared in London ten years later, lending some tenuous credence to the whimsy that Mother Goose was Fleet's mother-in-law, the widow of one Isaac Goose, or Vertigoos, and that she sang the songs to her six grandchildren.

Fleet printed penny song sheets until his death in 1758, long after he had become a prosperous Bostonian, publisher of the *Evening Post,* the city's best and most popular newspaper, and a successful auctioneer dealing in slaves, household merchandise, and other trade items. When a British ship once came into Boston Harbor with a cargo that included bales of papal indulgences taken off a Spanish man-of-war, he bought the full lot of these printed exemptions from punishment for personal sins and advertised the "INDULGENCES of the Present Pope Urban VIII . . . either by the single Bull, Quire, or Ream, at a much cheaper rate than they can be purchased of the French or Spanish priests, and yet will be warranted to be of the same advantage to the Possessors." Reserving some of his catch, he printed two half-sheet ballads on the clean side of each indulgence. Among the songs he is known to have printed in the 1740s are Gay's "Black ey'd Susan" (written with Leveridge); "Teague's ramble to the camp," one of many current ballads mocking the Irish; and "Handsome Harry," the sailor carried to a watery grave in the arms of the dead woman he had seduced and then abandoned.

James Franklin's most significant involvement with American music, the printing for Gerrish of Thomas Walter's *Grounds and Rules for Music Explained,* was merely another job-printing order, secured through his father's friendship with the bookseller. The connection came to an abrupt end when Franklin published *The New English Courant,* a weekly newspaper espousing anti-Puritan views picked up during his stay in England. He had also been producing the city's first newspaper, and that, too, was taken away, and returned to a churchgoing member of the Green family. New Church of England friends found James's shop a splendid place for socializing and the *Courant* a welcome medium in which to publish their anonymous personal views. Twenty-three numbers were issued, but James found himself increasingly in trouble with the government and the Congregational church, headed by his editorials' chief targets, the Mathers and their friends, including Thomas Walter. His rash journalism got him into the Boston jail, from whose windows he could see his shop, where his brother Ben was issuing a tamer and more acceptable journal, with his own name on the masthead as publisher, hoping thus to temper government proscription against the freedom of editorializing. Once released, James sought to restore the master-apprentice relationship, despite Ben's new role at the *Courant.*

One night in September 1723, after one beating too many, seventeen-year-old Ben sneaked away from his brother's authority and slipped aboard a ship bound for the Southern colonies. He had convinced the vessel's master that stealth was necessary because the parent of a young maiden he had seduced and rendered pregnant was in hot pursuit of her virtue's despoiler.

Ben's work was then done by another apprentice, though his name continued to appear on the *Courant* until 1726, when an ailing James accepted the Rhode Island colony's offer to set him up in business as official printer. After some years there, during which he established a short-lived newspaper, James died, leaving his shop to a family of printing Franklins, his wife, two daughters, and a son.

Destiny intended a different future for Ben Franklin, and he was on his way to embrace it. He stayed overnight in New York, a city he did not enjoy, and then sailed for Philadelphia, where he found work as a journeyman printer and a ready market for the skill in maintenance and repair of aging printing presses learned and sharpened under James's tutelage. Within seven months, dressed in a genteel new suit and owning a watch and five pounds of the sterling-silver money Philadelphia used, rather than paper currency, Ben presented himself to his father, hoping to borrow sufficient money to go to London, buy a press and equipment, and then set himself up in business as a master printer. He was well qualified, but failed to persuade Josiah to make the investment of one hundred pounds sterling needed.

Some Philadelphians provided the fare and expense money to the blossoming teen-ager, who had learned how to win friends by a display of attention and on whom he used the gift of story-telling that charmed all who heard him throughout his life. A new friend sailed with him, the clerk James Ralph, who was leaving everything, including a wife and newborn child, to make his way to London, where he hoped with Franklin's funding, to join the literary world. They had a splendid time in the world's largest city, living on very little, climbing to the Haymarket's gallery to look down on Italian opera sung by the castrati and prima donnas Handel imported, hearing Leveridge sing in a tobacco-smoke-filled tavern, joining in ribald catches, strolling past St. Paul's and hearing the masters of the day try the great organ, swimming in a Thames River from which one could drink the water, and watching the great city throb with a vitality infused by the people's certain sense of their destined role in world affairs. Most of all, the two young Americans enjoyed the city's least expensive attraction, "foolish intrigues with low women" and their freely given favors.

Franklin worked as a journeyman typesetter while Ralph looked for work at the theater and failed. He could not sell his poetry. For a time he played at being a provincial schoolmaster, but inevitably London drew him back. Gaining some reputation as a maker of verses, enough to earn a couplet in Pope's *Dunciad,* which, as Franklin wrote, "cured him," he turned to writing for the theater. An unfortunate and ill-received attempt by Ben to take his friend's place in a mistress's bed put and end to their friendship, a breach considered by Ralph sufficient to discharge him of all debts owed the young printer.

Ralph made his way in the London playhouses, revising scripts, serving as a man-of-all-work to managers, and in 1728, under the pseudonym A. Primcock, finished *The Touchstone, or Essays on the Reigning Diversions of the Town.* This witty book satirized Italian opera and proposed as subject matter for the British musical stage that "Tom Thumb would be a delightful Foundation to build a pretty little Pastoral on." Henry Fielding made a burlesque tragedy of it in 1730, set to music by Arne in 1733 as *The Opera of Operas, or Tom Thumb the Great,* the first full-length, all-sung English opera burlesque. Ralph also suggested that the "noted combat betwixt Moore of Moor-hall and the Dragon of Wantcliff" was suitable for a libretto. Henry Carey's play and John Frederick Lampe's score produced *The Dragon of Wantley* in 1737, a prodigiously successful stage work, surviving for decades.

In 1730, Ralph's own *Fashionable Lady* rode to success on the wave of public interest in ballad opera. Following Gay's lead, he asserted that "some whores, a chorus of whores, a gang of street-robbers" were the "only proper subjects fit for an opera," but peopled his work with the sort of characters London's upper classes quickly recognized—coquettes, naval officers, beaux and social climbers. There were sixty-eight tunes, some of them by Sir Thomas Overbury, John Eccles, and D'Urfey, and others so old their authors had been lost in time.

Turning to political writing, Ralph irritated British statesmen so unmercifully that he was bought off with a government pension on condition he retire from the activity. Franklin saw him again in 1757, married to an Englishwoman and eager to hear about his American grandchildren, but fearful that his new wife might learn from his old friend that she was the victim of bigamy. The secret was preserved, for Franklin was now a man of the world who had himself fathered illegitimate offspring.

The young Ben Franklin with whom Ralph broke in 1725 was a most unusual printer by standards of the London trade. He could write a book as well as set it in type, and did the latter with considerable speed. Whereas other printers carried only one heavy form upstairs to the pressroom, Franklin carried two, and he was no victim of drink. The British printer appeared to exist on ale, "a pint before breakfast with his bread and cheese, a pint at dinner, a pint in the afternoon about six o'clock, and another when he had done his day's work," spending most of his weekly thirty shillings on drink. Consequently, Franklin had no difficulty in getting work as one of John Watts's fifty employees in his printing and publishing office near the Lincoln's Inn Fields theaters. A Stationers' freeman and partner with Jacob Tonson, in various congers, Watts was one of the first to discern William Caslon's abilities. With Tonson Watts printed many playscripts, usually delivered to playhouse subscribers and hawked in lobbies before curtain time. The young American's pride in his work and keen intelligence brought him to Watts's attention, and Franklin was given special chores and extra pay for his increasing mastery of the trade.

Some eighteen months after Franklin left England, the Watts printing office became a major figure in English music publishing. Immediately after *The Beggar's Opera* began its successful run, Tonson and Watts purchased the new stage hit's copyright and published the text, with the songs, words, and music together. For twenty years, this minor conger owned exclusive rights to the most successful theatre music, buying virtually all new ballad operas, printing them with music cut into wooden plates and indicating the names of tunes borrowed by the playrights. It also issued collections of songs "set for the violin and flute by the most eminent masters," in six editions by 1731, which established a contemporary standard for quality by their beautiful design.

Ben Franklin's career as a merchant back in Philadelphia lasted only a few months. His financial backer died, and he resumed the printing trade, working as a journeyman for a remarkably inept master, in whose shop he found his future partner, Hugn Meredith. Franklin ran the business, taught the apprentices, who were kept on only until they had to receive wages, made ink, handled special orders, and cut engravings when needed. He also made new letters, contriving a mold and using the letters in stock to make punches, then striking the matrices in lead, and "thus supplied in a pretty tolerable way all deficiencies." He duplicated the copperplate rolling press on which he had helped to produce Walter's music book six years before and ran off an issue of paper money for the New Jersey colony.

Meredith's father raised a hundred pounds to buy a press and type for the new firm of Franklin & Meredith, which opened its doors in 1728. The partnership did not last long. Meredith was an incipient drunkard who spent more time in the nearby alehouse than in the shop, where an abstemious Franklin carried on alone. Assisted by friends, who seemed all his life to appear when needed, Franklin purchased the equipment and ended the partnership. Among his early publications was the 1729 *New Version of the Psalms of David* by Isaac Watts, about which he complained two years later that it remained unsold on his shelves in that Quaker-dominated city whose Protestant denominations were still dubious about the moral efficacy of singing man-written psalms. The collection of "delightful songs showing the noble exploits of Robin Hood and his yeomanrie," offered by another Philadelphia printer, was in far greater demand. In 1732, Franklin printed the first German hymnbook issued in America for Seventh-Day Baptists who had settled in Lancaster County in 1720. There was no trouble disposing of this item, because the German colonists were firm believers in the use of melodic tunes, eventually creating their own literature of some 750 original hymns.

The Franklin shop also printed the first American "songster." In *A Bibliography of Songsters Printed in America Before 1821*, Irving Lowens writes:

> I define a songster as a collection of three or more secular poems intended to be sung. Since a songster is primarily a collection of song lyrics, under ordinary circumstances it would contain no musical notation. However, since it is a collection of poems *intended to be sung* it may well contain frequent references to the names of the tunes the compiler had in mind when he chose the lyrics. More often than not, these tunes were those the average purchaser reasonably could be expected to recognize and sing from mention of the title alone.

Franklin's 1734 *Constitution of the Free-masons* qualifies as a songster, containing as it does the words to five Masonic songs, printed on eleven pages.

From the start, the Franklin printing office and bookstore carried imported music among its own publications of German hymnals, Watts's hymns, the 1730 *Singing Master's Guide*, written by Daniel Warner, the first of the city's itinerant music teachers, and many broadside ballads. Once the taste of the local cultural elite was stimulated by concerts of European music given by immigrant German musicians, Franklin stocked imported printed music, Corelli sonatas, and Geminiani's concertos, the type of melodic instrumentals he himself enjoyed now that he was learning to play the violin and the guitar. Franklin's taste never ran to Italian operatic music of the sort that "disguised and confounded the language by making a long syllable short, or a short one long, when sung." Music like that, he wrote his brother Peter, "neglects all the proprieties and beauties of common speech and in their place introduces its *defects* and *absurdities* as so many graces." He illustrated that contention with a list of the defects and improprieties of common speech in Handel's "favorite" song from *Judas Maccabaeus,* "not one of his juvenile performances before his taste could be improved and formed; it appeared when his reputation was at the highest."

He liked those songs in which "melody and harmony are separately agreeable and in union delightful," like the Scottish popular songs and dance tunes that had captivated England after they first appeared in print. These would live forever, Franklin thought, "if they escape being stifled in modern affected ornament . . . they are really compositions of melody and harmony united, or rather that their melody is harmony. I mean the simple tunes sung by a single voice."

Wherever Franklin traveled in later years, he carried a portable musical instrument in his luggage, the Sticcado-Pastrale, a kind of wooden xylophone with three octaves of glass bars which were struck with a mallet to sound "the old, simple ditties," to which he occasionally wrote words and possibly the little suite for three violins and cello attributed to him.

Musicologists may dispute the authenticity of that work of chamber music, but few question the achievement which earned the American universalist a place in a 1782 German musical almanac, long before any other American was perceived by Europeans to be of any cultural importance. Franklin's *Glassychord,* an improvement of the musical glasses known in the Near East during the fourteenth century, was inspired by the Irish "gay wine music" virtuoso Richard Pockreach, who toured England with a set of glasses of different sizes tuned by placing different quantities of water or wine in them and played by passing the fingers around their rims. Charmed by the music's sweetness, Franklin, practical mechanic that he was, determined to improve the instrument. He demonstrated his "armonica" for the first time around 1761, after creating an instrument whose tones were "imcomparibly sweet beyond those of any other." He had ordered seven-dozen goblets of varying sizes to be blown, with a whole in the middle of each, the largest nine inches in diameter and the smallest three. Thirty-seven of these were mounted on an iron spindle, as close together as possible, and placed in a long case resting on four legs like a harpsichord, with only the rims visible. The player sat before the case and revolved the spindle by moving a treadle like that of a spinning wheel while he kept moistening his fingers with a sponge. The music could be "swelled and softened at pleasure by stronger or weaker pressures of the fingers and continued at any length." Once well tuned with a harpsichord, the instrument never again required tuning. A London instrument maker built these to Franklin's specifications and sold them for forty guineas. Their vogue lasted until about 1800. Many composers wrote for the instrument, the most sublime piece being Mozart's *Adagio and Rondo*, K. 617.

Benjamin Franklin, the extraordinarily versatile American public servant and printer, is remembered better than B. Franklin, the music lover, possible composer of chamber music, inventor of instruments, lover of old English tunes, and songwriter. He understood the appeal of song melodies that had been loved for centuries by Englishmen and their American offspring. When his brother Peter composed a ballad and sent it to him in London, hoping to have some "eminent master" set a tune for it, Franklin wrote that "if you have given it to some country girl in the heart of Massachusetts who has never heard any other than psalm tunes or 'Chevy Chace', 'The Children in the wood' or 'Spanish lady' and such old simple ditties, but has a naturally good ear, she might more probably have made a pleasing popular tune for you than any of our masters here and more proper to your purposes." The lyrics he himself wrote, and sang in taverns for friends after he came to know and love rum and madeira, were set to the old tunes. Only a handful of them remain, two about the joys of the vine and one for the common-law wife, Deborah, he married in 1730. She served him as another hired hand in the printing office, "folding and stitching pamphlets, tending shop, purchasing old linen rags for the papermakers," while raising the illegitimate son fathered shortly after his return from England. She was illiterate and invaluable, her devotion permitting him to indulge the simultaneous careers he enjoyed. For years she kept the house clean and made the clothing he wore.

The popular "wishing song," as he called it, that Franklin sang "a thousand times when I was young," was written as a broadside in the 1680s by the Catholic astronomer Walter Pope and later appeared with music by John Blow in Playford's *Theater of Music* and in all editions of *Wit and Mirth or Pills to Purge Melancholy*. Its first chorus asked

> May I govern my Passion with an absolute sway,
> And grow wiser and better, as my strength wears away,
> Without gout or stone by a gentle decay.

## John Peter Zenger, Broadside Ballads, and Freedom of the Press

One printer-publisher who established himself in a major American city before the Revolution learned that the civil government was, as in Great Britain, an enemy of the free use of a printing press in the dissemination of "naughty ballads." Having no Stationers' Company to do its work and censor and repress dissent, New York royal authority took action, threw him into prison, and confiscated and burned his work.

John Peter Zenger was a Palatinate German who came to New York in 1710, at the age of thirteen, as one of Queen Anne's charity children and was apprenticed to the printer-publisher of New York's only newspaper. He never lost his accent and his English was poor, but he became a capable printer and went into business for himself, sometimes printing broadsides and ballads for their authors. Much like the only newspaper in other colonies, the New York *Ga-*

*zette,* still published by Zenger's former employer, was obliged to serve as the government's mouthpiece or lose its right to print, and certainly never gave space to opposing views. A group of citizens, headed by the real-estate operator whose holdings included the new theater on Broadway, Rip Van Dam, subsidized Zenger to bring out a second paper, the *Weekly Journal.* In addition to the usual fare of reprinted selections from Addison, Steele, Fielding, and other contemporary British writers, the small four-page weekly carried the community's only dissent, some in prose and some in broadside ballad form, to be sung to specified music.

The successful election to the magistracy of two opposition candidates was hailed with two ballads of triumph. City taverns pulsated with laughter as they were sung again and again. A reward for the name of their author was offered, but Zenger maintained his silence, refusing to cooperate. Copies of his paper were publicly burned by official order, and he was arrested for "printing and publishing several libels" and confined to jail, while the city enjoyed a new broadside devoted to the "funeral pile and execution of a ballad or ballads burnt by public authority."

After languishing in prison for nine months, Zenger was put on trial. His chief counsel was Andrew Hamilton, one of the continent's most distinguished lawyers. The aged attorney admitted that his client was indeed guilty of publishing the *Weekly Journal,* and with it the alleged libels, but submitted that "the words themselves must be libelous, that is, false, scandalous and seditious, or else we are not guilty." Turning to the jury, he pleaded "not for the poor printer, nor for New York alone . . . [but for] every freeman that lives under a British government on the main of America . . . [for] the cause of liberty . . . the liberty both of exposing and opposing arbitrary power by speaking and writing Truth."

The jury returned quickly with a verdict of "not guilty." Zenger was freed, and the cause of freedom of the press in America moved forward another step, the result of a broadside ballad.

## "Ingenious, public-spirited gentlemen, who have time to spare . . ."

Like Zenger, the average colonial printer-editor was a man of little formal education, few ever attaining Franklin's range of scientific and cultural perception, though many of them had more formal education than that man of many parts received as a boy in Boston schools. Pragmatic businessmen, they dabbled in the economic opportunities presented by a growing nation, running the postal service, starting newspapers, extending their interests to encompass the classic function of the stationer—publication and sale of pamphlets and books— as well as offering job printing at reasonable rates. They opened the columns of their small weekly papers to intellectuals possessed of a thirst to see their own words in print, and played on the vanity of would-be littérateurs by printing their poetic contributions. Some found themselves, as had James Franklin and Zenger, the victims of repressive legal actions after providing a forum for dissent. With the increase of public sentiment for meaningful self-government, even separation from the mother country, newspaper printers joined the conflict, boldly allying themselves with one side or the other, often to their financial ruin and exile.

Drawn to one another by similar cultural tastes, middle- and upper-class colonials met in public houses and formed social groups or literary clubs. Many members kept local journals supplied with verse, satire, tavern songs, fiction, and philosophy, and editors who recognized the potential increase in circulation stemming from publication of these contributions printed virtually everything offered. In the process, the only literary marketplace for contemporary men of letters was created. Because the ballad form was used for many of these poetic effusions, the American newspaper became a repository for songs that in an earlier time would have been hawked through city streets and on village greens.

American colonists were as much a singing people as the British from whom most of them sprang. The German Lutheran cleric Henry Mühlenberg marked this propensity in his diary. In 1752, after spending a stagecoach journey in the raucous company of singing and drinking New Yorkers, he noted:

> [They] have a kind of songs which are set to melodic music and describe all sorts of heroes and feats of arms on land and sea. Respectable people sing them as pastime and regard it as a serious invasion of their liberties if one protests against these songs. Now, if one rebukes them on account of their amorous songs, they believe they can justify themselves by referring to those songs about heroes. The musical settings and melodies of these songs of heroic deeds are very similar to those which our Germans use for church music.

Much as had the founder of Mühlenberg's religious denomination, Martin Luther, American poetasters and lyric writers believed good tunes and good rhyme schemes were common property, and they set to them their own doggerel verse and occasional poetry that mirrored the times and the poets' own response to the complexities of modern life. Joseph Dumbleton, who saluted a new paper mill in 1744 with verse contributed to the Virginia *Gazette,* was read in England as well as in the colonies, and his "Rhapsody on rum" was reprinted in the eminent London *Gazette,* offering proof to Englishmen that American farmers were possessed of more than a modicum of culture.

The Tuesday Club, founded in Annapolis around 1745, limited membership to twenty-five and attracted the colony's leading writers, men of wealth, musicians, wits, and good drinkers. Politics was never discussed, the only subject forbidden; "fiddlers, fools and farces" was its motto. The Scottish-born Dr. Alexander Hamilton, lover of Handel's and Corelli's music, was its founder, and among the leading members was Jonas Green, of the Boston printing family.

Trained by Franklin and then sent south as a partner with funds to buy a printing business, Green was appointed official Maryland printer in 1738, at an annual stipend of £500. Seven years later, he began the region's second newspaper, and issued a call to Marylanders for literary contributions to the *Gazette*'s first issue, asking for "ingenious productions . . . consistent with sobriety and good manners." The earliest offering printed was a forty-five-line ballad, "To the ladies of Maryland," by a bard who identified himself as "Juba," the earliest recorded use of the word that was identified with black dancing a century later. Green served as master of ceremonies at the club's regular meetings and was the official "poet, printer, punster, purveyor, punchmaker and poet laureate, of a most happy clubbical nature." He added to the group's purposes the obligation "to converse, laugh, differ, sing, dance and fiddle," bringing together Maryland's leading amateur musicians and music lovers. Charged with the composition of annual odes and drinking songs, Green wrote many pieces of light verse, in one of which there was a listing of the members' instruments:

> sackbuts, cymbels, timbrels, lutes,
> banjos, dulcimers and flutes;
> bagpipes, drones and snuffling bellows,
> pipes and tabors, kettledrums;
> trumpets shrill and deep humstrums;
> harpsichords and the hautboy sharp;
> Irish, Welsh and Jewish harp . . .

The colony's first music dealer had arrived in 1730. He sold Bibles, prayer books, psalters, minuets, overtures, songs with notes printed on copperplates at his Annapolis store, providing fare for the area's musicians, who graduated to the Tuesday Club and its musical evenings. Robert Morris, the wealthy father of the even wealthier financier of the Revolution, was part of the string quartet that played for Ben Franklin when he made a tour of inspection of his printing properties owned in partnership with Jonas Green.

The most talented club member, the Reverend Thomas Bacon, curate of St. Peter's, in Talbot County, best violinist in Maryland, and one of America's earliest and forgotten composers, was charged with setting Green's words to music. Bacon was born about 1700, presumably on the Isle of Man, and worked at a dockside coal depot in Dublin as a young man. There he met and married a widowed coffeehouse owner. He served an aprenticeship with the Dublin Company of Stationers and, on attaining his freedom, published a newspaper. Having gotten to know the British master printer Samuel Richardson, whose novel *Pamela* had just been issued, Bacon contracted with the author to furnish sheets as they came off the press so that the book could be reprinted in an authorized Irish edition, thus preserving the copyright. The first book of this tale of the dangers facing a virtuous young woman in service to a London household became an overnight sensation throughout the British Isles. When another Dublin stationer stole copies and printed the book, Richardson sent 250 copies of "the genuine edition" for sale at Bacon's bookstore, causing great financial damage to the pirate. When Handel conducted a public rehearsal of *Messiah* prior to its Dublin world premiere, Bacon was in the audience, and reported to friends that the work "far surpassed anything of that nature which had been performed in this or any other Kingdom."

Two years later, Bacon began studying for the Anglican priesthood and was ordained as a missionary to Maryland in 1745. He arrived with his wife and son, and made friends quickly, impressing everyone with his ability to play the violin, cello, and bass and with the collection of music he brought from Dublin. With his minuets and string music, he "soon topped the 'tip top' " musicians of Maryland, one of them remembering a half century later that "he was an exquisite performer, and several pieces of his composing, under the humorous signature Signior Lardini [given by Dr. Hamilton on admission to the Tuesday Club] are still preserved and much esteemed in Maryland."

Among Bacon's friends was the Oxford-educated merchant Henry Callister, who came to America as an indentured servant, won his freedom, and could now spend his evenings playing the spinet, oboe, flute, and cello that graced his home. With Bacon now writing it, the quality of the Tuesday Club's music improved greatly, and in 1750 members felt so proud of the fifth anniversary *Ode* that it was sent to London's *Gentlemen's Magazine* for reprinting, an offer that was rejected. The following year, Green printed the annual musical salute, complete with Bacon's "arias, allegros and strathspeys," written for an ensemble of three violins, flute, drummer, and a mixed chorus of ten.

Having come into what his wife termed "a very considerable income," Bacon turned his energies to a favorite project, a charity work school, and traveled about Maryland and Virginia, raising funds and offering music concerts for the school's benefit. As one of the few permanent groups of organized musicians, the Tuesday Club members often performed at these concerts. Jonas Green, who had learned to play the French horn with sufficient skill to appear before his fellow members in a solo, as founder of Maryland's first lodge of Freemasons sponsored a performance of *The Beggar's Opera* in Annapolis. The "set of private gentlemen" playing the opera's musical accompaniment was also made up of club members.

"The most delightful concert America can afford" helped assuage Bacon's pain from his son's death in action against the French in Ohio. Bacon wrote to Callister about two evenings of music during October 1756, during which he played his violin, accompanied by the "famous Signor Palma on the harpsichord . . . a thorough master on that instrument and his execution surprising." Juan di Palma was one of many foreign musicians eking out a living by instructing Americans. He lived in Philadelphia but served other communities, including the Maryland-Virginia region, where he found other music masters, among them Peter Pelham, come to install the new church organ in Williamsburg. In Philadelphia, Francis Hopkinson was a pupil of Palma, and George Washington attended one of Palma's concerts, an occasion carefully noted in the Virginian's ledger book.

Before his death in 1768, Bacon was named minister to Maryland's richest and largest parish. Serving as Lord Baltimore's chaplain, he compiled the *Laws of Maryland at Large* with Green, producing the most beautiful piece of typography printed in the colonies prior to 1776. He was elected to the American Philosophical Society, and he fought to stay rising public clamor for separation from England. Little of Bacon's music survives—some half-dozen pieces in all—though letters reveal that he often presented his compositions to acquaintances in America and in England.

The "ingenious public-spirited gentlemen, who have time to spare" as the Tidewater printer William Parks characterized these Southerners, rarely wrote music; instead, they indulged the passion for creativity by writing innumerable verses—patriotic, romantic, religious, humorous, courtly, classical, and descriptive—and usually called for an English melody, but sometimes original music by some neighboring musician or visiting music master, a Bacon or a Palma. What they thus created, if it is recognized for what this body of literature and music really was, is among the earliest native-born popular music of the eighteenth century. These creations have been found in old letters and diaries, nineteenth-century collections of fugitive American poetry, microfilmed copies of old newspapers, and bound volumes of *Gentlemen's, Imperial, Scots, London,* and other British magazines. American verse was often reprinted in these last, sent by colonial subscribers who expected publication, for much of what they wrote was universally English in character.

New England's poets, being nearer the center of Puritan religious and social authority, were more sober and decorous than their Southern contemporaries. Yet in their verse lies a subtle Yankee humor and a passion for puns. The broadside tradition began in Massachusetts shortly after the first printing press was put in place, producing a lamentation in rhyme upon the death of a friend, and thus transplanting from the Old World an elegiac tradition that survives in present-day obituary pages. Indian raids and massacres, kidnappings, deaths by shipwreck and murder, the earthquake that shook Boston in 1755, the appearance of Halley's comet, drought in the Merrimack Valley, George Whitefield's sermons—all were subjects.

Street-song literature embraced the region's own exploits and problems: narrative verse about battles fought and won by local volunteers, marching songs, and after enactment of the repressive stamp tax, songs of protest and of patriotism. The earliest surviving broadside sheet began with the report of a battle, according to Ola Elizabeth Winslow, in *American Broadside Verse.* The author is known, Walt Winthrop, son of Connecticut's governor, sent into action in 1675 commanding volunteers against King Philip's Narragansetts. In thirty-two four-line verses, he recounted the story of a bloody battle that meant nothing outside the valley in which it was fought. No copy exists of James Franklin's 1724 broadside "The rebels, rewards, or English courage displayed," the "full and true account" of another victory over the red man, sung to a melody traced back to Elizabeth's time and used in *Wit and Mirth or Pills to Purge Melancholy.* The following year Franklin printed "The volunteer's march," sometimes known as "Lovewell's flight," for more than a century New England's best-loved song. Reportedly composed by Franklin's uncle, the broadside was a whitewash of a recent massacre in which white bounty hunters who collected ten pounds for each red scalp delivered were themselves ambushed and all killed or wounded. Thomas Symmes, always on the hunt for a crowd-pleasing theme, glamorized the incident and Captain Lovewell, leader of the vigilantes, in a highly colored sermon delivered to bloodthirsty Indian-hating Christian Sunday congregations and Wednesday-night-meeting groups.

As loyal Englishmen, Yankee poets cheered the stout red-coated British soldier and his every victory on the North American mainland until he became the symbol of London oppression and an object of vilification. Broadsides preserved in words and music triumphs over the French, the Indians, and Spain: the storming of Cartagena by a fleet of 115 ships and 25,000 soldiers, many of them from the northern colonies; the capture of Cape Breton, which commanded the approach up the St. Lawrence to Canada; the 1755 victory of 3,000 colonials and their Indian allies over an army of French regulars at Lake George. They gave evidence of a new nationalistic spirit being born in the American soul, buoyed by its own contributions to victory over France and deeply rooted in religious conviction and tradition.

## The Ballad Writers Go to War

It was in the colonial newspapers, chiefly those in Boston, that the broadside-ballad war against England was finally joined. Boston had five four-page weekly journals to serve its fewer than 15,000 citizens. When the British Army marched on Lexington and Concord in April 1775 in search of contraband military supplies, nineteen American newspapers were still in business, out of the forty-one that began publication after John Campbell started his *News-letter* in 1704. Philadelphia, which had taken Boston's place as America's largest printing center, offered six, one of them, in German, issued twice weekly. There were four in New York, three in Charles Town, and one in Newport. Print runs were from 700 to 3,000, and they were delivered by hand or post courier to local residents and by boat to subscribers as far removed as the Scandinavian countries. Taverns and coffeehouses added to their circulation and readership making available for perusal without charge copies of both local and foreign papers.

Most broadsides printed in the newspaper were signed only with initials or some phrase such as "A Gentleman of Massachusetts." Rarely was an author's name known to any but the printer or the writer's friends. One man stands out in all this anonymity for the unmistakable quality of his wit and his gift for satire: Joseph Green, a Harvard graduate who made his fortune distilling rum. Green published collections of his own classical verse in the 1740s, but intimates knew him best for his robust and bawdy letters and ballads, written for their amusement. One of his ballads, "The death of old Mr. Tenor," sung to "Chevy Chace," was regarded as subversive, and a royal proclamation offered a reward for arrest of the hawkers who sold it on the colony's streets.

When Boston was rent by controversy over the propriety of using words written by a mere mortal to replace those of the great harpist David, Green took part. As a pewholder of the First Church and a member of its standing committee, but also an admirer of good writing, he deplored such hymn verses as

> Ye monsters of the briny deep,
> Your Maker's praises spout;
> Up from the sands, ye codlings, peep,
> And wag your tails about

and

> The race is not always got
> By him the swiftest runs,

> Nor the battle by those people
> That shoot the longest guns.

Green parodied the whole school of Massachusetts hymn writers in signed broadsides that deflated their considerable egos and made Bostonians chuckle. He died in London, driven there for his Loyalist sympathies. An apt epitaph, which he wrote as a young man, marked his now-forgotten grave:

> Siste Viator, here lies one
> Whose life was whim, whose soul was pun,
> And if you go too near his hearse,
> He'll joke you both in pun and verse.

All American printers faced economic hardship after passage of the 1765 Stamp Act, which placed a penny tax on every four-page newspaper and two shillings on every advertisement, costs that were sometimes as much as fifty percent on the widely read papers. This challenge to a meaningful source of income brought printers, conservative and liberal alike, to a militant editorial campaign against the legislation, and newspaper owners were able to manipulate the issue into a matter of the gravest national concern. The public was aroused to defy a law that would have taken only a single shilling from every American; boycotts were enforced; mob action was fomented under the auspices of the newly formed Sons of Liberty as colonists of every economic class found common cause. Within the year, the crown was forced to withdraw the legislation.

A handful of editors was seduced by official subsidy, becoming paid government organs on this issue. Among them was James Rivington, publisher of what was often acknowledged to be the best newspaper in colonial America. When Rivington opened his London Book Shop, New York's fourth, in Hanover Square, near the lower end of Wall Street, in 1760, he brought to America an expertise in contemporary English book-business practices stemming from a long involvement in the trade. His father was a Stationers' freeman and a member of a major conger. At the age of eighteen, in partnership with an older brother, Rivington took over the family business. Some twelve years later, he opened his own bookshop in London and published a few volumes of religious music and hymns. He made his greatest profit, £10,000, from Tobias Smollett's *History of England,* by means of shady business methods that earned him the enmity of London's book trade.

Rivington spent money lavishly, owned a carriage, and consorted with the nobility. A lusty and sensual man, he passed his nights in the company of London's demimonde and his days at the Newmarket racecourse, surrendering much of his profits to both. Among his acquaintances was the president of King's College of New York, who later wrote urging him to to come to New York, where opportunity abounded for an enterprising bookman. While assuring his British creditors that an appetite for profligacy had brought him to the edge of ruin, Rivington engaged secretly in negotiations for the purchase of a house and land in New York. The creditors permitted an application for bankruptcy, settling for twenty shillings on the pound and leaving Rivington free to sail for

America with a stock of books and printed pages he had retrieved after disposition of his presumably tangled affairs.

Rivington opened his shop and immediately advertised books for sale to libraries and collectors, and a new publication, *The American Mock Bird,* a collection of 336 of the "most favorite songs now in vogue." This elaborate book, the first of its kind to be published in America, was probably among the cargo he brought to America. His catalogue was also available in branch stores, those in Philadelphia and Boston being the first of a proposed new chain. The contents of other song books issued by him during the next twenty years, though ostensibly produced locally, were probably printed in England and then cut and bound in America. For example, the 1763 *Clio and Euterpe* was identical to a three-volume edition of the same name published in London.

By the early 1770s, Rivington had closed all his branch stores, to concentrate on the New York operation, which had become the largest bookstore in the colonies. It offered printed works, paintings, reproductions, prints, music, dice, "the handsomest shaving equipages, fit for persons of the first rank," tickets to the John Street's concerts and plays, "racquets for tennis," and a line of patent medicines. Among the last were Doctor Bateman's Drops, John Hooper's Female Pills, and British Oyls, "extracted from a flinty rock for the cure of rheumatick and scorbutick and other cases," nostrums imported by the bookstore owner and transshipped to the other colonies.

Rivington acquired an American wife, the daughter of a wealthy local merchant, and, with her, a printing office, where he produced programs for touring theater companies, theater tickets, editions of best-selling English books, and broadsides of popular appeal, written by gentlemen who found the cultivated Englishman a splendid companion in conviviality. The major work coming off his press was *Rivington's New York Gazetteer, or The Connecticut, New Jersey, Hudson's River and Quebec Weekly Advertiser.* The editorial policy, stated in an early edition, promised that the *Gazetteer* would never print reports of "any performance calculated to injure virtue, religion or other public happiness, to wound a neighbour's reputation, or to raise a blush on the face of virgin innocence." "Copiously furnished with foreign intelligence," it served 3,500 regular subscribers "in every colony of North America, most of the English, Spanish, Dutch and Danish West India Islands, the principal cities of Great Britain, France, Ireland and the Mediterranean."

Regularly advertised in the *Gazetteer,* Rivington's music stock was equal to that of any but London's most important music stores. It contained stage works and concert music by names still known today, as well as by others who, with their music, have disappeared from all but the dusty volumes of nineteenth-century encyclopedias.

As America's leading voice for the Loyalist cause, the *Gazetteer* printed pro-British editorials, news items, and ballads. The anti-American gossip, scandal, and rhymes appearing in its pages roused the Sons of Liberty to such a pitch that in early 1775 Rivington was kidnapped and forced to sign a pledge of support of the Whig cause. The following November a group of Connecticut Minute Men rode into New York, broke into his printing office, and destroyed the presses while fifers piped "Yankee Doodle." The fonts of type were carried off to make bullets. Rivington left New York, returning only when the British cause there appeared to go well. He had a new press and type and an appointment as royal printer. Publication of his newspaper, now known as *Rivington's New York Loyal Gazette,* later the *Royal Gazette,* resumed and once more Americans found themselves and their struggle the butt of editorial humor, scorn, and distortion. George Washington was a regular target, the innocent victim of forgeries involving him in graft and scandal. On one occasion, Rivington printed a dispatch purporting to detail Franklin's death in Paris during an amorous bout with one of the many Frenchwomen who found the ambassador irresistible.

Among the Loyalist ballad writers and song-writing propagandists whose work was regularly printed in the *Gazette* were Jonathan Odell and John Stansbury, probably the most effective of their breed. Odell was born in Newark, New Jersey, to a family whose Puritan forebears had settled in Massachusetts a century before. He learned sufficient medicine to qualify as a British Army surgeon in America, a post asking little more than an undiscriminating use of saw and knife and the liberal dosing of patients with alcohol to render them insensate. Turning from bodies to souls, Odell studied in England for the ministry and was assigned to a New Jersey parish, where he practiced medicine weekdays and preached Anglican dogma on the Lord's Day. When revolution tore the colony apart, he opted for the Loyalist cause, proclaiming his dedication in ballads and ponderous verse. After Tories celebrated King George's birthday with public readings of Odell's ballad marking the occasion, authorities sequestered him to an eight-mile circle around his pastorate. He escaped behind British lines and became a military chaplain and part-time propagandist, whose favorite target was General Washington.

James Stansbury had none of Odell's gloominess about him; he delighted in the lilt of the latest popular tune and his sentiments to music enjoyed by Tory and patriot alike. He came to America from London at the age of twenty-five and opened a shop dealing in china tableware. His warm baritone voice, a gift for music, and his friendly manner won the friendship of young Philadelphians active in theatrical readings and music making. After the First Continental Congress gathered there, Stansbury sent information about it to the British. When this was discovered, he was placed in prison, and was released only after the English returned to occupy the city.

Stansbury's bubbling Loyalist lampoons, delivered by military postal service, found a welcome in the pages of the Tory press. When the British moved north to New York, he remained in Philadelphia and swore allegiance to the Yankee cause, but he continued his clandestine activities. With the secret help of Odell, who was stationed with the British in New York, Stansbury played a role in the Benedict Arnold affair. After the plot was exposed, he was arrested, held for a short time, then turned over to British authorities for lack of any real evidence against him. He found a place among the entertainers who enlivened life's tedium in Philadelphia. Among his new acquaintances was James Rivington, whom he enchanted with his sparkling wit and his frequent contributions to the *Royal Gazette.*

The general commanding George III's armed forces in America, Sir Henry Clinton, was a music-loving man who shared an enthusiasm for song, dance, and the playhouse with his fellow officer "Gentleman Johnny" Burgoyne. When Clinton moved into New York early in 1777 at the head of some 17,000 troops, his personal baggage contained the violin and bass viol he turned to in time of anxiety. Rivington struck up an immediate business relationship, supplying Clinton's small personal orchestra with fifty pounds' worth of sheet music and binding for the general's use twenty-seven volumes of orchestral and vocal music.

The Rivington bookstore was again open, carrying a supply of musical instruments and accessories among its usual stock. The *Royal Gazette* printed notices of concerts, performances by the military acting companies, and appearances by John Street actors who had been stranded by the war, and Rivington's store was again the central agency for all entertainment tickets. Except for the annoyance of a war whose outcome was steadily becoming more apparent, British officers stationed in the city enjoyed several seasons of competent musical and theatrical diversions.

In late 1779, Clinton sailed out of New York to take over the campaign in the South. Left alone in a city whose patriots wished to vent their anger upon the traitor Rivington, the bookstore owner sought to repair relations. Only because of the garrison left behind by Clinton did he survive, but when the war ended, he had to face the inevitable. An American poet who had just been returned to freedom after weeks aboard a British prison ship lumped Rivington with the British who had tortured him in captivity and castigated both in sensational verses. New York's patriots were then not to be denied. Rivington was pressured into a public apology for his conduct during the war and protested that he had always been loyal to his adopted country. His printing office and newspaper were closed, and he was often attacked in the streets.

With only his bookstore left and with a large family to support, for a time he was able to make a bare living, but debts and the past eventually caught up with him. In 1798, he went to debtors' prison, where he remained until a few weeks before his death, July 4, 1802, at seventy-eight.

In 1959, John Bakeless revealed, in *Turncoats, Traitors and Heroes,* that Rivington had been an American spy during the entire period. Among other contributions to the American cause was the British Royal Navy's signal codebook, stolen through his friendship with English officers. It was a decisive factor in the French victory at sea that led to the final victory at Yorktown.

The vast majority of American printers allied themselves with the cause of revolution, dedicating their pages to the forging of public opinion in its support. There were no more ardent patriots than Benjamin Edes and John Gill, the printers of William Billings's first collection, *The New England Psalm-singer* (1770), and none more amenable to the pressures of His Majesty's colonial government than John Mein and John Fleming, the Scottish-born printers of the Boston *Chronicle,* who, ironically, printed the words and music to America's earliest patriotic song, "The Liberty Tree."

John Dickinson, author of the original nine-verse broadside, wrote it to the then popular seven-year-old "Heart of Oak," a hit song from the William Boyce–David Garrick stage success *Harlequin's Invasion*. Dickinson made clever use of the catchy refrain

> Heart of oak are our ships,
> Jolly tars are our men;
> We will always be ready,
> Steady, boys, steady,
> We'll fight and we'll conquer again and again!

in the cause of liberty:

> In freedom we're born
> And in freedom we'll live;
> Our purses are ready,
> Steady, boys, steady,
> Not as slaves but as freemen our money we'll give!

Believing "songs are frequently very powerful on certain occasions," and that the brilliant seventeenth-century French politician Cardinal de Retz "always enforced his political operations by song," Dickinson wrote his broadside to support American freedom in the early summer of 1768. The previous year, this conservative Philadelphia lawyer and gentleman farmer won fame with a series of twelve *Letters from a Farmer in Pennsylvania,* advocating peaceful and legal resistance to English laws like the Stamp Act. His authorship became known, and he quickly emerged as spokesman for the middle-of-the-road attitude favoring all action short of war. Samuel Adams was diametrically opposed to the politics of watchful patience, but he immediately adopted the broadside as another "opportunity for the inculcating of sedition" and encouraged its use in the streets, the open fields, and at fund-raising occasions. The Sons of Liberty marked its first anniversary of resistance to the Stamp Act in 1768 with an outdoor celebration at which "the music began at high noon, performed on various instruments, joined with voices; concluding with the universally admired American song of Liberty, the grandeur of its sentiment, easy flow of its numbers, together with an exquisite harmony of sound."

The new song was immediately printed in papers throughout the colonies. The August 29 edition of Mein and Fleming's *Chronicle* advertised

The New and Favorite
  Liberty Song
In Freedom we're Born, etc.
Neatly engraved on Copper-plate, the
size of half a sheet of paper
Set to MUSIC for the VOICE
And to which is also added
A Set of NOTES adapted to the
  GERMAN FLUTE and VIOLIN
Is just published and to be sold at
the LONDON Book-store King Street, Boston
Price Sixpence, lawful, single and
Four Shillings, lawful, the dozen.

The bookstore was owned by Mein, who had been a book dealer in Scotland before coming to the colonies in 1764 to open a shop selling Irish linens and a good assortment of books. He found an excellent market for British literature and bought out Rivington's Boston bookstore the following year. Realizing that pirated American editions of English publications, even when bearing false imprint notices, could be sold for less than the originals, he sent John Fleming to Scotland to purchase printing equipment and bring back trained workmen. The house of Mein & Fleming was opened with a stock of 10,000 volumes, including a circulating library of over 1,200 books, which made a profit of forty to fifty pounds a week.

Mein began the Boston semiweekly *Chronicle* in 1767 and issued the first *Bickerstaff Boston Almanac*. This was edited by Benjamin West, the mathematician and astronomer, who compiled such books for colonial printers and used the pseudonym Isaac Bickerstaff for the almanac. The "Liberty Song," probably made from the original single-sheet copperplates, appeared in the 1769 edition. The *Chronicle* proved to be another moneymaker for its publisher. Printed on a sheet of paper larger than its competitors, it carried news, articles from the best European periodicals, and original essays. In 1769, the Massachusetts customs commissioners paid Mein to publish accounts of smuggling by leading Boston merchants, and the *Chronicle*'s intercolony reputation was thereby destroyed. Mein was hanged in effigy by the Sons of Liberty, the verse "Mein is his name / Mean is the man" fixed to the crude figure. Eventually, the publisher of America's first patriotic song disguised himself as a British foot soldier and shipped to London, where he worked as a propagandist against the colonies during the revolution his publication had encouraged.

Tory parodies of the "Liberty Song" appeared almost immediately after its initial appearance, the first in the Boston *Gazette*, owned by the fiery Ben Edes, who personally stuffed effigies of Boston Loyalists, Mein among them, to be used by the Sons of Liberty. "In folly you're born, in folly you'll live" went a parody inspired by a parody. It was written by Dr. Benjamin Church, another Harvard graduate, and shared the original's popularity. Church's unquestioned social and patriotic credentials brought him membership in the secret Boston Committee of Correspondence. It came as a shock to American leaders when the physician was exposed as a British spy. A former lover of Church's mistress chanced upon the woman in Newport and found in her possesssion a letter containing information about committee business she was to deliver to agents of the royal governor. Church was tried and exiled, John Adams lamenting, "Good God! A man of genius, of learning, of family, of character, a writer of Liberty Songs, and good ones too!"

The 1770 edition of Samuel Stearn's *North American Review and Massachusetts Register*, printed by Edes & Gill, carried both Dickinson's and Church's patriotic ballads, as well as a parody of the English marching tune "The British Grenadiers," which had first been heard in Boston streets when played by the red-coated fife-and-drum corps. The melody was an old one, tracked back to Thomas Morley, although its first appearance with the words "Some sing of Alexander, and some of Hercules" was around 1750. The new patriotic words were by Dr. Joseph Warren, Boston physician, orator, and grand master of the

Freemasons of North America, whose oratory mourning the Boston Massacre victims brought great crowds to tears. Warren was named president of the provincial Congress just before his death in the Battle of Bunker Hill.

In 1770, political agitation resulted in the withdrawal of all revenue-raising measures designed to enforce American contribution to the British defense budget. Many factors were responsible, among them a rising tide of nationalism resulting in no small measure from the feeling of involvement encouraged by the broadside-ballad patriotic songs.

King George chose a levy on tea imported from British holdings in Asia, hoping the measure would aid his failing economy as well as serve as a token of royal power. Tea became the enemy, and the shipping bearing it to America the target for action. Three vessels anchored in Boston Harbor in late 1773, and on December 16 a group of 150 men, some of them in Indian dress, boarded them and dumped overboard 15,000 pounds of tea as watchers on shore cheered. The papers carried word of "this most magnificent movement of all" to other colonies, and a ballad appeared in the *Pennsylvania Packet,* to be sung to Handel's "Hosier's Ghost." Only New York emulated the Boston action; other cities merely seized the cargoes and eventually sold them at auction, the proceeds going to the cause of revolution.

Britain retaliated by closing Boston Harbor to all but military traffic and in the next year passed the Quartering Act, making all the colonies responsible for the support and maintenance of royal troops garrisoned in them. This led to the First Continental Congress, which met in Philadelphia in September 1774. Once again, Thomas Arne's "Rule! Britannia" served as a message to king and Parliament.

In New York, the newspapers took different directions. Two appeared to support the Yankee cause, the *Journal,* founded by Zenger and now John Holt's property, and the *Mercury,* established in 1752 by Hugh Gaine, a printer who had been an Irish stationer's apprentice before coming to America. The third, Rivington's *Gazetteer,* had long since put on the king's colors. Holt, once mayor of Williamsburg, was a zealous Virginian who sacrificed purse and property to the cause of freedom, and with them the press from which Zenger's illicit ballads came. Immediately after the Boston Tea Party, he replaced the traditional king's arms device on his masthead with the severed snake Franklin had created, bearing the slogan "Unite or Die!"

Gaine, on the other hand, was an opportunist, who allied himself with whatever side seemed to have power. His shrewd perception of popular taste, particularly in well-illustrated books for the young (he was the first to publish *Robinson Crusoe* in America), books of verse, the classics, and music (he printed *The American Mock Bird* a year after Rivington's initial edition), made Gaine one of the colonies' most prosperous book publishers and printers. Arriving in the city in 1745, at the age of twenty, "with neither basket or burden" Gaine worked for New York printers until he set up his own press and began printing the *Mercury.*

In February 1770, his paper reported the raising of a liberty pole to replace one cut down the previous month by redcoats. The incident gave opportunity to a Loyalist sympathizer to enlist the music of a not-yet-published British marching song in a broadside that was shoved under the doors of New Yorkers during the night of March 15, 1770. *The Procession,* a "cantata," used four popular melodies in its mockery of New York's Sons of Liberty, the second being "Yankee Doodle."

The traditional history of "Yankee Doodle" 's origin attributes it to Richard Shuckburgh, an English-born doctor attached to colonial regiment in the 1750s. His verses, written to ridicule the provincial riflemen supporting British troops in the attack from Albany on the French Fort Carillon (now Ticonderoga), were promptly taken up by the redcoats. "The Yanky Doodle song" was among the tunes played by an army band aboard one of the troopships that appealed to regulars on their way to garrison Boston in September 1768. There were many instances of its popularity among the English in the seven years before Lexington and Concord. Officers staged a near-riot during a Boston concert by calling to the band to play the "Yanky Doodle" tune and forcing an end to the music. On another occasion, redcoats stripped, tarred, and feathered a patriot and marched him through Boston streets to fife-and-drum playing of the lilting tune. When British troops moved out of Boston in search of military stores at Concord, they marched to "Yanky Doodle." The new Worcester *Gazette,* owned by Isaiah Thomas, reported of the raid and the threat that "upon their return to Boston, one of them asked his brother officer how he liked the tune now? 'Damn them! (he retorted) they made us dance it until we're tired.' Since then Yankee Doodle sounds less sweet to their ears." The British returned the insult during the attack on American troops entrenched on Breed's Hill in June, playing "Yanky Doodle" as they killed, wounded, or captured 459, while losing half of their own forces.

During the summer, Thomas Skillern, a London music dealer who was employed as an engraver by John Walsh, Jr., issued the first printed publication of the words and music:

YANKEE DOODLE or
(as now christened by the SAINTS of New England)
THE LEXINGTON MARCH
NB: The Words to be sung thro the Nose & in the
North Country drawl & dialect

The well-known "Yankee Doodle keep it up" refrain was familiar to Americans before 1767, when it was used in the ill-fated first American ballad opera, *The Disappointment,* for a solo sung by a white rustic comedy figure.

Ten years later, after their defeat at Saratoga, where the British learned no longer to fancy the "doodle dances" of "The Lexington March," the tune was dropped from English military-music literature, leaving it to become the colonists' own for songs deriding their enemies. When at last the war was done, a military band, commanded to do so by the Marquis de Lafayette, struck up "Yankee Doodle" as the British laid down their arms and presented their swords at Yorktown.

The song became so loved by the new nation's citizens that when the theater came back to America during the 1790s it was used in lieu of an official national anthem. Many instances of violence and near-riot occurred when theater bands, generally made up of immigrant Europeans, failed to begin the program properly with its rendition. The first American music publishers, most of them with some experience in the British music trade, brought out instrumental versions to meet the demand from theaters, taverns, and other places of amusement. By the beginning of the nineteenth century, many printed versions were on sale in music and book stores.

A critical analysis of "Yankee Doodle" and its origins by J. A. Leo Lemay is a well-reasoned and persuasive argument for the song's purely American origins. Shuckburgh, he points out, was born in England but came to America before 1735, "lived nearly all his adult life in America, married and had a family in America, spent most of his time on the frontier, was acknowledged by his contemporaries as an Indian expert." He concludes that it was a New England folk song, that its verses first celebrated the astonishing victory at Cape Breton in 1745, and that "their intention is to burlesque the English attitudes toward the American militia, and that they were in oral circulation in a song by the end of the 1740s. . . . From the seventeenth century to the mid-twentieth, Americans have been keenly aware of English criticism of their supposed barbarism. Colonial Americans learned to reply to British snobbery by deliberately posturing as unbelievable ignorant yokels." "The Lexington March," then, was one of many examples of such shamming.

## Thomas Paine, Ballad Writer

"The Fireband of the Revolution," English-born Thomas Paine, whose little paper pamphlet *Common Sense,* calling for complete independence from England, appeared in early 1776, and became the greatest seller to appear in the first 130 years of American publishing, made little money from its sale of 150,000 copies, equivalent to a present-day distribution of over ten million copies.

Paine first won acclaim as a versifier in the small English country town where he served as a tax collector and was a regular habitué of the local tavern. He wrote short ballads for his drinking companions and sharpened his political talents in barroom debates. The campaign song he wrote for the local Whig candidate for the House of Commons got him three guineas. The death in 1769 of the popular general James Wolfe in action against the French on the Plains of Abraham was a blow to both Englishmen and Americans, and Paine added to the outpouring of songs about that gallant soldier. His song, known as "In a mouldering cave," became a favorite of British musical societies. When Paine got into trouble with government authorities after he was named spokesman for his fellow townsmen in a dispute over wages, he went off to America. He had letters of introduction from Benjamin Franklin, whom he had met in London. Franklin's recommendation that the "ingenious, worthy young man"—he was thirty-six—deserved employment impressed Robert Aitken, a Scottish bookbinder who had come to Philadelphia in 1769 as a bookseller and auctioneer and had opened a printing office in 1774. In January 1775, Aitken issued the first number of his *Pennsylvania Magazine*. Recognizing that he was no editor, he immediately hired Paine as editor and contributor, for 50 pounds a year. Paine required only a decanter of brandy, and by the time he had swallowed a third drink was writing rapidly, with clarity and precision, material fit for the press without any alteration or correction.

That simple and direct style won a circulation of 5,000 an issue for contents that were mostly by Paine, including the ballads and poetry. In the March 1775 issue, he published Wolfe's song. When Paine had first arrived in America, he had submitted the piece to a committee engaged in raising funds to erect a statue to Wolfe's memory and offering a cash prize for the best song honoring the fallen general. When the project ran out of money, the committee disbanded, and no prize was ever awarded. Paine now published the four verses, "set to music by a gentleman of this country," in the *Pennsylvania Magazine*, using a pen name he had adopted, Atlanticus.

The broadside "Epistle to the Troops in Boston," which appeared in the *Pennsylvania Magazine* in May 1775, was probably also by Paine, as were the number of variations on that text that circulated during the next several months. However, none of Paine's ballads, either those written in England or subsequent ones penned in America, ever achieved the long-lived popularity of "In a mouldering cave," which continued to appear in American songbooks for years.

In addition to his chores for Aitken, Paine clerked for Robert Bell, another local bookseller, who had been a partner in Dublin of the British actor and popular songwriter George Alexander Stevens. Bell's catalogue was outstandingly diverse, ranging from Chesterfield's *Letters* and the first American edition of Blackstone's *Commentaries on the Laws of England* to the medical text serving professional and amateur American surgeons during the Revolution, John Jones's *Plain, Concise, Practical Remarks on the Treatment of Wounds and Fractures*, part of a stock advertised in every one of the American newspapers extant.

In 1776, Bell brought out his clerk's most famous work, *Common Sense,* which quickly became his best-selling publication. Most publishers had to dispose of a usual first edition of 3,000 copies before any profits were realized, but Paine's work was a runaway seller, requiring paper Bell had stored in anticipation of severe shortages. He also dipped into that precious paper supply for several editions of a 260-page collection of *Songs, Satirical and Sentimental,* by his former business partner in England G. A. Stevens. A remarkably versatile songwriter, Stevens, who wrote "Nancy Dawson" and other current hit songs, was acknowledged to be the greatest master of the popular song art in Europe.

The *Pennsylvania Gazette,* published by William Bradford, the third of that distinguished name in Philadelphia printing, opposed the Stamp Act immediately after its passage, and appeared in full mourning when the law became effective. A death's-head and crossbones were printed over the paper's title, and at the bottom of the fourth and last page was a coffin bearing the periodical's age, its death attributed to "an illness called the Stamp Act." Bradford appealed for patriotic material for his Poet's Corner, but the important contributions were made to rivals: Dickinson's *Letters* appeared in the *Gazette,* Paine's

"American Crisis" editorial, beginning with "These are the times that try men's souls," was first printed in the *Journal* in late 1776, when Washington's frozen meager forces were in full retreat through New Jersey, and the popular "Pennsylvania March," a three-verse ballad sung to a Scottish tune, was reprinted throughout the colonies after the *Journal* ran it.

"In praise of Saint Tammany," a popular song written in 1776 by the Philadelphia wine maker and goldsmith John Leacock for his play *The Fall of British Tyranny,* was published in the *Gazette.* The ballad was described by its writer as part of a "truly dramatic performance, interspersed with wit, humor, burlesque and serious matter," and was intended to be read, rather than performed, in the anti–public entertainment atmosphere of the capital city. Despite the Congressional ban, the song became a hit in Philadelphia and in New York, where Sons of Saint Tammany had been gathering on each May 1 to feast in memory of their patron saint, a Delaware chieftain. The rest of the year they engaged in charitable works for relief of the distressed in Tammany's name.

In early 1775, Philadelphia's first evening paper, the *Evening Post,* began, published three times weekly by Benjamin Towne, an English printer who had worked his way up from immigrant journeyman to the ownership of several printing offices. During the paper's first two years, Towne worked hard to prove the *Post* a pillar of patriotism, once publishing "The King's own regulars," alleged to have been written by Benjamin Franklin, a myth dispelled by recent research. Its melody was "The Queen's old courtier," written in the early seventeenth century, a single psalmlike refrain following four lines sung on a single note, giving the song a strong flavor of church music.

When the British arrived, however, Towne turned the editorial policy completely around. Then, in 1778, after the government returned to Philadelphia, Towne announced publication of some anti-British songs. Whether any of his efforts to ingratiate himself with local authority succeeded or not, the songs never appeared except as titles mentioned in advertisements, but Towne was allowed to keep the *Post* going until the early 1780s. In 1783, he embarked on a history-making project: publication of the first daily American newspaper. He sold it himself on the streets of Philadelphia, offering "all the news for two coppers."

## "Gentleman Johnny" Burgoyne and Other Writers of Popular Music

Popular street songs dealing with the hostilities in America appeared in print chiefly in broadside form or on the pages of American newspapers. One of them attained a circulation of 8,000. As had broadsides in England, chronicles of victory and defeat, of villains and heroes, of gossip and truth circulated long after printed accounts had disappeared. Military requirements for speedy delivery of important orders and papers reduced the availability of express riders for civilian commerce, but three "advice boats" did keep the southernmost colonies informed of current events. News of the encounter at Lexington and Concord appeared in the *Savannah Gazette* six weeks after the event, and songs about it and other events suffered equal delays in transmission to the nation.

After the post of inspector of dead letters was established in 1777 to oversee censorship, the quality of intercolony mail fell even farther, forcing Americans to rely on the press to keep them abreast of the latest news, though it, too, was often weeks behind.

An interesting history of those years of struggle can be compiled from ballads narrating significant occurrences that appeared in newspapers of the period. Many of those who wrote these bits of poetry and doggerel remain unknown, but a few of them, persons of achievement in other capacities, are sometimes remembered for their accomplishments in the world of popular music. One was that unwitting architect of the blunders that led to the Yankee victory at Saratoga, General John Burgoyne.

Burgoyne's triumphs in the English musical theater and his talent for writing the librettos and lyrics of many popular musical plays are usually forgotten. His affection for the stage started early and grew into a passion. In 1774, he wrote and produced a "new dramatic entertainment," *Maid of the Oaks,* a masque he wrote for a wedding celebration. He hired François Barthelemon, a French-Irish soldier turned musician, leader of Marylebone's musicians, and one of the best violinists in Britain, to write the music for the lyrics and the dance spectacles created for the festivities. Because of its enthusiastic reception, Burgoyne adopted it for the stage and sent it to David Garrick. This socially ambitious actor was impressed enough to help him with revisions. It was put on at the Drury Lane in November and was a great success. The score was published, but without all of Burgoyne's songs, remedied by publication at his expense of *Songs and Choruses from The Maid of the Oaks.*

There was no similar opportunity to print his next effort, a farce, *The Blockade of Boston,* written for presentation by British officer and soldier amateur players on January 8, 1776. While the piece was in rehearsal, the *New England Chronicle* commented that it might never be seen before "a tragedy called *The Bombardment of Boston*" was presented by the patriots. Washington was played as "an uncouth figure, awkward in gait, wearing a large wig and rusty sword, attended by a country servant carrying a rusty gun." The premiere was interrupted by an announcement that the rebels were attacking the Charlestown outposts, putting a halt to the performance as officers and men rushed to join their regiments. Burgoyne's songs, which were encored by the various leading characters after the play ended, were printed on a broadside.

In 1780, Burgoyne borrowed a plot from the French stage and wrote a full-length comedy, *The Lord of the Manor,* to music written by the Exeter Cathedral organist, William Jackson, in his first musical-theater venture. Their play was a success from its first performance at the Drury Lane in December 1780, and continued to appear in revivals as late as 1853. Jackson's music and Burgoyne's words were published in full score in 1782, one of only two such publications in the last half of the eighteenth century. Rising production costs were responsible for this small output of theater music in full score, brought about by the increasing sophistication of orchestrations. The play script, without any music, was reprinted in America several years after the London opening, published by William Spottswood, of Philadelphia.

In his preface to the English publication, Burgoyne spoke his mind on the long controversy over all-sung opera, revealing a professional's awareness of the process of wedding words to music.

Adopting what is called recitative into a language, to which it is entirely incongruous, is the cause of failure in an English serious opera much oftener than the want of musical powers in the performers . . . vocal music should be confined to express the feelings and passions, but never to express the exercising of them. Song in any action in which reason tells us it would be innatural to sing, must be preposterous. . . . The idea of five or six fellows with fusils in hand, presented as a gentleman's head, and their fingers resting upon the triggers, threatening his life in bass notes, he resisting in tenor, and a wife or daughter throwing herself between them in treble, while the spectator is kept in suspense, from what in reality must be a momentary event, till the composer had run his air through all its different branches, and to a great length, always gave me a disgust to a great degree. . . . [Music] should always be the *accessory,* not the principal subject of the drama. . . .

*The Lord of the Manor* contained two hit songs, ''Encompass'd in an angel's frame,'' better known to nineteenth-century Americans as the popular ''Anna's urn''—anticipating the flood of Victorian popular ballads dealing with death and loved ones—and ''The dashing white sergeant,'' which won its greatest popularity after Henry Rowley Bishop wrote new music for it in an 1812 revival of the play.

''The best new comedy since *The School for Scandal,*'' as one critic hailed it, Burgoyne's next play, *The Heiress,* opened in January 1786, and was immediately added to the Drury Lane's permanent repertory, playing nearly a hundred times by the end of the century. That same year, Burgoyne adapted an André Grétry opera, as *Richard the Lion-hearted.* Two new melodies by Thomas Linley were added to the original score. The one-time commander of British forces in America was engaged in writing a musical version, in Georgian English, of Shakespeare's *As You Like It* when he died.

The new nation's first, and self-proclaimed, ''native of the United States who has produced a musical composition,'' Francis Hopkinson entered the world of popular music during the Revolution with a number of broadside ballads. He was an eager amateur of the arts from boyhood, painting watercolors, writing poetry, playing the harpsichord and organ, and hiding his own art songs in a 200-page manuscript book, among words and music of airs, songs, hymns, and other vocal music by Europe's best-known masters, Handel, Arne, Purcell, and lesser-known Italians. ''My days have been so wondrous free,'' usually catalogued as ''the first known secular song written by an American,'' used words by Thomas Parnell, an early-eighteenth-century Irish poet and granduncle of the Dublin patriot. The manuscript book was discovered among papers donated by the Hopkinson family to the Library of Congress. The little ditty undoubtedly was heard by members of the immediate family, but it was so little esteemed by the composer that it was not included in his first printed collection of original songs, published in 1788. The vast majority of his contemporaries never heard this ''first song,'' delighting instead in familiar popular English melodies and the spiritual songs of more talented American compilers and songwriters.

He wrote "The battle of the kegs," which first appeared in the *Pennsylvania Packet* and was introduced in Washington's winter camp by a chorus of gentlemen singers. Its reference to Sir William Howe, "snug as a flea in bed with Mrs. Loring," was an unusually unbuttoned sentiment from Hopkinson's pen, even in an age when blunt and coarse humor was common. The woman was the wife of an American Loyalist who became commissioner of prisoners for the British Army after the general took her as a mistress. Another song, "The Toast," dedicated to his friend Washington, was far truer to the genteel cultural tradition of which Hopkinson was a leading American advocate. The song appeared in an April 1778 edition of a Philadelphia paper, made its way through the colonies quickly, and some twenty years later was among the many musical expressions of grief mourning the dead Washington.

## The Printer–Music Publisher in Federal America

When the British surrendered in 1781, Ezekial Russell, printer of best-selling broadsides usually dealing with tragical events and decorated with cuts of coffins, was at work on the new *Bickerstaff Boston Almanac*. He had moved from Boston during the British occupation, returning when it was safe for a man of his political persuasion. His household included the woman who composed his ballads, one of which, "Washington and de Grasse," sung to "The British Grenadiers," was "designed to add mirth to the Day of General Thanksgiving, Rejoicing and Illumination" declared after the happy news arrived from Yorktown. Having learned during the early 1770s that publication of a newspaper was impossible without government support, Russell did what was most profitable—he produced ballads for sale to peddlers.

The papers founded to serve as mouthpieces for political leaders striving to take control of the new government, many printers quickly learned, were not as profitable as job printing and the publication of almanacs, pamphlets, and books. More than 400 news publications were introduced during the Federal era, sixty of them immediately after the Revolution, to support the diametrically opposed attitudes of those fighting to mold the new constitution as a reflection of their social concerns. Most of these new papers eventually disappeared, winnowed by the pressures of rising production costs and the failing support of patrons. Only a baker's dozen of the wartime papers survived the century, as printers died or went into the more profitable side of the craft, to which was slowly being added publication of music books. Russell, for example, published the fifth edition of William Billings's *Singing Master's Assistant,* as well as a *Collection of Songs* "designed for entertainment and edification," which contained eleven "sacred" songs.

In Philadelphia, the *Gazette*'s new owners, Hall & Sellers, printed 2,000 copies for the state's Grand Lodge of Masons of the 170-page *Ahiman Rezon,* a collection of the group's official songs and some popular music associated with them, one of the books going to George Washington. William Spottswood published the first American edition of *The American Jest-Book* in 1789, pirating the famous English publication *Joe Miller's Jests,* a collection of jokes and funny stories compiled by that semieducated comedian from books printed through two centuries. Miller died in the mid-eighteenth century, just before the book bearing his name appeared, but "Joe Miller" became a synonym for ancient wheezes and venerable humorous stories. Among Spottswood's books for "instruction and amusement of children" was the 1786 *Little Pretty Song Book.* Popular Spottswood songbooks for adults were *The Apollo,* which sold more than 8,000 copies in three editions, *The Charmer,* a "select collection of English, Scotch and American Songs, including the modern," and a *Vocal Remembrancer.*

Daniel Bowen, a New Haven printer and bookseller, employed the brilliant local silversmith and engraver Amos Doolittle to make the music plates for a 1790 publication of *The Select Songster,* popular contemporary songs compiled by Chauncey Langdon, a Yale senior, member of the college's Musical Society, and future congressman from Vermont. Langdon was a student of the classics, but he combed current music literature for Thomas Paine's "Death of General Wolfe," "Delia" by the French cellist Henri Capron, recently arrived in America, and "The Shepherd's Complaint" by Timothy Swan, a twenty-seven-year-old singing teacher in nearby Suffield, who later won renown as a hymn tune composer. In 1796, Langdon compiled *Beauties of Psalmody* for Bowen, a collection of popular psalm tunes and anthems, with an essay on the rules of singing.

Amos Doolittle was, with John Norman, among the country's few skilled craftsmen making music plates. He left his silversmith shop near Yale after the fighting at Lexington and went off in the militia company formed by Benedict Arnold. He spent the next month near Boston, where he talked to men who had participated in the first battle and made notes and sketches of the location. At the end of 1776, when his service agreement ended, Doolittle returned to New Haven and cut four line engravings of the action, offering them to Americans as accurate eyewitness picture accounts of the time when the war for freedom truly started. After the war, he went into partnership with Daniel Read, a local book dealer and gifted composer, even though he had had no musical training. In 1784, the partners brought out the nation's first music journal, *The American Musical Magazine.* Each issue of the four-page monthly contained music predominantly of a religious nature, written by the "Best American and foreign masters," who also produced the secular songs included. Next, Read and Doolittle issued *The American Singing Book,* a psalm and gospel tune collection that had gone through six editions by 1796. A supplement, with twenty-five additional tunes by Read and others, was issued in 1787 and enjoyed sales to pupils of Read's school and to many throughout New England. Read's *Introduction to Psalmody* (1790), with copperplate illustrations for the music lessons, which offered training in church music to young people, was followed two years later by *The Columbian Harmonist,* which had run through four editions by 1810. It was intended chiefly as a source of lighter music, though some religious songs were included. Two years after the *Harmonist* had sold most of the 5,500 copies of its second edition, Doolittle's plates were damaged, and Read was obliged to use the services of a nearby typesetter. The problems that had vexed composers since music type's first appearance immediately arose, Read complained: "Some obvious blunders of the printer have excited my notice, viz such as printing all the pages wrong side up . . . misarranging some of the tunes—breaking them into pieces—leaving out the name of one tune or more in the index—and inserting wrong pages for others, but what is most unpardonable is that some of the tunes appear to be taken from copies very different from what I furnished." Correspondence such as this, in the possession of the New Haven Colony Historical Society, offers an insight into the problems of music publishing in a period when its business was beginning to take shape in America.

Read's publications represent the popular gospel music of that vast majority of Americans with neither cultural pretensions nor access to the art music represented by Hopkinson. Lower-class New Englanders sang the music of William Billings and Daniel Read and that from other tune books. Read offered complimentary copies of his books to singing-school teachers and to prominent citizens whose interest "might open a way to the sale of these." He had visions of editions of tens of thousands, believing that graduates of his and other singing schools might, when traveling, open up the middle-South market to his music, having heard stories of the money itinerant music masters were making there.

Distribution became easier for music publishers after government action established a federal system for "the communication of intelligence with regularity and despatch from one part to another of the United States." A newly appointed postmaster general improved the lagging mail system, whose chief interest had been the quick dispatch of government mail, supplemented by private express-rider service. Stagecoaches carried government mail after 1782, and four years later there was a postrider and coach mail service from New Hampshire to Georgia. In 1789, seventy-five post offices serviced 2,000 miles of post roads, over which letters were carried, with the recipient paying charges based on mileage involved and the number of sheets in the envelope. Service in the western states was provided by boat until the mid-1790s, when post roads were built. By the end of the century, 16,000 miles of these roads existed, serving Cincinnati, western Kentucky, middle Tennessee, and all of the South. Although not part of the official service, packages could be carried on intercoastal shipping and stages.

Read shipped his books to the larger cities, doing business in New York with Cornelius Davis, the city's leading bookseller, who bought printed sheets on consignment at wholesale and had agents in Virginia and as far south as the Carolinas. Scrupulous in his choices of tunes, Read offered suggestions to songwriters, urging revisions to make their work more appealing, and always asking permission to use the pieces. He did sometimes include music that did not "appear to me the best tunes that ever was but still they may be popular . . . the Collection is for use of the Public, the public opinion is always to be respected."

Except in states where copyright protection had been legislated, though it affected only local publication, books published before Noah Webster succeeded in promoting national copyright were usually in the public domain, free to all for the copying. After some of Read's songs had appeared without permission in Isaiah Thomas's successful *Worcester Collection,* he wrote to a fellow composer that he was

> irritated beyond measure at the unprovoked robbery committed upon the *American Singing Book* by the editor of the *Worcester Collection* and having no redress but by retaliation there being no law in existence to prevent such abuses I have availed myself of the opportunity to publish some pieces from the *Worcester Collection* to which I had no right. But since the Statutes of the United States made for the purpose of securing to authors the copyright of their work, I do not mean to give any person cause to be offended in that way, on the other hand I think it my duty to prosecute any person who prints my music without my consent, as much as if he were a common thief or housebreaker.

The new major center of American printing, Philadelphia, witnessed a flurry of secular and art music publication beginning in 1787 with the appearance of William Brown's Three Rondos for keyboard. This immigrant German musician, whose name was probably Braun, dedicated his six-page engraved work to Francis Hopkinson, then Pennsylvania's admiralty judge and a leading patron of the musical arts. Sold by subscription for two dollars a copy, the book was engraved by John Aitken, of the Scottish bookselling and binding family that had settled in the city before the Revolution. One of them, Robert, became a printer in 1775 and produced the first American Bible in English in 1782. This publication was immediately sanctioned by the United States Congress, which approved the pious and laudable undertaking "as subservient to the interest of religion, as well as an instance of the progress of the arts in this country." John Aitken migrated to Philadelphia sometime in the mid-1780s and set up his silver and goldsmithing business, adding copperplate printing to his activities when he became "the first engraver on metal in America to engage in the publication of music in a serious and continuing way and the first to employ steel punches for the purpose," as Richard J. Wolfe points out in *Early American Music Engraving and Printing.* Aitken issued some twenty pieces of music before he retired, though he returned to music printing in 1807. Many of his early publications were most ambitious—for example, his compilation, with an unknown but not Catholic editor, of *Litanies, Vespers Hymns and Anthems* used in the Church of Rome, which "not only surpassed in size and appearance the best such work that had appeared in England but constituted a landmark in the history of printing in the United States," according to Wolfe.

The majority of Aitken's Federal-period publications were composed and/or edited by Alexander Reinagle, the most talented of those European masters who flocked to the newly created United States after the Peace of 1783. Philadelphia's rapidly rising economy encouraged the opening of musical-merchandise stores and their sale of the increasingly popular pianoforte to wealthy merchants and businessmen, whose daughters concentrated on the music of Haydn and their own instructors, principally Reinagle and Brown. The Scottish musician and great pianoforte player issued his own collection of music for that instrument for sale to students, the *Select Collection of the Most Favorite Scot's Tunes*, engraved by Aitken and sold at his and other leading stores. It was soon followed by Reinagle's *Collection of Favorite Songs,* divided into two books.

Responding to his own question "Ought not a new nation to have new songs?," Francis Hopkinson gathered together from his manuscript book and library material for *Seven Songs for the Harpsichord,* precisely the type of art music men of his background might be expected to create. Advertising by the collection's publisher, Thomas Dobson, printer and bookseller, in November 1788 papers called attention to this "first work of this kind attempted in the United States," Aitken punched and engraved the music. Writing to his friend Thomas Jefferson, Hopkinson said: "I have amused myself with composing [the book actually had eight songs, the last being engraved after the title page was completed] easy & simple songs for the harpsichord—words and music all my own . . . the best of them is that they are so easy that any person who can play at all may perform them without trouble."

Among the 10,000 pieces of popular music published between 1800 and 1825, only one Hopkinson song was reprinted. That was neither "My days have been so wondrous free," still buried in the pages of his manuscript book, nor any of the eight songs published in 1788, but the "Battle of the Kegs," which he may have considered vulgar and trivial.

Three music books printed in Philadelphia during this period were more attuned to majority tastes: *The Charms of Melody* (1788), published by Thomas Seddon; Reinagle's *Twelve Favorite Pieces* (1789), a compilation of popular concert pieces and theater music engraved by Aitken and printed by Dobson at the compiler's expense; and *The Philadelphia Songster* (1789), assembled by Absalom Aimwell, a pseudonym favored by Andrew Adgate, president of the local Uranian Academy of Music. Among the songs in the last was Burgoyne's "Anna's urn," well on its way to becoming one of the country's best-loved songs, but never associated in print with its writer. The book was published by the Scottish printer John McCulloch, whose *Introduction to the History of America* (1787) contained the first appearance in book form of the complete text of the new Constitution, signed only five days before the book came off the press, a feat of publishing history.

## Ratifying the Constitution with Music

From May 14, 1787, Philadelphia throbbed with excitement over the presence of delegates to a convention called to revise the Articles of Confederation. George Washington presided over the deliberations, enlivening the days of debate over the national future by attending concerts by Reinagle and other Europeans and going to the theater while his colleagues labored. They eventually agreed to plan a new national government, and on September 17, agreed to the Constitution, which then went to the states for ratification. The issues involved were taken to the people by the use of popular music.

The still-popular "Heart of Oak" melody was impressed into duty for one of the earliest Federalist broadsides:

Our freedom we've won
And the prize let's maintain
Huzzah for the Convention again and again.

Francis Hopkinson, the major musical talent among the Federalists, lent his experience to the cause, for which he was eventually rewarded with appointment to the United States Court, predecessor to the Supreme Court. In a song, "The Raising, a new song for mechanics," aimed at the workingmen whose support the Federalists clearly needed, Hopkinson made clever use of those similes that would affect them most. Its thirteen verses, one for each state, likened the Constitution to a new roof over the new nation. It first appeared in a February 1788 issue of the *Pennsylvania Gazette,* and then in papers throughout the country.

The musical theater was also impressed into service for national ratification when New York's John Street Theatre presented *The Columbian Father,* a pastoral in two acts, provided to the theater by "a citizen of the United States." The first act, called "The Convention," offered "a procession of the Thirteen States, from the Temple of Liberty." The street "procession," in which the various trades were represented by craftsmen bearing their tools and marching behind banners and groups of musicians, was used by all factions during the dispute, and was used later to mark each state's approval of the Constitution. In New Hampshire, such a parade included six caparisoned horses drawing an open coach from which copies of a new song honoring the state's action were distributed to spectators as the band played. Philadelphia's celebration included a Grand Federal Procession organized by Hopkinson. Reinagle's new "Federal March" was played by civilian and military bands accompanying the eighty-seven divisions of floats, delegations, and representatives of the trade guilds, fraternal societies, and professions. A wagon sponsored by the local printers, bookbinders, and stationers displayed a printing press, on which masters of the ancient mystery ran off copies of an ode written by Hopkinson, which were thrown to the crowds. Ten carrier pigeons, one for each of the states that had ratified thus far, were sent off the float bearing copies of the composition. New York's day-long parade brought out representatives of every social, trade, and labor group. They marched to music and sang pro-Federal songs, copies of which had been printed for distribution to the spectators. When evening came, thousands sat in a giant tent designed by Pierre L'Enfant, future planner of Washington, D.C., drinking, eating, singing, and toasting the new document.

Among the cheering Manhattanites was a young man from Germany, John Jacob Astor, who had left his home around 1780 to join a brother in his London flute-making business. In 1783, he sailed to Baltimore, to visit another brother, taking him him a parcel of flutes valued at about five pounds. After selling them locally, he invested all his assets in fur pelts, which he took back to England, and made a substantial profit. Now fully aware of America's business opportunities, Astor, with a large stock of musical wares, went to New York, where another brother, Henry, was a successful butcher. John Jacob clerked for a time in a baker's store, and in 1786 opened the city's first full-service music store, not far from Rivington's foundering establishment. Hitherto, instruments and printed music had been sold in bookstores and by other commercial enterprises.

But there were few opportunities as dazzling for a young man as the fur trade, and he sold his stock to a German immigrant and embarked on the career that made him and his descendants one of America's richest families.

## Isaiah Thomas, Full-Service Music Publisher

The printing of music was generally a part-time activity for most press owners. Exceptions were John Aitken and Daniel Read, and soon Isaiah Thomas, of Boston and Worcester, joined them, making that business part of the first major publishing enterprise in America. Born to a Welsh family that had come to New England in 1640, Thomas was the grandson of a woman who had been hanged as a witch in Salem. By the time of his birth, in 1749, the Thomases had fallen upon hard times, and the boy was apprenticed to Zechariah Fowle, who specialized in ballad printing and had one of Boston's best stocks. Isaiah's first typesetting chore was printing the bawdy ballad "The lawyers' pedigree," one that took the seven-year-old boy, who could neither read nor write, two days to complete. In time, Thomas taught himself by studying a dictionary and the Bible and became a highly literate man, founder of the American Antiquarian Society, and author of the indispensable *History of Printing in America.* At sixteen he was involved in a serious fracas with the master printer who had taken over his articles of indenture and, like Franklin, ran away, taking ship to London by way of Halifax. He stopped there for a few months and worked as a journeyman printer, then ventured south to the Carolinas and returned to the Boston at the age of twenty-one.

With his original master, Fowle, he began publication of a weekly newspaper, the *Massachusetts Spy,* and when the two divided their business interests, he went out on his own and made the paper one of New England's most important, with the largest local circulation, which was attained by his unflagging support of the Sons of Liberty.

In January 1774, Thomas started the first monthly magazine of any significance yet to appear in America, the *Royal American,* modeled after leading British journals. It borrowed heavily from London originals, but also used articles, love stories, poetry, and engravings by Americans and was the first native publication to print the words and music of a popular song. "The hill tops," a hunting song, appeared in the April 1774 issue, with an elaborate copperplate illustration.

Thomas found himself, in April 1775, with Paul Revere, a part of a group of horsemen riding to raise the countryside, warning that the British were coming. He then joined his militia compatriots on the field at Lexington. Expecting the worst, he had ferried his equipment across Boston Harbor to Charlestown, where Sons of Liberty friends sent it by wagon to Worcester, some fifty miles west of Boston, which became the base for his printing and publishing complex.

During the war, Thomas did some printing for the provincial Congress, and when Benjamin Franklin was named postmaster general for the colonies, he was appointed to the postmastership at Worcester, in charge of a single mail east and west each week. He continued publishing the *Spy*, though operating under lease to various owners. The *Spy*'s profits, if any, went to creditors. The type from which it was printed came from a vessel captured by American privateers, and the paper was the period's typical poor quality. Fortune turned for him in 1781. The *Spy* was back in his hands, paper was in plentiful supply, and he had purchased a new and elegant type.

He advertised in the *Spy* for December 1784 that he "had just received from England, a beautiful set of Musical Types; by which he is enabled to print any kind of Church or other music, in a neat and elegant manner and can afford to do it cheaper than such work has heretofore been done in this country from copper or pewter plates." Type specimens were available at Boston's leading bookstores for inspection by potential clients. This Caslon type was the round music-note font that became standard in America, replacing the lozenge-shaped notation in use since the mid-sixteenth century. Operating from a growing and self-contained plant in Worcester, Thomas now added music-book printing to the book publishing, binding, and merchandising he had begun two years earlier.

With a keen awareness of public demand, Thomas never concentrated on any single aspect of the book trade. His catalogue ranged from the substantial and respected *Thomas' New England Almanac*, still prepared for him by Benjamin West, of Providence, and Blackstone's *Commentaries* to such titillation as *The Amours and Adventures of Two English Gentlemen in Italy* and the downright eroticism of *A Woman of Pleasure [Fanny Hill]*, whose pirated first American edition Thomas brought out under a false imprint in order to keep unknown his ownership of the copyright.

He learned early that people were always ready to buy ballads, and he turned them out in quantity. When he acquired the music type, it was set to immediate use for children's books that contained music and collections of popular sacred songs, beginning with *New Hymns on Various Subjects*, compiled by Silas Ballou in 1784. He also pirated from John Newbery's London chapbooks the first of six editions of *Mother Goose Melodies*, "sonnets for the cradle . . . the most celebrated songs and lullabies of the old British nurses . . . calculated to amuse children and to excite them to sleep." The second part of these three-by-five-inch paperbacks contained a single page of music and sixty-eight songs, sixteen of them by that "sweet songster and nurse of wit, Master William Shakespeare," the first American printing of any of the Bard's work. Songs and music in the same format appeared in the 1786 *Little Robin Red Breast*, with thirty-five juvenile songs; the 1787 *Pretty Pocket-book*, with forty-two songs and "a new attempt to teach children the use of the English alphabet by way of diversion"; and the 1788 *Poetical Description of Songbirds*, with twenty-two songs. Selling for about twenty cents, the books were highly successful, their contents finding a place in the culture of countless generations of young Americans. Scrubbing them clean of any references to their British sources that might offend the sensibilities of a proud new nation, Thomas substituted suitable Americanisms.

Thomas's new publications and his type specimen books were available for examination at Boston's newest bookstore, owned by Colonel Ebenezer Battelle, who had served with distinction throughout the war. Available there were best-selling music books aimed at singing-school pupils, Andrew Law's *Select Harmony* and *Rudiments of Music,* and Billings's collections. The evident market for these and similar works led Thomas to issue his own series. In 1786, he brought out the first edition of *Laus Deo! the Worcester Collection of Sacred Harmony,* New England's first music publication made entirely with music type. In the introduction, Thomas apologized for the price, which was more than anticipated due to production costs.

Thomas, whose first experience of printing anything to do with music took place in 1773, when he printed a Boston singing master's lecture, "Religion productive of music," served as editor for this and the following four editions. Responsibility for the book's contents and musical accuracy were then turned over to Oliver Holden, a carpenter, who, after prospering in the real-estate business, began to publish popular hymn collections. Copyright laws in Massachusetts and Connecticut failed to trouble Thomas, who borrowed freely from others, rarely crediting composer, compiler, or source. Nineteen of Billings's tunes and eighteen of Andrew Law's were printed in the first edition and other compiler-composers suffered in later printings. His cavalier attitude toward Noah Webster's *Blue-Backed Speller* was one of the many larcenies that prompted the lexicographer's crusade for national copyright legislation.

In 1788, Thomas entered into partnership with his former apprentice Ebenezer Andrews, forming the Boston-based Thomas and Andrews business, whose five presses added to the seven in Worcester made it America's major printing enterprise. Branch offices, managed by former apprentices trained for the purpose, took the firm's imprint into most of the New England states and as far south as Baltimore. Andrews ran the Boston office and engaged in a voluminous correspondence, which provides an insight into Thomas's abrupt dealings with the composers whose music he used, among them William Billings, down on his luck and struggling to keep his family fed and warm; in order to have his 1794 *Continental Harmony* published, a mortgage had to be taken out on his house.

Some 900 books were put out by the many Thomas partnerships. These included the majority of roughly three dozen tune books printed in the United States prior to 1800, many of them ambitious works of more than a hundred pages, printed in editions of between 3,000 and 4,000 copies. With ready access to the majority of new hymns, many of which came off his own presses, Thomas could easily change the contents of each new edition of his *Worcester Collection.*

Possessed of the country's largest stock of music type, permitting production cheaper than copper- or pewter-plate engraving, Thomas and Andrews became the obvious printer for New England's singing masters and tune-book compilers, who were generally obliged to supply the paper, pay for printing costs, labor, and binding. Thomas had no compunction in suing for nonpayment of bills or abandoning the publication of a volume for which the subscription fees fell short of production costs.

The composers from whom Thomas borrowed were an amazing cross section of New Englanders infatuated with music, who had learned their craft in singing schools and fused Yankee know-how to elements of genteel European music, and were now determined to bring their creations to anyone who would buy them.

Supply Belcher, "the Handel of Maine," learned his music from Billings in Stoughton, Massachusetts. He moved to Maine in his mid-twenties and served in the Massachusetts legislature, representing his hometown, Maine being a part of that state until 1820. In the tavern he kept, he taught people how to sing, and he wrote *The Harmony of Maine,* published by Thomas and Andrews in 1794.

Abraham Wood served as a drummer at Washington's Cambridge headquarters in 1775, when he was in his early twenties. He was a clothes dresser, whose chief interest was church singing. In 1789, Thomas published *Divine Song,* Wood's collection of hymn settings for verses by the fiercely Calvinist London preacher Joseph Hart.

Samuel Holyoke, who wrote his most famous tune, "Arnheim," when he was a sixteen-year-old Harvard student, became a music teacher and taught his pupils to dislike Billings's dancelike melodies, saying that they confused the senses and rendered the performance a mere jargon of words. Thomas published Holyoke's first two collections, the 200-page *Harmonia Americana* in 1791 and *The Massachusetts Compiler* in 1795. The latter was the first composition manual printed in America and was put together by Holyoke with Thomas's editors Hans Gram and Oliver Holden. When Henry Ranlet, of Exeter, New Hampshire, bought New England's second font of music type, from which he printed *The Village Harmony* in 1795 and cut into sales of Thomas's publications, Holyoke went to Ranlet with his new manuscript. He learned that publishers were all the same. Ranlet wrote an agreement that gave Holyoke half the printed edition of 1,500 copies, made on paper supplied by the author, and fixed the price at which Holyoke could sell his portion of the printing.

Other Thomas and Andrews authors included Daniel Belknap, an unlettered farmer and mechanic, who became a singing teacher at eighteen and compiled *The Harmonist's Companion* of church songs (1797); the Hartford singing and writing master Amos Bull, author of the 1795 *Responsary,* one hundred pages of church music; the blacksmith's son Jacob Kimball, who was a boy drummer with the patriot army, studied for the law at Harvard, but learned that he loved music more and continued to teach it all his life throughout New England. His *Rural Harmony* (1793) sold well, but his 1800 *Essex Harmony,* printed by Henry Ranlet, was considered a "catch penny production [resulting] from the promise of cash for the compilation." When Yankee singing master Amos Pilsbury moved to South Carolina, he took a stock of his 1799 *United States Sacred Harmony,* and it became a great influence on the course of southern Methodist hymnody.

None of the tunesmiths whose books Thomas issued made any significant profits from their sales, particularly after other printers—Thomas's apprentice Andrew Wright, in Northampton; Manning and Loring, in Boston, whose senior partner had been a principal employee of Thomas and Andrews; and Herman Mann, of Dedham—purchased music type, entered the market, and almost saturated it. The sale of books to their pupils and the consignment of their share of editions to postmasters, book and music stores, local grocers, and rural merchants helped put food on their tables and left their names to prospective scholars. Only Holden died in better than moderate circumstances, the result of his gains in real-estate sales.

From 1789 until 1793, Thomas and Andrews published the *Massachusetts Magazine*, "a monthly museum of knowledge and national entertainment, poetry, music, history, biography, physics, geography, morality, criticism, philosophy, mathematics, agriculture, architecture, chemistry, novels, tales, romances, translations, news, marriages and death, meteorological observations, etc. etc." Andrews contracted with Hans Gram, the Danish-born organist at the Brattle Square Church and the teacher of Kimball, Holden, Holyoke, and many other New England musicians, to provide new music for the magazine at one dollar a piece. Gram supplied ten selections, some of them his own, before the autumn of 1792, when the "best magazine in America" was running an annual deficit of one hundred pounds, with a print order of 800, a hundred of which were usually defective and thrown away. Included in the music Gram provided was the first printed orchestral score published in America, his "Death song of an Indian chief," printed in the March 1791 issue. The words were by Sarah Wentworth Apthorp Morton, of Boston, taken from her narrative poem *Ouabi*. Mrs. Morton was one of a scandalous trio that titillated New England society and served as the inspiration of the "first American novel," William Hill Brown's *The Power of Sympathy*, a best seller for Thomas and Andrews. Mrs. Morton's husband, Perez, author of the text used by William Billings for "When Mary wept," had seduced his sister-in-law, driving her to suicide.

Regular publication of engraved American music and songs in the sixty-four page monthly *Massachusetts Magazine* served to introduce its several hundred subscribers and their families to many New England composers and to promote sales of the music books.

When he retired from active participation in the business in 1802, Thomas estimated his personal wealth at $151,340.91. In 1825, six years before his death, this had been reduced, through the incompetence of a son to whom he had turned over much of the business, to $39,000, his remaining stock in the Worcester plant, where in the 1780s 150 people operated seven presses, a paper mill, and a bookbindery.

## Noah Webster and American Copyright

The *Blue-Backed Speller*, an American version of John Day's profitable Elizabethan *ABCDarium*, compiled by twenty-four-year-old schoolmaster Noah Webster, began to win wide attention in 1784. Isaiah Thomas sought to purchase exclusive rights in Massachusetts but failed. Webster had already secured copyright in Connecticut, his native state. Thomas therefore prepared his own speller, *The New American Spelling Book*, an outright plagiarism of Webster's. It sold over 300,000 copies in the first five years, though it never matched the sale of Webster's book, which had sold in excess of 70 million copies by the early twentieth century.

The rising of an exuberant national consciousness following independence fostered a determination to strip public education of all British influence. All grammars, histories, and arithmetic texts had been imported from England or pirated from British editions, so schoolbooks now required replacement by works containing American pronunciation and spelling. Recognizing the commercial appeal of a work that combined geography, history, and the American language, Webster proposed to issue a *Grammatical Institute of the English Language* in three parts, a speller, a grammar, and a reader. The first part later called the *Blue-Backed Speller,* was printed in 1783, at Webster's expense, and an exclusive license to print subsequent Connecticut editions was given to its printers, the publishers of Hartford's *Connecticut Courant.* In addition, Webster petitioned the Connecticut General Assembly for the exclusive right to print, publish, and vend his book in that state, a grant similar to that Andrew Law had received the year before. Protection came to Webster in January 1783, when an act ''for the encouragement of literature and genius'' was passed, lobbied through the state body by a group of local literary figures. Webster's petition had been greatly assisted by a similar one from a fellow Connecticut writer, John Ledyard, who had written an account of his travels with the British explorer Captain James Cook. In passing the first copyright law in any of the original states, Connecticut created a model from which the federal Congress fashioned its own law in 1791.

Under the Articles of Confederation, the national government had had no power to enact binding legislation, but could recommend action to its constituents, which, in this case, it did on May 2, 1783, urging that authors be granted copyrights for a period of not less than fourteen years, which could be extended, if they survived, for a similar term; this was modeled after English law. An early proponent of this and of federal copyright protection was Noah Webster.

This remarkable man was born in East Hartford in 1758, to a British family whose American roots went back one century, to when his ancestors helped found what became Connecticut. At sixteen Webster was admitted to Yale College to prepare for the law, at considerable sacrifice to his father, who mortgaged the family farm to meet tuition expenses. Exempt, as a student, from military duty Webster put his musical abilities to patriotic use by helping to form an infantry company that trained with the local New Haven militia, both marching to drums and Webster's flute. When George Washington passed through in the spring of 1775 on his way to take command of the forces around Boston, Webster marched at the head of the student military escort, playing ''Yankee Doodle.''

After graduation in 1780, Webster read for the law, earning his keep as a schoolmaster, and worked late into the night on his grand plan for the *Grammatical Institute*. Little honor accrued to a public schoolteacher, most being failed scholars, causing wealthy families to buy indentured servants to instruct their offspring. Webster abandoned his teaching post in mid-1782, and traveled about the northeast to bring his speller to the attention of leading educators and agitating by pen and tongue for a national copyright law. He was admitted to the Connecticut bar in 1781 and supplemented his income by trying cases in that state. This training sharpened his writing skills, and he began to circulate memorials to the state legislatures, urging passage of Congress's recommendation. By the end of 1785, nine states had copyright laws and insisted on reciprocity for their citizens.

The first Connecticut edition of 5,000 *Blue-Backed Spellers* sold out almost at once, and a second and third went by 1784. Webster's grammar was completed that year and his reader in the next. Webster then turned to promotion and merchandising. He sent copies to every college in the country, asking for testimonials to its quality and worth, and received many. Whenever he had the opportunity, he traveled by horseback to small villages, to talk with teachers and citizens about his concept of protection of intellectual property, and generally left copies of his books on consignment with postmasters and teachers. During these years, he also taught "vocal music in as great perfection as is taught in America," opening schools wherever he went, charging one dollar a lesson for instruction "in the regular scientific manner," and an additional seventy-five cents for music books, which he had purchased from their compilers in job lots. During one summer in Baltimore, he led a class of ten for six weeks and then presented his pupils in concert at a local church. Response was great, doubling his next class, where he found pleasure in the company of young ladies come to learn from the charming Yankee singing master.

In early 1786, Webster worked as a Philadelphia part-time schoolmaster and renewed his friendships with Benjamin Franklin, who argued with him about education; young James Madison; the Pennsylvania Farmer, John Dickinson, whose "Liberty Song" was still being sung; the tune writer and music publisher Andrew Law, and other leading politicians. When the Constitutional Convention gathered to frame a new way of operating the business of government, Washington visited Webster in his rooms. The young grammarian had been a valuable ally to the General's followers, aiding them in lectures, articles, and the pages of his *American Magazine*.

In the twelve issues Webster brought out before the magazine fell victim to the poor times and sales, he argued for a strong central government and continued his fight for national copyright. "The productions of genius and the imagination are if possible more really and exclusively property than houses and lands, and are equally entitled to legal security," he wrote. Throughout the nation, printers were violating copyrights guaranteed by local legislation, enriching these American pirates with the fruits of his and others' wisdom and genius. To raise funds for his efforts, Webster sold exclusive rights in various states to local publishers, turning down a penny a copy royalty for ready cash. New York book dealer Samuel Campbell paid $500 for a five-year contract allowing exclusive rights to the *Speller* in New York, New Jersey, the Carolinas, and Georgia, and then sold 20,000 copies a year, stocking an additional 100,000 just before the contract lapsed.

Webster brought action against a Connecticut printer, who responded by offering the state legislature "a proposal to save three hundred and thirty pounds, six shillings and eight pence annually to the inhabitants of Connecticut," which asked that Webster reduce the *Speller*'s price or that the state-granted privilege for printing it be awarded to the defendant, who could print it at a cheaper price.

Webster's cares and struggles were made easier by recourse to the flute. "What an infinite variety of method have men invented to render his life agreeable," he wrote in his diary. "What a wise and happy design in the human frame that the sound of a little hollow tube of wood should dispell in a few moments, or at least alleviate, the heaviest cares of life."

With final acceptance of the new Constitution in sight, Webster stepped up litigation against violators of his copyrights and lectured, wrote, and campaigned even more strenuously. Although the Constitution, passed September 17, 1787, and ratified during the following year, bore this provision in Article 1, Section 8: "The Congress shall have Power . . . to promote the progress of Science and useful arts, by securing, for limited Times to Authors and Inventors the exclusive Right to their respective Writings and discoveries," it was not until May 1790 that a public law relating to copyright was passed, requiring more of Webster's personal involvement in the process. The result, the original copyright law "for the encouragement of learning, by securing the copies of maps, charts and books, to the authors and proprietors of such copies, during the time herein mentioned," did not include music specifically among the materials cited. This did not occur until the 1831 revision.

The law was modeled on the English law of Queen Anne, which limited the first term to fourteen years, with a similar renewal period if the creator remained alive. A printed copy of each work was to be deposited with the Secretary of State and another with the local U.S. District Court, rather than the Stationers' Company, and notice of publication was to be made in a local newspaper. Failure to observe any of these provisions resulted in a fine of fifty cents for each page of unregistered material. Musical works qualified only when included in a book, or if registered as maps, charts, or engravings. They were also covered under a provision that maps and charts and books not printed were protected when the "sole right and liberty of printing, reprinting, publishing or vending."

In another section, which affected the course of book and music publishing for many decades, Congress provided that "nothing in this act shall be construed to extend to prohibit the importation or vending, reprinting, or publishing within the United States of any map, chart, book or books, written, printed, or published by any person not a citizen of the United States, in foreign parts or places without the jurisdiction of the United States," which gave printers and publishers carte blanche to print foreign music without any obligation to secure permission or pay royalties, enabling them to dip without hindrance into the giant pool of contemporary creativity around the world. As a result, the cause of American composers and songwriters suffered and the vast preponderance of music published in the United States was of foreign origin.

In spite of Noah Webster's long and loud agitation for protection, most Americans were slow to take advantage of the law during the first years of its existence. Some 13,000 titles were published, but only 556 entries were registered; many of these were textbooks. Thomas and Andrews extracted the copyright and the cost of paper from Jeremy Belknap, whose *The Foresters* was the first American novel registered for copyright protection.

Though he owned untrammeled copyright to his textbooks after passage of the federal law, Webster did not realize the profits that poured in when his *Blue-Backed Speller* sold more than five million copies by 1818 and fives times that before the Mexican War. As owner of an exclusive printing and sales agency for the book in New Hampshire, Massachusetts, and Rhode Island, Thomas and Andrews sold hundreds of thousands of copies and gave Webster a royalty income larger than that of any other of their authors. Other printers and booksellers to whom he assigned rights generally sent him short-count statements. When the initial copyright expired in 1814, Webster was obliged to add new material in order to make obsolete the editions already in existence or being pirated widely by many printers. Thomas and Andrews refused to accept his new and higher terms and brought out their own spelling book, based on copyright-free British materials. Only a vastly improved edition, called *The American Spelling Book,* with an appropriate blue cover, kept Webster on the bestseller lists.

Tricks like that practiced by Thomas and Andrews drove Webster to a lifetime effort to improve the laws. ''I do not see,'' he wrote in 1804, ''why an interest in original literary composition should stand on different ground from all other personal property. . . . Literary composition is a species of property more peculiarly a man's own than any other, being the production of his mind or inventive faculties. A horse or an acre of land, which a fool may obtain by muscular exertions, is a permanent inheritable state.''

The problems of fraudulent royalties, fair compensation, and property rights faced by such a well-placed, influential, and articulate man as Noah Webster pale into relative insignificance in relation to the situation among the unsophisticated tunebook compilers, immigrant musicians, and hopeful songwriters who fed the popular music business during the following century.

# CHAPTER 22

# Black Music in America

## Black Secular Music

After more than 150 years of the black presence in America, Thomas Jefferson observed of blacks' musical potential in 1784: "In music they are more generally gifted than the whites, with accurate ears for tune and time, and they have been found capable of imagining a small catch. Whether they be equal to the composition of an extensive run of melody, or of complicated harmony, is yet to be granted." He himself was an energetic violinist of some skill and a man who found high baroque and classical music a "resource . . . against ennui." His library at this time included popular ballads from the London stage, fiddle tunes, drinking songs, and publications imported from England and France that reflected the interest of one who attended concerts, the opera, and theater. His brother, Randolph, a less complicated man, was content "to come among the black people, play the fiddle and dance all the night." Jefferson, who questioned the black man's natural capacity, asked of him a sophistication possessed by few of his own acquaintances. Randolph tolerated the role of black music in a regional culture that was influencing its course far beyond his brother's hopes for it.

This acculturative process was more advanced in the north, for a variety of social and economic reasons. Heavy labor in large northern communities was done by both black and white workers, and the streets were filled with shouting, singing men who unloaded cargo, carried produce to market, cleaned the streets, and did most of the manual labor. Not yet branded as unteachable, slave and free blacks mended boots, cut hair, dug oysters, caught and sold fish, assembled barrels, and worked at other trades necessary to a growing nation. White and black slaveowners rented out their property by the day or on long-term contract and retained all money earned. Concentrated in port cities, blacks formed less than ten percent of the population north of Maryland. Out of the controlled homogeneity had grown a kind of social acceptance. Black and white poor shared the dram and beer shop, joined on the streets to watch Muster Day parades, in which black men often took part as musicians or militiamen, flocked to outdoor fairs and gathered to watch street sports played by youngsters of both races. Virtually every local community boasted of a black fiddle player whose prowess was a matter of neighborhood pride. In the large cities, black musicians played for pennies and leftover food in taverns and on the streets around hostelries and rooming houses.

Blacks early learned that their antics at open-air markets, on street corners, and wherever liquor was consumed earned shillings from people of all classes. The most talented developed the song and patter that won coins. Scarcely aware they were in bondage, they became local favorites, dancing on five- or six-foot-square boards called "shingles" to hand-clapped rhythms or the music of homemade percussive instruments and the audience's shouted encouragement. In fine weather, spectators watched blacks from the Long Island and New Jersey farm country vie with slick home-grown Manhattan talent in dancing, singing, and cutting up for the customers at the Catherine Street Market. The New York tavern, in which black and white men and women mingled, dancing to a fiddle's music, where the 1741 slave outbreak was planned, was little better or worse than most such establishments catering to the lower class of both races and richer whites who came to see. After George Whitefield's first crusades, Americans with a taste for mixed dancing resorted to "Hell Towns" that sprang up in the leading cities.

As a result of such exhibitions, the black man's gliding, dragging shuffle steps were incorporated into country dances, and, with them, the music and song of the street performers and musicians. The lines run straight from this early music making to the dances that grew out of the twentieth century's ragtime, blues, jazz, swing, rhythm and blues, rock 'n' roll, and disco, all come into the white life style by reverse acculturation.

Free northern blacks and house servants alike were more affected by the white culture to which they had daily access than were Southern blacks, except for those who worked inside plantation houses. Until the Revolution, one-third of the population south of Maryland was black, ranging from that region's three out of ten, to the Carolinas' nearly seven out of ten. At least 200,000 whites lived where slaves outnumbered them, bringing about the enactment of codes regulating conduct. Blacks were restricted to the plantation on which they lived, except with written permission to be abroad. They could not bear arms, and such gatherings of large groups as the northern blacks' holidays were unthinkable. Whether real or imagined, the threat of insurrection and its slaughter was a constant deterrent to any improvement in racial relations. Because many whites lived all their lives in fear of a torch in the night, a blade to the throat, any black gathering was presumed to be conspiratorial, and laws were passed to put an end to public dancing and the slaves' private message carrier, the homemade drum, as well as to most black music making in the slave quarter.

Contact in Africa with Muslim culture had already added the Arabic lyre, guitar, and fiddle to an indigenous store of stringed instruments, of which the best known on the plantation was the bania or banjar. A popular ditty ran:

> Negro Sambo played the banjar
> Make his finger go like handsaw

Jefferson observed that instrument's place in black life: "proper to them is the 'banjar' which they brought thither from Africa and which is the original of the guitar, its chords being precisely the four lower chords of the guitar." Northern and southern household servants and slaves alike came into contact with the European guitar only after the English vogue for the instrument was exported to the colonies. The white man's improvement of this originally Near Eastern instrument and his technical mastery of it added further to black music-making capabilities.

A southern black culture preserving its own identity was born, merging into an entity made up of various tribal influences. A private language, brought from Africa, was spoken, a secret code that served as the foundation of black English. Phrases from the white man's language were added in order to make the patois comprehensible to whites who needed or cared to understand. Restricted to the slave quarter, the transplanted culture evolved a communal music, rooted in basic African elements, the rhythmic hand-clapping supported by percussive and melody instruments, improvised from available materials, duplicating those remembered from a long-lost Africa.

Access to the white man's music-making devices, many of which were similar to African instruments, was restricted to blacks deemed sufficiently bright or prepossessing to work inside the master's house. The accurate "ear for tune and time" noted by Jefferson, served in mastering the guitar and fiddle. "Negroes prefer the violin," a diarist noted, adding that they possessed good ears and once they heard a tune it was never forgotten. For much of the century, few plantation owners who loved the guitar or fiddle would demean themselves by playing to accompany dancing. That was work for servants, and any skill on the instruments became a prized asset in black slaves. Newspaper advertisements for runaway slaves sometimes added something like "Shoemaker Jack is fond of the violin and has taken away a new one of which his master lately gave him" or that a fugitive made violins and "could play on them."

The nature of the crop economy from which their wealth came often made it necessary for upper-class colonists to live in rural areas away from concentrations of people, leaving them to improvise their diversions. In many a house, black fiddlers provided music for family parties after supper, to entertain the visitors who brought the outside world nearer and were thus much prized, and for occasional formal balls. Contemporary records and eyewitness accounts are filled with details of impromptu gatherings, balls, and assemblies at which black fiddlers provided music for the latest minuet, cotillion, rigadoon, allemande, or reel imported from England. These musicians often had taught themselves or learned from other blacks, who showed them only the proper position of fingers on strings and left them to their own devices. Others learned the Playford and

Walsh collections' lilting tunes, which continued to be heard by generations of white Southern dancers.

On his death at an advanced age in 1820, Sy Gilliat, the leading member of Richmond's black community, was memorialized in the local press as the "court fiddler" at the Virginia governor's mansion in pre-Revolution days and for decades after as the state's favorite society bandleader. Not all black musicians achieved Gilliat's reputation, but they did influence the course of white music and dance. Playing for dancing in the slave quarters, on rowdy, homemade banjos and fiddles, they created music for the "African jig" that found its way into the mansion house and for a century or more was a white Southerners' dance.

Its black ancestry was sometimes acknowledged, as in this 1877 recollection by a South Carolinian:

> The jig was an African dance and a famous one in old times, before more refined notions began to prevail . . . it was always called for by some of the older ones who had learned the steps and never failed to raise shouts of laughter, with applause for the performers. The fiddle would assume a low monotonous tone, the whole tune running on three or four notes only. . . . The step, if it may be called so, was simply a slow shuffling gait, in front of the fiddler, edging along by some unseen exertion of the feet . . . the feet moved about in the most grotesque manner, stamping, slamming and banging the [sanded] floor, not unlike the pattering of nail on the housetop.

The hornpipe that brought John Durang fame throughout the states had many elements of this jig in it, as did the jig and reel steps that enlivened the disco phenomenon.

## Black Music and Twentieth-Century Country Music

Not all black music makers achieved the place in their own society or the white acceptance of Sy Gilliat, but they did influence the course of popular music among poor whites and made a contribution that created much of what is known today as "country music." As Alan Lomax has noted: "Negro fiddlers played the instrument with great percussive effects, bowing heavily and developing the rough and rhythmic style which one hears among both white and Negro in the south today." That musical cross-fertilization was neither as rapid nor as direct as in eighteenth-century upper-class white Southerners' dance music and song.

The earliest English pioneer families to leave the lower Tidewater were victims of the growth of large plantations made possible by increased dependence on cheap black slave labor. No longer able to compete with big landholders, they moved, from lands claimed for generations, into the backlands of the western Carolinas and northern Georgia. Runaway slaves, black and white, made a similar trek, many of them winning the red man's respect and some being put into places of authority in the tribal structure. Others set up solitary wooden shelters on crags overlooking the green valleys below, and eventually came into contact with poor Carolina whites and roving Scots from Ireland in search of a place where they would wear no man's collar. Beginning in the early 1730s, these devout Presbyterian refugees from ruinous taxation imposed on their woolens and farm produce by an Anglican Tory government trying to placate London entrepreneurs began to pour into middle America at the rate of 6,000 a year. They were joined later by Scots who had supported the young Charles Stuart in his try for the English throne and were now fleeing Hanoverian justice.

The earliest Scottish migrations represented the futility of still another of the solutions to the eternal Irish problem. Early in the seventeenth century, James I drove Ulster Irish rebels off their lands and repopulated the territory with his own people, 60,000 hard-working lowland Scottish farmers and weavers, who produced cloth of a quality that competed favorably in price with London factory-made materials. Responding to protests by their merchant constituents, Parliament imposed an embargo on Ulster cloth and higher rates of taxation on all Ulster produce. Finally the lands were expropriated and the Scottish Ulstermen driven into exile.

William Penn's shrewd public-relations campaign to attract worthwhile settlers to his colony offered Scots a haven and freedom of worship. By the mid-1730s, 12,000 refugees were making their way each year to Pennsylvania, where they claimed land in its fertile western portion. By tradition, the Scots were border people and by nature private persons. When, within a few decades, good Pennsylvania land was running out, they looked south, toward the greenery beyond the Cumberland Gap. This open door to tens of thousands of miles of unpopulated land had been discovered in 1750 and led to the opening of trails to central Kentucky and the Blue Ridge and Alleghenies beyond. Much of this, Daniel Boone and his business associates purchased for £10,000 from Cherokees in 1775. When the Revolution ended, the Scots joined the movement through the Gap into Boone's vast holdings and beyond. With them went an occasional Scottish fiddle and an age-old tradition of vocal ballad music, creating a vast pocket of music in the isolation they found.

In the late nineteenth and early twentieth centuries, a new body of American music emerged, produced by the impingement of black-influenced popular music upon the traditional Celtic "mouth music" and abetted by the availability through mail-order catalogues of instruments new to the inner mountain settlements—the banjo, the Hawaiian guitar, and instruments developed from them. Once the banjo's ringing rhythmic voice was mastered and added to the solitary moan of the fiddle, the last elements of "hillbilly," or country, music were in place. Technology and a rising economy added new instruments and a wider audience.

## Black Music and the Music of a White God

A principal ingredient in introducing American black music to European was British Protestantism's growing concern for the souls of the enslaved. During the previous century, American slaveowners resisted all efforts to baptize their property, arguing that to do so made ownership of a Christian soul a sin in God's eyes. Southerners, particularly, fought mass conversion and the basic education of slaves, maintaining that both tended to diminish their value, reduced productivity, brought about questioning by blacks of their place in the social order, and other dissatisfactions. At the root of this opposition was a general tendency to believe that the black man, being an unteachable and unbaptized barbarian, could not learn or be taught.

During the seventeenth century, there were isolated incidents of blacks being accepted into white worship, principally in New England: the baptism in 1641, two decades after the first black arrived in Plymouth as a bondservant, of a slave woman belonging to the Reverend Stoughton, of Dorcester, and her admission into the congregation as a "well-approved" woman with a "sound knowledge and true Godliness"; and the 1648 Massachusetts requirement that "all masters do once a week cathechize their children and servants in the grounds and principles of religion."

Cotton Mather was among the first Bay colonists to argue that blacks were entitled to a more important presence at God's table. In 1689, he wrote: "their souls, which are as white and good as those of other nations, their souls are not look'd after, but are Destroyed for lack of Knowledge. . . . But are they dull? Then instruct them the rather. This is the way to sharpen them." Five years later, he followed his conscience when a group of poor blacks came to him for ministry and organized the Society of Negroes, to meet early on Sunday evenings in order to obey the curfew. They met to pray, listen to Mather's sermons, and sing psalms, possibly using the newly printed ninth edition of the *Bay Psalm Book,* the first one with printed music. If they did not use a book then, they like other churchgoers, memorized the words and music. The following year, 1695, the Massachusetts legislature was petitioned to enact a law permitting baptism of blacks, but with a statement confirming that baptism did not arbitrarily bring freedom.

Some Boston churches allowed slaves to attend Sabbath Day services when chaperoned by their masters, but segregated them in special sections, just as poor white church members were seated in the building's rear pews. The black section was sometimes marked with a BM, and BW for their women. In 1701, Samuel Sewall, a Boston moneylender and foe of slavery, arranged a church wedding for a slave couple. Twenty years later, such an event was considered newsworthy only because a white man stood for and gave the woman in marriage. The wedding service did, however, include the usual admonition to the nuptial couple that "you remain still, as really and truly as ever, your master's property."

Despite such seeming progress, the ultimate segregation went on. Cemeteries maintained a separate area for baptized blacks, even among the Quakers, whose founder, George Fox, was one of slavery's most outspoken antagonists, espousing preaching of the gospel to people of all colors. Philadelphia's Quakers were the earliest colonists to advocate sharing of worship and religious education with black people, and to consider wholesale manumission and the return of all blacks to Africa.

The first step in the creation of black gospel music was the Church of England's determination to restore backsliding Virginia and Carolina Episcopalians to the fold and to bring the blessings of white Christianity to black and red Americans. The Carolinas had no Anglican churches in 1700, and those in Virginia and Maryland accommodated only half their avowed communicants. The new churches were built and dominated by slaveowners, who felt that their safety depended on total subjugation of their property. They could not accept the bishop of London's pronouncement that black slaves and red Indians must be baptized. With sole jurisdiction over Anglican churches beyond the seas and responsibility for licensing their ministers and schoolmasters, he issued the 1701 order that all missionary work in America would be under direction of the Society for the Propagation of the Gospel. The work of some of the 390 SPG missionaries during the following eighty years was of monumental significance to American blacks.

New York's first Anglican church, New York's Trinity, opened its doors a few years later to the community's blacks when a Huguenot trader, Ellis Neau, offered to instruct such new members in appropriate religious and musical training. Churches in other communities followed, in one degree or another, with similar treatment. But for the first forty years of the work, SPG missionaries were most active among Southern blacks, and had little more success with them than with whites. Slaveowners who could not picture a heaven shared with blacks objected to sharing Communion with their servants.

The fight for black conversion received great impetus from the national purgation following the Great Awakening and Whitefield's evangelism for a revival of the Christian spirit as perceived by the Wesleys. There were many black faces among the crowds flocking to hear the master orator in Boston, New York, and Philadelphia. Blacks became voices of the Lord and were caught up in the mass hysteria that erupted wherever the English cleric spoke.

Many northern blacks, both freedmen and slave, were fifth-generation Americans by the 1750s, with no memory of an African past and no culture other than the American experience in which they were part participant, part spectator. Some possessed an education equal to that of their economic and social white equals, having been taught the necessary basics alongside the children of white families that owned them. Some operated their own businesses, were craftsmen or artisans, and, thinking themselves little different, except in color, from whites with whom they worked and lived, included black slaves among their assets.

Whitefield's message had won converts in England's open fields, where the poor were moved to tears. Now it touched the hearts of both white and black lower-class colonials. They responded to a doctrine that condemned the pleasures—dancing, fox hunting, card playing—of their masters or employers, and found jubilation when Whitefield told them "Jesus loves you." For the first time, northern blacks heard a public declaration in front of white crowds that, as children of God, they, too, were entitled to public conversion, baptism, and the gospel's blessings, although Whitefield never advocated complete abolition of slavery. Buoyed by the message, blacks joined Protestant churches.

Before his death in 1763, Whitefield repeated that message to several generations of black people. The veneration in which he was held by blacks found voice in the pen of the African-born prodigy Phillis Wheatley. Her white Boston owners discovered her genius when she was seven. They helped her to learn to read and write before her own fanatical determination to learn took over. She won international fame when she was seventeen, with the elegiac broadside ballad "On the Death of the Rev. George Whitefield."

Whitefield's insistence on acceptance of blacks into the church, even without a demand for an end to slavery, sat poorly with Southern whites and contributed to evangelical Protestantism's slow progress among them. Many in the South blamed the evangelist for every uprising by discontented blacks, thought therefore to be educated. A 1739 revolt in South Carolina was laid at the door of those who insisted on Negro education, and the 1741 New York conspiracy, hatched in a low-down tavern where blacks and whites mingled to dance to the music of a slave fiddler, was attributed to Whitefield's "rantings."

One long-lived element in Protestantism's appeal to American blacks lay in the coincidental explosion of English hymnody. Men for the first time found an opportunity to sing God's praises in contemporary language that expressed their thoughts and feelings, through the Watts and Wesley brothers' texts. The first successful American edition of Watts's *Hymns and Spirituals* was published during Whitefield's initial American visit and went through twenty editions in as many years. Wesley hymnals did not enjoy any major popularity in the colonies until after the Revolution, when Methodism began its great concerted drive to gain American adherents.

Heartened by signs of changing religious attitudes, clergymen of other dissenting denominations went into the field, encroaching on what was long considered SPG territory. In Virginia, where its efforts had been most effective, only about 1,000 of 150,000 slaves had been baptized. One of the most remarkable of the new young Protestants venturing into the South was Samuel Davies, who arrived in Virginia in 1747. A "New Side" Presbyterian who championed Watts's psalm versions, Davies was among the earliest to introduce the controversial new hymnody to singing black worshipers, who then loved Watts's hymns with great fervency throughout two centuries of dedicated Protestantism. Concern for both the temporal and the spiritual advancement of blacks is manifest in all of Davies's correspondence, as in the following:

> Heaven and earth seem to conspire to afflict me and my fellow-laborers in this remote corner of the world in promoting Christianity among the out-casts of mankind. The large collection of books sent by the Society and other benefactors have been distributed to various parts of the country by my own hands. The spelling books have been a new excitement to the Negroes to learn to read; and many of them are making good progress in it. I can hardly express the pleasure it affords me to turn to that part of the Gallery where they sit, and see so many of them with their Psalms or Hymn books, turning to the part then sung, and assisting their fellows who are beginners, to find the place, and then all breaking out in a torrent of sacred harmony, enough to bear away the whole congregation to Heaven.

In his *Three Centuries of American Hymnody,* Henry Wilder Foote asserts that Davies also used his own hymns in Virginia and that he was "the earliest American native-born writer whose songs had any general acceptance." Several hymns from a manuscript sent by Davies to England two years before his death were published there in the 1769 *Hymns Adapted to Divine Worship*, a book that continued in use until the late nineteenth century.

The victories against great odds described to his financial supporters in the north and in England were not unique. A Cumberland County missionary told of Virginia "slaves at worship in the Lodge, singing Psalms and Hymns in the evenings and again in the morning, long before the break of day. They are excellent singers and long to get some of Dr. Watts' Psalms and Hymns.'' In South Carolina, where SPG people had been preaching the gospel to whites and blacks since 1709, an Anglican reported that after fifty years "the vital part of religion among us at this time seems chiefly to be among them [the blacks]. I am extremely glad of the books, for their sakes, especially with the Bibles, Dr. Watts' Psalms and Hymns and the Compassionate Address. . . . Several of them meet once a week and spend some time in singing, praying and reading of the Bible, or some of those good books.''

The dedication of Southern blacks to a new-found God required even greater fortitude when the thrust of missionary work changed from acceptance of the institution of slavery necessary to gain permission to work among the slaves. The new line was a zealous concern for the right of freedom of the human body. "Contented and joyful, the sooty sons of Africa forgetting their bondage, in chorus sung the virtues and beneficence of their master in songs of their own composition,'' the same missionary wrote, a whisper that the slave song had already made an appearance.

The union of white folkways with a dimming African tradition produced a storehouse of song, functional and emotional at the same time, shaped by the restrictions of the new religion. To set it to the use of the powerful white God, blacks borrowed the melodies of those whose sovereignty they were forced to accept until true music of their own emerged.


The Baptist Invasion

Taking advantage of the opportunity for expansion created by the Great Awakening, the dissenting sect of Baptists, which had emerged early in the century from beneath a century of Puritan repression, began to establish churches in the South. Philadelphia, whose Quakers had shared their abuse and molestation in England, was the major Baptist center at the opening of the century. Now Baptist missionaries moved south to challange the Anglicans' fifty-year monopoly of Southern blacks and their relapsed masters. Baptist field workers spread a new doctrine; they urged baptism by immersion for those adults who had undergone personal religious experiences as the prelude to sharing the Communion of the Lord's Supper. Laying on hands, personally washing converts' feet, rejoicing in love feasts, Baptist preachers manifested their faith to astonished Southerners of all races.

Left the choice offered them by passionate missionaries between formalistic Anglicanism and the Baptist gospel, with its Watts songs, plantation slaves opted for the latter's dramatic and emotionally charged revivalistic ritual. Like them, their neighbors in economic and social oppression, the poor white farmers, also embraced that faith. Another factor was the Baptists' use of "born again" converts to serve as ministers, to which even those uneducated and untrained in theology were admitted, among them, eventually, blacks.

The first of these black Baptist preachers, David George, born in 1742, had run away in his twenties from a Virginia owner to live among South Carolina Indians. After two years, he was sold by them to a plantation owner at Silver Bluff, South Carolina, and underwent immersion by a traveling white Baptist minister. He learned, as many others were doing, to read from the Bible and from Watts. When he felt ready, he gathered together a small group of fellow slaves to form the first black Baptist church in America, exhorting them in worship and teaching them songs.

After the British overran the Carolinas in 1778, George and his flock, grown to almost seventy from the initial eight, went to Savannah, seeking the freedom promised by British authorities in return for service in their army. Many black Baptists and their slave preachers made this trip, among them George Leile. He was the slave of a white Baptist deacon, who had encouraged Leile's call to preach, and so impressed other whites with his work among slaves that he was asked to speak before the white membership at a quarterly meeting and won a probationer's license.

When the British were driven out of Savannah in 1782, George and Leile were among the black families taken along as indentured servants. George went to Nova Scotia, Leile to Jamaica. For a decade, in the face of French Catholic prejudice, the Silver Bluff Baptist preacher ministered to mixed white-and-black congregations. In 1792, he sailed with 1,200 American blacks to settle in Sierra Leone, on Africa's west coast, where British abolitionists had persuaded the government to grant a haven to slave-trade victims. There, George established the first Baptist English-speaking church in Africa and assisted in forming the colony's first government.

George Leile ministered to a Jamaican flock of whites and blacks, baptizing them in the sea and training parents and children to read from the Bible. He never lost contact with the Savannah black church he had started during the British occupation, which now numbered several hundred and was headed by Andrew Bryan, a slave brought to Christ by Leile. Now in his forties, uneducated and unlettered, Bryan had undergone tribulations rivaling those of the Roman martyrs. He was imprisoned twice and publicly beaten before he bought his freedom and moved his Ethiopian Church of Jesus into a plantation barn. Hundreds of free and slave blacks came to be baptised, and as the century neared its end, 700 black Baptists enjoyed the "rights of conscience" under Bryan's guidance in a new edifice built with white support. The group was so large he was required to preach three times each Sunday. When Bryan died in 1812, his congregation had grown so large that it splintered into three branches, each with its own building.

The Baptist church made its greatest inroads between 1776 and 1800, often under licensed black preachers, and when the Louisiana Purchase opened the West, it was a black Baptist from Virginia who preached the first Protestant sermon beyond the Mississippi River, in 1804.

Other denominations were slower to ordain black clergy, the Presbyterians not until 1800, and the newly reorganized Anglicans and Methodist Episcopalians only after black members broke away to form their own churches. There was little in the new American Anglican church music to attract blacks. The revised 1786 *Book of Common Prayer* reflected the musical aesthetic of Frances Hopkinson, one of its compilers, who argued that

> in general, the organ should ever preserve its dignity, and upon no account issue light and pointed movements which may draw the attention of the congregation and induce them to carry home not the serious sentiments which the church services should impress, but some very pretty airs with which the organist hath been so good as to entertain them. It is as offensive to hear lilts and jigs from a church organ, as it would be to see a venerable matron frisking through the public streets with all the fantastic airs of a Columbine.

## The New Wesleyan Methodism

The war effected major changes in Wesleyan Methodism in America. John Wesley had pleaded for colonial loyalty to the crown, and all but one of the English preachers personally selected by him for service in America returned home once the fighting began. The remaining one, Francis Asbury, was most active in the South, where 12,000 Methodists were located in the early 1780s, among them some 3,000 blacks. Throughout his ministry Asbury traveled on horseback, often with a black assistant, as he visited and preached to white and black worshipers and appointed local preachers to carry on the work. As Wesley's only duly ordained representative in America, in 1784 he called sixty preachers to meet in Baltimore to form an Episcopal Methodist church and to appoint superintendents, elders, and deacons. Asbury was elected bishop, and the Wesleyan liturgy, prayer book, and hymnal were adopted. During the deliberations, the conferees, some of whom were black, debated the proposition "How shall we reform our singing," agreeing finally that the printed sheets of a small collection of Wesley's *Psalms and Hymns,* sent with his *Sunday Service for Methodists in North America,* be bound and distributed. Rulings aimed at reform were adopted, urging that "all our preachers who have any true knowledge in the notes, improve it by learning to sing true themselves." Methodists were urged to go only to singing schools operated by fellow adherents, original hymns were banned, and although it was agreed that fugue tunes of the sort William Billings wrote were neither sinful nor improper when used for private entertainment, they were not to be used in congregational singing. This imposition of a majority musical taste on the character of Methodist music, like Hopkinson's dictum and a general insistence on "keeping close to Mr. Wesley's hymns and tunes," flew in the face of a growing taste among both white and black Americans for a more contemporary hymnody. A few years later, it overwhelmed the past in the frontier camp meetings of America's second Great Awakening.

The black participants in the conference readily subscribed to the majority musical judgment. As northerners, living in a white culture whose musical, literary, and religious tastes they accepted, even though they fought against its racial policies, the judgment reflected a world of which they wished to be part. Like them were the two earliest-known black singing-school teachers, both trained by Andrew Law. Little is known of Frank the Negro, who taught "about 40 scholars" in his New York school during the 1780s, except that Law complained his pupil was taking away paying pupils.

Published music by the other, the Rhode Island musician and missionary to Africa Newport Gardner, still exists: of the large number of tunes he composed, the song "Crooked Shanks," which appeared in an 1803 collection, and "Promise," an anthem published in 1826. Gardner received his family name from the merchant who had bought him, a fourteen-year-old boy fresh from Africa, in 1760 from the captain of a sailing ship. The child taught himself to read and write and revealed an early talent for music. Mrs. Gardner was proud of her young slave's accomplishments and encouraged him, paying for studies with Andrew Law when that wandering music teacher passed through Newport. The youth progressed quickly but showed an interest only in religious music. He never did learn to master an instrument, and taught Newport students the rudiments of music and singing using only a pitch pipe and the ivory-headed walking stick sometimes used to rap disobedient pupils on the head.

Gardner was one of the first black men with a still-fresh memory of Africa and a working knowledge of tribal language that the Reverend Samuel Hopkins met in the early 1770s when he accepted a call from the Congregational church. Hopkins believed that trained black missionaries should be sent to Africa to convert the natives, and to that purpose began to train the young music-loving slave. Because of the Revolution, the clergyman never achieved his goal.

Gardner was among the group of Newport blacks who organized the African Union Society in 1780, in order "to refute the objections that have been made against [the city's blacks] as rational and moral characters." The fraternal organization busied itself recording births, marriages, and deaths in the black community, assisted the indigent, and helped young men find work. Using his share of proceeds from a lottery ticket purchased with nine other slaves, Gardner bought his freedom and that of most of his family in 1791 and opened his own singing school.

When Hopkins died in 1803, Gardner organized the Colored Union Church and Society, dedicated to African repatriation. Twenty-two years later, he sailed with sixteen Colored Union members for the new settlement of freed Americans in Liberia. During a farewell party in Boston, he was serenaded, with one of his anthem settings of Bible text, by a chorus of white and black singers. "I go to set an example to the youth of my race; I go to encourage the young," he exclaimed in farewell. "They can never be elevated here: I have tried it for sixty years—it is vain."

Six months after he arrived in Africa, Newport Gardner was dead.

## Richard Allen: Father of Black Hymnody

Within a few years after the Revolution's end, the shining spirit of man's equality, regardless of race or religion, which had played an inspirational role in winning the conflict, was waning, particularly in connection with the place of northern blacks in society. While the excitement surrounding democratic principles still prevailed, abolition laws were passed, usually after pressure from Quaker-organized antislavery groups. Vermont was the first state to bar the institution, in its 1777 Constitution. Pennsylvania, in 1780, and Rhode Island and Connecticut, four years later, followed, with laws promising freedom to the succeeding generation of black children. Court decisions ended slavery in Massachusetts by the early 1780s, and, after considerable argumentation, slavery was forbidden after 1787 in the Northwest Territory, formed out of lands ceded by New York and Virginia that eventually became the states of Ohio, Illinois, Indiana, Michigan, Wisconsin, and part of Minnesota. The dream of immediate manumission in the South died quickly. Jefferson mourned its passing in 1805, when he wrote, "I have long since given up the expectation of any early provision for the extinguishment of slavery among us."

Even as antislavery laws were enacted in the north, deliberate racial separation was growing there, often initiated by blacks themselves in response to white actions. Americans were preoccupied with financial recovery from the most recent depression and an argument over reorganization of the national government when a new kind of separation of the races appeared in the church.

In later life, the black minister Richard Allen recalled that significant day in 1787 when a separatist movement started after his white fellow Methodists let him know that blacks were not their equals, at least in Philadelphia, and cast them out of the Fourth Street Methodist Episcopal Church.

Born a slave, in 1750, Allen was the property of Philadelphia's wealthy Chew family and was converted to Christianity at the age of seventeen, after joining the Methodist Society, which met in the woods at night near the Delaware farm to which he had been sold. With his brother, Allen bought freedom from a "good master" by paying about 2,000 continental dollars, or 60 pounds in hard cash, money raised by cutting cordwood and making bricks. Once free, he bought a wagon to haul salt and began wandering around the countryside, exhorting on Sundays and at night. The blacks he confronted had never heard such preaching before, and quickly accepted him as a chosen man of God.

He was one of the few blacks present at the Baltimore conference, where he attracted Bishop Asbury's attention and was offered a post as traveling assistant in the slave states. The twenty-five-year-old black preacher aspired to other things and refused the offer. He continued, without orders or authority, as an unordained Methodist cleric until February 1786, when the elders of St. George's, in Philadelphia, hired him to preach the first and last Sunday services, at 5:00 A.M. and 5:00 P.M. Allen learned that many of the city's blacks felt rejected by the white congregation, and he began to work among his own people exclusively, preaching four or five times a day, establishing prayer meetings, and raising a group of forty-two, who joined the church in a body.

Northern white Methodist clergymen were, like their Anglican and Presbyterian brothers-in-Christ, quite different from those in the South. As an unknown nineteenth-century black preacher wrote:

> While the good Presbyterian parson was writing his discourse, rounding off the sentence, the [southern] Methodist itinerant had traveled forty miles with his horse and saddle bags; while the parson was adjusting his spectacles to read his manuscript, the itinerant had given hell and damnation to his unrepentant hearers; while the disciple of Calvin was waiting to have his church completed, the disciple of Wesley took to the woods, and made them re-echo with the voice of free-grace, believing "The groves were God's first temples."

Unlike his white superiors in Philadelphia, Allen was of the Southern itinerant stripe. His black converts provided the money needed to finish St. George's gallery and laid a new floor. With free black parishioner Absalom Jones, Allen accepted Quaker funding to organize the cooperative Free African Society of Philadelphia. Shortly after, the St. George's congregation cast its black members out of the church.

The Free African Society launched a crusade for an all-black church, beginning in a store. It soon bogged down over which doctrine to accept, with which sect to affiliate. In August 1791, $360 was raised, and work began on a new building, one block away from the city jail. As construction went on, a denominational split grew, and the majority voted to join the Protestant Episcopal Church, with Absalom Jones as a pastor. Allen remained true to Methodism, the first people or denomination, he said, that "brought glad tidings to colored people."

Work went slowly on the church, interrupted by the epidemic of yellow fever that killed one-tenth of the city's inhabitants. During the disaster, Allen and Jones worked side by side to nurse the ill and bury the dead. In gratitude, wealthy Philadelphians contributed to the blacks' building funds.

Allen had built up a profitable shoemaking and repairing business, employing journeymen and apprentices, and when a group of Methodist-inclined blacks came to him for guidance, he bought an old building once housing a blacksmith shop, moved it to the lot he had purchased for the purpose, and began to make it fit for worship. In July 1794, Bishop Asbury held a ceremony in the completed house, called "Bethel," the first African Methodist Episcopal church in Philadelphia, the first independent black church in America. During the same summer, Jones's St. Thomas African Episcopal Church was also dedicated, and ten years later, Jones became the first ordained black Episcopalian preacher in the United States.

Emboldened by the Philadelphia black community's success, those in other cities instituted similar activities. In New York, black Methodists moved in 1799 from the white-dominated John Street Church to their own African Methodist Episcopal church, called "Zion." Their leader was Peter Williams, a cigar maker who had learned the trade as a slave and bought freedom with his savings and extra income earned as the John Street sexton. Later, other black Methodist churches were formed in South Carolina, Maryland, Delaware, Pennsylvania,

New York, and New Jersey, and by 1820 there were more blacks than whites in the denomination. A general conference held in Baltimore in 1818 elected Richard Allen bishop of the national AME Church Bethel. A second national black church, springing out of a New York schism, the AME Zion was organized four years later.

They were completely segregated from white Wesleyans, but black Methodists continued to use Wesley's *Psalms and Hymns* until Bishop Allen completed the compilation of a hymnal for his Philadelphia flock. Two editions appeared in 1801 of the first *Collection of Spiritual Songs,* selected by Allen from various authors. Fifty-four verses, without musical notation, were included, to which ten were added for the second edition. The hymns included verses by Watts, Charles Wesley, John Newton, the American Indian hymnist Samuel Occom, Augustus Toplady, and other British writers, as well as some believed to be by Allen himself. As a participant in American Methodism's first organizational meeting, Allen had subscribed to musical principles that influenced his collection, the two volumes showing a heavy reliance on Watts and Wesley, their innovations and followers.

A prominent nineteenth-century white clergyman wrote that Methodists were the most "spirited and attractive" of all singing Protestants, "always of such popular cast and spirit as would easiest please the ear and enchain the attention; and it well succeeded with all those who were unsophisticated." They had "a quicker and more animated style of singing all times than prevailed in the slower cadences of other churches." The most "stirring and attractive" of them all, according to foreign visitors and white Americans who came to hear their worship, were the black Methodists and Baptists.

# Bibliography

## General

Barck, Oscar T., and Hugh T. Lefler. *Colonial America*. New York: Macmillan, 1958.

Batterbery, Michael and Ariane. *On the Town in New York: A History of the Eating, Drinking and Entertainment from 1776 to the Present*. New York: Scribner, 1973.

Blom, Eric. *Music in England*. Baltimore: Penguin Books, 1942.

Boorstin, Daniel J. *The Americans: The Colonial Experience*. New York: Random House, 1958.

Boyd, Morrison Comegys. *Elizabethan Music and Musical Criticism*. Philadelphia: University of Pennsylvania Press, 1962.

Bridenbaugh, Carl. *Cities in Revolt: Urban Life in America 1743–1776*. New York: Oxford University Press, 1971.

———. *Cities in the Wilderness: The First Century of Urban Life in America, 1625–1742*. New York: Oxford University Press, 1966.

———. *Vexed and Troubled Englishmen*. New York: Oxford University Press, 1967.

Brooke, Iris. *Pleasures of the Past*. London: Odhams Press, 1955.

Burney, Charles. *A General History of Music*. 2 vols. London: G. T. Foulis, 1935.

Bush, Douglas. *English Literature in the Earlier Seventeenth Century, 1600–1660*. New York: Oxford University Press, 1945.

Camus, Raoul F. *Military Music of the American Revolution*. Chapel Hill: University of North Carolina Press, 1976.

Carson, Gerald. *The Polite Americans: 300 Years of More or Less Good Behaviour*. New York: Macmillan, 1966.

Chase, Gilbert. *America's Music*. New York: McGraw-Hill, 1955.

Crewdson, H. A. F. *The Worshipful Company of Musicians*. London: Constable, 1950.

Demos, John. *Remarkable Providences*. New York: Braziller, 1970.

*Dictionary of National Biography*. Edited by Leslie Stephen and Sidney Lee. 21 vols. with suppl. London: Oxford University Press.

Dolan, J. R. *The Yankee Peddlers of Early America*. New York: Clarkson N. Potter, 1965.

Dulles, Foster Rhea. *A History of Recreation: America Learns to Play*. New York: Appleton-Century-Crofts, 1965.

Duncan, Edmondstoune. *The Story of Minstrelsy.* New York: Scribner, 1907.

Durant, Will. *The Age of Faith.* New York: Simon & Schuster, 1950.

———. *The Reformation.* New York: Simon & Schuster, 1957.

———. *The Renaissance.* New York: Simon & Schuster, 1953.

Durant, Will and Ariel. *The Age of Louis XIV.* New York: Simon & Schuster, 1963.

———. *The Age of Napoleon.* New York: Simon & Schuster, 1975.

———. *The Age of Reason Begins.* New York: Simon & Schuster, 1961.

———. *The Age of Voltaire.* New York: Simon & Schuster, 1965.

———. *Rousseau and the Revolution.* New York: Simon & Schuster, 1967.

Emmerson, George S. *A Social History of Scottish Dance and Celestial Recreation.* Montreal: McGill-Queens University, 1972.

Evans, Tom and Mary. *Guitars—from the Renaissance to Rock.* New York: Paddington Press, 1977.

Farmer, Henry George. *A History of Music in Scotland.* New York: Da Capo Press, 1970. Reprint of 1947 Hinrichsen, London, ed.

Franks, A. H. *Social Dance: A Short History.* London: Routledge & Kegan Paul, 1963.

Furnas, J. C. *The Americans: A Social History of the United States.* New York: Putnam, 1969.

Garraty, John A. *The American Nation.* New York: Harper & Row, 1971.

George, Dorothy M. *London Life in the Eighteenth Century.* New York: Capricorn Books, 1965.

Grattan-Flood, W. H. *A History of Irish Music.* Dublin: Brown & Nolan, 1913.

*Grove's Dictionary of Music and Musicians.* Edited by Waldo Selden Pratt. 6 vols. New York: Macmillan, 1928.

Grunfeld, Fred. *The Art and Times of the Guitar: An Illustrated History of Guitars and Guitarists.* New York: Collier Books, 1959.

Harley, John. *Music in Purcell's London: The Social Background.* London: Dennis Dobson, 1968.

Hitchcock, H. Wiley. *Music in the United States.* Englewood Cliffs, NJ: Prentice-Hall, 1969.

Hixon, Donald L. *Music in Early America: A Bibliography of Music in Evans.* Metuchen, NJ: Scarecrow Press, 1970.

Hodstadter, Richard. *America at 1750: A Social Portrait.* London: Jonathan Cape, 1972.

Hogarth, George. *Musical History: Biography and Criticism.* New York: Da Capo Press, 1964. Reprint of 1848 ed.

Hogwood, Christopher. *Music at Court.* London: The Folio Society, 1977.

Hoover, Cynthia A. *Harpsichords and Clavichords.* Washington, D.C.: Smithsonian Institution Press, 1966.

Howard, John Tasker. *Our American Music. Three Hundred Years of It.* New York: Crowell, 1954.

Kraus, Michael. *The Atlantic Civilization: Eighteenth-Century Origins.* Ithaca, NY: Cornell University Press, 1966.

Lane, Margaret. *Samuel Johnson and His World.* New York: Harper & Row, 1975.

Lang, Paul Henry. *Music in Western Civilization.* New York: Norton, 1941.

Legman, Gershon. *The Horn Book.* New Hyde Park, NY: University Books, 1964.

Lloyd, A. L. *Folk Song in England.* New York: International Publishers, 1967.

Loesser, Arthur. *Men, Women and Pianos: A Social History.* New York: Simon & Schuster, 1954.

McCue, George, ed. *Music in American Society, 1776–1976: From Puritan Hymn to Synthesizer.* New Brunswick, NJ: Transaction Books, 1977.

Mackerness, E. D. *A Social History of English Music*. London: Routledge & Kegan Paul, 1964.

Marrocco, W. Thomas, and Harold Gleason. *Music in America: An Anthology from the Landing of the Pilgrims to the Close of the Civil War*. New York: Norton, 1964.

Marzio, Peter, ed. *A Nation of Nations: The People Who Came to America as Seen Through Objects, Prints and Photographs at the Smithsonian Institution*. New York: Harper & Row, 1976.

Morison, Samuel Eliot. *The Intellectual Life of New England*. New York: New York University Press, 1933.

Nettel, Reginald. *The Englishman Makes Music*. London: Dennis Dobson, 1952.

———. *Seven Centuries of Popular Song: A Social History of Urban Ditties*. London: Phoenix House, 1956.

———. *Sing a Song of England: A Social History of Traditional Song*. London: Phoenix House, 1954.

Nevell, Richard. *A Time to Dance: American Country Dancing from Hornpipes to Hot Hash*. New York: St. Martin's Press, 1978.

Newburg, Victor. *The Penny Histories*. New York: Harcourt, Brace & World, 1968.

———. *Popular Literature: A History and Guide*. London: Woburn Press, 1977.

North, Roger. *Roger North on Music: Being a Selection of His Essays Written During the Years 1695–1728*. London: Novello, 1959.

Notestein, Wallace. *The English People on the Eve of Colonization*. New York: Harper Torchbooks, 1954.

Nye, Russell Blaine. *The Cultural Life of the New Nation, 1776–1830*. New York: Harper Torchbooks, Harper & Row, 1963.

Orde-Hume, Arthur W. J. G. *Clockwork Music. An Illustrated History of Mechanical Musical Instruments from the Musical Box to the Pianola; from the Automaton Lady Virginals Players to the Orchestrion*. New York: Crown, 1973.

Parker, John Rowe. *A Musical Biography*. Detroit: Information Coordinators, 1975. Reprint of 1825 ed.

Rayner, Henry. *A Social History of Music: From the Middle Ages to Beethoven*. New York: Schocken Books, 1972.

Richards, Maurice. *The Public Notice*. New York: Clarkson N. Potter, 1973.

Roche, Jerome. *The Madrigal*. New York: Scribner, 1972.

Roche, T. W. E. *The Golden Hind*. New York: Praeger, 1973.

Rourke, Constance. *American Humor: A Study of the National Character*. Garden City, NY: Doubleday, 1953.

———. *The Roots of American Culture*. New York: Harcourt, Brace, 1942.

Sachs, Curt. *A History of Musical Instruments*. New York: Norton, 1940.

Sampson, George. *Concise Cambridge History of English Literature*. New York: Macmillan, 1941.

Sands, Mollie. *Invitation to Ranelagh 1742–1803*. London: John Westhouse, 1946.

Scholes, Percy A. *The Puritans and Music in New England*. New York: Oxford University Press, 1934.

Silverman, Kenneth. *The Cultural History of the American Revolution*. New York: Crowell, 1976.

Singleton, Esther. *Social New York Under the Georges, 1717–1776*. New York: Ira Friedman, 1969. Reprint of 1902 ed.

Sonneck, O. G. *Early Concert Life in America, 1731–1800*. Leipzig: Breitkopf & Haertel, 1907.

————. *Report on The Star Spangled Banner, Hail Columbia, America and Yankee Doodle*. New York: Dover, 1972. Reprint of 1909 ed.

Spillane, Daniel. *History of the American Pianoforte*. New York: Spillane, 1890.

Spink, Ian. *English Song from Dowland to Purcell*. New York: Scribner, 1974.

Warwick, Alan R. *A Noise of Music: The Music of London 1422 to the Present*. London: Queen Anne Press, 1968.

Wertenbaker, Thomas J. *The Golden Age of Colonial Culture*. New York: New York University Press, 1949.

Wood, Gordon, S. *The Rising Glory, 1760–1820*. New York: Braziller, 1970.

Woodfill, Walter L. *Musicians in English Society from Elizabeth to Charles I*. Princeton: Princeton Unviersity Press, 1953.

Woodward, W. E. *The Way Our People Lived: An Intimate American History*. New York: Dutton, 1944.

Wright, Louis B. *The Cultural Life of the American Colonies, 1607–1763*. New York: Harper, 1957.

————. *Everyday Life in the New Nation*. New York: Putnam, 1972.

————. *Middle-Class Culture in Elizabethan England*. Ithaca, NY: Cornell University Press, 1958.

Wright, Richardson. *American Wags and Eccentrics: From Colonial Times to the Civil War*. New York: Frederick Unger, 1939.

————. *Hawkers and Walkers in Early America*. New York: Lippincott, 1927.


## Black Americans' Music

Bennett, Lerone, Jr. *Before the Mayflower: A History of the Negro in America, 1619–1964*. Baltimore: Penguin Books, 1966.

Botkin, B. A. *Lay My Burden Down: A Folk History of Slavery*. Chicago: University of Chicago Press, 1945.

Brawley, Benjamin. *A Social History of the American Negro*. New York: Collier Books, 1970.

Bridenbaugh, Carl. *Myths and Realities: Societies of the Colonial South*. New York: Atheneum, 1963.

Butcher, Margaret Just. *The Negro in American Culture, Based on Materials Left by Alain Locke*. New York: Knopf, 1956.

Courlander, Harold. *Negro Folk Music USA*. New York: Columbia University Press, 1963.

Cuney-Hare, Maude. *Negro Musicians and Their Music*. Washington, D.C.: Associated Publishers, 1936.

Curtin, Philip D., ed. *Africa Remembered: Narratives by West Africans from the Era of the Slave Trade*. Madison, WI: University of Wisconsin Press, 1969.

Dalby, David. *Black Through White: Patterns of Communication in Africa and the New World*. Bloomington: Indiana University African Studies Program, 1971.

Davidson, Basil. *The African Genius*. Boston: Little, Brown, 1969.

Dillard, J. L. *Black English: Its History and Usage in the United States*. New York: Random House, 1972.

Dowd, Jerome. *The Negro in American Life*. Chicago: Century, 1926.

Epstein, Dena J. "The Folk Banjo: A Documentary History." *Ethnomusicology*, 19, September 1975.

————. *Sinful Songs and Spirituals: Black Folk Music to the Civil War*. Urbana: University of Illinois Press, 1977.

Gaines, Francis Pendleton. *The Southern Plantation: A Study in the Development and the Accuracy of a Tradition.* New York: Columbia University Press, 1924.

Genovese, Eugene D. *Roll, Jordan, Roll: The World the Slaves Made.* New York: Pantheon Books, 1974.

Grissom, Mary Ellen. *The Negro Sings a New Heaven:* New York: *Dover, 1969. Reprint of 1930 ed.*

Gutman, Herbert G. *The Black Family in Slavery and Freedom, 1750–1925.* New York: Pantheon Books, 1976.

Kaplan, Sidney. *The Black Presence in the Era of the Revolution, 1770–1800.* New York: New York Graphic Society, 1973.

Katz, Bernard, ed. *The Social Implications of Early Negro Music in the United States.* New York: Arno Press, 1969.

Levine, Lawrence W. *Black Culture and Black Consciousness: Afro-American Folk Thought from Slavery to Freedom.* New York: Oxford University Press, 1977.

Lomax, Alan. *Folk Songs of North America.* Garden City, NY: Doubleday, 1960.

Lovell, John, Jr. *Black Song: The Forge and the Flame. The Story of How the Afro-American Spiritual Was Hammered Out.* New York: Macmillan, 1972.

Murdock, George Peter. *Africa: Its Peoples and Their Culture.* New York: McGraw-Hill, 1959.

Ottley, Roi, and William J. Weatherby, ed. *The Negro in New York: An Informal Social History.* New York: New York Public Library, 1967.

Roberts, John Storm. *Black Music of Two Worlds.* New York: Morrow, 1972.

Southern, Eileen, *The Music of Black Americans.* New York: Norton, 1971.

————, ed. *Readings in Black American Music.* New York: Norton, 1971.

Tannenbaum, Frank. *Slave and Citizen: The Negro in America.* New York: Knopf, 1947.

Walker, Wyatt Tee. *Somebody's Calling My Name: Black Sacred Music and Social Change.* Valley Forge, PA: Judson Press, 1979.

## British Music Publishing

*Amaryllis: Consisting of Such Songs as Are Most Esteemed for Composition and Delicacy and Sung at the Publick Theatres or Gardens.* New York: Benjamin Blom, 1968. Reprint of 1778 ed.

Ball, Johnson. *William Caslon, Master of Letters.* Warwick: Roundwood Press, 1973.

Bickman, George, engraver. *The Musical Entertainer.* London: Harrap, n.d. Facsimile of 1757 ed.

Blagden, Cyprian. "Notes on the Ballad Market in the Second Half of the 17th Century," *Studies in Bibliography,* Vol. 6. 1954.

————. *The Stationers' Company: A History, 1405–1959.* Stanford: Stanford University Press, 1977.

Blagden, Cyprian, and Norma Hodgson. *Notebooks of Thomas Bennet and Henry Clement: With Some Aspects of the Book Trade, 1686–1717.* New York: Oxford University Press, 1956.

Day, Cyrus Lawrence, ed. *The Songs of Thomas D'Urfey.* Cambridge, MA: Harvard University Press, 1933.

Day, Cyrus Lawrence, and Eleanore Boswell Murrie. *English Song Books 1651–1702.* London: The Bibliographical Society, 1937–1940.

————. "English Song Books and Their Publishers 1651–1702." *The Library,* March 1936.

D'Urfey, Thomas. *Wit and Mirth: Or Pills to Purge Melancholy.* 6 vols. Facsimile ed. New York: Folklore Library, 1959.

Evans, Willa McLung. *Henry Lawes, Musician and Friend of Poets.* New York: Oxford University Press, 1941.

Fellowes, Edmund H. *William Byrd.* New York: Oxford University Press, 1936.

Fraenkel, Gottfried S. *Decorative Title Pages: 201 Examples from 1500 to 1800.* New York: Dover, 1968.

Gamble, William. *Music Engraving and Printing.* New York: Da Capo Press, 1971. Reprint of 1923 ed.

Greg, W. W. *Some Aspects and Problems of London Publishing Between 1550 and 1650.* New York: Oxford University Press, 1956.

Handover, P. M. *Printing in London from 1476 to Modern Times.* Cambridge, MA: Harvard University Press, 1960.

Harris, Charles. *Islington.* London: Hamish Hamilton, 1975.

Hind, Arthur M. *A History of Engraving and Etching from the Fifteenth Century to the Year 1914.* Boston: Houghton Mifflin, 1923.

Hindley, Charles. *Curiosities of Street Literature.* New York: Augustus Kelley, 1970. Reprint of 1871 ed.

———. *The History of the Catnach Press.* London: Hindley, 1887.

———. *The Life and Times of James Catnach, Ballad Monger.* London: Reeves and Turner, 1878.

Humphries, Charles, and William C. Smith. *Music Publishing in the British Isles from the Beginning until the Middle of the Nineteenth Century.* London: Cassell, 1954.

Kidson, Frank. *British Music Publishers, Printers and Engravers.* New York: Benjamin Blom, 1967. Reprint of 1900 ed.

———. "Handel's Publisher, John Walsh, His Successors and Contemporaries." *Musical Quarterly,* July 1920.

———. "John Playford and Seventeenth Century Music Publishing." *Musical Quarterly,* October 1918.

King, A. Hyatt. *Four Hundred Years of Music Publishing.* London: British Museum, 1964.

Krummel, D. W. *English Music Printing 1553–1700.* London: The Bibliographical Society, 1975.

———. "Graphic Analysis: Its Application to Early American Engraved Music." *Notes* 2, 1959.

Lawrence, Vera Brodsky. *Music for Patriots, Politicians and Presidents: Harmonies and Discords of the First 100 Years.* New York: Macmillan, 1975.

Painter, George D. *William Caxton.* New York: Putnam, 1977.

Pattison, Bruce. "Notes on Early Music Publishing." *The Library,* March 1938.

Pinkus, Phillip. *Grub Street Stripped Bare.* Hampden, CT: Archon Books, 1968.

Ravenscroft, Thomas. *Pammelia, Deutormelia, Melismata.* Philadelphia: American Folklore Society, 1961. Reprint of 1609, 1611 eds.

Robinson, Clement, and Divers Others. *A Handful of Pleasant Delights.* Edited by Hyder E. Rollins. New York: Dover, 1965. Reprint of 1584 ed.

Rollins, Hyder Edward. *An Analytical Index to the Ballad Entries (1557–1709) in the Registers of the Company of Stationers of London.* Chapel Hill: University of North Carolina Press, 1924.

———. "Martin Parker, Ballad Monger." *Modern Philology,* January 1919.

———. "William Elderton, Elizabethan Actor and Ballad Writer." *Studies in Philology* 17, 1920.

Rollins, Hyder Edward, ed. *Tottel's Miscellany 1557–1587.* 2 vols. Cambridge, MA: Harvard University Press, 1929.

Sharp, Cecil. *One Hundred English Folk Songs,* New York: Dover, 1975. Reprint of 1916 Ditson ed.

Shepard, Leslie. *A History of Street Literature: The Story of Broadside Ballads, Chapbooks, Proclamations, News-sheets, Election Bills, Tracts, Pamphlets, Cocks, Catchpennies and Other Ephemera.* Detroit: Singing Tree Press, 1973.

———. *John Pitts, Ballard Printer of Seven Dials, London 1765–1844: With a Short Account of His Predecessors in the Ballad and Chapbook Trade.* Detroit: Singing Tree Press, 1969.

Smith, William C. *A Bibliography of the Musical Works Published by John Walsh during the Years 1695–1720.* New York: Oxford University Press, 1948.

———. "John Walsh, Music Publisher: The First Twenty-Five Years." *The Library,* June 1946.

———. "John Walsh and His Successors." *The Library,* March 1949.

Steele, Robert. *The Earliest English Music Printing: A Description and Bibliography of English Printed Music to the End of the Sixteenth Century.* London: London Bibliographical Society, 1903. Reprint.

Weiss, Harry B. *A Book About Chapbooks.* Trenton: Harry B. Weiss, 1942.

## British Theater Music Before the Stuarts

Albright, Evelyn May. *Dramatic Publication in England 1580–1650.* New York: Gordian Press, 1971.

Altick, Richard. *The Shows of London.* Cambridge, MA: Harvard University Press, 1978.

Baskerville, Charles Head. *The Elizabethan Jig and Related Song Drama.* Chicago: University of Chicago Press, 1929.

Bell, Robert, ed. *Songs from the Dramatists.* New York: Dodd, Mead, n.d.

Boas, Frederick S., ed. *Songs and Lyrics from the English Masques and Light Operas.* London: Harrap, 1949.

Boulton, William B. *The Amusement of Old London. Being a Survey of the Sports and Pastimes, Tea Gardens and Parks, Playhouses and Other Diversions of the People of London.* New York: Benjamin Blom, 1969. Reprint of 1901 ed.

Bush, Douglas. *The Earlier Seventeenth Century.* Oxford History of English Literature. Oxford: Oxford University Press, 1924.

Chambers, Edmund K. *The Elizabethan Stage.* New York: Oxford University Press, 1923.

Chute, Marchette. *Ben Jonson of Westminster.* New York: Dutton, 1960.

———. *Shakespeare of London.* New York: Dutton, 1949.

Clunes, Alec. *The British Theatre.* London: Cassell, 1964.

Cowling, G. H. *Music on the Shakespearian Stage.* Cambridge: Cambridge University Press, 1913.

Evans, William McClung. *Ben Jonson and Elizabethan Music.* New York: Da Capo Press, 1965.

Hartnoll, Phyllis. *The Oxford Companion to the Theatre.* New York: Oxford University Press, 1951.

Lawrence. W. J. "Music in the Elizabethan Theatre." *Musical Quarterly,* July 1920.

———. *Pre-Restortion Stage Studies.* Cambridge, MA: Harvard University Press, 1927.

Lewis, C. S. *English Literature: The Sixteenth Century.* Oxford History of English Literature. Oxford: Oxford University Press, 1954.

Long, John H. *Shakespeare's Use of Music: The Final Comedies*. Gainesville: University of Florida Press, 1961.

———. *Shakespeare's Use of Music: A Study of the Music and Its Performance in the Original Production of Seven Comedies*. Gainesville: University of Florida Press, 1955.

———. *Shakespeare's Use of Music: The Tragedies*. Gainesville: University of Florida Press, 1971.

McKechnie, Samuel. *Popular Entertainment Through the Ages*. New York: Frederick Stokes, 1931.

Mellers, Wilfrid. *Harmonious Meetings: A Study of the Relationships Between English Music, Poetry and Theatre*. London: Dennis Dobson, 1965.

Noyes, Robert Gale. *Ben Jonson on the English Stage, 1660–1776*. New York: Benjamin Blom, 1969. Reprint of Harvard University Press 1935 ed.

Partridge, Eric. *Shakespeare's Bawdy*. New York: Dutton, 1960.

Pearsall, Derek. *John Lydgate*. London: Routledge & Kegan Paul, 1970.

Pollard, Alfred W. *Shakespeare's Fight with the Pirates and the Problems of Transmission of His Text*. Cambridge: Cambridge University Press, 1920.

Smith, Irwin. *Shakespeare's Blackfriars Playhouse: Its History and Design*. New York: New York University Press, 1964.

Wallace, Charles William. *The Evolution of the English Drama Up to Shakespeare*. Port Washington, NY: Kennikat Press. Reprint of 1912 ed.

———. *Pre-Restoration Stage Studies*. Cambridge, MA: Harvard University Press, 1927.

Wilson, F. P. *The English Drama, 1485–1585*. Oxford History of English Literature. Oxford: Oxford University Press, 1969.

## British Theater Music After the Restoration

Allen, Ned Bliss. *The Sources of John Dryden's Comedies*. Ann Arbor: University of Michigan Press, 1973.

Avery, Emmett L. *The London Stage 1660–1700: A Critical Introduction*. Carbondale: Southern Illinois University Press, 1968.

Boas, Frederick S. *Songs and Lyrics from the English Playbooks*. London: Cresset Press, 1965.

Cibber, Colley. *An Apology for the Life of Colley Cibber*. Edited by B. R. S. Fone. Ann Arbor: University of Michigan Press, 1968.

Clinton-Baddeley, V. C. *The Burlesque Tradition in the English Theatre After 1660*. London: Methuen, 1952.

Dent, Edward J. *Foundations of English Opera: A Study of Drama in England During the Seventeenth Century*. New York: Da Capo Press. Reprint of 1928 Oxford ed.

Deutsch, Otto Erich. *Handel: A Documentary Biography*. New York: Norton, 1955.

Fiske, Roger. *English Theatre Music in the Eighteenth Century*. New York: Oxford University Press, 1973.

Gagey, Edmond M. *Ballad Opera*. New York: Benjamin Blom, 1968. Reprint.

Gay, John. *The Beggar's Opera*. New York: Dover, 1973. Reprint of 1922 ed.

———. *The Beggar's Opera*. Edited by Peter Lewis. New York: Harper & Row, 1973.

Greene, Graham. *Lord Rochester's Monkey*. New York: Viking, 1974.

Heriot, Angus. *The Castrati in Opera*. London: Martin Secker, 1966.

Highfill, Philip H., Jr., Kalman A. Barnim and Edward A. Langhans. *A Biographical Dictionary of Actors, Actresses, Musicians, Dancers, Managers and other Stage Personnel in London 1660–1800*. Vols. 5, 6. Carbondale: Southern Illinois University Press, 1978.

Kidson, Frank. *The Beggar's Opera.* Cambridge: Cambridge University Press, 1922.

Landon, H. C. Robbins. Liner notes for London Records' complete edition of Haydn's symphonies. HN48.

McQueen-Pope, W. *The Haymarket: Theatre of Perfection.* London: W. H. Allen, 1948.

———. *Theatre Royal, Drury Lane.* London: W. H. Allen, 1951.

Mander, Raymond, and Joe Mitchenson. *Pantomime.* New York: Taplinger, 1973.

———. *The Theatres of London.* New York: Hill and Wang, 1975.

Nettleton, George Henry. *English Drama of the Restoration and Eighteenth Century, 1642–1780.* New Haven, CT: Yale University Press, 1913.

Nicoll, Allardyce. *A History of Early Eighteenth Century Drama, 1700–1750.* Cambridge: Cambridge University Press, 1929.

———. *A History of English Drama, 1750–1800.* Cambridge: Cambridge University Press, 1952.

———. *A History of Restoration Drama, 1660–1700.* Cambridge: Cambridge University Press, 1940.

O'Keeffe, John. *Recollections of the Life of John O'Keeffe.* New York: Benjamin Blom, 1969. Reprint of 1826 ed.

Oman, Carola. *David Garrick.* London: Hodder and Staughton, 1958.

Pearce, Charles E. *Polly Peacham: The Story of Lavinia Fenton and the Beggar's Opera.* New York: Benjamin Blom, 1968. Reprint of 1913 ed.

Sheldon, Esther K. *Thomas Sheridan of Smock-Alley.* Princeton: Princeton University Press, 1967.

Stead, Phillip John, ed. *Songs of the Restoration Theatre: Edited from the Printed Books of the Time.* London: Methuen, 1948.

Sutherland, J. R. *English Literature of the Late Seventeenth Century.* Oxford: Oxford University Press, 1969.

Thorp, Willard, ed. *Songs from the Restoration Theatre.* Princeton: Princeton University Press, 1934.

Wardroper, John, ed. *Love and Drollery: A Selection of Amatory, Merry and Satirical Verse of the Seventeenth Century.* New York: Barnes & Noble, 1969.

Wiley, Autrey Nell, ed. *Rare Prologues and Epilogues.* Port Washington, NY: Kennikat Press, 1970. Reprint of 1940 ed.

Williams, C. F. Abdy. *Handel.* London: Dent, 1901.

Wilson, John Harold. *All the King's Ladies: Actresses of the Restoration.* Chicago: University of Chicago Press, 1959.

## Circus History

Chindall, George L. *A Story of the Circus in America.* Caldwell, ID: Caxton Printers, 1959.

Fried, Frederick. *Artists in Wood: American Carvers of Cigar Store Indians, Show Figures and Circus Wagons.* New York: Bramhall House, 1970.

Greenwood, Isaac J. *The Circus: Its Origins and Growth Prior to 1835.* Washington, D.C.: Hobby House Press, 1962. Reprint of 1898 ed.

Wykes, Alan. *Circus: An Investigation into What Makes the Sawdust Fly.* London: Jupiter Books, 1977.

## Copyright

Birrell, Augustine. *Seven Lectures on the Law and History of Copyright in Books.* London: Cassell, 1899. Reprint: New York: Augustus M. Kelley, 1971.

Clyde, William M. *The Struggle for Freedom of the Press from Caxton to Cromwell.* New York: Oxford University Press, 1934.

Collins, Arthur Simon. *Some Aspects of Copyright from 1700 to 1780.* New York: Oxford University Press, 1925.

Copyright Office. *Copyright Enactments: Laws Passed in the United States Since 1783 Relating to Copyright.* Washington, D.C.: Copyright Office, Library of Congress, 1978.

Frank, Joseph. *The Beginnings of the English Newspaper.* Cambridge, MA: Harvard University Press, 1962.

Greg, W. W. *Some Aspects and Problems of London Publishing Between 1550 and 1650.* New York: Oxford University Press, 1956.

Johnson, John, and Strickland Gibson. *Print and Privilege at Oxford to the Year 1700.* Oxford: Clarendon Press and Oxford Bibliographical Society, 1946.

Morgan, John S. *Noah Webster.* New York: Mason/Charter 1975.

Morris, Thomas B. "The Origins of the Statute of Anne." *Copyright Law Symposium (ASCAP).* Vol. 12. New York: ASCAP, 1936.

Peterson, Lyman Ray. *Copyright in Historical Perspective.* Nashville: Vanderbilt University Press, 1968.

Ransom, Harry W. *The First Copyright Statute: An Essay on an Act for the Encouragement of Learning, 1710.* Austin: University of Texas Press, 1956.

Warfel, Harry R. *Noah Webster, Schoolmaster to America.* New York: Macmillan, 1935.

## Darling Songs of the Common People

Allingham, William. *Songs, Ballads and Stories.* New York: AMS Press, 1972. Reprint of 1877 ed.

Anderson, Gillian B., ed. *Freedom's Voice in Poetry and Song.* Wilmington, DE: Scholarly Resources, 1978.

Andrews, Edward Deming. *A Gift to Be Simple: Songs, Dances and Rituals of the American Shakers.* New York: Dover, 1962. Reprint of 1940 ed.

Ashton, John. *Humour, Wit and Satire of the Sixteenth Century.* New York: Dover, 1968. Reprint of 1883 ed.

———. *Modern Street Ballads.* New York: Benjamin Blom, 1968. Reprint of 1888 ed.

———. *Real Sailor Songs.* New York: Benjamin Blom, 1972. Reprint of 1891 ed.

Ault, Norman. *Seventeenth Century Lyrics from the Original Texts.* New York: William Sloane, 1928.

*The Bagford Ballads: Illustrating the Last Years of the Stuarts.* New York: AMS Press, 1968. Reprint of 1878 Ballad Society ed.

Bell, Robert, ed. *Early Ballads and Songs.* London: George Bell, 1877.

Bradley, S. A. J., ed. *Sixty Ribald Songs from Pills to Purge Melancholy.* Selected and edited, with a glossary. New York: Praeger, 1967.

Brand, Oscar. *A Folksinger's History of the Revolution.* Philadelphia: Lippincott, 1972.

Brooks, Henry M. *Olden-Time Music: A Compilation from Newspapers and Books.* New York: AMS Press, 1973. Reprint of 1888 ed.

Burns, Robert. *The Merry Muses of Caledonia: A Collection of Bawdy Folksongs, Ancient and Modern.* New York: Putnam, 1964.

———. *The Merry Muses of Caledonia.* Copy of first edition. Edited by Gershon Legman. New Hyde Park, NY: University Books, 1965.

Carey, George B., ed. *A Sailor's Songbook: An American Rebel in an English Prison 1777–79.* Amherst, MA: University of Massachuseets Press, 1976.

*The Catch Club or Merry Companions. Being a Choice Collectiion of the Most Divert-ing Catches for Three and Four Voices.* 2 vols. New York: Da Capo Press, 1965. Reprint.

Chappell, William. *Old English Popular Music.* New ed. with Preface and Notes by H. Ellis Wooldridge. New York: Jack Brussell, 1961.

———. *Popular Music of the Olden Time.* 2 vols. New York: Dover, 1965. Reprint of original edition, 1855–59.

Craigie, William A. *A Primer of Burns.* Port Washington, NY: Kennikat Press, 1970. Reprint of 1896 ed.

Davis, Richard Beale, C. Hugh Holman, and Louis D. Rubin, eds. *Southern Writing 1585–1920.* New York: Odyssey Press, 1970.

deSola Pinto, Vivian and Rodway, and Allen Edwin, eds. *The Common Muse: An An-thology of Popular British Ballad Poetry XVth to XXth Century.* New York: The Philosophical Library, 1967.

Dixon, James Henry. *Ancient Poems, Ballads and Songs of the Peasantry of England.* East Ardsley, Wakefield: EP Publishing, 1973.

Dobson, R. B., and J. Taylor, eds. *Rymes of Robin Hood: An Introduction to the En-glish Outlaw.* Pittsburgh: University of Pittsburgh Press, 1978.

Duffy, John, ed. *Early Vermont Broadsides.* Hanover, NH: University Press of New England, 1973.

Duncan, Edmondstoune, ed. *Lyrics from the Old Song Books.* London: Routlege & Sons, 1927.

D'Urfey, Thomas. *Wit and Mirth: Or Pills to Purge Melancholy.* Facsimile ed. New York: Folklore Library, 1959.

Edmunds, John, ed. *A Williamsburgh Songster: Songs, Convivial, Sporting, Amorous, &c. from 18th Century Collections Known to Have Been in the Libraries of Colo-nial Virginians.* New York: Holt, Rinehart & Winston, 1964.

Engel, Carl, and Oliver Strunk, eds. *Music from the Days of George Washington.* New York: AMS Press, 1970. Reprint of 1931 Ditson ed.

Fowler, David C. *A Literary History of the Popular Ballad.* Durham, NC: Duke Uni-versity Press, 1969.

Friedman, Albert F. *The Ballad Revival: Studies in the Influence of Popular on Sophis-ticated Poetry.* Chicago: University of Chicago Press, 1961.

Frith, G. H., ed. *An American Garland: Being a Collection of Ballads, Relating to America 1563–1760.* London: Blackwell, 1915.

Gerould, Gordon Hall. *The Ballad of Tradition.* New York: Oxford University Press, 1967.

Gibson, John Murray. *Melody and the Lyric: From Chaucer to the Cavaliers.* New York: Haskell House, 1964.

Haufrecht, Herbert. *Folk Songs in Settings by Master Composers.* New York: Funk & Wagnalls, 1970.

Hecht, Hans. *Robert Burns as a Songwriter.* London: William Hodge, 1950.

Hodgart, M. J. C. *The Ballads.* London: Hutchinson, 1950.

Holliday, Carl. *The Wit and Humor of Colonial Days.* Williamstown, MA: Corner House, 1975. Reprint of 1912 ed.

Jackson, George Stuyvesant. *Early Songs of Uncle Sam.* Boston: Bruce Humphries, 1933.

Jenkins, Herbert. *The Broadside Ballad: A Study in Origins and Meaning.* London: Her-bert Jenkins, 1962.

Kidson, Frank, and Mary Neal. *English Folk-song and Dance.* Totowa, NJ: Rowman & Littlefield, 1972.

Kittredge, George Lyman, ed. *English and Scottish Popular Ballads*. Boston: Houghton Mifflin, 1902.

Laws, G. Malcolm. *American Balladry from English Broadsides: A Guide for Students and Collectors of Traditional Song*. Austin, TX: American Folklore Society, 1957.

———. *Native American Balladry: A Descriptive Study and a Bibliographical Syllabus*. Austin, TX: American Folklore Society, 1964.

Leach, MacEdward, ed. *The Ballad Book*. New York: A. S. Barnes, 1955.

Legman, Gershon. *The Horn Book*. New Hyde Park, NY: University Books, 1964.

Lloyd, A. L. *Folk Song in England*. New York: International Publishers, 1967.

Loesser, Arthur. *Humor in American Song*. Detroit: Gale Research, 1974. Reprint.

Logan, W. H. *A Pedlar's Pack of Ballads and Songs*. Edinburgh: William and Patterson, 1869.

McCulloh, Judith. "Some Child Ballads on Hillbilly Records." *Folkore and Society*. Hatboro, PA: Folklore Associates, 1966.

Meserole, Harrison T., ed. *Seventeenth Century American Poetry*. New York: New York University Press, 1968.

Miner, Louie M. *Our Rude Forefathers: American Political Verse 1783–1788*. Cedar Rapids, IA: Torch Press, 1937.

Moore, Frank. *Songs and Ballads of the Revolution*. New York: Appleton Century, 1855.

Prescott, Frederick C., and John H. Nelson. *Prose and Poetry of the Revolution*. New York: Crowell, 1925.

Rabson, Carolyn. *Songbook of the American Revolution*. Peak's Island, ME: NEO Press, 1974.

Rollins, Hyder Edward. *Cavalier and Puritan: Ballads and Broadsides Illustrating the Period of the Great Rebellion, 1640–1660*. New York: New York University Press, 1923.

———. *Old English Ballads 1553–1625*. Cambridge: Cambridge University Press, 1920.

———. *The Pack of Autolycus or Strange and Terrible News, 1624–1693*. Cambridge, MA: Harvard University Press, 1927.

———. *A Pepsyian Garland: Black-letter Broadside Ballads of the Years 1595–1639*. Cambridge, MA: Harvard University Press, 1971.

Rubin, Louis, ed. *The Comic Imagination in American Literature*. New Brunswick: Rutgers University Press, 1973.

Seng, Peter J., ed. *Tudor Songs and Ballads from Ms Cotton Vespasian*. Cambridge, MA: Harvard University Press, 1978.

Shepard, Leslie. *The Broadside Ballad: A Study in Origins and Meaning*. London: Herbert Jenkins, 1962.

Silber, Irwin. *Songs of Independence*. Harrisburg, PA: Stackpole Books, 1973.

Silverman, Kenneth, ed. *Colonial American Poetry*. New York: Hafner, 1968.

Simpson, Claude M. *The British Broadside Ballad and Its Music*. New Brunswick: Rutgers University Press, 1966.

*The Universal Songster or Museum of Mirth*. 3 vols. London: George Routledge, n.d.

Wardroper, John, ed. *Love and Drollery: A Selection of Amatory, Merry and Satirical Verse of the Seventeenth Century*. New York: Barnes & Noble, 1969.

Wells, Evelyn Kendrick. *The Ballad Tree: A Study of British and American Ballads, Their Folklore, Verse, and Music*. New York: Ronald Press, 1950.

White, Helen, Ruth Wallerstein, and Ricardo Quintana, eds. *Seventeenth Century Verse and Prose*. New York: Macmillan, 1969.

Winslow, Ola Elizabeth, ed. *American Broadside Verse from Imprints of the Seventeenth and Eighteenth Centuries.* New Haven, CT: Yale University Press, 1930.

Yerbury, Grace. *Song in America.* Metuchen, NJ: Scarecrow Press, 1971.

## Music of God's Englishmen and Americans

Ahlstrom, Sydney E. *A Religious History of the American People.* New Haven, CT: Yale University Press, 1972.

Barbour, J. Murray. *The Church Music of William Billings.* East Lansing: Michigan State University Press, 1960.

Benson, Louis F. *The English Hymn, Its Development and Use in Worship.* New York: George Doran, 1915.

Brice, Douglas. *The Folk Carol of England.* London: Herbert Jenkins, 1967.

Broadwood, Lucy. *English Traditional Songs and Carols.* Totowa, NJ: Rowman & Littlefield, 1974.

Bucke, Emory Stevens, ed. *Companion to the Methodist Hymnal.* Nashville: Abingdon Press, 1970.

Cremin, Lawrence A. *American Education: The Colonial Experiment 1607–1783.* New York: Harper & Row, 1971.

Curti, Merle. *The Growth of American Thought.* New York: Harper & Row, 1964.

Daniel, Ralph T. *The Anthem in New England Before 1800.* Evanston, IL: Northwestern University Press, 1965.

Douglas, Charles W. *Church Music in History and Practice.* Revised by Leonard Ellinwood. New York: Scribner, 1962.

Ellinwood, Leonard. *The History of Church Music.* New York: Morehouse-Gorham, 1953.

Fox, Adam. *English Hymns and Hymn Writers.* London: Collins, 1947.

Hall, Jacob Henry. *Biography of Gospel Song and Hymn Writers.* Chicago: Fleming H. Revell, 1914.

Julian, John. *A Dictionary of Hymnology.* New York: Dover, 1957. Reprint.

Le Huray, Peter. *Music and the Reformation in England.* Cambridge: Cambridge University Press, 1978.

MacDougald, Hamilton C. *Early New England Psalmody: An Historical Appreciation, 1620–1820.* Brattleboro, VT: Steven Daye, 1969.

Metcalf, Frank. *American Psalmody 1721–1820.* New York: C. F. Hartmann, 1917.

———. *Writers and Compilers of Sacred Music.* New York: Metcalf, 1925.

Ochse, Orpha. *The History of the Organ in the United States.* Bloomington: Indiana University Press, 1975.

Parrington, V. L. *The Colonial Mind, 1620–1800.* Vol. 1 of *Main Currents in American Thought.* New York: Harcourt, Brace, 1927.

*Performance Practice in Early American Choral Music.* Suppl. of *Journal of the American Choral Foundation,* October 1976.

Polack, W. G. *The Handbook to the Lutheran Hymnal.* St. Louis: Concordia Publishing House, 1942.

Reese, Gustav. *Music in the Middle Ages.* New York: Norton, 1940.

———. *Music in the Renaissance.* New York: Norton, 1959.

Reynolds, William Jensen. *Companion to the Baptist Hymnal.* Nashville: Broadman Press, 1976.

———. *A Joyful Sound: Christian Hymnody.* 2d ed. New York: Holt, Rinehart & Winston, 1978.

Routley, Eric. *The Music of Christian Hymnody: A Study of the Development of the*

*Hymn since the Reformation, with Special Reference to English Protestantism.* London: Independent Press, 1958.

Sallee, James. *A History of Evangelistic Hymnody.* Grand Rapids, MI: Baker Book House, 1978.

Scholes, Percy. *The Puritans and Music in England and New England: A Contribution to the Cultural History of the Two Nations.* New York: Oxford University Press, 1934.

Stevenson, Robert. *Protestant Church Music in America: A Short Survey of Men and Movements from 1584 to the Present.* New York: Norton, 1966.

Sweet, William Warren. *Religion in Colonial America.* New York: Scribner, 1942.

————. *Religion in the Development of American Culture.* New York: Scribner, 1952.

Tamke, Susan. *Make a Joyful Noise Unto the Lord: Hymns as a Reflection of Victorian Social Attitudes.* Athens, OH: Ohio University Press, 1978.

Walker Williston. *A History of the Christian Church.* New York: Scribner, 1959.

Wienandt, Elwyn A., and Robert H. Young. *The Anthem in England and America.* New York: Macmillan, 1970.

## Music Publishing in the American Colonies

Aitken, John. *A Compilation of the Litanies, Vespers, Hymns and Anthems as Sung in the Catholic Church.* Facsimile of 1787 ed. Philadelphia: Musical Americana, 1956.

*The American Musical Miscellany.* New York: Da Capo Press. Reprint of 1798 ed.

*American Printmaking: The First 150 Years.* Washington, D.C.: Smithsonian Institution Press, 1969.

Ayars, Christine Merrick. *Contribtutions to the Art of Music in America by the Music Industries of Boston, 1640–1936.* New York: H. W. Wilson, 1937.

Carr, Benjamin. *Federal Overture.* Philadelphia: Musical Americana, 1957.

————. *The History of England.* Philadelphia: Musical Americana, 1954.

Crawford, Richard A. *Andrew Law, American Psalmodist.* Evanston, IL: Northwestern University Press, 1969.

Dichter, Harry, and Elliott Shapiro. *Early American Sheet Music, Its Lore and Lure.* New York: R. R. Bowker, 1941.

————. *Handbook of Early American Sheet Music, 1768–1889.* New York: Dover, 1977. Reprint of 1941 Bowker ed.

Fisher, William Arms. *Notes on Music in Old Boston.* Boston: Oliver Ditson, 1918.

————. *One Hundred and Fifty Years of Music Publishing in the United States, 1783–1933.* Boston: Oliver Ditson, 1933.

Franklin, Benjamin. *Autobiography.* Many editions.

Gerson, Robert A. *Music in Philadelphia.* Philadelphia: Theodore Presser, 1940.

Goldman, Richard Franko, and Roger Smith. *Landmarks in Early American Music, 1760–1800.* New York: AMS Press, 1974. Reprint of 1943 ed.

Hastings, George Everett. *The Life and Times of Francis Hopkinson.* New York: Russell & Russell, 1968.

Hixon, Donald L. *Music in Early America.* Metuchen, NJ: Scarecrow Press, 1970.

Jackson, H. Earle. *Musical Interludes in Boston 1795–1830.* New York: Columbia University Press, 1943.

Keefer, Lubov. *Baltimore's Music: The Haven of American Composers.* Baltimore: J. J. Furst, 1962.

Krummel, D. W. "Graphic Analysis: Its Application to Early American Engraved Music." *Notes* 2, 1959.

————. "Philadelphia Music Engraving and Publishing 1800–1820: A Study in Bibliography and Cultural History." Diss. University of Michigan, 1958.

Lemay, J. A. Leo. *Men of Letters in Colonial Maryland*. Knoxville: University of Tennessee Press, 1972.

Lowens, Irving. *A Bibliography of Songsters Printed in America Before 1821*. Worcester, MA: American Antiquarian Society, 1976.

————. *Music and Musicians in Early America: Aspects of the History of Music in Early America and the History of Early American Music*. New York: Norton, 1964.

McKay, David, and Richard Crawford. *William Billings of Boston, Eighteenth-Century Composer*. Princeton: Princeton University Press, 1975.

Mangler, Joyce Ellen. *Rhode Island Music and Musicians 1733–1850*. Detroit: Information Service, 1975.

Maurer, M. "A Musical Family in Colonial Virginia." *Musical Quarterly*, July 1948.

————. "The 'Professor of Musicke' in Colonial America." *Musical Quarterly*, October 1950.

Mott, Frank Luther. *American Journalism: A History of Newspapers in the United States through 250 Years, 1660–1920*. New York: Macmillan, 1941.

Nathan, Hans. *William Billings: Data and Documents. Bibliographies in American Music #2*. Detroit: College Music Society, 1976.

Oswold, John Clyde. *Printing in the Americas*. New York: Hacker Art Books, 1968. Reprint of 1937 ed.

Pichierri, Louis. *Music in New Hampshire 1624–1800*. New York: Columbia University Press, 1960.

Redway, Virginia Larkin. "The Carrs, American Music Publishers." *Musical Quarterly*, January 1932.

Scheele, Carl H. *A Short History of the Mail Service*. Washington, D.C.: Smithsonian Institution Press, 1970.

Shipton, Clifford K. *Isaiah Thomas: Printer, Patriot and Philanthropist*. Rochester, NY: Leo Hart, 1948.

Silver, Rollo. *Aprons Instead of Uniforms: The Practice of Printing 1776–1783*. Worcester, MA: American Antiquarian Society, 1977.

————. *Typefounding in America 1787–1825*. Charlottesville: University Press of Virginia, 1965.

Sonneck, Oscar G. *A Bibliography of Early American Secular Music*. Revised and enlarged by William Upton. New York: Da Capo Press, 1964.

————. *Francis Hopkinson/James Lyon*. New York: Da Capo Press, 1967.

Stoutamire, Albert. *Music of the Old South: Colony to Confederacy*. Madison, NJ: Farleigh Dickinson University Press, 1972.

Strunk, Oliver. "Early Music Publishing in the United States." Papers of the Bibliographical Society, Vol. 31, pt. 2, 1937.

Tebbel, John. *The American Magazine: A Compact History*. New York: Hawthorne Books, 1969.

————. *A History of Book Publishing in the United States: The Creation of an Industry, 1630–1865*. New York: R. R. Bowker, 1975.

Thomas, Isaiah. *The History of Printing in America, with a Biography of Printers and an Account of Newspapers*. New York: Weathervane Books, 1970. Reprint of 1810 ed.

Tourtellot, Arthur Bernon. *Benjamin Franklin: The Shaping of Genius, the Boston Years*. New York: Doubleday, 1977.

Wagner, John Waldorf. "James Hewitt: His Life and Works." Diss. Indiana University, 1969.

Winterich, John T. *Early American Books and Printing*. Boston: Houghton Mifflin, 1935.

Wolfe, Richard J. *Early American Music Engraving and Printing: A History of Music Publishing in America from 1787 to 1825 with Commentary on Earlier and Later Practices*. Urbana: University of Illinois Press, 1980.


## Theater in America

Bernheim, Alfred L. *The Business of the Theatre: An Economic History of the American Theatre 1750–1932*. New York: Benjamin Blom, 1964. Reprint of 1933 ed.

Coad, Oral Sumner, and Edwin Mimms. *The American Stage*. New York: U. S. Publishers Association, 1929.

Dannett, Sylvia G. L. *The Yankee Doodler*. South Brunswick & New York: A. S. Barnes, 1973.

Freedley, George, and John A. Reeves. *A History of the Theatre*. New York: Crown, 1968.

Grimsted, David. *Melodrama Unveiled*. Chicago: University of Chicago Press, 1968.

Havens, Daniel F. *The Columbian Muse of Comedy: The Development of a Native Tradition in Early American Social Comedy, 1787–1845*. Carbondale: Southern Illinois University Press, 1973.

Henderson, Mary C. *The City and the Theatre: The History of the New York Playhouses—A 235-Year Journey from Bowling Green to Times Square*. New York: Clifton Publishers, 1973.

Hill, West J. *The Theatre in Early Kentucky*. Lexington: University Press of Kentucky, 1971.

Hodge, Francis. *Yankee Theatre*. Austin: University of Texas Press, 1964.

Hornblow, Arthur. *A History of the Theatre in America: From Its Beginnings to the Present Time*. 2 vols. New York: Benjamin Blom, 1965. Reprint of 1919 ed.

Mates, Carl. *The American Musical Stage Before 1800*. New Brunswick: Rutgers University Press, 1962.

Molnar, John, ed. *Songs from the Williamsburgh Theatre: A Selection of 50 Songs Performed on the Stage in Williamsburgh in the Eighteenth Century*. Charlottesville: University of Virginia Press, 1972.

Moody, Richard. *America Takes the Stage: Romanticism in the American Drama and Theatre 1750–1900*. Bloomington: Indiana Unviersity Press, 1955.

O'Dell, George C. D. *Annals of the New York Stage*. Vols. 1 and 2. New York: Columbia University Press, 1927.

Quinn, Arthur Hobson. *A History of the American Drama: From the Beginning to the Civil War*. New York: Appleton-Century-Crofts, 1923.

Rankin, Hugh F. *The Theater in Colonial America*. Chapel Hill: University of North Carolina Press, 1965.

Seilhammer, George O. *History of the American Theater During the Revolution and After*. 3 vols. New York: Benjamin Blom, 1968. Reprint of 1889–91 ed.

Sonneck, Oscar G. *Early Opera in America*. New York: Benjamin Blom, 1963. Reprint of 1915 ed.

Vernon, Grenville, eds. *Yankee Doodle-doos: A Collection of Songs of the Early American Stage*. New York: Payson & Clarke, 1927.

Walser, Richard. "Negro Dialect in Eighteenth-century American Drama." *American Speech*, December 1955.

Wemyss, Francis. *Chronology of the American Stage from 1752 to 1852.* New York: Benjamin Blom, 1968. Reprint of 1852 ed.

Wright, Richardson. *Revels in Jamaica 1682–1838: Plays and Players of a Century: Tumblers and Conjurers, Musical Refugees and Solitary Showmen, Dinners, Balls and Cockfights, Darky Mummers and Other Memories of High Times and Merry Hearts.* New York: Benjamin Blom, 1969. Reprint of 1937 ed.

# Index